RICHARD J. ALDRICH
and RORY CORMAC

THE BLACK DOOR

SPIES, SECRET INTELLIGENCE
AND BRITISH PRIME MINISTERS

WILLIAM
COLLINS

William Collins
An imprint of HarperCollins*Publishers*
1 London Bridge Street
London SE1 9GF
WilliamCollinsBooks.com

First published in Great Britain by William Collins in 2016

2

A catalogue record for this book is
available from the British Library

ISBN (HB) 978-0-00-755544-4
ISBN (TPB) 978-0-00-755546-8

Printed and bound in Great Britain by
Clays Ltd, St Ives plc

To Joanne and Libby

(two espionage experts)

Contents

Illustrations

Herbert Asquith with Lord and Lady Allenby. (*US National Archives*)

Lloyd George on the Western Front. (*US National Archives*)

Grigory Zinoviev, the alleged author of the 'Zinoviev letter'. (*US National Archives*)

Special Branch officers intercept mail couriers during the 'Arcos' raid in 1927. (*US National Archives*)

Ramsay MacDonald. (*US National Archives*)

MI5 reluctantly eavesdropped on Edward VIII and Mrs Simpson at the insistence of Stanley Baldwin. (*US National Archives*)

Neville Chamberlain and Hugh Sinclair. (*Authors' private collection*)

Laurence Hislam is led away by police after throwing a suitcase-load of 'bombs' outside Downing Street in August 1939. (© *Corbis*)

British troops practise rounding up a 'Nazi parachutist' in a 1940 exercise. (*Imperial War Museum*)

Winston Churchill inspects a commando dagger. (*Library of Congress, Prints & Photographs Division*)

Anthony Eden with a Lysander aircraft used to drop SOE and MI6 agents into France. (*Imperial War Museum*)

Klaus Fuchs. (*Imperial War Museum*)

Clement Attlee. (*Cleveland Press Collection, Michael Schwartz Library*)

John Thornton Stanley and Charles Pittuck after their release from prison by Nasser in the wake of the Suez fiasco. (© *Keystone Pictures USA/Alamy Stock Photo*)

Castro and Nasser – twin survivors of assassination plots by Eden and Eisenhower. (*US National Archives*)

Julian Amery and Archbishop Makarios. (© *Keystone Pictures USA/ Alamy Stock Photo*)

A Special Branch officer keeps an eye on the 1956 visit to London by
   Khrushchev and Bulganin. (*Cleveland Press Collection, Michael
   Schwartz Library*)
Harold Macmillan visits Khrushchev in Moscow in 1959. (© *Keystone
   Pictures USA/Alamy Stock Photo*)
Christine Keeler during her trial in 1963. (© *Corbis*)
The IRA attacked Westminster repeatedly during the 1970s and 1980s.
   (*US National Archives*)
Forensic specialists pick bullets out of the Jordanian ambassador's car in
   London in 1971. (© *Keystone Pictures USA/Alamy Stock Photo*)
Edward Heath. (© *Keystone Pictures USA/Alamy Stock Photo*)
KGB officer Oleg Lyalin caught on a hidden camera. (*Authors' private
   collection*)
Harold Wilson. (*Marvin Lichtner/The LIFE Images Collection/Getty
   Image*)
Cecil King and Hugh Cudlipp, two of the many anti-Wilson plotters.
   (© *Keystone Pictures USA/Alamy Stock Photo*)
Margaret Thatcher accepting the Donovan Medal from Bill Casey,
   director of the CIA. (*By permission of the OSS Society*)
The 'Super-Gun', one of the many Iraq episodes that swirled around John
   Major and his successors. (*US Department of Defense*)
Tony Blair and Donald Rumsfeld in Downing Street. (*US Department of
   Defense*)

The author and publishers are committed to respecting the intellectual
property rights of others and have made all reasonable efforts to trace the
copyright owners of the images reproduced, and to provide appropriate
acknowledgement within this book. In the event that any untraceable
copyright owners come forward after the publication of this book, the
author and publishers will use all reasonable endeavours to rectify the
position accordingly.

Abbreviations and Acronyms

'C' – Chief of the British Secret Intelligence Service (SIS)
CCC – Churchill College Cambridge
CIA – Central Intelligence Agency [American]
CIGS – Chief of the Imperial General Staff
CND – Campaign for Nucleur Disarmament
Comint – Communications intelligence
Comsec – Communications security
COS – Chiefs of Staff
CPGB – Communist Party of Great Britain
CSC – Counter Subversion Committee
CX – Prefix for a report originating with SIS
DCI – Director of Central Intelligence, the head of the CIA
DIS – Defence Intelligence Staff
DMI – Director of Military Intelligence
DNI – Director of Naval Intelligence
D-Notice – Defence Notice to the media covering security issues
DOPC – Defence and Overseas Policy Committee
Elint – Electronic intelligence
FBI – Federal Bureau of Investigation [American]
FCO – Foreign and Commonwealth Office
GC&CS – Government Code and Cypher School
GCHQ – Government Communications Headquarters
GOC – General Officer Commanding
GRU – Soviet Military Intelligence
IRD – Information Research Department of the Foreign Office
ISC – Intelligence and Security Committee
ISI – Inter-Services Intelligence [Pakistan]
ISP – Internet Service Provider

JAC – Joint Action Committee
JIC – Joint Intelligence Committee
JTAC – Joint Terrorism Analysis Centre
LHCMA – Liddell Hart Centre for Military Archives
MI5 – Security service
MI6 – Secret Intelligence Service (also SIS)
MIT – Turkish Intelligence Service
MoD – Ministry of Defence
NATO – North Atlantic Treaty Organisation
NSA – National Security Agency [American]
NSC – National Security Council [American]
NUM – National Union of Mineworkers
OSS – Office of Strategic Services [American]
PKI – Indonesian Communist Party
PLO – Palestine Liberation Organisation
PSIS – Permanent Secretaries' Committee on the Intelligence Services
PUSC – Permanent Under-Secretary's Committee of the Foreign Office
PUSD – Permanent Under-Secretary's Department
PV – Positive vetting
RAW – Research and Analysis Wing [Indian]
RUC – Royal Ulster Constabulary
SAS – Special Air Service
SAVAK – Iranian Security Service
SBS – Special Boat Service
Sigint – Signals intelligence
SIS – Secret Intelligence Service (also MI6)
SOE – Special Operations Executive
TASS – Soviet Press Agency
TUC – Trades Union Congress
Ultra – British classification for signals intelligence
UKUSA – UK–USA signals intelligence agreements 1948
WMD – Weapons of Mass Destruction

Introduction

This is my own true spy story ...
WINSTON CHURCHILL[1]

On Saturday, 6 September 1941, Winston Churchill stood on a pile of bricks outside the newly built Bletchley Park. Here, in the Buckinghamshire countryside, the mysteries of the German Enigma encryption machine were being patiently unravelled. Each day the codebreakers' product was fed to a prime minister in Downing Street who was beside himself with anticipation. Now, with some emotion, Churchill expressed his profound gratitude and explained to the codebreakers how they had already transformed decision-making at the highest levels, and with it the course of the Second World War. A decade later – and now approaching his eightieth year – Churchill was back in Downing Street. His keen interest in intelligence had not diminished. In 1952, top-secret spy flights took pictures over Moscow at the express instruction of the prime minister. Over Minsk and Lvov, his airborne intelligence emissaries were greeted by a formidable wall of Soviet anti-aircraft fire.

Churchill also relished covert action. In 1953, he positively purred with enthusiasm over a joint CIA–MI6 plot that had overthrown the government of Iran. This underlines the way in which intelligence was not just a secret window on the world for Britain's leaders, but also a discreet means of manipulating it. In 1956 Churchill's successor, a furious Anthony Eden, neurotic and plagued by ill-health, barked into a telephone that he wanted Egyptian President Nasser destroyed by MI6. Harold Macmillan's government drew up what he called a 'formidable' plan for Syria which involved assassinating several leaders. Alec Douglas-Home added Indonesia's President Sukarno to the list of foreign leaders that prime ministers wished to see toppled using Britain's intelligence agencies. However, when Harold

Wilson asked for the liquidation of the Ugandan dictator Idi Amin, officials responded with horror, and refused to investigate the options. When secret intelligence took extreme risks, it was usually at the direction of Downing Street.

Harold Wilson evoked the dark side of intelligence. He was convinced that plotters within MI5, MI6 and especially renegade generals in the Ministry of Defence were out to undermine his government. Notably terrified of the South African secret service, known as 'BOSS', he chose to develop close personal relations with the Israeli secret service Mossad instead. Speaking with American officials who were inquiring into illegal activities by the CIA in the wake of Watergate, he agreed with them that the CIA failed to tell British authorities everything it did in London. Yet he remained fascinated by the secret world, and valued the intelligence machinery in Downing Street, engaging in academic debate with his intelligence analysts on points of detail like the Oxford junior research fellow he once was.

Intelligence imperilled more than one British prime minister. Within weeks of her arrival at Downing Street, Margaret Thatcher insisted on sitting in with the Joint Intelligence Committee to better understand how intelligence was prepared for those at the top. Only three years later, a major intelligence failure by the same mechanism over the Falkland Islands almost ended her government. John Major found himself confronted by the Arms to Iraq affair, in which ministers had sought to cover up the control of arms export companies by MI5 and MI6. The subsequent inquiry by Lord Scott revealed only part of the murky tale, and brought Major's government close to defeat in the House of Commons. Tony Blair's era was defined by vicious public arguments over intelligence. Despite his successful use of secret service during the creation of the Good Friday Agreement in Northern Ireland, it was accusations of the misuse of intelligence over Iraq that would leave his reputation in tatters. His bold decision to use intelligence publicly to justify the war on Iraq quickly backfired, and by 2005 the missing WMD fiasco threatened to end his government prematurely. Blair's administration also left a toxic legacy of allegations about complicity in torture with which Gordon Brown and David Cameron have both struggled. Most recently, the deluge of secrets revealed by NSA contractor Edward Snowden has reshaped relations between David Cameron, Barack Obama and other world leaders including Angela Merkel. In an era when secret services are increasingly kept in check by whistleblowers and their remarkable revelations, British prime ministers live in constant fear of intelligence 'blowback'.

For good or ill, intelligence matters to prime ministers. It may be only one factor shaping their thinking, but it can be critical and very personal, often revealing what their opponents think about them.[2] Intelligence can provide warning of dangerous future events, and has certainly averted major terrorist attacks on London. It can help to prevent wars, or – once they begin – mean the difference between victory and defeat. Yet it can also be misused to justify preconceived policy desires. The secret world can help to resolve a prime minister's most difficult dilemmas by providing a hidden hand that shapes events behind the scenes. It can also become a seductive apparent panacea, whereby secret service is employed to carry out a leader's dirty work, at home and abroad. In its darkest moments, intelligence can consume prime ministers.

The relationship has become ever closer. The link between Number 10 and Britain's intelligence agencies, as intimate as it is secret, lies at the heart of the British establishment. For almost a century, a stream of secret boxes – red for MI6 material and blue for intercepted communications from GCHQ – made their way to 10 Downing Street. Sifted by the cabinet secretary, the best material was placed in a special striped box, nicknamed 'Old Stripey', for the early attention of the prime minister. Since the creation of Britain's intelligence agencies in 1909, the relationship between prime ministers and the secret world has moved from circumspection to centrality. One thing is clear from this story. Intelligence is not about rogue agents operating wildly and freely; nor is it an unaccountable business far removed from the corridors of political power. Many of the most hair-raising intelligence activities and many of the most dangerous covert operations have involved Number 10 directly. Intelligence is part of the beating heart of Britain's core executive, and has long held a special place behind the famous black door of 10 Downing Street.

The use of secret intelligence is one of the dark arts of statecraft. Yet during the early years of the twentieth century, British prime ministers were notably inept practitioners. Relative strangers to the murky world of espionage and clandestine warfare, they treated the subject with either indifference or outright suspicion. When prime ministers did draw on intelligence, they demonstrated remarkable inexperience and naïvety in its use. While Herbert Asquith presided over the creation of the modern British intelligence services in 1909, he had little interest in secret matters other than his mistress. David Lloyd George and Stanley Baldwin enjoyed the first fruits of Britain's revived wartime codebreaking operations, but squandered them by publicising not only German but also American and Russian intercepts, compromising the source and causing anguish among the denizens of secret service. Ramsay MacDonald, Britain's first Labour prime minister, distanced himself from the secret services, fearing they may have been out to plot the demise of his government; while Neville Chamberlain arrogantly ignored invaluable secret intelligence provided by brave Germans who personally visited Downing Street at the risk of their own lives. Instead, he preferred to rely on diplomatic reports from those sympathetic to Hitler, which reinforced his own preconceptions.

In 1940, Churchill changed all this. Indeed, a Churchillian revolution in intelligence occurred during the middle of the twentieth century. For five years Britain's fate hung in the balance, and intelligence, especially Ultra material provided by Bletchley Park, often proved the operational advantage. Churchill placed a premium on intelligence chiefs telling truth to power: he believed that craven intelligence officers accounted for some of Sir Douglas Haig's failings during the First World War. 'The temptation to tell a Chief in a great position the things he most likes to hear,' Churchill later observed, 'is one of the commonest explanations of mistaken policy.'[3] As prime minister he developed close links with the secret world, especially through Stewart Menzies, chief of MI6, whom he sometimes summoned to his bedside in the middle of the night. The prime minister was obsessed with secret intelligence, and – more importantly – strained every sinew to make sure that the government used it to efficient purpose.

Churchill was impulsive, and so constituted a mixed blessing. As David Reynolds argues in his magisterial study, there were reasons why both Baldwin and Chamberlain had kept him out of office. He had imagination, industry, energy and eloquence, but he lacked judgement and wisdom. Lloyd George was of much the same opinion, arguing that in an emergency Churchill's vision and imagination were essential, and should be used to the full, but at the same time he should be kept under a 'vigilant eye'.[4] Churchill's over-enthusiasm led to friction with the chiefs of staff, who had the onerous duty of vigilance, and indeed to occasional blunders. Yet his determination to harness the power of intelligence transformed not only the centre of government, but also the very nature of British statecraft.[5]

Uniquely, Churchill brought with him vast intelligence experience. In charge of the Admiralty during the First World War, he had seen the work of Britain's most proficient codebreakers at first hand. In the interwar years he had been deeply interested in intelligence, and repeatedly shaped its development. Once he became prime minister in May 1940, he was finally empowered to change procedure at the top. He demanded raw intelligence fresh from MI6 agents in the field or from Bletchley Park. This annoyed the chiefs of staff, and triggered a revolution in Whitehall's intelligence assessment machinery – the Joint Intelligence Committee moved centre stage – laying the foundations of the successful body which still operates today. Moreover, the impetuous Churchill loved action. He not only nurtured Number 10's direct connection with espionage, but also encouraged a new focus on special operations and covert warfare. His personal interest in 'funnies' and oddball units – ranging from the Chindits and the Commandos to the Special Operations Executive and most famously the SAS – changed how Britain approached warfare for decades to come.[6]

Churchill's wartime government was itself a school for secret service. Around him, Britain's future leaders learned the business of intelligence and its importance to the practice of statecraft. Thereafter, Britain's next few prime ministers – all veterans of Churchill's wartime government – understood the value of secret sources and the event-shaping power of intelligence. Trained in the sophisticated integration of intelligence and policy, his successors realised that it formed a crucial instrument for any leader in a perilous period of British decline. Secret service was part of the 'fancy footwork' of retreating empire that could potentially turn the tide in colonial bushfire wars, gain an upper hand in manoeuvrings against the Soviets, and even deceive Washington or Brussels.[7]

Churchill constituted an improbable double act with Clement Attlee. Serving as Churchill's wartime deputy, Attlee took a quiet interest in intelligence from the very first week he entered office, including the sensitive matter of interning Nazi sympathisers.[8] As early as the autumn of 1940, he was arguing for a single authority to coordinate and improve intelligence.[9] Later, he led an inquiry into one of darkest episodes of the war, the Gestapo penetration of Britain's resistance efforts. Despite his public reputation for timidity, Attlee hid an inner toughness. After 1945, he quietly sanctioned numerous covert operations behind the Iron Curtain and across the Middle East. He also recognised the importance of MI5, of positive vetting and of domestic counter-subversion – even at the risk of frustrating his own backbenchers. Most importantly, he completed Churchill's project, developing new mechanisms that improved Downing Street's control over secret service. Indeed, by 1951, deliberately seeking to capture corporate memory and learn the lessons of the preceding ten years, Attlee completed the Churchillian revolution, harnessing the power of the hidden hand to state policy and creating a connected British intelligence community for the first time.[10]

Anthony Eden and Harold Macmillan had also learned about the growing power of secret service during the war. Eden in particular had endured a series of vexatious confrontations with SOE, which appeared at times to be conducting a parallel foreign policy. In 1942, confronted with yet another improbable episode, he peevishly exclaimed, 'Am I foreign secretary or am I not?' Yet once ensconced in Downing Street, both Eden and Macmillan recognised the value of secret service. They also realised that the CIA was quietly being used to expand American influence while bypassing the political, economic and military constraints associated with overt intervention. Accordingly, as well as launching their own covert operations, the prime ministers' relations with presidents Eisenhower and Kennedy often involved selling cooperation on Anglo–American secret wars against figures like Nasser and Sukarno to the White House.[11]

More recent prime ministers did not, of course, serve under Churchill or Attlee. But all experienced their legacy inside Number 10. Churchill brought the intelligence machine more firmly into Downing Street, while Attlee, as his partner and immediate successor, greatly strengthened the central control of the cabinet secretary over the secret world and began the creation of a refined national security apparatus. Together, they created an intelligence community and made it a familiar part of the working lives of prime ministers for the first time. Thereafter, intelligence became part of the growing 'presidentialism' of the British prime minister. While Harold Wilson may have nurtured a curious love–hate relationship with intelligence, Burke Trend, his cabinet secretary, continued Churchill's drive to connect secret service with the centre. Under Wilson, the involvement of the Cabinet Office with the intelligence services became so great that Trend created a new post of Cabinet Office Intelligence Coordinator to help manage their business. To Wilson's pleasure, Dick White, who had served as a much-admired director-general of MI5 and then chief of MI6, was the first incumbent.

The growing power of premiers, presidents and prime ministers in the twentieth century went hand in hand with secret service. In Britain, this meant the rise of special policy advisers, spin doctors and the increasing tendency of Downing Street to impinge on the territory of cabinet ministers. Typically, Edward Heath created a Central Policy Review Staff under Victor Rothschild, a wartime MI5 officer who also served as a back channel to the secret services. Margaret Thatcher took this further, appointing Percy Cradock to serve simultaneously as her personal foreign policy adviser and also as Chair of the Joint Intelligence Committee. Unhappy with the reluctance of the 'wets' in MI5 and the Foreign Office to confront what she saw as Britain's enemies, Thatcher even created a network of private secret services around Downing Street that paralleled Ronald Reagan's piratical adventures with the US National Security Council during Iran–Contra. In Whitehall and Washington, secret service now bestowed upon Western leaders their own hidden and deniable foreign policy.[12]

The twenty-first century witnessed the final convergence of intelligence and political leadership. Tony Blair waged wars from Bosnia to Iraq, Sierra Leone to Afghanistan. Doing so required the support of Britain's secret services. Ironically, his failure to understand intelligence, his determination to exercise personal control and the calamities that followed prompted a further reshaping of the way in which secret service connects with British foreign policy. Gordon Brown and David Cameron formally institutionalised their relationship with the intelligence community, the latter using an American-style National Security Council. For the first time, Cameron meets with the three agency chiefs once a week, together with key decision-makers, in an environment that promotes action. Moreover, he announces himself as 'minister for the intelligence services'.[13]

One of the things that frightens British prime ministers most is the ghost of secret service past. A special security squad of weeders and censors constantly patrols the boundaries of Britain's official past in the hope of protecting Downing Street from embarrassment. The intention is that intelligence scandals will only emerge slowly and in a controlled fashion, as the result of papers being opened after an embargo of seventy-five or even a hundred years. Eventually, in the National Archives at Kew, amid crumbling paper and crumbling academics, the sensations of yesteryear can be safely examined, since any possible witnesses who might speak out of turn have long passed away. But occasionally, premiers have had to confront skeletons rattling in the secret service cupboard of their immediate predecessor. None was as noisy or as dangerous as the 'Arms to Iraq' episode that came within a whisker of ending John Major's government.[14]

'Scandals are the nastiest experiences in politics,' noted Bernard Donoughue, senior policy adviser to both Wilson and Callaghan. In September 1977, reflecting on the latest press revelations about alleged attempts by the intelligence services to subvert or even overthrow the prime minister, the so-called 'Wilson plot', he added that these affairs brought together 'scared politicians, hysterical and self–righteous civil servants and hypocritical lying journalists'.[15] Intelligence scandals have long caused sleepless nights in the flat above 10 Downing Street. Almost as soon as he entered office, Attlee was confronted with revelations about the 'atom spies', Alan Nunn May and Klaus Fuchs, two wartime scientists employed by the British who had seemingly passed the secrets of the West's new wonder weapon to Moscow. When Stalin detonated an atomic bomb ahead of the British in August 1949, there were awkward public questions in Parliament, made worse by the mysterious flight of Donald Maclean and Guy Burgess to the Soviet Union in 1951. Security scandals had an alarming habit of appearing out of a clear blue sky, as Anthony Eden discovered just a few years later. In 1956, he clumsily attempted to bat away questions about the mysterious death of the navy frogman 'Buster' Crabb, who during a state visit to Britain by the Soviet leadership had embarked on a hazardous secret operation that MI6 had failed to clear properly with the political authorities. The Crabb fiasco triggered a major review of prime ministerial clearance for clandestine operations and new mechanisms for assessing attendant political risk.

The 1963 Profumo affair was a defining moment for Downing Street. It not only helped prompt Macmillan to terminate his premiership early, it also heralded a new attitude by the press towards matters of secrecy. Hitherto, the long shadow of the Second World War had ensured a degree of circumspection and security-consciousness by journalists when addressing intelligence matters. But by the 1960s, propelled by a range of scandals around CIA special operations, the press was hungry for stories about espionage. The shooting down of Gary Powers' U-2 spy plane in May 1960 reverberated personally for Macmillan, collapsing a Cold War summit with Khrushchev that he had worked hard to create. This was followed by the CIA's disastrous Bay of Pigs escapade, which marred the first months of Kennedy's presidency and raised questions about his personal judgement. Profumo too had an Anglo–American dimension, with anxious FBI officers arriving in London to probe the delicate question of whether Kennedy had met Christine Keeler. For Macmillan, always keen to project the persona of Edwardian stability, the increasing connections made by the press between premiers, politics and the secret world became deeply disconcerting. It was a wind of change he did not welcome.

Harold Wilson had enjoyed tormenting Macmillan over Profumo. As leader of the opposition in 1963, he recognised that this episode was about sex and high society as well as secrets – a gift in terms of media coverage. Entering Downing Street in 1964, he was determined to protect himself against the same fate, and noted that his predecessor, Alec Douglas-Home, had already established a Security Commission to which he could refer malodorous matters when they came before Parliament, giving the prime minister the welcome appearance of actually doing something. For Downing Street, the tactic of creating long-running inquiries into secret matters gradually became a central mechanism for containing toxic security issues. But Wilson also wanted his own 'security enforcer', and appointed his paymaster general, George Wigg, to sniff out potential scandals within government. Cabinet ministers and MI5 loathed the freewheeling security inquiries that Wigg made into the most sensitive parts of Whitehall. All this failed to protect Wilson from hideous embarrassment over the interception of telegrams during the 'D-Notice affair' in 1967, and then the public flaunting of MI6 secrets by Kim Philby in his waspish memoirs published in 1968.

Labour leaders faced a peculiar predicament. They often found themselves publicly defending domestic security services that they privately feared might be seeking to undermine them. Attlee faced the awkward position of being a socialist prime minister at the onset of the Cold War. The Labour Party and MI5 were not, at this point, natural bedfellows, and Attlee had to balance issues of positive vetting with backbench accusations of launching an anti-communist witch-hunt. Attlee was always conscious of the tension between intelligence, security and liberty. He agonised over investigation into the personal backgrounds of Whitehall officials, and introduced it only under the American threat of ceasing nuclear cooperation, passing this into law as almost the last act of his administration. By the 1970s, Labour prime ministers were inspecting MI5 files on their own MPs and wondering what level of risk was involved in appointing them to government. It was now known by Downing Street that some MPs – like John Stonehouse – had actually worked for Eastern bloc intelligence services. Indeed, one of the longest-serving MPs in the House of Commons, Labour's Bob Edwards, who represented Wolverhampton South-East until 1987, was a fully-paid-up KGB agent. Other MPs had worked closely and enthusiastically with the CIA or Mossad.[16]

Jack Straw, one of the most prominent cabinet ministers of recent years, recalls his initial security vetting when he first joined the government. 'A man in a mac, with a skin disease which meant he could not shake my hand ... came to interview me ... for three hours.' Later the same man came back for another three hours, and in this second interview he suddenly leaned across the desk, looked his subject in the eye and asked, 'Mr Straw, do you like men?' This reflected the fact that historically, several people who had spied for the Soviets had been trapped by sexual black-mail. In 1974, when Straw was an adviser at the Department of Health and Social Security, his file was already two inches thick, and from their questions it was clear that MI5 had been collecting material on his family members since he was fifteen. Straw reflected on the scale of the surveil-lance operation that this implied. But, he recalls, this 'neither surprised nor shocked me'. He saw it as part of everyday life on the strange planet that was Cold War Britain, where the KGB had to be kept at bay. Years later, when Straw became home secretary, MI5 was nervous that he might wish to see his own file. But he did not request this privilege, taking the view that he had no more right to see this secret material than any other citizen – and he gave the same response to Peter Mandelson, who was characteristically eager to peruse his own MI5 dossier.[17]

In the 1970s, Downing Street also lived in the shadow of Watergate, and was engulfed by growing paranoia about grand political conspiracy. Plots and bugging seemed to be almost normal. In March 1976, during the last days of the Wilson government, Tony Benn, then secretary of state for energy, attended a reception at the American embassy at which he chatted amiably to Cord Meyer, head of the CIA station in London. They reviewed the continuing fallout from Watergate, and Benn offered the opinion that Nixon was in fact quite charming, and that the media had been 'unfair to him'. Meyer countered that Nixon was a 'terrible man', and had done a lot of damage to his service. But Benn took the wider view that given the catalogue of human error that went with the political experience, 'bugging your opponent wasn't so bad'.[18] A year later, James Callaghan and the cabi-net secretary were debating whether Benn himself could be trusted to see intercepts and 'sigint' material from GCHQ.[19]

Labour prime ministers also worried about plots. Ramsay MacDonald famously feared that MI5 was working against him. During the 1930s, Neville Chamberlain employed a former MI5 officer, Joseph Ball, to spy on both the Labour Party and his own rivals within the Conservative Party, using human agents and telephone taps. The Harold Wilson government rightly feared that a number of secret elements – both domestic and foreign – were seeking to destabilise his regime. For reasons yet unknown, Harold Macmillan had insisted that Downing Street be wired for sound to allow recording of conversations, much in the same style as the Kennedy White House. The extent to which this was used or abused during his time in office and subsequent administrations remains a mystery. The sensitivity of this subject was such that the Cabinet Office insisted that all references to it be cut out of what was otherwise a remarkably candid authorised history of MI5 published in 2009.

Harold Wilson was not the only senior figure who feared bugs. In 1973, in the final days of Edward Heath's Conservative government, William Armstrong, the head of the home civil service, turned up in the Cabinet Office and demanded to speak to the cabinet secretary somewhere that was 'not bugged'. Ushered into a suitably secure room, he took off his clothes, lay on the floor chain-smoking and talked 'very wildly' about the whole system collapsing and 'the world coming to an end'. The next day he summoned a meeting of all Whitehall permanent secretaries and told them to prepare for 'Armageddon'. 'He was babbling incoherently', and was 'taken off to hospital for treatment'. He later spent a month recovering at Lord Rothschild's private villa in Barbados. Although Wilson said almost nothing about the security services in his first volume of memoirs, penning a bizarre chapter of just two and a half pages on the subject, he later said much more to the press. Cabinet Office officials were by turns amused, embarrassed and then dismissive when these stories first appeared. But by 1979, evidence of interference by South African intelligence in London was mounting, and officials gradually came to accept that there was real substance to Wilson's fears.[20]

Wilson's public ramblings on intelligence required a new approach by Downing Street. Since the early 1960s, prime ministers had been forced to confront a new era of exposure. Now, a decade later, they had begun to manage their own gentle counter-offensive. Encouraged by the cabinet secretary, Burke Trend, with whom Wilson had enjoyed a good relationship, the intelligence agencies initiated a deliberate policy of emerging from the shadows. The Cabinet Office presided over the writing of the official history of wartime intelligence, and approved the release of the papers of Bletchley Park. This project was expressly about intelligence at the top, and traced the interaction between secrets and high strategy. Throughout the 1970s, British prime ministers were feeling their way towards a more public profile for the security agencies and their own engagement with them, pondering the possibility of public avowal of their existence and activities.

Margaret Thatcher hated this. Even as opposition leader in the late 1970s, she had repeatedly attempted to veto any public revelations about intelligence, however carefully controlled. Once she entered Downing Street, she was immediately confronted by the media frenzy surrounding the revelation that Anthony Blunt, Surveyor of the Queen's Pictures, was the 'Fourth Man'. Tasked with explaining the decision not to prosecute him, she went against her instincts and, rather than saying as little as possible, made a detailed statement to the House of Commons. She soon regretted it. Each morsel of detail was picked over, and seemed to draw out further press revelations. Now confirmed in her personal commitment to absolute secrecy, Thatcher's later years were partially defined by the absurd battle with MI5's supreme mole-hunter Peter Wright, whose *Spycatcher* memoir she sought to suppress. Her cabinet secretary endured public humiliation in the Australian courts in a futile attempt to hide what was already in the public domain.

By contrast, John Major found himself surrounded by modernisers. Not only were the intelligence chiefs of the 1990s happy to adopt an avowed legal identity, they were also keen to emerge from the shadows. In 1994 the new director-general of MI5, Stella Rimington, gave the BBC Dimbleby Lecture on 'Security and Democracy' – despite the intense unease of Home Office officials. MI6 opened an extraordinary new building at Vauxhall Cross, on the south bank of the Thames, that looked like something out of science fiction. Not to be outdone, GCHQ then commissioned its own new headquarters that looked like a flying saucer, and became the first British agency to have a presence on the internet. Yet the press still seemed determined to turn success into scandal. In 1999, when MI6 revealed the treasures of the Mitrokhin archive, compiled by a KGB archivist who had given his secrets to Britain, surely one of the most magnificent intelligence successes of the late Cold War, the press instead focused on the failure to prosecute some of the espionage 'small fry' this had revealed. Government spin doctors puzzled over how MI6 had managed to turn a golden story to ashes, and Duncan Wilson of the Cabinet Office agreed that the secret services now needed assistance from Downing Street in managing their public image.

Tony Blair exuded confidence in all areas of public affairs, including secret service. When asked about MI6 operations in Moscow he quipped to a waiting band of journalists, 'We never comment on intelligence matters ... except when we want to, obviously.'[21] Even before 9/11, his public relations team were fascinated by the media operations of MI6 and the interface between openness and secrecy. After the attacks on the World Trade Center in New York, secret matters were on the front pages of the newspapers each week during a decade-long 'War on Terror'. This raised important questions. To what extent should prime ministers place intelligence in the public domain to explain policy? And how should this be done? In two notorious Downing Street dossiers, Tony Blair and his press secretary Alastair Campbell did this badly, and paid a considerable price in terms of trust and public confidence. In the background, senior MI6 officers, some of them modernisers like Richard Dearlove and some old-school types like John Scarlett, argued over issues of public image and the proximity of their own service to Number 10. None of them had any idea how disastrously this episode would explode in their faces.

Yet David Cameron retraced Blair's footsteps. In early 2013, faced with the issue of the use of chemical weapons against its own people by the government of Syria, Cameron released JIC material to the press, going even further than Blair in the public use of intelligence. He realised that prime ministers must balance intelligence's inherent need for secrecy with their public duties leading the government. If this was an effort to reassert control and confidence, it surely failed. After Blair's Iraq fiasco, the public were deeply sceptical about intelligence as a justification for pre-emption, and Parliament voted against military action in Syria. Moreover, Downing Street was about to discover that it did not have control over what became public in this realm. Even as it agonised over the release of a two-page letter from Jon Day, the chair of the JIC, to Cameron, an unknown figure called Edward Snowden was preparing to release a deluge of secret material that amounted to thousands of documents. Much of this was British, and each remarkable revelation was more eye-wateringly secret than the last.[22]

Cameron said almost nothing about Snowden. This was because much of the material shone a harsh light on the personal interaction between premiers and espionage. In a world in which diplomacy has become increasingly personal, characterised by G7 summits and mobile-phone calls, spies and statesmen rub shoulders with increasing frequency. For wealthy and powerful states, Snowden's revelations were a story of hacked emails and rude words. GCHQ was specifically accused of hacking into the Belgian telecoms firm Belgacom, which includes EU institutions as clients. Cameron refused to answer questions about whether he had been able to reassure allies that British intelligence had not been involved in any bugging.[23] In fact, this was hardly news. Generations of British cabinet ministers have been amazed by the scale of Britain's surveillance of its European partners.[24] But what Snowden, and previously Bradley Manning, also revealed was the jostling of less powerful states, such as Chile and Mexico, which suffered not only stolen briefcases, but also bullying and bribery by the West. This rather raw business of personal espionage has now been exposed, and to the surprise of many, we have realised that James Bond often takes his orders in these delicate matters direct from the prime minister in Downing Street, rather than from 'M' in MI6 headquarters.

In the summer of 2007, the British embassy in Baghdad received five bloody index fingers through the post. They were claimed to be the body parts of five British citizens who had recently been kidnapped by a pro-Iranian offshoot of Hezbollah in Baghdad. On 29 May that year, Shia militants disguised as policemen had conducted a violent raid on the Iraqi Ministry of Finance. Their main target was Peter Moore, a British consultant who had been installing software designed to prevent fraud surrounding the billions of dollars of aid flowing into the new government's accounts. Downing Street was determined to secure Moore's release. SAS and MI6 representatives attended four separate cabinet-level security conferences to plan his rescue with ministers, and as a result special forces conducted more than two dozen house assaults seeking persons involved in the kidnap. Gordon Brown came within minutes of ordering a raid on the kidnappers, but the intelligence on their location was judged to be too thin. Eventually, in December 2009, after 946 days of captivity, Moore was swapped for Qais Khazali, a Shia militant leader, and his brother, who had been seized by the SAS on the streets of Basra at around the same time he was kidnapped. The negotiations were carried out by an MI6 officer operating in Baghdad. The other four Britons, who had served as his security guards, had all been executed the previous year.[25]

The dirtiest diplomacy is talking to terrorists, kidnappers and insurgents. This has to be deniable, since even if governments are willing to admit their part, terrorists frequently are not, and all parties ultimately fear being perceived as 'weak'. This can place prime ministers in a difficult position, potentially forcing them to mislead the House of Commons. Harold Wilson kept his MI6 back channel with the IRA incredibly secret – many in his own cabinet did not know what was going on. Similarly,

Margaret Thatcher publicly insisted that Britain did not talk to terrorists, and yet, as under her predecessors Wilson, Heath and Callaghan, various back channels remained open. In fact, Thatcher was personally involved in some exchanges. She made handwritten comments on one statement sent to the IRA as part of negotiations over the hunger strikers in 1981, and personally amended and approved Britain's negotiating position.[26] Her successor, John Major, faced a similar dilemma. Despite stating in the House of Commons that he did not negotiate with terrorists, he had approved precisely that, and his emissaries were secret service officers whom the IRA regarded as 'untouchable'. But when the secret talks leaked, Major and the IRA descended into a welter of accusation and counter-accusation, with each side publicising its version of the hitherto secret communiqués.

Bizarrely, even as Thatcher and Major talked to terrorists, they were also their top targets. Both came within inches of being eliminated by the IRA, and one of the darker stories of intelligence, security and 10 Downing Street is the ever greater level of protection required to prevent assassination. Margaret Thatcher, characteristically, had just finished rehearsing a speech with her private secretary, Robin Butler, at ten to three in the morning when a bomb destroyed a large part of the Grand Hotel in Brighton during the 1984 Conservative Party Conference. One minister recalled the security shambles in the immediate aftermath, as injured politicians made their way out of the rubble with barely a policeman in sight. Two IRA gunmen could have 'got the whole Government as they blearily emerged', and made their getaway unimpeded. The IRA also purposely eliminated two of Thatcher's closest advisers, with the assassinations of Airey Neave in 1979 and Ian Gow in 1990, bracketing her arrival and her departure from office.[27]

As a result, Downing Street was turned into a fortress. Large reinforced black gates prevented public access. Harold Wilson had resisted elaborate gates when they were suggested in 1974, but now they arrived, together with armed policemen.[28] Several levels below Downing Street, technicians were putting the final touches to 'Project Pindar', a command bunker deep beneath the Ministry of Defence on Whitehall to which selected denizens of Downing Street could retreat in times of peril, at a cost of £126.3 million.[29]

By 2005, threats against the life of the prime minister had become an almost daily occurrence. The intelligence warnings of assassination attempts often landed on the desk of David Blunkett, the home secretary, who observed with delightful *sangfroid* that these plots did not worry him unduly – unless they related to an event at which he was likely to be sitting next to Tony Blair. Towards the end of Blair's administration, simply moving outside the Whitehall government complex became a problem. Alastair Campbell gazed at the vast prime ministerial convoy of armoured vehicles proofed against nerve gas, the motorcycle outriders stopping the traffic amid a cacophony of wailing sirens, and wondered how many votes were lost every time this baroque parade of vehicles took the prime minister to the airport.

The personal threat to the prime minister is at its worst overseas. In October 2001, Blair set off on a trip to Russia, India, Pakistan, Saudi Arabia and finally Egypt. The BBC ignored security guidance and announced the prime minister's destinations to the world, thereby increasing security concerns. As a result, Blair's entourage had to be 'surrounded by outriders with machine guns and tanks carrying anti-aircraft missiles'.[30] On their return to the UK, Blair's team told the BBC director of news that Number 10 was 'exasperated by their continued reporting of his movements'.[31] Blair remains a high-profile target. In 2014, MI5 planted a listening device in the car of one terrorism suspect and listened in on his conversations for two weeks after searching the vehicle and finding Blair's home address on a scrap of paper folded inside a Versace glasses case.[32] MI5 had previously established covert surveillance of Ishaq Kanmi, the self-proclaimed leader of al-Qaeda in Britain. His stated aims included 'the elimination of political leaders and capitalists Blair and Brown'.[33] In the twenty-first century, British prime ministers value their intelligence and security services partly because they keep them alive.

No less worrying are the threats to visiting heads of state. Each premier on a state visit to Downing Street, whether from Russia, Israel, Sri Lanka or Saudi Arabia, has brought in his wake an exotic trail of would-be assassins. The grim prelude to every visit is the backstairs diplomacy of death. As the leaders make their way around London, they are shadowed by ambulances carrying copious supplies of their blood group. The most vexed discussions concern the intelligence precautions involved in each visit, with every drain and culvert along the routes taken by visiting dignitaries being searched for explosives. Defensive weaponry is an issue, with each American president asking to bring with him an increasingly formidable array of automatic weapons and ground-to-air missiles. George W. Bush was denied permission to bring an SUV containing an M134D minigun in an armoured pop-up turret. MI5 routinely regard the US president's secret service as a more dangerous threat to the British public than potential assassins.[34]

Death has hovered over Downing Street for more than a century. While attacks and plots have become steadily more serious in recent years, enterprising amateurs have always abounded, and earlier prime ministers were more accessible to the public. On 28 August 1939, panic swept through a crowd of protesters immediately outside the door of 10 Downing Street when a London clerk called Laurence Hislam opened a small suitcase and scattered its contents, which resembled the deadly devices beloved of bearded bomb-throwing anarchists. Mayhem ensued, until the crowd realised that the 'bombs' were actually large black rubber balls inscribed with the message 'Peace Conference Now'. Hislam was in fact a pacifist protesting against the mounting international crisis and the spectre of another major war in Europe. The police led him away, and despite his defence that he acted 'in the cause of peace', the court sentenced him to six months' hard labour.[35]

No prime minister illustrates this interface between premiers and personal hazard more than Churchill. Britain's wartime leader accepted the advice of the Special Operations Executive that assassinating Hitler would be counter-productive, since his strategy was increasingly incompetent and damaging to Germany. However, in 1943 Churchill did approve an assassination attempt against Mussolini, with female agents being dropped into Italy, together with aggressive kill missions against Rommel and other senior German generals. Meanwhile, lesser fascists were earmarked for mere bribery, with an initial £100,000 personally approved by Churchill and then passed over in a large bag to members of Franco's circle on a Spanish golf course as an inducement to keep Spain out of the Second World War.[36] Eden was appalled by the operation, but when more money was required for Franco, Churchill eagerly minuted in red ink: 'Yes Indeed. WSC.'[37]

Britain's wartime leader was oddly relaxed about his own personal safety, despite more than a dozen serious attempts on his life. Hitler certainly ordered his multiple secret services to target Churchill, the oddest such operation being a plot to attack Allied leaders at the Tehran Conference in 1943 using a team of Nazi agents transported by camel.[38] Much of Churchill's remarkable ability to survive the attempts on his life must be attributed to good fortune and his ever-vigilant bodyguard, Detective Inspector Walter Thompson. Occasionally Churchill insisted on carrying his own revolver, but for the most part brazen and carefree with only a single bodyguard, he travelled over 200,000 miles across Europe, America and the Middle East in the course of the war. No British prime minister will ever do that again, so in many ways Churchill stands at the turning point of security and intelligence in Downing Street, representing both the first of a new wave of premiers who exploited intelligence properly, but also the last of a dying breed.

Nineteen prime ministers have led Britain since 1909. From Herbert Asquith to David Cameron and from Ramsay MacDonald to Gordon Brown, these premiers have held diverging political views, possessed wildly different leadership styles, and have confronted the full spectrum of problems, threats and crises. This book examines each prime minister in turn. It traces their personal approaches to intelligence and uses each premiership as a vehicle to explore the most pressing national security issues of the day. It reveals that despite the vagaries of personality and politics, intelligence has become increasingly central to all prime ministers. This was not always the case. Back in the first decade of the twentieth century, the secret world was alien to Asquith. Churchill and Attlee addressed this problem together, and forged a quiet revolution. Now, as a result, David Cameron presides personally over an organised intelligence community operating at the heart of Whitehall. This book traces that secret service journey from the periphery to the centre of power.

PART ONE

CREATING SECRET SERVICE

1

Herbert Asquith, David Lloyd George and Andrew Bonar Law (1908–1923)

A rumour spread next day in true war-time fashion that Lord Chetwynd had caught three German spies trying to signal the Zeppelin with lights, and had shot them out of hand.
DAVID LLOYD GEORGE[1]

The British intelligence system was already immense by the dawn of the twentieth century. The entire British Empire, sprawling across more than half the globe, served as an intelligence machine – a veritable 'empire of intelligence'.[2] It depended on information of every kind to project British rule in remote places. Romanticised in the works of Rudyard Kipling, intelligence was about amateur imperial adventurers, revelling in deceit and subterfuge. Unlike today, espionage was conducted informally by local agents, eccentric travellers and scholars. Lawrence of Arabia and the legendary team of British archaeologist-spies at Carchemish, working across the Turkey–Syria border, typified the way great-power rivalry in the Middle East and Asia mixed with academic debates about how archaeology might change understandings of the Bible. Importantly, scholarly research was not merely a cover for secret service work. Intelligence was considered to be every kind of information, including that obtained by peculiar scholars who spoke many languages, collected eggs, bulbs and butterflies, and mixed 'comfortably and innocently' with the local population. Indeed, at the turn of the twentieth century, British officials in Mesopotamia feared an archaeologist-gap and urged the India Office to contact learned societies which could send more scholar-spies to buttress British interests.[3] India itself, the vast jewel of the empire, depended on spies too. It became an extraordinary 'empire of information', allowing just over a thousand British civil servants to superintend close to 280 million people.[4]

An empire of information, in some form, existed at home too. New public health initiatives and social programmes meant the state knew much more about its people than ever before. Meanwhile Irish nationalists and bomb-throwing anarchists from the Continent had forced the Metropolitan Police to develop the world's first 'Special Branch' in 1883. Inevitably perhaps, by the first decade of the twentieth century, Special Branch had broadened its net beyond Fenians and anarchists to collect intelligence on possible foreign spies, anti-colonial agitators, suffragettes, union leaders, pacifists, and even those with radical views on sex.[5]

Nevertheless, these developments were more about keeping authoritarian surveillance at arm's length from the British public. Mysterious battles with Russian spies in Central Asia were reassuringly remote, while the creation of a small Special Branch of intrepid detectives to counter terrorism was seen as a low-key alternative to the sort of harsh and repressive security legislation preferred in Europe. Accordingly, intelligence remained a matter for distant vice-consuls travelling to Samarkand, or detective sergeants in Whitechapel. It rarely resonated at the centre of British government. More rarely still did a prime minister take a personal interest in espionage.

All this began to change over the next decade. Bizarrely, it was literary fashion which drove the transformation of British intelligence, thrusting it towards the heart of government for the first time. A wave of popular Edwardian 'invasion literature' forced Herbert Asquith, an otherwise uninterested Liberal prime minister more focused on progressive domestic reforms, to take notice of foreign espionage. Acting only under pressure, Asquith set in train a course which would fundamentally alter the landscape of British intelligence forever. The intelligence revolution may have been forged by Churchill and Attlee, but the first sparks came through the unlikely Asquith. Nonetheless, despite the expansion of espionage during the First World War and greater interest on the part of Asquith's successor David Lloyd George, it took time and endless trouble before successive prime ministers learned to use intelligence effectively.

Fiction paved the long pathway to the creation of a modern British intelligence service. During the nineteenth century, a stream of often sensational crime novels fed a growing public fascination with detection, police work and science. This generated cultural change, gradually eroding anxieties about government surveillance. Created by writers as diverse as Edgar Allan Poe and Arthur Conan Doyle, fictional detectives gradually became heroic figures to be worshipped, rather than bogeymen associated with distasteful and un-British authoritarianism.[6] Journalists, who often exchanged information with real policemen, accelerated this transformation, helping to create real-life detectives who enjoyed a similar cult status.[7] William Melville, who became head of Special Branch, was one example. He famously foiled several anarchist attacks, including the 'Jubilee plot' against Queen Victoria in 1887 and another dastardly scheme known as the 'Walsall plot', in which anarchists from the West Midlands sought to manufacture a bomb. Many now believe that he created the latter plot himself for mere self-glorification.[8]

Over three hundred spy novels went into print between 1901 and 1914, mostly focused on the 'German Menace'. This new fiction effectively rebranded itself as a barely concealed form of 'true crime' writing, supposedly based on the patriotic leaking of government secrets. In 1903, Erskine Childers published *The Riddle of the Sands*, which narrated the summer sailing adventures of two young British men along the East Frisian coast who stumble upon a German plot to invade England with a flotilla of barges. Childers claimed to be offering the British people nothing less than a warning of what was to come, and Rudyard Kipling urged the public to support him in taking a firm stand against the 'shameless Hun'.[9] The story was improbable – the German admiralty had long written off the possibility of an invasion from East Frisia – but the hapless Royal Navy was forced to investigate the claims regardless.[10]

Members of Parliament from constituencies on the east coast, the closest part of Britain to Germany, bombarded the First Lord of the Admiralty, Lord Selborne, with difficult questions. In response, he ordered the Naval Intelligence Division to write a detailed report on the invasion plan outlined by Childers. After reconnaissance of the Frisian coast, the report concluded that the lack of railways and roads, together with the shallowness of the water and general lack of facilities, made a secret invasion from there impossible. 'As a novel it is excellent; as a war plan it is rubbish,' insisted Lord Louis Battenberg, the director of naval intelligence. To Childers' barely disguised delight, the Kaiser banned the book in Germany. Childers also claimed that when he next went sailing in the Baltic, German spies dogged his every move.[11]

Spy fiction developed a darker side, shifting its focus closer to home, portraying immigrants and foreign visitors as the hidden hand of subversion. The new trope was Germans as a hidden fifth column already *within* Britain. Most active of all was a mischievous thriller-writer called William le Queux. He almost single-handedly created a fifth-column panic and then demanded the creation of a domestic security service to combat the undercover 'German Menace', with which the day of reckoning would surely come.[12] Le Queux's *The Invasion of 1910* became the most influential of these books. Published in 1906, it told of German armies overrunning the country with the help of spies and saboteurs. Le Queux admitted to a political purpose, explaining his intention to illustrate how poorly British defences would stand up to this sort of sneak attack. He also insisted that the content of his book was factually correct, and had been informed by conversations with 'the authorities'.[13]

William le Queux posed as an international espionage expert, but was in fact nothing of the sort. Instead, he was a tireless and well-paid pulp-fiction writer who produced five novels a year until his death in 1927.[14] *The Invasion of 1910* sold more than a million copies, and publicists at the *Daily Mail*, which possessed serialisation rights, sent columns of men marching up Oxford Street dressed in Prussian uniforms, complete with bloodstained gloves, carrying sandwich boards that advertised the book.[15] An inevitable flood of literary emulators hit the presses as le Queux's royalties rolled in. Not to be outdone, le Queux responded in 1909 with *Spies of the Kaiser*, which insisted that no fewer than 5,000 German undercover operatives were at work in Britain. This was a new idea. A whole undercover army, not just a few spies and saboteurs, were apparently biding their time until the Fatherland told them to retrieve their weapons from a series of arms dumps in the British countryside. No less important, the novel also claimed to offer the inside story of intrepid British detectives working with agents to uncover these foreign networks.[16]

The British public were whipped into a frenzy. Politicians who wanted to expand Britain's relatively small peacetime army jumped on the bandwagon. In 1908 Lord Roberts, Britain's most distinguished soldier, claimed there were 80,000 trained undercover German soldiers in England ready to assist in the event of an invasion.[17] Newspapers offered £10 to members of the public who reported sightings of suspicious activities that they could pass on to le Queux so he could 'supplement his investigations'. Unsurprisingly, they were inundated with information, and soon it seemed a supposed German saboteur had been spotted in every town in the land,[18] including some unfortunate Foreign Office clerical staff holidaying on the east coast.[19] The government was annoyed by the obvious political scheming by advocates of increased arms spending. In 1906, Asquith's predecessor as prime minister, Henry Campbell-

Bannerman, rose to his feet in Parliament to denounce le Queux as a 'pernicious scaremonger' whose stories risked provoking an unnecessary war with Germany.[20]

Despite prime ministerial condemnation, several key figures in government worked hand in glove with le Queux. James Edmonds, head of a fledgling military intelligence unit called MO(5), maintained that Berlin had an extensive ring of operatives in Britain. Edmonds had long been nagging a dismissive Richard Haldane, secretary of state for war under both Campbell-Bannerman and Asquith, about the shortcomings of British counter-espionage. He therefore found le Queux's activities more than welcome.[21] Indeed, much of the evidence that he presented to his masters came from le Queux, who in turn said that he had received it from concerned members of the public. There had only been five cases of German espionage reported in 1907, but unsurprisingly by 1908 this had risen to forty-eight. Edmonds created a helpful map of agent sightings. Perhaps equally unsurprisingly, this was soon leaked to the press. He also recruited William Melville, the former head of Special Branch, who while a talented agent-runner, had a reputation for embellishing his stories.[22]

By 1909, nefarious German agents were apparently hiding behind almost every bush in Britain. Asquith, however, had other things on his mind. His overwhelming, and rather challenging, priority was to take on and reform the House of Lords, which had consistently blocked his progressive agenda. The time and energy he devoted to this issue only increased further when the Lords famously rejected his government's budget in 1909. But with the public suffering from spy-fever, the prime minister now had to take note of intelligence matters. As chancellor of the exchequer and in his early months as prime minister, Asquith had already chaired a senior committee to consider the invasion threat in response to pressure from Roberts and le Queux. His report demolished their theories, and showed a surprise attack to be impossible.[23] Nonetheless, still under immense public pressure, in 1909 Asquith asked the Committee of Imperial Defence to consider the danger of foreign agents operating in the UK. All this accelerated an important cultural change away from the idea that counter-espionage at home was authoritarian and un-British.[24]

Although flawed and bogus intelligence reports shaped its ultimate findings, Asquith swiftly sanctioned the committee's recommendation to establish a new Secret Service Bureau. This top-secret decision – very few people knew about the bureau's existence – fundamentally altered the landscape of British intelligence forever. British espionage was nothing new, but its formalisation and growing proximity to Downing Street marked the beginning of a more organised and centralised intelligence system. It was not yet, though, an intelligence community linked to Downing Street, and early prime ministers remained unable or unwilling to engage with the secret world particularly closely.

The Secret Service Bureau was comprised of two branches. MO5(g) was the domestic branch, responsible for counter-espionage, and would soon come to be known as 'MI5', or the security service. It inherited a number of army counter-intelligence officers, and was led by Captain Vernon Kell, deputy to James Edmonds at MO(5). Kell went on to serve continuously in the role for more than twenty years. Ever present around intelligence matters for nearly half a century, Winston Churchill, as home secretary, oversaw Kell's appointment. Adding a symmetry to Kell's long career as spymaster, Churchill, when prime minister, would remove him from office in 1940.[25] The Secret Service Bureau also had a foreign branch. Initially called MI1c, it soon restyled itself MI6, and was headed by the remarkable figure of Sir Mansfield Cumming, a retired naval officer. Despite losing his leg in a traffic accident in France, Cumming continued to run MI6, speeding down the corridors of Whitehall by planting his wooden leg firmly on a modified child's scooter. MI5 was a small organisation and MI6 even smaller, but a key change had occurred. Hitherto, individual government departments, especially the India Office, had gathered intelligence locally and conducted espionage for their own purposes. Now Whitehall had an interdepartmental intelligence machine at the centre, delivering a 'service' to all government departments and anointed with the cult of specialness.[26]

After 1909, Asquith's government went further. Harassed by continued public concern about nefarious German activities, it introduced the trappings of a secret state that previous successive governments had resisted for a century. Between 1909 and 1911, Asquith not only created the Secret Service Bureau, but also passed a draconian Official Secrets Act and allowed for much wider mail interception, something a Liberal government had banned as a diabolical infringement of liberties some fifty years before.[27] The new Official Secrets Act, encouraged by Edmonds of MO(5), also helped the government to crack down on the press.[28] Asquith, a facilitator rather than a dictatorial prime minister, also set up a new committee under Winston Churchill to consider how Britain would tackle 'Aliens in Time of War'. With foreigners and exiles at the heart of this scare, the government created a register of aliens living in Britain. By 1913, it would have 11,000 Germans on this list, and had already prepared internment legislation.[29] Notwithstanding domestic spy-fever, on the eve of the First World War much British intelligence activity lay elsewhere. Intrepid consuls, attachés and military officers carried out most of the spying on German armament programmes, while MI6 relied on the collection of specialist journals by travellers, or open observations, rather than actual espionage. Despite a lack of coordinated assessment, this material gradually filtered up into the higher reaches of government and influenced Britain's diplomatic and strategic behaviour.[30]

The most immediate physical threat to Asquith came not from swarms of German spies, but from other quarters, notably the suffragette movement. In September 1909, two women were busy improving their shooting skills at a rifle range at 92 Tottenham Court Road with the rather improbable name of 'Fairyland'. They intended to assassinate the prime minister, who was a firm opponent of votes for women. The two would-be assassins planned to join a group of suffragettes who had been picketing the gates of Parliament for eight weeks. Asquith passed them frequently, and therefore presented a tempting close-range target. Fortunately for the prime minister, the police received a tip-off. The informant was a Mrs Moore, a member of the Women's Freedom League, but also a close friend of Asquith's sister-in-law. She was an advocate of peaceful protest, and spent a great deal of time trying to dissuade her fellow suffragettes from violent acts.

Moore produced a letter from one of the two women who had been practising with a revolver.[31] She refused to name names, but the police made enquiries at the shooting range, whose owner, Henry Morley, told them that two suffragettes had indeed been practising with a Browning automatic pistol. Their alarm was increased by the knowledge that the same range, and the same type of pistol, had been used only months earlier by an assassin who had killed Sir William Curzon-Wylie, aide to the secretary of state for India. Although undercover officers hung about for some days afterwards, neither woman returned. This left Asquith's government with a dilemma familiar to later administrations dealing with terrorist threats. They knew full well that there would be serious recriminations if they did nothing and the prime minister was assassinated. The police did not remove the protesters from outside Parliament, but increased the number of officers there instead. They did not wish to give prominence to the idea of assassination, fearing that publicity might 'act on the minds of these half-insane women, and might suggest effectively the commission of the very act which we wish to prevent'. Moreover, the removal of the pickets would be looked on by the women as an act of violence and injustice, and would 'make them furious and more ready to commit such a crime'. In addition, the government thought that if there was an assassin, it would be easier to stop her if police knew she would be amongst the picketers, rather than walking 'up and down between the House of Parliament and Downing Street at the hour when the P.M. may be expected to drive down'. Thanks to Mrs Moore, the prime minister remained able to pass in and out of Parliament unscathed.[32] Recent research shows that the suffragettes included some notably dangerous groups, who fire-bombed churches and later sent a letter-bomb to Lloyd George. Some of the more violent women would go on to become active supporters of the extreme right, including Oswald Mosley's blackshirts.[33] Yet, remarkably, Asquith and all his successors through to the Second World War remained largely unprotected.

It was an act of assassination that finally triggered the outbreak of war in August 1914. Intelligence now had a more crucial – and real – role to play. The new secret services quickly pounced upon the small German espionage network in London, and rounded up all twenty-two known agents. The authorities had been assiduously following this spy ring, run from a barber shop in London by a naturalised German, since 1911. In an early intelligence success story, close monitoring had prevented the ring from passing useful information on to Berlin. Several hundred people were placed under surveillance. Predictably, the biggest problem was public paranoia. In the first two weeks of the war, the Metropolitan Police were forced to investigate thousands of people, with little to show for it. The newspapers followed this eagerly, and noted with satisfaction that by the end of November 1914 there had been over 100,000 reports of espionage, with 6,000 homes entered and searched.

Popular enthusiasm for war, combined with paranoia about spies, forced the Asquith government to look tough. Eleven German spies were shot at the Tower of London, a location chosen for its sinister appearance and reputation. More people were executed there during the First World War than under the Tudors. The amateurish German spies were not difficult to capture. They used lemon juice and peppermint oil instead of ink to render their reports to Berlin invisible, but were often arrested in possession of pen nibs corroded by the acidic lemon juice.[34] Such tales allowed le Queux to continue to pump out his pulp-fiction spy thrillers.

He maintained his phoney reputation as a spymaster to the end, and even now some of his relatives insist that he was assassinated by Russian agents in 1927.[35]

No one was safe from the paranoid public. Not even Charles Rennie Mackintosh, the Scottish architect and designer, who dared to sketch in the Suffolk village of Walberswick, close to the sea; or the composer Ralph Vaughan Williams, who sat down with a notebook to write 'The Lark Ascending' on cliffs near Margate. Both attracted vigorous police attention. Any Continental connection became a form of contagion. A Polish girl, who was a friend of the Asquith family, was fired from her teaching job simply out of fear that she might be mistaken for a German spy.[36] The Asquith government stepped up internment, rounding up some 60,000 Germans living in Britain.[37] Under popular pressure, and perhaps against his better judgement, the prime minister personally emphasised that all non-naturalised adult males 'should, for their own safety, and that of the community, be segregated and interned, or, if over military age, repatriated'.[38]

The First World War triggered Britain's tangible intelligence changes. MI5 had only fifteen staff prior to the conflict, but it soon expanded. The Post Office also assumed an intelligence function. It grew into a Censor's Office that employed over 2,000 officials, each steaming, scanning and resealing some 150 letters per day. Britain now boasted a serious domestic surveillance apparatus.[39] By the last year of the war, censorship employed 4,871 people, a sizeable engine of surveillance.[40] In the empire, MI5 worked closely with security agencies in Delhi to thwart German plots to promote revolts amongst imperial subjects. With good intelligence to hand, Asquith's government allowed the German Foreign Ministry to continue its ludicrously ambitious plans to promote insurrection on the subcontinent, content that they were unlikely to succeed.[41]

Overseas, MI6 remained weak. The majority of important international intelligence instead came from a revival of codebreaking. For at least a decade before 1914, the War Office had plans to recreate a codebreaking centre if a military crisis occurred, and both the army and navy did so independently in August 1914. Although they initially cooperated, differences developed in both personality and approach, rendering any harmony short-lived. Nonetheless, they still managed to break German, French and American codes, alongside a host of other streams of high-level communications. Starting from scratch in 1914, this was an amazing feat. The Admiralty's famous codebreaking unit, codenamed 'Room 40', was the more effective; directed by Reginald 'Blinker' Hall, it pioneered many of the scientific methods used by Bletchley Park two decades later.[42]

The First World War may have transformed British intelligence collection, but Asquith still took little interest. The prime minister was in fact deeply uninterested in war, strategy or intelligence, although he found time for bridge, lavish dinner parties and country weekends. He was not lacking in energy or application, but his focus was elsewhere, not least on his mistress Venetia Stanley, more than thirty years his junior. Asquith wrote to her over five hundred times during his period as war leader, sometimes as often as three times a day. The qualities that had made him a good peacetime prime minister were unhelpful in wartime. He was an affable chairman of the board, able to reconcile differences of opinion and find compromises. But he failed to appreciate the value of some of his partners in the wartime Liberal–Conservative coalition, and above all he failed to take hard decisions that were required for the vigorous prosecution of the war. He offered little guidance and support to the military, which was then led by Field Marshal Lord Kitchener.[43]

Intelligence proved important in the context of Ireland. Again, however, Asquith seemed broadly unaware of troubling developments, and instead engaged intermittently with particular incidents. The British had failed to properly penetrate the dissident movement, so human sources inside Ireland were few, and their reports fragmented and contradictory.[44] Consequently, little warning of the 1916 Easter Rising came through these channels. Room 40 provided more solid intelligence. Decrypted secret German cables from America gave important intelligence on the international activities of Irish nationalists, including details relating to the Rising, during which Berlin assisted the exiled Irish nationalist Roger Casement in fomenting rebellion. Casement's dealings were not news to the prime minister. Although the flow of intelligence to Downing Street was patchy, Asquith had enjoyed a stream of incriminating material on Casement.[45] What appeared to be an intelligence bonanza turned out to have come from an untrustworthy source, Casement's bisexual manservant and lover, who was 'a liar, a blackmailer and a fantasist'. When Casement found out about his betrayal he publicly (but falsely) alleged a British plot to murder him. Although the incident embarrassed Asquith's government, it was enough for MI5 to open a file on Casement and unearth more details of his nationalist scheming – and ultimately his German connections.[46]

Room 40 intercepted more than thirty cables dealing with German assistance to Ireland during the first two years of the war.[47] The codebreakers not only gave full warning of the Easter Rising, but also revealed Germany's plans to send weapons to Ireland in an attempt to divert British attention from the Western Front, allowing the Royal Navy to intercept a German U-boat carrying Casement to Ireland and the arms shipment to be captured. The signals intelligence, though, was only sent to a small military circle. It seemingly did not reach the politicians, even Asquith.[48] Nor did it reach the authorities in Dublin. The sorry episode reflects the perennial problem of using signals intelligence: it is difficult to do so without compromising the source, thereby leading to a reluctance to share, even inside Westminster. More intriguingly, there is evidence that the British authorities deliberately allowed the Easter Rising to go ahead in order to justify repression of the Irish dissidents. Under interrogation, Casement offered to publicly call off the rebellion, but this was declined. Instead, he was told that 'it's a festering sore', and it was 'much better it should come to a head'.[49] Either way, the Easter Rising failed.

Despite the work of Room 40, Asquith experienced the rebellion as 'a real bolt from the blue' – albeit one with a 'comic side'.[50] His wife Margot confessed in her diary that 'none of us had any idea what had really happened'.[51] Upon hearing the news of the Easter Rising, and in the midst of a conscription crisis, the prime minister simply said, 'Well, that's something,' and went to bed. Intelligence seemingly had little impact in Number 10. Such nonchalance belies Asquith's growing interest in Irish affairs, which had been a key issue in the months prior to war. He subsequently took on the office of Irish secretary himself, and headed off to Dublin to try unsuccessfully to sort things out.[52] General John Maxwell, appointed by Asquith to force a military solution on a political problem, drew on Special Branch intelligence to persuade the prime minister that the case against every executed rebel leader had been overwhelming.[53]

They included Roger Casement. Partly because signals intelligence had thoroughly convinced the authorities of his treacherous links with Germany, Casement was hanged in Dublin in August 1916. To counter calls for clemency, the 'Casement Diaries', containing what were regarded as shocking descriptions of Casement's homosexual exploits, were leaked by Blinker Hall to influence the trial. Previously, many Irish nationalists had mistakenly insisted that these diaries were forgeries.[54] This episode underlines the long history of the selective use of intelligence to influence public opinion.

Meanwhile, the seemingly directionless war strategy left the cabinet unimpressed. Discontent also arose over the quality of information reaching them. Asquith had formed an ultimately unpopular coalition government, with Andrew Bonar Law as his Tory partner. In early September 1915, Bonar Law pressed the prime minister to make changes to the leadership of the war effort. He sought the resurrection of a General Staff at the War Office, with the hope that this would result in better strategic advice to cabinet. Nothing was done until 22 September, when Kitchener was conveniently absent. The Tories then took the lead and insisted on a smaller and more active War Council, together with the provision of better intelligence to cabinet by the General Staff. Asquith was finally forced to write to Kitchener, insisting on an improved flow of intelligence to the centre. He appointed General Archibald Murray as the new Chief of the Imperial General Staff, but beyond that none of the suggested reforms were implemented, and Asquith did not follow up on the cabinet's requests for more intelligence.[55]

The Asquith coalition government disintegrated in late 1916, as a result of its own incompetence and disorder. Lacking personal authority, Asquith had spent much of his time assembling factions and alliances. There was little planning, and astonishingly, letters sent by the prime minister to the King after each meeting formed the only record of cabinet discussions. When Bonar Law joined the coalition in 1915 he had been amazed by the lack of any method or even agenda for cabinet meetings. The failure of the Gallipoli campaign at the start of 1916 accelerated the decline of the Asquith government. Mercifully for the war effort, in June 1916 Lord Kitchener, the aged secretary of state for war, died at sea off the Orkneys in mysterious circumstances, an event that many attributed to a bewildering mixture of German, Irish or Russian saboteurs. He was replaced by the energetic David Lloyd George. At the end of the year, however, both Asquith and Lloyd George resigned in short order, while Bonar Law declined to form a government. Lloyd George became head of a new coalition two days later, establishing a Supreme War Council. Neither Asquith nor Bonar Law was mentally equipped to handle the range of decisions required by modern war. The main challenge for Lloyd George, now and for the rest of the war, was to try to wrest strategic control of the conflict from the military chiefs, a task that he never quite completed.[56]

Asquith had been notably detached from the business of war. He may have presided over the creation of the Secret Service Bureau and the rapid expansion of every kind of intelligence after 1914, but it had interested him very little. By contrast, in December 1916, David Lloyd George became the first prime minister to embrace intelligence, albeit often in an amateurish manner. This was partly to do with his nature, for he was by temperament a man of enormous energy and sudden impulses. But his initial mistakes also reflected the fact that British intelligence lacked a central brain. No system existed for sifting and interpreting intelligence for top policymakers. Despite a quantum leap in the organisation of Downing Street, and the creation of the Cabinet Office in late 1916, intelligence was deliberately left out. As a result, Lloyd George lacked context and made emotional responses to the raw intelligence he received – with unhappy results.[57]

His previous interactions with intelligence had been in the context of the ongoing spy-mania. In May 1915, as minister of munitions, he sought to confront the problem of factory explosions. Such disasters were almost invariably the result of primitive manufacturing processes, running at maximum capacity, which did not privilege safety. Like many others, however, Lloyd George was obsessed with the danger of the German 'hidden hand', and blamed saboteurs. His staff were allowed to set up a counter-intelligence unit to ferret out these imaginary enemies. Given the name P.M.S.2, it failed to find any spies, and slowly shifted its attention to trade union activity in the munitions factories.[58]

Lloyd George later admitted that he and some of his friends had deliberately encouraged rumours of saboteurs within the British munitions programme. This included the vast shell-filling factory at Chilwell on the banks of the River Trent in Nottingham, the largest concentration of high explosives anywhere in Britain. In January 1916, a Zeppelin was reported to be hunting up and down the Trent, supposedly hoping to bomb the factory. The next day, rumours circulated that Lloyd George's friend Lord Chetwynd, who ran the huge complex, had caught three German spies in the act of trying to guide the Zeppelin to its target with hand-held torches and had shot them. Chetwynd exploited the false rumour by asking a labourer to dig three graves on the hillside by night, placing an anonymous black post at the head of each. This, recalled Lloyd George, 'turned the rumour into unquestioned history' and discouraged the curious from prying around the factory. Predictably, when it suffered a catastrophic explosion later in the war, it was blamed on yet more spies.[59]

In late 1916, shortly before Lloyd George became prime minister, the Germans asked the American ambassador in Berlin to explain to President Woodrow Wilson that they were 'anxious to make peace'. But they did not wish to appear weak, so they secretly asked the United States, which was then neutral, to make a 'spontaneous' offer of mediation. Unfortunately for Germany, Britain's Room 40 had decrypted the American message. When Lloyd George read it, he wrongly assumed that it signified collaboration between America and Germany. With the cabinet in disarray, and lacking intelligence-assessment machinery, the impulsive Lloyd George decided to act alone. He warned the American press against interference by Washington, and asserted that the war must be a 'fight to the finish'. In reality, President Wilson was immersed in an election campaign and had no interest in peace initiatives at this point. Either way, diplomacy was not Lloyd George's responsibility. When rebuked by the foreign secretary for meddling, he used the decrypts to defend himself. Far worse, he also alluded to secret information when explaining his actions in Parliament. Even as he assumed office in Downing Street in December 1916, more decrypts crossed his desk which he wrongly – and amateurishly – assumed suggested that the Kaiser and Wilson were still working together. This was not an auspicious beginning, and pointed to a wider failure around the assessment of intelligence at the centre of government.[60]

Lloyd George brought his undoubted talents for planning and organisation to the highest level of government. The most important part of this reform was the creation of a professional secretariat by Maurice Hankey, a former Royal Marine officer who became the first cabinet secretary. His background was in intelligence – as a junior officer assigned to HMS *Ramillies*, the flagship of the Mediterranean Fleet, he had engaged in unofficial reconnaissance. By 1902, he had joined the staff of the Naval Intelligence Department in Whitehall. An outstanding officer who spoke many languages, he was the perfect administrator. In 1909, he had written a report for the Committee of Imperial Defence that proposed a Secret Service Bureau.[61] Now, in the newly created Cabinet Office, he was joined by Thomas Jones. Once described as 'a disguised Bolshevik whom Lloyd George had discovered somewhere in a Welsh coal pit', Jones was nevertheless an equally formidable organiser. It is difficult to capture the chaos that surrounded cabinet affairs before their arrival, and it is no exaggeration to say that they invented modern cabinet government.[62]

Hankey's reforms were a triumph. They became central to the development of a modern British interdepartmental coordination system, with its labyrinthine sub-committees and orderly minutes focused on Downing Street. Cabinet meetings were no longer rambling conversations amongst twenty-three people, with no agenda. Instead, they became businesslike discussions at which decisions were made and properly recorded. Yet the reforms were a tragedy for secret service. Hankey created a central mechanism for everything except intelligence. Jones, his deputy, recalled that he had been insistent that the new Cabinet Secretariat should not become 'an Intelligence department',[63] and although the design of the war cabinet at first envisaged 'a comprehensive and regular gathering of intelligence', this never happened.[64] The lack of a central clearing house for assessing intelligence had been a constant criticism of government for some time, so while Hankey is celebrated as a moderniser of the government machine, he simultaneously retarded the British intelligence community by twenty years. The idea of a central intelligence machine located alongside Downing Street had to await a further world war, and the arrival of Winston Churchill as premier.[65]

Lloyd George's personal record as a user of decrypts did not improve during the war. He was often left to deduce the story from individual intercepts, or 'flimsies' as they were called, because of the thin paper on which they were recorded, that arrived without context or comment. He was also given little guidance on the need for security. Thus in February 1917, when the American ambassador, Walter Page, visited Downing Street to convey a message from President Wilson, the prime minister could not restrain himself. He boasted that he had already seen Wilson's message, attributing this to a leak. Page thought it possible that the telegram had been obtained by a 'British spy service' from an unreliable American official. In any case, knowing Wilson's hatred of leaks, he did not inform Washington. Indeed, the president was obsessively secretive, and actually insisted on deciphering his more sensitive telegrams himself, sometimes with the help of his wife. The realisation that Lloyd George was reading his every word would not have endeared London to him.[66]

Surprisingly, even as Lloyd George put their work in peril, British codebreakers delivered the greatest intelligence coup of the First World War. They had intercepted what would soon become famous as the 'Zimmermann telegram'. In this amazing message, Germany's foreign minister, Arthur Zimmermann, promised Mexico the reward of three of America's southern states if she joined the German cause and declared war on her northern neighbour, the US. The message was one of the most secret of the war, and was supposed to have been taken by safe hand on a German submarine. But the vessel broke down before leaving port, forcing Berlin to trust the safety of its ciphers.

The Zimmermann telegram is a rare example of a single piece of intelligence changing the course of history. The way in which the British exposed it was elegant, but had nothing to do with Downing Street. Instead, it was a cooperative venture between Room 40 and the Foreign Office – and perhaps for that reason it was not bungled. Lloyd George, doubtless kept abreast given his strong interest in American orientations, was a mere observer. President Woodrow Wilson had won his recent election campaign on the slogan 'He kept us out of war'. But, provoked by the Zimmermann telegram, alongside Berlin's aggressive submarine policy, he declared war on Germany in April 1917.[67] In his memoirs, Lloyd George records his gratitude to the codebreakers of Room 40 and their 'uncanny efficiency in the unearthing of German secrets'.[68]

By the end of the war everyone seemed to be aware of the British secret service. The famous German philosopher Hannah Arendt, for example, was fascinated by the rise of Britain's professional spies. She wrote that after the First World War, British secret services 'began to attract England's best sons, who preferred serving mysterious forces all over the world to serving the common good of their country', adding that as a result 'the stage seemed to be set for all possible horrors'. However, she noted that with the British, unlike the Russians and Germans, 'a minimum of human rights was always safeguarded'.[69] Bertolt Brecht wrote that Britain controlled detective fiction and also controlled the world, clearly feeling that these two things were connected in some subterranean way.[70]

Room 40 was created as a wartime emergency. Nevertheless, its product proved too valuable for it to disband once the guns fell silent, and in peacetime Britain continued to read the secret communications of many countries. As the armistice talks opened in France, President Wilson sent his trusted confidant Colonel Edward House to join the negotiations. Lloyd George was able to read everything sent between House and Wilson. Yet strangely he had not been bitten by the intelligence bug, and useful as he found it, was not an enthusiast. Intelligence spending dwindled dramatically after the war, and the prime minister was happy to leave the reorganisation of peacetime intelligence matters to his cabinet colleagues. Accordingly, although Lloyd George established a governmental committee to review secret service in 1919, he did not join it. Instead, Churchill, an avid intelligence enthusiast, was the leading light in this important reordering.[71] Its most important decision would be to maintain the wartime codebreaking effort and focus all resources in one unit: the Government Code and Cypher School, or GC&CS.[72]

Nonetheless, in February 1920, Lloyd George was required to revisit intelligence matters. He sought to end the festering conflict with the Bolsheviks, viewing Britain's support for the White Russians as an unhappy extension of the First World War, and therefore a chapter that should now be closed. Although reluctant to offer recognition to the revolutionaries, the prime minister offered Moscow trade agreements as a path to restoring relations. His cabinet colleagues Churchill and Curzon were horrified, not least because of mounting evidence of Bolshevik subversion against the British Empire. Indeed, although there was clear evidence of Soviet funds going directly to the increasingly communist-dominated Labour Research Department during the early 1920s, it was Moscow's interference in areas such as India that really got the British cabinet excited.[73] MI6 had been active in this clandestine conflict too, and many military intelligence officers who had been heavily involved in the Russian Civil War were also dismayed.[74]

Once more, Lloyd George had access to his opponents' decrypts. Not for the last time, a British leader was able to read the derogatory terms in which his opposite numbers discussed him. Lenin denounced the prime minister as a deceiving 'swine' and a man without scruples, and urged the Soviet trade delegation in London to repay him with even greater levels of deception. This, of course, was difficult, given that every line of Lenin's instructions was being decoded by the British. Lloyd George declared himself 'unruffled by Bolshevik intrigues', which he considered amateurish and unimportant. He was also prepared to turn a blind eye to the war between Russia and Poland that developed in late 1919. But Moscow was a highly political and divisive issue, and by early 1920, some senior military chiefs had begun to question Lloyd George's motives. On 15 January General Henry Wilson, the Chief of the Imperial General Staff, wrote in his diary: 'I keep wondering if L.G. is a traitor & a Bolshevist, & I will watch him very carefully.' Wilson was especially paranoid about Bolshevik plots, and made several similar entries to the same effect over the next few months.[75]

The activities of Soviet negotiators in Britain were inflammatory. In August 1920 Leonid Krasin, a Soviet trade representative, had arrived for talks accompanied by Lev Kamenev, head of the Moscow Communist Party. Decrypts clearly showed that Kamenev was establishing secret contact with the embryonic British Communist Party, and subsidising the far-left newspaper the *Daily Herald*, using smuggled diamonds. Every move was visible to the codebreakers, and General Wilson was incredulous that Lloyd George had not immediately ejected the trade mission. On 18 August, Wilson confided his worries to Winston Churchill and the director of military intelligence, General Sir William Thwaites. Over the next few days he did the rounds of the security chiefs, including Lord Trenchard, who commanded the RAF, Sir Basil Thompson from the Home Office, and Rear Admiral Hugh 'Quex' Sinclair, director of naval intelligence, and received a sympathetic hearing.[76] On 24 August he noted in his diary: 'Trenchard with whom I discussed the matter later and to whom I showed … the intercepts thinks like Basil Thompson, that Lloyd George is a traitor.'[77]

On 2 September, with Lloyd George away in Lucerne, his coalition partner Bonar Law summoned a meeting at Downing Street that included Balfour, Churchill and Basil Thompson. Thompson circulated the latest material from the codebreakers. Thomas Jones, the deputy cabinet secretary, recalled that 'Everyone felt that the last intercept from Lenin where he lays down propaganda as *the* business of the Russian Delegation put the lid on and that there was nothing for it but to clear them out as quickly as possible.'[78]

Hankey, who had accompanied Lloyd George to Lucerne, argued exactly the opposite. He insisted that Wilson was absurdly alarmist, and that the activities of the Soviets in London were silly and easy to counter. His main worry was that if they ejected the Soviets they would have to publish the decrypts to justify their actions, placing the prime minister in a very difficult position. Britain would then lose its 'most valuable and trustworthy source of secret information', as no matter what they did to try to disguise the fact, Moscow would probably realise its communications were being read. He continued: 'This particular cypher is a very ingenious one which was discovered by great cleverness and hard work. The key of the cypher is changed daily and sometimes as often as three times in one message. Hence if it becomes known that we decoded the messages all the governments of the world will probably discover that no messages are safe.'[79]

Back in London, Lloyd George forced a showdown with his critics. He freely admitted that the Soviets were engaged in 'perfidy' and 'trickery', but argued that good intelligence could be obtained by keeping the trade mission in place. Although he thought their activities ineffective, he could see that political opinion in cabinet was turning against him, and probably regretted not having taken a closer interest in secret service matters, since the intelligence chiefs had been part of this pressure to act. An opportunity to do so arose in early September, when Kamenev decided to return to Moscow and came to Downing Street to pay his respects. He walked into a diplomatic ambush. Lloyd George met him accompanied by Hankey, Jones and Bonar Law. The prime minister opened with a tirade about 'gross bad faith' and interference in British internal affairs, including Soviet attempts to recruit labour leaders and secretly subsidise the *Daily Herald*. He also accused Kamenev of attempting to turn Poland into a client Soviet state – but did not mention the decrypts. There was obviously a double game going on here, with the prime minister trying to clear himself of suspicions of being overly sympathetic to Bolshevism.[80] Perhaps for audience effect, he warned Kamenev that if he did not leave Britain he would be deported.[81]

Lloyd George's hard line resulted in his also being criticised by the left, so he was eventually pushed into publishing eight of the intercepts. He used a rather thin cover story, claiming that they had been provided by a neutral country. Churchill, showing his characteristic impulsiveness and little nuanced appreciation of the value of intelligence, had led the charge demanding publication. Amazingly, blinded by their ideological hatred of Moscow, the intelligence chiefs had agreed. Quex Sinclair, now head of MI6, who had superintended the best wartime codebreakers, insisted that 'even if the publication of the telegrams was to result in not another message being decoded, then the present situation would fully justify it'. Intelligence officials leaked further decrypts to newspapers three weeks later. Lloyd George fired Basil Thompson shortly afterwards, leading some to suspect that it was he who was responsible for the leak. His departure was a positive move, and ensured that the Foreign Office and MI6 extended full control over foreign intelligence.[82]

The prime minister maintained his policy regardless, and secured an Anglo–Soviet trade agreement in 1921. Although a further surge of Soviet subversive activity was discovered in 1922, Lloyd George was overtaken by political scandal before he could respond, accusations of selling seats in the House of Lords forcing him to resign in October. In the summer his colleagues, led by Bonar Law, had chosen to make more Soviet decrypts public. Moscow predictably changed its cipher system, and an important stream of high-grade intelligence disappeared.[83] Despite the deliberate and foolish revelations of 1920, 1922 and 1923, GC&CS continued to read much high-level Soviet traffic.[84]

Astoundingly, Soviet incompetence was even greater than that of the British. As early as July 1920, Kamenev and his colleagues had requested a replacement for their 'Marta' cipher system, believing it to be insecure.

But their superiors resisted this request as requiring too much effort. They not only ignored the revelations in *The Times* but also strident warnings from senior Red Army commanders that their most secret correspondence in Europe 'is known word for word to the English, who have organised a network of stations designed particularly for listening to our radio'. By the end of 1920, Georgy Chicherin, the long-serving Soviet foreign minister, seemed to have got the message, and warned his mission in London that very sensitive material should be sent only by courier. But many secret communications continued to be intercepted by GC&CS.[85]

GC&CS therefore remained the star in Britain's interwar intelligence firmament. Between 1920 and 1924, it issued over 13,000 intercepted signals, approximately 290 a month, including more than half of all French traffic. Yet little of this went to Downing Street. If the prime minister was not regularly in receipt of these gems, where did they go? The answer is to the Foreign Office, which aggressively clawed back control over foreign intelligence from the military following the end of the war. Intercepts informed the negotiation of complex post-war settlements and treaties that followed the First World War, such as those at Sèvres and Lausanne, often giving British diplomats the upper hand. One of the most important customers was the foreign secretary, Lord Curzon. By 1922, Curzon also enjoyed power over distribution, deciding what secrets should go to the prime minister or to members of the cabinet. Unfortunately, the decrypts often revealed the fact that Lloyd George was pursuing a separate and secret foreign policy, entirely undeclared to Curzon, and was sometimes backing the Greeks in treaty negotiations against his own foreign secretary. Curzon was an emotional individual, and knowledge of the 'dirty' activities of his friends and allies stirred apoplectic outbursts. In 1922, meeting with the French prime minister Raymond Poincaré, Curzon had to be led weeping from the room, and refused to return until Poincaré apologised for his behaviour.[86]

Curzon deliberately kept much intelligence away from Downing Street. Things were made worse by the lack of a system for synthesising intelligence material and presenting it to leaders in a way that would allow it to inform strategy. Instead, attention often focused on single documents. This was typified by the impact of intelligence on talks about the future of Britain's alliance with Japan during the early 1920s, a decision that would cast a long shadow. Intelligence focused less on Japan's intentions and capabilities than on plots and nefarious activities: Lloyd George told cabinet that other friendly powers did things that were 'infinitely worse' than the Japanese secret service. Curzon argued for a renewal of the alliance, despite the fact that he considered the Japanese 'insidious and unscrupulous'. Churchill opposed a continued alliance with Tokyo, and to back up his argument showed his cabinet colleagues a secret Japanese map of Gibraltar that had come into the hands of MI5. Intelligence was often about alarms and incidents, and rarely informed national assessments.[87]

Meanwhile, the Irish problem had been rumbling on. The Easter Rising and the First World War were swiftly followed by the Irish War of Independence in 1919. Peace negotiations began in 1921, culminating in the formation of the Irish Free State the following year. This time Lloyd George lacked signals intelligence, but he did draw upon other forms of intelligence to aid the British position. Unfortunately, the material reaching him and his ministers came from military intelligence officers who opposed the truce. Consequently, they offered biased worst-case scenarios in which Sinn Féin and especially the IRA intended to play for time before resuming their offensive, including 'fantastical reports' of chemical weapons. Fortunately for the peace process, a more confident outlook emanated from the civilian authorities in Dublin, and the 'two opposing interpretations of the Irish situation battled it out from July to December 1921'. Lloyd George fell into the optimistic camp, and was determined to reach peace, but the alarmist intelligence came perilously close to collapsing the negotiations altogether. By early December, the prime minister had had enough. He issued a dramatic ultimatum: accept the peace or resume war in three days. This was a gamble. Contradictory and inaccurate intelligence meant that he had no idea whether Sinn Féin would accept – and Britain was in no position to resume war so soon. However, the starkly pessimistic intelligence coming out of Ireland offered enough warning about IRA rearmament to convince Lloyd George to set a strict deadline. The negotiations hung in the balance, and there was 'palpable relief' when the Irish signed the deal.[88]

Prime ministers must celebrate when they can; success is often short-lived. In May 1922, Lloyd George was livid when he was shown the new Irish government's draft constitution, despairing that it represented 'a complete evasion of the treaty' he had gambled on securing. Intelligence uncovered numerous plots, some more real than others, against Northern Ireland and the British mainland, in which the Dublin government was complicit. Frustrated, Lloyd George feared that the Irish 'may have to face re-conquest'. When IRA men assassinated Field Marshal Henry Wilson in London the following month, the government found itself under pressure to wipe out the IRA headquarters in Dublin. A single piece of intelligence wrongly linked the murder to a Dublin conspiracy, and an attack on the IRA headquarters by British troops would have wrecked Britain's Irish policy 'at one stroke'. Nevertheless, led by Churchill, the cabinet approved the strike. Once more, Churchill failed to appreciate the nuances of raw intelligence and exhibited his famous impetuousness. All this frustrated the prime minister, but fortunately for Lloyd George and his Ireland policy, the army refused to obey the order.[89] This marked Lloyd George's final dealings with the Ireland problem, but Churchill would have to return to it during the Second World War. More ominously, it was merely a taste of the troubles to come for future prime ministers, from Harold Wilson onwards.

Bonar Law, who replaced Lloyd George in 1922, was the shortest-serving prime minister of the twentieth century, spending only 211 days in office. He died of a throat tumour shortly afterwards, and was buried in Westminster Abbey near the Tomb of the Unknown Soldier. During the funeral, Asquith described him as 'the unknown prime minister'. Hankey noted in his diary: 'Poor Bonar never had the nerve for the job of prime minister. The responsibility preyed on his mind and, I feel sure, hastened on his cancer.' Turning to Bonar Law's successor, he added, quite correctly, 'Baldwin has the nerve but scant capacity and I fear will not last long.' Stanley Baldwin's first term in office indeed lasted only eight months, and he stepped down in January 1924. Alongside these figures, Lloyd George appeared a political giant, and it was under him that British intelligence took its most adventurous step forward.[90]

A connected British intelligence community was not created in 1909, but it had already begun to centralise and professionalise. Indeed, it has been suggested that Asquith's government changed the very meaning of the word 'intelligence'. At the turn of the century, intelligence was something that existed in the far-flung service of empire, and meant information of almost any kind, so long as it impacted upon policy or made colonial rule more efficient. Much of it was supplied by an army of enterprising amateurs serving on 'special duties', supplemented by eccentrics who divided their time between collecting rare beetles or tulip bulbs and sketching Turkish fortifications. By 1918, intelligence was about secret work, and incorporated a strong emphasis on counter-intelligence. Most importantly, it had also become increasingly militarised, and had embraced the science of codebreaking. Room 40 had produced astonishing intelligence in just four years, but as yet no one knew how to interpret it or to use it securely.[91]

Lloyd George, perhaps assisted by the wise counsel of Maurice Hankey, had begun to learn his trade. In contrast to his early years as prime minister, by 1920 he knew that context was everything in interpreting decrypts. Accordingly, Lenin's hot language had not alarmed him. He also came to understand that access to decrypts was acquired with difficulty, and given away easily – a lesson quickly forgotten in Number 10. Therefore, although he eventually discussed codebreaking in his memoirs, he said no more than had already appeared in the public domain, and worked closely with Hankey on the agreed text.[92]

By contrast, his cabinet colleagues performed poorly – even those with more intelligence experience. Lord Curzon, foreign secretary between 1919 and 1924, should have been a master of intelligence, having presided over a sophisticated espionage system in his previous existence as viceroy of India. Yet personal insults from the French, revealed in all their glory by intercepts, literally drove him to tears of rage. Churchill's performance was even worse, and despite boundless enthusiasm for intelligence he was impulsive in its use. Moreover, when he rushed out his own history of the First World War in 1923, he made many references to British codebreaking capabilities. The Germans were soon avidly reading his account, and it is no coincidence that shortly afterwards they began to take an interest in a new and effective cipher machine called Enigma. In the mid-1920s, however, Germany had not yet resurfaced as a problem. The First World War was over, and a young man named Adolf Hitler had only recently established a nascent Nazi Party. Instead, it was the Russians who attracted the attention of Britain's secret service. An early cold war of subversion and subterfuge was emerging, in which incoming prime ministers would need to use intelligence subtly and wisely. Inexperienced in handling the secret world and lacking an integrated intelligence assessment community, this may have been asking too much.

2

Stanley Baldwin and Ramsay MacDonald (1923–1937)

How can I avoid the suspicion …
that the whole thing is a political plot?
RAMSAY MACDONALD[1]

We were completely misled on that subject
STANLEY BALDWIN[2]

The interwar years were a time of international subterfuge; of clandestine struggles between intelligence agencies only recently created. As Britain and Bolshevik Russia faced off in a global war of subversion and counter-subversion, a fear of communism swept the Whitehall establishment. A smear plot allegedly sought to topple a Labour prime minister, while another prime minister publicly misused intelligence for political expediency. Remarkably, these things happened twice in the space of a decade. The history of secret intelligence and Downing Street has an intriguing habit of repeating itself, and many of the issues that emerged in the interwar years would resurface to confront later prime ministers.

Two prime ministers dominated the 1920s and 1930s: Stanley Baldwin and Ramsay MacDonald. Both entered office as inexperienced and unsophisticated consumers of intelligence. Both faced a steep learning curve. Stanley Baldwin was a hands-off prime minister. A master of delegation, he allowed his ministers maximum freedom – to the extent that he drew charges of complacency and laziness. Baldwin expended most of his energies developing personal relations with MPs, and so spent a great deal of time sitting in Parliament: sometimes on the green benches of the Commons resting his eyes through some dreary debate, at other times slouched in an armchair somewhere soaking up the political atmosphere; but always in conversation. It was a working style that did not please everybody. One exasperated colleague complained, 'What can you do with a leader who sits in the smoking room reading *Strand* magazine?'[3]

Beneath the surface, Baldwin was a highly-strung individual. He exhibited a range of nervous habits, from a subtle eye-twitch to compulsively smelling any object that fell into his hands. He was particularly keen on putting books to his nostrils and enjoying a long, loud sniff.[4] Yet he worked well in a crisis. These are intriguing, almost contradictory, characteristics which bear directly upon a prime minister's use of intelligence. His proclivity for delegation hints at a lack of interest in detailed intelligence material, while his nervous demeanour suggests an unsuitable constitution for dealing with the periodic crises of the secret world. In fact, Baldwin did draw steadily on intelligence throughout his time in office, although he did so in a blundering and unsophisticated manner which frustrated the intelligence community. He compromised GC&CS's best intelligence source on the Soviets, publicly accused Air Ministry intelligence reports of misleading him, almost cost an MI6 analyst his job, and fell out with MI5 over surveillance of King Edward VIII.

In theory at least, Baldwin should have had an easier ride than Ramsay MacDonald. The illegitimate son of a farm labourer and a housemaid, MacDonald was an outsider. As the first ever Labour prime minister, he was also the first prime minister to hail from a working-class background. He was not part of the establishment; not one of the old boys. MacDonald had never even held a ministerial position before entering Downing Street. There can have been very few prime ministers as inexperienced in the workings of the secret world – or indeed of Whitehall in general – as he.

Despite his energy, good looks and personal magnetism, MacDonald was prickly, guarded and introverted. Unlike Baldwin, he had an impressive capacity for hard work. His working day began at seven, and would drag on until the early hours of the following morning. Poor at delegating, he served as his own foreign secretary in his first government throughout 1924. Returning as prime minister for a second time in 1929, MacDonald only appointed someone else, Arthur Henderson, as foreign secretary for political reasons, and sought to keep as much control over foreign policy himself as possible.[5] One might expect that this would have increased his access to intelligence, and made him a particularly active consumer compared to other prime ministers. But in reality, he generally kept the intelligence community at a distance, and had little intention of ever meeting an MI5 or MI6 officer. At one point, in order to remain detached from the intrigues of the secret world, he even forced a senior MI6 man to stand in an adjoining room, and would only speak to him using the permanent secretary at the Foreign Office as an intermediary.[6]

Yet MacDonald was a Labour hero, the party's man of destiny. He served as prime minister in 1924, and again between 1929 and 1931. In politics, as in much of British public life, however, heroes exist only to fall. Things inevitably soured for MacDonald in 1931 when he agreed to serve as head of a national coalition government designed to see Britain through the international economic crisis. Deemed a traitor by his erstwhile supporters, he was unceremoniously sacked from the Labour Party which he had done so much to turn into a credible force in British politics. Although he remained prime minister until 1935, the Conservatives, including Stanley Baldwin and Neville Chamberlain, increasingly dominated the government. Ravaged by insomnia and ill-health, the ageing prime minister 'slowly faded away'.[7] A sea voyage was recommended to restore his health, but he died on board an ocean liner in November 1937. By then, many of the European crises that would trouble his successors were already visible.

The election of the first ever Labour government raised a whole host of questions about the relationship between Number 10 and the intelligence establishment. King George V wondered what his 'dear Grandmama', Queen Victoria, would have made of a Labour government, and the same can be said for the intelligence services. MacDonald had long been on MI5's radar: the service had actually recommended prosecuting him for delivering seditious speeches during the First World War. Elements within the intelligence elite continued to view MacDonald and his first government with 'suspicion, alarm and in some cases contempt'. The mistrust was mutual, and Vernon Kell, the long-serving director-general of MI5, knew full well of Labour suspicions towards his service.[8]

The Foreign Office deliberately waited several months before showing any signals intelligence to the new prime minister. When he was finally inducted, MacDonald was probably the only member of his cabinet informed of the activities of GC&CS. The diplomats feared that Labour ministers would be horrified at the idea of intercepts and espionage, and, in Churchill's words, kept MacDonald 'in ignorance'. Even once he had gained experience, intelligence officers still kept him ill-informed. In the early 1930s, important reforms meant that MI6 confined itself to operations on foreign territory, while MI5 took over responsibility for countering communist subversion from Scotland Yard. Seeking to ease coordination and reduce overlap, these reforms shaped both organisations for decades to come. Yet it seems that MacDonald was not even told about them.[9] Similarly, Arthur Ponsonby, his parliamentary under-secretary at the Foreign Office, was refused all access to signals intelligence and MI6 reports, despite directing the government's Russia policy. Whenever Ponsonby mentioned intelligence, his officials became rigid. Not that Ponsonby particularly minded; he thought intelligence was a 'dirty' business.[10]

Few Labour ministers were intelligence enthusiasts. In 1929 Robert Vansittart, the senior official at the Foreign Office, had to defend the Secret Service Vote, from whence came funding for clandestine activity, against the new foreign secretary, Henderson. Britain's most senior diplomat, Vansittart was an extraordinary polymath and aesthete – during his time as a young diplomatic trainee in Paris he had written a play in French, entitled *Les Parias*, which was a great success at the Théâtre Molière. He went on to produce several volumes of poems fêted by figures such as T.E. Lawrence. A romantic soul, full of passionate loves and hatreds, he adored intelligence.[11] 'Van', as he was known, bemoaned how Henderson, a tee-totaller, 'rated Secret Service like hard liquor, because he knew, and wanted to know, nothing of it'. Although this is perhaps unfair, given that even senior Labour ministers were given limited access to it, Vansittart felt frustrated because the government indulged in intelligence 'all too little'.[12] MacDonald's administration took 'a jaundiced view' of the orientation of the intelligence establishment as a whole. There was a 'climate of mutual mistrust', with MI6 officials wary of discussing anything within earshot of MacDonald's ministers.[13]

As prime minister, MacDonald did receive a weekly summary of British revolutionary movements written by Special Branch. He was not impressed, thinking the reports suffered from political bias and added little insight. To the anger of Special Branch, he refused to circulate them to cabinet. His attitude towards intelligence did soften over time, especially when dealing with growing problems of industrial unrest, and he came to realise that domestic intelligence provided by MI5, Special Branch and even MI6 could help to determine government responses.[14] His hard work won respect amongst the Whitehall establishment. The cabinet secretary Maurice Hankey, for example, liked MacDonald 'very much', and got on with him 'like a house on fire'.[15] MacDonald was no Soviet stooge, and indeed was disliked by the Soviet ambassador in London, who called him fickle and vain. Throughout his premiership, MacDonald remained committed to monitoring Soviet activities just as much as did his

Conservative counterparts.[16] But the notorious 'Zinoviev letter' delivered a fatal blow to MacDonald's burgeoning relationship with the secret world, and cast a dark shadow over relations between Labour ministers and secret service for decades to come.[17]

MacDonald found himself in a precarious position in 1924, perched delicately atop an unstable minority government. The fact that his was the first ever Labour administration made his position even more perilous. He, and his young party, had a lot to lose. Rather like Harold Wilson half a century later, MacDonald had been elected early in the year, but faced another general election in October. MacDonald too found enemies among right-wing sections of the establishment, eager to smear the prime minister and destabilise his nascent Labour government.

Days before the election of October 1924, the *Daily Mail* published a sensational story: 'Civil War Plot by Socialists: Moscow Order to our Reds'.[18] The newspaper had somehow obtained a copy of a letter purportedly written by Grigory Zinoviev, head of the Comintern, to the Communist Party of Great Britain. So close to an election, this 'revelation' inevitably had damaging implications for MacDonald and his Labour government – which was exactly why the *Daily Mail* published it so gleefully. Addressed 'Dear Comrades', the letter sought to 'stir up the masses of the British proletariat' and instigate rebellion. It mentioned 'agitation-propaganda work' inside the armed forces, and urged communists to penetrate 'all the units of the troops'. Perhaps most damaging to MacDonald, it referred to a group inside the Labour Party 'sympathising' with closer Anglo–Russian relations.[19] This implied that the government was soft on Bolshevism – an injurious charge, given the enduring paranoia about Moscow.

Although MacDonald had sought to distance Labour from the British communists, as prime minister he had already offered *de jure* recognition of the Soviet Union and signed two treaties with the new state. Like Lloyd George before him, he hoped simply to improve bilateral trade and bring the Soviet Union into the international community. Unfortunately, his approach 'seemed nothing less than treachery' to establishment figures fearful of the relentless march of communism. The popular press were critical too, dubbing one of the treaties 'Money for Murderers'. To make matters worse, the Labour cabinet had also resisted prosecuting John Campbell, a communist journalist accused of subverting the armed services, on the grounds that he had an excellent war record.[20] Personally,

MacDonald had some reservations about that decision, and rightly worried that 'more will be heard of this matter'.[21]

Questions over the role of the intelligence community in the notorious Zinoviev affair lingered for almost a century. Did intelligence officers deliberately forge the letter to bring down a democratically elected prime minister? If not, did they at least publicise the letter in order to achieve that end? Was the secret civil service during the 1920s simply anti-Labour? MI6's official historian, Keith Jeffery, sums up the suspicions nicely: 'Right-wing elements, with the connivance of allies in the security and intelligence services, deliberately used the letter – and perhaps even manufactured it – to ensure a Labour defeat.'[22] These questions are crucial. They raise issues of accountability and political legitimacy at the heart of the secret world.

The Zinoviev letter was almost certainly a fake. Gill Bennett, the Foreign Office historian with access to MI6 sources, concludes that it was 'highly unlikely' to have been written by Zinoviev. Instead it was most likely a forgery produced by someone with links to the international intelligence community and a decent knowledge of Comintern. Bennett adds that the mystery forger was also probably 'aware that there were interest groups in Britain who would make use of the forgery to further their own cause by damaging the Labour Government and derailing the ratification of the Anglo–Soviet treaties'. It is more than possible that information about the proposed forgery could have reached British intelligence officers looking to aid the Conservatives in the forthcoming election.[23]

White Russians, the exiled supporters of the tsar, were the most likely culprits. Those based in Britain certainly possessed motive, given their vehement opposition to MacDonald's Anglo–Soviet treaties. They also had the means, including a sophisticated intelligence network and forgery capabilities in Europe. It is likely that the forger was based in Riga – some of the individuals passing intelligence to MI6 in that city were certainly involved with White Russian circles.[24] One of a team of four key White Russian suspects in the forgery, Alexis Bellegarde, had close links with MI6, and went on to become one of the service's most successful wartime double agents working against the Nazis.[25] Others would exaggerate the authenticity of the letter as it was passed upwards – eventually to MacDonald himself.[26]

On 2 October 1924, MI6's Riga station obtained the letter and despatched an English version to London. A week later, MI6 headquarters sent copies to the Foreign Office with a covering note asserting that 'the authenticity of the document is undoubted'. It was, they insisted, by Zinoviev. In fact, MI6 conducted no checks on the authenticity of the letter. Nobody inside MI6, for example, had asked how Riga had obtained it; nor did anybody enquire as to whether it was the original or a translation.[27]

The Foreign Office rightly sought 'corroborative proofs' before showing the letter to the prime minister. MI6's Desmond Morton supposedly provided these on 11 October. His report, apparently based on information received from an agent who had infiltrated the Communist Party of Great Britain, stated that the British communists had held a meeting at the start of October to consider a letter received from Zinoviev, thereby validating the Riga letter. Intriguingly, however, the agent's original written report made no mention of any letter from Moscow at all. Morton claimed that the extra information had been gained after he met the agent on 10 October for further discussion. Morton appears guilty of, at the very least, asking leading questions to generate information to fit the Zinoviev story. At most, he knew the letter was a forgery, but realising the implications for MacDonald, intended it to be treated as genuine. He certainly disliked both the Bolsheviks and the Labour Party.[28]

Morton's rather weak 'confirmation' was good enough for the Foreign Office. The permanent secretary observed: 'We have now heard definitely on absolutely reliable authority that the Russian letter was discussed at a recent meeting of the central committee of the Communist Party of Great Britain.'[29] The prime minister was duly informed. Upon first reading the letter on 16 October, MacDonald was suspicious. He 'did not treat it as a proved document', and asked that 'care should be taken to ascertain if it was genuine'. 'In the storm of an election', it never crossed his mind that this letter 'had any part to play in the fight'.[30] He requested more proof, but his instructions were ignored, and none was sought.[31] MacDonald was both right and wrong: the letter was of dubious authenticity, but it would play a role in the election.

MI6 realised the letter was a fake: Morton privately told MI5 towards the end of November – long after the damage was done – that 'We are firmly convinced this actual thing is a forgery.'[32] But he refused to admit this in wider circles. Quex Sinclair, the head of MI6, even wrote a list of reasons, probably drafted by Morton, explaining why the letter was genuine. Each, however, was rather weak. First, Sinclair argued that the source's reliability strengthened the authenticity, even though MI6 did not know the identity of the ultimate source – an agent's agent. Second, Sinclair pointed to various 'corroborative proofs', but these too were unreliable.

Third, MI6 noted that the Soviets had frantically arrested two Comintern officials – a circumstantial point at best. Fourth, Sinclair arrogantly avowed that the possibility of MI6 being taken in by White Russian forgers could be 'entirely excluded'. This was complacent, to say the least. He then falsely asserted that MI6 knew the identity of all hands through which the letter had passed. Again, this was simply not true, since MI6 did not know the original source. Finally, Sinclair argued that the letter's contents were consistent with other genuine documents – but this proved nothing. Morton had something to hide. He had long prided himself on being able to spot forgeries, and most likely knew all along that the letter was a forgery.[33]

A leak was probably inevitable, especially once MI5 had circulated the letter widely to senior military personnel. There were also anti-MacDonald factions within MI6, with contacts in the press, who would have been glad to see him fall and who rubbed their hands with glee when the letter arrived in London. Given the overlapping nature of intelligence circles at the time, it is difficult to prove the identity of the culprit.[34] There were many suspects, all rather devious. Within MI6, suspicion falls on Desmond Morton and Stewart Menzies, a future chief. In fact, Morton later accused Menzies of posting the letter to the *Daily Mail*. Joseph Ball of MI5 is another candidate. He later went on to work for the Conservatives and, liaising with his former intelligence colleagues, ran a campaign of dirty tricks against the Labour Party, including infiltration, press manipulation and the tapping of phone lines.[35] Others include Reginald 'Blinker' Hall, the naval intelligence chief turned politician, who had lost his Conservative seat in Parliament when MacDonald came to power.[36]

All of these suspects have three things in common: they had served with the intelligence services; they were allied closely with the Conservatives; and they would have firmly believed that they were acting in the national interest by unofficially publicising the letter in an attempt to destabilise MacDonald. Remarkably, by 22 October Conservative Central Office also had a copy of the letter. Whoever leaked it, it certainly found its way 'to those vested interests who could best make political capital out of it at the government's expense'.[37] Meanwhile, similar people, including 'Blinker' Hall, were exploiting the Conservative–intelligence nexus to play similar tricks against the nascent Irish Free State. Stanley Baldwin too was not above suspicion, regarding Ireland at least, given that he became an honorary member of a secretive group of former intelligence officers presided over by Vernon Kell and known as the IB Club. The

Zinoviev affair can easily be seen as part of a broader campaign by the establishment to undermine opponents.[38]

Ramsay MacDonald was away in the final stages of electoral campaigning when the *Daily Mail* broke the story. Hoarse and audibly tiring, the last thing he wanted so close to a second election was a scandal which threatened to prematurely end the Labour dream. Although sceptical of the letter's authenticity, he asked the Foreign Office to draft a protest to the Soviet ambassador. It had to be 'so well-founded and important that it carried conviction and guilt'.[39] Unsatisfied by the draft of this response, he substantially rewrote it in a hotel room at Aberavon on 23 October, but ran out of time before having to rush off to another election meeting. He therefore returned the unfinished draft to London without initialling it, indicating that he wanted to see it again before it was sent. Upon hearing that the *Daily Mail* had a copy of the Zinoviev letter and was about to publish, the Foreign Office sent MacDonald's unfinished protest off to be printed alongside it. MacDonald was not consulted.[40] He was therefore naturally 'dumbfounded to be asked by a pressman attending one of my meetings that evening if I had authorised publication'. Caught off guard, he 'felt like a man sewn in a sack and thrown into the sea'.[41]

MacDonald considered the matter carefully, and concluded that 'in my absence, the anti-Russian mentality of Sir Eyre Crowe, the senior official at the Foreign Office was uncontrolled. He was apparently hot. He had no intention of being disloyal, indeed quite the opposite, but his own mind destroyed his discretion and blinded him to the obvious care he should have exercised.'[42] Although undoubtedly disappointed with Crowe, MacDonald saved the blame for the *Daily Mail* and the Conservative Party. He ranted in his diary that 'nothing untoward would have happened had not the *Daily Mail* and other agencies including Conservative leaders had the letter and were preparing a political bomb from it'.[43] Rather naïvely, perhaps, he was 'genuinely dumbfounded' that the paper had obtained a copy.[44]

On 27 October, MacDonald finally gave a public explanation during an election speech in Cardiff. Feeling bruised and suspicious, he vehemently denied that he had delayed the publication of the Zinoviev letter, slammed the 'Tory propagandists' who 'know nothing', but loyally defended the Foreign Office and Crowe's decision to publish his protest. He then attacked the press for obtaining a copy of the letter and seeking to 'spring it upon us'. He implicated the Conservatives for smearing him and, to laughter from the crowd, alluded to 'another Guy Fawkes – a new

Gunpowder plot'.[45] The speech failed to deal with the threat posed by the letter. With the election just hours away, the press continued to hound the beleaguered prime minister. The *Daily Express* and the *Daily Mail* both saw him at odds with the civil service. The *Manchester Guardian* joined the chorus, arguing that if the letter was a hoax MacDonald's department had made an 'egregious blunder', but if it was genuine the prime minister could hardly accuse his enemies of fabricating a plot. MacDonald was livid at the 'scoundrels of the press', and increasingly saw the whole affair as a personal vendetta.[46]

The election was held on Wednesday, 29 October. Although MacDonald held his constituency, the Conservatives enjoyed a resounding victory, gaining 155 seats. Electoral experts suggest that the Zinoviev letter was not the cause of the Labour defeat, as the Conservatives, in all likelihood, were going to win regardless. But the following day MacDonald returned to London convinced that the letter was a forgery and a plot was afoot. He now sought proof.[47] One of the first things he did was to visit Eyre Crowe. Instead of finding him at the Foreign Office, Crowe was ill in bed, heartbroken at having published the protest letter without approval. On 31 October MacDonald met with his outgoing cabinet. A long and heated discussion developed, with some calling for an inquiry into the role of the intelligence services in the Zinoviev affair. MacDonald resisted the idea, explaining that Crowe and the Foreign Office had not tried to sabotage the Labour Party. Instead, MacDonald appointed a cabinet committee to examine the authenticity of the now notorious letter. But with little firm evidence, no conclusion was possible. And with that MacDonald resigned and departed for a walking holiday in the West Country.[48]

Stanley Baldwin had been disturbed by the Zinoviev saga. Taking the helm on 4 November 1924, he convened the prime minister's Secret Service Committee and ordered a review of the whole system, asking for recommendations for 'greater efficiency'. At the end of 1925, the committee reported to Baldwin that had they been designing the intelligence system from scratch, a single unified department would have been desirable. As it was, however, they advised the prime minister to leave it as it was: imperfect but functioning.[49] Baldwin cannot have been entirely satisfied. Two years later, he convened the committee again, this time tasking them with an investigation into the state of affairs at Scotland Yard – he feared that Labour might seize on the 'political work' of the Yard to argue that a government department was engaging in party politics.[50] His anxieties about the intersection of ideology and intelligence, fuelled by Zinoviev, were prescient, given that he soon ordered a politically controversial security raid on Soviet premises which backfired spectacularly.

The 1926 General Strike increased the obsession of the authorities with Soviet subversion and the hidden hand of Moscow. Baldwin remained calm, but the Beaverbrook and Rothermere press portrayed the strike as an attempted revolution. MI5 and Special Branch intercepted the mail of leftist leaders and sampled public opinion directly by eavesdropping under railway platforms. The resolution of the General Strike in May 1926 was perhaps Baldwin's most triumphant moment: he was mobbed in the streets and cheered in Parliament. But the security services and the military remained nervous, especially about sedition in the armed forces. In October 1926, at the behest of the excitable home secretary William Joynson-Hicks, a dozen prominent communists were arrested on transparently trumped-up charges.[51]

Britain's intelligence services now had their collective eyes firmly fixed on the same building in Moorgate. It housed 'Arcos', or the All-Russian Co-operative Society, a body which orchestrated Anglo–Soviet trade. The intelligence community rightly perceived Arcos as a front for Soviet propaganda and subversion against Britain. MI5 ridiculed the Soviet description of Arcos – 'the sole purchasing and selling agency in Great Britain for the Government of the U.S.S.R.' – as naïve and childlike: 'They believe that if they say a thing often enough most people are bound to believe it in the long run.'[52] To complicate matters, Arcos shared offices with the Soviet Trade Mission, making the line between the two organisations rather blurred. Nonetheless, MI5 had traced the first major Soviet espionage ring to be deployed in Britain back to the offices of Arcos.[53] MI5, MI6 and Special Branch all watched and waited, trying to build up a bigger picture of an international communist network.

In March 1927 a new lead emerged. A human source informed MI6 that a classified British military document had been copied at Arcos. Quex Sinclair promptly passed this information to Vernon Kell, given that, in Sinclair's words, 'it concerned an act of espionage against the Armed Forces', and therefore was not MI6's responsibility. With Zinoviev a fresh memory, Kell and MI5 prudently spent a few weeks validating the evidence before alerting the director of public prosecutions. It was then felt to be time for action. Kell attempted to see John Anderson, permanent secretary at the Home Office – but Anderson was at a conference and unavailable. Undeterred, Kell instead sought a meeting with the director of Military

Operations and Intelligence. Also unavailable, out of London. To complete an unhappy hat-trick, Kell was also knocked back by the Chief of the Imperial General Staff; also away for a couple of days. After mulling over the problem during lunch, lamenting his lack of traction in Whitehall, Kell was ambling back towards the office when he bumped into the secretary of state for war, Laming Worthington-Evans, in the street, and managed to secure an appointment at the House of Commons for 5 p.m. Worthington-Evans kept Kell waiting for fifteen minutes, but having heard the evidence he sent Kell to see the home secretary. At 5.40 p.m., and after a frustrating day, Kell finally found a receptive audience in the fervently anti-communist home secretary. Joynson-Hicks, or 'Jix' as he was popu-larly known, immediately interpreted the evidence as proof of dangerous sedition. Leaving the MI5 boss in his office, he took Kell's statement straight to the prime minister. Baldwin, who was with his foreign secretary Austen Chamberlain at the time, agreed that Arcos should be raided in order to obtain evidence of a breach of the Official Secrets Act. An animated Jix returned less than thirty minutes later, saying, 'Raid Arcos. Do you want it in writing?'[54]

Baldwin's haste surprised Kell. The prime minister was not known for quick decisions or decisive action, but Jix had been pressing him to take a tougher line against the Russians for a while, and had long been angry about Soviet financial support for the miners during the General Strike. Kell's evidence from Arcos forced Baldwin's hand.[55] As with the Zinoviev affair, the fact that this evidence focused on subversion of the armed forces, a serious government concern, made it all the more compelling.[56] Neither Baldwin nor the foreign secretary, however, was made aware of the full diplomatic implications: that a raid on Arcos would mean a *de facto* raid on the Soviet Trade Mission.[57] Remarkably, Sinclair and MI6 were barely informed of the proposed raid, despite the fact that it was Sinclair who had passed the evidence to Kell in the first place. On 12 May, as was often his way, Sinclair, a *bon viveur*, enjoyed a long lunch some-where in clubland. He only found out about the raid at three o'clock – just one and a half hours before it commenced. Understandably angry at Kell, he later used the incident as ammunition in his ill-fated attempt to unify the intelligence services into a single organisation.[58]

The raid itself was utterly inept. Ham-fisted policemen brandished guns and ordered employees to empty pockets and handbags, but didn't seem to know what they were looking for. Nobody was in charge. To make matters worse, a lack of Russian-speakers prevented the police from translating the piles of documents in order to uncover incriminating evidence. Meanwhile, two Arcos employees frantically burned a stack of secret papers in the basement.[59] Although the prime minister had personally authorised the raid, MI6 were livid. They too had an interest in Arcos, and Baldwin's foray had ruined their continuing operations against an international espionage ring. Sinclair cursed that it was an 'irretrievable loss of an unprecedented opportunity'.[60] The raid had broader ramifications for MI6 operations: it would compromise their espionage efforts in Moscow if the Soviets sought retaliatory action against the British mission there, given that it quietly acted as a letterbox for MI6.[61]

That was not the worst of it. Under pressure from Jix, Churchill and a group of baying backbenchers to take a tough line against Soviet subversion, Baldwin's government decided to sever diplomatic relations with Moscow. They had hoped to find incriminating evidence in the Arcos raid with which they could publicly justify this move. Unfortunately, none was forthcoming, and opposition MPs taunted the government that the supposed seditious document was 'merely a figment of the imagination'.[62] The security services lamented that the documents they had captured 'do not appear to be of very great value'.[63] Specifically, there was nothing which proved that the Soviet Diplomatic Mission had been conducting sedition or propaganda.[64] Panicking, Baldwin drew on top-secret intercepted GC&CS material to prove Soviet guilt. On 24 May, in an unprecedented move, he rose to his feet in the House of Commons and read from signals intelligence intercepts – or, as the cabinet put it delicately, from 'secret documents of a class which it is not usual to quote'.[65]

The harassed Baldwin falsely presented the Arcos raid as an intelligence success, claiming that 'both military espionage and subversive activities throughout the British Empire and North and South America were directed and carried out from Soviet House'. Moreover, he added that 'No effective differentiation of rooms or duties was observed as between the members of the Trade Delegation and the employees of Arcos, and both these organisations have been involved in anti-British espionage and propaganda.'[66] These two charges were accurate, but could not be adequately backed up by documents found at the scene. Instead, Baldwin began reading the highly classified signals intelligence intercepts. He quoted a startling intercept sent from the Soviet chargé d'affaires to Moscow, stating: 'I very much doubt the possibility of a raid on our Embassy. I would, however, consider it a very useful measure of precaution to suspend for a time the forwarding by post of documents of friends, "neighbours" and so forth from London to Moscow and vice versa. Telegraph your decision immediately.' Uproar broke out when the opposition asked how Baldwin had obtained the documents, and only the speaker's intervention saved the prime minister from having to answer.[67] Baldwin even published the texts of top-secret telegrams intercepted by GC&CS in a White Paper.[68] Two days later the House of Commons reconvened to debate the issue. Following the prime minister's earlier lead, both the foreign secretary and Jix gleefully divulged yet more intercepted material. As Christopher Andrew, MI5's authorised historian, has observed, the debate 'developed into an orgy of governmental indiscretion about secret intelligence for which there is no parallel in modern parliamentary history'.[69]

GC&CS, and by extension Baldwin's cabinet, had long had access to all Russian traffic, including diplomatic and intelligence material. GC&CS also monitored communications between Comintern and the British Communist Party from, for example, an unmarked intercept station located in south London targeting a transmitter based in Wimbledon.[70] After the Arcos fiasco, however, the Russians realised that their codes had been broken. Predictably, they replaced the system with a better, seemingly impenetrable, encryption scheme, known as the one-time pad.[71] The one-time pad system, as the name implies, used a new cipher for each message, creating huge problems for the codebreaker. As a result, intelligence dried up. Over the next few years GC&CS had access to few Soviet diplomatic messages, and the only high-grade Soviet traffic available was that of Comintern.[72]

Sinclair, his deputy Stewart Menzies, and Alastair Denniston, the operational head of GC&CS, were all furious about Baldwin's use of signals intelligence in Parliament. They pointed out the inestimable value of the source, and rightly predicted the detrimental consequences of parliamentary revelation. It was to no avail. Given the Soviet threat, the suspicions about the USSR's connections to the left wing of the Labour Party, and, most importantly, the political reputations now at stake, intelligence had become temporarily expendable.[73] Sinclair lamented how decrypts had been read 'as a measure of desperation to bolster up a case vital to Government'. He bemoaned the lack of coordination within the intelligence services, and once again pressed for all three agencies to be united under one roof.[74] Denniston also attacked Baldwin for having 'found it necessary to compromise our work beyond question'.[75]

Baldwin should not shoulder all the blame. As we have seen, in the immediate aftermath of the First World War, intelligence chiefs had grown so alarmed about Soviet subversion that they too had advocated publishing intelligence in order to make the public aware of the scale of the threat. In fact, even Sinclair had changed his tune. Just seven years before, confronted with fears of the Bolshevik Revolution stretching its tentacles into Britain, he had argued that 'Even if the publication of the telegrams was to result in not another message being decoded, then the present situation would fully justify it.'[76] Moreover, Baldwin had tried to learn the lessons of the secret past. He consulted cabinet minutes from 1923, when the government had faced a similar issue. Amazingly, they recommended full disclosure: 'The advantages of basing the published British case on actual extracts from the despatches which had passed between the Soviet government and its agents, outweighed the disadvantages of the possible disclosure of the secret source from which these despatches had been maintained.'[77] The whole decade of the 1920s proved a learning experience for both the intelligence agencies and the politicians, who still lacked a central intelligence machine to guide them in the use and practice of this important weapon of statecraft.

The Arcos story – told and retold – eventually became the symbol of security failure for secret services around the world. New recruits to GC&CS were warned that senior politicians, including the prime minister himself, could be horrendously indiscreet when the political stakes were high. The episode strained the trust between the secret world and Number 10. It demonstrated that intelligence officers needed to be careful about how their product was used.[78] The lesson would prove crucial during the Second World War regarding the use of Ultra decrypts. Menzies, the wartime head of MI6, never forgot that nobody in government understood the importance of protecting the source as much as the intelligence professionals.[79] The lessons were not lost on a future prime minister, either. With the Arcos fiasco perhaps in mind, Churchill would personally insist that the circle with whom he shared his Bletchley Park material was limited to only half a dozen of his closest ministers.[80] Even in the 1970s, when cabinet ministers were being indoctrinated into the arcane mysteries of 'sigint', they were visited by a mysterious figure from the Cabinet Office whom they called 'the Man from UNCLE'. This official, in fact the Cabinet Office Intelligence Adviser, proceeded to recount the story of Baldwin's blunder – by then politely referred to as a 'mistake' – to reinforce the importance of never breathing a word about sigint.[81]

By the summer of 1929, Ramsay MacDonald was back inside Number 10. This time, however, he headed a national coalition government with Stanley Baldwin, who chose to occupy the traditional residence of the chancellor of the exchequer next door at Number 11. He became increasingly influential as MacDonald aged, withered, and became an ever more marginalised figure. Although not prime minister between 1931 and 1935, Baldwin, as lord president of the council, in practice wielded as much power as, if not more than, MacDonald. Churchill referred to him as 'the virtual prime minister'.[82]

Throughout the 1920s, the intelligence community had focused on Russia, communism, and what can perhaps be seen as a First Cold War, often fought out on the fringes of empire in locations as distant as Hong Kong and Shanghai. By contrast, the cabinet ignored Ireland during the second half of the decade. When MacDonald returned to power, though, attention turned briefly to the rise of the Irish leader, Éamon de Valera, who had been involved in the Easter Rising, had fought in the War of Independence, and had opposed the settlement that created the Irish Free State. Since then he had led the nationalist party Fianna Fáil into the Dáil, and went on to win the 1932 election. The government sensed trouble, and sought to bring de Valera down. In the absence of effective intelligence-gathering machinery in Ireland, MacDonald was informed by biased, outdated and alarmist intelligence which insisted on portraying de Valera as a violent IRA man rather than a democratic statesman. MacDonald bought this line, and believed de Valera was 'undoubtedly a complete prisoner to the Irish Republican Army'. This flawed intelligence also confirmed the prejudices of Baldwin, who had increasing sway over MacDonald and was a diehard unionist with bitter contempt for Irish nationalism. Although London was jittery about overreacting to inflammatory intelligence, MacDonald and particularly Baldwin embarked on a campaign of economic sanctions to undermine de Valera. Based on an exaggerated threat of Irish subversion, the strategy was misjudged, and merely allowed de Valera to gain 'immense political mileage'.[83]

For now, though, Ireland was a red herring. The real threat seemed to be coming from the east rather than the west. Eyes began to turn towards Adolf Hitler and the ominous rise of Nazi Germany. Yet secret intelligence did not inform strategic policy on Germany, or indeed Japan, particularly closely during the late 1920s and early 1930s. Especially in the empire across the Middle East, India and Malaya, intelligence officers remained unduly focused on Bolshevism.[84] Moreover, partly because Hankey had failed to create a central intelligence 'brain' in the Cabinet Office, secret information remained tactical and operational, with little impact on discussions about the next major threat. Instead, policymakers relied on conventional and open sources – or, as in Ireland, biased locals. As Germany, Italy and Japan all began to make noises about revising the international order during the mid-1930s, intelligence on capabilities and industrial capacity became a priority. However, there was still no central machine for using intelligence to assess the strategy or intentions of these new enemies.[85] Added to this, British impecuniousness and memories of the tragic devastation of the First World War fostered a reluctance in MacDonald and Baldwin to address the issue. MacDonald, perhaps unsurprisingly, remained more focused on economic recovery in the aftermath of the 1929 Wall Street Crash.[86]

Rearmament remains a controversial issue – one breath away from 'appeasement'. Baldwin was long paraded alongside Ramsay MacDonald and Neville Chamberlain as one of the 'Guilty Men' who had failed to deter Hitler. More recently it has become apparent that, in a difficult economic context, he did much to improve Britain's defences – albeit not enough to provide convincing deterrence.[87] In March 1934, Baldwin announced that Britain would retain parity in air strength with Germany, hoping that this public commitment would deter Hitler's aerial ambitions. Later in the year, he announced an expansion of the RAF to keep pace with the German programme. Nevertheless, Baldwin wanted to avoid an all-out arms race, and sought to rearm at a pace the public could accept, rather than at the optimum speed to counter Hitler.[88]

Intelligence was central to these complex rearmament debates. Both MacDonald and Baldwin knew Britain could not afford rapid, large-scale rearmament. Intelligence therefore became crucial in understanding exactly how much rearmament was necessary to counter the Nazi threat, and what kind of weapons were needed. Everyone was obsessed with air power. For the fascists it was symbolic of a modernist future, for others it was the likely harbinger of urban destruction at the very outbreak of war. Downing Street wanted an accurate picture of the current size of the Luftwaffe and the speed of future expansion. This, of course, was rather difficult to achieve in what was increasingly a Nazi police state. New technologies are often developed in secret and misunderstood even by those who develop them. Moreover, Hitler maintained strict control of the German press, and exaggerated Nazi strength. In other countries, especially Japan, 'horrible deaths awaited those suspected of spying'.[89]

Britain lacked hard intelligence – especially on German intentions. The decline of the codebreakers at GC&CS made matters worse still. In the 1930s the Germans made increasing use of the Enigma encryption machine and electro-mechanical ciphers that generated millions of possible solutions to any secret message, and could not at the time be broken. Progressively through the 1930s, GC&CS lost the ability to read the codes of other important powers, including Russia, Italy and Japan. By the end of the decade the only major power whose traffic they were regularly reading was the United States. Baldwin and MacDonald never enjoyed the insight into German thinking that Churchill was later to gain from Bletchley Park.[90]

Intelligence capability cannot be increased overnight. Successive governments had slashed public spending in an attempt to deal with the aftermath of the First World War and then the Great Depression. As part of this, MacDonald's national government had imposed deep cuts on army, naval and particularly air intelligence. Strikingly, Robert Vansittart, the permanent under-secretary at the Foreign Office, later admitted that the head of one section of the intelligence services 'was so short of funds that at times he was reduced to relatives for assistance'.[91] Lack of funding proved particularly detrimental given the increasing focus on the size and strength of the German air force, which was one of the great unknowns of the 1930s and which, as a new and frightening form of warfare, needed to be better understood. Interwar developments in air power had dramatically increased British feelings of vulnerability. Baldwin captured the mythical status of air power in his 1932 speech 'Fear for the Future' when he insisted 'the bomber will always get through'.[92]

Air intelligence now fell into a range of mental traps which generated complacency about the pace of Luftwaffe growth. Analysts believed that the Germans sought quality over quantity, and so thought it would take some time before Hitler could build enough planes to constitute a real threat.[93] Accordingly, intelligence was made to fit into a preconceived model, with the German air force 'expanding in neat and well-ordered steps from the creation of one air division to the next'.[94] Even when offered excellent intelligence by France which indicated greater German ambitions, the Air Ministry refused to budge from its fixed mind-set.[95] The ministry's dogged underestimation of the Germans is still a puzzle, not least because back in the 1920s it, alongside the Admiralty, deliberately exaggerated the strength of the French air force and the Japanese navy to argue for more resources.[96] Obsessed with the national stereotype of

German efficiency and order, analysts thought the Nazi approach would be slowed by the need to train air crew, create support services and build barracks. According to the Deputy Chief of the Air Staff, 'a nation so admittedly thorough as Germany will not be content with a mere window-dressing collection of aircraft and pilots'. The Air Ministry happily predicted that the Germans would not be able to match the RAF until 1945.[97]

Meanwhile, at the centre of government a slow revolution was beginning. In 1931 Desmond Morton, an impish MI6 officer, had been allowed to create the Industrial Intelligence Centre. Beginning as a modest clearing house for economic intelligence on arms production capacity, something that no one seemingly wanted to own, it offered accurate assessments based on all source intelligence. More importantly, this unit was also the seed of centralised intelligence analysis that the Cabinet Office and Downing Street so badly needed. Although less sanguine than those of the Air Ministry, Morton's assessments lacked impact, not least because he himself was unpopular, and did little to 'promote interdepartmental harmony'.[98] Detailed and extensive, the reports apparently 'raised a riot each time' they were read, since 'neither Baldwin nor Chamberlain wanted to believe them', and nor did MacDonald.[99] Despite the improving intelligence on industrial matters, Baldwin woefully underestimated the speed of German rearmament throughout 1934 and much of 1935.[100] With Robert Vansittart and the Foreign Office joining the argument, intelligence on the state of the German air force became Whitehall's hottest potato.[101]

In March 1935, Hitler himself joined the debate, dramatically lifting the veils of secrecy from the Luftwaffe. In doing so, he bewildered British planners by claiming air power parity with the UK. This was bad news for Baldwin. Firstly, Churchill had long argued that Germany would soon overtake Britain if rearmament of the two countries continued at their present rates. Secondly, he had also warned that once Hitler had got the lead, Britain would be unable to catch up.[102] Thirdly, poor Baldwin had unequivocally promised the House of Commons in November 1934 that 'it is not the case that Germany is rapidly approaching equality with us'.[103] Overnight, Hitler's claims seemed to prove Baldwin wrong and Churchill right. Churchill was not guessing, and had secretly been supplied with the more hawkish intelligence estimates by Morton.

Baldwin publicly admitted to intelligence failure, explaining to the House of Commons that his forecast of German air power expansion, given the previous year, was off the mark.[104] In a dramatic confession, he continued, 'Where I was wrong was in my estimate of the future. There I was completely wrong.' He also admitted that there was simply a lack of good intelligence. 'I tell the House so frankly, because neither I nor any advisers from whom we could get accurate information had any idea of the exact rate at which production was being, could be, and actually was being speeded up in Germany in the six months between November and now.' He did not stop there. Going beyond lamenting a dearth of facts, he added: 'We were *completely misled* on that subject.' This was a damning judgement of the intelligence assessments, and amounted to an admission that the British secret services had been defeated by a German deception. 'I will not say we had not rumours,' the prime minister continued. 'There was a great deal of hearsay, but we could get no facts' – aside from those which came from Hitler himself: hardly the most reliable source.[105]

Baldwin was refreshingly unafraid to admit mistakes.[106] Like so many prime ministers publicly discussing intelligence, however, his performance was 'dishonest, if politically expedient'.[107] The Foreign Office and the Industrial Intelligence Centre had offered a less complacent view. By publicly blaming intelligence, Baldwin had put at least one MI6 officer's job on the line, while Christopher Bullock, the permanent secretary at the Air Ministry, also worried about his future – after all, he had provided Baldwin with the soothing air intelligence estimates. In the end, though, Baldwin used the opportunity to sack Lord Londonderry, the secretary of state for air.[108] The prime minister had misused the intelligence débâcle publicly in the House of Commons for political purposes and to effect ministerial change. It soon became apparent that Hitler had exaggerated his air power parity claims anyway.

The failure of British intelligence on the key question of air power actually makes Baldwin look rather better. He deserves more credit for increasing rearmament, given the weak intelligence support he received on this vital matter, and it could be argued that his decisions helped ensure victory in the Battle of Britain in 1940.[109] Yet, as the historian David Dilks has argued, had intelligence been stronger, and had 'the British appreciated the magnitude of their peril at an earlier date, had they embarked on an ambitious rearmament programme in 1934 instead of 1936', Hitler might have been deterred altogether.[110] Weak British intelligence in the 1930s, and the lack of any central assessment mechanisms, probably contributed to appeasement. Conversely, good intelligence 'might have been the only means possible to tear the blinkers' from ministerial eyes.[111]

For both MacDonald and Baldwin, intelligence services became entangled with matters of the heart. A former lover allegedly blackmailed MacDonald with compromising letters during the latter stages of his final premiership in the mid-1930s. Various accounts exist as to what happened next, but some suggest MacDonald used secret service funds to pay her off, or even asked MI6 to swoop in and seize the offending letters. Either way, somehow the blackmailer, one Mrs Forster, was prevented from sending her evidence to the press. MacDonald's biographer sees some truth in the story, but maintains that it was 'out of character for MacDonald himself to have authorised – much less ordered – the use of public money for such a purpose. But desperate men do sometimes act out of character.'[112]

For Baldwin, the stakes were higher. In 1936, increasingly frail and looking to retire, he confronted the abdication crisis. King Edward VIII was determined to marry the American Wallis Simpson. Baldwin considered her completely unsuitable, since she had divorced her first husband and was seeking a divorce from her second. The security service also knew of her Nazi sympathies, and for this reason Baldwin and his foreign secretary Anthony Eden had decided that the new King should no longer be supplied with secret documents.[113] Baldwin staunchly believed that it would be better for the whole government to resign than to allow any such marriage to proceed. Running on phosphorus pills prescribed by his doctor, he was ready for this final challenge, and wondered whether destiny had kept him in office solely for the task. Oddly, this delicate piece of constitutional management was perhaps the prime minister's most concerted effort as a personal user of intelligence.[114]

Edward VIII became King in January 1936. Baldwin liked the new monarch on a personal level, and met Wallis Simpson in May. By the autumn, having shown the King gossip about the couple's relationship from American newspapers, Baldwin felt 'the ice had been broken'. He was comfortable warning the King to be careful and discreet.[115] Although the affair received front-page coverage in America, remarkably the King persuaded the British press to say nothing. The crisis erupted in November, when Edward summoned the prime minister and declared that he intended to marry Mrs Simpson. Unsurprisingly, he was used to getting his own way, and was immune to appeals to duty from Baldwin.[116] In addition to creating tension between Buckingham Palace and Number 10, the crisis brought Baldwin into direct conflict with Vernon Kell at MI5. In December 1936, the prime minister demanded that MI5 investigate Mrs Simpson, but Kell declined. Baldwin certainly disliked the American socialite, once stating 'I have grown to hate that woman.' He felt she had done more to harm the monarchy 'in nine months than Victoria and George the Fifth did to repair it in half a century', and noted approvingly that a friend of the King had referred to her as 'a hard-bitten bitch'.[117] It was more than personal, though – Baldwin feared a constitutional crisis of sovereignty. He also felt 'no other suitable machinery existed' to conduct such a sensitive operation.[118]

In what was a rare confrontation with a prime minister, Kell disagreed. He argued that the proposed marriage would not threaten the realm, and was consequently no business of MI5's. The prime minister refused to give up. He pressed Kell further, and the director-general felt compelled to discuss the issue with his deputies. They were seemingly persuaded, and reluctantly agreed to conduct telephone and physical surveillance. MI5 consequently made 'certain delicate enquiries'. Surveillance of Mrs Simpson's phone revealed that she had another secret lover, a Ford car dealer in Mayfair. The King was never informed. Special Branch also apparently watched Mrs Simpson, and drew up a file documenting her liaison with the car dealer, whom they described as 'very charming, very good looking, well bred and an excellent dancer'. Even while the King was considering abdication, Mrs Simpson was seeing her other beau, upon whom she lavished expensive gifts and money.[119]

Baldwin's government also targeted the King. Horace Wilson, the prime minister's adviser at Number 10, asked the head of the General Post Office, Thomas Gardiner, to intercept all phone calls between the King's addresses, including Buckingham Palace, and certain addresses in both Continental Europe and London where Simpson was likely to be staying. Five days before the abdication, the Home Office put the 'most secret' request in writing.[120] 'Tar' Robertson, an MI5 officer better remembered for his wartime role in the Double Cross deception operations, claims to have been involved. He apparently entered Green Park at night to access a GPO junction box hidden in the bushes and tap the phone line between the King and his brother, the next in line to the throne, in order to 'see how the situation was moving'.[121]

Intelligence gathered by such means not only helped Baldwin to deal with the King by providing context, it also enabled him to monitor and control the international press during the crisis. Several unhelpful stories were intercepted by cable monitoring and then squashed by the home secretary.[122] However, it seems that the process of abdication, Baldwin's favoured outcome, would have been under way by then in any case. It also seems unlikely that MI5 found anything further against Mrs Simpson through its telephone-interception operation. Nonetheless, Baldwin got his way, although he believed that 'no more repugnant task has ever been imposed on a prime minister'.[123] The King abdicated on 10 December 1936. Baldwin's appearance at the Houses of Parliament that day was greeted by 'loud cheers' from the public, and only a small and insignificant 'little burst of booing'.[124] The prime minister himself would resign less than six months later, making way for his chancellor of the exchequer, Neville Chamberlain.

Between them, MacDonald and Baldwin had faced a wide array of complex secret service issues. These included Soviet subversion, the Ireland problem, the rise of Nazi Germany and the abdication crisis. Inexperienced, driven by political motivations, and for the most part lacking a centralised 'brain' to bring intelligence into policymaking, they fared poorly and made costly mistakes. By contrast, Chamberlain's premiership faced just one overriding issue which intelligence targeted: the Axis between Adolf Hitler and Benito Mussolini. Yet few prime ministers, if any, endured a more disastrous relationship with intelligence than he.

PART TWO

THE WINDS
OF WAR

3

Neville Chamberlain
(1937–1940)

Phew! What a week, the place buzzes with rumours and
our own Secret Service continually reports information
'derived from an absolutely reliable source' of the most
alarming character. I don't know how many times we
have been given the exact date and even hour when the
Germans would march into Poland.

NEVILLE CHAMBERLAIN[1]

It is easy to forget that Britain had not one, but three prime ministers
during the Second World War. Neville Chamberlain presided until the
invasion of France in May 1940, and Clement Attlee arrived in Downing
Street shortly after the general election of July 1945, overseeing crucial
end-of-war settlements and the final weeks of the war against Japan. Yet
the story of intelligence and the Second World War overwhelmingly
remains a mythologised Churchillian romp. Newly released documents
show Attlee to have been an improbable action hero, or at least a fan of
covert operations, quietly learning the intelligence trade alongside Eden
and Macmillan in Churchill's wartime training school for future occupants of Downing Street. By contrast, Chamberlain remains something of
a cipher.[2] Amongst a mountain of books about Chamberlain and the road
to Munich, the interaction between intelligence, appeasement and rearmament is hard to find. Despite significant intelligence disasters in the
first six months of the war, Chamberlain's own impact on intelligence
through to May 1940 is almost unknown.[3]

Chamberlain took little interest in British intelligence before 1939. He
eschewed it partly because it was weak. MI6 had suffered budget cuts, and
was underperforming against Nazi Germany. It had ceased to recruit
agents in Mussolini's Italy, while its representatives in the Far East were a

standing joke. Britain's small band of talented codebreakers had valiantly and successfully filled the intelligence void for much of the interwar period, but during the late 1930s they progressively lost access to the high-level communications of Russia, Italy and finally Japan, while never gaining access to German ciphers. Japanese communications, the last substantial insight into Axis activity, were lost in late 1938 when Tokyo radically improved its communications procedures, probably as a result of its thorough penetration of the British embassy there. But this was not just a failure of spies to collect. Those responsible for assessments at the centre of government concentrated on counting aircraft and tanks, rather than thinking seriously about Hitler's intentions. During the intense argument over appeasement, intelligence could not speak truth to power simply because it did not know what the truth was.

Chamberlain made a bad situation worse by filling this intelligence void with his own arrogance and assumptions. Although hampered by the slow pace of British rearmament, he nevertheless made some real choices among a range of alternative policies, deliberately using his wilful and obstinate personality to prevent a serious debate about these options. He had an overwhelming confidence in his own judgement, and believed that his personal skills in diplomacy would overcome any problems and allow him to make robust agreements with untrustworthy leaders. Worst of all, he punished those who purveyed negative intelligence assessments of Hitler, and with MI5's connivance used his own private system of surveillance to destabilise his political rivals.

Although lacking effective intelligence or a proper assessment machine, Chamberlain did have a range of information sources on Hitler available. He chose to rely on Sir Nevile Henderson, the British ambassador in Berlin, who was close to Herman Goering and believed Hitler's assurances of good faith concerning his intentions for Czechoslovakia. Robert Vansittart, the able permanent under-secretary at the Foreign Office, took the opposite view. Understanding that MI6 was struggling, Vansittart had taken pains to develop his own 'private detective agency', which delivered surprisingly good, if sporadic, reports from secret contacts inside Germany. Instead of patiently evaluating these competing views, Chamberlain chose to persecute and marginalise Vansittart. In the inter-war period very little MI6 material and very few intercepts from GC&CS were circulated to the Treasury, which may help to explain why Chamberlain, despite considerable government experience, was so naïve about intelligence.[4]

Nevertheless, Chamberlain loved conspiracy. He sent endless secret diplomatic missions behind the backs of his foreign secretaries. He also used his family as emissaries to outwit his own Foreign Office. New and secret documents have recently come to light that show just how far Chamberlain was prepared to go in using the hidden hand against members of his own party, and even his cabinet colleagues. He also manipulated public opinion to artificially create the impression that his views were widely supported. During the 'Phoney War' of late 1939 and early 1940, some of the most intricate games of espionage were not focused on Germany, but around Chamberlain's immediate circle.

The greatest intelligence failures are those of the imagination. Chamberlain and his government underestimated Hitler because it was difficult to conceive of someone who was bent on world domination and genocide – doubly so given that the horrors of the First World War were only a decade or so in the past. Yet for those willing to listen, Hitler calmly set out his plans in some detail. In the summer of 1933, for example, John F. Coar, a retired American professor specialising in German literature, reported to the American ambassador in Berlin a conversation he had had with Hitler and his deputy Rudolf Hess: 'Hitler talked wildly about destroying all Jews, insisting that no other nation had any right to protest and that Germany was showing the world how to rid itself of its greatest curse. He considered himself a sort of Messiah. He would rearm Germany, absorb Austria and finally move the capital to Munich.'

Even hearing these words, no one believed that Hitler meant literally killing millions of people. Many assumed that his talk of 'destroying all Jews' meant merely removing them from influential jobs and limiting their economic power.[5]

Although Britain appears to have been deeply divided about intelligence in the late 1930s, there was broad consensus on strategy. Everyone wanted to avoid war, not least because British leaders realised it would expose the nation's weakness as an imperial power. Faced with threats from both Germany and Japan, and latterly from Italy and Russia, they had agreed to prioritise Germany, quite simply because this enemy was closest to Britain's shores. Many also agreed with Chamberlain's grand strategy, which was based on deterrence and diplomacy, not fighting. The prime minister, however, wrongly assumed that the dictator states feared conflict as much as he did. In reality, those around Hitler, Mussolini and Hideki Tojo, the Japanese prime minister at the time of Pearl Harbor, were

looking for war. As a former Treasury man, Chamberlain brought an actu-
arial approach to intelligence that involved counting guns and assessing
military capabilities, not political intentions.[6]

British intelligence amplified Chamberlain's misunderstandings. On
the raw size of German forces it was quite accurate, but more importantly,
it did not understand Blitzkrieg. Having lost the First World War, Hitler
chose a military doctrine emphasising highly mobile conflict. In 1936, he
began a second and more rapid phase of rearmament – so rapid that the
German armed forces found it hard to spend all the additional money.
British intelligence began reassessing the German military's power, and
grew increasingly worried between 1936 and 1938 about growing Nazi
capabilities. After 1939, however, the intelligence community became
more optimistic about the balance of numbers, and this 'bean-counting'
approach, which so appealed to Chamberlain, helped to persuade the
prime minister to declare war, because he thought Britain was now relatively stronger. In reality, the Wehrmacht's real capability did not lie in its
size but in its new doctrine. Hitler's audacity and his use of surprise were
far more important.

Britain's biggest intelligence problem was codebreaking. It had lost the
battle over secret communications, and so lacked deep insight into Hitler's
intentions. Although GC&CS numbered only two hundred staff between
the wars, it was still perhaps the world's biggest codebreaking organisation. Up until 1935 it was also the most effective. But just as Britain
confronted the crises of the late thirties, its rivals adopted modern electro-
mechanical cipher machines, and British codebreaking, then still a
bespoke handicraft activity rather than an industrial organisation, went
into a sharp decline. By 1937, GC&CS had lost access to Russian and
Italian diplomatic messages. The following year, the Japanese improved
their code systems, shutting Britain out there too. Political communications between the four revisionist powers, Russia, Germany, Italy and
Japan, would have been especially revealing regarding enemy intentions.
Intercepts would have made Chamberlain's appeasement strategy hard to
sustain, and would also have prevented Mussolini from manipulating the
prime minister with such pathetic ease. Axis diplomacy was a sealed box,
and it was only opened in 1940, when the Americans began to break high-
level Japanese diplomatic ciphers, and generously shared this secret with
Britain.[7]

Human spies could not fill the gap. The years of economic crisis in the
early 1930s cast a distinct shadow over MI6. Its chief, Quex Sinclair,

explained that although his main task was to provide raw intelligence for the services against all potential enemies, the lack of funds meant only partial coverage of secret fascist plans to rearm. Heeding the exhortations of the Foreign Office, Italy was designated 'friendly', and there had been no MI6 agents there when Mussolini invaded Abyssinia in 1936. MI6 concentrated on Germany, but there was little work on either her allies or the neutrals in Europe. This meant an underestimation of German total long-term industrial capability.[8]

Britain's embassy in Berlin was worse still. The ambassador, Nevile Henderson, a close friend of Herman Goering, head of the Luftwaffe, took German reassurances at face value. For their part, the Germans treated Henderson and his staff as idiots. During the *Anschluss* of 1938, Henderson asked his military attaché to call up German military intelligence and ask what was going on. Senior staff officers there assured him that no unusual troop movements were planned for that day, and everything was calm. The attaché was suspicious, and decided to go on a private reconnaissance expedition out into the countryside. He had only reached the outskirts of Berlin when his car became embroiled in a huge traffic jam caused by a column of 3,000 soldiers, police and SS 'moving towards Austria in buses, bakers' vans, pantechnicons and a mass of other miscellaneous vehicles'.[9]

Britain's weak intelligence was not just about collection. Whitehall lacked a central analytical brain that could assimilate and assess material from all sources. The resulting fragmentation, combined with the focus on capabilities, allowed Chamberlain to manipulate or ignore intelligence. As early as late 1933, Sir Warren Fisher, head of the home civil service, had decided that Germany was the 'ultimate potential enemy' against which long-term defence planning had to be directed.[10] But subsequent efforts to determine Germany's strength were frustrated by interservice rivalries between army, naval and air intelligence. 'Bitterness and mistrust' – especially between the Air Ministry and the Foreign Office – dominated relations. The British intelligence apparatus was not yet a community, but rather a number of factions at odds with each other. In 1936, the first glimmerings of central intelligence appeared with the creation of a Joint Intelligence Committee, or 'JIC', but this was then a lowly body, and only served the chiefs of staff. Surprisingly, it did not at this point include representatives from MI5, MI6 or GC&CS.[11]

Intelligence work accelerated after Germany's occupation of the Rhineland in 1936. All the service ministries boosted their assessment efforts accordingly. Yet there was 'remarkably little discussion or collaboration between them'. As we have seen, the only effective cross-Whitehall body was Desmond Morton's Industrial Intelligence Centre, undertaking detailed study into the German war machine. Morton, therefore, might well be credited with the whole idea of central intelligence machinery that would eventually support Downing Street and the Cabinet Office. Even had this existed at the time, Chamberlain was such an incompetent and wilfully blind consumer of intelligence that it would have made little difference. The impact of Morton's work on Chamberlain was to generate anxiety, then paralysis, and ultimately to accelerate appeasement.[12]

Despite not understanding intelligence, the prime minister spied shamelessly upon his cabinet colleagues. He also appreciated the value of covert propaganda and manipulating the press. Nothing underlines this more clearly than his personal friendship with the mysterious figure of Sir Joseph Ball, an MI5 officer who became Director of the Conservative Research Department in the 1930s, when Chamberlain was party chairman. Ball secretly controlled a weekly journal that engaged in what the leading historian of the Conservative Party has called the 'venomous anti-semitic character assassination' of Chamberlain's enemies.[13] One of his colleagues recalled that he was 'steeped in Service tradition, and has as much experience as anyone I know in the seamy side of life and the handling of crooks'.[14] Ball was so determinedly secret that he destroyed most of his own papers in an attempt to vaporise himself from the historical record. Devoted to Chamberlain, he not only ran spies inside the Labour Party but also spied on the prime minister's enemies within his own party, especially the anti-appeasers led by Churchill and Eden, even claiming to have had some of their telephones tapped.[15]

Chamberlain also used Ball to conduct a separate overseas policy behind the back of his first foreign secretary, Anthony Eden. Rightly suspecting Mussolini of being a thug and a double-dealer, Eden preferred to look to the United States for support. Chamberlain, however, paid little attention to Washington, believing that he could reach a binding agreement with Hitler and charm Mussolini into alliance. He sought to cultivate Dino Grandi, the Italian ambassador in London, who had previously been Mussolini's foreign minister. Grandi's power base came from the most radical and violent Italian fascists; he was also an adept covert operator. Knowing that his masters in Italy had a low regard for the British, he enthusiastically encouraged the secret channel in order to poison relations between Eden and Chamberlain, reportedly meeting Ball in the back of London taxis.[16]

Ball's many London friends included a Maltese barrister called Adrian Dingli. A lawyer for the Italian embassy, Dingli knew Grandi well, and was also a member of the Carlton Club in St James's, the oldest and most important of all Conservative clubs. Chamberlain and Ball therefore decided to use Dingli to try to open talks with Italy behind Eden's back.[17] In early 1938, they concocted a letter, purporting to be from the Italians, addressed to Eden offering talks, and gave it to Grandi to pass to Eden. Grandi was nervous, and insisted that if the letter were made public he would have no choice but to reveal Chamberlain as the real author 'in order to protect Italy's honour'. The scheme went ahead, and when Grandi finally met Chamberlain and Eden on 18 February he greatly enjoyed the open disagreement between them, recalling the 'two enemies confronting each other like two cocks in fighting posture'.[18] There was a fearsome row, and further meetings between cabinet colleagues over the weekend could not mend the subsequent crisis. Eden grew annoyed that exchanges with the Italians increasingly came secretly via Ball rather than via the Foreign Office. To Grandi's impish delight, Eden resigned on 20 February 1938 and was replaced by Lord Halifax.[19]

Chamberlain had been using his sister Ida as a further secret conduit to Mussolini. Visiting Rome in early 1938, she was enthralled by the Duce, who 'took both my hands and kissed them'. She reported that he was 'kindly & human', and only wanted peace. Italian diplomats told her they liked Chamberlain, but nurtured a deep dislike and distrust of Eden. Mischievously, they promised to call off their anti-British propaganda if only London recognised Italy's conquest of Albania. In further meetings with Mussolini and his foreign minister Galeazzo Ciano, Ida read out long private messages from Chamberlain. After getting rid of Eden, Chamberlain thanked her for her 'invaluable help'.[20]

The Eden resignation was a potential source of embarrassment. Ball's influence over the Conservative press, however, helped to limit the damage. The BBC barely mentioned the resignation at all, and Ball assured the prime minister that he had 'taken certain steps privately' to manage the story. Amazingly, in the following months Ball watched for counter-attacks on Chamberlain by tapping 'the telephones of the Eden group' and of staff working on their journal the *Whitehall Newsletter*.[21] Various Conservative groups had their own news-sheets and outlets. Ball secretly took control of one named *Truth*, and developed it as both a mouthpiece for appeasement and a weapon with which to discredit his opponents outside and inside the party. Chamberlain was well aware of this, happily confiding to his sister that *Truth* was 'secretly controlled by Sir J Ball!'[22] Remarkably, *Truth* was not only anti-Eden and anti-Churchill, it was also overtly pro-German and pro-Italian. Most striking was its anti-Semitism, attacking mainstream journalists with phrases such as the 'Jew-infested sink of Fleet Street'. Even after the outbreak of war in 1939 and the formation of the national government, *Truth* conducted attacks on behalf of Chamberlain against his cabinet colleagues.[23]

Chamberlain's subsequent visit to Italy was a failure. The Italian secret service had free run of the British embassy in Rome, and used their burglary team, the 'P Squad', to gain access to British communications.[24] They therefore knew what cards the British held. In addition, Chamberlain played his hand badly, and his excessively polite approach seemed craven to the Italians. Ciano rightly concluded that Chamberlain would make almost any concession to avoid war, which underlined the value of a German military alliance. With Hitler's support, Ciano now felt the Italians 'could get whatever we want' from the British.[25] Chamberlain continued to communicate with Rome via the Dingli 'secret channel' until the outbreak of war.[26] Thereafter, Ball, ever attentive to detail, continued for years to tidy up the evidence of his and Chamberlain's spectacular failures. Their go-between, Adrian Dingli, died unexpectedly and violently in Malta on 29 May 1945. Two days later, British security agents seized copies of his highly compromising diary.[27] Fortunately, his wife preserved an extra copy to tell the real tale. Dingli officially died of a self-inflicted gunshot wound to the head. But writing to a friend after the war, Ball explained how he had employed a double agent to work on Italian policy. He added casually that this agent became 'untrustworthy', and so 'I arranged for M.I.5 to look after him in the usual way'.[28]

On 14 May 1938, an odd incident underlined Chamberlain's desire to appease Hitler. The England football team was playing Germany at the Olympic Stadium in Berlin. Hitler missed the match, but Goebbels, Goering, Himmler and Ribbentrop sat amid a crowd of 110,000. Controversially, before kick-off the England captain led his team in giving the Nazi salute during the German national anthem. The instructions for this came direct from the Foreign Office, and were delivered to the players in the dressing room just before the game.[29] Stanley Matthews, who was a member of the team that day, felt that this was no mere football match, and that the Nazis saw it as a test of the New Order: 'This day as never before we would be playing for England.' England won 6–3, with Aston Villa trouncing another German team in Berlin the following day.[30]

The Czechoslovakia crisis dragged on throughout the year. Hitler demanded that the Czechs cede the Sudetenland to Germany, and it fell to a private intelligence network to shake Chamberlain's complacency. In the 1930s, such networks thronged within Europe's capitals. The most important was run by Robert Vansittart, who as we have seen understood how intelligence worked inside Whitehall. Having served as private secretary to two prime ministers and a foreign secretary, and being on extremely good terms with Quex Sinclair, Vansittart had more experience in this field than almost anyone else.[31] Chamberlain, however, removed him as permanent under-secretary at the Foreign Office in 1937, on account of his strong anti-German views. The prime minister privately rejoiced that he had managed 'to push Van out of the F.O.', adding that this was 'deathly secret at present'.[32]

Vansittart had forecast doom and destruction almost as soon as Hitler swept to power. He consistently pressed cabinet ministers to encircle and isolate Germany. These warnings reflected thinly disguised prejudice against Germans generally rather than hard intelligence, and Vansittart's shrill voice often proved his own worst enemy.[33] His replacement, Alexander Cadogan, considered Vansittart to have a one-track mind, exclaiming: 'He's an idiot with an *idée fixe* – a very simple one. He's all façade and nothing else.' Vansittart may have had a fixed idea, but it was essentially the right idea. Now sidelined as a mere 'diplomatic adviser' at the Foreign Office, he nevertheless understood that the key intelligence question was German intentions rather than capabilities.[34]

MI6's own intelligence capability was badly damaged in the mid-1930s. The key MI6 station in Europe for watching Germany was based in The Hague, and was an indirect casualty of the Nazi persecution of the Jews. MI6 operations there, as in much of Europe, were hidden behind the Passport Control Office, which issued visas. These now became flooded with Jews escaping Germany and seeking permits for Palestine. The MI6 head of station, Major Dalton, took sizeable bribes in return for visas and was then blackmailed by one of the clerks, subsequently committing suicide in 1936. The blackmailer was sacked after an inquiry, and sold his services to the German secret service, which allowed it to uncover Britain's best human source reporting on the German navy. Inexplicably, Dalton's MI6 replacement in The Hague took the blackmailer back onto the payroll, along with another German agent. Unsurprisingly, the station was soon flooded with German deception material.[35]

Further disasters followed. On the morning of 17 August 1938, Captain Thomas Kendrick, the MI6 station chief in Vienna, was arrested near Salzburg when he became unacceptably close to German army manoeuvres while driving towards Munich. He was taken to Gestapo headquarters at the Hotel Metropole in Vienna. After being subjected for three days to non-stop harsh interrogation carried out by security teams in eight-hour relays, he was expelled from Germany on grounds of espionage. His staff shut down the station and burned all their papers. Sinclair recalled all the remaining MI6 personnel back to London from Vienna, Berlin and Prague – the key cities in central Europe. If the Germans' intention had been to blunt Britain's operational capacity to gather intelligence on military operations against the Czechs, this was a resounding success.[36]

Vansittart's greatest asset was his 'private detective agency', established by his friend Malcolm Graham Christie. Serving as air attaché in Washington in the 1920s, Christie had come to Vansittart's attention because of his technical and commercial espionage against the Americans. He developed contacts in journalism, government circles and the aircraft industry, and used 'grey methods' alongside borderline illegal techniques. Vansittart knew exactly what to do with Christie, and sent him to Berlin as air attaché. Because Christie had a degree in science from a German university and was an experienced pilot, he immediately made friends high up in government and industrial circles. In January 1930, he left government service and became an international businessman, using his German connections. He deliberately socialised with the German political right, and reported back to London. Like Vansittart, Christie loathed the Nazis, but he was skilled in the collection and interpretation of intelligence. He not only used Nazis as sources, but also courted political rebels, and was close to the dissident Nazi leader Otto Strasser, as well as German Catholic circles. The virtue of the Vansittart–Christie network was therefore its broad base, including both Nazis and different types of opposition. True to the tradition of the best spymasters, Christie's most useful sources remain anonymous, but they included 'Agent X' in the German Air Ministry, 'Agent Y' in the Catholic Church, and 'Agent Fish' who was close to Hitler himself.[37]

Vansittart and his 'private detective agency' jubilantly rode the waves of the Czechoslovakia crisis. Hitler's increasing belligerence served to improve their standing. On 10 August 1938, Halifax, the new foreign secretary, met Christie to hear his reports of another imminent crisis over Czechoslovakia. But the constant reports of Nazi plotting still seemed fantastic, and neither Halifax nor Cadogan knew what to believe. Cadogan later recorded, 'There's certainly enough in the Secret Reports to make one's hair stand on end. But I never quite swallow all these things, and I am presented with a selection.' Like Chamberlain, they still could not imagine the leader of a major European country undertaking the violent course of action that was now predicted.[38]

Vansittart's most remarkable achievement occurred on 6 September 1938. A shadowy figure slipped noiselessly through the garden gate of 10 Downing Street to pay a secret visit. This was Theodor Kordt, chargé d'affaires at the German embassy and one of Vansittart's 'private detectives'. He met Horace Wilson, head of the civil service and Chamberlain's most trusted adviser, to warn him that whatever agreements were made on paper, Hitler intended to invade all of Czechoslovakia. Wilson was unimpressed. The next day, Kordt returned to give the same message to Halifax in a private audience. Whether or not Halifax was convinced was immaterial. Chamberlain had increasingly taken personal control of foreign policy together with Wilson. Similar messages from German generals opposed to Hitler had already been dismissed. Instead of listening to Vansittart's private network, their main alternative source of 'intelligence' came from the straight diplomatic reports of the credulous Nevile Henderson.[39]

Henderson had been appointed as ambassador to Berlin in April 1937 because of his uncanny ability to 'hit it off with dictators'. In the early 1930s, he had formed a close friendship with King Alexander of Yugoslavia. Ironically, it was Vansittart who had identified him as a rising star and promised him a place in the Foreign Office 'first eleven'. Before Henderson departed for Berlin, Chamberlain sent for him, and after this meeting Henderson became convinced that he was the prime minister's personal representative rather than a mere diplomat. His positive reporting of Hitler's assurances underpinned the Munich Agreement that autumn. Early in the morning of 30 September 1938, Hitler, Chamberlain, Mussolini and French prime minister Édouard Daladier agreed to German acquisition of the Sudetenland and postponed the issue of other areas. The Czechs had no choice but to capitulate. Chamberlain returned to a tumultuous welcome, and spoke of 'peace for our time'.[40]

Halifax now stepped away. He had initially agreed with Chamberlain that Hitler merely sought a racially coherent Germany, had no real ambitions beyond areas of German population, and would not aggravate Britain by using military force. But the increasingly angry arguments within Whitehall over the Czechoslovakia crisis changed his mind. The foreign secretary eventually confronted Chamberlain and told him that although Hitler had not won a conflict, the Führer was effectively dictating terms. Chamberlain hated being contradicted. 'Your complete change of view since I saw you last night,' he said, 'is a horrible blow to me.' Lacking in official and reliable intelligence, the prime minister continued to use his own personal estimation in his attempts to predict Hitler's intentions. He believed he had established a personal connection with Hitler when the two had met, and so invested strongly in Hitler's promise that he had no intention of invading all of Czechoslovakia if an arrangement could be made about the Sudeten territories with majority German populations. In September 1938, Chamberlain noted that 'In spite of the hardness and ruthlessness I thought I saw in his face I got the impression that here was a man who could be relied upon when he had given his word.' The prime minister assured his cabinet colleagues that he had secured 'some degree of personal influence over Herr Hitler' – but they were increasingly sceptical.[41]

From Christmas 1938 to the invasion of Czechoslovakia in March 1939, Vansittart's circle were on the rise. Their main weapon was intelligence on Hitler's future intentions. Although Cadogan found Vansittart's reports from Germany 'bloodcurdling', their growing number forced him to conclude that Britain had to assume that Germany was now aggressive. In January 1939, Vansittart was suddenly invited to join the Cabinet Committee on Foreign Policy. He patiently explained to Horace Wilson and Samuel Hoare, two of Chamberlain's most trusted allies, that his intelligence now indicated that Hitler planned an invasion of the Netherlands. But although he was winning the intelligence argument about the German threat, his prescription was unpalatable and he was never welcomed back into the fold. He recommended an alliance with Russia, something about which even his friends in MI6 were sceptical. Many argued that such an alliance would simply drive Germany into the arms of Japan.[42] Indeed, there was some evidence of this from GC&CS. On 14 September 1938, it distributed one of its last successful Japanese intercepts, which showed that Tojo had received a proposal from Berlin for precisely this kind of full offensive military alliance.[43]

Throughout the Munich episode, Joseph Ball continued to spy on Chamberlain's political rivals. Chamberlain even boasted of this in a letter to his sister Ida, gloating that Churchill and the Czech minister in London were 'totally unaware of my knowledge of … their doings and sayings'.[44] Most observers suspect that these telephone taps would have been hard to arrange without some assistance from elements within MI5.[45] Yet the senior officers inside MI5 were vigorously anti-appeasement, and busily informed Cadogan and Halifax of Chamberlain's private diplomacy with Germany.[46] Bizarrely, while all of this was going on, Churchill was receiving secret intelligence on rearmament from the former MI6 officer Desmond Morton. Ramsay MacDonald, Stanley Baldwin and then Neville Chamberlain had approved this arrangement in more peaceful times, but Chamberlain had forgotten his own instruction, and was horrified when Morton reminded him that Churchill was on the circulation list for some of the most sensitive intelligence circulating in Downing Street.[47]

At the centre of all this absurd internal political espionage and counter-espionage was the young Harold Macmillan. Although only a backbench MP, he was the key link between the various anti-appeasement factions, including Eden's 'Glamour Boys' and Churchill's 'Old Guard'. Their supposedly secret meetings at Conservative MP Ronnie Tree's house in St Anne's Gate seem to have been bugged by Ball and his team. Meanwhile, Harold Macmillan, a passionate opponent of Hitler, had taken in forty refugees from the German Sudetenland at his country estate, Birch Grove. In early November 1938, his new Czech guests had joined in the Bonfire Night celebrations, replacing Guy Fawkes with an effigy of Chamberlain. An enthusiastic Macmillan had personally donated his black homburg hat and a rolled umbrella to ensure a perfect likeness of the prime minister.[48]

By Christmas 1938, few in the cabinet shared Chamberlain's confidence in his ability to divine Hitler's intentions. MI5 had recruited further sources inside the German embassy in London, including the former military attaché.[49] The Foreign Office also understood that the majority of the Nazi Party saw Great Britain as 'Enemy No. 1', and that a full-scale military confrontation was likely. A blizzard of rumours, often picked up by military attachés, suggested that Hitler's generals had been told to plan an attack in the west. Halifax noticed a troubling consistency in the myriad fragmentary intelligence. Chamberlain, by contrast, preferred to believe Henderson's assurances from the embassy in Berlin that these were all 'stories and rumours'. The absence of reliable sigint meant there was little decisive material to help.[50] At one point, MI5 resorted to highlighting Hitler's personal insults about Chamberlain in order to shock him out of his complacency. Playing on Chamberlain's vanity, Hitler's use of the word *Arschloch*, or 'arsehole', to describe the prime minister was underlined. It made a 'considerable impression'.[51] At the same time, however, Hitler's regime was genuinely chaotic, with different groups continually developing plans and cancelling them. German exiles and opposition groups, including elements of the German secret service itself, deliberately invented stories in the hope of inspiring action by London or Paris. There were constant rumours and continual mobilisations, making it very hard to distinguish between 'signals' and 'noise'. All of those earnestly warning about German plans, including MI6, worried about the danger of crying wolf and sowing confusion.[52]

In January 1939, perhaps encouraged by Halifax's visible defection from the Chamberlain camp, MI6 changed its tune dramatically: 'Germany is controlled by one man, Herr Hitler,' it reported, 'whose will is supreme and who is a blend of fanatic, madman and clear-visioned realist.' It added: 'his ambition and self-confidence are unbounded, and he regards Germany's supremacy in Europe as a step to world supremacy', and offered the somewhat belated warning that Hitler might well come west in 1939. Of the Führer himself, MI6 assessed that he was 'barely sane, consumed by an intense hatred of this country, and capable both of ordering an immediate aerial attack on any European country and of having his command instantly obeyed'.[53]

The last valuable sigint from GC&CS underpinned this new certainty. At the end of 1938, the German foreign minister, Joachim Ribbentrop, explained to the Japanese ambassador in Berlin, Baron Ōshima, that Hitler wanted to transform the Axis from a mere ideological pact against communism into a platform for a joint war on Britain. Ōshima immediately telegraphed the news back to Tokyo. These were some of the last Japanese messages that GC&CS read during Chamberlain's administration before Tokyo improved its cipher security. Diplomats in the Foreign Office panicked when they read this new intelligence on Hitler's intentions. It suggested that he was planning nothing less than global war.[54]

Remarkably, Chamberlain chose to disregard this definitive sigint, which, taken with the material collected by MI5 in London, pointed only one way: to impending war. The prime minister continued to do so right up until the German attack on Czechoslovakia in March 1939. Although the Foreign Office loathed Chamberlain because of his private diplomacy, diplomats had still held out hopes that he was right about Germany. But with the crushing of the Czechs there could be no doubt. Alexander

Cadogan, who had been appointed at Chamberlain's instigation to replace the violently anti-German Vansittart, conceded that he and the prime minister had been wrong. The story was turning out 'as Van predicted and as I never believed it would'. Meanwhile, he continued, Nevile Henderson, the prime minister's single source in Berlin, had been 'completely bewitched by his German friends'.[55]

British intelligence failures came thick and fast after the German troops marched into Prague in March 1939. On 7 April, Italy invaded Albania, to the general bewilderment of Whitehall and Westminster. Chamberlain, who had sent another craven message to Rome via the 'secret channel' using Ball and Dingli only four days previously, was especially shocked. 'Musso has behaved to me like a sneak and cad,' he moaned. 'He has carried through his smash and grab raid with complete cynicism.'[56] Although MI5 had given a direct warning as the result of its excellent sources in the German embassy in London, Halifax had absurdly then gone to a cabinet meeting two days before the invasion and insisted it was unlikely.[57]

In the subsequent debate in the House of Commons a familiar backbencher rose to speak. Winston Churchill chose the British secret service as his subject, praising it as the 'finest service of its kind in the world'. The subject was an unusual one for an MP, but Churchill was uncommonly expert on the subject. He attacked the government for failing to use the service's excellent product properly, insisted that it had received plenty of intelligence about both Czechoslovakia and Albania, and wondered aloud if some sinister 'hidden hand' was at work, withholding intelligence from ministers. On balance, however, he thought it more likely that Chamberlain's obsession with appeasement and striking a peace deal with Germany had blinded him:

> It seems to me that Ministers run the most tremendous risk if they
> allow the information collected by the Intelligence Department,
> and sent to them I am sure in good time, to be sifted and coloured
> and reduced in consequence and importance, and if they ever
> get themselves into a mood of attaching importance only to
> those pieces of information which accord with their earnest
> and honourable desire that the peace of the world shall remain
> unbroken.

Churchill's accusation that Chamberlain had ignored good intelligence in his blind search for peace was true, but in reality was only one of several problems. As yet, Britain lacked a central brain to undertake proper analysis of intentions as well as capabilities. Although this machinery was emerging in the JIC even as Churchill spoke, the challenge for intelligence analysts everywhere at this time was to abandon pre-formed notions about the way civilised world leaders generally behaved. Policymakers of every persuasion would be surprised by the political events of the next few months.[58]

On 23 August 1939, Britain was hit by a bombshell. Ribbentrop met Molotov, his Soviet counterpart, in Moscow to sign the Nazi–Soviet pact. This was not only an intelligence failure of the first order, since no one had even begun to contemplate such a possibility, it was also a disaster for British foreign policy. Talks aimed at producing an Anglo–Franco–Soviet alliance were in progress, and a joint British–French military mission was in Moscow for this very purpose even as the Germans and Soviets embraced. The result was abject and public failure. Chamberlain had never been keen on these talks in the first place, confessing in his private diary that he felt 'a profound distrust of Russia' and doubted its military capabilities. He believed that Stalin's objective was to absorb the small states around the edge of the Soviet Union – or, in his words, 'getting everyone else by the ears'. But he had been forced to pursue a deal, because Halifax and the chiefs of staff now saw containment as the only rational alternative given the bankruptcy of appeasement.[59]

The Nazi–Soviet pact was a classic case of surprise despite many warnings. Chamberlain and his senior colleagues did not believe these because they did not fit in with their preconceived stereotypes and assumptions about the world. But those with inside knowledge of Moscow had warned publicly of precisely this eventuality. Walter Krivitsky, formerly a senior officer in Soviet military intelligence, dramatically predicted the agreement. He had fled the Soviet secret services the previous year, and taken refuge in America. In April 1939, he wrote a remarkable article for the *Saturday Evening Post* alleging that Stalin had long been contemplating an understanding with Nazi Germany. When Stalin dismissed his foreign minister, Maxim Litvinov, in early May, Krivitsky knew what was coming next, perhaps because Litvinov's Jewish heritage had served as a potential obstacle in negotiations with Hitler. Krivitsky then predicted the Nazi–Soviet pact. But London was sceptical, and indeed Daniel Lascelles, who superintended relations with Russia at the Foreign Office, dismissed Krivitksy's prediction as 'twaddle'.[60]

Oddly, the invasion of Czechoslovakia in the spring of 1939 triggered a surge of British intelligence optimism, even belligerence. Combined with the invasion of Albania, these various shocks resigned Whitehall to the increasing likelihood of war. The JIC perceived Britain's military chances as improving, especially in terms of air power, and London suddenly offered military support to countries as far afield as Poland, Greece and Turkey. The strategy formed a belated attempt at Vansittart's Eastern Front plan to encircle Germany, but now without the vital addition of Russia. It was this very effort, with its guarantee to Poland, that would bring Britain and France to declare war in September 1939. During the summer of that year, MI6 predicted, confidently and correctly, that if war broke out it was most likely to begin with a German strike on Poland. Although MI6 did not predict the Nazi–Soviet pact, it did observe that there was some evidence that many in Germany sought better relations with Stalin. By late August 1939, the JIC assessed that it was now a question of *when* war came, rather than *if*.[61]

Even at this late hour, Chamberlain still ignored the facts and remained preposterously hopeful. MI6 had reported that Herman Goering wanted to come to London for talks, and Sidney Cotton, an extraordinary airman and pioneer of advanced aerial photography, together with the deputy head of MI6 made intensely secret preparations for a meeting with Chamberlain at Chequers.[62] Quex Sinclair then brought news of a possible revolt by the German high command. But both of these rumours were probably elaborate Nazi deceptions designed for Chamberlain's consumption.[63] A week later, on 1 September 1939, Germany invaded Poland.

At exactly eleven o'clock on 3 September, Britain declared war on Germany. One cabinet minister later reminisced about how Chamberlain said quietly, 'Right, gentlemen, this means war.' The rain was pouring down outside, and hardly had he said it than there was a most enormous clap of thunder and the whole Cabinet Room was lit up by a blinding flash of lightning. 'It was the most deafening thunderclap I've ever heard in my life.'[64]

The outbreak of war had an equally startling effect on intelligence. The many secret service and analytical elements in Britain instinctively started to behave like a community. A diplomat began to chair JIC meetings, and the committee now considered political intentions rather than mere capabilities. The new chairman Victor Cavendish-Bentinck, heir to the Duke of Portland, had the advantage of having served in the military before becoming a diplomat in 1918. He was renowned for crossing St James's

Park accompanied by his pet dog Angus, who would spend all day with him in the office, and soon became known as 'the Intelligence Dog'. Unfortunately, Angus did not last long. Crossing Hyde Park Corner one day he noticed another dog coming up Constitution Hill. Leaping forward and barking, he ran under a taxi, making him one of the few British casualties of the 'Phoney War'. Dog accidents aside, Cavendish-Bentinck was an excellent chairman, and played a key role in the JIC's wartime rise.[65]

The only person who appeared not to be shaken by the events of 1939 was Chamberlain. His mental concepts were so fixed that he seemed to see the 'Phoney War' as an extension of appeasement. Four weeks into the war, the prime minister told his sister that he thought Hitler would not push beyond Germany's western borders, and would carry on with a peace offensive. Mysterious emissaries came and went between Britain and Germany throughout the entire year to discuss possible truces, and there is evidence that Chamberlain launched several further secret attempts at backstairs diplomacy shortly after Munich.[66] Meanwhile, there was no real fighting. 'I may be quite wrong', Chamberlain predicted, but 'however much the Nazis may brag and threaten I don't believe they feel sufficient confidence to venture on the Great War unless they are forced into it by action on our part'. 'It is my aim,' he naïvely continued, 'to see that that action is not taken.' Alluding to the national government he had formed at the outbreak of war, containing both Churchill and Eden, Chamberlain believed he had 'the unanimous consent of my colleagues, including Winston'.[67]

Chamberlain 'gave his personal approval' for MI6 to 'continue discussions with the Germans'. Early in October 1939, two MI6 officers in The Hague, Richard Stevens and Sigmund Payne Best, informed London that they were reasonably confident of persuading two dissident senior German officers, one of whom was General von Rundstedt, to visit Holland. They wanted to talk about overthrowing Hitler and establishing a regime run by the army. Best was intoxicated with excitement, and 'saw in this a possibility of literally winning the war off his own bat'. This affected his operational judgement, and also that of those around him. They rushed forward impetuously. The person who should have stopped the ill-fated mission was Sir Nevile Bland, the British minister at The Hague. Having previously served as the go-between for MI6 and the Foreign Office, Bland had considerable experience, and a few years later would serve as a strategic reviewer of all of British intelligence. On 7 November, the MI6 officers excitedly reported that 'a coup would definitely be attempted'. But the

German SD, or security service, had in fact used a double agent to lure Best and Stevens into a superbly executed trap. On 9 November, when they went to meet their contact again at Venlo, near the German border, the agent gave the prearranged signal by taking off his hat. A German snatch squad immediately ran forward firing machine guns into the air and took the two MI6 officers prisoner. What became known as the 'Venlo incident' compromised many British agents and damaged relations with the Dutch government.[68] Even ten years later, the intellectually mediocre Stewart Menzies, chief of MI6, still believed that the overtures from the German army via The Hague had been genuine.[69]

The 'Venlo incident' is symbolic of a wider credulity at this time. Chamberlain failed to understand that a global war was imminent. It was typical of his overconfidence that the longer the Phoney War went on, the more he disregarded intelligence reports and believed that he was right. In fact the war was widening. The Soviet Union joined Hitler in his invasion of Poland, occupying the east of the country and liberating German soldiers captured by the Poles in the first days of fighting. Two months later, Stalin embarked on his disastrous 'Winter War' with Finland. British intelligence saw things more clearly, viewing the conflict as a struggle between the British Empire and a four-headed monster that consisted of Nazi Germany, Soviet Russia, fascist Italy and militarist Japan. Its answer was to plan secret missions and covert actions against Russia as well as Germany.[70]

While MI6 busily planned special operations, including a team of 'volunteer' commandos that they intended to despatch to Finland, Hitler sprung his next surprise: the invasion of Norway. On 3 April 1940, German vessels secretly headed out in advance of the main force, and with shameful Swedish complicity, all of Scandinavia was soon under German control. In a further embarrassment for Chamberlain, a beautiful Russian ballerina turned Nazi spy, Marina Lie, managed to acquire British plans for Norway's liberation, allowing the Germans to claim another victory.[71]

Again Britain had no warning of the invasion, and even Chamberlain recognised that this was a classic case of intelligence failure. He ordered an investigation. It turned out that the Air Ministry had suspected something was up as a result of reconnaissance flights, and that MI6 had passed on some general hints, but had no specific information about timing. The problem was explained to Chamberlain by Arthur Rucker, his principal private secretary: 'The position is that we were fully warned of the preparation by the Germans of an Expeditionary Force on a big scale.' But, he continued, 'we could not, of course, foretell where that Force would be sent'. Senior officials began to realise that even when good intelligence was collected, it was not being assimilated. The JIC needed to be strengthened further. Discussing the matter with Horace Wilson and cabinet secretary Maurice Hankey, Chamberlain agreed that the JIC should be instructed to maintain 'a running and connected story based upon such Intelligence material as seems to point to the need for action'.[72] Norway had sounded a warning that even Chamberlain could not ignore, but although he had now begun to think about substantive intelligence reform, the invasion of France in May 1940 swept his government away.[73]

Neville Chamberlain did not have as much room for manoeuvre as his detractors suggest.[74] He faced enormous challenges, but his elementary error of 'mirror-imaging' his enemies as civilised leaders naturally averse to war made them much worse. So often, premiers disregard intelligence, preferring to believe that the enemy shares their values and thinks like them. Chamberlain was also an intelligence bungler. Not only was he a reluctant consumer of intelligence that did not concur with his world view, he was also a poor manager, and the central machinery did not develop much during his time in Downing Street. His incompetent efforts to use a private secret service to open diplomacy with Rome and Berlin radiated weakness and contributed to an emerging Axis triple threat. At the same time, he marginalised the most experienced intelligence professionals and went shopping for 'intelligence' that would confirm his preconceived ideas, fixing on single-source reports from Berlin.

Chamberlain was not the only bungler. In the higher echelons of government, few understood intelligence or had any idea how it might organise collectively to meet the challenge of fast-moving Blitzkrieg warfare. Halifax, a deeply intelligent and capable man, was bemused by the contradictory stream of material coming out of Germany, on scraps of paper pinned beneath the collars of secret agents. His senior official, Cadogan, was uncomfortable with the secret world and gladly delegated such matters to Gladwyn Jebb, his private secretary. Jebb recalled how his boss seemed to have 'the impression that the reports of the SIS which are circulated in the office are obtained by "hired assassins" who are sent out from this country to spy out the land'. The fact that such a naïve view was entertained at the highest level is revealing.[75]

Hitler was inherently unpredictable. German historians who have immersed themselves in the archives for their entire careers still disagree about whether he was at the outset merely a German nationalist like Bismarck, or whether he always had diabolical plans for world domination. In any case, Hitler loved springing surprises, not least upon his own long-suffering generals. Britain's codebreakers, so celebrated in the context of the Second World War, simply could not read Hitler's intentions. Had they been able to decipher even a sliver of top-level German communications in 1939, Chamberlain could not have sustained his arrogant commitment to a personal appeasement policy. But ironically, the weakness of the codebreakers in 1939 became their future strength. Thereafter, a vast influx of young civilians, irreverent students and unorthodox thinkers forced change, powering the intelligence revolution that became Bletchley Park.[76] With Winston Churchill at the helm, the relationship between intelligence and Downing Street could finally undertake the long-awaited revolution.

4

Winston Churchill
(1940–1941)

Once I was convinced about the principles of this queer and
deadly game, I gave all the necessary orders that very day.
WINSTON CHURCHILL[1]

Winston Churchill was obsessed with intelligence. He arrived in Downing
Street in May 1940 with unparalleled experience of the secret world. For
almost half a century, he had seen intelligence in action in both peace and
war. Churchill was there at the very creation of MI5 and MI6 in 1909.
Most importantly, he understood the importance of intelligence – and
especially sigint – in wartime operations, as he had been First Lord of the
Admiralty from 1911 to 1915, and then secretary of state for war and air
in the last year of the First World War. He then became involved in the
minutiae of the post-war reorganisation of British intelligence. Later, he
immersed himself in the subterranean connections between domestic
surveillance, Irish terrorism and communist subversion. Despite this
remarkable wealth of government experience in the realm of national
security, he remained an outsider. Regarded as a renegade, he had changed
political parties twice, and did not hesitate to challenge conventional
wisdom. He transferred these impulsive tendencies to the world of
intelligence, accelerating the British secret service community as never
before.

Churchill believed passionately in the transformative power of intelligence, and knew it could play a central role in government policy. An
incurable romantic, he loved the craft of espionage and all the paraphernalia of secrecy, and was an enthusiastic advocate of undercover activity
for its own sake. More than this, he also believed in conspiracy, covert
action and special operations – what we might call the power of the hidden
hand. Churchill has been celebrated as one of the great champions of

British intelligence, but his impulsiveness and unpredictability often caused exasperation on the part of his intelligence chiefs. The British intelligence community undoubtedly expanded, innovated and became more connected to policy during the Second World War as a result of his boundless enthusiasm, but it also had to protect itself from his meddling and his impulsive desire to control its detail.

Most importantly, Churchill's wartime government served as a school for future prime ministers. Just as he had learned the craft of intelligence in several previous administrations, so his own wartime ministers, including Clement Attlee, Anthony Eden and Harold Macmillan, all future denizens of Downing Street, saw intelligence at first hand. Senior figures in their governments such as Ernest Bevin, Hugh Dalton and Duncan Sandys had also been members of Churchill's wartime government. Unlike previous prime ministers, Churchill taught his pupils that intelligence was of the utmost importance. His entourage were able to see for themselves the transformative power of secret activity at the top.

Churchill was ahead of his time in his conception of Downing Street. He anticipated a more presidential style of government, gathering around himself a cluster of special advisers and personal staff able to respond instantly to his sometimes whimsical enquiries. Desmond Morton served as his intelligence adviser and linked Number 10 with MI5, MI6 and GC&CS – as well as the volatile world of special operations. Although this style would later be adopted by Harold Wilson, Margaret Thatcher and Tony Blair, it did not always prove popular with Churchill's ministers. As foreign secretary, Anthony Eden found Morton's interventions with Charles de Gaulle and the French resistance especially vexatious, noting in November 1942, 'I wish Morton at the bottom of the Sea.'[2]

Paradoxically, Churchill's weakest suit was secrecy, which he applied stringently to everyone except himself. In 1923 he had 'blown' the secrets of signals intelligence during the First World War in his account of that conflict, and after the Second World War publishers offered him eye-watering sums to write about that global conflict in which he had played such an important part. Once again he was determined to tell all, including the story of secret service, and initially he fought the efforts of the Cabinet Office to enforce secrecy. Sir Stewart Menzies, the chief of MI6, had to be despatched to bring him to heel. After the war, Morton was debating at length with a friend what constituted the 'essence of Winston's life and spirit'. Morton thought 'freelance newspaper correspondent-adventurer' was the best possible description. Churchill loved secret service, but he also loved to tell stories. He was not a man naturally inclined to keep secrets for very long.[3]

He was also abrasive. From the moment he entered Downing Street he wanted to see raw intelligence, not just summaries and appreciations. Most of all he wanted to see all the intercepts provided by the codebreakers at Bletchley Park in their original form. Churchill became Britain's war leader just as the flow of intelligence from Enigma expanded. It would soon become a torrent. Only with great reluctance was he persuaded that he could not see everything. Instead, Menzies personally delivered selections of Ultra to the prime minister in a buff-coloured box.[4] Churchill was proactive, too. At moments of extreme tension, such as the Japanese attack on Pearl Harbor, he would ring Bletchley Park 'at all hours of the day and night' to get the latest news.[5] This allowed him to become a 'do-it-yourself analyst' of raw intelligence, and he often leapt to the wrong conclusions. The misreading of Ultra or the selective use of intelligence underpinned some of his more hare-brained schemes. As the war progressed, Alan Brooke, the Chief of the Imperial Staff, found more and more of his energy expended on containing Churchill's ill-judged enthusiasms. From July 1941 the chiefs of staff were given updates on the latest sigint from Bletchley three or four times a day, to help them deal with the prime minister's 'proddings'.[6]

Yet, it was precisely because of these vexing tendencies that Churchill transformed intelligence at the top. Under him, Whitehall developed the first modern system for incorporating intelligence into strategy and operations, not least with the expansion of the Joint Intelligence Committee. The development of the JIC as the central brain of British intelligence was one of the Churchill government's most important contributions. As we have seen, throughout the interwar period the Foreign Office and the three ministries of the armed services had battled over the control and interpretation of intelligence. This began to be addressed in 1936 with the creation of the JIC, which then worked for the chiefs of staff. But it had remained underpowered and weak. All that changed with the advent of Churchill and his insatiable desire for a daily diet of raw decrypts.[7]

In May 1940, twin disasters catapulted Downing Street into action. The Germans had shocked Europe with their surprise occupation of Norway and the successful invasion of northern France. The lack of warning bothered Churchill, and he ordered the chiefs of staff to rethink how intelligence connected to high-level strategy and operations. As a result, on 17

May, only a few days after Churchill had arrived in Number 10, the JIC was elevated in importance, being given sole authority for producing strategic and operational assessments, alongside a new warning function. Major General Hastings 'Pug' Ismay, Churchill's senior staff officer, was ordered to bring JIC intelligence 'to the notice of the prime minister at any hour of the day or night'.[8]

This was less about creating a good government machine than about personal control. In August 1940, Churchill told Ismay that he was fed up with receiving 'sifted' intelligence from the various authorities. He renewed his demand for raw material that he could analyse himself, and insisted that Morton 'be shown everything', and should then 'submit authentic documents to me in their original form'.[9] A few months later he asked to see a list of all those who were allowed to see this special material from GC&CS. He expressed horror at the 'vast congregation', and ordered that it be cut drastically. By November 1940, there were very few recipients of raw Ultra, although many more received the information in a disguised or digested form.[10]

Churchill constantly surprised the chiefs of staff with questions derived from specific Ultra decrypts. His own understanding of them was often at odds with that of the JIC. He used Ultra to underpin his own eccentric approach to strategy, which was romantic, inspirational, loquacious and often fuelled by alcohol. Talking late into the night, he used intelligence and his alarming ability to orate spontaneously at inordinate length to wear down his opponents in the war cabinet. Both Brooke and Alexander Cadogan, the senior official at the Foreign Office, used their diaries to let off steam by recording the vexations that Churchill caused his immediate circle. Cadogan asked how they ever managed to run the war 'with the PM spending hours of his own and other people's time simply drivelling, welcoming every red herring so as only to have the pleasure of more irrelevant, redundant talk'.[11]

The reinforced JIC was there to help the chiefs of staff resist Churchill. It expanded to include MI6 (which also had responsibility for the codebreakers of GC&CS), MI5 and the Ministry of Economic Warfare (which oversaw special operations), and more personnel joined the analytical team drafting the assessments. Increasing the amount of assessed intelligence would, it was hoped, prevent the prime minister from engaging in DIY analysis. Yet Churchill was sometimes right in his reading of the decrypts, and was far ahead of the 'professional analysts' in spotting one of the most remarkable turning points of the war, Hitler's stunning decision to launch an attack on Russia on 22 June 1941.

Churchill forced Whitehall and Westminster to wake up to the importance of intelligence in modern war. This not only included intercepts, but extended to scientific developments. Indeed, the prime minister backed the creation of entirely new forms of electronic intelligence and the acceleration under R.V. Jones of the 'Wizard War', a field that would constitute an entirely new secret world by the 1950s. Most importantly, he understood the strategic importance of special forces and covert action. Britain's most famous secret armies owed their existence to Churchill's enthusiasm for wild characters. This included the SAS, the Commandos and the Chindits. Conventionally-minded staff officers detested this sort of unconventional activity. Brigadier Orde Wingate, who led a successful guerrilla revolt against the Italians in East Africa 1940, was actually demoted by his superiors at GHQ Middle East because of his maverick ideas. Churchill rescued him from his military exile and forced the chiefs of staff to take him seriously, allowing him to create the Chindits in Burma, who then inspired a generation of behind-the-lines enthusiasts who believed passionately in what they called the 'fourth dimension of warfare'.

This was not mere romanticism. Churchill understood the importance of unconventional thinking about warfare, and so was the first to connect organisations like SOE and MI6 to national policy. His inner circle learned these dark arts, and began to conceive of a whole new secret way in warfare – which later extended to peacetime. Churchill's adherents and associates, including some improbable converts like Clement Attlee, his deputy prime minister, ensured that this revolutionary approach to secret statecraft, in which bribery, blackmail and other kinds of subterfuge were used to exercise British power, extended over the next fifty years.

Churchill's most immediate concern was closer to home. He worried that Britain might be overwhelmed by Nazi secret warfare. During late 1939 and early 1940, this fear focused specifically on Ireland as 'England's back door', and anxiety about Irish–German links reached fever pitch. In May 1940, MI6 despatched a veteran Anglo-Irish intelligence officer called Charles Tegart to Dublin to investigate. His fantastic reports would not have been out of place in a William le Queux novel of 1913. He claimed that IRA leaders had allowed 2,000 Nazi agents to be landed by submarine, and that they were already at work preparing hidden aerodromes for a surprise German invasion from the west. Churchill and his new cabinet accepted this at face value and panicked, extending a rather desperate offer of Irish unity to Éamon de Valera, who skilfully played up the fifth-column menace. Secretly, the British military prepared for a pre-emptive invasion of southern Ireland.[12]

Churchill's long association with both India and Ireland underpinned his views on subversion. During the First World War, Germany had launched elaborate plots conniving with rebels in imperial locations as far apart as Canada, Ireland, India and Singapore. As early as 1937, MI6 warned Robert Vansittart, then still the top official in the Foreign Office, that Germany was advancing similar plans for Ireland in the event of war. All of Britain's secret services began to turn their attention across the Irish Sea. The IRA, who had been allies of the Soviet Union in the previous decade, sensed an opportunity and began to explore a secret alliance with Hitler. In early 1937, the IRA chief of staff, Tom Barry, visited Germany to discuss opportunities for wartime sabotage. Several other high-level visits followed, and by 1939 even the Irish government were of the opinion that Sean McBride, the IRA's director of intelligence, was working more eagerly for the Germans than for his own organisation.[13]

During the summer and autumn of 1939, German emissaries visited Dublin, proving their identities by matching a pound note that had been torn in half with one carried by their contacts. In August, the Abwehr, Germany's overseas secret service, actually informed the IRA that war was coming – 'probably in one week'. Meanwhile, MI6 had learned, at least in outline, of further meetings between the IRA and the head of the Abwehr, Admiral Canaris. At this point de Valera denied that there was any connection between the IRA and Nazi Germany, but MI6 knew otherwise.[14]

British intelligence overestimated the 'backdoor' threat because of an IRA bombing campaign on the mainland. The IRA was a small and divided organisation in the late 1930s and early 1940s, with innumerable splits between those who wanted to do little, those who wanted a guerrilla war against Ulster, and those who wished to bomb the British mainland. In 1939, the faction that advocated bomb attacks on England triumphed. Their plans were somewhat eccentric, and included blocking London's sewers with two tons of quick-drying cement. Many of their explosives were homemade and most of their attacks failed. Even so, in June 1939 there were seventy-two IRA attacks in England. The worst came two months later, when a bomb exploded in a busy shopping street in Coventry, killing five people and injuring a further fifty-one. In early 1940, two IRA operatives, James McCormick and Peter Barnes, were hanged for their role in the bombing, after much debate in cabinet over their possible reprieve. In another incident, five hundred pounds of explosives were discovered in a raid on a chip shop in Manchester. De Valera refused intelligence cooperation against the bombers.[15]

There were a further fifty IRA attacks in the period up to May 1940. Churchill was particularly exercised, which formed the personal background to the panic about a German fifth column as he arrived in office. It clearly loomed large in the new prime minister's imagination, and he sought the views of the chief of MI6 on German activity on the west coast of Ireland, asking, 'Are there any signs of succouring U-boats in Irish creeks or inlets?' He urged that more be spent on building up a better force of agents in Dublin. Sidney Cotton, an eccentric businessman who cooperated with MI6 and who pioneered aerial reconnaissance, was despatched on a survey of the west coast of Ireland in search of U-boats.[16]

Churchill arrived in Downing Street on 10 May 1940. Five days earlier, Hermann Görtz of the Abwehr landed by parachute in County Meath. A hardened spy who had been jailed for four years for his espionage activities in Britain in the 1930s, Görtz's task was to establish a more permanent liaison with the IRA and develop detailed plans for attacks on Northern Ireland.[17] The Garda raided one of his safe houses a few weeks later and recovered Görtz's uniform, his parachute, documents referring to 'Plan Kathleen', and £20,000 in cash. The Dublin government brought some of those arrested before the courts, and the affair received considerable publicity.[18] Görtz managed to evade the authorities for another eighteen months, and after his capture he committed suicide by biting on a glass phial filled with prussic acid.[19] Guy Liddell, a senior MI5 officer, eventually came to regard the Görtz case as 'fairly conclusive proof' that the Germans were working in close conjunction with the IRA.[20]

In reality, the IRA was small and ineffective in May 1940. It admired Hitler no more than it had admired Stalin in the previous decade. These were merely opportunistic explorations on its part.[21] But its expansive bombing campaign in England, together with some genuine instances of Nazi agents with secret radios and subventions of cash, gave substance to the largely fictional fifth-column menace. Hermann Görtz and his associates transferred some £50,000 to the IRA in this period. This was more than enough to alarm Downing Street. In May 1940, the nascent JIC warned that the IRA could rapidly grow to 30,000 members, and that German aircraft parts and spares had already been smuggled into Ireland.

Churchill ordered plans for an invasion of southern Ireland to be drawn up using newly arrived Canadian troops.[22]

By the summer of 1940, the fifth-column menace appeared terrifying. The Netherlands and France had surrendered after only limited resistance. For Churchill, and indeed President Roosevelt, the most plausible explanation for this surprising turn of events was an insidious 'enemy within'. In reality, Hitler's thrust into Holland, Belgium and France was informed by excellent signals intelligence derived from the intercepted messages of the French high command, which also revealed British plans.[23] Nevertheless, in July 1940, with Churchill's approval, Roosevelt sent William J. Donovan, chief of America's embryonic intelligence service, to Britain to investigate 'fifth column methods'. He found a receptive audience. Churchill was now obsessed with the idea that a large fifth column was preparing the ground for a German invasion of Britain.

Donovan found hard facts difficult to come by. The British public were infected with what Churchill himself called a 'spy mania' – just as they had been in the First World War. German spies were seemingly everywhere. In one odd case, locals assumed a cattle stampede on the island of Eilean Shona off western Scotland was the work of German agents.[24] The police, the army and the security services were inundated with reports about mysterious foreign men on trains, flashing lights assumed to be signals to the enemy, and above all the menace of carrier pigeons, which were seen as the main means for spies sending secret messages to Germany. An army of British birds of prey was marshalled to bring down the pro-German pigeons on their way back to the Fatherland.[25] MI5 took the pigeon threat seriously, and even had its own anti-pigeon section under Flight Lieutenant Richard Melville Walker.[26]

The idea of a fifth column captured the popular imagination. One woman, a rare voice of scepticism, recorded the everyday experience: 'From every part of the country there came the story of the Sister of Mercy with hobnailed boots and tattooed wrists whom somebody's brother's sister-in-law had seen in the train.' Every unusual occurrence was explained by the hidden hand of Nazi agents. Remarkably, the newly formed Ministry of Information dismissed any doubts as further evidence of subterranean activity. Anyone who thought it could not happen in Britain, it insisted, had 'simply fallen into the trap laid by the fifth column itself', adding that the top priority of the fifth column was of course 'to make people think that it does not exist'. In a perfect climate of conspiracy, doubters were themselves part of the vast plot. The police and security agencies were flooded by absurd reports of suspicious Nazi doings.[27]

Churchill had personal reasons for fearing subversion. Pro-German sentiment, often converging with virulent anti-Bolshevism, was rife amongst the British aristocracy. Lord Londonderry, Churchill's own cousin and the government minister responsible for the RAF in the early 1930s, was notoriously pro-German. Although not a fascist himself, he sought to pursue friendship with the Nazis at any cost, flying to Germany to meet Hitler and Goering, and repeatedly hosting Ribbentrop and 'a noisy gang of SS men' in his stately home during 1936.[28]

Evidence of real Nazi spies in important places confronted Churchill within days of his arrival in Downing Street. On 18 May 1940, the Tyler Kent espionage case exploded, shaping the new prime minister's immediate views on subversion and increasing his fears. Tyler Kent was a lowly cipher clerk at the American embassy in London, but he had close links with the Right Club, a pro-German and anti-Semitic group. He used an intermediary to pass top-secret documents, including summaries of conversations between Churchill and Roosevelt, to the Germans and the Italians. MI5 raided his flat and found 1,929 official documents, as well as Churchill's cables and a notebook containing the names of people under surveillance by Special Branch and MI5. The haul also included agreements on Anglo–American intelligence cooperation. Kent's espionage only came to light because MI5 had managed to penetrate the Right Club and the codebreakers at Bletchley Park were now able to read Italian communications.[29] Churchill and Roosevelt had no way of knowing how far this subterranean network had spread. Both were horrified by the presence of someone with profoundly Nazi beliefs at the centre of the nascent transatlantic relationship. Guy Liddell noted in his diary: 'It seems that the PM takes a strong view about the internment of all 5th columnists at this moment and has left the Home Secretary in no doubt about his views. What seems to have moved him more than anything was the Tyler KENT case.'[30] Kent never abandoned his beliefs. After serving his prison sentence and returning to the United States he became the publisher of a newspaper with links to the Ku Klux Klan, and spent his time asserting that President John F. Kennedy was part of a communist conspiracy.[31]

Precisely because of the German offensive in Europe, refugees and 'enemy aliens' were now a growing issue at home. Churchill wondered who among them were German or Italian agents. The Chamberlain government had worked hard to avoid mass internment, which had gone badly wrong in the First World War. That said, at least thirty men and women were interned even before Chamberlain declared war.[32] In 1939 the procedure had been for local tribunals to screen suspects, and less than one in a hundred, mostly Nazi sympathisers, were interned as 'Category A' risks. These now amounted to 5,600 people. Around 6,800 received ambiguous 'Category B' status, and 64,000 people, mostly fleeing Nazi oppression, were deemed 'Category C' and were left at liberty. In the febrile atmosphere of May 1940, Churchill gave the stark order to 'Collar the lot.' In practice this meant interning all male aliens and all women in 'Category B'. The authorities rounded up some 27,000 people, including 4,000 women, most of whom were Jewish refugees. Because this was a panic measure, many went to temporary camps, including the racecourse at Kempton Park, where conditions were appalling.

Churchill was so anxious about the fifth-column danger that he thought the detention camps might themselves become launch points for insurrection, possibly reinforced by the arrival of German parachutists. Officials tried to address the problem by deporting some of the internees to Canada and Australia. On 2 July 1940 the liner *Arandora Star* was torpedoed off the Irish coast with the loss of several hundred lives. Many of the dead were Jewish refugees in 'Category C'. Churchill's policy had backfired, and caused a furore in Parliament. Under pressure, the prime minister performed a dramatic U-turn, and by August 1941 only about 1,300 refugees were still interned, mostly on the Isle of Man.[33] Many of these were dedicated fascists, and on Hitler's birthday in April 1943 they celebrated by coming together to sing the Nazi Party anthem 'The Horst Wessel Lied' in the camp canteen. Importantly, many of those initially interned by Churchill should not have been, while others, often with society connections, escaped detention. One columnist for *The Times* wondered, if they interned all the pro-Germans in Britain, 'how many members of ... the House of Lords would remain at large?'[34]

MI5 found itself in a mess in 1940. Spending most of their time investigating aliens and refugees, staff soon became overwhelmed by the huge numbers involved. Because home secretaries had been consistently squeamish about issuing warrants for phone tapping, or intercepting the mail of British citizens, MI5 had no clear idea whether there was a connection between German secret service operations, Nazi sympathisers and enemy aliens. Moreover, while it was tied up with the alien problem it had little time to address other important issues.[35] Having moved from the top floor of Thames House to new wartime headquarters at Wormwood Scrubs Prison, and then decamped to Blenheim Palace to escape the Blitz, MI5 described itself as being in a 'chaotic' state.[36]

Unfairly perhaps, this prompted Churchill to sack Vernon Kell, the long-serving MI5 director-general. He moved the control of MI5 from the Home Office to a new Home Security Executive under Lord Swinton, formerly secretary of state for air, and ordered him to 'find out whether there is a fifth column ... and if so eliminate it'. Oddly, Sir Joseph Ball, a Chamberlain henchman and one of Churchill's detractors, was chosen to run its shadowy Intelligence Committee. Meanwhile, the prime minister's anxiety about 'the enemy within' flitted from aliens to communists and IRA terrorists. But he understood that MI5 badly needed reform. In early 1941, he chose as director-general Sir David Petrie, who had done the same job in India. Petrie restored confidence, and MI5 went from success to success.

Although Churchill had overestimated the number of fifth columnists in Britain, his fears were not entirely unwarranted. Real traitors did exist, and MI5 set up a clever 'false flag' operation to catch them. Working from the basement of a London antique shop, it attracted more than a hundred would-be pro-Nazi spies into its web with excited talk of invisible ink and secret plots. Assuming they were aiding Berlin, these individuals, including both foreigners and British fascists, unwittingly offered plans of military defences, reports on amphibious tanks and details of experimental jet fighters to undercover MI5 officers. British security officers even acquired a stock of replica Iron Cross medals to award to especially zealous members of the network for their good work and prove that they really were working for Hitler.[37]

Churchill did not only fear subversion; he also saw it as a useful offensive weapon. Indirect warfare, including subversive propaganda and economic sabotage, fascinated him. Accordingly, he conceived of an anti-Nazi fifth column in Europe that would beat the Germans at their own game.[38] Morton was no less enthusiastic. On 27 June 1940, he told Churchill that anti-sabotage was well in hand under Swinton, but 'offensive underground activities' against the Axis were neither centralised nor vigorous. Agreeing with the prime minister, Morton argued that 'strong underground action ... if carefully thought out and coordinated can play an important part in helping to defeat the enemy'. Indeed, Morton now believed that this sort of event-shaping activity was more important than gathering intelligence.[39]

Churchill acted quickly. On 16 July he gave Hugh Dalton, a Labour MP who had long opposed appeasement, responsibility for what he called 'the Ministry of Ungentlemanly Warfare'. This was the new Ministry of Economic Warfare, which encompassed propaganda, economic sabotage and special operations, including what would soon become the Special Operations Executive, or SOE. Having served as under-secretary of state at the Foreign Office in the 1920s, Dalton understood intelligence, and had experience of dealing with GC&CS intercepts. Churchill also thought that Labour politicians were more suited to underground work because it included the promotion of economic sabotage and labour unrest.[40] Nonetheless, subversion was a hot potato in Whitehall. Prior to Churchill's arrival, it had been owned by a small department of MI6 under Major Laurence Grand. MI6 was underperforming, and this section was especially weak. Although Grand was flamboyant, gregarious and well-liked, everyone knew he was not up to the task, and he had become a universal figure of fun – Dalton nicknamed him 'King Bomba', after Ferdinand II of Sicily, who bombarded his own cities in 1849.[41] Even Grand's senior official remarked that to have him in charge of subversion was 'like arranging an attack on a Panzer division by an actor on a donkey'.[42]

Dalton's Ministry of Economic Warfare was essential. But Churchill's passion for forming new organisations caused trouble. MI6, the Foreign Office and the chiefs of staff all hated SOE for cutting across their jurisdictions, and for two years it remained ineffective while Dalton presided over an unholy amount of bureaucratic infighting. Menzies fought doggedly to resist its growth, insisting that SOE's desire to stir things up imperilled the safety of his own traditional intelligence networks. Conversely, Dalton's chief of staff complained that MI6 had 'a "false beard" mentality ... especially those who have been in the show for a very long time'. 'Times have changed,' he continued, 'and "secret" activities are now the rule rather than the exception.' Precisely because secret activities were now everywhere and seemed to touch everything, Whitehall was ablaze with arguments over subversion. The extraordinary interdepartmental warfare over SOE between 1940 and 1942 was a symptom of Churchill's determination to change how Britain thought about warfare and to fully embrace subterranean techniques. The infighting only decreased in 1942, when Lord Selborne replaced Dalton. Quietly effective and close to Eden, Selborne enabled some of the frictions that SOE had created to subside.[43]

SOE was a widely known secret within Whitehall. By contrast, Bletchley Park was not – with a few exceptions, even the inhabitants of Churchill's private office knew nothing of Ultra: his various private secretaries who handled the mysterious boxes of intercepts only became aware that they had contained Ultra material in the 1970s. The boxes arrived in Number 10 with a strict notice: 'Only to be opened by the prime minister.' The secretaries placed them on the prime minister's desk, 'and left [them] for him to re-lock'. The Ultra secret really was ultra-secret – even in Downing Street.[44]

Bletchley Park was only one part of the vast sigint operation presided over by GC&CS. The British codebreaking empire, which numbered some 10,000 people by the end of the war, also intercepted diplomatic traffic ('flimsies', also known as 'BJ's, or 'blue jackets', after the colour of their folders) from dozens of countries. This material was full of political gossip, and Churchill characteristically found it irresistible. His favourite reading included seemingly obscure stuff, such as messages from the Brazilian ambassador in London. The volume was incredible – reaching 13,000 messages in 1941 and increasing dramatically thereafter. It was Morton's job to sift through this material, selecting those messages that he knew would interest the prime minister.[45]

Stewart Menzies also brought Churchill human agent reports, known as 'CX', from MI6. On the whole, though, MI6 and its human intelligence – or 'humint' – underperformed, and Menzies found the flow of decrypts from the codebreakers vital in terms of both maintaining his personal standing and defending the reputation of MI6 within Downing Street. In Europe he was also able to piggyback to some degree on the governments-in-exile by trying to restore their agent networks in Europe, but in other regions, including the Far East, MI6's wartime performance was weak. In August 1940, a teleprinter circuit connected the MI6 headquarters at Broadway Buildings in St James's with Downing Street, where Group Captain F.W. Winterbotham helped Menzies to select the 'headlines' for Churchill.[46] One MI6 agent, codenamed 'Knopf', did provide Menzies and Churchill with valuable intelligence on Hitler's plans for the Eastern Front and the Mediterranean – including the location of the so-called 'Wolf's Lair', Hitler's headquarters in eastern Prussia. Knopf and his sub-network provided access to the upper echelons of the Third Reich, informing London that, for example, the Führer was 'determined to capture Stalingrad at all costs'.[47] For the most part, however, Menzies relied on sigint.

Unlike Menzies, Churchill adored science, and depended heavily on his scientific adviser 'Prof' Frederick Lindemann. Meeting Churchill almost daily, Lindemann enjoyed more influence than any other civilian adviser. Together they helped to create an entirely new form of scientific spying that would come to be called 'electronic intelligence'. On 12 June 1940, one of Lindemann's protégés, a young Oxford scientist working for MI6 called R.V. Jones, was asked by the head of the RAF element that worked with Bletchley Park about a puzzling reference to something called a 'Knickerbein', or 'crooked leg'. No one could understand what it was for. Jones developed a theory that the Germans were using radio beams to guide their bombers. The bizarre theory, unsurprisingly, made its way back to Churchill. Shortly afterwards, a captured German flier gave some details of the system under interrogation: when two radio beams intersected, the bombs were dropped automatically and found their target.

On 21 June, Churchill summoned Jones to Downing Street. Ushered into the Cabinet Room, he found himself sitting with the prime minister, his former Oxford tutor Lindemann, and an array of advisers. Jones was only twenty-eight, but was unabashed by the company – he knew the business was simply 'too serious'. He sensed a lack of comprehension around the table, and decided to tell his tale like a detective story. Churchill, predictably, was captivated, and he described the collective fascination in the room as 'never surpassed by the tales of Sherlock Holmes'. Without informing the cabinet or the chiefs of staff, he ordered that the existence of the German radio beams be assumed, 'and for all countermeasures to receive absolute priority', before adding that the 'slightest reluctance or deviation ... was to be reported to me'. Churchill later recalled that 'in the limited and ... almost occult circle obedience was forthcoming with alacrity, and on the fringes all obstructions could be swept away'.[48]

The prime minister's response to the inspired deductions of Jones brilliantly captures his effect on intelligence. Impulsive and romantic as he was, his interventions could be critically important, and often inspired immediate action when the machine had become slow. The RAF created an entire special unit called '80 Wing' to jam the German beams with a counter-weapon codenamed 'Aspirin'. Sometimes this simply bent the beams, causing the Luftwaffe to drop their bombs in the wrong place. In September 1940 the Germans came up with a new system called the 'X-beam', and Jones had to create a new jamming system, codenamed 'Bromide'. Churchill is often associated with the now heavily debunked story that he allowed Coventry to be bombed to save the secret of Ultra.

In fact, the reverse is true. He was at the forefront of deploying a new form of intelligence that saved many of Britain's cities from greater bombardment just before the onset of the Blitz in the autumn of 1940.[49]

A year later, the prime minister visited Bletchley Park. On 6 September 1941, he was escorted into the famous huts, and Alan Turing was asked to tell him about the remarkable mathematical triumphs that had been accomplished there. Being a rather shy character, Turing allowed his colleague Gordon Welchman to take over. Before he could finish, the director, Alastair Denniston, interrupted and moved Churchill on. Welchman later fondly recalled: 'whereupon Winston, who was enjoying himself, gave me a grand schoolboy wink'. The prime minister moved on to tour the machine room in Hut 7. His bodyguards tried to follow him in, but the sentries shouted 'Not you!' so they waited obediently outside. Here Churchill could see intelligence being produced on an industrial scale, with forty-five machine operators in action.

He stood on a pile of bricks and gave an impromptu address to some of the codebreakers. 'You all look very innocent; one would not think you knew anything secret.' He explained that he called them 'the geese that lay the golden eggs – and never cackle!' With deep emotion, he explained how grateful he was for all their work, and how important it was. Privately, he was struck by the informality of the place and its eccentric inhabitants: it reminded him more of a university common room than a military camp. Winding down the window of his car, he said to Denniston, 'About that recruitment – I know I told you not to leave a stone unturned, but I did not mean you to take me seriously.'

Churchill would have been shocked to know that all was not well at Bletchley Park. Managed by MI6, some of whose officers struggled to understand technology, the codebreaking operations were starved of resources. With Germany's new Enigma keys coming on stream and a vast amount of fresh material to process, the situation soon reached breaking point, and some of the codebreakers Churchill had met on his visit elected to write to him personally. On 21 October 1941, the anniversary of the Battle of Trafalgar, Stuart Milner-Barry, a chess champion turned Bletchley cryptanalyst, was given the unenviable task of conveying their letter to the front door of 10 Downing Street and handing it to a bemused official. The letter thanked Churchill for his visit, and continued:

We think, however, that you ought to know that this work is being held up, and in some cases is not being done at all, principally because we cannot get sufficient staff to deal with it. Our reason for writing to you direct is that for months we have done everything that we possibly can through the normal channels, and that we despair of any early improvement without your intervention ... it is very difficult to bring home to the authorities finally responsible either the importance of what is done here or the urgent necessity of dealing promptly with our requests.

They offered him several alarming examples of bottlenecks and hold-ups. One concerned the decoding of German Army and Air Force Enigma in Hut 6, which was especially close to Churchill's heart, given his obsession with Rommel and developments in the Western Desert:

We are intercepting quite a substantial proportion of wireless traffic in the Middle East which cannot be picked up by our intercepting stations here. This contains among other things a good deal of new 'Light blue' intelligence. Owing to shortage of trained typists, however, and the fatigue of our present decoding staff, we cannot get all this traffic decoded. This has been the state of affairs since May. Yet all that we need to put matters right is about twenty trained typists.[50]

Churchill was apoplectic. The result was one of his famous messages headed 'Action This Day'. He insisted that Bletchley Park's needs be met in full, and with extreme priority. As a result, throughout 1941 the British were able to read all German air and army intercepts in collaboration with an American liaison group working at Bletchley Park. The Americans had not made headway with Enigma, but had achieved an equivalent triumph against Japanese diplomatic ciphers. Thus, during the summer of 1941 the British were also reading the secrets of Germany's Japanese allies, including the vital messages of Baron Ōshima, the Japanese ambassador in Berlin, to whom Hitler liked to talk at length, and who was regarded as his Japanese confidant.[51]

In October 1941, Churchill and Roosevelt held a top-secret meeting off Newfoundland on board the US Navy ship the USS *Augusta* to discuss military matters, including America's then top-secret assistance to the British fight against Germany. On his way to the meeting, Churchill made special arrangements for Ultra to reach him 'in a weighted case, so that they will sink in the sea if anything happens to the plane'.[52] A few weeks later, British codebreakers intercepted a communiqué from the Japanese embassy in London to Tokyo with a remarkably detailed account of the secret meeting. The news stunned Churchill. Even worse, it transpired that one of those who passed the information to the Japanese was not only a highly regarded member of the House of Lords, but a long-time Churchill associate.

In 1919 William Forbes-Sempill, a pioneering commander in the Royal Flying Corps whose father had been an aide to King George V, led a mission to Japan – then a British ally – to help it develop naval air power. When Britain terminated the alliance with Japan in the 1920s, Sempill secretly continued assisting Tokyo, providing it with the designs of the latest engines, bombs and aircraft carriers. He also encouraged the development of Japanese naval air power as a national strategy. In 1924, MI5 had begun watching Sempill and intercepting his correspondence, but it hesitated to act because of his status as a war hero at the heart of the British aristocracy. By the mid-1930s, Sempill had become a member of the House of Lords, and joined a number of British pro-Nazi groups. He believed that Britain should have allied with Germany and Japan against Russia and the communists.[53]

Sempill avoided internment because of his status. He would visit Churchill, and then relay the content of their conversations to the Japanese embassy. When the prime minister realised the severity of the leak in October 1941 he ordered: 'Clear him out while time remains.' A few days later, Morton wrote: 'The First Sea Lord … proposes to offer him a post in the North of Scotland. I have suggested to Lord Swinton that MI5 should be informed in due course so they may take any precautions necessary.' At one point, the attorney general secretly considered prosecuting Sempill. But when the Admiralty confronted him and pressed for his resignation, Churchill interceded and required only that Sempill be 'moved'. This is a classic case of the prime minister protecting himself. 'If Sempill had been revealed as a spy, it would have been politically calamitous for Churchill at a low point in the war.' Even when he was caught calling the Japanese embassy several times in the week following the attack on Pearl Harbor, Sempill still escaped arrest. After the war, he was decorated by both the Japanese and the British. The latter award was widely regarded as an effort to cover up his activities.[54]

Towards the end of March 1941, Churchill read one particular Ultra report 'with relief and excitement'. It showed a major transfer of German armour from Bucharest in Romania to Cracow in southern Poland. 'To me,' he recalled, 'it illuminated the whole Eastern scene like a lightning flash. The sudden movement ... could only mean Hitler's intention to invade Russia in May.' The armoured units returned to Bucharest, but this, he correctly surmised, simply meant a delay from May to June because of local trouble in the Balkans caused by an SOE-inspired coup. 'I sent the momentous news at once to Mr Eden.'[55]

Churchill observed with some satisfaction that it was not until 12 June – only ten days before the attack – that the Joint Intelligence Committee agreed that Hitler had definitely decided to invade Russia. The idea that he would voluntarily begin fighting on a further front when he was already busy in Western Europe and North Africa seemed improbable. The prime minister's DIY analysis had triumphed on this occasion, and he added jubilantly in his own account: 'I had not been content with this form of collective wisdom,' depending instead on Morton's 'daily selection of tit-bits, which I always read, thus forming my own opinion, sometimes at much earlier dates'.[56]

Unsurprisingly, Churchill's account of the Second World War often portrays him in a favourable light. Yet newly opened archives confirm that he indeed predicted the German attack on Russia before almost anyone else. On 26 March, Ultra showed that Hitler had indeed moved a vast force, including two whole army headquarters, from the Balkans to southern Poland. Only a few days later, Churchill informed Stalin of this directly, disguising the source by hinting that the intelligence came from 'a trusted agent'. Stalin did not believe Churchill, and neither did the Russian chiefs of staff.[57] Frustrated, Churchill repeatedly pressed Stewart Menzies to send Ultra-based material to Moscow in 1941. However, Menzies worried about both the volume of material going to Stalin and its security. He warned Churchill personally and repeatedly not to let the Russians know about Ultra, and to heavily disguise any intelligence as coming from other sources. Menzies knew from reading Ultra that the Russian ciphers were insecure, and anything Churchill told them might well make its way to Berlin.[58]

Soviet intelligence agents performed brilliantly in early 1941. Secret reports poured in from Germany, Eastern Europe and even Japan, showing in detail Hitler's massive preparations for invasion. Stalin received more than eighty separate warnings, but ordered his forces to do nothing.

The Luftwaffe was permitted to fly reconnaissance missions deep into Soviet territory – some of the aircraft crashed, spilling thousands of feet of film from their underbelly spy cameras. German commando units crossed the Soviet frontier to plan forward routes for the attack. Stalin, however, wanted to signal to Hitler that the Soviet Union was not about to attack Germany, and so avoided mobilisation. He was certain that Hitler would do nothing until he had conquered Britain. This belief was underpinned by an impressive German deception operation that involved two letters to Stalin, directed by Hitler himself. Therefore, Stalin ignored the massive military build-up on his borders, and dismissed every warning of a German attack as disinformation or provocation right up until the morning of 22 June 1941.[59]

Stalin regarded Churchill's offer of British intelligence on German troop movements as a crude attempt to entrap him in the war in Europe. For years, London and Moscow had each thought the other was on the verge of a deal with Berlin. Most importantly, for Stalin the dramatic flight to Britain in May 1941 by Rudolf Hess, Hitler's deputy, was not the erratic act of an unbalanced individual, but firm proof that British talks with Hitler were well advanced. He was obsessed with the idea of a British deal with Hitler, so much so that in October 1944 he was still asking Churchill why British intelligence had brought Hess to Scotland.[60] Ironically, Churchill had insisted on Stalin being fully briefed about the arrival of Hess, but this only fed his paranoia.[61]

Churchill passed his warning to Stalin on 9 April, but there were many other efforts to warn the Soviets. In February 1941, Eden told Ivan Maisky, the Soviet ambassador in London, that the Germans were moving troops into Bulgaria, and had taken over the airfields. Churchill was constantly in touch with Eden about what Stalin might be told and how he might receive it.[62] Similarly, Stafford Cripps, Britain's ambassador to Moscow, passed on a letter from Churchill in which he wrote, 'I have at my disposal sufficient information from a reliable agent [a disguised reference to Ultra] that when the Germans considered Yugoslavia caught up in their net, that is, after March 20, they began transferring three of their five tank divisions from Romania to southern Poland.'[63] Cripps did so reluctantly. He did not know the information was based on Ultra, and underrated its importance, assuming the warning was mere supposition. We now know that Churchill was wise to disguise the source of his intelligence, since German diplomats in Moscow quickly learned the contents of the letter handed over by Cripps.[64]

By early June, Ultra had provided forensic detail about German troop concentrations on the Soviet border. The Foreign Office passed this intelligence to Maisky, and ultimately on to the Soviet foreign minister Molotov. Cadogan gave Maisky a detailed briefing of more information obtained through Ultra on 16 June, but again disguised its source. By then the German attack was only a week away.[65] Churchill later complained to Lord Beaverbrook about the earlier foot-dragging by Cripps, insisting that 'if he had obeyed his instructions' his relationship with Stalin would have been better. But in fact, the message was vague, and only told Stalin what others had already told him many times over.[66]

Churchill did not give up sending Ultra to Stalin. In early 1941 Bletchley Park's window on 'the War in the East' mostly came from Luftwaffe Enigma decrypts. But by the autumn, it was also reading a German Army Enigma key codenamed 'Vulture' that carried messages from the German Eastern Front headquarters to particular army groups. This gave wonderful operational information, especially on the drive towards Moscow in October. Churchill sent nine separate warnings to Stalin in the space of a week conveying disguised Ultra information. On the day the Germans launched their October offensive, he ordered a reluctant Menzies to show him 'the last five messages that had been sent to Moscow'.[67] He was unaware that John Cairncross, one of the KGB's top spies in Whitehall, was sitting only yards away in the Cabinet Office during 1941, and was himself about to transfer to Bletchley Park. Predictably, Stalin only believed Bletchley Park material when it was stolen, and not when it was freely given.[68]

Did Churchill have advance warning of Japan's attack on Pearl Harbor? More precisely, did he withhold this intelligence from President Roosevelt as part of a plot to draw the United States into the war? This question has been debated endlessly, and historians have firmly concluded that he did not. In fact the British passed several intriguing batches of intelligence about Japanese intentions to the Americans, which they ignored. For example, British intelligence sent a wealthy Yugoslavian playboy named Dusan 'Dusko' Popov to New York in 1941. Codenamed 'Tricycle' due to his fondness for 'three in a bed' sessions, he served as a double agent feeding false reports to the unwitting Germans.[69] Popov claimed to have warned both the British and the Americans of the impending Japanese attack on Hawaii. Although two senior British intelligence officers, John Masterman and Ewen Montagu, supported him, J. Edgar Hoover, director

of the FBI, was unimpressed, and failed to convey any of the information
to Roosevelt.[70] Hoover distrusted British intelligence, and believed that he
was fighting not only Axis espionage and subversion, but also the plots of
British agents meddling in American domestic politics and trying to
manoeuvre the United States into war. He concluded that Tricycle's intelligence was a forgery created by the British intelligence office in New
York.[71] Within Roosevelt's supposedly 'Anglophile' administration, assistant secretary of state Adolf Berle also harboured extensive suspicions of
British intelligence.

Churchill's intelligence relations with Roosevelt were complex. Indeed,
Hoover and Berle were partially justified in their suspicions. Although
Tricycle's intelligence was not a British plot, Churchill did authorise a
remarkable range of risky schemes in order to draw America into the
conflict. He read intercepts of private phone calls between Roosevelt, his
secretary of state Cordell Hull, and Joe Kennedy, the US ambassador to
London, during which they discussed options 'if Europe is overrun' by
Nazi Germany. The British also compiled a dossier four inches thick on
the isolationist group America First, and then set out to smear it.[72]

British activities involved not only espionage within the United States,
but interference in American domestic polity. Churchill and Menzies
chose Sir William Stephenson as their special representative in America.
Although Stephenson was head of MI6 in the USA, his organisation,
British Security Coordination, was more of a department store, representing the myriad secret services, including MI5, SOE and those engaged in
propaganda.[73] The British Security Coordination Office in New York occupied two whole floors of the Rockefeller Center, and employed close to a
thousand people. Berle was not exaggerating when he claimed that
Stephenson was operating a 'full size secret police' inside the United States,
and he knew that interventionist organisations such as the Fight for
Freedom Committee were closely linked to this undercover British apparatus.[74] He tried to persuade Roosevelt to ban Stephenson's agents, who
responded by attempting to gather 'dirt' on him.[75]

As Roosevelt edged closer to war, Berle correctly concluded that British
intelligence was seeking to manipulate US foreign policy by creating 'false
scares'.[76] Historians now have full accounts of a range of remarkable high-
risk British operations, often conducted in connivance with pro-interven-
tion Americans. Churchill authorised a complicated influence operation
designed to offer secret support to interventionists and to vilify isolation-
ism. Meanwhile, Britain offered remarkable support to interventionist

bodies including the Committee to Defend America by Aiding the Allies and Fight for Freedom. Churchill also authorised secret operations to generate support for the 'destroyers-for-bases' deal and lend-lease, in which the Americans agreed to supply Britain and Free France with oil, food and military equipment from 1941. Most remarkably, Britain encouraged a hostile US government probe into the prominent New York congressman Hamilton Fish, the leader of the isolationists on Capitol Hill. Unquestionably, British intelligence forged a so-called 'secret German map' that set out a German plan to attack South America. In October 1941, Roosevelt gave this map prominence in a public speech, and the document, actually created in an MI6 forgery laboratory in Canada, was placed on public display.[77]

More than fifty years later, some of the most significant black propaganda operations conducted by British intelligence are still emerging. In 1941, two of the top ten best-selling non-fiction books in the United States were accounts of the Second World War in Europe. One of them was William Shirer's *Berlin Diary*, kept by a CBS correspondent who covered Hitler and his regime during 1940.[78] The other was the diary of a young Dutch boy, Dirk van der Heide, who recorded the experiences of his family under the first days and weeks of German occupation. Owing to their innocent portrayal of the immediacy and trauma of war, children's diaries are often amongst the most moving testimonies produced by any conflict.

Dirk was a 'twelve-year-old blue-eyed Dutch boy with taffy coloured hair' who lived in Rotterdam with his mother, father and younger sister, Keetje. When the Germans invaded in 1940, his mother encouraged him to begin a diary and make a family record of their extraordinary experiences. Rotterdam was heavily bombed, and his mother was killed. His father had already departed to fight the invaders, and so their uncle Pieter arranged for the two children to make a dramatic escape to England. Arriving in London only to encounter a renewed German Blitz, they then embarked on a further adventure, evacuated on a ship that makes a hair-raising voyage through minefields and submarine attacks in the North Atlantic to eventual safety in America.

Dirk van der Heide's diary is a fabulous evocation of small people caught up in the vastness of war. It is also a complete fake. Neither Dirk nor any member of his family ever existed. The diary was created for the purposes of anti-Nazi propaganda and published in Britain with the connivance of the publisher Faber & Faber – although this fact was not revealed to its American publisher, Harcourt Brace. It was part of the vast disinformation campaign launched by Churchill and the British secret services.[79] The real author remains a matter of speculation.[80] Remarkably, this work of propaganda is so good that it continues to be read and commented upon as if it were real. Tellingly, however, it is one of the few wartime diaries in which the child adopts a pseudonym, and no records or photographs of the family have ever surfaced.[81] We may never know the full extent to which other plots are waiting to be unearthed. Nicholas Cull, the most important historian of this secret programme, has remarked that the British government seems to have tried to destroy the evidence of its war propaganda in the United States.[82] British agents even resorted to putting dead rats in the water tanks of American Nazi sympathisers – a less subtle means of manipulating opinion.[83]

Churchill also manipulated intelligence himself in an attempt to play the Americans. In July 1940, Ultra revealed the dismantling of German special equipment that was to be used for an invasion of Britain. Photo-reconnaissance confirmed that invasion barges in France were being towed away. Churchill chose not to share this information with Roosevelt or Harry Hopkins, the president's special envoy. Instead, he sought to keep the Americans' sense of threat high enough for them to want to support Britain, but not so high that they thought it a lost cause. In November 1940 he ordered that the amount of intelligence passed on to the US be cut back, and 'padding should be used to maintain bulk'. Controlling Ultra was vital, and this partly explains why Churchill and Menzies were cagey about cooperation with the Americans on that front. Nevertheless, the first American mission arrived at Bletchley Park in February 1941. In return, the Americans gave the British the power to read Japanese diplomatic communications.[84]

By the end of 1941, the Soviet Union and then the United States had joined what was now a global war impacting on every continent. Increasingly, the international media talked about the 'Big Three' (Britain, the USA and the Soviet Union) and how they would shape the future of the world as the war progressed. Churchill, more than anyone, understood that in such a conflict one had to watch one's allies no less closely than one's enemies. Deploying the power of intelligence would be even more vital as the war moved towards its climax.

5
Winston Churchill
(1942–1945)

*... the part your naughty deeds in war play, in peace cannot
be considered at the present time.*
CHURCHILL ON SOE[1]

Downing Street was now facing a world war. What had begun with minor
Italian and Japanese adventures as early as 1936 was now conjoined into a
vast global struggle. Britain and the US had declared war on the Japanese;
Hitler had declared war on America; and the Soviets had begun a coun-
ter-offensive to stem the Nazi march on Moscow. Having been prime
minister for nearly two years, Churchill understood the transformative
impact of intelligence on strategy and operations on this scale. It would
continue to prove vital as the Allies edged towards victory.

For Churchill, the Second World War was a struggle not only against
Britain's Axis enemies, but also against its new allies, including Russia and
the United States. In 1942, he discovered that some Foreign Office officials
had been talking to Moscow about the post-war settlement without his
approval. He 'emitted several vicious screams of rage'.[2] In particular, he
hoped to educate the Americans about what he saw as the problem of
growing Soviet power, but he knew this would take time. Pressed to
discuss troublesome issues with Roosevelt in 1944, Churchill stalled, and
replied, 'The war will go on for a long time.'[3] Intelligence and careful
timing were part of this delicate game of influence and empire.

Nonetheless, Churchill's detailed control over intelligence declined
during the second part of the war. This was an inevitable outcome of the
priority he had placed on its expansion. The flow of special intelligence
from GC&CS increased massively: by the middle of 1942 Bletchley's codebreakers produced between 3,000 and 4,000 decrypted German messages
a day, as well as Italian and Japanese material. Churchill could not inspect

and interpret even a fraction of this material. The torrent of sigint forced the government machine for central assessment to become ever stronger and better-organised. Intelligence was now being produced on an industrial scale, defeating the prime minister's preference for personal involvement.

This was especially evident in his acerbic discussions with his Middle Eastern commanders, whom he constantly goaded to attack the enemy. In early 1942, Bletchley Park's Hut 8 cracked a medium-grade Italian cipher. This new material showed that Rommel was desperate for supplies. Convinced that Rommel had built his successes on a perilously thin supply of armour and air power, Churchill exhorted his commanders in Cairo to attack. Demonstrating his proclivity towards personal intervention, he summoned Claude Auchinleck, the Middle East commander, back to London and unleashed a classic five-hour haranguing in the Defence Committee. Auchinleck refused to launch an immediate offensive, and demanded more tanks.[4] By the end of the year, and despite his remaining an avid consumer of the decrypts that passed across his desk, the vast flow of Enigma material to both Downing Street and the commanders in the Western Desert made it increasingly difficult for Churchill to insert himself into such debates.[5]

Churchill had less to do with MI5. His main intervention had been sacking Vernon Kell and appointing David Petrie as its new director after the great 'spy scare' of 1940, and MI5 and the chiefs of staff tried to keep it that way. They regarded domestic security as a sensitive area, and feared Churchill's impetuous meddling. While Stewart Menzies, the chief of SIS, worked hard on his relationship with Churchill, meeting him perhaps over a thousand times during the course of the war, MI5 shied away from personal contact. Petrie, despite being a Churchill appointee, made no attempt to sell the increasingly important triumphs of his organisation 'at the top'. This only changed because Duff Cooper, who had taken over from Lord Swinton as head of the Home Security Executive, urged it upon him in March 1943.

Guy Liddell, a senior officer in MI5, summed up the dilemma: 'There are obvious advantages in selling ourselves to the PM who at the moment knows nothing about our department. On the other hand, he may, on seeing some particular item, go off the deep end and want to take some action, which will be disastrous to the work in hand.'[6] For example, 'When told that a clerk at the Portuguese Embassy in London was spying for both the Germans and the Italians, Churchill scrawled: "Why don't you just shoot him?'"[7] Accordingly, internal security issues rarely reached Churchill. Petrie remained reluctant to see the prime minister personally, but considered sending him monthly bulletins with summaries of MI5's best operations as a compromise.[8] Churchill loved these bulletins, noting in prime ministerial red ink that they were 'deeply interesting'.[9]

In the spring of 1944, plans for D-Day finally connected Churchill with MI5 and deception in detail. On Wednesday, 8 March, Menzies joined Churchill, Eden and the chiefs of staff at a special meeting at Downing Street to discuss 'certain aspects' of the D-Day preparations that could not be revealed even to the war cabinet. They went backwards and forwards over the deception plans, especially the vast dummy works, supply depots and aerodromes that were being built to misdirect Hitler about the direction of the assault and to persuade him to place his reserves in the wrong location. The conundrum was whether to ban the diplomats of neutral countries based in London from using enciphered messages to report home. The Spanish had passed a great deal of material to the Germans by this means, while the Swedish air attaché had been especially active in spying for the Nazis. Yet Menzies was against a ban. Two years previously, during the invasion of North Africa, the vast volume of conflicting information emanating from Britain through these channels had actually 'misled the enemy', and German intelligence officers in Spain had proved delightfully incompetent at sifting 'true from false information'. Unintentionally, the reports of various spies had also 'helped us greatly' in building up aspects of the cover plan and knowing what to stress. Menzies was confident, and rather relishing the deception battle ahead.[10]

As D-Day approached, the prime minister was increasingly obsessed with the plans and the accompanying cover operations. Again, senior MI5 officers were concerned that he might take some rash initiative of his own. But some activities were high-risk, and required Downing Street's approval. Thus, at ten in the morning on 15 April 1944, Colonel Bevan of the London Controlling Section, the secret unit charged with coordinating deception plans, arrived at 10 Downing Street. Churchill was sitting in his pyjamas smoking a cigar and reading boxes of secret papers. Bevan had come seeking his personal permission to execute one of the most ingenious deception operations of the Second World War: 'Operation Mincemeat'. The deception planners wished to create a fictitious 'Major William Martin' of the Royal Marines, supposedly on the staff of Vice Admiral Lord Louis Mountbatten, Chief of Combined Operations. They would eventually use the body of a homeless Welshman, Glyndwr

Michael, who had died after swallowing rat poison, and which had been purchased from a hospital morgue for £10. Dressed in the appropriate uniform, and with minute attention to detail, the corpse was to have a briefcase chained to its wrist containing top-secret plans that suggested the main Allied attack would come through the Mediterranean. Churchill was thrilled, and with his enthusiastic blessing 'Operation Mincemeat' went ahead.[11]

Two weeks later the body was dropped into the sea on an incoming tide. Spanish officials recovered it and, very properly, handed it over to the British authorities. But first they opened the briefcase, photographed the documents and handed the evidence to German intelligence. The outline plan carried by 'Major Martin' pointed to an Allied attack through Greece and the Balkans in an operation codenamed 'Husky'. The fact that the Germans swallowed the bait was later revealed in Ultra decrypts.[12] Churchill took great satisfaction in further intercepts showing that Hitler had bought the broader deception plan completely.

Sitting with Menzies at Chequers, Churchill gestured in the direction of his cat, 'Nelson', who was looking intently out of the window. He remarked that the cat was 'in touch with the pelicans on the lake', adding, 'and they're communicating our information to the German secret service!'[13] One of the prime minister's perpetual arguments with Menzies was about the extent to which Ultra should be exploited, or protected. He cared deeply about its security, but also directly exploited it on occasion. During the battle of El Alamein in October 1942, for example, GC&CS informed Churchill of an intercept reassuring Rommel that a convoy of Italian ships was on its way with fresh ammunition and fuel. Hesitating for only a moment, Churchill ordered an attack on the convoy. Rommel's deep suspicions about the security of Enigma were only alleviated when the British sent a deliberately insecure message congratulating a group of fictional Italian agents on their information and for their help in sinking the convoy. Ultra later revealed that the Germans had intercepted the signal and set off in hot pursuit of the fictional Italians.[14]

Upon hearing about Axis successes against British communications during 1943, Churchill demanded an immediate inquiry into the security of British ciphers.[15] As the Allies made their way through Italy and France they rounded up Axis codebreakers, and were shocked to find that many British embassies had been penetrated. Although the Italians had not attacked Britain's top-grade cipher machine, the Typex, they had broken many other systems. Bletchley Park boffins held prolonged 'conversations' with Commander Cianchi, head of the Italian Cryptographic Bureau in Rome, and his staff. Cianchi enthusiastically set out the triumphs of the Italians, especially against British Admiralty communications. The catastrophic Dieppe raid of August 1942 had gone badly because the Germans had been reading Royal Navy messages and had seven days' warning of this 'surprise' attack. Convoy message security had also been weak. The findings of the inquiry did not make for comfortable reading, leaving Churchill at his explosive best. He insisted on the immediate creation of a new body, the Cypher Security Board, to underline the importance he attached to this subject. Soon it had extended its authority over the design, production and operation of all British cipher machines, most of which were made at Bletchley Park's outstations or at a secret Foreign Office factory at Chester Road in Borehamwood. Ten years later, this had developed into the London Communications Security Agency, a hidden fourth British secret service that worked alongside MI5, MI6 and GCHQ and managed some of the UK's most sensitive projects.[16]

Churchill was less bothered about his personal security than about ciphers. Yet MI5 learned of more than a dozen attempts on his life during the war. Some of them were bizarre or childish, including an attempt in May 1943 to kill him or members of his entourage using exploding chocolate positioned among the snacks laid out for the war cabinet. This plot was uncovered by Lord (Victor) Rothschild, MI5's bomb disposal expert. It was not the only such attempt scuppered by Rothschild, and Churchill personally insisted on his decoration.[17]

Germany launched numerous attempts to kill Churchill, many of which were more serious. In late May 1943, Menzies received information from Bletchley Park that it had decoded a most alarming message from a German secret service agent in the Spanish port of Algeciras. The agent had observed the arrival of Churchill and de Gaulle by air, and noted that they had headed eastwards. Churchill was travelling to see General Eisenhower in Algiers to make a passionate case for the invasion of Italy and Sicily. He was joined by Eden, General Montgomery and the chiefs of staff. Menzies rightly feared an attempt to eliminate Churchill on his return. The fact that the secret German watchers were themselves being watched protected Churchill. But events unfolded more quickly than Menzies had expected.[18]

On 1 June, BOAC's flight 777 took off from Lisbon at 9.35 a.m. and headed towards the Bay of Biscay. Nazi spies were convinced that Churchill

was on board. In fact, among the passengers was a man called Alfred
Tregar Chenhalls, who unfortunately for himself resembled Churchill,
dressed like him and even smoked large cigars. It was clear that the Nazis
believed Chenhalls was the prime minister. In fact, he was the business
manager of the film star Leslie Howard, who was travelling with him.
Three hours after take-off an entire squadron of German warplanes
attacked the aircraft. Punctured by shells and bullets, it plummeted into
the sea, killing all on board. The attacking aircraft circled the flaming
wreckage, and their crew took pictures that were sent to Berlin. Three days
later the *New York Times* reported: 'It was believed in London that the Nazi
raiders had attacked on the outside chance that Winston Churchill might
have been among the passengers.' Churchill too subscribed to the mistak-
en-identity thesis, and referred to Leslie Howard's death – which was a
severe blow to British morale – as 'one of the inscrutable workings of fate'.
Despite rumours to the contrary, it is overwhelmingly likely that the
shooting down of the plane was merely an unfortunate coincidence, and
that Chenhalls was not a decoy deliberately sent by Menzies to protect
Churchill.[19] Meanwhile, Churchill's RAF York aircraft was given an especially strong escort of P-38 fighters to Gibraltar, and then accompanied by
a veritable phalanx of Spitfires on the final leg back to England. The prime
minister insisted on helping to fly the plane, to the consternation of senior
RAF officers.[20]

Even as Churchill landed back in Britain, the Nazis were planning
another operation against him. 'Operation Long Jump' was one of their
most ambitious. The NKVD, the Soviet internal security agency, boasted
to the British about having uncovered a plot in which Churchill, Roosevelt
and Stalin would be simultaneously assassinated during the November
1943 Tehran Conference, at which the principal item on the agenda would
be the opening of a second front in Western Europe. The Abwehr,
Germany's military intelligence service, had learned of the time and place
of the conference, having deciphered the American naval code, and put
the operation to assassinate the Allied leaders in the hands of one of its
most trusted special force commanders, Otto Skorzeny. Although the
British had troops in southern Iran to guarantee the flow of supplies to
Russia via the Persian Gulf, the conference was principally the responsibility of the Soviets, who had sent troops into the north of the country in
August 1941 to shut down German influence. This was the only time
Stalin left Russian-occupied territory during the war, precisely because he
was paranoid about assassination attempts.

Some have remained sceptical about whether 'Operation Long Jump' was a real plot, or merely a Russian propaganda ploy. It did, however, create consternation in London, and Roosevelt was clearly briefed on the episode.[21] It has since transpired that from 1941 a team of NKVD intelligence officers known as 'the light cavalry', on account of the fact that they constantly whizzed around Tehran on bicycles, identified more than four hundred Nazi agents.[22] Some of their operations were conducted with the assistance of the British, as Churchill had authorised careful but effective cooperation with the NKVD – rather to the distaste of Menzies. Their final success was the arrest of Franz Meyer, a top German agent in Iran, in August 1943. By the time of the conference three months later, German intelligence was thin on the ground, albeit the last German parachute team was not rounded up by the British until early the following year.[23]

Skorzeny later admitted that there had been an assassination plot, but he had thought it hare-brained, and refused any part of it for his commandos.[24] In 1968, he recalled irritably, 'My part in the whole damn thing was to turn it down rather bluntly', adding that the basis of a successful commando operation was always good intelligence. 'We had no information.' The Germans only had two remaining agents in Tehran, and so 'had nothing to go on'.[25] The plan was taken up by Walter Schellenberg, the brigadier general in charge of the Waffen SS. Schellenberg sent Germany's top expert on Iran to prepare secret landing sites and conduct the commandos. This was Major Walter Shultz of the eastern section of the Abwehr, who would travel under the alias of a Swiss businessman. Shultz – whose real name was Ilya Svetlov – was actually a long-term agent of the Soviet secret police who had been infiltrated into Germany in 1928 under an assumed identity. His application for the Nazi Party was signed by none other than Rudolf Hess. Therefore the Soviet secret service commander in Tehran, General Vassili Pankov, was informed of precisely when and where the assassination squad would be arriving. An unmarked German J-52 was shot down by the Soviets as it crossed into Iran. The wreckage, littered with the plane's load of automatic weapons, mortars and ammunition, continued to explode for some time after it went down.[26]

Gevork Vartanyan, one of the NKVD officers, recalled that the Germans nevertheless dropped a team of assassins by parachute near the city of Qom, eighty miles by road south-west of Tehran: 'We followed them to Tehran, where the Nazi field station had readied a villa for their stay. They were travelling by camel, and were loaded with weapons.' All the members of the group were arrested and forced to contact their handlers under

Soviet supervision. Vartanyan claimed that in this revised version of the plot, Churchill and Stalin were to be killed, while Roosevelt would be kidnapped. He claimed that the NKVD arrested hundreds of people prior to the conference, and unearthed a German secret service team of six, including radio operators. The Allied leaders were certainly safe by the time of the conference, with some 3,000 NKVD troops saturating the streets.[27]

Soviet claims that Germany launched an elaborate plot sit uncomfortably with the involvement in it of Schellenberg. He was about to take over most of Germany's foreign intelligence from the Abwehr, and it has recently emerged that in the same year he launched a covert operation codenamed Modellhut, or 'Model Hat', which sought to get a message to Churchill from the SS stating that a number of leading Nazis wanted to break with Hitler and negotiate a separate peace with England. The channel of communication was to be the infamous collaborator Coco Chanel, with whom he had a close relationship, and who remained in Paris throughout the war.[28] His plan was to send her to neutral Madrid to meet the British ambassador and former MI6 officer Sir Samuel Hoare, whom both she and Churchill knew well. Although Chanel was brought to Berlin, the plan failed, and Churchill never received the letter. In any case, MI6 was tired of receiving such missives, and Churchill, scenting eventual victory, was certainly in no mood to negotiate.[29]

If the assassination plot at Tehran had not progressed very far, why did the Soviets make such a fuss about it when Churchill and Roosevelt arrived in Iran? Perhaps it was part of an elaborate Soviet ruse to persuade Roosevelt to move his personal accommodation into the Soviet diplomatic compound, to facilitate bugging. The conference itself, codenamed 'Eureka', was held in the Soviet embassy. This gave the Russians the opportunity to bug everything, and transcripts were handed to Stalin personally by Lavrentiy Beria, his intelligence chief, by eight o'clock each morning.[30] At one point during the conference, Stalin observed Roosevelt passing a handwritten note to Churchill, and was desperate to know what it said. He ordered his NKVD station chief in Tehran, Ivan Ivanovich Agayants, to get hold of a copy. He succeeded, and reported the message to Stalin. It read: 'Sir, your fly is open.'[31]

Further assassination attempts are still coming to light. Newly declassified MI5 documents reveal that one of the last assassination plans of the war was launched by Zionists in Palestine, where the militant Jewish Stern Gang wanted to end the British mandate and establish the state of Israel.

One member, Eliyahu Bet-Zuri, decided in 1944 to send an agent to Britain to assassinate Churchill. MI5 soon became aware that 'he proposed a plan for assassination of highly placed political personalities, including Mr Churchill, for which purpose emissaries should be sent to London'. The Stern Gang were indeed training their members for assassination attempts, and Bet-Zuri was later executed for the murder of Lord Moyne, the British minister resident in the Middle East, in November 1944. Moyne was a close confidant of Churchill.[32]

Churchill, who was often cavalier about his personal safety, had finally got the message. In December 1944, he visited Athens to have preliminary talks with the various Greek factions, including the prime minister Georgios Papandreou and the Orthodox Archbishop Damaskinos, in what was an emerging civil war between left and right. Some locals worked for the British by day and for ELAS, a militant leftist partisan movement, at night. The women reportedly carried hand grenades in their shopping baskets or under their black dresses. The British delegation drove through areas controlled by the ELAS guerrillas escorted by heavily armed troops, and Churchill opted to sit in an armoured car 'with a giant 45 Colt revolver on his knees and a look on his face that suggested he would love to fire it'.[33]

Churchill was willing to pay the Germans back for their plots. The military were more cautious. 'Pug' Ismay, Churchill's senior staff officer, warned the prime minister that 'The Chiefs of Staff were unanimous that, from the strictly military point of view, it was almost an advantage that Hitler should remain in control of German strategy, having regard to the blunders that he has made, but that on the wider point of view, the sooner he was got out of the way the better.'[34] Nonetheless, in June 1944 Churchill approved a vague plan for Hitler's assassination by a French sniper. In parallel, SOE had developed detailed plans for the liquidation of Hitler, codenamed 'Operation Foxley'. Like Ismay, however, Colonel Ronald Thornley, head of SOE's German Section, warned that Hitler's direction of the war effort was helpful to the Allies, since he often dismissed the sound advice of his generals. Thornley insisted, 'his value to us has been equivalent to an almost unlimited number of first-class SOE agents strategically placed inside Germany'. In any case, SOE was aware that both the Russian NKVD and the Polish resistance had studied the possibility of assassinating Hitler and concluded that it would be absurdly difficult.[35]

Churchill loved clandestine activities, sometimes almost regardless of consequence. Unlike his personal support for Bletchley Park, his enthusiasm for SOE and for encouraging resistance has attracted much criticism. John Keegan, one of Britain's foremost military historians, denounced SOE as 'a costly and misguided failure', and the actions of individual agents as 'irrelevant and pointless acts of bravado'.[36] Max Hastings, among the most assiduous and persuasive scholars of Britain's wartime leader, has gone further. He has denounced Churchill's interventions in this field as resembling those of a 'terrorist', adding that his 'hunger to take the fight to Hitler made him send thousands of heroes to needless death', and concludes that SOE exerted a malign influence across Europe by arming local factions that were keener to fight each other than to fight the Germans. There is a growing sense that Churchill was emotional, even irrational in indulging his love of immediate action through SOE, while wasting military resources and promoting needless political trouble in Whitehall.[37]

This is not the case. Churchill was remarkably astute in his management of SOE. He had appointed Hugh Dalton as its head in part to keep the Labour partners in his coalition government happy. When it became apparent that Dalton's main talent lay in annoying other interested parties, Churchill rescued SOE by replacing him in March 1942 with Lord Selborne, a steady and effective Tory ally who had previously been director of cement at the Ministry of Works. The calm Selborne was the opposite of the temperamental Dalton. Over the next two years, whenever SOE fell out with Stewart Menzies, Churchill prevented Desmond Morton, an ally of MI6, from manipulating the ensuing inquiries, and ensured that they were led by intelligent and open-minded people such as John Hanbury-Williams, managing director of Courtaulds. Selborne rewarded Churchill by sending him edited highlights of SOE's successes, which the prime minister found 'very impressive'. In the summer of 1943 Churchill waded in to support SOE's demands for more RAF special duties aircraft in the Balkans, arguing that the uprisings there reinforced the need for strategic deception, and also gave 'immediate results'.[38]

SOE's activities in the Balkans are often seen as one of Churchill's biggest blunders. During 1940 and 1941 all the Balkan countries had come under increasing pressure to collaborate with the Axis. In March 1941, Yugoslavia signed the Tripartite Pact, formalising its alliance with Germany, Italy and Japan. Churchill was furious, and enthusiastically backed an SOE coup d'état that deposed the ruler, Prince Paul. He and SOE basked in the momentary glory of apparent success as an anti-Axis regime took over. Hitler responded by invading not only Yugoslavia but also Greece. On 6 April, German, Italian and Hungarian forces poured into both countries. Belgrade surrendered within a week, and SOE's protégé King Peter fled the country. Ten days later, the Wehrmacht marched into Athens. In the short term this looked like a disaster. But Hitler had been forced to delay 'Operation Barbarossa', his invasion of Russia, by three months in order to secure his southern flank. This had profound consequences for the Russian campaign, which were visible when the German armies stalled in the snow outside Moscow at the end of the year.[39]

SOE now had a choice of Yugoslavian resistance movements to back. Churchill initially urged it to support the Serbian royalist General Draža Mihailović. However, by early 1943 his support had shifted to Josip Tito, who led the rival communists. The Yugoslav section of SOE sent intelligence about resistance activities to their colleagues in London and to the Foreign Office. James Klugman, deputy chief of SOE's Yugoslavia Section and a Cambridge-educated communist, ran down Mihailović's efforts against the Germans and overstated Tito's.

Churchill and much of Whitehall seem to have been misled by Klugman's trumpeting of Tito's effectiveness as a resistance leader. Downing Street certainly had an exaggerated view of the contribution of Tito's partisans, insisting that they were tying down twenty-four crack German divisions. In fact, only eight under-strength German divisions were in Yugoslavia at this time, and the partisans spent much of their effort on factional infighting. Tito even sent a delegation to German headquarters at Sarajevo proposing a truce so they could both concentrate their efforts against the Royalists.[40]

Yet the idea that Churchill was misled by a single middle-ranking SOE officer with Moscow connections is little more than a conspiracy theory. The prime minister had many other sources, including his own special envoy to Tito, the redoubtable Fitzroy Maclean. Churchill chose him personally, writing to Eden: 'What we want is a daring Ambassador-leader with these hardy and hunted guerrillas.' Maclean, an adventurer after Churchill's own heart,[41] was asked to keep an open mind and to find out, in Churchill's words, which faction was 'killing the most Germans'. He parachuted into Yugoslavia in September 1943, and quickly built up a good personal relationship with Tito which persisted for decades. He told Churchill that Tito's partisans were doing most of the fighting against the Germans.

Much of the criticism of Churchill has been made with the benefit of hindsight. Some of it reflects post-war 'mole-mania', brought on by revelations about Soviet spies such as Kim Philby. But it is clear that Tito would have prevailed in Yugoslavia with or without SOE assistance. In the end, British intelligence, and Maclean in particular, became important once again when Tito broke with Stalin in 1948 to develop anti-Soviet communism. Mihailović and his Chetniks were the advance guard of Serb nationalism – with all that this would entail after 1989. In both the long and the short run, Churchill was right to back SOE and support Tito in 1943.[42]

There was one further source of information for Churchill on Tito. When Maclean parachuted into Yugoslavia with his mission in September 1943, his subordinates were a curious mixture. They included Churchill's own son Randolph and his friend the novelist Evelyn Waugh. Randolph, a hard-drinking and boisterous officer, had served with the SAS. Admired for his exceptional bravery, he was nevertheless rather tiresome company. Franklin Lindsay, an American who later planned the Bay of Pigs operation and who served with him in Yugoslavia, described him as 'one of the most aggressively rude men I ever met'. But Maclean valued him for his courage, endurance, and of course his political connections.[43]

Waugh was also a difficult character, and his superior officers were often desperate not to work with him – when his Commando unit sailed for Italy he was given leave to stay behind and complete *Brideshead Revisited*. In mid-1944, Randolph Churchill told him that he was going out to work for Maclean in Yugoslavia, and asked Waugh to join him. Both were almost killed on arrival when their plane crashed, killing eleven of the twenty on board.[44] Evelyn Waugh and Randolph Churchill were a comic couple. Both professional drunks, they were bound together because most people found them insufferable. Waugh noted in his diary: 'Further "tiffs" with Randolph ... he is simply a flabby bully who rejoices in blustering and shouting down anyone weaker than himself and starts squealing as soon as he meets anyone as strong.'[45] But Randolph was fearless, and survived an enemy raid on his camp, fleeing into the mountains without shoes. The prime minister received long and detailed reports direct from his son, fighting with the partisans deep in the heart of the Balkans.[46]

Critics of Churchill's attempts to promote secret resistance rarely think beyond Europe. Much has been written about SOE in France and the Low Countries, a great deal of it highly critical. But Churchill encouraged SOE to think of itself as a global organisation operating on every continent, resulting in success as far afield as Brazil, Madagascar and Papua New Guinea. Remarkably, almost nothing has been written about its biggest success, which lay in Burma. During the last year of the war, SOE in Burma carried out its most spectacularly successful campaign of the entire conflict. The main focus was a series of operations employing the fiercely loyal Burmese hill tribes, codenamed 'Nation' and 'Character'. Churchill was instrumental in promoting a wide range of special forces activity in Burma, including the Chindits. This force was led by Orde Wingate, one of Britain's most eccentric wartime leaders. He was so odd that Churchill had to compel his generals to give him a role, but thereafter he achieved remarkable things. Churchill collected eccentrics precisely because they shook things up, and he thought Wingate 'a man of genius'. At one point the prime minister considered making Wingate overall commander in India, to the absolute horror of the chiefs of staff.[47]

From late 1944, the guerrilla levies recruited from the Burmese hill tribes scented victory. Guerrilla intelligence also multiplied the effect of Allied air attacks. Japanese casualties of 'Operation Nation' were estimated at between 3,582 and 4,650, with Allied casualties between sixty-three and eighty-eight.[48] 'Operation Character', conducted in the Karen tribal area, met with even greater success. It consisted of three main groups under Lt. Colonel Tulloch, Lt. Colonel Peacock and Major Turral. By 13 April 1945, Tulloch's Northern Group commanded a tribal force of 2,000. As the 50,000-strong Japanese 15th Division tried to move south through the Karen areas in a race with the British for the key town of Toungoo, which controlled the strategic road south to Rangoon, it was ambushed.[49] Extended fighting developed, and continued into July. Remarkably, on 21 July, General Stopford, commander of the British 33rd Corps, conceded that SOE's locally-raised Karen forces had inflicted more casualties in the previous month than the regular army.[50] Churchill loved secret service, but even more than that he loved empire. Here, in the hills above the Irrawaddy River, they came together.

When Roosevelt and Churchill met off Newfoundland in 1941 they drew up an agreed statement of war aims called the Atlantic Charter. Few people realise that this charter was never signed. To Churchill's horror it contained clauses offering self-determination to everyone – including Britain's impe-rial subjects. He saw the war as a struggle to save the British Empire, and was already thinking about the impact of the post-war settlement on imperial territories. Fearing Roosevelt's anti-imperialism, he turned the lens of British intelligence on the country's closest ally, the United States.

Churchill was far from merely defensive when it came to imperial territory, believing that the empire needed to become larger if it was to become safer. After Britain's ignominious defeat at Singapore in 1942, which he called 'the greatest disaster in our history', he was determined to restore British rule to Burma and Malaya, and if possible to expand their territory by annexing parts of Thailand. He told Eden that this could be presented to the world as 'some sort of protectorate'.[51] But the American Office of Strategic Services, or OSS, engaged in special operations behind enemy lines, thwarted the plan by taking the lead in working with the Thai resistance. In April 1945, it was reporting that Thailand should become an 'incubator of Americanism' in the Far East.[52]

Churchill envisaged the Far Eastern war as an exercise in imperial recovery. By contrast, Roosevelt believed that the European empires were a major contributing factor to the outbreak of war. The president was a devout anti-imperialist on ideological grounds, but he also saw the European empires as a barrier to post-war American trade. Some of his secret services were even backing Ho Chi Minh against the French – the future of French Indochina was an issue so divisive that by 1944 Churchill and Roosevelt had refused to discuss it. Instead, they simply spied on each other and sought to subvert each other's projects.[53]

SOE was the most powerful British secret service in Asia. It was run by Colin Mackenzie, a friend of Lord Linlithgow, the Viceroy of India, and a director of the textile company J&P Coats. In the early twentieth century, this was the world's third largest company after US Steel and Standard Oil, and it had vast imperial interests. Its main business rivals were American. Similarly, John Keswick, the senior SOE officer in China, was with the Hongkong and Shanghai Bank, while MI6's Asian operation was run by Geoffrey Denham, a director of Anglo-Dutch Plantations. Like Churchill, they were determined to perpetuate the post-war empire.

The main focus of Churchill's paranoia was the Indian independence movement. Churchill's views on India can seem shocking. His private secretary recorded how 'The P.M. said the Hindus were a foul race', and wished that Bomber Harris could 'send some of his surplus bombers to destroy them'.[54] British intelligence followed every move of Indian nationalists, and also discovered covert OSS activity in India. Anglo–American spy rivalry was rife in Delhi. From 1942 onwards, Gandhi's 'Quit India' movement had left the British in the awkward position of trying to fight a war in Asia from a base that was itself effectively occupied territory. India presented a major internal security problem, and the OSS was seen as siding with the subversives. The Americans were not unaware of the ironies. Donald Downes, an OSS officer watching events in Bombay, recalled: 'I saw the great Gandhi himself come to visit his British dentist in a green Rolls-Royce on which was mounted a sign in five languages saying "boycott British goods".'[55]

William Stephenson's British Security Coordination continued its operations in New York, and busily spied on Indian nationalists in the United States. In return, Roosevelt deliberately provoked Churchill by appointing William Phillips, head of OSS London, as his personal representative in India. OSS officers arriving in Delhi were warned that 'the British are past masters at intrigue and had planted spies in all American agencies to piece together information'.[56] In fact, the British had gone even further, and from early 1943 were intercepting all mail addressed to American consulates in India.[57] General Al Wedemeyer, the most senior American officer in India, was told by his staff that the British had tapped his telephone.[58]

Hong Kong lay firmly in the American sphere of military operations. Although occupied by Japan during the war, everyone expected it to be liberated by American and Chinese nationalist forces. Churchill feared that this prize piece of British real estate would be handed to Chiang Kai-shek. He therefore approved the insertion of a British SOE group under John Keswick conveniently close to Hong Kong to watch events there. In April 1942, the head of the Chinese secret service had them expelled. But SOE was greatly helped by the fact that the Chinese nationalists were fighting the Chinese communists, while the OSS were fighting a rival intelligence outfit run by the US Navy. By 1944, SOE had made its way back into China under the cover of a mission to recover and rescue escaping prisoners of war from Hong Kong. It developed a plan to arm and train 30,000 British-paid guerrillas to ensure that a British force played a part in liberating Hong Kong at the end of the war. Also assisting Britain's return to Hong Kong was a massive SOE black-market currency-smuggling exercise so large that it paid for all of SOE's operations in every theatre during the Second World War.

French Indochina had considerable symbolic value for Roosevelt. In conversations with Stalin he remarked that after a century of French rule, 'the inhabitants are worse off than before'.[59] As a result, he tried to prevent French special forces operating in the region under Mountbatten. Unbeknown to the president, Churchill lifted his veto on French secret service operations into Vietnam in late 1944. SOE's Indochina section had been completely handed over to French control, and essentially became a platform for France's efforts to restore colonial rule. Colin Mackenzie recalled that the French were a law unto themselves – 'We let them get on with their own business.'[60] By 1944, SOE was dropping French colonial governors and policemen by parachute over the Mekong delta. At exactly the same time Roosevelt's OSS was assisting and arming the Viet Minh. At one point, an OSS medical team seems to have saved Ho Chi Minh's life.[61]

By 1945, SOE and the OSS were parachuting rival paramilitary teams into Indochina to support opposite sides in a messy conflict. Both were under pressure from their governments to inch ahead in a secret race over restored empire in Asia. In this febrile atmosphere, accidents were bound to happen. Accordingly the British operated a 'ban on informing the Americans' about their secret flights, meaning there was a very real danger that they might be mistaken for Japanese aircraft. Just before midnight on 22 January 1945, two RAF Liberator aircraft from No. 358 Special Duties squadron set off to drop operatives into Indochina. They never returned, and soon questions were being asked. Air Vice Marshal Gilbert Harcourt Smith eventually reported: 'It now seems certain that two of the Liberators missing from No. 358 Squadron on the night of 22/23 were destroyed by American fighters.' He added, 'I am convinced that it will be in the best interest of all concerned if we adopt sealed lips on these incidents and drop all idea of any investigation.'[62]

Churchill watched these imperial issues closely. He employed Gerald Wilkinson, an MI6 officer, as his secret contact with General Douglas MacArthur, the American commander in the South-West Pacific. MacArthur loathed Roosevelt, and was a potential Republican candidate for the next US election. When Wilkinson made return trips to England he reported first to Menzies in MI6 headquarters, and then went round to Downing Street to brief Churchill directly.[63] One key issue was MacArthur's prospects as a potential presidential candidate. Wilkinson described him as 'ruthless, vain, unscrupulous and self-conscious', but 'a man of real calibre'.[64] On his visits to London, Wilkinson was often summoned by telephone to brief Churchill in the middle of the night.[65] His main theme during these midnight conversations was the 'Wall Street imperialists' and the danger they presented to British imperial interests in the Far East. Wilkinson visited Alan Brooke, who found him 'very interesting',[66] and also briefed the editor of *The Times*, the secretary of Imperial Tobacco, the head of Imperial Chemical Industries and the senior staff from Anglo-

Iranian Oil.[67] Late in the war, at the suggestion of Ian Fleming, then a naval intelligence officer, he was posted to Washington, where he continued to monitor the American and Chinese threat to British commercial interests in the Far East. As William Stephenson noted, this work was 'somewhat outside the charter of British Security Coordination's activities'.[68]

British covert action in the service of empire was even more remarkable in the Middle East. Recent research in French archives has shown how the British tried to keep the Middle East quiet by means of a vast programme of bribery undertaken by both SOE and MI6.[69] As the war drew to an end and the future of SOE came under scrutiny, Lord Killearn, the ambassador to Egypt, reflected that its main job in the Middle East had been the bribery of senior political figures, what he called 'the payment of baksheesh'.[70] At this point, Lord Selborne, the last head of SOE, wrote a veritable essay to Churchill on how SOE defended his beloved empire:

> SOE can lend valuable aid to top-hatted administrators by
> unacknowledgeable methods. Lord Killearn in Egypt and Sir
> Reader Bullard in Persia have already employed SOE to important
> effect in nobbling personalities who can make themselves
> inconvenient to HMG. A 'loan' here, a directorship there, pay
> dividends out of all proportions, and may save battalions ...
> this can be done in conformity with Foreign Office policy, but,
> it can only be done by those who understand the technique,
> potentialities, and limitations of subterranean work.[71]

It is only now becoming clear, with the recent discovery of documents which MI6 hoped had long been destroyed, that the wartime Middle East in particular served as a playground for the British secret service, perfecting their techniques of bribery and covert political influence. Many senior figures, including leaders in Egypt, Iraq, Syria and Lebanon, were on the payroll. The British not only bribed an astonishing number of ministers, officials and newspaper editors across the region, they even forced them to sign receipts to underline that they were on the take.[72]

In 1941, Churchill had viewed William Donovan, the head of OSS, as an ally. But by the end of the war, because of these colonial issues, he saw him as a dangerous enemy trying to subvert the British Empire. In April 1945, when asked about the role of guerrillas and the liberation of Hong Kong, Churchill warned Eden, 'I incline against another SOE–OSS duel, on ground too favourable for that dirty Donovan.'[73] Donovan was in much the same mood. He visited London in July 1945 to hold discussions with the large OSS station there, but US intelligence and security officers reported that 'he did not desire to see "any damn British".[74] Donovan's vexation in the summer of 1945 may have reflected a sense that he was losing the anti-colonial war against the British in Asia. Russia was on the rise, and Roosevelt, the great evangelist of anti-colonialism, died in April 1945. One of Donovan's very last missives to the White House as America's intelligence chief was to insist that the Viet Minh were fundamentally nice people but naïve, and were being 'misled' by 'agents provocateurs and Communist elements'.[75] Other OSS officers in Washington disagreed, and were already warning the new president, Harry S. Truman, that the US should be supporting the European colonial empires, not undermining them, as they would be needed to help contain the post-war Soviet Union. British and American intelligence agencies were increasingly talking the language of anti-communism and an emerging Cold War.

For Churchill, the Cold War had begun in earnest with the arguments over Poland in early 1944. Dismayed at Stalin's brutal treatment of the Polish resistance, he told Eden: 'I fear that very great evil may come upon the world … the Russians are drunk with victory and there is no length they may not go.' He added that this time, at any rate, 'we and the Americans will be heavily armed'. Clearly he was already thinking about a military confrontation with Stalin – and perhaps even about nascent nuclear weapons.[76] Churchill mused that there would soon be nothing 'between the white snows of Russia and the white cliffs of Dover'.[77]

A year later, within days of Germany's defeat, the prime minister contemplated the 'elimination of Russia'. He ordered plans for war with the Soviets to be drawn up, codenamed 'Operation Unthinkable'. This called for hundreds of thousands of British and American troops, supported by 100,000 rearmed German soldiers, to unleash a surprise attack upon their war-weary eastern ally. Meanwhile the RAF would attack Soviet cities from bases in northern Europe.[78] The military lacked enthusiasm, not least because Hitler had failed to achieve this objective even with more than a hundred divisions.[79]

Brooke and his fellow chiefs of staff were horrified by Churchill's idea. The prime minister perhaps felt that nuclear weapons would provide the answer to the question of how to defeat Stalin. Such thoughts and discussions are not ordinarily recorded in formal minutes, but Brooke captured the reality of these intensely secret and private discussions in his diary.

Churchill, he recorded, now saw 'himself as the sole possessor of the bombs and capable of dumping them where he wished, thus all-powerful and capable of dictating to Stalin'.[80] This was so secret that it was never taken near the main intelligence machine. The JIC, which had not been told about America's plan to use the atomic bomb on Japan, remarkably undertook very little work on the issue of the Russians after late 1944, precisely because Stalin's future course was such a hot potato in Whitehall.[81] Only in January 1946 did it feel able to revisit the explosive issue of Russia.[82] By this time, Attlee, who became prime minister shortly before the nuclear bombing of Japan, had sought joint action with Russia to stave off an 'imminent disaster' in Allied relations. Taking over the helm at the Potsdam Conference of July–August 1945, Attlee wrote, 'The time is short … I believe that only a bold course can save civilisation.'[83]

Churchill's impact on intelligence at the beginning of the war had been formidable. At the end of the war it was negligible. He was simply exhausted, and increasingly overwhelmed by the complexity of post-war settlements. Many important questions about the future of British intelligence were now being pondered. They included the possible merger of MI5 and MI6, together with the future of SOE and sabotage. For over a year, Churchill and Eden had also discussed whether it might be a good idea to merge SOE and MI6, in an attempt to end their squabbling. Churchill had decided not, concluding that the 'warfare' between the two secret services was 'a lamentable, but inevitable, feature of our affairs'.[84]

By 1945, senior officials were anxious to keep these discussions away from Churchill, judging him too tired to make sensible decisions. Alexander Cadogan, the senior official at the Foreign Office, agreed with the military that there should be a report on relations between MI5 and MI6. The logical person to do this was the cabinet secretary, but then it would come to the notice of the prime minister, who would 'have wanted to know all about it'. Guy Liddell discussed this review with Peter Loxley, a young diplomat who helped Cadogan with intelligence matters, and said that 'In my experience once things of this sort reached cabinet level it was the toss of a coin whether they went right or wrong.' Loxley entirely agreed, and mentioned 'off the record' the bizarre atmosphere in which SOE's future was being discussed. Churchill received minutes on these subjects at the end of a rather tiring day, and scribbled across them: 'Let Major Morton look into this and advise. SIS [MI6] I know but who are SOE? I know S. Menzies. He is head of MI5.'[85] Menzies was, of course, the chief of MI6. By this time, Churchill was in no state to be making important decisions about the future of intelligence.

With Churchill fading fast, square-minded individuals and bureaucrats did their level best to kill off SOE. Diplomats and staff officers, people who saw the world from behind a collar-stud, instinctively feared special forces and 'funnies' just as much as Churchill loved them. As the war drew to a close, Sir Esler Denning, Britain's most senior diplomat in the Far East, insisted that some order must now be brought to the sprawling secret empire, adding tersely, 'Reforms will be much appreciated by all of us who for our sins are in frequent contact with these organisations.'[86] One senior staff officer lamented that SOE had been created outside the regular military, in a place 'where imagination was welcomed and allowed to have full play, and where resources were readily obtainable. It is to be hoped that this will never occur again.'[87]

Over the course of the war Churchill had done much to expand and accelerate Britain's secret state. He had personally driven the creation of most of the nation's new raiding, sabotage and special operations forces, from SOE to the Commandos to the Chindits. He had boosted Bletchley Park, providing additional resources the instant they were needed. He had encouraged new mechanisms for distributing and integrating Ultra into British decision-making. It was under him that the JIC, the central machine of intelligence, came of age and was relocated close to Downing Street. Above all, he understood the importance of 'intelligence at the top', and was the first prime minister to have a special assistant dealing only with intelligence. Impressively, he reined in his impulsive love of immediate action to protect the twin secrets of Ultra and deception.

Ironically, Churchill's last great Second World War battle involved crossing swords with his own security officials. In the interwar period, he had been deeply dependent on writing to stay afloat financially. As David Reynolds has shown, in the 1930s Churchill's earnings from literary activities brought him about half a million pounds a year at current values. But it was never enough: he was always mortgaging ahead, and employed an army of accountants and legal advisers to help him avoid tax. Even with extraordinary deals for film rights, somehow he was always in deficit. Accordingly, his six-volume history of the Second World War was begun eighteen months after the end of the conflict by a syndicate of ghost writers and assistants, including R.V. Jones. The prime minister's official salary in 1945 was £10,000, while this project earned around £600,000.[88]

Churchill omitted Ultra from his personal account of the war, and touched only lightly on deception and resistance work. But he enjoyed pushing the boundaries, giving detailed accounts of subjects like the 'Wizard War' and the passing of intelligence to Stalin. He discussed the Joint Intelligence Committee, something no other prime ministers would do in their memoirs for another half-century. He wanted to include the original texts of telegrams sent to leaders like Stalin, Roosevelt and Truman. This raised the immediate problem of cipher security, for verbatim texts could, in theory at least, compromise much of the other British cipher traffic sent on the same day. Bletchley Park had used just such 'cribs' to help break Enigma. Stewart Menzies had dinner with Churchill on the night of 9 June 1948 and explained the problem, trying to 'tie him down' to a formal arrangement for changes. Churchill was 'not impressed' by his arguments, but eventually caved in.[89]

As prime minister, Churchill had overseen an intelligence revolution. He had recognised the transformative power of intelligence both in support of policy and in shaping events themselves. He brought intelligence to the heart of government in a manner unknown to earlier occupants of Downing Street. However, his impetuosity at times bedevilled his relations with the secret world. He presided over an informal and personal system rife with impulsiveness. It could work well. But it could also lead to recklessness and acrimony. Churchill could therefore only take the revolution so far. To fully harness the power of intelligence, a prime minister needed to be better organised, to inject a sense of order and rationality into what was becoming an intelligence community. Churchill's revolution required a straight man to form all this new activity into a central machine. Enter Clement Attlee.

PART THREE

THE HOT
COLD WAR

6

Clement Attlee
(1945–1951)

Are they not possibly for sale?
CLEMENT ATTLEE[1]

Clement Attlee spent his time in office busily scuttling between competing priorities. Labour's first post-war prime minister is best remembered for successful domestic reform in the face of severe impecuniousness, and for engineering Britain's miraculous 'Escape from Empire' while under pressure from nationalist unrest in India. Crucially, however, Attlee also presided over the early Cold War – a burgeoning conflict that would dominate the second half of the twentieth century. His choices, especially on security, had ramifications for generations to come. Following the Soviet detonation of an atomic bomb in August 1949, the Cold War created increasingly serious responsibilities for the new prime minister. With the advent of the Korean War the following year, all-out confrontation seemed only weeks away.

The Cold War placed a high premium on intelligence. Successive prime ministers needed to know the Soviet Union's capabilities and intentions, including its nuclear arsenals and technological developments – and, crucially, whether it would use them. A great deal was at stake. Intelligence also had a more active, and potentially explosive, role to play. It became crucial in fighting a large-scale underground struggle. With open warfare now too dangerous to contemplate, conflict was forced into a lower key. Subversion, espionage, insurgency and propaganda became the weapons of choice. Clement Attlee was the first prime minister to be forced to adjust to this 'hot peace', and to recognise its implications for the active use of intelligence in peacetime. He was well aware of the difficulties. Spoilt by the Ultra material during the war, the new government had to adapt to a lack of high-grade intelligence, since it was not reading many Soviet communications. GCHQ, as GC&CS had become in 1946, could not provide direct insights into the mind of the enemy. Attlee himself privately acknowledged that 'The difficulties in dealing with Communist activities are far greater than anything which we have had to face before, for the iron curtain is very hard to penetrate.'[2]

Attlee's premiership was sandwiched between two governments led by Winston Churchill, an enthusiastic – even flamboyant – advocate of secret service. By contrast, Attlee is remembered neither as a natural Cold Warrior nor as an avid consumer of intelligence. He was a modest and sensible man; the last ever prime minister to be challenged to a duel – which he declined, telling the accuser not to be so silly.[3] Yet, unlike prime ministers who had served during the interwar period, Attlee and his colleagues did not arrive in office ignorant of the workings of the secret world. As an integral part of the wartime coalition he had been aware of MI5 and MI6 long before being elected prime minister.[4] As Winston Churchill's deputy prime minister, he had been discussing reform of the secret services as early as 1940, and also experienced the vital contribution made by 'most secret sources', especially signals intelligence, first hand.[5] During the war, Stewart Menzies had picked out Bletchley Park decrypts not only for Churchill, but also for Attlee.[6]

Churchill had asked his deputy to preside personally over some of the most sensitive wartime issues. In December 1943, Attlee had chaired a staff conference that looked at the 'highly disturbing' issue of German penetration of SOE in Holland.[7] And he was not alone. His own deputy prime minister, Herbert Morrison, had been wartime home secretary, while his chancellor of the exchequer, Hugh Dalton, had run SOE. Attlee was therefore quite right to assert that he 'had had full experience of high and responsible office', and 'understood the machinery of government'.[8] As a consummate committee man, machinery was his strength. Churchill may have boosted Britain's intelligence community, but it was Attlee who refined the secret structures that ensured its smooth running over the next half-century.

Clement Attlee had endeared himself to Churchill personally as Labour's most vocal enemy of appeasement in the late 1930s. Indeed, it was his refusal to join a coalition government led by Chamberlain that had ushered in Churchill as premier in May 1940. Thereafter, Attlee, together with Anthony Eden and Harold Macmillan, completed the Churchillian intelligence revolution. Schooled in the importance of secret service during the long years of conflict with Nazi Germany, the need to integrate intelligence into the core business of government was second nature to them. The amazing achievements of MI5, MI6, SOE and especially Bletchley Park resonated with Britain's rulers over the next two decades, a period during which 10 Downing Street was consistently run by ministerial figures from Churchill's wartime coalition. Already well-versed in the clandestine workings of intelligence, as prime minister Attlee oversaw the growth of an intricate secret state prosecuting the Cold War both domestically and overseas.[9] As Britain faced severe economic decline, intelligence was an area in which it could perhaps still lead the world, while secret service provided opportunities for fancy footwork that dodged imperial retreat.[10]

The new prime minister was no stranger to domestic counter-subversion. Churchill had inducted Attlee into this sensitive area almost as soon as he joined the coalition government in May 1940.[11] Owing to his intense fear of fifth columnists, Churchill had wished to progress with the internment of enemy aliens, and he instructed Attlee to liaise with MI5 on the matter. Attlee agreed with its senior counter-espionage officer, Guy Liddell, that 'the liberty of the subject, freedom of speech etc were all very well in peace-time but were no use in fighting the Nazis'.[12]

As prime minister, Attlee continued to value MI5, not least to 'detect attempts to penetrate our defence organisation'. He also believed that MI5 should be free from political control, separate from government and police machinery.[13] Yet upon his election in July 1945, he was cautious in his dealings with Britain's security agencies. They were not natural bedfellows.[14] Aside from Philby, Burgess and Maclean, senior British intelligence officers were hardly renowned for their love of socialism. According to one barbed remark in Liddell's diary, the state socialism pursued by Attlee's government 'differed little if at all from Communism by evolutionary means'.[15] Conversely, the Labour Party's opinions of MI5 were framed by historic antagonism dating back to the Zinoviev affair. More recently, memories of internment, censorship and other infringements of civil liberties perturbed the new Members of Parliament who filled the government benches following Labour's landslide victory – a victory which took MI5 by surprise.

Attlee was being watched carefully by both left and right. During an election broadcast in July 1945, Churchill had rather cruelly suggested that if Labour was elected, his former wartime colleagues would create 'some form of Gestapo'.[16] Where would ordinary people be, he asked, 'once this mighty organism had got them in their grip?'[17] Attlee feared accusations from the Labour left that he was mounting a witch-hunt if he took obvious measures to keep British communists away from sensitive material.[18] His understandable caution over domestic security during the early years of his premiership frustrated senior figures in MI5. Within just months of the election, they began moaning about government prevarication.[19]

Towards the end of his first year in office, Attlee expressed strong concerns about MI5's files on individuals, and demanded that they be kept clean of anything that did not come under the service's terms of 'defence of the realm'. In his usual brusque manner, he made it abundantly clear to all concerned that MI5 was not to have the names of anybody on its index cards who was not considered a threat to national security. The issue played heavily on Attlee's mind over the early summer of 1946. After some weeks he summoned MI5's director-general to his office to check if the records had indeed been cleared of irrelevant material. Despite the fullest assurances, Attlee remained concerned. Churchill's pointed comment had clearly stung, and the prime minister 'was still afraid that the Opposition might accuse him of running a Gestapo'.[20]

Everyone expected the talented Guy Liddell to be next in line for the top job at MI5. When David Petrie retired as director-general in spring 1946, however, Attlee controversially appointed an external candidate. After an impressive career in the police, Percy Sillitoe had hoped for a gentle retirement running a sweetshop in Eastbourne. He clearly did not expect to be catapulted into the murky world of international espionage, but Eastbourne's loss was Britain's gain. Sillitoe accepted the position, and the relationship between Downing Street and MI5 swiftly improved.[21]

Attlee and Sillitoe developed an excellent – if unlikely – personal rapport. 'Little Clem' was famously a slight man of few words. Loathing small talk and blushing easily, he radiated a shyness which he imparted to his visitors. Even the King privately referred to him as 'Clam'.[22] By contrast, Sillitoe was a burly, no-nonsense policeman who had cut his teeth suppressing hooliganism in Sheffield and fighting gangs on the mean streets of Glasgow. Despite physically towering over his new boss, Sillitoe also had a streak of shyness, apparently stemming from his lack of a university education. One therefore wonders how painfully awkward their meetings may have been.[23] But meet they did – and on the 'special instructions' of Attlee himself.[24] In fact the prime minister met Sillitoe more often than any other prime minister has met the director-general of MI5 before or since – perhaps with the exception of David Cameron.[25] Sillitoe had 'trenchant views on the danger of police states and the importance of restrictions on police powers', and is a rare example of a director-general who inspired greater confidence in Number 10 than he did in his own service.[26]

Understandably, Guy Liddell, then deputy director of MI5, was less impressed. In his invaluable diaries, so secret that they were kept locked in a safe and had their own codename of 'Wallflowers', Liddell, perhaps deliberately, consistently misspelled 'Shillito's' name in the weeks following his appointment.[27] A once considerable man, 'a great mimic, dancer and teacher of the Irish jig', Liddell cut a sadder figure after his wife left him during the war. He increasingly found solace only in the cello, and spent his time working or in the clubland company of male friends.[28] Given that the latter included various traitors and Soviet spies, including the bibulous Guy Burgess, his reputation became somewhat tarnished.[29]

Somebody within MI5 gave the new boss the wrong papers for his first meeting with Attlee, which Sillitoe furiously interpreted as a deliberate attempt to embarrass him. Other MI5 staff deliberately spoke in Latin to ridicule Sillitoe's lack of intellectual pretension. After retiring from MI5, Sillitoe would work for De Beers investigating diamond smuggling. At their London headquarters he repeatedly briefed Ian Fleming on his adventures, and his exploits went on to inform the best-selling James Bond novel *Diamonds are Forever*.[30]

Attlee kept MI5 under his personal control. He delegated responsibility neither to the minister of defence nor, as would become customary, to the home secretary. This arrangement also suited MI5. Not only did it keep interfering ministers out of the day-to-day running of its affairs, it also allowed the service to have a 'very convenient' right of direct 'appeal to the P.M.' if attacked.[31] Towards the end of Attlee's premiership, MI5's privileged position was challenged by Norman Brook, the tall, discreet and ever-unruffled technician of government who as cabinet secretary played an integral part in advising successive prime ministers on intelligence.[32] At one point Attlee even considered merging the three intelligence and security services under his direct command. He knew that 'in the past there was a good deal of friction and a tendency for separate empires to grow up', and was 'not yet satisfied that we get full value for our expenditure'.[33] He would later return to this question.

The close relationship between the prime minister and his head of domestic intelligence would soon become paramount. The early Cold War was characterised not only by the tightening of the Soviet grip on Eastern

Europe, but by fears of communist subversion within Western states. In September 1945, Whitehall linked fear of Soviet espionage with domestic Communism as a result of the defection of a humble Soviet cipher clerk called Igor Gouzenko. Gouzenko, who had been working for Soviet military intelligence in Ottawa, both exposed a Canadian spy ring and revealed that the Soviets had planted agents inside the top-secret Manhattan Project, the wartime programme that produced the first atomic bomb. His defection brought home the dangers of Soviet infiltration to the British, and also the use of local communist parties to recruit agents. It triggered a chain of events which saw Britain's Alan Nunn May, one of the first atom spies, exposed and arrested; the arrest of the scientist Klaus Fuchs for passing top-secret information on the British nuclear programme to Russia; and the introduction of a controversial new government vetting process.[34]

Intelligence proved a vital factor in spurring Attlee into action.[35] Drawing on revelations from MI5 and MI6 about the growing underground threat to Britain, the prime minister founded a Committee on Subversive Activities in spring 1947, and went on to personally organise counter-espionage collaboration between the UK and various Commonwealth allies.[36] Although the new counter-subversion body was initially chaired by A.V. Alexander, the minister of defence, Attlee took personal charge when security matters grew in importance. Subversion was simply too dangerous to be delegated outside Downing Street. Discussing the need for vetting individuals who might have access to classified information, the prime minister's security advisers came down in favour of a hard line. It was impossible to distinguish between those British communists who would spy for Russia and those who would not. Security arrangements therefore had to be tightened. After prevaricating for a few months, Attlee agreed that Communist Party members should not be allowed to work in such positions. Counting on public support, he decreed that 'We cannot afford to take risks here.'[37] A purge of the civil service based on 'negative vetting' – a simple check against existing records of communist or fascist affiliation – was accordingly announced to the House of Commons in March 1948.[38] There was relief when MI5 found a closet fascist lurking in the War Office.[39]

Perversely, Attlee's purge worried MI5. Despite instinctively wanting it, senior intelligence officers were concerned that their valuable sources on the inside would be fatally compromised if a target was removed for having links to the Communist Party or fascists. Worried that Attlee was not adequately considering this issue, MI5 felt the need to ask Edward Bridges, head of the home civil service, to 'ram home' the point to the prime minister.[40] The impact of Attlee's purge on MI5's relations with the rest of Whitehall proved a further sticking point. Other departments did not like being pushed around by what they saw as 'a bunch of autocrats' with no authority. MI5 consequently came in for 'a good deal of abuse'. Attlee had little sympathy, responding to Liddell's protestations by saying, 'I doubt whether you would ever get it out of peoples [sic] minds that your Department has overriding powers and is not subject to ministerial control.' Liddell left feeling that Attlee 'was his usual self, uncommunicative and unresponsive, but quite pleasant'.[41]

Still haunted by Churchill's Gestapo accusations, Attlee blew hot and cold on the vetting issue. Fretting that it might be going too far, he set off from Downing Street late one afternoon for cocktails at MI5 headquarters. Talking through the issue over drinks, he was uncharacteristically on 'extremely good form', entertaining the spooks by 'firing questions at everybody and telling stories'.[42] The accelerating pace of the Cold War carried him along, and in July 1949 he made a particularly bullish public speech slamming the 'sickening hypocrisy' of communists accusing him of executing a purge.[43]

What had hardened Attlee's position? In 1949, he dealt ruthlessly with a major strike by London dock workers, deploying the armed forces and emergency powers. This strike, he claimed, was secretly orchestrated by the British Communist Party, and was intended not only to unhinge the delicate post-war economic recovery, but to overturn social democracy. Because of MI5's reports, he increasingly saw the Communist Party as doing the Kremlin's bidding, and deliberately increasing Cold War tensions. The strike came against a broader international backdrop of intensifying acrimony. The previous year, the local Communist Party in Prague had, with backing from Moscow, taken control of Czechoslovakia in a shocking coup which served to highlight the ambitions and dangers of Stalinism. Back in Britain, Attlee was suspicious that this strike coincided exactly with other strikes in the Commonwealth, and saw it as part of a plot by international communism targeted against him. On 11 July 1949, he declared a state of emergency, and at the end of the month sent in 12,792 troops, effectively a declaration of war on the British Communist Party.[44]

'We are in a state of affairs quite unlike anything we have previously known in peacetime,' Attlee said. He agreed with the JIC that Soviet foreign policy aimed to establish communism, directed from Moscow, throughout the world, and that Soviet leaders sought to 'achieve this by methods short of open war'. Virtually quoting MI5 documents, Attlee stated that 'the Russian technique in all countries is to infiltrate their sympathisers into key positions in all circles, official and non-official, and by this means to influence policy'. He convened an annual London conference of senior representatives of security services from Commonwealth countries 'to counter the skilful and extensive infiltration measures which Russia is now carrying on'.[45]

Remarkably, Attlee also encouraged the monitoring of Members of Parliament. He instructed Sillitoe to tell him, and only him, the name of any MP who was 'a proven member of a subversive organisation'. Going further than later prime ministers, he also 'expected to be kept informed about signs of subversion amongst ministers' families'.[46] This opened a can of worms: what should be done if an MP had a clean bill of health, but their spouse was a communist and thought to be in touch with, say, the Romanian secret service? Once again, Attlee was taking counter-subversion extremely seriously, and making full use of his relationship with Sillitoe. It was he who began the long-standing tradition that after every general election, 'MI5 informs the incoming prime minister whether there is evidence that anyone nominated for ministerial office is a security risk.'[47]

These sensitive topics were usually reserved for Attlee and Sillitoe alone. However, once or twice when Sillitoe was away, it fell to Liddell to have the conversation with the prime minister. On one such occasion, Liddell entered the Cabinet Room and found the sixty-three-year-old Attlee huddled in his chair and looking exhausted. Liddell asked the prime minister what action he wanted to take regarding Members of Parliament who had close contact with subversive movements. After an uncomfortable pause, Attlee brusquely stated that he, and he alone, should be informed in every case – regardless of the MP's party affiliation. Another awkward silence followed, with the prime minister straining to avoid eye contact with Liddell. The conversation turned to the activities of British communists in the event of war with Russia. Again Attlee offered little reaction. He was, according to Liddell, 'an extremely difficult man to talk to'. After a further painful pause Liddell got up to leave, and Attlee 'bundled out of his chair in a somewhat confused state.'[48]

The outbreak of the Korean War heightened anxiety. Whitehall grew increasingly nervous about communist encroachment into the armed forces, the education system, industrial movements and the scientific community.[49] In Parliament, Attlee's front bench was being asked what steps it had taken 'to ensure that Communist teachers are not employed by local education authorities'.[50] In early 1951, in the dying days of Attlee's administration, he agreed to establish a new and extremely secretive body of senior officials whose existence has only very recently become known. Its mission was to 'focus all available intelligence about Communist activities in the United Kingdom, and to recommend to Ministers what action can be taken to counter such activities'. Demonstrating a more proactive approach, it was also tasked 'to co-ordinate any anti-Communist activities in this country which may be approved by Ministers'.[51] Known as the Official Committee on Communism (Home), it led the charge against domestic subversion into the 1960s, and formed another of Attlee's important legacies in the intelligence and security sphere.[52]

Working closely with MI5, Attlee built the machine of Cold War counter-subversion. He was always painfully conscious of the tension between intelligence, security and liberty, acknowledging that the problem 'bristle[d] with political difficulties', and that 'infiltration can regularly be defended by appeals based on democratic conceptions of freedom'.[53] Possibly still haunted by the Gestapo fears, he emphasised that 'we feel it essential to develop effective precautions' against communist infiltration 'whilst doing everything possible to maintain democratic liberties'.[54] He later publicly wrote that the director-general of MI5 'has to have a very lively appreciation of the rights of the citizen in a free country'.[55] Meanwhile, he spurned regular requests from Conservative backbencher Sir Waldron Smithers to establish a House of Commons select committee on 'un-British activities', similar to the McCarthyite movement gathering pace in the United States.[56]

Attlee was right to take domestic security and counter-espionage seriously. In addition to the wartime atom bomb spies, Stalin had other eyes at the heart of the British establishment. Now known as the notorious Cambridge Five, they included Donald Maclean, Guy Burgess, Kim Philby, Anthony Blunt, and a fifth man – thought by many to be John Cairncross, who had worked at Bletchley during the war. Recruited at Cambridge University in the 1930s, they went on to become influential in secret and foreign policy circles, passing secrets to the Soviets throughout the Second World War and into the Cold War. Maclean and Burgess worked for the Foreign Office and MI6 respectively before defecting in 1951. Philby, who became known as 'the Third Man', was a high-flier inside MI6, at one point heading its anti-Soviet section before defecting in 1963. Blunt, revealed as the Fourth Man in 1979, had been an MI5 officer during the Second World War, and alongside Philby had helped Maclean and Burgess to escape.

'Stalin's Englishmen', as they have also become known, managed to hide their communist pasts because they came from the right class. This smoke-screen worked in Britain, but it held little sway in America. J. Edgar Hoover was amazed at some of their antics. Donald Maclean, for example, who had been in charge of the code room at the British embassy in Washington, 'broke into the apartment of two American girls' before being placed under the care of a psychiatrist in London. Dwelling at some length on Guy Burgess's personal behaviour, Hoover told one of President Truman's closest advisers that during his time in Washington Burgess had shared a house with Kim Philby, 'a representative of MI6', adding that Philby's first wife Alice 'was at one time a Communist'. Truman was getting better information on the British moles than Attlee.[57] It was pressure from the Americans that finally persuaded Attlee to introduce a more proactive and intrusive system of 'positive vetting', which went further than merely checking names off against existing files.[58]

Attlee was stunned by the defections of Burgess and Maclean in 1951, and demanded to know why they were never turfed out of the Foreign Office for their debauchery and drunkenness. Understated as ever, he predicted 'a lot of public criticism'. The Foreign Office responded that Maclean had an outstanding record before a drink-induced breakdown. He was moved to Washington because it was the 'least heavily loaded' of all the political departments. By contrast, it informed Attlee that Burgess had indeed been 'irresponsible, displaying indiscreet behaviour with loose talk about secret organisations'. Attlee never did receive a reasonable answer as to why the Foreign Office did not eject these unsuitable charac-ters earlier,[59] but he was increasingly concerned about the 'moral fibre' in the Foreign Office and its implications for national security.[60]

Issues of vetting were intimately connected to the Klaus Fuchs espionage case, the impact of which on internal security and transatlantic relations was enormous. More importantly, Attlee was not given the full truth about the intelligence failure by MI5 concerning Fuchs. The prime minister consequently defended the service's performance to Parliament and the public under false pretences.

Klaus Fuchs was a brilliant theoretical physicist. Quiet and withdrawn, he wore round spectacles and had an uncanny ability to attract female sympathy. He was also a dedicated communist, and the most important atomic spy of the post-war period. Born in Germany, Fuchs settled within the British university system after fleeing Nazi Germany before the war. Becoming a British citizen and signing the Official Secrets Act in 1942, he worked on the atomic bomb as part of the Manhattan Project in America. He was one of the few scientists with an overview of the whole project, including the perplexing problem of trigger design for detonation of the main device. After the war, he returned to the UK to work at the Atomic Energy Research Establishment at Harwell. But unbeknownst to the government, Fuchs had long been passing secret information to the Soviets. In America he would drive around in his second-hand blue Buick with a stash of papers on the passenger seat, containing closely guarded secrets about the most devastating weapon ever created. Still he was not caught. In England, he used prearranged signals to meet his Soviet contacts in pubs. To one he offered: 'I think the best British heavyweight of all time is Bruce Woodcock.' On cue, the contact replied: 'Oh no, Tommy Farr is certainly the best.' Following a 'complete dog's breakfast' of an investigation by MI5 in late 1949, Fuchs finally confessed early the following year.[61]

According to Sillitoe, suspicions about Fuchs first arose in August 1949 as a result of 'Venona', a programme by British and American codebreakers to unravel wartime messages sent by the KGB that were proving uniquely vulnerable. The following month, J.C. Robertson, head of counter-espionage at MI5, and Arthur Martin, the MI5 liaison with GCHQ, began working with security officers at Harwell to investigate Fuchs's background. Jim Skardon, an MI5 interrogator, questioned Fuchs, while MI5 listened in on his phone calls and followed him with teams of 'watchers'.[62] As is so often the case, intercept material, this time gathered from Venona, was too sensitive to be openly used in court. Under pressure from the FBI to act, MI5 needed to gather its own physical evidence, ideally based on his contacts with Soviet handlers.

Percy Sillitoe grew frustrated. By his own admission, the 'investigation produced no dividends'. Running out of options and unable to use Venona, he even resorted to asking the senior official at the Ministry of Supply 'to quietly arrange for Fuchs [sic] departure from Harwell as soon as decently possible'.[63] Doing so, however, would have raised suspicious eyebrows from Fuchs's colleagues and friends, since he was Britain's star nuclear weapons scientist.

Sillitoe was furious when he learned how long Fuchs had been operating as a spy for the Soviets. Together with Dick White, a future head of MI5 and then MI6, he had to make the short but uncomfortable journey to Downing Street to break the bad news to the prime minister. White insisted that they had been thorough – four separate investigations had failed to find anything incriminating – but Attlee was unimpressed. The prime minister 'could only reflect that, if MI5's four investigations had produced no evidence, it was a reflection upon the investigation not the evidence'.[64]

In early 1950, Sillitoe delivered a brief to Attlee. It was described by the service as 'merely factual', but was clearly designed to defend MI5's actions. A month later, when Sillitoe saw the prime minister again, he found him in 'fighting form' and proposing 'to defend the department'. To aid the prime minister with this defence, Sillitoe left some 'debating points' in Number 10 and went away satisfied that he had Attlee's support, that the prime minister 'had no intention of allowing an enquiry into the activities of the Security Service', and was 'entirely satisfied with the work of the department'.[65] He had guessed right. Just three days later Attlee stood in front of the House of Commons and stalwartly defended MI5, confidently asserting to the nation that 'I do not think there is anything that can cast the slightest slur on the Security Services.'[66] This was the first time a prime minister had discussed intelligence and security at such length in Parliament.

There was one snag. Sillitoe later admitted that he had not given Attlee the whole story. The MI5 brief was written in part by Roger Hollis, MI5's expert in Soviet espionage and the man who had repeatedly cleared Fuchs.[67] It contained certain strategic inaccuracies and misrepresenta-tions, and these flaws shaped Attlee's speech to Parliament. Unsurprisingly, it portrayed MI5 as having been proactive and vigilant by conducting numerous checks on Fuchs and unearthing no evidence. Fudging key dates, it tried to pass the buck to other government departments, includ-ing the Ministry of Aircraft Production and the Ministry of Supply.[68] MI5 hoped to weasel out of its central role by insisting to the prime minister that 'the responsibility of the Security Service is limited to tendering advice'.[69] Yet the advice tendered was that Fuchs posed only a 'very slight' security risk.[70]

MI5's brief informed Attlee that Fuchs had become 'a close friend' of a German while interned in Canada in 1940. Significantly, however, it stopped short of revealing the identity of this German friend. He was Hans Kahle – 'such a notorious Communist that his name may well have been known to Attlee'.[71] The significance of this had previously been dismissed by Roger Hollis.[72] The fact that he strangely 'over-looked' the connections between one of Britain's most damaging post-war spies and one of the decade's most active communists would later become one of the drivers for lingering suspicions about the loyalties of Hollis himself, with some alleging that he had spied for Moscow. Moreover, the prime minister was informed that until 1949 there was no confirmation of Fuchs's membership of the German Communist Party. Once again, this was not the full story – Attlee was not told that MI5 had 'access to the Gestapo records since 1946 but had failed to consult them'.[73]

Sillitoe and his subordinates pointed to everyone except MI5. They went on to blame the police, the constraints of parliamentary democracy, and the importance of using skilled foreigners during the war. These arguments seemingly held weight with the prime minister, who adopted the parliamentary democracy line in his address to the House of Commons. Directly summarising MI5's suggestions, he told MPs, 'I am satisfied that, unless we had here the kind of secret police they have in totalitarian countries, and employed their methods, which are reprobated rightly by everyone in this country, there was no means by which we could have found out about this man.'[74]

MI5 also urged Downing Street to counter criticism of its performance in the press, Sillitoe complaining to Attlee, 'There has been a great deal of uninformed criticism of the Security authorities in relation to the FUCHS case.' In the circumstances, he felt, the prime minister 'may consider it advisable that some statement should be made in the House of Commons putting the facts into their proper perspective'. MI5 even went on to suggest exactly what the prime minister should say.[75] Arguably, MI5 was rather better at public relations than at security. Behind the scenes, it was successfully persuading documentary-makers not to make films about Fuchs.[76] Influenced by his brief, Attlee did indeed argue that 'there is a great deal of loose talk in the Press suggesting inefficiency on the part of the security services. I entirely deny that.' He praised MI5 for acting 'promptly and effectively as soon as there was any line which they could follow'.[77]

When the Fuchs case broke in late 1949, Attlee knew it could not have come at a worse time for the British.[78] The test of a Soviet nuclear bomb in August that year had been a defining moment in Anglo–American intelligence collaboration on nuclear weapons – the most sensitive area of post-war spying. Until the Soviet bomb test was detected, the United States and Britain had exchanged a considerable amount of intelligence on the Soviet programme. More important, during the investigations that led to the detection of the Soviet test, American and British officials had co-operated not only in collecting radioactive samples but also in analysing them. As a result, talks on resuming full atomic technical exchange in the area of their own bomb production began in earnest in late September 1949. The discussions went so well that US secretary of state Dean Acheson explained to the British ambassador that 'it should be possible to get Congress to make the necessary changes', and the cabinet were told to expect a resumption of full cooperation. At that very moment, the Fuchs case broke. One American diplomat recalled: 'We were getting very close to really going into bed with the British, with a new agreement. Then the Fuchs affair hit the fan and that was the end of it.' The case destroyed any British hopes for a resumption of the wartime nuclear partnership, and even Attlee's artful performance before Parliament could not rescue it.[79]

The Fuchs episode was actually a case of double deception. Although Attlee was not in possession of all the facts when he publicly defended MI5, neither was Percy Sillitoe. Indeed, Sillitoe was highly irritated that he had not been informed at the time when MI5 re-examined the Fuchs case back in 1947. He was angrier still when he learned that he had not given the prime minister the full story. Sillitoe called together his senior staff and asked some tough questions. He was particularly upset that he had not been shown the full file before he briefed Attlee. Guy Liddell believed that had his boss been in possession of all the facts, he 'would have been extremely apprehensive' about the prime minister's response. If an inquiry had been ordered, Sillitoe felt 'that he would probably have lost his job and the Department would have been split from top to bottom'. Furious, he privately criticised MI5's performance during the investigation, and argued that his colleagues should have done more. He assured his staff that when he saw the prime minister nothing he imparted was 'intended to be inaccurate or misleading'. But MI5 officers appear to have concealed the whole truth from their boss in order to escape scrutiny and recrimination.[80]

Klaus Fuchs was a genius who had done much to advance the British nuclear bomb project after Anglo–American atomic cooperation had tapered off at the end of the war. He was so admired by the American defence scientist Edward Teller, known as 'the father of the H-bomb', that in April 1946, less than a year after the attacks on Hiroshima and Nagasaki, Teller had invited Fuchs to a highly secret scientific conference, called to explore the possibility of creating something called a 'Super', which was in fact the hydrogen bomb. Within six weeks, Fuchs and an American scientist, John von Neumann, had come up with a new implosion device to ignite the H-bomb, ignition being one of the most technically difficult issues. When interrogated in early 1950 Fuchs 'laughingly' claimed that the Soviets might well already be working on the hydrogen bomb, since he had passed all this information to them. Predictably, this information was omitted from Attlee's MI5 briefings.[81]

In late 1950, Attlee was misled again. The story was becoming depressingly familiar: another nuclear physicist, another Cold War defection. This time it was Bruno Pontecorvo. An Italian-born scientist working at the Atomic Energy Research Establishment, Pontecorvo disappeared on his way back to Britain from a family holiday in Finland. It seems likely that Philby had tipped off Moscow that the net was closing in on yet another atom spy.[82] Growing increasingly concerned, Attlee had to endure another uncomfortable briefing with MI5. This time the task fell to Sillitoe's deputy. Liddell tried to reassure the prime minister that, contrary to inflammatory press reports, Pontecorvo had in fact had very little contact with secret work. In doing so, he was simply parroting the views of Michael Perrin, the director of Whitehall's Department of Atomic Energy. But Perrin, and perhaps MI5, knew this was not true, and that Pontecorvo's ongoing access to classified information had earlier caused MI5 to recommend his dismissal.[83] Sillitoe assured Attlee that detecting Pontecorvo's actions had been impossible, because MI5 'had no magnet to find the needle in the body'. Attlee seemed unconvinced.[84]

In June 1951, Britain's top nuclear scientists at Harwell and Aldermaston writhed in horror as the US Congress produced a report that threw 'all the blame for leaks on British security'. American politicians lamented that the British had indeed been responsible for two out of the three known atomic spies and for one very probable spy. The exception among the known spies was Julius Rosenberg in New York, who had just been sentenced to die in the electric chair, along with his wife Ethel. MI5 earnestly hoped that the Americans would unearth a few more 'dubious cases' of their own, but conceded that espionage activities by US citizens did not seem to amount to very much: 'They may well have had some real top-line atomic spies but there is no evidence at all of it.'[85]

Clement Attlee also embraced secret work overseas by MI6. Traditionally, he has been painted as a reluctant Cold Warrior, and certainly in the first two years of his government he needed persuading that Joseph Stalin, his wartime ally, was bent on world domination.[86] The prime minister tended to resist the hawks in the military, and sided with intelligence assessments that the Soviets would not be in a position to risk a major war until the mid-1950s at the earliest.[87] He consequently has a reputation for being cautious when it came to covert operations overseas – keeping MI6 on a tight leash. He liked to be kept updated about MI6 activities, and received a weekly report from its chief, Sir Stewart Menzies – something not matched even by his close relationship with Sillitoe.

In the post-war world, MI6 was sometimes referred to as Whitehall's 'pirates'. But it knew that Attlee was not in any sense a buccaneering figure. In the words of one disgruntled former deputy director of MI6, George Young, Attlee was 'a sphinx without a riddle'.[88] But there was more to 'Little Clem' than met the eye. He was not averse to using MI6 in covert pursuit of foreign policies abroad, especially when Britain was under severe pressure. In 1946 and 1947 he approved a scheme to kidnap German scientists, technicians and businessmen from the British-controlled zone of Germany. The aim was either to steal business information or to force them to work in Britain in an attempt to boost British industry. Herbert Morrison informed the prime minister: 'It is most important at this formative stage to start shaping the German economy in the way which will best assist our own economic plans and will run the least risk of it developing into an unnecessarily awkward competitor.'[89]

In 1947 the Soviet press published a grotesque cartoon of a multi-headed beast that was part Ernest Bevin, Attlee's bullish foreign secretary, and part Churchill. It was the work of a new and aggressive Moscow propaganda department called the 'Cominform'. In response, Attlee and Bevin persuaded the cabinet to agree to the creation of a secret propaganda unit, the Information Research Department, which worked with MI6 to counter such attacks. Events in Eastern Europe, notably the Prague coup and the Soviet blockade of Berlin between 1948 and 1949, considerably stiffened Attlee's attitude, making him increasingly convinced about the Soviet threat and the necessity of energetically prosecuting the Cold War.[90] He gradually became willing for MI6 to play the communists at their own covert game of subversion and political warfare. Soon, however, the Information Research Department became a general covert tool beyond the Cold War, attacking by means of unattributable propaganda anything that was hostile to Britain. In its own words, it was the 'anti-anti-British' department.[91]

It was in the colonial sphere that Attlee felt most willing to apply the cosh. In the immediate aftermath of the war, Palestine became one of the worst trouble spots for the prime minister and his colleagues. In October 1946 the Zionist group Irgun bombed the British embassy in Rome, destroying half the building. Six months later, it placed a bomb in the Colonial Office in London, but it failed to detonate. Attlee himself had received death threats from Zionist extremists, and had already authorised the use of firearms against Jewish immigrants trying to escape from camps in Cyprus,[92] because the accelerating flood of illegal emigration from southern Europe to the British Mandate appeared to be feeding a troublesome insurgency. He now sought more direct action, and authorised a covert war on the emerging state of Israel. Leading from the very top, Attlee asserted that 'it is essential that we should take all possible steps to stop this traffic at source'. Recognising that any 'general protests' would be futile, he insisted that officials come up with 'practical measures' to stem the flow.[93]

Implementing Attlee's directive, senior officials first looked at black propaganda. Devious ideas included clandestinely introducing leaflets into the refugee camps, spreading rumours, and 'perhaps even setting up secret radio stations'. The plan was to paint such a dire picture of conditions in Palestine, and of the dangerous voyage across the Mediterranean, that potential immigrants would think twice before setting sail. This was soon abandoned as too complex and too slow; Attlee wanted quick results.[94] An even more secret and controversial operation, however, was under way. In early 1947, a top-secret MI6 team was created to engage in deniable action to slow the flow of illegal immigration. Demonstrating a hangover from SOE activities, these measures included sabotage. Wartime veterans in special operations were quietly plucked from the clubs of Belgravia and despatched to the Mediterranean to launch 'Operation Embarrass'.[95]

Initially, under the cover story of a 'yachting trip', they headed for the ports of France and Italy with limpet mines and timers. Joined by Colonel David Smiley, a former SOE officer who had only just recovered from burns inflicted by an exploding briefcase at the end of the war, they were soon marauding all over the Mediterranean in motor torpedo boats.[96] Over the summer of 1947 and into early 1948 they attacked five ships in Italian ports, three of which were badly damaged. British-made limpet mines were found on the other two vessels, but Italian security assumed they had been planted by Arabs using stolen British stores. MI6 even considered blowing up the Baltimore steamship *President Warfield* – later hailed as the 'Exodus' ship that launched the Israeli nation – at its anchorage in France. Deniability was crucial. If captured, the operatives were ordered 'under no circumstances to admit their connection with HMG'. They were to say they had been recruited in New York by international industrialists. To increase plausible deniability, these attacks were combined with black propaganda and deception measures. Overall, the operation was deemed a success.[97]

Attlee also supported 'Operation Valuable', an ill-fated scheme to penetrate Albania, incite rebellion and ultimately detach the country from the Soviet orbit.[98] Although it is remembered as a notorious failure, 'Valuable' formed a significant advancement of Britain's use of covert operations in the post-war world. Liberation operations against the Soviet bloc were seen as dangerous business, but Albania supposedly offered a ripe target. The ongoing civil war across the border in Greece formed one important reason, as operations against Albania would prevent Greek communists from acquiring safe haven in, and supplies from, the north. The split between Marshal Tito's Yugoslavia and Moscow was another key factor. Developing in June 1948, this had isolated Enver Hoxha's Albania geographically from the rest of the Soviet bloc. There was little danger of a counter-invasion by the Red Army, because the Russians no longer enjoyed land access to the country. With Albania seemingly vulnerable, the hawks in Whitehall smelled blood.

In 1948, William Strang, the studious new permanent under-secretary at the Foreign Office, put an idea for covert action to Bevin. The foreign secretary requested that it be sent to the prime minister himself for approval – despite his reputation for single-handedly dominating the foreign policy of the Attlee government, Bevin valued the support of Downing Street.[99] By spring 1949, Attlee and Bevin had approved the setting-up of an intelligence system in southern Albania to test the possibilities for action. If this proved encouraging, they were willing to infiltrate guerrilla-warfare instructors to train anti-communist groups. However, they held off on any decision about actually trying to liberate Albania until the success of phase one was known.

Phase one was an unqualified disaster.[100] Attlee initially advocated bribery, and asked for 'an appreciation of Albanian personalities', wondering, 'Are they not possibly for sale?'[101] William Strang replied that, sadly, they were not: the leading members of the regime were 'probably irrevocably' committed to the communist cause, and would only be open to defection if they believed they were about to be purged by their own party. Similarly, the less hardcore party members were unlikely to be swayed unless open resistance, which counted on external support, had broken out and was achieving some success.

Perhaps most importantly, MI6 simply lacked the necessary intelligence. It was unable to identify whom to bribe or with whom to establish contact.[102] Strang assured Attlee that bribery remained a possibility for the future. If, as planned, an intelligence organisation could be set up in southern Albania, then information would become available that would 'provide us with some basis for calculating the possibilities of bribery' – 'This is certainly one of the covert methods which we would bear in mind for possible use in due course.'[103] Meanwhile, Attlee and Bevin were thinking big, and hoping to see their own proxy take over in Albania. Discussing the operation just prior to its launch date with Dean Acheson, Bevin pondered 'what government would replace Hoxha' as Albanian leader. He was sceptical of the CIA-backed National Committee for Free Albania, believing that what was needed was 'a person they could handle'. He asked, 'Are there any kings that could be put in?' Acheson dodged the question, replying that the present situation was 'too fluid' for him to decide.[104]

Although the Albanian operation failed, Attlee had now embraced covert action. He had done so perhaps even more than Churchill, since he wanted it to be integrated into mainstream foreign policy in an orderly way. For Attlee, this meant committees: no problem was too big or too secret to be tackled by such very British means. In February 1950, he set up the Ministerial Committee on Communism as part of his desire to turn 'towards the idea of competing with the Kremlin in the matter of subversion'.[105] Labour heavyweights including Morrison, Bevin, Dalton and Alexander joined Attlee in highly secretive meetings on covert anti-communist activities.[106] Arguably, Attlee would have liked to have done this rather earlier, but Bevin, just like Eden during the war, saw the central direction of sabotage and subversion as an unbearable trespass on the territory of the foreign secretary.[107]

By December 1950, Bevin was in decline, suffering from the illness that would kill him a few months later. Attlee's committee now surged ahead, and approved a new strategy of 'pin pricks' outlined by Stewart Menzies. A range of measures, including subverting Red Army troops in Germany and Austria, sought to chip away at Soviet authority behind the Iron Curtain.[108] Economic sabotage was also planned, with disruptive operations focusing on Czechoslovakia as an important industrial target.[109] The prime minister was kept updated by the omniscient Norman Brook, who assured him that MI6's plans were 'the most likely activities to produce a reasonable return for the money and effort expended on them'.[110]

Ironically for a Labour government committed to escape from empire, Attlee's growing enthusiasm for covert action was as much about sustaining British power in the Third World as the Cold War. In early 1951, Mohammed Mossadeq was appointed prime minister of Iran, marginalising the shah. When he nationalised the vast new British refinery owned by the Anglo-Iranian Oil Company shortly after coming to power, London decided that he was not a man with whom it could do business. The Exchequer judged the loss of £170 million of oil revenue from Iran to be disastrous, and British companies wanted him removed. Meanwhile, and complicating matters, Mossadeq's rise was in part sponsored by the CIA, because American oil interests, which already dominated Saudi Arabia, were circling like vultures hoping to take British assets.[111] C.D. Jackson, who was running one of the CIA's largest European operations in the summer of 1951, complained that the British were still 'living in the days of colonial supremacy', and thought the only way to win was to 'frighten the niggers'.[112]

The coup plan was originated by Herbert Morrison, who had replaced Bevin as foreign secretary. A one-time opponent of capitalist wars, Morrison suddenly became 'rather a fire eater' over Iran. A pugnacious character, known for his quiff and his taste for bow ties,[113] Morrison first advocated aggressive gunboat diplomacy to resolve the crisis, but this was vetoed by President Truman. Attlee acknowledged: 'Such action would no doubt have been taken in former times, but would in the modern world have outraged opinion at home and abroad.'[114] With overt military action ruled out, Attlee again pursued the covert route, developing the secret plot to overthrow Mossadeq alongside a small circle of his most senior ministerial colleagues.[115] The idea was first proposed by Professor Ann Lambton of the School of Oriental and African Studies, who had been based in Tehran during the war, and moved seamlessly between intelligence work and her academic post. She recommended her wartime MI6 colleague 'Dr Z' as the operator on the ground, adding that he 'knows almost everyone in Tehran and is a man of great subtlety'.[116]

'Dr Z' was Dr Robert Zaehner, an Oxford academic, although rarely in Oxford, who had been employed by MI6 on the Albanian operation the previous year. Sporting pebble glasses, a squeaky voice and all sorts of academic eccentricities – he kept all his money in his sock drawer, as he had 'no particular use for it' – he did not look like James Bond. But in the summer of 1951, Zaehner was despatched to Tehran, reporting direct to Morrison. He was close to Ernest Perron, the shah's private secretary and general fixer, and together they spent a great deal of money buying support in the bazaar.[117]

Nothing reveals the secret continuity between the various British governments in mid-century better than the fact that Attlee and Morrison personally gave Zaehner his first brief for the Iran coup.[118] Zaehner launched a campaign of political action and manipulation against Mossadeq throughout the dying days of the Attlee administration, with a mission to foster regime change and promote the return of the shah. While the eventual coup of 1953 was approved by Churchill, who was better placed to persuade the Americans to change sides and back the shah, it was Attlee who set this quasi-imperial adventure in motion.

Even as Attlee launched an improbable Churchillian adventure on the very frontiers of empire, the decade-long joint project of this unlikely duo to improve secret service was coming together. Britain had enjoyed modern intelligence services since 1909, but it was only under Churchill and Attlee that we see the creation of a real intelligence community. Churchill had served as the innovator, requiring the JIC to take a bigger role, accelerating covert action, developing propaganda and initiating entirely new fields such as electronic intelligence. Attlee was the integrator, making sure that everything worked together as a connected community. Towards the end of his government it was, above all, a series of security shocks, including the exposure of Klaus Fuchs, Guy Burgess and Donald Maclean, that prompted him to ask whether this elaborate machine was working quite as well as it should.

Immediately after the conviction of Fuchs, Attlee contacted his old wartime friends Philip Swinton and William Jowitt, and asked their advice on reforming the British intelligence community. In doing so he was going back to his intelligence roots, for one of his first wartime jobs had been to superintend Swinton's work as head of the Home Security Executive in 1940. Swinton now told him that the besetting sin of the British secret services was their refusal to work together. Obsessed with secrecy, each service lived in 'water-tight compartments'. Although this had been addressed to a degree under Churchill, Swinton still sensed 'below the surface among some of the subordinates a hankering for the old secretive ways and their own little isolated housemaids' closets'.[119] It was 'essential to amalgamate MI5 and MI6 under one chief', he insisted.

William Jowitt, who had been wartime solicitor general and was now lord chancellor, had come to the same conclusion. They both wanted an intelligence and security overlord who would ensure proper coordination. Swinton also advised Attlee not to be bamboozled by officials who would press 'experts' upon him. Instead, the sort of overlord he needed was an outsider with vision and management skills, someone who could 'see the wood for the trees'.[120] Attlee confided to Swinton that, while things had improved in the past five years, there was still some way to go. He and Swinton resolved to talk further over Easter 1950.[121] Later, Swinton was able to give Attlee feedback from a visit to discuss intelligence matters with Truman's key advisers, Stuart Symington and Walter Bedell Smith. They had been especially focused on 'stimulating activity behind the Iron Curtain'. Attlee was pleased to hear about the thoughts of 'our American friends' on covert action and how to coordinate it across government.[122]

It was typical of Attlee that he brought paperclips and cost-effectiveness to covert action. In April 1950, he considered restructuring the whole British intelligence community. After talking with Swinton, he ordered Norman Brook to carry out a full-scale inquiry into MI5, MI6 and GCHQ, together with the JIC. He had already arranged one such investigation in 1947, but Brook's was more substantial, and was triggered by a general sense that British intelligence was underperforming.[123] This was under-lined not only by the Fuchs affair, but by the failure to anticipate the first Soviet A-bomb test in August 1949, and – even as Brook's inquiry got under way – the JIC's failure to predict the outbreak of the Korean War.[124]

In October 1950, Brook gave Attlee an early view of his conclusions. The big question was whether there should be an overall director for all three secret services.[125] This suggestion had been prompted by poor coop-eration between MI5 and MI6, but Brook advised against it, observing that the three agencies were now so large that it was inadvisable for them to have a single head. Attlee agreed with him that what was really needed was improvement in strategic direction and planning. Instead of an overall director, they went for a high-level planning group that would, for the first time, determine 'whether the total effort expended on intelligence is being allocated in the right proportions between the different organizations concerned'. For this, Brook proposed a group of key permanent secretaries sitting with the JIC chairman. He believed that such a body would become 'a source of authority and direction for the various intelligence organisa-tions, and an instrument on which the prime minister of the day would come to rely for advice on intelligence matters'. Attlee agreed.[126] Created on 5 June 1951, and eventually called the Committee of Permanent Secretaries on the Intelligence Services, or 'PSIS', this super-secret committee would plan the over-arching development of Britain's intelligence community for the next fifty years.[127] The chiefs of staff confessed that previously no one had actually known what Britain was spending on intelligence; now, for the first time, a team of permanent secretaries tried to work it out.[128]

In June 1951, as Burgess and Maclean fled across the English Channel, the three secret services were still fighting against the imposition of an intelligence and security overlord. With Parliament debating 'security' failures yet again, Swinton led another charge arguing for some sort of secret service supremo. Recent events seemed to show that the security side in particular was not being properly coordinated. He suggested that both an overall coordinator and a review of how security connected across Whitehall were needed.[129] But the inner circle of officials and former officials from the Cabinet Office resisted these proposals. On the idea of an overall coordinator, John Maude of MI5 warned Swinton that it would be 'one hell of a job', and that to impose the wrong man 'would be disastrous'. He added:

> I should have thought that the PM (any PM) of today should get someone like you, who went through it all before, to have a good look at what was going on. But I think this frightfully difficult for him to do without antagonising his Security Service – unless they can be shown to have made a complete balls of something. Being 'investigated' is most unpleasant and I found slows up work in every direction.[130]

With the Korean War now in full swing, Attlee certainly could not afford to slow things down. Notwithstanding this, his review ensured that British intelligence entered the fifties as a coordinated community, in stark contrast to that of its American allies.[131]

By 19 October 1951, some surprising things were afoot under Attlee's direction. MI5, together with the Information Research Department, or IRD, his new propaganda department in the Foreign Office, was working domestically with sympathetic trade unionists like the TUC's Vic Feather to counter 'Communism in the British Trade Unions'. Officials were careful to emphasise that this was being done 'by the authority of the prime minister'. Such interference in political matters at home was potentially explosive, and underlined how far Attlee had travelled in his journey towards anti-communism over the previous six years. For now, he was content that the new PSIS was busy refining and reordering the secret machine that he and Churchill had developed together over the past decade.

Just a week later, Attlee passed the baton back to his wartime partner.[132] He had channelled Churchill's wartime intelligence enthusiasm into an orderly system fit for the Cold War. The key question now was whether or not Churchill, returning to office as he approached his seventy-seventh birthday, would let his impetuousness get the better of him and disrupt Attlee's good work.

Winston Churchill
(1951–1955)

Tangle within tangle, plot and counter-plot, ruse and
treachery ... were interwoven in many a texture so
intricate as to be incredible and yet true.
WINSTON CHURCHILL[1]

On 26 October 1951, Winston Churchill entered Downing Street as prime minister for the second time. Anthony Eden stepped up as foreign secretary for the third time. Harold Macmillan arrived in the cabinet. Although he was now back in familiar surroundings, the world had moved on in the six years Churchill had spent as leader of the opposition. The Cold War was turning hot in Korea, Vietnam and the Taiwan Straits – which at times threatened the possibility of a devastating nuclear exchange. Under this looming shadow of conflict, Churchill longed for a summit meeting with Soviet leaders in an attempt to bring about an end to the Cold War, or at least a period of European détente.[2]

Churchill too had changed. No longer the heroic wartime leader, the old man had grown increasingly frail. He suffered a minor stroke within months of returning to office, and spent much of the next four years trying to convince those around him that he was fit to carry on. In truth, the ailing prime minister was no longer up to the job, and increasingly relied on the tireless service of faithful officials such as the cabinet secretary Norman Brook.[3] Churchill was, in the words of one sagacious observer, 'gloriously unfit for office', and had become preoccupied with 'being someone' rather than 'doing something'. His was a mere 'pageant of a premiership'.[4] This raised important questions regarding the top-level management of intelligence. Was Churchill still up to the task, or would his still-boyish enthusiasm for provocative intelligence operations lead to catastrophe, and unravel Attlee's reforms?

On 3 May 1953, Churchill held a long lunch at Number 10. Over three hours he drank 'a great deal' of 'a varied and noble procession of wines' alongside champagne, port, brandy and Cointreau, 'and ended with two glasses of whisky and soda'. A month later he suffered a second and more serious stroke. Miraculously, the government kept it a secret, partly because Churchill's deputy, Anthony Eden, was also out of action, undergoing a bile-duct operation in Boston.[5] Churchill's illness severely diminished his mental and physical capacities, and he now attempted to run the country from his bedroom. Even before the stroke, he had regularly remained under the covers until shortly before lunch. From there he would dictate to one of his secretaries with an unlit cigar in his mouth, a halitosis-ridden poodle (Rufus) at his feet, and a noisy, occasionally incontinent budgerigar (Toby) perched atop his head.[6] This unusual scene greeted the parade of ministers and officials summoned to Number 10. During his slow demise, Churchill either sat silently through cabinet meetings or rambled verbosely.[7] In the words of Peter Hennessy, that most experienced of Whitehall watchers, 'it was a rich, eccentric, selfish ... and shamelessly personal way of heading a government'.[8]

Harold Macmillan, who served as defence minister from late 1954, now believed Churchill to be an almost 'monomaniac', and lamented, 'All of us, who really have loved as well as admired him, are being slowly driven into something like hatred.'[9] Churchill became obsessed with being the man who would end the Cold War, and this ambition to be remembered as the great peacemaker underpinned many of his policies. Much mythology has developed around Churchill and the Russians. Some of it is true: Churchill and Stalin once shared a seven-hour drinking binge which was 'merry as a marriage bell' and allowed both leaders to make a personal connection.[10] Above all, he deeply coveted the Nobel Peace Prize. In 1953, he could barely conceal his excitement when contacted by the Nobel committee. Alas, his face fell upon realising that he had been awarded the Nobel Prize in Literature for his six-volume account of the Second World War, 'as well as for brilliant oratory in defending exalted human values'.[11]

The Cold War was waged by espionage. If Churchill was to end it and find real peace with the Russians, he would have to rely heavily on the secret services. 'Churchill's passion for intelligence endured to the very end of his political career.'[12] The Cold War, however, was not the Second World War. He had grown accustomed to the supply of golden eggs from Bletchley, but enjoyed no post-war equivalent. GCHQ was still reading little high-level Soviet traffic, and therefore, much to the prime minister's frustration, intelligence on the Soviets was sparse. Nonetheless, he constantly demanded updates about Soviet intentions and capabilities from all quarters. At one point, the Foreign Office, perhaps with the connivance of Anthony Eden, conspired with MI6 to ensure that only anodyne intelligence reached the hungry prime minister. Demonstrating parallels with vexations during the Second World War, diplomats did not want Churchill 'overinformed', and thus 'more prone to interfere'. Unfortunately for the plotters, Anthony Montague Brown, his private secretary, soon detected this, and dutifully informed his boss.

Churchill exploded. Furious, he demanded, 'Send for "C" and I'll sack the shit.'[13] This was unfair, and Montague Brown calmly tried to explain that blame lay with the Foreign Office rather than with John Sinclair, the new chief of MI6. 'Sinbad' Sinclair was a 'tall, lean Scot with the angular, austere features of a Presbyterian minister, blue eyes behind horn-rimmed spectacles and a soft voice giving him a kindly demeanour'. He was also out of his depth, and 'not overloaded with mental gifts'. Nor was he Churchill's first choice. Despite Stewart Menzies designating Sinclair as his successor, Churchill had favoured Sir Ian Jacob, controller of the BBC's European Services, who refused the role.[14] Notwithstanding Montague Brown's advice, Churchill soothed his anger by sending a deliberately petulant note to Sinclair, ordering that 'the disagreeable information' sent to Number 10 be written in black ink, as befitted its subject, rather than the blue ink used by MI6.[15] Differentiating between ink colours was a carefully calculated slight that only a seasoned secret service expert like Churchill could have delivered. His relations with MI6 deteriorated as, in pursuit of his vision of détente, he repeatedly vetoed operations against the Soviet Union, preferring covert action against colonial enemies in the Middle East and Africa.[16]

A similar problem hampered his relations with MI5. In 1953, officials in Number 10 busily prepared to welcome Josef Tito, the Yugoslav leader, to London on a historic visit – the first ever by a communist head of state. Security was always going to be tight, but then Churchill received a telegram warning of an assassination attempt. MI5 did not rate the intelligence at all highly, but given that it had reached Churchill, the incident caused a 'frightful flap'. Despite attempts to soothe the prime minister's anxieties, he still insisted on dealing with it personally, summoning the commissioner of police to Downing Street the next day.[17] Churchill's interventionist spirit was well-known, but now his judgement was in decline.

His impulsive enthusiasms risked provoking the Soviets into a tragic escalation of hostilities of the very kind he was so desperate to avoid.

Churchill's first months in office took place in the shadow of Soviet espionage. Klaus Fuchs had just begun to serve a fourteen-year sentence for atomic espionage, and Guy Burgess and Donald Maclean had fled to France, leaving a trail of embarrassing parliamentary questions in their wake. Thankfully for Attlee, perhaps, he was able to bequeath the thorny issues of communist traitors and Whitehall purges to his successor.

Churchill had expressed surprising indifference to the damaging defections of Burgess and Maclean. According to his private secretary John Colville, he 'merely wrote them off as being decadent young men, corrupted by drink and homosexuality'. If they had taught him anything, Colville believed, it was that his already 'not very high' opinion of the Foreign Office was correct.[18] Churchill's ambivalence extended to MI5. Dick White, who became director-general in 1953, felt that the prime minister had gained a 'jaundiced' impression of the service during the war.[19] Others have described it as 'lingered antipathy', deriving in part from his misplaced enthusiasm for internment back in 1940 and in part from 'suspicion of MI5's potential as a threat to parliamentary democracy'. The mistrust was mutual: 'MI5 had quietly sabotaged Churchill's attempts to limit its powers during the latter stages of the war.'[20] In short, while the prime minister enthused about intelligence employed against foreigners, he saw it as a more dubious instrument when used at home.[21]

Percy Sillitoe failed to perpetuate the rapport he had established with Attlee. He had been overseas when Churchill won his election victory, and returned in mid-November expecting a meeting with the new incumbent at Number 10. Met off the plane by his deputy, Guy Liddell, Sillitoe was informed that there had been no word from the prime minister's office.[22] Churchill had crossed paths with the burly ex-policeman before. In 1943, Sillitoe transferred from Glasgow to Kent to serve as chief constable. Two of the residents on the new patch of 'the big fellow', as his men called him, were Winston and Clementine Churchill who lived at Chartwell, their beloved country home nestled in woodland and hillside gardens.[23] Towards the end of the war, Sillitoe had aided Churchill in the curious case of his missing fish. After finding out that President Roosevelt collected tropical fish, Churchill had promised to send over some rare breeds from his pond. Unfortunately, he then discovered that the fish had vanished. As Churchill desperately threw fish-food into the pond, Sillitoe, who was more used to busting Glaswegian gangs, spotted a grey heron. 'I think, sir,' he suggested, 'we have just seen one of the thieves.'[24]

Churchill's interest in security was most piqued by the possibility of scandal. His intervention when suspicions arose about Kim Philby was driven largely by worries that Philby might escape abroad like Burgess and Maclean, causing an unwelcome press sensation. When Sillitoe came to Downing Street to discuss the case with Eden and William Strang, still the senior official at the Foreign Office, he was struck by how badly briefed they all were. Sillitoe attempted to reassure them that Philby was unlikely to abscond, as MI5 had little concrete evidence against him. Eden and Strang, who seemed unaware that Philby had already been interrogated three times, were convinced that a forthcoming interrogation would lead to his prosecution. Sillitoe had to tell them that this was a remote possibility, as the evidence against Philby was entirely circumstantial. At this point, Churchill offered a typically impatient interjection. He could not see why the interrogation, scheduled for two weeks' time, could not take place 'at once'. Although Sillitoe protested that the interrogating counsel were not prepared, Churchill wanted it done within a week. Like Eden, the prime minister feared that Philby would abscond in the meantime. Sillitoe begrudgingly acquiesced, but noted that it was a pity Churchill 'had been so badly briefed'.[25] Philby admitted nothing in the rescheduled interrogation, and did not defect for more than a decade.[26]

If Churchill did not meet Sillitoe particularly often, his rapport with Dick White, who succeeded him in 1953, was worse. In stark contrast to Attlee's model, the two met rarely, and the relationship became strained.[27] At one meeting, White unwittingly expressed his profound dislike of one of Churchill's friends, and the mood grew tense as the old man shot a 'special glare' towards him: 'It was not my finest hour I fear.'[28] It is, however, unfair to compare Churchill's relationship with director-generals to that of his predecessor. MI5 now reported to the home secretary rather than the prime minister. David Maxwell Fyfe, co-author in 1950 of the European Convention on Human Rights, was a quietly conscientious House of Commons man, and it has been suggested that this new arrangement, recommended by Norman Brook, was intended to discourage interference from Churchill.[29] Unexpectedly, Churchill agreed, stating, 'This should lie with the Home Secretary – get on with it.'[30]

Neither MI5 nor Maxwell Fyfe was entirely happy with this situation. The new home secretary, a large bald man with heavy eyebrows and an unhealthy pallor,[31] informed Sillitoe that he regarded himself as merely 'deputising for the Prime Minister'. Sillitoe, used to direct contact with Attlee, promptly reeled off a list of sensitive matters which he believed should be for the prime minister's ears only, including the embarrassing personal affairs of government ministers. Maxwell Fyfe agreed that direct access to Number 10 would have to be maintained for 'delicate issues'. He also promised that MI5 would not become part of the Home Office, thereby alleviating any worries about politicisation.[32] Sillitoe worked hard at the new relationship, and a couple of weeks later threw a cocktail party at MI5 headquarters for Maxwell Fyfe and his closest staff – but under the previous government his guest on such occasions had been the prime minister.[33]

One of Churchill's first security tasks was to publicly announce Attlee's expanded positive vetting system in January 1952. Because this involved watching British citizens, he was ambivalent. Determined to avoid the witch-hunt being spearheaded by Senator Joseph McCarthy across the Atlantic, he gave public assurances that purges of the civil service would be 'limited and discreet'.[34] Nonetheless, Guy Liddell noted that MI5 had privately been told by others to 'operate the P.M.'s purge to the utmost of our ability'.[35]

Churchill himself had been probed. When he returned to Downing Street, MI5 had taken an interest in his Swiss valet. Fearing security and political implications, Liddell believed it 'a bad thing for the P.M. to be employing an alien'.[36] Churchill promptly summoned Liddell to Downing Street – and then kept him waiting as he finished his 'customary siesta'. Eventually an aide ushered him into the Cabinet Room, where Churchill sat alone contemplating his papers. As if to underline his unhappiness, Churchill sat in silence a while before asking about MI5's various inquiries. He then sternly reminded Liddell that it was not MI5's decision whether the valet stayed or went. Having been assured that nothing incriminating had been found, Churchill characteristically indulged himself in a long and irrelevant wartime story about Stalin and the Swiss. As Liddell got to his feet to leave, Churchill asked, 'How are you getting on over there' at MI5? 'We were getting on all right,' Liddell responded non-committally, before adding that 'We were extremely pressed with work and had a really hard nut to crack, due to a large extent to the excellence of Russian security.' Warming to the theme of defending Britain against foreign agents, Churchill explained that he wanted the KGB to see it as 'the back of a hedgehog and not the paunch of a rabbit'. Liddell smiled to himself, but did not linger.[37]

In June 1952, Churchill summoned Dick White, then head of counter-espionage, to Chartwell to discuss the recent arrest of another British traitor, a cipher clerk called William Marshall who had previously handled MI6 communications, and had been recruited by the KGB while serving at the British embassy in Moscow. White found Churchill in bed with the Sunday newspapers spread out around him, a cigar in his mouth, and a large box containing more cigars at his bedside. The prime minister immediately asked for the facts about 'the Marshall case', which was all over the papers. For thirty-five minutes White provided a detailed account of this latest espionage saga.

He explained that MI5 routinely followed KGB officers based in London to see who they met, and that the Russians would jump on and off the famous red London 'Routemaster' buses to try to lose their tails. MI5 had successfully trailed a KGB officer called Pavel Kuznetsov, whom it suspected of receiving information from a British source. In April 1952, Kuznetsov had made an elaborate journey across London in an attempt to shake off any surveillance, and eventually met William Marshall, who had been a radio officer for MI6 and now worked for the Diplomatic Wireless Service, outside a cinema in Kingston. MI5 would see him meet Kuznetsov a second time, at the Dog and Fox pub in Wimbledon. After the two had met at least three more times, MI5 instructed Scotland Yard to make an arrest. The police did so in Wandsworth Park on 13 June, and the press gleefully published the details.[38] This was the first time MI5 had caught a KGB officer 'ready to receive information' on the streets of London, and traced his contact through a 'successful watching operation'. Liddell, however, worried that future KGB operations would become more watertight as a result.[39]

Churchill greatly enjoyed White's account, and asked a series of questions. He did not raise any aspects of policy, but simply sought to know the full story. First, he asked what had happened after Kuznetsov's arrest. White told him that the Russian was carrying a notebook containing the number plates of cars used by MI5's 'shadowing organisation', sinisterly known as 'the Watchers'. This, White and his colleagues felt, indicated that he was a 'professional espionage agent'. Second, Churchill wanted to know whether it was unusual to name a Russian diplomat involved in charges such as those listed in the press. It was, White conceded, but it was also unavoidable under the circumstances. Third, and particularly importantly, Churchill asked whether Marshall had had access to secret material, including decoded diplomatic messages. White assured him that this was unlikely, but said that it could not be ruled out. This was far from the truth: MI5 well knew that Marshall had purposely been supplied with the latest batch of British codes, to ensure that he possessed compromising material at the moment of his arrest. MI5 told the ageing prime minister what it felt he wanted to know, rather than the full truth.[40]

MI5 may have felt that it was increasingly being asked to pander to the whims of confused old men. Before dismissing White, Churchill offered him a cigar and a drink, then sent him off to talk with his friend 'the Prof', Frederick Lindemann, Lord Cherwell – who had 'a bee in his bonnet' about the recent Fuchs case. Cherwell, now Lord Privy Seal with responsibility for nuclear weapons, had developed a 'pet theory' that communists had planted a story in the press about Fuchs, with the intention of sabotaging ongoing Anglo–American talks. After a lengthy discussion, White feared that he had failed to convince Cherwell to abandon his conspiracy theory.[41] A week later, Churchill's private secretary phoned White after midnight, and explained apologetically that the prime minister had read the evening papers and again grown 'rather excited' about various espionage stories. Once more, in the early hours of the morning, White sat in Number 10 trying to calm Churchill down.[42]

By 28 July 1952, Churchill's butterfly interest in press reports had transferred itself to the problem of UFOs. Mercifully, this was not in Dick White's area of responsibility. Instead, he asked several of his wartime friends, including Cherwell, who still had responsibility for atomic intelligence, 'What does all this stuff about flying saucers amount to? What can it mean? What is the truth?' Various scientific and air-intelligence authorities were consulted, and it turned out there had been a 'full intelligence study' of the matter the previous year. Churchill was advised that, like the Americans, British intelligence had concluded that the vast majority of UFO sightings were meteors, optical illusions or hoaxes. One gets the sense that he was at times being humoured by officials in his final years as prime minister.[43]

Defectors travelled in both directions. Although Britain lost the likes of Guy Burgess and Donald Maclean to the Soviets, a number of intriguing defectors came the other way. Prime ministers and the intelligence services obviously feared British defections to Moscow. They created press scandals, prompted awkward questions in the House, undermined confidence in security, and above all jeopardised American faith in British intelligence. Surprisingly, attitudes towards Soviet bloc intelligence operatives coming westward were not as welcoming as one might have expected. Certainly, intelligence officers inside MI5 and MI6 longed for defectors. MI6 concocted numerous elaborate ploys to help encourage defections from the Soviet bloc, ranging from black propaganda to instigating whispering campaigns. Defectors, especially those at a high level, could provide MI5 with invaluable intelligence about Soviet moles inside the Whitehall hierarchy – conclusive proof of Kim Philby's guilt, for example, only emerged as a result of Anatoliy Golitsyn's defection from the KGB in 1961.

But Churchill did not like defections, and many senior politicians expressed reservations too. They had diplomatic side-effects. While the frenzied press coverage held propaganda value, it also fed the growing appetite for spy stories from whatever quarter. Moreover, such publicity risked damaging British relations with the Soviet Union. As an old man in a hurry to achieve an improved relationship with Moscow, Churchill feared that defectors could jeopardise his bid to end the Cold War. In 1954, Britain received five significant defectors from the Soviet bloc. Unfortunately, the timing was politically awkward. Stalin had died the previous year, and Churchill had hoped to use the opportunity to establish peaceful co-existence with the dictator's successors. He pinned his hopes on the Geneva Conference, scheduled for April 1954, at which Britain, America, France, Russia and China were to discuss the accelerating Cold War in Asia.[44]

The KGB officer Nikolai Khokhlov, who was picked up by MI6 in Germany a few months before the conference, was just what Churchill feared. Of the five defectors, Khokhlov was the nastiest specimen. He had been ordered to assassinate Georgi Okolovich, the leading Russian émigré living in exile in West Germany, whom Moscow deemed a high-profile traitor. In February 1954, Okolovich opened the door of his apartment in Frankfurt. Khokhlov calmly explained that he was from the KGB, and that 'I am here because the Central Committee of the Communist Party has ordered your liquidation.' His murder weapon was disguised as a cigarette packet. The cigarettes were only butt-length tips; hidden behind them was a mechanism designed to fire a charge of poison into a victim with the gentle squeeze of a finger. Completely silent, it could penetrate a wooden plank three inches thick from a distance of ten feet. In case the device did not work, Khokhlov carried two miniaturised KGB pistols with which to finish the job.[45]

Khokhlov did not fire. Before he left for West Germany his wife had warned him that she could not remain married to a murderer, and urged him not to go through with it. Agonising to the very last moment, he lost heart on Okolovich's doorstep. His intended victim said, 'You'd better come in and have some tea,' then rang his contact in MI6. Officials in the Information Research Department such as John Rennie, alongside Anthony Nutting, a junior Foreign Office minister, smelled a golden opportunity. They planned to hold a press conference to tell Khokhlov's remarkable story and show off his secret assassination armoury. This, they hoped, would generate public excitement and encourage more defections. They met the prime minister to make their case. Churchill was 'totally opposed', and blocked the plan without even consulting Eden. He argued that allowing Khokhlov a press conference would 'make a hero out of a traitor', and was also 'tantamount to arousing anti-Russian hate'. In truth, he simply feared ruining the Geneva Conference. This was not the time to 'stir up anti-Russian feeling'.[46]

In the event, it appears that MI6 and the propagandists of the Information Research Department carried out their own deception against Churchill. They passed Khokhlov on to the Americans, who presented him as a defector to the CIA. The US had the opposite Cold War policy to Churchill, and wanted to ruffle some Russian feathers. Just as the Geneva Conference opened on 26 April, the CIA held a press conference in Germany featuring Khokhlov hugging his intended victim. All his ghastly KGB weaponry was laid out for the benefit of the world's press, which delighted in the drama of this story. On 1 May the *Illustrated London News* devoted a full page to the story of 'the Khokhlov case', with numerous photographs of what it called 'A Russian Secret Agent's Fantastic Weapons'.

Churchill had been completely circumvented, but he proved to be quite right about the degree of Russian irritation. In 1957, the KGB attempted to poison Khokhlov with thallium slipped into his coffee. Remarkably, he survived, and recalled feeling that his body was 'convulsed in a terrible struggle with some strange force', and his 'bursting eyelids were oozing blood'. The poison burned through his stomach lining and entered his bloodstream, but had he died the coroner would have found no trace of it. His wife, who had remained in Russia, was sent to prison for five years.[47]

Reluctantly, Churchill did agree to the expulsion of two service attachés from the Soviet embassy in London on charges of espionage, but asked for it to be 'delayed as long as possible'. This seemed to backfire when the Soviets responded in kind by expelling the British assistant military attaché from Moscow on the same charges, although Churchill assumed he was innocent. The prime minister took full responsibility for the original decision, and acknowledged that the Russian response was 'fairly obvious'. It is perhaps odd, therefore, that he had not previously considered this issue.[48] In an indication of the Cold War game of tit-for-tat expulsions, the minister of state for foreign affairs Selwyn Lloyd informed Churchill that the British expellee 'can be replaced without inconvenience and we think it likely that the Russians feel that the score is settled'.[49]

Defectors presented prime ministers with uniquely personal issues. At the end of 1954, long after the Geneva Conference, the defection issue arose again. The foreign secretary Anthony Eden informed cabinet that the Soviets wanted the return of a soldier who had sought asylum in the British zone of Germany. According to Eden, Britain would usually decline to return such deserters, but this case was more serious. The soldier, Sergeant Nikolai Kupstov, had killed a fellow sergeant who had tried to stop him defecting. This complicated matters. The situation was made more awkward because Russia had been behaving well in terms of returning British soldiers who had gone over, or who had been arrested for minor offences. Again, Churchill worried about the potential negative impact on East–West relations, and argued that 'refugees', as he called them, should not be murderers. After some discussion, the cabinet sought legal advice before making a final decision. If Kupstov was returned to the Soviets, he probably faced the death penalty. Six weeks later, Churchill must have had a change of heart. Eden agreed to keep Kupstov, justifying the decision by claiming that the murder had been in self-defence.[50]

Churchill faced a bigger dilemma with special operations. Even more than intelligence, the prime minister adored action, and had long been fascinated by the power of the hidden hand to shape international events. His support for special operations to attempt to overthrow Lenin's Bolsheviks in 1917, and, more famously, his personal backing of SOE, testify to his boundless enthusiasm for irregular warfare. An incurable romantic, he even drew ideas from the plot of a John Steinbeck novel, *The Moon is Down*, about arming underground resistance movements which he had read during the war.[51]

In the late 1940s, Churchill had drawn on his wartime resistance contacts in Europe to help found the European Movement, and then used his friends in the embryonic CIA, like Walter Bedell Smith, to secure sizeable secret subsidies for this organisation.[52] By 1951, because Churchill's stature in Europe was so great, MI6 officers had placed him at the centre of a bizarre plan for stay-behind operations and sabotage in Western Europe in the event of a Russian invasion. With the advent of the Korean War, MI6 preparations for a hot war with Russia accelerated, and were placed under Colonel 'Monty' Woodhouse. MI6 was also sending technical advisers to countries like Austria to offer advice on strategic demolitions should Russia invade.[53]

Woodhouse was attached to the NATO military staff in Europe, where his job was to plan for 'the revival of Special Operations after the Russian conquest of Western Europe'. Intelligence forecasts suggested that in a future war, the Red Army would reach the Channel ports in sixty days. Woodhouse's idea was that thereafter, the Allies would borrow Hitler's idea of an Alpine retreat in the centre of Europe as a physical base for resistance. He envisaged nothing less than a 'European fortress' in the Alps, supplied by air and 'forged on the anvil of heroic but highly skilled resistance'. Instead of effete governments-in-exile, the heart of European resistance would be in this 'mountain redoubt'. Woodhouse added, 'Mr Churchill might decide to leave the government of Britain to Mr Eden, in order to personally preside over the government of Europe.' Churchill's immediate circle found this idea 'zany', not least because Hitler's Alpine retreat had in fact been largely an urban myth.[54]

Nonetheless, MI6 helped to fund a special section of the European Movement that focused on the 'captive nations' of the East under Soviet domination, and also supplied its secretary. Harold Macmillan was close to the Czech and Polish members of this body, and a particular enthusiast for the idea of liberation, noting the recent creation of a 'vast American radio organisation' in West Germany to promote resistance, and the availability of endless resources for secret struggle. But neither Churchill nor Eden would allow them to stir up trouble inside the Eastern bloc in peacetime.[55]

This was because Churchill knew deep down that there was no such thing as 'secret warfare', and that any effort to arm rebel groups inside the Soviet bloc, something the CIA boldly advocated and even boasted of, would be risky and inflammatory. Therefore, according to Evelyn Shuckburgh, Eden's principal private secretary, Churchill prohibited such operations for 'fear of upsetting the Russians'. Again, his desire was not to provoke Moscow, and he insisted on being 'consulted ... about every individual "intelligence" operation'.[56] Instead, Churchill prioritised the propaganda activities of IRD, which was now run by his old wartime private secretary, John Peck.[57]

During the 1951 election campaign, Labour had sought to portray Churchill as leading 'a gang of war mongers', and in late 1951, Patrick Reilly, chair of the JIC, cautioned his American counterparts that the Conservatives could be 'hauled up in Parliament' on these matters. Reilly wagged his finger at the enthusiastic Americans, warning that at this dangerous time Moscow should not be 'pushed too far' in the satellite states, as this would cause 'violent reactions by the USSR'. The new Conservative government needed to be 'extremely careful'.[58] Almost immediately, Churchill ordered Reilly to undertake a review of the whole issue of liberation and Cold War fighting in Eastern Europe. Officials concluded that it was paramount 'to deflect the Americans from unwise and dangerous courses'.[59] Visiting Washington in early 1952, Churchill warned Truman not to instigate any operations in Eastern Europe that could not be backed up, physically if necessary, by conventional force. He put forward an alternative proposal to stop arming rebel groups and instead focus on psychological warfare, which the Americans dismissed as 'feeble'. Annoyed at this American resistance, Churchill abruptly cancelled his scheduled meeting with his old friend the director of the CIA, Walter Bedell Smith. Ironically, Bedell Smith too was trying to apply the brakes on risky paramilitary operations, aware that they were failing badly in the face of tight KGB security.[60]

Yet, Churchill actively supported special operations in the cause of empire. As we have seen, soon after being elected as prime minister of Iran, Mohammed Mossadeq nationalised the Anglo-Iranian Oil Company, including its new refinery at Abadan. Born to a salty-tongued Qajar princess in 1882, the year Britain occupied Egypt, Mossadeq was a curious character. His mother was the dominant character in his early life – she once said to another family member, 'I'd prefer to be sexually abused, than to be fucked [as] you have been by the papers.' Mossadeq combined a free-thinking family background with an international education, studying in Paris in 1910 and earning a doctorate in law from the University of Neuchâtel in Switzerland. As a politician, he sought economic and political reforms, including women's suffrage, but he is best remembered as an anti-colonialist. The British press caricatured him as 'a bald, huge-nosed, tearful, bedridden maniac'.[61] He was prone to melo-dramatic bouts of emotion during speeches, to wearing pyjamas in public, and to working from his bed, which was wheeled into the Iranian parlia-ment. This, rather than as a progressive elected reformer, is how the British saw him.

Infuriating Whitehall, Iran's nationalisation severely threatened Britain's oil revenues at a time when the economy was in a dire state and rationing remained in force. Labour had started subversive operations against the Iranians, but with little result. Churchill's wish to push harder reflected his emotional commitment to Britain's continued role in the Middle East. Raised on romantic tales of imperial adventure, the prime minister 'had been an enthusiastic participant in the process of late Victorian empire building'.[62] He also had a deep interest in and admiration for the region and its culture. His soon-to-be sister-in-law even wrote to him imploring, 'Please don't become converted to Islam; I have noticed in your disposition a tendency to orientalise, Pasha-like tendencies, I really have.'[63] This was a worry too far. According to his private secretary Anthony Montague Brown, Churchill 'firmly' believed that it was Britain's duty to 'rule and guide'.[64] He also nurtured a personal interest in the Anglo-Iranian Oil Company. In 1914, as First Lord of the Admiralty, he had been instrumental in acquiring the government's 52 per cent ownership of the company.[65]

President Truman spent most of 1952 telling Churchill to accept Iranian nationalisation. Resistance, he warned, could provoke a leftist revolution, sending the country 'down the Communist drain'. Churchill tried to persuade Truman that in fact Mossadeq was pro-communist, and that the Abadan refinery had been stolen. Using a mid-west metaphor that he hoped would appeal to the Missourian president, Churchill urged that Britain and America must 'gallop together', and asked 'why two good men asking only what is right and just should not gang up on a third who is doing wrong'. Truman finally agreed to a revised proposal that included $10 million of US aid – but Mossadeq enjoyed publicly rejecting this obvious bribe.[66] Aware that the British were still plotting, he expelled the entire staff of the British embassy, forcing MI6 to hand its local agents over to the CIA. Churchill was unflappable and bided his time, knowing that by the end of the year Truman would make way for his old friend Eisenhower. MI6 had secured the support of General Fazlollah Zahedi, the former chief of police in Tehran and head of the retired officers' associations, most of whom hated Mossadeq.[67] The new president Eisenhower liked coups as much as Churchill, but he sought to charge a high price for American involvement, suggesting that 'a number of our major oil companies might buy out British interests and start afresh in the region'. Churchill stoutly resisted, and the eventual division of the spoils reflected the emerging CIA–MI6 operation. A new international oil consortium gave British and American oil companies each a 40 per cent interest.[68]

MI6 worked with the CIA to overthrow Mossadeq using bribery to incite protests. Monty Woodhouse, in charge of MI6 planning, was literally trying to buy mobs on the streets of Tehran – after one shadowy conversation he reported, 'His price is a bit stiff: he asks for about £2 million.'[69] Emissaries on the ground were asked to explore the possibility of working with a faction of the army, but they concluded that 'a military "coup" may be a dangerous venture', since the junior officer grades were thought to be 'badly Communist infested'.[70] By early 1953, they were ready, but London now vacillated. The senior diplomats at the Foreign Office, according to MI6's chief of station in Tehran, had become 'thoroughly alarmed by what had started'.[71] Anthony Eden, ever the neurotic worrier, was in two minds, and Pierson Dixon, one of his senior officials, shuddered at the thought of an 'underhand action of uncertain effectiveness and doubtful morality'.[72] At one point in early 1953, they called the whole operation off. Then, in April, Eden nearly died after a failed operation to remove gallstones, when the surgeons accidentally cut his bile duct. The following month, a life-saving operation in Boston repaired some of the damage, but left the foreign secretary out of action.

Churchill now took control. He wrote to Walter Bedell Smith, who had just stepped down as director of the CIA, explaining that 'in Anthony's unfortunate illness I have had to take over the Foreign Office'. He added that he had been given word of Bedell Smith's recent talks with British officials 'about the Persian tangle', adding that 'I like the news.' Churchill felt that the new Eisenhower administration was more amenable to action against troublesome Middle East leaders, so he also expressed his hopes for American help in the Suez Canal zone against 'any Egyptian dictator who may jump or crawl into office overnight'. Bedell Smith had been Eisenhower's chief of staff and 'hatchet man' during his time in London in 1944, and he and the prime minister knew each other well. Indeed, he was about to check the proofs of Churchill's last volume of war memoirs for him.[73] Eisenhower's new secretary of state, John Foster Dulles, famously tough on communism, pressed Churchill's emissaries about Mossadeq and his relationship with the left, and observed that 'In dealing with wily Orientals, one ought not to make the mistake of treating them as if they were straightforward westerners.' Everyone was now speaking the same language.[74]

The idea of Churchill in direct charge of Iran pleased Monty Woodhouse, who had known him from his SOE days, and even attended the odd prime ministerial birthday party. Woodhouse, a breed of MI6 officer as much

interested in ancient Greek scholarship as special operations, recalled that
'The idea of launching a coup against Mossadeq was much less distasteful
to Churchill than to Eden, and he was also much less inclined than Eden
to accept the pessimistic judgment of officials.'[75] Churchill viewed the
Foreign Office as 'a lot of scuttling rabbits'. He was also keen to remove
Mossadeq, whom his staff at Number 10 dismissed as 'permanently pyja-
ma'd and weeping' – a rather ironic criticism given Churchill's own
proclivity for governance from the bedroom.[76] The prime minister swiftly
gave the green light for MI6 to act in conjunction with the CIA to instigate
the coup. Churchill offered final operational approval on 1 July, with
Eisenhower concurring a few days later.[77] However, Churchill had suffered
his debilitating stroke just a week earlier, so it is likely that his final author-
isation was actually the work of Norman Brook, reflecting the prime
minister's previously expressed views.

The plan was risky, so much so that the CIA head of station in Tehran,
who had been there for five years, insisted it would fail. The CIA overcame
this resistance by placing the operation in the hands of an officer called
Kermit Roosevelt. The grandson of former American president Theodore
Roosevelt, he was a 'circumspect' man, 'soft-spoken, careful and not wildly
expansive'. Kim Philby once said Kermit Roosevelt was 'the last person
you'd expect to be up to his neck in dirty tricks'. Nonetheless, he and
Churchill were cut from the same cloth; both were 'nineteenth-century
warriors', brought up in the tradition of the Great Game.[78] On 11 July,
Roosevelt began a perilous drive from Damascus to Tehran carrying
several suitcases filled with $100,000 in small denominations to pay for the
rent-a-crowd who would riot in the streets in favour of a new prime minister.[79] Meanwhile the shah, head of state in Iran's supposedly constitutional
monarchy and wary of Mossadeq's rise, was a natural coward who needed
a signal that Britain really did support the coup plans. Given that Mossadeq
had expelled the British diplomatic and intelligence presence in 1952, this
proved difficult. In the end, Churchill managed to persuade the BBC
World Service to alter its usual signal on its Persian-language broadcast.
Instead of 'It is now midnight,' the announcer stated, 'It is now [pause]
exactly midnight.' The subtle change served as a secret confirmation that
Britain was on board, and the shah finally agreed to sack Mossadeq and
replace him with Zahedi. Unfortunately, the plan soon began to unravel.
Mossadeq evaded arrest, his supporters flooded the streets, and the shah
fled. Waiting attentively for updates in London, Churchill apparently 'hit
the ceiling'.[80] A combination of propaganda, initiatives by both local

Iranians and the CIA, and mob violence eventually turned the tables and ousted Mossadeq. Thereafter, the shah ruled as an autocrat.

Two months later, after the operation had been successfully executed, Churchill met privately with Kermit Roosevelt. The American found the ailing prime minister in bad shape physically. He could not hear well, had occasional trouble articulating his words, and apparently could not see to his left. Nonetheless, the meeting was a touching occasion. From his bed, the prime minister reminisced with his visitor and wistfully told him that had he been a younger man, he would dearly have liked to participate personally in 'this great venture'.[81] If the success of the operation could be maintained, it would be 'the finest operation since the end of the war'. He referred to MI6 as *his* service, and it was clear that intelligence remained a topic very close to Churchill's heart.[82]

Roosevelt apologised for the sporadic reporting from Tehran during the tense days of the coup. Had the CIA officers reported what they were doing, he explained, London and Washington would have thought them 'crazy', and ordered them to stop immediately. But if Roosevelt had reported at length on why he felt justified in taking such action, the officers would not have had time to actually execute it. Therefore, Roosevelt had played the man on the spot, and reported practically nothing back to London or Washington. It could have been different had the operation failed, but this was wholly in the Churchillian spirit of action, and the prime minister fully endorsed Roosevelt's decision, alluding to Lord Nelson's blind eye.[83] He hoped that the long-term impact of the coup would 'enable the West to turn things around in the Middle East'. As the CIA later acknowledged, Western influence in the region 'steadily declined', but for three decades the CIA and MI6 were especially close to the new regime in Tehran.[84]

Roosevelt was dismayed by Churchill's physical and mental deterioration. Confined to his bed and with fading faculties, the prime minister had difficulty in remembering the name of the chief of MI6, John Sinclair. As for American intelligence, he had no idea what the abbreviation 'CIA' stood for, although he had a hunch that it had something to do with the wartime Office of Strategic Services.[85] It was just as well that Attlee, his predecessor and wartime deputy, had put such robust new intelligence-management structures into place in 1951. Britain now needed them badly.

Churchill may have vetoed SOE-type operations to liberate the Eastern bloc, but he did recognise the need to carry out intelligence-gathering operations behind the Iron Curtain. GCHQ was still breaking little in the way of high-level Russian communications, despite a massive injection of extra funds for the codebreakers within months of Churchill returning to office.[86] Moreover, despite anxiety about rising Cold War tensions and the possibility of nuclear confrontation, the old man could not resist a good escapade. In fact, precisely because he feared that the ongoing Korean War might escalate into nuclear conflict, intelligence that would help the RAF to strike at key Soviet cities if necessary became his top priority. For the last six years Britain had laboured, without American assistance, to build its own atom bomb, and this was successfully tested, to Churchill's considerable delight, in October 1952. But without good target intelligence, Britain's new deterrent lacked credibility.[87]

The RAF had been given American RB-45C aircraft especially for this purpose by the US Air Force, because the White House, horrified by the risk, had banned any American flights over Moscow. The US Strategic Air Command knew it was a gamble, and gave Churchill the codename 'the betting commissioner'.[88] Churchill personally approved the first dangerous spy flights deep into Russia, and on one occasion in March 1952 he discussed the mission directly with one of the pilots involved at Downing Street. The young officer warned the prime minister that the Russian air force would be well aware of the mission's progress due to air-defence radar, and that there was a good deal of political risk, given that a Russian MiG-15 might well shoot the planes down if Moscow had any inkling of the planned flights. A smiling Churchill retorted, 'The Russians already know, just don't let the MPs in the House of Commons find out.'[89]

The RB-45C was vulnerable to the high-performance MiG-15 by day. But the Russian fighter did not have its own onboard radar and could not find its quarry by night, so these secret RAF reconnaissance flights became night-time 'radar photography' missions. In early May 1952, three RAF spy flights simultaneously took different routes through the Russian night-time sky and escaped without incident, but the Russians had seen the intruders come and go on their ground radar. In 1954, when Churchill approved further flights over Russia, the story was rather different. Wing Commander Rex Saunders recalls a wall of anti-aircraft fire lighting up the sky over Kiev as he approached his target.[90] Churchill's wartime experience had taught him that aerial photography could be as useful as Bletchley Park intercepts, so he prioritised these overhead programmes. It was under him that the RAF deployed its revolutionary Canberra aircraft in 1953, setting a new world altitude record of 63,668 feet. This was well above the 50,000 feet of which the MiG-15 was capable, and for the next few years the British Canberra became the spy plane of choice for operations over Russia.[91]

Churchill also approved a rapidly expanding programme of so-called 'ferret flights'. The RAF and GCHQ had jointly created special aircraft that were virtually flying laboratories to map the electronic patterns of Soviet air defences. But, flying along the perimeter of the Eastern bloc, there was every chance of the planes being shot down. Procedures for the approval of special intelligence operations at this time were somewhat haphazard, but for these dangerous missions Eden and Harold Alexander, the defence minister, were keen to secure the approval of Downing Street. This was because in order to capture the emissions of the Russian air defence, the 'ferret flights' sometimes crossed the border, provoking their enemy into launching fighters in response. Given the inherent dangers of a shoot-down, Eden and Alexander sent a regular top-secret list of proposed intelligence missions to Churchill for his personal approval.[92] Not for the first time, a prime minister was misled on an issue of intelligence. Alexander disingenuously told Churchill that Britain and America had conducted only a few flights with special intelligence aircraft near Russia. In reality, a veritable fleet of aircraft equipped to gather electronic intelligence had been flying around the Soviet perimeter for over five years.[93]

Fearing American overreaction to the Russian threat, Churchill saw the CIA as a problematic partner. Nevertheless, in the spring of 1954 he approved an especially risky intelligence escapade codenamed 'Operation Gold'. Completed in February 1955, just months before Churchill left office for the last time, this mission involved the CIA and MI6 jointly tunnelling from beneath the American sector of Berlin into the Russian sector in order to tap the landlines used by the Soviet military and intelligence headquarters. Although the operation had been betrayed early on by George Blake, an MI6 officer recruited by the KGB, the Russians dared not respond quickly, for fear of exposing their last remaining prize agent within British intelligence. Accordingly, the KGB did not tell the Russian military or diplomats of the subterranean security breach, and so for a year vast volumes of communications were stolen from beneath Berlin's streets. Because they were sent by landline and were assumed to be immune to interception, they were mostly not in code. The quantity was so great that GCHQ had to open a new building in London near St Paul's, with five floors of translators, to handle the deluge. For a golden year, before the KGB 'accidentally on purpose' discovered the tunnel and shut it down, Churchill had a glimmer of Bletchley Park all over again.[94]

Churchill also accelerated work on the latest radio microphones, or 'bugs'. Like the Berlin tunnel operations, these were a way of getting around the fact that Russian codes remained impregnable. In 1952, a British technical team discovered that the KGB had been bugging George Kennan, the American ambassador in Moscow. More alarmingly, they had been using particularly sophisticated technology, activated by microwaves. Churchill saw the development as 'most important', as it showed 'how far the Soviets have got in this complex field'. In response, the prime minister instructed both MI5 and MI6 to 'take all necessary action'. He ordered an active programme of research into both defensive security measures and offensive bugging techniques which Britain could use against the Russians. The chief scientific adviser to the Ministry of Defence, Sir Frederick Brundrett, coordinated a technical investigation into bugging possibilities for MI6 – especially using new transistor-band devices. Brundrett's secret team had soon developed four prototype bugs which MI6 gratefully deployed in early 1955.[95] At around the same time MI6, under John Sinclair, pressed for other scientific advances. Worried that the Russians had developed mind-control drugs, MI6 sought to do the same. Scientists operating under the strictest secrecy applied LSD to subjects – without their consent. On hallucinogenic trips, one man recalled seeing distorted 'Salvador Dalí-style faces and cracks in people's faces'.[96] Whether Churchill knew about this is unclear. As we have seen, the prime minister was, however, an advocate of technological and scientific 'progress' in espionage.

On 4 April 1955, Churchill hosted a dinner party at Downing Street attended by the young Queen Elizabeth, Prince Philip, and his political colleagues past and present. He beamed with happiness, and his eloquence was undimmed. 'I have the honour,' he announced, 'of proposing a toast which I used to enjoy drinking during the years when I was a cavalry subaltern in the reign of Your Majesty's great-great grandmother, Queen Victoria.'[97] The following day Churchill went to Buckingham Palace and resigned. For all his flaws and his failing powers, in his eighty-first year he retained the sheer enthusiasm for secret service of a young cavalry officer pursuing adventure on the outer fringes of empire. The intelligence services had lost a powerful advocate who had, more than any other prime minister, moved them from the periphery to the very centre of govern-

Herbert Asquith (*seated left*) with Lord and Lady Allenby. Carrier-pigeon paranoia was part of the German spy scare that gripped Britain during the First World War.

Lloyd George on the Western Front. British codebreakers in the First World War achieved many of the amazing feats later repeated by Bletchley Park after 1939.

Grigory Zinoviev, the alleged author of the 'Zinoviev letter', most likely a forgery, that was published by the *Daily Mail* just before the British general election of 1924.

Special Branch officers intercept mail couriers during the 'Arcos' raid in 1927.

Ramsay MacDonald in 1930. The intelligence debate in the 1930s was increasingly about air power and the dangers of city destruction by bombers.

MI5 reluctantly eavesdropped on Edward VIII and Mrs Simpson at the insistence of Stanley Baldwin.

Neville Chamberlain exits Downing Street followed by a camera-shy Hugh Sinclair, the chief of MI6. Chamberlain only wanted intelligence that pleased him.

Peace protester Laurence Hislam is led away into police custody after scattering a suitcase-load of 'bombs' outside Downing Street in August 1939, causing general panic.

Fact or fantasy? Winston Churchill was obsessed with the German fifth column in Britain in 1940. Here troops practise rounding up a 'Nazi parachutist' in an exercise; but few actually arrived.

Churchill, who loved irregular warfare and special forces of all kinds, inspects a commando dagger.

(*Opposite*) Anthony Eden was circumspect about subversion, but here shows enthusiasm for a Lysander aircraft used to drop SOE and MI6 agents into France.

Klaus Fuchs, who was central to both the British and the Soviet atomic bomb programmes, and whose espionage activities prompted the introduction of positive vetting in Whitehall.

Clement Attlee was a quiet and orderly enthusiast of intelligence. In contrast to his predecessor, he focused on bringing organisation and process to Churchill's expanded intelligence community after 1945.

ment. More importantly, Churchill's immediate successors, Anthony Eden and Harold Macmillan, had been part of this intelligence transformation, serving closely with him in both war and peace. Cemented by the diligent work of Attlee, his uncharismatic deputy, successor and predecessor, the relationship between Number 10 and the secret world was now more robust and orderly. It would need to be, for despite these impressive foundations, the unfolding events of the next decade would threaten to tear the relationship apart.

8

Anthony Eden
(1955–1957)

I have no recollections of any such discussions … I certainly
never talked about murdering anyone.
ANTHONY EDEN[1]

Although his time in office was short, Anthony Eden's eventual accession
to the premiership came as no surprise. He had had plenty of time to
prepare for it. In increasingly ill health, Winston Churchill had stubbornly
clung to power, vainly hoping for a final peace summit with Moscow, leaving Eden, the crown prince, impatiently pacing the grand corridors of the
Foreign Office where he had been almost perpetually since 1935. The two
had at least one fiery exchange about the old man reneging on a secret deal
to stand down in late 1954.[2] After years of serving ably as a respected
foreign secretary and waiting resentfully for Churchill to step aside, Eden
finally achieved his apotheosis in April 1955. Churchill may have nurtured
a 'cold hatred' of Eden for forcing him out, but in reality the whole
Conservative Party were convinced they would lose the next election if he
remained as leader.[3]

Entering Downing Street on 6 April, Eden had endless experience of
world affairs in peace and war. He had spent three terms and no less than
ten years as foreign secretary. With this came a detailed knowledge of the
role and functions of intelligence, special operations and black propaganda overseas. Although lacking the imagination and sense of history
possessed by Churchill before him and Macmillan after him, he was clever,
meticulous and hard-working. Quick-witted, he was able to disentangle
complex problems, and had long mastered the art of delicate personal
diplomacy.[4] Having served in Churchill's wartime cabinet, he enjoyed the
same intelligence upbringing as the rest of the early post-war prime ministers, from Attlee to Macmillan. Eden's premiership should have become

the textbook example of how a prime minister uses secret service. Sadly, this was far removed from the tempestuous reality.

Eden and his circle of friends in the House of Commons were known as 'the Glamour Boys', and he remained a handsome man. As prime minister, though, he became a tragic figure, still vain but riddled with neuroticism and ill-health. When it became apparent that Churchill was planning his overdue retirement, doubts about Eden's own health, mercurial character and petulance surfaced. Lord Moran, for example, Churchill's doctor, feared that the incoming prime minister would have difficulty withstanding the strains of the office. Eden was a fusser, with frayed nerves. He constantly meddled in the affairs of his ministers, sending his poor foreign secretary, and subsequently chancellor of the exchequer, Harold Macmillan up to twenty notes a day. He phoned Selwyn Lloyd, who had just replaced Macmillan as foreign secretary, thirty times over the Christmas weekend of 1955. It is no wonder that, as head of MI6, Dick White always felt answerable to Eden directly rather than to the foreign secretary.[5]

'Eden is a queer man,' noted Macmillan after an explosive cabinet meeting.[6] His jealousy and volatile temper unsettled his colleagues. Fearing a notoriously thundering chastisement, they sometimes withheld information from Number 10.[7] His neurotic behaviour extended to his handling of secret service. That intelligence officers need to be able to 'speak truth unto power' is an axiom bordering on cliché. It is, however, true. Similarly, prime ministers must not meddle in the daily affairs of the intelligence services. Although regular contact enhances the relevance and utility of intelligence, interference degrades objective reporting. Prime ministerial meddling leads down the dangerous pathway towards the politicisation of intelligence. On both counts, Eden's temperament raised serious doubts. Potential recruits into the intelligence services must undergo psychological tests to examine their ability to handle secrets. Many of the incumbents of Downing Street, including Eden, would have failed them.

Over the previous ten years, in matters of spies and subversion, Churchill had often been the voice for tough action. Eden counselled restraint. No episode captures this better than the post-war fate of the comic writer P.G. Wodehouse, who had naïvely broadcast for the Nazis during the war. MI5 files show he spent two years of the war living in an expensive fourth-floor suite at the Hotel Adlon in Berlin, before fleeing to Paris to escape Allied air raids in 1943.[8] There, his friend the traitor John Amery introduced him to Dr Ameln of the Abwehr, who was preparing stay-behind operations against the expected D-Day landings.[9] At the end of the war, Malcolm Muggeridge of MI6 was moving Wodehouse around Paris.[10] Eden was keen to bring him home, for fear that the French might execute him as a collaborator. But Churchill asserted that Wodehouse's name 'stinks here', and so decided to keep him in France under MI5 surveillance: 'We would prefer not ever to hear about him again and this would be best in the general interest.' Churchill clearly hoped that Wodehouse would come to a sticky end, and added coldly that he 'could go to hell as soon as there is a vacant passage'.[11] While Amery was hanged, Wodehouse was allowed to flee to America with his wife and his beloved dog 'Wonder'.[12] Likewise, as we have seen, Eden had dragged his feet over tough action by MI6 against the Iranian prime minister in 1953. But by 1955 Eden was a different person. Illness, anger and irritation overtook him, and he now called upon his secret services for executive action.

Eden was no stranger to the murky worlds of counter-subversion and counter-espionage. During the latter stages of the Second World War, he held responsibility for MI5 and received copies of the service's intelligence reports. In this role he had policed all sorts of colourful episodes, including the French secret service torturing suspected collaborators in the dungeon-like basement of its London headquarters and generally behaving as if it were 'beyond the law'.[13] Together with MI5, Eden had sought to curb Churchill's enthusiasm for 'the execution of women spies', arguing politely and at length that 'Leniency is usually the wiser policy'.[14] Impressed with the audacious 'Doublecross' deception operation in the run-up to the D-Day landings, he gratefully told its director-general David Petrie that MI5 'could take legitimate pride in what has been achieved'.[15]

Eden was shadow foreign secretary when Guy Burgess and Donald Maclean defected to the Soviet Union in May 1951. He sympathetically declined to place too much blame on his Labour counterpart and former cabinet colleague Herbert Morrison. Instead, he hoped to draw a line under what he regarded as a sensitive and embarrassing matter. Interestingly, Eden had known Guy Burgess briefly. Burgess had been sent to the British embassy in Washington in 1950 as second secretary for Far Eastern affairs, where he lodged in the basement of Kim Philby's house. One of his duties included chauffeuring Eden, as shadow foreign secretary, during a visit to America. Despite Burgess's erratic driving and uncanny ability 'to lose the car keys at crucial moments, they had got on well'.[16] Eden, however, was unaware that the KGB had instructed Burgess to marry Churchill's niece Clarissa, a bizarre order with which he felt he could not comply. Instead, Eden married her in 1952, shortly after becoming foreign secretary for the third time.[17]

Unfortunately for Eden, the Burgess and Maclean saga did not go away. The defection in 1954 of a KGB officer called Vladimir Petrov revived these tales of treachery. Petrov had served in the Soviet embassy in Canberra before agreeing to defect in Sydney, but his dramatic defection had ramifications far beyond Australia. Rumours and then revelations about Philby and other members of the Cambridge circle would haunt seven prime ministers down the decades. The 'Sixth Man' was only revealed in 2015: Wilfred Mann, a top MI6 atomic scientist and friend of both Philby and Burgess.[18]

Petrov knew a great deal. One of his KGB colleagues had been a cipher clerk in London after the war, and had then been put in charge of a special section in Moscow that housed all the secrets supplied by Burgess and Maclean. Petrov's authoritative account explained that the pair were dangerous long-term spies, not just defectors, and had handed over 'briefcases full' of secret documents.[19] He rightly alleged that someone – a 'Third Man' – had tipped them off that they were under suspicion, allowing them to flee. A few years later, with Petrov's intelligence, the race was on to identify this mystery traitor.

In some intelligence circles it was already an open secret: Kim Philby, the most notorious of the Cambridge Five, who had successfully spied for the Soviets for over a decade. Oozing charm, Philby loved cricket, exclusive clubs and throwing parties. Like Anthony Blunt, he was infected with snobbishness, which sat awkwardly with a chilling certainty in his communist ideology; a certainty that betrayed his country and condemned many to ignoble deaths. Philby had been forced to resign from MI6 in November 1951 after the Americans grew suspicious of his close association with Burgess in Washington. Increasingly frustrated by British inaction, J. Edgar Hoover and certain CIA officers began to leak his name to the American press.[20] On Tuesday, 25 October 1955, the Labour MP Colonel Marcus Lipton rose in Parliament and accused Eden of a 'cover up' of the 'dubious third man activities of Mr Harold Philby'.[21] There was an audible gasp – and a predictable sequel. Parliamentary privilege having been used to name Philby, a media 'feeding frenzy' ensued.[22] MI6 went into shock.

Roger Hollis from MI5 privately visited Lipton at the House of Commons to unearth his source. Lipton had been tipped off by the CIA, but refused to reveal this to Hollis. Undeterred, Hollis now launched a disinformation operation. Fearing that the Soviets would soon parade

Burgess and Maclean in Moscow and spill more secrets, he arranged for officials to contact Chapman Pincher, the leading spy-writer on the *Daily Express*. Pincher then met the head of MI5's legal department, and was persuaded that the KGB would use the defectors to sow distrust between London and Washington. He helpfully wrote a front-page splash, head-lined 'Beware the Diplomats!' insisting that any statements emanating from Moscow were lies constructed by the KGB. Hollis was delighted. The KGB responded by commissioning a sympathetic biography of Burgess by the colourful journalist and Labour MP Tom Driberg, and soon the secret organisations were engaged in barrage and counter-barrage in which more and more secrets spilled out.[23]

Eden simply hated it. In November 1955, he reluctantly faced a debate in the Commons. He chose to focus on his beloved Foreign Office, and lamented a 'very sad day for the Foreign Service, and a very sad day for our country, too, because the reputation of the Foreign Service is part of our national reputation'. He rejected suggestions that the Foreign Office was too 'high and mighty' to follow security procedures, and went on to give a spirited and personal defence of the department and its staff. In particular, he made sure to emphasise the unique stresses and strains posed upon the foreign secretary, and argued that it had not been wrong to give Maclean a second chance even after his heavy drinking had caused concerns.[24]

Eden then left it to Harold Macmillan, as foreign secretary, to address the toxic subject of Philby. He was, for once, happy to delegate on this most sticky of subjects. Macmillan was embarrassed by the public airing of what he considered a 'sordid' and 'terribly shaming story'. He took the criticism personally, noting in his diary that the 'gutter press', especially the *Daily Mirror*, had made 'violent attacks on me today', and adding, 'I shall be glad when the debate is over.'[25] Philby's friends Nicholas Elliott and Richard Brooman-White, who had served with him in MI6 during the war, helped to draft Macmillan's statement. They exonerated him completely. Macmillan assured the House that Philby had carried out his duties 'ably and conscientiously. There was no reason to conclude that he had been a traitor or the "third man"' – adding, 'If, indeed, there was one.' Eden and Macmillan just wanted the whole business to go away.[26]

Philby did his best to assist them. On 8 November he gave the perfor-mance of his life at his mother's flat in Drayton Gardens, Chelsea. Appearing before the press in a beautiful grey pinstripe suit, he lectured them on official secrecy, and having assured the journalists that he was certainly not the 'Third Man', he gave them a parting glass of sherry. Philby was a deceiver, a great actor. Unlike Maclean and Burgess, nobody really knew him. Yuri Modin, his KGB controller, watched it all unfold on television, and thought it a 'breathtaking' performance.[27]

Behind the scenes, Eden was also stonewalling. Dick White urged him to publish the Petrov revelations. White, by now well experienced in counter-espionage, was blessed with a huge amount of common sense, and was rarely hoodwinked. He had also become Philby's nemesis. 'It will undermine Philby,' White argued. 'It will create uncertainty for Philby. We'll lure him into a new interview and try to get a confession.' But Eden repeatedly refused, not least because the hapless MI6 chief, John Sinclair, argued that White had a vendetta against Philby which was best ignored.[28] White's frustration at Eden's intransigence turned to fury when he discovered this. He later dismissed the prime minister as 'a very vain man'.[29]

Above all, Eden hated the defections of Burgess and Maclean because he loathed disorder. As prime minister, he developed an appetite for MI5 and Joint Intelligence Committee briefings on internal security and counter-subversion matters, and was 'punctilious about keeping abreast' of their intelligence material.[30] Despite blocking White's desire to probe Philby, he actually respected the constabulary correctness of MI5, and believed its officers were more disciplined than the 'robber barons' at MI6 headquarters, and much less likely to take risky action without ministerial authority.[31] Eden's misgivings about MI6 were soon confirmed. The following year, a seemingly routine spying operation went wrong, dealing a severe blow to the prime minister's authority and finding him paraded in front of Parliament on spy issues once again.

Eden's self-image was that of a global statesman. Well-versed in international affairs after a long and successful career as foreign secretary, he inherited Churchill's ambitions to be the man who eased Cold War tensions. He therefore devoted a great deal of time to improving diplomatic relations with the Soviets. In April 1956, a planned visit to Britain by the Russian leaders Nikita Khrushchev and Nikolai Bulganin was intended to be the culmination of Eden's hard work and proof of Britain's right to a place at the top table.[32] Khrushchev would not visit America for another three years, and this was the first visit by a high-profile Russian delegation to the West since 1917. It was a real coup for Eden.[33]

Nothing was to go wrong. To ensure this, Eden personally and explicitly banned risky or provocative intelligence-gathering operations against the

Russian delegation. The secret services had fallen over themselves to propose pantomime operations, including the bugging of Claridge's hotel in Mayfair, where the Soviet delegation would be staying, and another mysterious ploy somehow involving a catamaran.[34] But Khrushchev and Bulganin came from the land of bugging, and the Russians were known for their formidable communications security discipline. Eden felt that little intelligence would be lost by keeping his spies at bay.[35] With this clear directive from Downing Street in place, the biggest remaining headache for Eden and the Foreign Office was deciding on a gift for the Russians. Jawaharlal Nehru, India's first prime minister, had just presented Khrushchev with two elephants as a gesture of goodwill. How, Whitehall's mandarins pondered, could they possibly top that?[36]

'B&K', as the headlines called them, were touring the world. Visiting India just prior to London, they had made rude remarks about Britain's colonial past which went down well in Delhi, but not in Downing Street. Some suggested that the visit should be cancelled but Eden insisted otherwise. Nevertheless, the Information Research Department, the top-secret propaganda unit housed in the Foreign Office, could not resist firing back. The Russian delegation included the head of the KGB, General Ivan Serov, who was officially serving as its chief of security. One journalist recalls how the IRD 'slipped me a copy of his curriculum vitae, as it were – a long list of decorations for oppressing, suppressing and/or terrorising unfortunate peoples'. As a result, for the entire visit Serov was 'hounded by reporters', who described him variously as 'Ivan the Butcher' and 'Ivan the Terrible'.[37]

Khrushchev and Bulganin arrived on the Soviet cruiser *Ordzhonikidze*, which docked in Portsmouth's large natural harbour on 18 April. On the first day of the talks, Eden reminded his guests that Britain and Russia had been allies in three wars, once against Napoleon and twice against Germany, and urged closer relations in peacetime.[38] Aware that the Russian leaders were nervous about their personal security, the government agreed to convey them around London amid the tightest security, flanked by fifty motorcycle outriders. When they visited the Royal Opera House, Special Branch officers watched from the rooftops to ensure their safety. There were plenty of wild émigré groups from Ukraine and the Baltic who would welcome taking a potshot at the Russian leaders, or indeed at Serov, so the British police deployed sharpshooters, controlled by radio cars, for the first time.[39]

There was other surveillance afoot that Eden had certainly not approved. The next day, a short, tubby, balaclava-clad MI6 frogman slipped quietly into Portsmouth's muddy waters to inspect the underside of the *Ordzhonikidze*, with the intention of finding what electronic wizardry lurked beneath the waterline. As Nicholas Elliott, MI6's London station chief, indelicately put it: 'We wanted a closer look at those Russian ladies' bottoms.'[40] Despite not being the strongest of swimmers, Lionel 'Buster' Crabb had served with distinction in the Second World War. He had fought against knife-wielding Italian submarine commandos in the Mediterranean, and torn limpet mines off the hulls of ships before they exploded.[41] These wartime exploits had earned him a certain cult status amongst the press, no doubt aided by his eccentric insistence on wearing a monocle and carrying 'a swordstick with a handle carved in the shape of a crab'.[42] He remained an occasional secret underwater odd-job man for MI6, but for all his bravery and fame, poor Crabb was past his prime. He was a depressive, a heavy smoker and drinker, and in ill-health. He had struggled to adapt to the mundanity of peacetime, and his personal life was a mess. He liked dressing up in his frogman outfit when taking women to dinner – 'this seldom had the desired effect' – and when tapped up for this particular MI6 job he was going through a divorce and selling tables to cafés.[43] The night before his ill-fated dive, Crabb downed five double whiskies – hardly ideal preparation for a secret mission. The next morning, as he set out on a lonely and difficult dive in cold, dark and murky water, there were some inside MI6 who doubted whether he was up to this most secret and dangerous task.[44] They were right.

Meanwhile, Eden's talks with his Soviet counterparts had been a success. Although uneasy at times, both sides enjoyed establishing personal connections.[45] Publicly proud of his diplomatic achievements and statesmanlike role, Eden expressed 'great pleasure', and felt that the visit had 'helped to remove suspicion'.[46] Privately, on 30 April he told his foreign secretary, Selwyn Lloyd, that now 'the Russian visit is over' he wanted a review of policy: 'I do not believe that the Russians have any plans at present for military aggressions in the West.' He wondered how Britain should respond to the new assumption that the Russians wanted to improve relations and increase contacts. Considering propaganda, he asked, 'Is there anything that IRD is doing that ought to be discontinued?' – at least until it could be proved whether or not the Russians 'really mean business'.

The prime minister's moment of glory was short-lived. The Soviets had spotted a frogman diving around the hull of their cruiser; a frogman who had now disappeared. When Crabb failed to resurface, Dick White was alerted. Despite this being an MI6 operation, espionage on British territory necessitated his attention. White summoned his most senior colleagues, who 'trooped upstairs' and were met by MI5's director-general in full schoolmaster mode. The usual charm and warm smile had drained from White's face as he sat rubbing his temples and shuffling his papers nervously. A ticking clock broke the silence from the corner of the room, and panic was etched across the faces of those present. Eventually, White decided to visit Eden personally 'and see if I can head this thing off'.[47] It is unclear whether he actually spoke to Eden, and if so, what he said. The first the prime minister heard of the botched operation was at a dinner party with Khrushchev when the Russian made a joking reference to lost property and the *Ordzhonikidze*. The next night a Soviet admiral reported the sighting of the frogman near the ship. The truth could no longer be concealed from the prime minister. Eden was finally formally briefed on what had transpired on 4 May. By then, press coverage was in full swing.[48]

Eden was livid. This was personal – a double slap in the face. Nobody had told him. Even more importantly, he had banned the operation in the first place. The Russians had long conducted underwater spying missions against British ships, and unsurprisingly the Admiralty thought it only fair that British intelligence should respond in kind. Back in October 1955, Eden had granted permission for operations against visiting warships, but when the First Lord of the Admiralty specifically requested permission to spy on the *Ordzhonikidze*, Eden firmly overruled it. He had prioritised good diplomacy, and politely responded, 'I am sorry but we cannot do anything of this kind on this occasion.'[49]

Unfortunately, MI6, which actually conducted the operation, seems to have ignored this ruling.[50] To make matters worse, communications between MI6 and the Foreign Office also broke down. Michael Williams was the diplomat responsible for liaising with MI6. His father had died on the morning of the day on which John Bruce Lockhart, MI6's controller for Western Europe, requested permission for the operation. Understandably distracted, Williams skimmed the file and passed it, without a word, back to Lockhart, who assumed that permission had been granted. It had not. Williams also failed to inform his own superiors, leaving Patrick Dean, overseeing intelligence and security matters at the Foreign Office, frustrated at being out of the loop.[51] Williams was removed from his post.[52]

Eden was furious, and summoned the various Admiralty chiefs to Downing Street to face the full force of his rage.[53] He knew it was the navy that had initially sought the intelligence,[54] but he was also unimpressed with MI6, and took its disobedience as a sign of disrespect.[55] Its weak chief, John Sinclair, a decent man but far out of his depth, was forced into early retirement. In fact, Eden had been planning to replace Sinclair with Dick White since before he became prime minister,[56] and the Crabb incident offered an opportune moment. White was summoned to Downing Street to be briefed on taking over from Sinclair, and was told to clean things up. Having devoted his life to counter-espionage, he had little enthusiasm for buccaneering special operations, and felt MI6 was full of 'patriotic officers, Establishment cowboys in his opinion, steeped in self-deluding mystery, convinced that SIS operations could influence the course of history'.[57]

Such a switch from MI5 to MI6 was unprecedented, but Norman Brook, Eden's cabinet secretary, believed White was the man to lead the service. 'We need you, Dick,' he gently urged, 'because you know what the British public will tolerate. You need to bring those qualities to SIS.' Brook also confided to White that Eden was 'neither fit nor the rational strategist he had known during the war', and warned that there would be 'great difficulties ahead'. With a heavy heart, White reluctantly accepted the post, and his place at MI5 was filled by his deputy, Roger Hollis.[58] Frank Newsam, the top civil servant at the Home Office, told White that his duty lay with whatever the prime minister requested.[59] This would soon place the new chief in a difficult position.

Eden had more pressing matters. Not for the first time as prime minister, he had to face questions on intelligence in the Commons. The disappearance of Crabb, a decorated war hero and minor celebrity, had naturally generated much media speculation. Just four days after his belated briefing, Eden found himself standing at the despatch box in front of a baying opposition. His opening statement was predictable: 'It would not be in the public interest to disclose the circumstances in which Commander Crabb is presumed to have met his death.' His next sentence, however, was astonishing: 'Whilst it is the practice for Ministers to accept responsibility I think it necessary, in the special circumstances of this case, to make it clear that what was done was done without the authority or the knowledge of Her Majesty's Ministers.' Further fuelling already rampant press conjecture, he then assured Members that 'appropriate steps are being taken' to discipline those involved.[60]

The Labour opposition had a field day. Amidst the gasps and howls rising from the backbenches, Eden was asked whether he realised 'that that is one of the most extraordinary statements made by a Prime Minister in the House of Commons'. If he was aware of his gaffe, he tried not to show it, stubbornly reiterating his stance: 'I thought it right to make the statement which I have made to the House, and I have nothing to add to it.' He braced himself for the onslaught, and was duly subjected to taunting questions from the Labour leader Hugh Gaitskell about his cryptic half-truths. 'There are certain issues,' Eden replied, hoping to close the debate down, 'which are the responsibility of the Prime Minister himself.' This attempt to play the prime minister card fooled no one. Enjoying himself, Gaitskell retorted, 'Is the Prime Minister aware that that answer is totally unsatisfactory?' The lack of information provided by Eden, Gaitskell jibed, made it look as if the government was trying to hide a 'very grave blunder'.[61]

Less than a week later, Eden had to face Gaitskell again. A courageous politician, principled in his convictions, who rarely took unfair advantage of the licence that opposition can exploit,[62] Gaitskell was nonetheless now enjoying baiting Eden. He picked up where he had left off, accusing the beleaguered prime minister of 'a very grave lack of control at home'. Eden clung stoically to the line that 'Parliament has preserved the long-estab-lished convention that a responsible Minister may decline to give informa-tion, if, in his judgement, it is not in the public interest to do so.'[63] Eden's approach, offering snippets of information about unapproved MI6 opera-tions, unsurprisingly provoked 'a media firestorm'.[64] Khrushchev clearly relished watching Eden's public discomfort, remarking that the *Ordzhonikidze* was an out-of-date vessel with no secret equipment. It was sold to Indonesia shortly afterwards.[65]

Lord Hailsham, who became First Lord of the Admiralty later that year, denounced the episode as one of the 'most foolish, unedifying and dishon-ourable' of the post-war period.[66] Yet although Eden looked weak, he had in fact behaved honourably. He had overruled a rather callous Foreign Office suggestion of lying to the House and besmirching Crabb's name by accusing the famously eccentric frogman of operating alone and 'in the spirit of adventure'. Eden refused to sanction a blatant cover-up and make the war hero a public scapegoat.[67]

Unsurprisingly, MI6 did not appreciate his decency. Bizarrely, Nicholas Elliott, whose fingerprints were all over the operation, argued that the fault for the entire Crabb saga lay with the politicians, notably Eden. Elliott insisted that 'a storm in a teacup was blown up by ineptitude into a major diplomatic incident which reflected unjustifiable discredit on MI6'.[68] Eden, he ranted, 'could simply have kept his head down and refused to comment "in the national interest". Instead, he flew into a tantrum because he had not been consulted, and a series of misleading statements were put out which simply had the effect of stimulating public opinion.'[69] Improbably, Elliott also accused Labour of making 'a meal of it', as if the opposition was not supposed to ask questions when presented with such a fiasco.[70] In reality, the buccaneering Elliott was lucky to survive with his job. Described as 'plug ugly' even by his own father, he compensated with a taste for mischief.[71] He was one of those MI6 officers who loved a good escapade, and the Crabb débâcle was, as one former colleague later described it, 'a one-man Bay of Pigs'.[72]

Prime ministers hate the blowback from bungled spy operations. Too much detail can jeopardise national security, no detail is a cover-up, while a few details merely feed the press's ravenous appetite for scandal. With Crabb, the speculation continued for many decades afterwards, partly as a result of a persistent refusal to declassify all available files. Explanations have ranged from a British government cover-up to Crabb being killed in a dramatic underwater knife-fight with a Soviet frogman – a retired Russian sailor claimed in 2007 to have slit Crabb's throat.[73] Wild stories of Crabb being arrested, taken to the Soviet Union and brainwashed also appeared, insisting that the headless, handless body found floating in Chichester harbour fourteen months after Crabb's ill-fated dive was not his.[74]

An angry Eden wanted answers. He instructed Edward Bridges, a former cabinet secretary, to conduct an investigation into the 'misconceived and inept operation',[75] demanding to know 'what authority was given for the operation', and 'why its failure was not reported to Ministers until 4 May'.[76] The prime minister read the resulting report closely, and scrawled furiously in the margins: 'ridiculous', 'against orders', 'forbidden'.[77] Eden was notably unimpressed by the report, which he regarded as yet another establishment attempt to close ranks and protect its own. In June, he summoned those involved to Chequers and berated them at length for not informing him sooner.[78]

Eden launched a second investigation, with a wider remit. Headed by Norman Brook as cabinet secretary, and Patrick Dean as JIC chairman, it examined the future of intelligence operations and the problem of assessing what Eden called 'political risk'.[79] This investigation ushered in a new era of close political control over operations of every kind. The days of robber barons and the initiatives of gentleman amateurs were consigned to history. As a direct result of the Crabb saga, Eden decided against allowing the CIA's latest U-2 spy planes to fly out of RAF Lakenheath in Suffolk, fearing that this had the potential for another international incident, and that the Soviets might not be quite so forgiving a second time. Similarly, he cancelled covert British submarine missions which had collected signals intelligence. While understandable, Eden's restrictions damaged Britain's intelligence prestige. He handed the initiative in the fast-developing fields of underwater espionage and high-altitude imagery to the Americans – at least until Harold Macmillan became prime minister, and resurrected these more intrusive operations.[80]

Eden had long been a cautious consumer of intelligence. More in the style of Attlee than Churchill, he was a diligent reader of reports, and keen to see rules and regulations followed. As foreign secretary, he constrained covert operations against the Soviets, and found the coup against Mossadeq in Iran 'distasteful'.[81] Above all he hated being sidelined, which arguably Churchill had done to him for more than a decade. So the failure to follow his orders during the Crabb incident appalled him, and he responded with a range of Attlee-type reviews and regulations to prevent such risky operations in the future. It is therefore bizarre that Eden is best remembered for Suez, an episode in which he abused intelligence and attempted to co-opt MI6 into launching his own secret foreign policy, underpinned by farcical assassination attempts. The driver was Eden's pathological hatred of Gamal Abdel Nasser, the Egyptian president, who nationalised the Suez Canal in late July 1956. Conjuring up the 'Hitler' analogy, Eden surrendered to his neuroses and succumbed to a manic obsession.

The tragedy of Eden's relationship with the intelligence community during the Suez crisis comes in two acts. The first is a story of a prime minister ignoring sombre warnings from the Joint Intelligence Committee. Despite his reputation as a punctilious consumer of JIC material, on the subject of Suez, Eden felt he knew best. The second act involves the prime minister using MI6 to do his private bidding direct from Number 10 – ironically subverting the new control structures he himself had just created in the wake of the Crabb affair. Geoffrey McDermott, who ran the permanent under-secretary's department in the Foreign Office that supervised MI6, recalled that his instructions were 'passed down by word of mouth by Eden'. Only three officials were to be 'in on all the intelligence and planning', and this number was 'reduced to two at a later stage'.[82]

During the chaos of the Suez crisis, Dick White, head of MI6, met Gerald Templer, Chief of the Imperial General Staff. Frustrated, they grumbled to each other about how 'Eden's barely consulting us.' It was a fair point. The prime minister had isolated the intelligence community over assessments, yet still expected MI6 to obey him loyally regarding covert action and collusion.[83] Ivone Kirkpatrick, the small, dapper and decisive permanent secretary at the Foreign Office, spent more and more time at Number 10 with Eden driving policy – but continuously ignored JIC input.[84] By contrast, Patrick Dean, the tall, well-built and rubicund JIC chair, was unaware of Eden's secret plans for collusion until the last minute.[85] Clearly, Eden was aware that the JIC worked closely with the Americans, and was anxious that 'no whiff of our planning activities' should reach them.[86]

Eden strongly believed that Nasser was becoming an instrument of the Soviet Union's strategy of encroachment in the Middle East.[87] He disliked the JIC's views on the Egyptian president precisely because they were balanced. Dean and his colleagues around the JIC table refused to demonise Nasser, despite occasionally joking about the 'petty Hitler'.[88] They advocated a 'steady line', while Eden by contrast became 'increasingly fixated on removing Nasser'.[89] The JIC was not therefore at fault for 'feeding Eden's anti-Nasser demons prior to the nationalisation of the Suez Canal Company'.[90] Even after the nationalisation, the JIC categorically warned Eden: 'We do not believe that threats of armed intervention or preliminary build-up of forces would bring about the downfall of the Nasser regime or cause it to cancel the nationalisation of the canal.' Dean, 'detached, cool, and highly intelligent',[91] gave Eden a clear warning: 'Should Western military action be insufficient to ensure early and decisive victory, the international consequences both in the Arab states and elsewhere might give rise to extreme embarrassment and cannot be forecast.'[92] The JIC had performed admirably. In bringing bad news to senior policymakers, it had behaved exactly as it should have done.

But Eden vainly brushed the JIC aside. In the words of one of the most formidable JIC chairs, Percy Cradock, 'While the prime minister was ready to call on individual officials or parts of the intelligence community to do his bidding, he and his colleagues were clearly not prepared to listen to the collective wisdom of its senior body.'[93] By the spring of 1956, there-fore, it appears that the JIC enjoyed little traction over Suez. There is 'clear evidence' that Eden and his small circle were intent on action, 'with the necessity to keep many senior individuals, including the JIC as a body, in

the dark'. Secret sources, some of them still classified, show conclusively
the 'JIC's accurate assessments based on intelligence reporting being disregarded' by Eden.[94]

Why did Eden cut the JIC intelligence out? First, he had seen at first
hand the dangers of appeasement regarding Hitler and Mussolini.
Policymakers often think by analogy, and this warped his judgement of
Nasserism.[95] Second, his views had been irrevocably coloured by his deep
and personal hatred of Nasser; all too often personal preferences can
prompt prime ministers to overturn hours of objective intelligence analysis. Third, and with the example of the wartime Churchill before him,
Eden believed he could do a better job than the intelligence machinery.
Not only was he vastly experienced in foreign affairs, he had specialised in
the Middle East since his days studying Persian and Arabic at Oxford.
Eden was therefore well-versed in the history and culture of the region, if
from a classical Orientalist perspective.[96] If anyone understood developments in the region, he believed, it was him. Viewing Nasser as a 'despot
seeking personal glory',[97] he set about selecting pieces of intelligence that
fitted that preconception.

Reminiscent of Chamberlain in the interwar period and Tony Blair
nearly fifty years after him, Eden neglected the JIC's best predictions and
picked his own bits of preferred intelligence. White, Templer and the rest
of the JIC had discounted material from a single MI6 agent supposedly in
Cairo. Codenamed 'Lucky Break', the agent emphasised Nasser's pro-So-
viet commitment, and predicted that Egypt would launch an attack on
Israel in June 1956. But Eden relished these reports, and drew heavily on
'Lucky Break' in conversations with President Eisenhower.[98] Eisenhower
knew that much of this was nonsense, and bluntly told the prime minister
as much: 'You are making Nasser a much more important figure than he
is,' adding that the picture was 'too dark and severely distorted'.[99] It turned
out that 'Lucky Break', far from being one of Nasser's inner circle, was
actually a member of the Czech intelligence service spreading disinformation. What remains unclear is whether MI6 allowed Eden to believe
that 'Lucky Break' was close to Nasser, or the prime minister deliberately
distorted and exaggerated the available intelligence.[100]

Suez may have failed to topple Nasser, but as a deception operation
against the Americans, it was superb. Allen Dulles, director of the CIA at
the time, later conceded that they only picked up on the British intervention in Egypt 'a matter of hours' before it was launched.[101] Washington was
perplexed and angry that Eden had slipped such a massive military oper-

ation past them. Dan Debardeleben, the CIA liaison officer with MI6 in London, was 'smartly removed' because 'he had not reported effectively on his allies'. Debardeleben was an anglophile old-stager who had served in London with the OSS in 1940. His replacement was Tracy Barnes, 'a very tough operator' who had been heading up the CIA's front line in Germany. His brief was that he should 'keep a closer watch on us in future'. There was plenty to keep an eye on.[102]

Eden tended to meet the new chief of MI6 only occasionally – and usually at Dick White's request. White, full of charm when needed, used the meetings wisely, being careful to remain pleasant and respectful, and to avoid any appearance of patronising the prime minister. But he knew that Eden, like most politicians, could be 'seduced by the intimacy' of such occasions and the 'exclusive revelation of "an exciting tit-bit"'.[103] White understood that despite formally reporting to the foreign secretary, he was in practice answerable to Eden. As a controlling former foreign secretary who had subsequently been confronted with the Crabb affair, it is hardly surprising that Eden demanded increasingly direct control over MI6.

Initially, he was rather impressed with MI6's covert operations. He was especially enthusiastic about its secret radio propaganda activities in the Middle East, designed to compete with 'Nasserism', and demanded that they be boosted. The old imperialist believed MI6's ability to secretly launch operations in forbidden territory offered the fancy footwork required to extend the life of empire and offset Britain's military and economic decline. At his first meeting with White, he told the new chief that Britain's foreign affairs required a 'first-class intelligence service' which would work effectively behind the scenes and never again 'embarrass the government'. For Eden, intelligence was a form of secret state power; albeit a dangerous one.[104]

From the outset, Eden prioritised covert action for empire. Alongside a select circle that included Harold Macmillan and Norman Brook, he devised a top-secret strategy for the Third World, where Britain's remaining influence faced the twin threats of communism and radical nationalism. The prime minister argued that 'we should be ready to make more use of counter-subversion in the smaller countries of the Middle East and in South-East Asia which are seriously threatened with Communist infiltration'.[105] Counter-subversion, according to Brook, included 'clandestine activities, whether by propaganda or by operations', directed against communism or subversive forms of nationalism.[106] The new strategy included covert political warfare to curtail Nasser's regional influence, and even a planned coup in Syria. Between 1955 and 1957, Anglo–American intelligence teams plotted to overthrow the Syrian government and assassinate inconvenient individuals there. Eden supported these secret attempts to 'attach Syria to the Iraqi state'.[107] In April 1956, senior MI6 officers even raised the possibility of regime change in Saudi Arabia. The Americans were horrified when George Young, a maverick in charge of MI6's Middle Eastern operations, and Nigel Clive, also with local experience, advocated covertly exploiting splits within the Saudi royal family and possibly using the British position in the Trucial States in order to hasten the fall of King Saud in revenge for his reneging on British oil interests.[108]

But Eden's top priority target remained Nasser. Theatrically, he demanded that the 'Muslim Mussolini' be destroyed, and afforded *carte blanche* to MI6 to secretly pursue its own foreign policy to remove Nasser.[109] He kept those in the know about plans to topple the Egyptian president to an absolute minimum. By December 1955, this meant just the foreign secretary, Kirkpatrick, and four other senior members of the Foreign Office, including Patrick Dean. The above-top-secret files were kept locked in Kirkpatrick's personal safe.[110] Eden encouraged discussions, including with the CIA, of how best to use a 'new revolutionary group' in Egypt to overthrow Nasser.[111] Influenced by the success of the coup in Iran in 1953, and a similar American operation in Guatemala in 1954, his plans centred on fomenting opposition, identifying and training a suitable replacement, and instigating a military coup.[112] The rest of the Foreign Office had a cautious policy of containment for Nasser, developed in blissful ignorance of Eden's secret plans. Seasoned diplomats who had served in the region feared that covert attempts to overthrow the president would prove ineffective, due to his grip on the population and the lack of an alternative regime.[113]

Eden demanded a new covert broadcasting station, based in Aden, to counter Nasser's growing influence in the region. Impatiently, he pressed Selwyn Lloyd about why this station had not opened speedily enough, and later complained about the limitations of an MI6-owned station in Cyprus, Sharq el-Adna, or 'the Voice of Britain'. He complained that Nasser's Voice of Egypt 'continues unchecked and pours out its propaganda into the area of our oilfields. We have simply got to take action as quickly as possible.'[114] Elsewhere, Eden drew on personal connections in his attempts to undermine his nemesis. Alongside MI6, the prime minister even developed his own privateer operations. He quietly asked the Conservative MP Julian Amery, an imperialist to the core with a lust for romantic adventure, to lead a shadowy group of unofficial figures to galvanise the Egyptian opposition. Amery, then secretary of the backbench Suez Group, with long experience of special operations dating back to the Second World War, was instructed to investigate the possibility of forming an alternative government to Nasser. He and his colleagues, who included SOE veteran Neil 'Billy' McLean, who had just recovered from a bible-clutching mental breakdown, and Norman Darbyshire, an MI6 veteran of Iran, held talks with Egyptian dissidents in France before travelling to Switzerland, where they met representatives from the Muslim Brotherhood in their small Geneva offices.[115] They thrived on conspiratorial activity, happily scheming before their efforts were overtaken by events.

There is growing but circumstantial evidence that Eden wanted Nasser murdered. This matter has been hotly debated for many years.[116] Michael Goodman, official historian of the JIC, has unequivocally stated that 'Nothing recorded in the open or closed papers indicates that assassination was ever considered as an option.' He also, however, notes 'significant gaps' in the Suez records, and the fact that the cabinet secretary, Norman Brook, admitted to taking 'damned good care' to ensure that 'the whole truth never does emerge'.[117]

Eden had form on the specific matter of Egyptian leaders. Despite his general caution regarding risky intelligence operations, Egypt seems to have long been an anomaly for him. Back in 1953, he plotted to assassinate the previous Egyptian nationalist leader, Mohammed Naguib. Having recently deposed the pliant, golf-playing, pro-Western King of Egypt in a coup d'état, Naguib threatened British interests in the Canal Zone region, declaring that British troops would remain in the area 'only over our dead bodies'.[118] However, Eden's officials persuaded him that assassination would have been pointless, because Naguib would only be replaced by Nasser, an even more fervent nationalist.[119]

Eden's patience finally snapped in March 1956, when King Hussein of Jordan dismissed John Glubb, the British commander of the Arab Legion and a visible symbol of surviving British influence in the region. Furious at what he saw as the hidden hand of Nasser, the highly-strung prime minister poured forth some of his most ferocious invective. On an open telephone line he called Anthony Nutting, his minister of state for foreign affairs, and shouted, 'What's all this nonsense about isolating Nasser, or "neutralising" him, as you call it? I want him destroyed, can't you understand? I want him murdered, and if you and the Foreign Office don't agree, then you'd better come to cabinet and explain why.'[120]

Bypassing Selwyn Lloyd, Eden went straight to Patrick Dean. Making a mockery of the channels of command and political responsibility that he claimed to value so highly, the prime minister and Dean then apparently bypassed the chief of MI6.[121] Instead they turned to George Young, who later described Suez as a last 'self-conscious fling of the old British style'. 'The collapse of the expedition,' Young lamented, 'left a malaise which has carried over into another generation.'[122] When White took over at MI6, Young apparently informed his new chief that he had been personally selected to implement Eden's orders to 'bump Nasser off'.[123] Young relished what he saw as a licence to kill, granted by no less than the prime minister himself, and excitedly drew up plans to assassinate Nasser both before and after the Suez conflict.[124]

Numerous alleged plots to assassinate Nasser have come to light over the past decade. Some proceeded further towards implementation than others. Some were borderline ludicrous. None were successful. The problem was that MI6 did not kill people very often. The KGB had a wonderful range of deadly devices, but the British were working from scratch. Firstly, having supposedly consulted an eighty-eight-page CIA manual on assassination methods, MI6's technical officers plotted to disseminate nerve gas throughout the ventilation system of Nasser's headquarters.[125] The scheme collapsed once officials realised that such an action would kill far more people than just the president.[126] Secondly, MI6 allegedly planned to use a cigarette packet modified to fire a poison dart, a direct attempt to copy the weapon carried by Nikolai Khokhlov, the faint-hearted but well-equipped KGB assassin who defected in 1954. A scientist at Porton Down, nicknamed 'the sorcerer', tested the device on an unfortunate sheep, which frothed at the mouth and slowly fell to the ground. Despite this success, Frank Quinn – the head of MI6's technical department and the inspiration for Ian Fleming's 'Q' – prevented the dart from being used on Nasser. Not because of ethical considerations, but because Quinn worried it could be traced back to MI6 too easily. Meanwhile, Quinn had acquired an odourless shellfish toxin from the biological and chemical warfare laboratory on the south coast. Hoping to exploit Nasser's love of a particular brand of chocolates, he cunningly developed a way of inserting the poison into the chocolate by temporarily detaching the base of each. He handed over a box of poisoned chocolates to his colleagues, but they were never sent. Outlandish contraptions continued to be developed even after the Suez débâcle. In 1957, for example, MI6 allegedly began experimenting with an exploding electric razor.[127]

Finally, MI6 also considered straightforward hit-men operations. This echoed the wartime practice of outsourcing such activity to third parties.[128] It considered offering Nasser's doctor £20,000 – nearly half a million pounds in today's money – to poison the president.[129] It also allegedly considered a parade of other candidates to do the deed. The Muslim Brotherhood had launched its own assassination attempt a couple of years earlier, and supposedly expressed a willingness to try again for £250,000.[130] Other possible footsoldiers approached by Nigel Clive and George Young included a group of dissident military officers; a three-man hit squad who supposedly got cold feet after entering Egypt; a German mercenary who fled the country after Egyptian intelligence was tipped off; and even the Special Air Service.[131]

The 'doctor plot' seemed to be the best of a range of improbable options. The task fell to a young MI6 officer called James McGlashan, nominally third secretary at the embassy in Cairo. As his 'cut out', or intermediary, he chose James Mossman, best known for his work with the BBC *Panorama* programme, who had served in MI6 during the war. Mossman, who was now the *Daily Telegraph* correspondent in Cairo, received an unexpected invitation for a cup of coffee. McGlashan explained that Britain was about to go to war with Egypt, but assassination would be an easier option for all, and would avoid endless bloodshed. Mossman's role was simply to take the money to the assassin. He drove twelve miles to a location outside the city and handed over a package containing £20,000 in used banknotes, then telephoned to confirm safe delivery – but he had handed it to the wrong man. Nothing more was heard of the money.[132]

Nasser proved to be a more effective and ruthless user of intelligence than his British opponents. In August 1956, the formidable Egyptian secret police, the Mukhabarat, aided and advised by former Gestapo officers, managed to roll up most of the MI6 network in Cairo. Its twenty-three operatives were soon behind bars, and James McGlashan found himself joining them despite his diplomatic status. The main MI6 network was being run by James Swinburn, the manager of the Arab News Agency, and included Charles Pittuck, under cover with Marconi Radio, and John Thornton Stanley, a wartime MI6 officer operating as the local representative of Prudential Insurance. All were arrested and interrogated in Cairo's fearsome Barrage Prison. The Egyptian prosecutors demanded the death sentence,[133] but the four Brits were released within a year, although the more numerous Egyptian agents in the network received long sentences, and in one case the death penalty.[134] The sight presented by some of these sorry figures exiting Egyptian custody, clutching their prison parcels and hoping to avoid the attentions of the press, sums up MI6's modest achievements during the Suez crisis. Indeed, its operations in Egypt were a metaphor for the imperial decline that Eden had so earnestly hoped to reverse.[135]

How much detail did Eden know of all these alleged activities? George Young's remark that he had *personally* been selected to execute Eden's wishes offers a clue. This was not being handled through normal MI6 channels; rather through a small team of like-minded people within MI6. The prime minister offered a 'toothy grin' at a chiefs of staff committee meeting when the matter of Nasser's hypothetical death came up and the MI6 representative remarked innocently that 'thuggery' was not on the agenda.[136] Similarly, Dick White claims to have told Eden directly that he would not sanction any further MI6 involvement in Nasser's assassination,[137] while the head of the Foreign Office, Ivone Kirkpatrick, bluntly informed the prime minister that MI6 did not have the sort of capability required to eliminate Nasser.[138] Interestingly, the same line would be used to deter Harold Wilson's desire to assassinate Idi Amin twenty years later.[139] The foreign secretary Selwyn Lloyd shared White's reservations, declaring that a secret file covering assassination plans had no business in the Foreign Office.[140]

To Eden's dismay, about a year before his death in January 1977, his assassination plots became public. Miles Copeland, a CIA officer who had been based in London, and later became London station chief, told a US Senate Committee inquiry about them, and the story erupted in *The Times*. Eden issued an indignant denial, calling it 'a load of rubbish', and 'a lot of wild stuff'. But Copeland remembered things differently, stating that he had 'frequently' discussed Nasser's assassination with Eden and top intelligence and security personnel, notably Young and Dean. 'Anthony Eden wanted me to shoot Nasser,' he recalled. Eden kept 'nagging' him about it. It seemed a plausible option, given that the military colonels with whom the CIA was in touch in Cairo also 'wanted to have him killed'.[141] Far from intending to expose a scandal, Copeland was merely describing these things to the Senate Committee to illustrate that they had been quite normal in the secret world, adding, 'You can't live in Togoland and not get involved in cannibalism.' He had not wanted to embarrass Eden, and later wrote to him to apologise, saying that he had been in 'serious trouble' with the CIA for speaking out. He felt his remarks had been taken out of context, but could not help telling Eden that at the CIA London station in 1956 a standing joke had been that they 'would have to restrain Sir Anthony physically to keep him from going down to Cairo to shoot Nasser himself'.[142]

Ultimately, Eden failed to topple Nasser. Once war broke out between Israel and Egypt in October 1956, Eden reverted to a slightly more conventional role. Like many prime ministers at war, he, along with the Queen, received a daily summary of events on the ground from the Joint Intelligence Committee. These supposedly helped him to stay on top of developments and oversee Britain's strategy – even if this was in a rather unusual and deceptive role as 'peacemaker'.[143] Both throughout the crisis and during the war, however, Eden, in the words of Peter Hennessy, offered an 'object lesson' in how not to run a war cabinet. The prime minister, under stress, exhibited 'tunnel vision' and, despite JIC input, failed to perform his most basic function as 'the daily overseer of military operations once the war had started'.[144] Unfortunately for Eden, these military operations failed, and under serious American pressure he agreed to halt the British invasion of Egypt at midnight on 6 November.

Anthony Eden had generally been a cautious and conscientious consumer of intelligence until he confronted Nasser. The Egyptian president's firebrand exploits brought out the worst aspects of Eden's fragile personality, transforming him into a poor consumer of intelligence, cherry-picking reports that supported his preconceptions while marginalising the collective wisdom of the JIC. Meanwhile, Eden bypassed Foreign Office channels to co-opt senior MI6 officers to do his personal bidding, in a move which undermined agreed cabinet policy. Ironically, this occurred at the very time he professed outrage about poor chains of command over the Buster Crabb affair and promised to keep intelligence operations on a tighter leash. After bungling his intelligence affairs, Eden fled to Ian Fleming's beautiful 'Goldeneye' estate in Jamaica, perched above its own coral bay, where many of the James Bond novels were written, to recuperate. Noël Coward, a neighbour, sent down Frank Cooper's marmalade and Huntley & Palmers biscuits. These treats failed to restore his spirits, and on 14 December 1956 he returned to London to resign.[145]

When Harold Macmillan succeeded Eden in January 1957, he had an unenviable task. The incoming prime minister had to rebuild confidence in the foreign policy machine, not least the relationship between the intelligence world and Number 10. Like Eden and Attlee before him, however, Macmillan was experienced in dealing with the secret world, and having served under Churchill, understood the transformative power of intelligence. Not that that had done poor Eden much good.

9

Harold Macmillan
(1957–1963)

I was forced to spend a great deal of today over a silly
scrape (women this time, thank God, not boys) into
which one of the ministers has got himself.
HAROLD MACMILLAN ON JOHN PROFUMO[1]

Harold Macmillan's seven-year premiership bridged the gap between the
fusty fifties and the swinging sixties. Yet, Macmillan himself thrived on
playing the part of the Edwardian gentleman. Nothing delighted him more
than being photographed in tweed plus-fours and a deerstalker. Part
poseur, he was 'stylishly self-ironic' and, in the words of one sagacious
political observer, 'marinated in a very personal sense of his country's
history and its place in the world'.[2] Lambasted as being old and out-of-
touch as his premiership faded in the aftermath of a string of security
scandals, it was unclear whether Macmillan had the ability to navigate the
new intelligence terrain in an era of journalistic exposure.

Behind the artfully contrived show of *savoir faire*, Macmillan was an
unhappy spymaster. Despite bringing his characteristic wit to the subject,
for the most part the prime minister found espionage exasperating and, in
contrast to Churchill, even questioned its overall value.[3] Espionage
conducted overseas, he argued, was 'clearly contrary to international law',
while he found domestic security episodes 'painful and frustrating'.[4] This
is perhaps unsurprising, given that his premiership was dominated by spy
scandals. It is little wonder that Macmillan at times thought intelligence
more trouble than it was worth. Despite close contact with Churchill and
recent periods as foreign secretary and minister of defence, once he
crossed the threshold into Downing Street he felt curiously unprepared for
the 'intricate and specialised' problems of the secret world. Ever the bibli-
ophile, often thumbing fine editions of Dickens and Thackeray late at

night, the prime minister confessed that they offered few clues to such mysteries: he lacked, by his own admission, 'a wide knowledge of detective fiction'.[5] He was also painfully aware that the security agencies had gradually come to be regarded as the special responsibility of the prime minister of the day. Given the 'widespread and hostile' public criticism evoked by periodic security scandals, other cabinet ministers happily subscribed to this emerging constitutional convention.[6]

Nevertheless, the central intelligence apparatus supported Macmillan well. He thought the Cabinet Secretariat had become 'a very efficient machine', and considered himself 'admirably served' by his private office.[7] Gently, both the cabinet secretary and the JIC chairman sought to 'bring the prime minister into closer touch with our intelligence matters'.[8] Macmillan certainly proved to be an attentive reader of intelligence summaries; he worried that despite the Joint Intelligence Committee moving to the Cabinet Office in 1957, intelligence targets remained too defence-orientated, and called for greater focus on political problems in Europe, Egypt and Cuba. He could also be ruthless, pressing for the continued expansion of the signals intelligence effort and for intelligence operations inside Commonwealth countries and neutral states.[9] To the delight of the JIC he often put specific questions to them, for example regarding French progress towards nuclear weapons, and used their assessments on the British nuclear deterrent thoughtfully in making major decisions over Blue Streak and Polaris missiles.[10] Moreover, he got on well with Dick White, chief of MI6, praising the contributions made by Russian double agent Oleg Penkovsky and by GCHQ.[11]

Yet, while dutifully developing the intelligence machine bequeathed by his wartime predecessors, Macmillan remained an intelligence sceptic. He may have served as Churchill's wartime minister in the Middle East, but he was in many ways Churchill's very opposite in disliking espionage. From the outset he was 'antipathetic to the whole subject of spies and spying', and subsequent events only seemed to confirm his view. On 1 May 1960, the shooting down over central Russia of a CIA U-2 reconnaissance flight piloted by Gary Powers caused the cancellation of an East–West summit with Khrushchev that Macmillan had been patiently preparing for two years. In private he exploded, accusing 'undisciplined American Generals' of 'blowing up the Summit Conference'.[12] He now required his cabinet secretary to organise a review of what he called 'buzzing' – reconnaissance flights over Russian naval exercises and secret submarine missions – and improved procedures for clearance of these special intelligence operations. 'All these involve <u>some</u> risk (remember always U2) but great gains.' It was 'a question of balance of the two', he mused. Eventually, he came to view these special activities as involving rather more risk than gain.[13]

The U-2 shoot-down put espionage on the front page. Macmillan disliked spying generally, but above all he loathed public discussions of such matters. He believed that matters of intelligence should remain out of the public domain, and later argued that the information passed to the Russians by Guy Burgess and Donald Maclean was less damaging than the demoralisation caused by the fact of their treachery becoming widely known. Publicly, in post-retirement interviews he attempted to downplay the importance of Burgess, Maclean and even Philby, on one occasion dismissing espionage and defection as 'not very important' and 'rather exaggerated.'[14] Trying to frame this as an administrative matter, he sought improved machinery and worked towards creating the Security Commission, to which these issues could be referred 'in case more spies are caught (as they will be)'. Privately, Macmillan knew that these were matters of life or death for his government. Towards the end of his premiership, he learned the full truth about Philby, and then about Anthony Blunt, and realised that if it got out, it would blow his government out of the water. While these ticking time bombs were contained for some years, it was another security scandal that pushed his administration towards the precipice in 1963.[15]

Paradoxically, Macmillan loved special operations and commando raids. This was notably odd, since these paramilitary activities, often implemented by mercenaries and other murky figures, carried the highest risk of all. In 1961, he watched President Kennedy, newly installed in the White House, writhe in discomfort over the CIA's failed Bay of Pigs episode. Macmillan had deemed this attempt to unseat Fidel Castro by storming the beaches with Cuban exiles foolish from the outset, noting, 'I have not great hopes of their winning,' and he later called the outcome 'a bad blow for Kennedy.'[16] Yet he greatly admired Allen Dulles, America's spy chief, and urged MI6 to join with the CIA on all sorts of improbable adventures. Four undeclared wars were fought by Macmillan and Kennedy in Cuba, Laos, Indonesia and all across the Middle East against Nasser. The most brutal was on the border between Aden and Yemen; here as elsewhere, Macmillan, an old imperialist of similar vintage to Churchill and Eden, recognised the power of covert action, of smoke and mirrors, in stemming decline. When the more cautious Dick White held back MI6 support for the Yemeni royalists in their war against Nasser's guerrillas, Macmillan formed his own groups of privateers to do the work. They reported gleefully: 'The Egyptians are getting short shrift from the Royalists. When they are caught they have their noses, ears and lips removed, and are then sent back to the Republican rebel leader naked.' Nasser took it all surprisingly well, and responded by sending the British leaders of this covert operation his official Christmas card.[17]

Macmillan's premiership enjoyed a honeymoon period. Two years passed without intelligence controversy. Then in late 1959, the CIA received information from one of its best agents, a mole in the Polish security services codenamed 'Sniper', that high-quality intelligence was being fed to the KGB from the Admiralty Underwater Weapons Establishment, much of it concerning nuclear submarines. MI5 was soon on the case. The key suspect was Harry Houghton, a former sailor who was a civil service clerk at the base. After he bought a fourth new car and a new house, and having gained a reputation for buying plentiful rounds for his friends in the local pubs and clubs, questions were asked about a lifestyle that went beyond his meagre salary.

The 'Watchers' of MI5 put Houghton and his girlfriend, Ethel Gee, under surveillance. They often went to London to meet Gordon Lonsdale, a Canadian businessman who dealt in jukeboxes and bubblegum machines. MI5 found that Lonsdale sometimes visited an antiquarian bookseller, Peter Kroger, and his wife Helen, at their home at 45 Cranley Drive, Ruislip, in north-west London. The Krogers were also put under close but discreet watch. On 7 January 1961, after patiently watching for more than twelve months, MI5 sprung its trap. Houghton and Gee were arrested in the act of passing a shopping bag to Lonsdale outside the Old Vic theatre near Waterloo station. It contained the secrets of *Dreadnought*, Britain's latest nuclear submarine. Roger Hollis, director-general of MI5, was thrilled, and expected Macmillan's gratitude. Not for the last time, he was to be disappointed. The public airing of a security failure made Macmillan highly uncomfortable, and concerned that the exposure of such a successful espionage ring inside Britain suggested that MI5 was incompetent. More worrying still, it would lead to press speculation about further moles burrowed elsewhere in the establishment. Macmillan was right on both counts.[18]

'Sniper' had further surprises in store. In 1961, the CIA's prize agent defected while visiting Berlin, and escaped to the United States with a large cache of documents. His real name was Michael Goleniewski, and he was in fact a remarkable triple agent. Deputy head of Polish security and then head of scientific intelligence, he was all the time spying on the Poles for the Russians. Unbeknown to the Russians, he was also reporting to the CIA. Remarkably, he had operated as his own case officer, and reported to the Americans anonymously while acting as a spy in Warsaw, because he knew there were many moles in the West who might reveal his identity. Safely arrived in Washington, he was intensely debriefed by the CIA and the FBI. A slightly mad figure with an enormous twirling moustache, he later lost a little credibility when he claimed to be the surviving son of Tsar Nicholas and heir to the Imperial Russian throne. But there was no denying the authenticity of the haul of documents he brought with him. It included three MI6 reports; careful investigation showed that only ten people could have seen all three. Suspicion fell on George Blake, an MI6 officer who had been incarcerated by the communists during the Korean War. He was recalled from Lebanon, where he was enrolled at Britain's 'school for spies', the Middle East Centre for Arabic Studies. Under interrogation, Blake hotly denied that he had been tortured or blackmailed by the North Koreans, boasting instead that he had switched sides voluntarily, and giving his MI6 interrogators a full confession of his ideological commitment to communism. Moscow's top remaining agent within the British intelligence and security establishment was now blown.[19]

Macmillan was horrified by the idea of a public trial, but MI5 managed to persuade him that most of it could be held in camera. In stark breach of the principle of judicial independence, Britain's most senior judge, Lord Parker, phoned Macmillan before passing sentence. After consulting the prime minister he sentenced Blake to an unprecedented forty-two-year stretch.[20] Nevertheless, the dramatic revelations shocked the public. It had, after all, only been a few years since the startling disclosures about Maclean and Burgess, yet here was another traitor within the establishment. With the eager press sniffing around another spy scandal, Macmillan desperately sought to keep Blake's MI6 links quiet: 'The public do not know and cannot be told that he belonged to MI6 – an organisation wh[ich] does not theoretically exist.' Macmillan's fear focused on 'terrible' journalists 'without any sense of responsibility' who seemed to glory in security failures. Following constitutional precedent, he personally briefed Hugh Gaitskell and a few other senior members of the opposition at Downing Street, including the shadow foreign secretary, George Brown. Macmillan noted that Brown was sober, as it was 11.30 in the morning, but he 'had clearly been pretty bad the night before'.[21]

Macmillan had not reckoned on Chapman Pincher, a pioneering investigative reporter on the *Daily Express* with unrivalled contacts. The prime minister's frustration at Pincher's dramatic scoops turned to outright anger when the journalist broke the news that Blake had worked for MI6, and had compromised the Berlin Tunnel operation. How had Pincher outfoxed the government yet again? He had simply enjoyed a 'bibulous luncheon' with George Brown. The incident heightened Macmillan's strong dislike of the 'common', 'ill-bred' and 'boorish' Brown. Macmillan had once asked his staff, 'Can nothing be done to suppress or get rid of Mr Chapman Pincher?' and now his hatred went off the scale.[22] To his further discomfort, the Blake saga was one of the first security matters he had to discuss with the new American president, John F. Kennedy, in early 1961.[23]

Spies now mixed with sex, another subject that sent shivers down Macmillan's spine. Hard on the heels of the Blake case came John Vassall. A homosexual who enjoyed an ostentatious lifestyle, designer clothes and long holidays in the sun, Vassall had nevertheless suffered from the snobbery of British diplomats and their wives when working as a cipher clerk in the claustrophobic atmosphere of the embassy in Moscow, where the social hierarchy was clearly defined.[24] Alienated, he became an easy target for Soviet intelligence. In an operation masterminded by KGB General Oleg Gribanov, who specialised in sexual honeytraps targeting Western diplomats, Vassall was photographed in 'a number of compromising positions'. He consequently handed over various secret documents over eight years as a KGB agent.[25]

Dennis Amy, the diplomat in charge of internal security at Britain's Moscow embassy, recalls that KGB tactics were 'really terrible'. Before taking up his post he had been sent on courses with both MI5 and MI6, but nothing prepared him for what he experienced in the Soviet capital. Technical surveillance was expected, and predictably he and his wife had 'eight microphones removed from our flat'. But the honeytraps were more upsetting, and no one was off-limits. The KGB 'would set up middle-aged old ladies, you know, in bed with people, take pictures of them, which was absolutely inexcusable. It blighted their lives.' They not only attacked diplomats but also distinguished visitors, and would 'go to any lengths'. A senior mathematics professor at Manchester University came out to a conference at Moscow University. 'They really gave him a hard time,' and soon after returning to Britain he killed himself. 'They would drug people,' Amy recalls, and many of his colleagues were sent home with their careers 'destroyed'. Increasingly, the British wanted to get back at the Russians for this. 'We were quite ruthless about it, because that was the game.'[26] Other prominent Britons caught by KGB sexual compromise operations during this period included the journalist Edward Crankshaw and the Conservative MP Anthony Courtney.[27]

When the Vassall case exploded in September 1962, Norman Brook broke the bad news to the prime minister.[28] Shortly afterwards, Roger Hollis apparently went to see Macmillan, triumphantly proclaiming, 'I've got this fellow, I've got him!' Macmillan sat stony-faced. The prime minister's sombre reaction puzzled Hollis, who had been expecting some much-needed praise for his beleaguered department. 'You don't seem very pleased, prime minister,' Hollis remarked disappointedly. 'No, I'm not at all pleased,' Macmillan sternly replied. 'When my gamekeeper shoots a fox, he doesn't go and hang it up outside the master of foxhounds' drawing room. He buries it out of sight.'[29]

Macmillan went on to lecture Hollis on the difficulties of dealing with spies in peacetime. 'You can't just shoot a spy as you did in the war. You have to try him … Better to discover him and then control him, but never catch him.' Like Thatcher after him, Macmillan loathed such public exhibitions involving spies and traitors. He pointed out that catching Vassall would lead to 'a great public trial', during which 'the security services will not be praised for how efficient they are but blamed for how hopeless they are', and theatrically prophesied that 'There will then be an enquiry … which will say … that no one was really to blame … There will be a row in the press, there will be a debate in the House of Commons.' He finished with a flourish: 'And the government will probably fall.' 'Why the devil,' he asked Hollis, 'did you "catch" him?' It was just as well that Hollis had decided to keep hidden from the prime minister the fact that they were hunting a second spy in the Admiralty.[30]

Humbled and downtrodden, Hollis was to be influenced by this bruising encounter – with damaging results for communication between MI5 and Number 10. In marked contrast to the Attlee period, meetings with the prime minister became less frequent. Macmillan made similar remarks to Dick White during their regular meetings, instructing the chief of MI6 to 'keep a lid on things'.[31] But he was especially antipathetic towards MI5. On one occasion he derisorily described it to Harold Wilson, Gaitskell's successor as leader of the opposition, as the 'so-called' security service. He reserved his greatest hostility for the hapless Roger Hollis, whom he criticised as being inept and insignificant.[32]

Macmillan was right about a row in the press. Although he set up an inquiry under Lord Radcliffe into the Vassall affair, this did not deflect attention.[33] Fleet Street, having discovered a public appetite for spies and scandal, published over 250 sensational articles about Vassall and the various rumours it generated. Many dwelled on his sexual orientation and were markedly homophobic. Journalists asked Downing Street why security officers had not noticed his trips to the West End dressed in women's clothes.[34] The fact that many of the stories were lurid, embellished or simply untrue alarmed the prime minister,[35] who confided to the home secretary, Henry Brooke, that he was 'surprised and indeed perturbed' about the amount of newspaper publicity. 'So far as I know,' Macmillan pondered, 'he has been in custody ever since he was first arrested. And yet newspapers are now printing what are alleged to be his memoirs.' Something did not add up, and the prime minister demanded answers.[36] Exasperated, he also asked Peter Carrington, First Lord of the Admiralty, to consider whether service attachés like Vassall actually performed any useful service at all in Moscow. Were they even worth the risk?[37]

Macmillan later sent Carrington a more comforting note, hoping that 'you are not worrying too much' about the burden of the Vassall case, 'since I share it as well'.[38] But the prime minister had no idea of the full burden that would eventually arrive on his shoulders. Vassall had been exposed by a further defector to the Americans, the KGB officer Anatoliy Golitsyn, who fled from Helsinki on 15 December 1961. Debriefed steadily and repeatedly through 1962, he claimed to know of an almost endless army of moles, spies and traitors in Whitehall and Westminster. A valued defector, he offered the first strong confirmation that Kim Philby was indeed a Soviet spy – so later that year the KGB launched a plan to assassinate Golitsyn.[39]

On Wednesday, 18 April 1962, Sir Harold Caccia, the British ambassador in Washington, flew to London to break the news about Golitsyn to Harold Macmillan at Chequers. Accompanied by Norman Brook, the cabinet secretary, his uncomfortable task was to explain 'the kind of information that is being obtained from a member of the Russian Intelligence Service who has recently defected to the Americans'. Macmillan was due to fly to Washington to meet Kennedy shortly, and they expected either JFK or his new CIA chief John McCone to raise the subject. Brook advised Macmillan to take Dick White with him on his visit to Washington. They explained that Golitsyn was only thirty-five, and that while his career had ranged over a wide field, 'nowhere has it any great depth', although Caccia noted that Golitsyn's interrogators regarded him as a 'reliable and accurate reporter'. Most of his information was 'imprecise', but, they added ominously, 'may be capable of being developed into bases for investigation'. Golitsyn had spoken of penetration of the British intelligence services, the Foreign Office and the Admiralty, and had claimed that five unnamed MPs 'accept tasks from the Russians'.[40] Like many defectors, he was determined to prolong his importance by suddenly 'remembering' new facts, and his narrative gradually became more inventive. Neither Macmillan nor Hollis yet knew just how much trouble this would cause.

In October 1962, embroiled in a series of domestic security scandals, Macmillan was unaware of a developing crisis in the Caribbean. On the evening of Sunday, 21 October, he was working quietly in the Downing Street study at around 10 p.m. when a duty clerk handed him an urgent message from President Kennedy informing him that: 'Photographic intelligence has established beyond question, in the last week, that the Soviet Union has engaged in a major build-up of medium-range missiles in Cuba. Six sites have so far been identified, and two of them may be in operational readiness. In sum, it is clear that a massive secret operation has been proceeding in spite of the repeated assurances we have received from the Soviet Union on this point.' The entire United States was now within range of a Soviet strike with only four minutes' warning. Kennedy warned Macmillan that 'This extraordinarily dangerous and aggressive Soviet step obviously creates a crisis of the most serious sort.'[41]

The next day, Macmillan saw the intelligence for himself when the American ambassador, David Bruce, and a senior CIA officer, Chester Cooper, brought him a dossier of U-2 photographs proving that the Soviets had secretly deployed a dangerous new armoury in Cuba.[42] As Macmillan examined the evidence, the handsome study fell silent except for the ticking clock and some nervous pipe-smoking. Barely audibly, Macmillan finally murmured, 'Now the Americans will realise what we here in England have lived through for the past many years.' Realising that this remark might have sounded somewhat acerbic and insensitive to his visitors, Macmillan looked up apologetically. 'I didn't mean that the way it sounded,' he said. 'I shall, of course, give President Kennedy my complete support.' The Americans were surprised that Macmillan only spent a few seconds looking at their precious intelligence. The pictures did not particularly excite the prime minister and he rapidly accepted their validity, perhaps feeling that if they convinced Kennedy then they were good enough for him.[43]

David Bruce, who had himself been head of American intelligence in London years ago, then showed Macmillan a more detailed account from Kennedy, in which the president emphasised the 'threat to the peace which imperils the security not only of this hemisphere but of the entire free world'. Interestingly, Kennedy again stressed the intelligence source, highlighting the 'incontrovertible military evidence obtained through photographic reconnaissance'. Here, intelligence played an important role in convincing leaders that the threat was real. Bruce may have been calm and detached, but he felt that the prime minister became uneasy as the meeting progressed. As soon as Bruce left, Macmillan called for the foreign secretary Alec Douglas-Home, with whom he worked particularly closely over the next few days. He later exclaimed in his diary: 'The first day of world crisis!' A period of sleepless nights had begun.[44]

The Soviets had indeed placed medium-range nuclear missiles on Cuba. The American joint chiefs of staff had advocated an immediate air strike followed by a ground invasion, but could only undertake to destroy 95 per cent of the missiles, and then only of those they had found. Imagining the Soviets launching the other 5 per cent at New York and Washington, Kennedy chose an alternative course. On 22 October he addressed the American public – and the world – about the crisis. For two weeks global security was on the brink as a naval blockade attempted to prevent the Soviets from delivering more military supplies to the island. Eventually, after fraught negotiations and a secret deal involving the removal of American missiles from Turkey, Nikita Khrushchev announced that all missile bases on Cuba would be closed.[45]

The very same day that Macmillan saw the photographic intelligence, the West lost its greatest human intelligence asset. Colonel Oleg Penkovsky, a dynamic and aggressive Soviet military intelligence officer, had been recruited by MI6 and run jointly with the CIA since April 1961.[46] Aware of both important clandestine activities and high-level gossip, Penkovsky had been passing high-grade nuclear intelligence to Whitehall and Washington. He had also devised a secret system of warning Western intelligence agencies of sudden dangerous developments by breathing down a telephone line. After a period of intensive surveillance, he was arrested on 22 October 1962 by the KGB for treason and espionage – at the very time Kennedy and Macmillan needed him most. He was executed in a Moscow prison the following year.

Penkovsky's importance during the nineteen days of the Cuban missile crisis has been much debated.[47] Macmillan certainly believed that his intelligence about the capacity of Soviet missiles, including those which had been installed on Cuba, had a stabilising effect.[48] He greatly appreciated MI6's success in recruiting and jointly running Penkovsky – in stark contrast to his perpetual disappointment with MI5's spy-catching capers. Dick White seems to have personally briefed Macmillan on Penkovsky's intelligence throughout the Russian's time as a double agent.[49] Moreover, when White had travelled to Washington with Macmillan earlier in the year, he had noticed that the prime minister was particularly impressed by the way Penkovsky's material had gradually but decisively altered Washington's attitude towards Moscow. During his election campaign, Kennedy had claimed that the Russians were ahead on missiles. Penkovsky's information proved the reverse. 'You see, Prime Minister,' White briefed Macmillan, 'the Americans accept that the Russians are going down, not up.'[50]

Photographic intelligence from U-2s alerted policymakers to the threat from Cuba. But human intelligence, through Penkovsky, provided the vital context, assuring the West that it had the strategic advantage, and did not need to panic. The extent to which intelligence guided Macmillan through the crisis, however, remains unclear. Despite seeming to accept the CIA's photographs during his meeting with Bruce and Cooper, he did ask the RAF to double-check them. He drew on his own intelligence services too, especially sigint from GCHQ collection stations on Cyprus.[51] Having done so, he was in 'no doubt as to the facts'.[52]

The prime minister spoke regularly with the president in a number of late-night telephone calls at the height of the crisis. On 24 October, Kennedy asked his older counterpart 'the $64,000 question': should the US 'take out' Cuba, or 'hold off and use Cuba as sort of hostage in the matter of Berlin?' Cautiously, Macmillan avoided answering directly, instead buying himself time to think things over. He did, though, inform Kennedy that British intelligence had revealed that 'Russian ships, not so far on in the queue, are returning via Baltic or Russian ports.' After further reflection, he counselled against military action.[53]

Kennedy implemented the blockade of Cuba on 24 October. At the same time, he asked Macmillan about releasing the intelligence reconnaissance photographs to the world's press. This was the first time that a prime minister had debated the public use of intelligence to support a policy designed to address a threat from weapons of mass destruction. As Tony

Blair and David Cameron would later find out, it is not an easy decision. Despite his distaste for press coverage of secret matters, Macmillan urged Kennedy to release the intelligence. Macmillan's private secretary, Philip de Zulueta, had been worried about 'the reception any strong Government statement would have in the absence of incontrovertible proof of the missile build-up', and argued that the White House should release the photographs. Macmillan agreed, feeling that the material 'disclosed that the work was continuing' and that 'this accumulation of proof was of vital importance'. The British ambassador in Washington, David Ormsby-Gore, also agreed, and suggested that the photographs be published with clear explanatory notes to allow the uninitiated to interpret the missiles as offensive, and this was how they eventually appeared. Not everyone was convinced. Senior opposition figures such as Denis Healey, already outraged by the Bay of Pigs fiasco, angrily denounced the intelligence as faked, and attacked US actions in Cuba.[54]

Aerial reconnaissance not only drove the whole crisis, it also rehabilitated the CIA on both sides of the Atlantic. Ormsby-Gore observed that the 'excellence of the photographs', the 'precision of the information obtained' from their examination, and the efficacy of the Western intelligence organisations in dealing with the crisis had done much to restore the reputations of the intelligence community. The CIA had 'now recovered from last year's disaster at the Bay of Pigs and from the U-2 incident of May 1960'. Moreover, the CIA's new director, John McCone, had enhanced his own status because he had voiced his suspicion that the Soviets intended to introduce offensive missiles at a time when the Office of National Estimates, Washington's equivalent of the JIC, considered this 'improbable'.[55]

Not knowing if the blockade would work, Macmillan heightened British readiness for war, placing the new British V-Bombers on alert and beginning preparations for evacuating key government officials to a secret bunker outside Bath, codenamed 'Turnstile'. One bomber pilot recalls being on constant alert and sleeping on a camp bed in flying kit at his war dispersal point, RAF Waddington: 'My Vulcan was parked about 20 yards away, fully fuelled, and loaded with nuclear weapons ... and I carried the key to the door on a string around my neck.' He thought he could be airborne in about seven minutes. Macmillan was not told how far discreet plans for rapid retaliation had progressed.[56] Just as a gloomy British cabinet had lunch prior to discussing evacuation plans, news came through that the crisis had ended. Khrushchev had agreed to dismantle the Cuban bases. Macmillan was exhausted, but delighted.[57]

With typical understatement, the prime minister reflected upon 'a fascinating week'.[58] Penkovsky's intelligence had been important, but above all Kennedy had valued Macmillan's avuncular advice as a man who had been through war, having been wounded in the First World War and been part of government during the Second. He remembered Munich, Dunkirk and most recently Suez. Kennedy frequently ended their conversations by saying, 'Right, Prime Minister, and I'll give you another telephone call tomorrow night and we'll discuss the situation again then.'[59] The crux of Macmillan's advice lay in psychological suggestions, rather than political or military details. He emphasised to Kennedy the importance of allowing Khrushchev to back down without damaging his reputation. Kennedy needed to create an 'exit strategy'.[60]

All these sensitive late-night phone calls between Macmillan and Kennedy were delivered by Britain's least-known secret service. This was the London Communications Security Agency, which worked closely with GCHQ to defend British communications against foreign eavesdropping. Since the late 1950s, it had been working on a new secure telephone link between Downing Street and the White House called 'Project Twilight'. This had been installed by May 1960 with the help of the NSA, which had overcome the obstinacy of American telephone companies and White House engineers. The resulting ostentatious red phone was available at Downing Street, Chequers, and also Birch Grove, Macmillan's private residence in West Sussex. However, Philip de Zulueta was forced to move Downing Street's shiny new red phone from the prime minister's desk to a more discreet location after visitors asked too many questions. It was becoming an 'unwelcome conversation piece'.[61]

The Cuban missile crisis focused minds on the problem of secure transatlantic telephone conversations. The newly installed 'Twilight' system performed well, but took more than two hours to set up, making it 'virtually useless' in a sudden crisis. If time was short, Downing Street had to use an older American system that only took half an hour to establish a secure connection. But its sound quality was so poor that officials referred to it as the 'Donald Duck' system, and Kennedy had refused to use it when a 'Twilight' call to Macmillan broke down.[62] Secure phones were essential because of KGB electronic eavesdropping in London. The Cuban crisis revealed Downing Street's infrastructure as antiquated, and improvements were now accelerated. All the communications equipment was inspected, new low-power teleprinters were installed, and a team of secret listeners carried out 'radiation test measurements' around the Cabinet Office using eavesdropping equipment in a dedicated monitoring vehicle.[63]

Oddly, while Macmillan loathed domestic security issues and the inevitable publicity that failures created, he liked covert operations. This long-held enthusiasm even threatened to strain his otherwise excellent relationship with Dick White. In opposition, Macmillan had favoured covertly supporting Eastern European émigrés. As minister for defence he had advocated fighting the Soviets with 'our brains', suggesting a Cold War minister to inject some drive into proceedings, and advocating MI6 'tricks' during the uprising in Cyprus.[64] As foreign secretary he lobbied strongly in favour of 'covert means' and 'indirect methods' to counter 'enemies of the Queen'. If Macmillan and Eden shared a Churchillian streak, it was an instinctive desire to protect the remnants of empire, especially in the Middle East and South-East Asia, at 'almost any cost'.[65]

Macmillan's passion for covert operations continued as prime minister. He was unafraid to launch daring special operations – often in conjunction with the US – and was keen to harness American secret power in order to uphold British influence on the global scene.[66] He considered Allen Dulles, director of the CIA, 'a very good friend', and noted that he 'gives us a very good position in the intelligence field'.[67] When Dulles left the CIA in November 1961, he visited London to say goodbye. Macmillan personally insisted on getting him a present. 'A signed photograph, or … a book?' de Zulueta asked. The prime minister chose the former, adding, 'You must put it in a frame of some kind.' Saying goodbye, Macmillan told Dulles, 'Your work has been of great and, I believe, lasting value and we are very grateful.'[68]

Macmillan endorsed covert actions across the world, from the Middle East to South-East Asia, Latin America to Africa. He authorised MI6 to work with the CIA to overthrow Patrice Lumumba in Congo, and after enjoying making Washington squirm for a while, finally allowed the CIA to run covert operations against Cheddi Jagan in British Guiana.[69] Remembering the trouble Eisenhower had given Britain over Suez, he took great delight in making the Americans 'repeat over and over again their passionate plea to us to stick to "Colonialism" and "imperialism" at any cost'.[70]

This was underlined by the changed American attitude to the liquidation of Nasser. Cairo was ever closer to Moscow, and was enjoying sweeping success across the Middle East. In 1958, a pro-Nasser coup in Iraq resulted in the murder of King Feisal and his prime minister. A bullet fired at three paces missed Sir Michael Wright, the British ambassador in Baghdad. Geoffrey McDermott, adviser to Dick White, recalls that MI6 had 'plenty of intelligence' pointing towards the impending assassination of King Hussein of Jordan, Britain's most staunch regional ally.[71] Unsurprisingly, then, Macmillan still sought the assassination of Nasser, and this idea was now received more warmly in Washington. Meanwhile, he established a secret US–UK Working Group to examine the covert overthrow of the communist-aligned government in Damascus – its plans included the assassination of several key Syrian figures.[72] British and American leaders communicated in coded language about such options, but they understood each other. Dulles told Macmillan that in Syria 'nothing looks particularly attractive', and the choices 'will be hard'. He added that 'Action, once begun, must, at even greater risk, be pushed through to success.'[73]

Covert action against Indonesia spanned the bulk of Macmillan's eventful premiership. Driven by a Cold War mind-set and fearing that Sukarno, the president of Indonesia, was moving irreversibly towards communism, Britain and America sought regime change. To achieve this MI6, working alongside the CIA, supported a rebellion against Sukarno's government in 1957 and 1958. Macmillan was initially sceptical, but Robert Scott, Britain's Commissioner-General for South-East Asia, directly lobbied him to covertly offer the rebels 'support from outside', arguing that 'The time has come to plan secretly with the Australians and the Americans how best to give these elements the aid they need.' Although acknowledging that it was a 'bold policy, carrying considerable risks', Scott believed it was justified, given that Sukarno had 'irredeemably identified' himself with the communists.[74]

Macmillan backed Scott against more cautious voices in the Foreign Office. The prime minister recognised that overt intervention would open Britain to accusations of aggression, while others advised that it risked escalating into a protracted war which might open the way to Soviet intervention.[75] Covert action offered a discreet solution. Aided by British officials in Washington, Macmillan established a further secret Anglo–American Working Group, this time focused on Indonesia. Wasting little time, the CIA–MI6 group met five times during January 1958 alone,[76] and officials spent the best part of the next four months devising plots to cause trouble. One idea involved acquiring, or creating, compromising photos of Sukarno with underage girls.[77] In the end, Macmillan went for a paramilitary option, discreetly supporting the rebels so long as the origins of that support remained concealed. He also agreed to respond 'where practicable to requests for help from the dissident provincial administrations', although he stopped short of activity 'to further the break-up of Indonesia',[78] emphasising that British involvement in the Anglo–American plan must remain 'disavowable'. Typically this involved refuelling undercover CIA planes engaged in the bombing, and using Singapore as a staging post for supplies sent to the rebels.[79] However, by March 1958 a rather glum Macmillan noted: 'The "rebels" are losing out in Indonesia, in spite of as much "covert" help as we and the US can give them quietly.'[80] Later that year, he was advised that the rebellion had 'failed militarily', so both the CIA and MI6 decided to stop helping the dissidents and to try instead to work through sympathetic elements in the Indonesian army.[81]

Macmillan and his officials actually tried to help American covert action function better. By the late 1950s, the Americans were pouring vast resources into silent warfare, but many different agencies wanted a piece of the action, and the result was confusion. Relations were especially bad between the State Department and the CIA, and Macmillan was told frankly that: 'Neither side trusts the other.' The head of propaganda at the CIA was so preoccupied with 'personal work for Mr Dulles' that he would not see other American agencies or the British, so 'black operations are in practice conducted independently'. This had led to a failure to mount effective joint operations during the recent Lebanon crisis. Macmillan urged Eisenhower to expand the working group principle that got everyone at the operational level – including the rival American agencies – around the table at 'frequent intervals'.[82]

Until 1960, Macmillan was encouraged in his covert escapades by the fact that he was working with Eisenhower, a wartime associate whose judgement he trusted. Kennedy was a new proposition. David Ormsby-Gore, the British ambassador in Washington, recalls that Macmillan was 'rather jarred' by the CIA's Bay of Pigs fiasco in April 1961, and it took him 'a longish time' to get over what he considered 'a gross error of judgement' by the new president.[83] British officials also warned that American covert action was not very covert. A motorist driving into Washington from the south, they observed, passed a large road sign that said 'Keep Right for the C.I.A.' They found this incredible, and felt that it underlined the fact that everything in America became public sooner or later – 'usually sooner': preparations for the Bay of Pigs operation had actually been widely reported in the American press beforehand. Kennedy, they noted, had tried to address the problem of American 'unsecrecy', but the press had responded with 'active hostility'.[84]

Nevertheless, within a year, Macmillan was working with the new White House on covert action. As the Indonesian problem intensified, he met Kennedy and urged that they should work together to 'liquidate' Sukarno.[85] In 1963, vigorously opposing Britain's creation of Malaysia from a range of neighbouring territories, Sukarno launched a policy of 'Confrontation', using political propaganda and minor military pressure. Couching their responses as defensive counter-attacks, British officials turned to covert measures to oppose Indonesian raids along the border with Borneo. Philip de Zulueta, Macmillan's private secretary, thought MI6 should be used to 'encourage a subversive movement inside Indonesia-Borneo'. This particular covert war would fall to Macmillan's successor Alec Douglas-Home, who had also been lobbying Macmillan to intensify British subversion.[86]

Successive Conservative governments had been engaging in special operations against Yemen throughout the 1950s. Harold Macmillan's was no exception, and activity expanded to include covertly sponsoring raids into the imamate by friendly tribes based across the border in South Arabia. Going further than either Churchill or Eden, Macmillan's government debated arming tribes inside Yemen, as opposed to merely in South Arabian territory. At one point, it even discussed instigating a coup.[87] As ever, covert action appealed owing to the constraints of world opinion. Military activity would have been seen as aggressive and colonialist, undoubtedly drawing international condemnation and recriminations in the United Nations.

In September 1962 a group of revolutionary officers from the Yemeni army overthrew the imam. Backed by Nasser's Egypt, they declared a Yemen Arab republic, plunging the country into a long and bitter civil war, which threatened the stability of the British position in neighbouring Aden. After the coup, Macmillan found himself caught between two Whitehall factions. On the one hand, the Joint Intelligence Committee doubted the royalist opposition's ability to win, and advised against covert action to aid it. Citing signals intelligence from GCHQ, they said that Egyptian morale was high. Similarly, Dick White said that MI6 was unconvinced about the ability of the royalists and disinclined to support aggressive operations against the Egyptians.[88] On the other hand, Julian Amery, Macmillan's son-in-law and an informal minister for Yemen, wanted action, and showed Macmillan a range of Saudi intelligence reports which romanticised royalist resistance. Amery recruited a number of piratical friends and colleagues, including Billy McLean, a veteran of the MI6 operation in Albania. Bypassing the JIC system, Amery and McLean directly lobbied the prime minister to engage in covert action, arguing that the JIC had underestimated the strength of the royalists and asking him to listen to Britain's fiercely anti-Nasser officials on the ground in Aden.[89]

A latterday Lawrence of Arabia, McLean toured the region during March 1963. He first visited King Hussein of Jordan, noting, 'I found an uneasy atmosphere of intrigue and plots at the Court of Amman.' Hussein had been backing the royalist resistance against Nasser's troops, but was losing heart because of American opposition, and was desperate for the British to show some leadership. In Riyadh, McLean reported, Prince Feisal was equally disappointed in London, and had also been under the 'strongest American pressure' to discontinue his efforts to help the royalists. McLean insisted that the successes of the opposition had been under-reported. Amery was the conduit through which this was conveyed to Macmillan.[90]

Macmillan embraced Amery and rejected Dick White. Unlike Amery, MI6 could not provide any eyewitness intelligence regarding developments in the region. Increasingly frustrated, the prime minister even resorted to press reports, lamenting that one particular newspaper article was 'better than anything we have got out of our people so far because it is a coherent account by someone who has obviously been there which we never get'.[91] He persuaded White to assist Amery in launching covert action in Yemen,[92] although he did heed the JIC's caution. Falling well short of the demands made by the likes of Amery, he offered only 'cautious support' for the royalists. This support was predominantly channelled indirectly through the British-protected tribes on the frontier.[93] Although Macmillan insisted to the Americans that his government was offering no assistance to the royalists, he had at the very least 'authorised minelaying in Republican areas along the frontier', and probably tit-for-tat tribal raids.[94] Like Churchill, Macmillan enjoyed a little imperial fantasy, and long after he retired he wrote to Billy McLean, praising him as 'one of those people whose services to our dear country are known only to a few'.[95]

The Profumo affair was the spy scandal of the decade. Yet despite the public sensation, it was actually less important from the point of view of intelligence or security than many others. MI5 later conceded that it must have been obvious to Russian intelligence that the 'attractive', but 'vacuous and untruthful' Christine Keeler had 'no information of significant value'.[96] Nonetheless, the affair summoned up Macmillan's worst fears, for it tapped into a growing public appetite for stories of security scandals and sexual deviance within the establishment. Orgies involving eight High Court judges – 'Seems a bit much', observed Macmillan – men in masks, explicit Polaroids showing a duchess fellating an unknown man, allegedly an MP, together with sex parties involving presidents and members of the Royal Family, all became part of an unfolding scandal.[97] The Profumo affair did Macmillan a great deal of damage, not least because he visibly mishandled it, although it did not topple his government. Perhaps the greatest damage was to the prime minister's state of mind. Privately aware that there were much greater spy scandals waiting to explode, an exhausted and bewildered Macmillan took extraordinary security precautions, and then hurriedly departed from office.

In 1961, John Profumo, secretary of state for war, had a brief affair with Christine Keeler, a model and call girl. He had been introduced to the semi-naked Keeler frolicking at a pool party hosted by Stephen Ward, a society osteopath with unrivalled London contacts. Ward, according to the subsequent government inquiry, was 'utterly immoral' and specialised in picking up sixteen- and seventeen-year-old girls for his influential friends. He also catered for those with 'perverted tastes', arranging whipping parties and 'sexual orgies of a revolting nature'. The security problem arose from Ward's friendship with Captain Eugene Ivanov. Operating under the cover of his position as assistant naval attaché at the Russian embassy in London, Ivanov was in fact a GRU intelligence officer. To make matters worse, he was 'something of a ladies' man', and also enjoyed relations with Keeler. The improbable foursome of Profumo, Ward, Keeler and Ivanov remained under the radar until March 1963, when Keeler sold her story to the press after another former lover, a drug dealer, shot at her with a pistol.[98]

At first, Macmillan did not take the Profumo affair seriously.[99] Preoccupied with French president Charles de Gaulle's veto of Britain's EEC membership bid, he dismissed it as merely 'a silly scrape'. Contrasting it with the Vassall case, he added, 'Women this time, thank God, not boys', and dismissed the rumours as 'gossip, grossly exaggerated no doubt if not altogether untrue'. Initially at least, he seems to have found the business rather funny, noting that 'What adds a certain spice of humour to this degrading story' was that MI5 'were hoping to use the lady to get intelligence out of the Russian', suggesting a honeytrap that had gone wrong.[100] But the wry smile soon melted from beneath Macmillan's moustache as the scandal heated up.

MI5 did have an interest in both Stephen Ward and the Russian intelligence officer, Ivanov. Back in August 1961, their intelligence revealed that a man named Ward was trying to strengthen his acquaintance with Ivanov by boasting of his society connections. Having placed him under surveillance and noted that the secretary of state for war was in his circle, MI5 worried that Profumo was straying dangerously into a murky world. Roger Hollis swiftly alerted Norman Brook who, without telling Macmillan, had a quiet word with Profumo warning him not to associate with Ward. Although MI5 did not in fact know of Profumo's affair with Keeler until January 1963, the minister misinterpreted Brook's warning as a covert indication that MI5 knew of the matter – and perhaps even condoned it.[101]

MI5's interest in Ward and Ivanov intensified. As a result of his society connections, Ward had been used by Ivanov as a backdoor intermediary with the Soviets during the Cuban missile crisis in 1962. The Foreign Office also saw him as a potentially useful intermediary with the Soviet embassy, due to his friendship with Ivanov. Indeed, there have been strong suggestions that MI5 employed Ward to try to discover more about Ivanov's military intelligence duties. It is clear that at some point MI5 considered using Keeler as a honeytrap to lure Ivanov into defection, in part as payback for the numerous honeytraps set by the KGB for British personnel in Moscow. Macmillan later noted that one of the most sensitive parts of the case was MI5's attempts at the 'winning over of Captain Ivanov … to be a defector' and the 'possible use of Mr Profumo for this purpose'. References to this were withheld from the subsequent public inquiry.[102] MI5 later disowned Ward when Macmillan became concerned that he might name ministers once he was charged with living off immoral earnings. Amid rumours that he was going to be assassinated at the hands of MI5, Ward committed suicide, and never heard the guilty verdict delivered at his court hearing.[103]

Rumours about Profumo had been circulating since the autumn of 1962, but the affair burst into the public consciousness on 22 March 1963. George Wigg, one of Harold Wilson's senior associates, chose to drop the bombshell during a parliamentary debate on press coverage of the Vassall case. Profumo's wife Valerie returned from the theatre to find her house surrounded by reporters shouting shocking questions. Profumo was not in the Commons, and long after midnight, as the debate drew to a close, he was summoned by Iain Macleod, the leader of the House of Commons and chairman of the Conservative Party. Together with the whips and several ministers, he proceeded to subject Profumo to a security-style interview. At three in the morning, flanked by his solicitor, Profumo was told that his choices were to deny everything or else to resign immediately. Macleod later told a journalistic friend on the *Spectator* that he had put the matter very directly: 'Look Jack, the basic question is: did you fuck her?' Profumo insisted that he had not – and followed up his denial with libel suits against *Paris Match* and several other magazines.[104]

The following day he made a personal statement to this effect in the House of Commons. Macmillan sat beside his beleaguered minister, and visibly offered his support by patting the defiant Profumo on the shoulder as he returned to his seat.[105] A few days later, Macmillan met Roger Hollis to discuss the security implications. Hollis told the anxious prime minister that according to Keeler, Ward had asked her to discover from Profumo the date on which certain atomic secrets were to be handed to West Germany by the Americans. He reassured Macmillan that Keeler denied doing so, and dismissed Harold Wilson's claim that Ward was a Russian agent. 'The security people', Hollis comforted Macmillan, believed that 'he was a pimp, not a spy'.[106]

In fact, Profumo's pillow talk may well have involved more than matters of the heart. Some years later the investigative journalist Chapman Pincher asked Keeler if she had indeed been told any real government secrets. She recounted that there had been one: in bed one night, Profumo had told her that on that very day 'there had almost been an explosion of a nuclear weapon because a rat had gnawed through some cable, exposing a wire or something'. Pincher rightly surmised that this was an improbable thing for Keeler to have invented out of thin air.[107] Historians have since discovered that the RAF's early hydrogen bombs were at the outer envelope of available British technology, and were indeed precarious items. The first production model, codenamed 'Yellow Sun', had a weak safety mechanism, and its primitive inner workings were alarmingly vulnerable to corrosion. It proved so unstable that within a few years it had to be taken out of service.[108] Keeler's story was not entirely unlikely, but was it true? Although Pincher wrote to the key defence figures of the time asking for confirmation, they maintained a wall of silence on the potentially embarrassing issue of rodents running amuck within Britain's nuclear arsenal.[109]

Once Keeler sold her story, mayhem erupted. John F. Kennedy took an increasing interest, and despatched his aide Arthur Schlesinger to investigate what effect the scandal was having on Macmillan's government. 'They are in very bad shape,' he told the president, 'and the whole party is falling apart.'[110] The journalist Ben Bradlee, who knew Kennedy well, noted his 'obsession' with reports of the case and how he 'devoured every word' – it combined so many things that fascinated him: sex, spying and British society. David Bruce at the US embassy was ordered to report on the case every twenty-four hours.[111] In early March, the Labour leader Harold Wilson visited Washington, and was booked in to see Kennedy for thirty minutes – but the president kept him for two hours. When Wilson finally came out he said, 'I couldn't believe it. The man just talked and talked about the Profumo business. He really grilled me on what I knew ...'[112]

Wilson was not told the underlying reason for Kennedy's interest. Behind the scenes, FBI men arrived in London to probe whether there had been any contact between the president and Ward's circle of women during any of his trips to London.[113] It is likely that Kennedy enjoyed a liaison with one of Ward's associates, Suzy Chang.[114] Macmillan had long been aware of Kennedy's colourful private life, noting that he was a 'strange character' and 'highly sexed'.[115] In fact, everyone seemed to know Ward – even Harold Wilson had privately brought additional information on him from Labour circles and handed it to Downing Street. Wilson believed that MI5 had subsequently leaked the material to the press.[116]

Macmillan now asked Lord Dilhorne, the lord chancellor, to quietly conduct an investigation. Despite Hollis's reassurances, the prime minister was growing increasingly concerned, to the extent that, according to one historian, 'he came close to interfering with the course of justice'.[117] Macmillan had hoped to postpone the arrest of Ward until after he had received Dilhorne's report and taken protective action against the tide of publicity about Profumo that would have been unleashed by Ward's incarceration.[118] Why had it taken so long for MI5 to brief the prime minister about the security implications? Macmillan's relations with Hollis were poor, moreover his 'shooting a fox' remark about the Vassall case had deterred MI5 from bringing its business anywhere near Number 10 – Hollis was 'not over eager to stick his neck out yet again'.[119] In any case, as MI5 thought Profumo posed no security threat, it was under no obligation to tell the prime minister about what basically amounted to the sexual conduct of one of his ministers. But in the days of Attlee and Sillitoe, the close and confident relations between Number 10 and MI5 would have led to an informal 'off the record' type warning, and the problem would probably have been averted.

Instead, Macmillan now had to face a fiery Labour Party in the House of Commons, and privately noted that Harold Wilson was clearly not going to leave the Profumo affair alone. 'He hopes,' Macmillan lamented, 'under the pretence of security, to rake up a "sex" scandal.' Distinctly unimpressed by the leader of the opposition's conduct, the prime minister bitterly added that 'Wilson, himself a blackmailing type, is <u>absolutely</u> untrustworthy.'[120] The showdown came in June 1963, when the House of Commons debated Profumo's eventual resignation. Macmillan later confessed that he had never been under such personal strain. Hundreds had queued overnight in the hope of seats in the public gallery, leaving Parliament Square gridlocked.[121] Wilson scented blood, and accused the prime minister of gambling with national security for political reasons. Dwelling on the way that a 'sordid underworld network' had 'shocked the moral conscience of the nation', he nevertheless focused mostly on security. His determined narrative was about a security threat negligently ignored by the prime minister.[122]

It was not the first time a prime minister had had to defend a spy scandal from the despatch box. Nor would it be the last. Macmillan's appearance was much more impressive than Eden's bungled performance in the aftermath of the Buster Crabb affair. Like Eden, Macmillan began with an emotional introduction which lamented the 'deep, bitter and lasting wound' created by the scandal. He then explicitly criticised Profumo for deliberately lying to the House, and offered a detailed account of Profumo's acquaintance with Ward, and Ward's relations with Ivanov. Unlike Eden's attempts at evasion, Macmillan's strategy was to offer a full and sympathetic account, posing as the loyal friend betrayed. He used this to explain why he had not tackled Profumo personally. An impressive debater, he stood his ground well, to cheers from the Tory benches.[123]

As with the Vassall case, Macmillan ordered an inquiry. Iain Macleod, the party chairman, was dead against this, arguing that 'we ought not to give an inch', but Macmillan 'was in a terrible state' and would not listen.[124] Such official proceedings are usually conducted by judges, and rarely make exciting reading. But Lord Denning, who headed the inquiry, interpreted his remit widely, understanding perhaps that this affair was more about sexual mores and social class than security. With salacious subheadings such as 'The Man in the Mask', the report swiftly became a best-seller. People queued for hours to obtain a copy, and the presses of Her Majesty's Stationery Office ran day and night. Some of Denning's papers remained classified for fifty years, since they documented the sexual peccadilloes of the establishment in considerable detail. Even Hollis was not allowed access to them.[125] Downing Street worried about what to do with the raw material that Denning had gathered. Under the legal provisions of the Public Record Office Act, it had to be preserved and eventually released to the public. 'Prime Minister,' exclaimed one horrified official, 'I hope they burn most of the Denning evidence. It contains some filth beyond imagination.'[126]

Denning did, however, exonerate Macmillan and MI5. He found that the prime minister genuinely believed Profumo's lie to the House of Commons: he and his advisers 'could not conceive that any of their colleagues would have the effrontery to make a false statement to the House'.[127] Denning also found that MI5 had confined itself to the defence of the realm: 'Once they came to the conclusion that there was no security interest in the matter, but only moral misbehaviour in a minister, they were under no duty to report it to anyone.'[128] Denning's lugubrious best-seller may have made money for the Stationery Office, but it also reaf-firmed Macmillan's conviction that a permanent commission of three judges should be created to investigate security breaches, an idea he had tried to press on Eden in 1955, but which had been rejected.[129] Harold Wilson was in agreement, and this was implemented shortly after Macmillan left office.[130]

Ironically, perhaps the largest security lapse coming from the scandal involved neither Keeler nor Ward. It appears that Ivanov did not necessarily need to rely on pillow talk with Keeler, nor on trying to recruit Ward as an agent or go-between. The Russian had actually managed to befriend Profumo directly. On one occasion he allegedly visited Profumo's home, was let in by his wife, and waited for the minister in his study. There, on the desk, lay secret files relating to American aeroplane technology, and perhaps even to tactical nuclear weapons. Ivanov apparently took plenty of photographs. It was as easy as that. With the authorities focusing on Keeler, Ward and sex, the real security risk seems to have slipped under the radar.[131]

Remarkably, the Profumo affair was actually the least of Macmillan's espionage worries. In July 1963, as the public eagerly followed the sexual antics of the secretary of state for war, the prime minister noted cryptically that 'Other "security" enquiries are proceeding.' In the greatest secrecy, Anatoliy Golitsyn, the CIA's star Soviet defector, had been invited to visit Britain to discuss possible moles. Macmillan was horrified when the story leaked and was published in the *Telegraph*, despite fervent protests by MI5. Golitsyn fled back to America convinced that KGB hit squads were scouring London for him. Kennedy was 'entirely relaxed' about the matter, but was more vexed about press stories that the British and American secret services were at loggerheads over the moles issue, and dismissed all this as 'foolish back-biting'.[132]

Macmillan was far from relaxed. He had only been told the truth about Kim Philby and Anthony Blunt in the past few months, and now the security agencies were in full pursuit of an endless trail of 'Fifth Men' and their accomplices. Blunt had been covered up, but Macmillan expected the news about Philby to come out, whereupon there would be 'a new row'. Remarkably, it was only now that Macmillan understood that Burgess and Maclean had not been mere defectors when they fled to Russia in 1951: 'they were spies, paid by the Russians, over quite a number of years'. Unsurprisingly, a weary Macmillan now mused, 'I am beginning to wonder whether all this game of espionage and counter-espionage is worth the candle.'[133] With increasingly frayed nerves, he began to fall prey to conspiracy theories, fearing that a red web had spread through Whitehall. Twelve days after Profumo's resignation he called for Dick White, and asked the chief of MI6 whether he himself was being set up by Soviet intelligence. Although White did not believe this was the case, he reassured the prime minister by establishing a joint MI5–MI6 working party to 'look into the possibility that the Russian Intelligence Service had a hand in staging the Profumo affair in order to discredit Her Majesty's Government'.[134]

Nothing could have prepared the prime minister for what came next. On 21 September 1963, less than a month before his resignation on grounds of serious ill-health, he received notice from the CIA of yet more information from Golitsyn. Macmillan recorded that the Russian had 'produced a story, supported by a good deal of evidence over the last 10 years, which he had given to the American authorities. It is that Harold Wilson has been, from 1951 for a number of years, working for the USSR and in effect, an agent!' The director of the CIA, John McCone, had asked Macmillan for his 'assessment' of the matter. 'I don't suppose, in all the history of this country – at least in modern history – a P.M. has had such an extraordinary question asked by an ally.' Macmillan's first thought was to 'just reply that it was absurd'. But reflecting on it through a long afternoon, he eventually felt 'we must <u>do</u> something about it', and so set in train consultations with White and Hollis, as well as the foreign and home secretaries – 'It's an odd world!' Ultimately, Hollis told McCone that the allegations were false.[135]

Before he left office, Macmillan played one last card. Downing Street was being modernised and refurbished: this offered an opportunity.[136] In the wake of the Profumo scandal, Philby, Blunt and now the suspicions about Wilson, the prime minister electronically bugged the Cabinet Room, its waiting room and his private study at Number 10. Although these bugs were temporarily removed when Macmillan left office, his successor Alec Douglas-Home reinstalled them following concerns about Soviet spies at the heart of government, indeed inside Downing Street itself. The highly secretive surveillance system then continued until 1977, when James Callaghan had it dismantled. It thus remained in place during the tenure of no fewer than five prime ministers, although it is unclear whether Harold Wilson and Edward Heath were ever aware of its presence.[137]

Harold Macmillan found spy scandals hard to handle. They not only threatened to end his government, they also promoted doubts about his ability to lead. John Biffen recalls that Profumo was the 'most memorable' event of his thirty-six years in the House of Commons. Conservative back-benchers had closed ranks in public, but at a private meeting of the 1922 Committee Macmillan was told firmly that it had been 'a culpable cock-up'. Suddenly, his Edwardian diffidence seemed out of place, and the party visibly yearned for a younger leader.[138] In late 1963, Macmillan wrote to the Queen to apologise for the 'injury' he had caused to the fabric of government as the result of what he thought was his mishandling of the Profumo affair. 'I had of course no idea,' he explained, 'of the strange underworld in which other people, alas, beside Mr Profumo have allowed themselves to become entrapped.' This was perhaps a discreet allusion to Anthony Blunt, Surveyor of the Queen's Pictures, about whom Macmillan had only been briefed by 'C' on 21 July 1963 – a further lurking security scandal which he thought might well have a 'shattering' effect and end his government prematurely.[139]

Why did Macmillan take the extraordinary step of bugging Downing Street? An Edwardian to the core, he found these covert matters subversive in a profound sense that encapsulated wider notions of social order as well as national security. In his letter to the Queen, he wondered aloud about the possibility of plots to destroy the 'establishment'. His own final response, worked into the very wiring of Downing Street itself, formed a fitting prelude to a period of institutional paranoia that persisted until the end of the Cold War. Over the next few years, more and more people who had become trapped in Macmillan's 'strange underworld' would be exposed, to the deep discomfort of his Downing Street successors.

10

Alec Douglas-Home
(1963–1964)

It is very easy to cross the line between a
free society and a police state.
ALEC DOUGLAS-HOME[1]

Harold Macmillan, bewildered by events and in failing health, resigned in October 1963. In doing so, he left his successor a legacy of messy intelligence issues to address. This unenviable task fell to Sir Alec Douglas-Home – one of the most decent and honourable prime ministers ever to set foot through the famous black door. Born to a wealthy landed Scottish family, Douglas-Home was the fourteenth Earl of Home, but set aside his peerage to serve in the Commons. A patrician figure, he had been popular at Eton and at Christ Church College, Oxford, where he completed a rather leisurely third-class honours degree in modern history in 1925. His main achievement was as a cricketer, playing for Middlesex and the MCC. If Macmillan had been somewhat Edwardian in his outlook, Douglas-Home seemed positively Victorian – Harold Wilson, leader of the opposition, dismissed the new premier as an 'elegant anachronism'.[2] Yet, once in office, he went about his business with a quiet competence, and was rarely ruffled by events. In power for only 363 days, Douglas-Home was one of Britain's most effective premiers, although today he is a largely forgotten figure.[3]

Secret service is the least-known aspect of his overlooked premiership. Yet, Douglas-Home believed passionately in intelligence, telling a NATO conference: 'When we policy-makers fail, as we so often do, it is generally because we have not got enough intelligence or because we have made the wrong use of what we possess.'[4] He was well-equipped to oversee secret service, having been a junior minister at the Foreign Office in the last months of the wartime government, and so perhaps qualifies as the last of Winston Churchill's wartime trainees. He had served as Commonwealth secretary and then foreign secretary under Macmillan, working closely with his deputy, Edward Heath. He was respected for his vast knowledge of world affairs, and later returned to the Foreign Office in the Heath government of 1970. In that role he went on to lead the expulsion of ninety Soviet intelligence officers from London, known as 'Operation Foot', advising the prime minister that 'a stand had to be taken on the scale of Russian spying in Britain'.[5]

Douglas-Home's brief tenure in Downing Street was remarkably action-packed. Scarcely a month after taking office, he was confronted by the Kennedy assassination, which had a considerable intelligence dimension and which some connected to a growing tide of covert action across the globe, eagerly pursued by both the CIA and the KGB. His overseas in-tray also included the waging of two of Britain's own secret wars. Domestically, he had to deal with the fallout from the Profumo affair and rising paranoia about Soviet subversion at home. The key question then is not whether Douglas-Home had much involvement with Britain's intelligence services: he had little choice. More interesting is the nature of the relationship, and whether a laid-back aristocrat could rise to the challenge of overseeing Britain's intelligence services in the turbulent 1960s.

Douglas-Home had scant experience of internal security upon becoming prime minister, and there is little record of his relationship with Roger Hollis, the director-general of MI5, once he was in office. He seems instead to have preferred unofficial consultations with John Cecil Masterman, a veteran of MI5's wartime deception operation and his former history tutor at Oxford, about security matters.[6] Circumstances forced him to turn swiftly to the defence of the realm. In doing so, he had to face the same dilemmas that confronted his predecessors in seeking to balance security, liberty and openness. Whilst acknowledging that, given the nature of cooperation between MI5 and the police, the security service should remain responsible to the home secretary, Douglas-Home knew that in effect the prime minister held overall control. Speaking in Parliament on the matter of MI5, he announced that 'The Prime Minister must be ready to answer questions if he himself judges that they involve the security of the state. No Prime Minister will ever shirk that duty, of that I am quite sure.'[7] The tumultuous events of the past few months had underlined the fact that the security buck stopped at Number 10.

Douglas-Home had dodged the unravelling Profumo affair in the summer of 1963. Travelling widely, he was busy negotiating a nuclear test ban treaty with the Americans and the Soviets. The new prime minister had, however, witnessed the damage the scandal had done to Macmillan's moribund premiership. Both he and his predecessor were painfully aware that ministers with security clearances did not go through the positive vetting process, and so did not always measure up to the highest standards of propriety; further embarrassing episodes were only a matter of time. Consequently, Douglas-Home was keen to avoid any media frenzies over security during his time in office which could cast a shadow over the Conservatives in the run-up to the 1964 general election.

The conventions around the secret agencies at the time were rather peculiar. The existence of MI5 was not formally admitted by the British government until 1989, yet it had acquired a raised public profile in the aftermath of the Profumo affair. The Denning report on the scandal, which became an instant best-seller, even divulged some of MI5's working practices and directives, and in 1963 John Bulloch, the diplomatic editor of the *Telegraph*, published an entire book about MI5's early history, having been passed a memoir by Vernon Kell's widow.[8] The heads of the agencies were divided on the question of avowal. Dick White favoured greater openness, as did the prime minister's unofficial security adviser, J.C. Masterman. But Roger Hollis preferred the tradition of absolute secrecy, and boasted of his 'excellent arrangements with the Press' which ensured that the newspapers did not make reference to MI5.[9]

While publicly welcoming Denning's report, Douglas-Home privately wondered if there was not a better mechanism for containing security scandals which would not offer such delicious targets for the press. From the despatch box in the House of Commons he pontificated about the importance of keeping MI5 'absolutely free from political bias or influence', and warned 'how very easy it would be to cross the line between a free society and a police state'. Nonetheless, 'no one', Douglas-Home continued ominously, 'can be complacent'. He reminded his parliamentary colleagues on both benches that 'the House has been warned many times of the constant pressure on our security system. This is likely, I am afraid, to continue for some time, because it is not likely that espionage will decrease at the same rate at which we hope that the cold war will evaporate.' 'The attack,' he warned, 'is always directed against the most sensitive parts of the Government service, and it throws up particular problems.'[10]

The prime minister was keen to distance himself from the approach of his predecessors, which had clearly failed. Firstly, he deliberately sought to broaden the burden of espionage and counter-intelligence beyond his immediate colleagues perched alongside him on the Tory front bench. 'They are problems, of course, primarily for the Government of the day,' he acknowledged, 'but, nevertheless, the security of the State is to some extent the responsibility of all and they are, therefore, problems for the Opposition, for Parliament, and, indeed, for society as a whole.'[11] Here he was quietly alluding to the tradition of considerable cross-party consultation behind the scenes on security matters and counter-espionage about which the public did not know.

Secondly, he worried about the inherent secrecy surrounding spy scandals. Perhaps having learned from the uneven parliamentary performances of his predecessors, he argued that secrecy 'tends to bring about a residual anxiety about the extent of the damage which may be caused by any particular spy or about the efficiency of operation of the security system as a whole'. Distancing himself from the neither-confirm-nor-deny mentality of both Eden and Macmillan, which essentially involved slamming the security shutters down at the first whiff of scandal, Douglas-Home argued that 'It has been said over and over again that the catching of spies is *prima facie* ground for saying that the security system is effective, but I do not think that it is right that Ministers and Parliament should always have to take that on trust.'[12]

Douglas-Home knew that times had changed. Profumo, the string of earlier scandals, and a decreasingly reverential press had irrevocably undermined successive governments' ability to play the 'trust us' card. As the Thames froze over and the snow fell deeply during the long, harsh winter of 1963–64, the new prime minister set about thawing party relations inside Westminster, seeking to elevate matters of security and intelligence above the backbiting and point-scoring of party politics. In doing so, he hoped to build trust between members of the government as well as between the government and the opposition, in order to prevent scandals from escalating and rumours from flourishing.[13]

To achieve this, Douglas-Home proposed a 'new' Security Commission. In fact, the idea had originally been put forward in 1962 by Lord Radcliffe, while conducting the Vassal inquiry, and the Macmillan government had already prepared the ground. Launched in January 1964, it investigated breaches of security, referred on a case-by-case basis by the prime minister in consultation with the leader of the opposition. Publicly, Harold Wilson remained frosty. He disagreed with the argument that 'If more spies and traitors are caught it means that everything is all right.' 'After all,' he logically argued, 'if a number of escaped prisoners were caught outside

Dartmoor tomorrow, we might say that it reflected great credit on the local police or warders but we might also ask why so many prisoners were at large.' Wilson's greater concern was that the new commission would only address incidents retrospectively – after the damage had been done. The government still needed to improve preventative measures.[14] But privately he gave his grudging support. Once in office himself, Wilson saw the political advantages of the proposal, and indeed in May 1965 he chose to expand the commission's remit, and considered the positive vetting of 'certain ministers'.[15]

Most importantly, Douglas-Home wanted to avoid giving a maverick judge like Lord Denning a licence to trawl through the dirty laundry of establishment figures. But the remit of the new Security Commission was narrow, limiting itself to a lessons-learned exercise designed to ensure a tightening-up of procedures where necessary after each new security incident. Its technical nature and sober membership reassured the Cabinet Office as much as it dismayed the headline-hungry reporters of Fleet Street.[16]

Douglas-Home's Security Commission had a long-lasting impact. Before Profumo, security incidents had often been handled by *ad hoc* intelligence committees composed of permanent under-secretaries, privy councillors or judges. These initially met under the Committee of Imperial Defence, before moving to the Cabinet Office. The public nature of the Profumo affair, however, necessitated a new approach, and the Security Commission stayed in place until 2010, with its last major piece of work being to investigate the penetration of royal palaces by unauthorised persons, after a figure dressed as Batman appeared on the balcony of Buckingham Palace.[17]

What Douglas-Home did not tell Parliament, or indeed Harold Wilson, was that he knew there were more security scandals in the pipeline. For over a year Downing Street had been pondering the improbable revelations of the KGB defector Anatoliy Golitsyn, passed on by the Americans. As we have seen, in the dying days of the Macmillan administration these included allegations against Harold Wilson. Although Golitsyn's extensive accusations of KGB penetration in Western capitals were in most cases met with bemusement and scepticism, he had his advocates in both London and Washington, and a fervent spy-hunt was already under way.

We now know that in the aftermath of the Profumo affair, and confronted with a cascade of further espionage scandals, Macmillan bugged Downing Street. The devices were removed at the end of his premiership, but it appears that Douglas-Home reinstalled them in the Cabinet Room, the Cabinet Room waiting room, and the prime minister's private study. The new prime minister therefore took an active decision to wire up Downing Street, and did not merely nod to the continuance of his predecessor's arrangement. The Security Commission offered a sensible institutional response to the general threat of Soviet espionage, while electronic monitoring at the heart of government offered the ultimate reassurance against Moscow's penetration at the very heart of British power.

Harold Macmillan knew all about electronic monitoring. On his visit to Moscow in 1959 he had been forcibly impressed by the way in which every conversation, even in gardens and squares outside buildings, was regarded as vulnerable. Inside the British embassy, the only safe location was a so-called 'secure room', a Perspex tent in which a gramophone record helped to frustrate the efforts of Soviet monitoring. He complained to President Kennedy that as a result of the ubiquitous bugging, serious diplomatic business was almost impossible in Moscow, and had clearly returned to London determined to turn the tables on the opposition.[18]

In the early 1960s, the entire Downing Street complex was effectively stripped out, modified and refurbished. When Macmillan took office the main staircase was sinking, and other parts of the building were thought to be close to collapse.[19] The Crawford Committee had recommended the modernisation of 10, 11 and 12 Downing Street, so the prime minister moved out to Admiralty House in August 1960, only returning in October 1963, after the Profumo affair and indeed only weeks before his departure.[20] As the works progressed, more problems were found and large-scale concrete underpinning was required. Number 10 was completely gutted, and the walls, floors and even the columns in the Cabinet Room were replaced. New rooms were added to both Number 10 and Number 11, with space being taken from the Whips' Office in Number 12. Connecting passageways to the Cabinet Office were also improved.[21] The renovations progressed slowly, dogged by endless industrial disputes – thirteen strikes and stoppages halted work during 1961 and 1962. The cause of four of these were recorded variously as 'limitation of tea break', 'abolition of paid tea break', 'tea points not reasonably warm and dry', and 'quality of tea'.[22]

Beneath Downing Street, connections were made to a growing warren of underground tunnels and doomsday bunkers. Work continued on and off as late as 1965. Some of the most sensitive elements concerned communications and audio surveillance. GCHQ and the Diplomatic Wireless Service tested the exterior of Downing Street for any leaky emanations from cipher machines or teleprinters, and a new telephone exchange was installed in a shielded room in the attic.[23] The most delicate subject was the wiring of Number 10 itself for sound. The cover for this was probably electrical work related to 'installation of television and radio facilities' for future BBC broadcasts. Building supervisors noted that all this was arranged 'in consultation with Prime Minister's Office and Security Officers'.[24]

In 2009, MI5 allowed the distinguished Cambridge historian Christopher Andrew to publish an authorised history that had been a decade in the making. The security service was liberal in its approach, permitting Andrew access to every file regardless of its sensitivity. However, when the book was approaching publication, the Cabinet Office blocked certain passages concerning the bugging of Downing Street in the 1960s. Some reports suggested that Gordon Brown forbade the disclosures himself. We only know the outline of the story, but even so, this is shocking given a succession of parliamentary statements over decades that no such bugging ever took place. MI5 files showed that three highly sensitive areas of Number 10 were microphoned.

Jonathan Evans, the MI5 director-general at the time of the book's release, confirmed that the rationale for blocking this material was not on grounds of national security, but for wider public interest reasons. MI5 therefore argued that the section should not be removed. But, just weeks before publication, the Cabinet Office insisted that it be excised, using the vague argument of 'public interest'. This arbitrary censorship triggered a confrontation with Professor Andrew, who later referred to 'one significant excision' which he felt was 'hard to justify'. The *Daily Mail* subsequently revealed that the excisions concerned the bugging of Downing Street in July 1963 on the order of Harold Macmillan. The MI5 files do not disclose why Douglas-Home too wanted the cabinet and officials put under surveillance, nor why he wanted his own study bugged.[25]

More than a decade later, James Callaghan probed the allegations that Downing Street had been bugged. The public assumption by then seems to have been that it was rogue activity by MI5, and not on the prime minister's orders. Callaghan made a statement to the House of Commons denying that Downing Street had ever been bugged: 'The Prime Minister is satisfied that at no time has the Security Service or any other British intelligence or security agency, either of its own accord or at someone else's request, undertaken electronic surveillance in No 10 Downing Street.' This was true. Technically, it was not MI5 that bugged the premises, it was Harold Macmillan. Apparently, the still-secret MI5 files indicate that it was Callaghan who finally asked for the surveillance devices to be removed in the 1970s, in the wake of Watergate.[26] When the furore erupted over dirty tricks authorised by the White House, US secretary of state Henry Kissinger privately remarked, 'The British can't understand us. Callaghan says that insiders there are routinely tapped.'[27]

Oddly, the details of microphones in Downing Street are available for all to see. While Gordon Brown and his Cabinet Office were busily suppressing some of the most interesting parts of Professor Andrew's magisterial and scholarly history, they forgot to send anyone down to the National Archives at Kew. There, in the long-neglected records of the Ministry of Works and the Property Services Agency, are hundreds of files on the refurbishment of Downing Street. Everything is recorded in minute detail. We know, for example, that the prime minister secured the very best fitments, including 'special Honduras mahogany lavatory seats' at £11 each, with an extra £2 for 'polishing'.[28] In April 1963 there are suddenly mysterious items that the officials clearly do not want to specify in detail, including £8,800 for something called 'Special requirements'.[29] Tucked away in another long-forgotten and dusty file are the magic words 'Install floor sockets for microphones'.[30]

Even as Douglas-Home stepped across the threshold of Downing Street, the spy-hunt was taking an improbable turn. In 1963, President Kennedy invited a distinguished American academic called Michael Straight to lead the Advisory Council on the Arts. This was a government post and, conscious that his background might be checked, Straight spoke to Arthur Schlesinger, one of Kennedy's security advisers who often dealt with intelligence matters. He told him that when he had been an undergraduate at Trinity College, Cambridge, in the 1930s, a figure called Anthony Blunt had recruited him as a spy. Soon, Straight was telling his story in detail to William Sullivan of the FBI.[31]

Arthur Martin, MI5's molehunter in chief, was quickly on a plane to Washington. Although Blunt's name had surfaced in previous investigations – most crucially, he had been mentioned by Golitsyn – his importance had not been recognised, and this was a 'decisive breakthrough' in MI5's attempts to sift the bewildering rumours and half-truths about Soviet penetration.[32] Macmillan, for example, had heard Blunt named as a spy, but assumed that it was Philby who was the arch-recruiter at Cambridge.[33] In fact, Blunt was an equally important 'talent-spotter' and recruiter.[34]

Peter Wright, who served as Martin's deputy at MI5, recalled that this development was highly political. Hollis and his senior colleagues had just witnessed the fallout from the Profumo scandal, but knew that this was far bigger – Hollis felt that 'a scandal on the scale that would be provoked by Blunt's prosecution would surely bring the tottering Government down.'[35] He was also aware that the man who would replace Douglas-Home was Harold Wilson, who had been fingered, however improbably, as a Soviet agent by Golitsyn. How much of this was discussed directly by Hollis and Douglas-Home will never be known, but unsurprisingly the home secretary Henry Brooke readily accepted the advice of MI5's director-general that Blunt should be offered immunity from prosecution in return for a full confession. 'Outing' him would have created yet another embarrassing spy scandal, threatened the government, and brought unwelcome attention on the Royal Family, for whom Blunt worked as Surveyor of the Queen's Pictures.[36]

On 23 April 1964, Blunt was interviewed by Arthur Martin at the Courtauld Institute of Art, of which he was the director. The initial conversation was polite, but Martin noticed that Blunt's right cheek twitched whenever he mentioned Michael Straight. Martin came to the point, and offered Blunt a firm assurance of immunity if he told the truth. After a stiff drink and several moments of reflection, he confessed. Judicious and selective in what he revealed, he nevertheless admitted to being a KGB agent and named twelve others, including John Cairncross.[37] Peter Rawlinson, the solicitor general, claimed that it was he who had formally extended immunity to Blunt, and that 'what he told them was immensely valuable.'[38]

Although Macmillan and Douglas-Home were told about Blunt on a number of occasions, it is quite possible that Downing Street never knew the full details about the assurance that had been given to him. Roger Hollis and Dick White persuaded Henry Brooke of the case for offering Blunt immunity, and Rawlinson and the attorney general, John Hobson, then authorised it. It is possible that Brooke, an increasingly unpopular pragmatist, did not tell Douglas-Home about it when he became prime minister in October 1963. But given that Macmillan, Douglas-Home and Brooke were part of a tight circle that had shared the secret of the investigation of Hollis himself, this seems unlikely.[39]

Either way, Douglas-Home and Hollis were perhaps unaware that this was a seminal moment in the history of British intelligence. Arthur Martin was disappointed by their decision not to put Blunt on trial. In retrospect, the political reasons are easy to understand – Henry Brooke had been particularly scarred by the affair, and the rationale was obvious. But for Martin, the decision seemed to confirm that there was still a KGB agent at a high level in the British establishment, protecting other agents. Hollis responded by ordering Martin to take a fortnight off to cool down. The two men continued to disagree on the subject, and eventually Martin left MI5. Remarkably, Dick White, who had been director-general of MI5 and was now chief of MI6, was inclined to agree with Martin, and felt that suspicions lingered around his former colleagues Hollis and his deputy, Graham Mitchell. In November 1964, White employed Martin, making him the MI6 officer on the 'Fluency Committee', the top-level group looking at KGB penetration which eventually reviewed over two hundred possible cases.[40] He was not the first outspoken officer to leave MI5 and be taken on by MI6.[41]

Douglas-Home's greatest fear was a scandal blowing across St James's Park to engulf Buckingham Palace: the prime minister was a personal friend of the Queen – both were landed aristocracy with a shared passion for country pursuits.[42] Blunt had served both the Queen and her father, George VI, as a distinguished royal art historian. But as early as 1951, the palace had raised suspicions. The King's private secretary, George Lascelles, telephoned Guy Liddell to express his concern about Blunt. After reassurances from MI5, Lascelles recalled that 'Blunt had on one occasion intimated to the Queen [Mother] that he was an atheist ... and that the Queen had been a little shaken by his remarks.' Lascelles 'was certain that if he now went up and told her that Anthony was a Communist, her immediate reaction would be "I always told you so."'[43]

All of them were aware of a more subterranean royal connection. Towards the end of the Second World War, Blunt was despatched on a secret mission for the Windsors. Hugh Trevor-Roper, wartime intelligence officer turned historian, asserts that Blunt had been asked to recover embarrassing documents that were thought to be in the hands of the Royal Family's many German relations, or even in Nazi archives. Blunt boasted to Trevor-Roper that his mission had been a success, and that his haul included letters from the Duke of Windsor to Adolf Hitler. Donald Cameron Watt, one of the world's most eminent professors of international history, examined the Duke of Windsor section of the German

Foreign Ministry files and asserted that important documents referring to the Windsors' meeting with Hitler at Berchtesgaden were missing.[44]

Blunt's clandestine archive trip for the royals has long intrigued investigators. In fact there were multiple trips. Travelling with the royal archivist, Sir Owen Moorhead, he made no fewer than three visits to the Continent during the summer of 1945, going through archives at numerous locations in Germany and also at the house of Kaiser Wilhelm II in Holland. He then briefed his KGB handlers about the material he found. Exactly what he recovered is still a matter of mystery: recently released FBI files that touch on the matter are full of second-hand gossip, including suggestions that the Duchess of Windsor slept with Ribbentrop. However, papers from General Franco's personal archive in Spain show that the Duke advocated that Germany bomb Britain in June 1940, insisting that this would bring about British capitulation, and result in peace between Britain and Germany. No one wanted this sort of thing to come out, and it appears that Blunt's immunity deal was crafted to ensure that royal secrets did not leak.[45]

Blunt had many ongoing royal connections. Occasionally, he would share a box at the Royal Opera House with the Queen Mother. There were also other secret missions. In the summer of 1963, shortly before the Profumo affair exploded, Blunt had acted for the Royal Family in a private matter. Stephen Ward was an accomplished artist who had some success drawing prominent society and aristocracy figures, using his talent to gain entrée into higher social circles. The Duke of Edinburgh had sat for him, and the drawings were about to be put on show in a Mayfair gallery. Michael Adeane, the Queen's private secretary, asked Blunt to discreetly purchase the portraits, which vanished into the royal collections on the first morning of the exhibition.[46]

Douglas-Home survived another near-miss the following year. In July 1964, a year after Profumo, another sex scandal threatened to bring down another government. Startling news broke that the reckless senior Conservative politician Lord Boothby was enjoying a homosexual affair with notorious East End gangster Ronnie Kray. Boothby was a promiscuous bisexual, and had already engaged in a passionate long-term affair with Harold Macmillan's wife, Lady Dorothy. MI5 had earlier noted rumours of links between Boothby and Kray, but deemed that any relationship lacked a national security angle, given that the politician had no access to sensitive classified material. Nonetheless, Douglas-Home feared that, with an election approaching, the scandal had the potential to turn into a second Profumo – with its potent mix of the establishment, illicit sex, and the sordid London underworld. Boothby denied the claims, and threatened to sue the *Sunday Mirror*, which paid him an out-of-court settlement. Further evidence confirming his bisexuality did not surface until after his death.[47]

The most bizarre threat to Douglas-Home's personal security came from neither the London underworld nor the communists. Instead, an attempt to kidnap the prime minister emanated from none other than a group of left-wing students at Aberdeen University. Shortly before the 1964 election, Douglas-Home was staying in Scotland with his friends John and Priscilla Tweedsmuir. John Tweedsmuir was the son of John Buchan, author of the famous spy thriller *The 39 Steps*. Douglas-Home had been briefly left alone at their home one evening when there was a knock at the door. The door was 'answered by PM in person'. To his surprise, the callers brazenly declared that they had come to kidnap him. True to form, Douglas-Home refused to be ruffled. 'I suppose,' he reasoned, 'you realise that if you do the Cons[ervatives] will win the election by 200 or 300.' He then politely requested permission to pack a few things before they took him away. The students acquiesced, and offered him ten minutes' grace. In what must go down as one of the more civilised kidnapping attempts, Douglas-Home proceeded to offer his would-be abductors some beer. They accepted, and sat about drinking until Douglas-Home's friends returned, at which point the kidnap had to be abandoned.[48]

What the prime minister did not know was that the students had tailed his car the previous afternoon as he drove to his friends' house from the Scottish Unionist conference he had attended. Their original plan was to contrive an accident on the road, blocking the path of his car, to seize him and take him to a house in Aberdeen before releasing him after a few hours. The whole area was covered in a heavy fog, so this was at the very least a rather dangerous scheme. But the students lost their nerve, and instead of attempting to take the prime minister on the road, opted to visit the house later that evening. In any case, this was one of the worst breaches of prime ministerial personal security in half a century.[49] Where was his personal bodyguard? He had headed into Aberdeen for an evening out, and after the incident he swore Douglas-Home to secrecy, fearing that his job would be in peril.[50] Ever the gentleman, the prime minister seems to have agreed to a code of silence.

Domestically, Douglas-Home's relationship with security was simply focused on containing further spy scandals. Overseas, by contrast, he followed Macmillan and went on the offensive with covert action. Foreign policy was his familiar territory, and his relationship with MI6 was certainly eventful. Upon his arrival in Downing Street, the new prime minister's in-tray included not one but two secret wars started by his predecessor – the first in Yemen and the other against Indonesia. Having transferred straight from the Foreign Office, neither took Douglas-Home by surprise. He was now in a position to influence Britain's secret foreign policy more substantially, and understood that he faced important choices in this realm. He could wind down these operations and revert to traditional diplomacy. He could opt for open warfare. Also, he could continue with covert action on a limited scale, similar to that authorised by Macmillan. Moreover, he could intensify the covert action in one or both theatres. He opted for the latter. His brief stint in Number 10 not only accelerated secret wars, but also transformed Whitehall's covert action machinery at home – reforms that would influence Britain's conduct of secret foreign policy for years to come.

Douglas-Home appeared mild and unassuming. Appearances can, however, be deceiving – indeed, Harold Macmillan famously described his successor to the Queen as 'steel painted as wood'. As prime minister, Douglas-Home was clearly unafraid to get his hands dirty or to resort to deniable and underhand methods to achieve Britain's policy goals. The historian Spencer Mawby has described how Douglas-Home's premiership 'spanned a period when a series of unconnected events around the globe impinged all at once' on Britain's overseas commitments. They exposed a dangerous overstretch in defence policy, with almost a third of Britain's defence strength deployed in an undeclared war in South-East Asia. Douglas-Home considered all available options, and deemed special operations the most cost-effective way of supporting important allies like Tunku Abdul Rahman of Malaysia and defending key bases in Singapore and Aden.[51] Like many prime ministers, he used the fancy footwork of covert action as a means of delaying imperial retreat, bridging the gap between perceived responsibilities and dwindling capabilities. Many of the practitioners he employed on these missions were oddballs and caricature enthusiasts of clandestine colonialism.

Even before stepping across Number 10's famous threshold, Douglas-Home had long been an advocate of covert action. Recently installed as foreign secretary, in 1960 he had wasted little time in promoting a covert agenda against Patrice Lumumba, the first democratically elected prime minister of the Democratic Republic of Congo. Lumumba had fatefully turned to the Soviet Union for help in dealing with rampant secessionism and a breakdown of law and order in his country. In doing so, he instantly alienated the West and sparked a degree of panic in the corridors of Washington and Whitehall.

In September 1960, Douglas-Home informed his cabinet colleagues that Lumumba, 'who claimed to be prime minister', had been 'successful in obtaining considerable support, probably including some military personnel, from the Soviet bloc'. How then should Britain respond? Douglas-Home was well aware that openly opposing Lumumba would be 'counter-productive'. He was, after all, an elected leader and a hero of Congolese independence from colonial rule. Douglas-Home therefore suggested that any action be undertaken 'privately'. Macmillan agreed, and authorised MI6 to work with the CIA to overthrow Lumumba.[52] High-level discussions with America followed. Douglas-Home led the charge. Replying to President Eisenhower's wish that Lumumba should fall into a river full of crocodiles, the new foreign secretary lamented how the West had lost many of the 'techniques of old fashioned diplomacy'. The following week, Douglas-Home stressed to Eisenhower the need to 'get rid of Lumumba'.[53] Howard Smith, a senior British diplomat – and future MI5 director-general – suggested 'ensuring Lumumba's removal from the scene by killing him'.[54] In January 1961, Lumumba died in mysterious circumstances at the hands of domestic political rivals, encouraged by Washington. John Stockwell, a local CIA operative, later reminisced about how he drove around Elizabethville one night with Lumumba's body in the boot of his car, trying to think what to do with it.[55] MI6's colourful and spirited local officer in Congo, Daphne Park, later confirmed that Lumumba had been 'murdered'. When asked who was responsible for his death she asserted, 'The CIA, of course.' Park felt the action was wholly justified. While in power, she said, Lumumba had given orders for his rivals to be beaten up or kidnapped – but she regretted that he had himself been tortured before he died.[56]

Douglas-Home was horrified by Moscow's recent successes in Africa. During the colonial period, the KGB had enjoyed only limited access to the continent, operating through front organisations such as youth movements. But independence had allowed the arrival of new Soviet and Eastern bloc embassies in a number of African countries, permitting a veritable assault by their intelligence services. Douglas-Home was keen to take action. In March 1964, as prime minister, he visited Sir Abubakar Balewa, the prime minister of Nigeria, and pressed upon him the dangers of Russian advances in Africa, following this up with a rather bloodcurdling personal message prepared at his request by the JIC and MI5, warning about nefarious Soviet activities. MI5 was already passing this material to the Nigerian security service, but Douglas-Home wanted it to reach the highest level. The Soviets and the Chinese, he explained, now had missions in twenty African countries, with some 1,500 staff. Ghana was the area Russian HQ, with 120 people; even the ambassador Gyorgy Rodionov was a KGB officer. In Nigeria, Douglas-Home warned, seven of the twenty Soviet embassy staff were intelligence officers. Their work was less spying than attempting 'to secure positions of influence by secret and devious means'. 'Flattery and bribery' were being used to create 'agents of influence'. Many African students were going to Moscow to study at the 'Lumumba Friendship University', whose rector was a KGB general.[57]

Patrice Lumumba was only one of a number of troublesome foreign leaders to meet an early death during Kennedy's presidency. President Ngo Dinh Diem of South Vietnam, who had roundly annoyed the White House, was deposed and killed on 2 November 1963. Numerous plots were launched in an effort to despatch Fidel Castro of Cuba, against whom Kennedy and his brother Robert both had a particular animus. On 11 March 1963, France executed French air force colonel Jean-Marie Bastien-Thiry, who had attempted to kill President de Gaulle a few months before. Assassination was in the air, and officials in London and Washington worried about the general precedent that was being set and its impact on the safety of all world leaders. Yet no one was ready for what came next.[58]

The assassination of President Kennedy on 22 November 1963 was one of Douglas-Home's first 'flaps' as prime minister. The whole week was a whirlwind for him. After being given the fateful news he was spirited from Scotland to London in order to make a television address – arriving with three minutes to spare, before getting stuck in a lift and nearly missing his slot. The president's funeral was equally hurried, as authorities in Washington had only three days to organise it. They inadvertently left the poor Duke of Edinburgh off the invite list, and he was only allowed to enter the cathedral when Douglas-Home's wife, Elizabeth, graciously surrendered her ticket. The atmosphere was tense – the prime minister later remembered the thousands of security personnel 'with their eyes and rifles firmly fixed upwards, because it was from a roof that the fatal shot which killed the president had come'.[59]

Douglas-Home felt he had lost a friend with whom he could speak frankly. He recalled his last meeting with Kennedy, 'when we walked in the garden in the White House' and discussed the problem of de Gaulle and his recent veto of Britain's entry into the EEC. Kennedy was typically direct, and said he felt that 'megalomania had taken charge', and French leaders now pursued only 'the selfish interests of France'.[60] Nevertheless, the president had been an impediment to British covert action, and so even while in Washington for Kennedy's funeral, the prime minister was pursuing new opportunities. He managed to squeeze in a brief talk with secretary of state Dean Rusk during a spot of rather hasty funeral diplomacy. Rusk quietly asked, 'Why could not something be done in Sumatra?' As Macmillan's government had found, Indonesia's President Sukarno had been launching operations against Malaysia from the island as the 'Confrontation' escalated. Douglas-Home replied that 'this had been an idea of his for two years but he had not been able to persuade others that it was a good one'.[61] Now he was in charge. He had been prime minister for less than five weeks, but he was already looking to intensify Britain's covert response to Indonesia.

The secret struggle in Yemen also accelerated. Four days before taking office, Douglas-Home had personally assured President Kennedy that Britain was not secretly helping the royalists in that country – a dubious assurance at best, that Kennedy then conveyed directly to Egypt's President Nasser.[62] Yet, after Douglas-Home had been in Downing Street for a few weeks, his policy began to harden. Covert action gradually intensified beyond Macmillan's approach to countering Nasser with mercenaries. Detailed briefings provided unofficially by special operations veterans Billy McLean and David Smiley proved influential in swaying opinions – especially those of the prime minister himself. Both men supported strengthening the covert campaign against Nasser. A pair of adventurers at heart, they had served with distinction in the Special Operations Executive during the Second World War, and had later undertaken post-war covert operations in Albania, with McLean also quietly involved in efforts to topple Nasser during the run-up to Suez. In Yemen, McLean had engaged in fact-finding missions since the revolution in 1962 and 1963, before recruiting Smiley to do the same. Both men then acted as unofficial advisers to the royalists and certain mercenaries.[63] In the background was Julian Amery, using his position as minister of aviation to promote his passion for covert warfare.[64]

Amery arranged for McLean and Smiley to enjoy direct access to the prime minister. Indeed, McLean sent a report to Douglas-Home in October 1963, almost as soon as he took up office. Smiley's access to Number 10 was 'undoubtedly helped by the fact that his wife was a distant relative of Douglas-Home'.[65] He returned from a two-and-a-half-week trip to Yemen in mid-December 1963, and briefed Douglas-Home in Downing Street on the political and military situation inside royalist-held areas. He was upbeat about royalist chances, and according to Smiley, 'The prime minister, Sir Alec Douglas-Home, listened carefully to my account, and asked me to contact him personally whenever I returned from future visits.'[66] A few months later, Smiley enjoyed another private audience with the prime minister, and found a 'much greater interest in the war, particularly among government circles'.[67] Like his predecessor, Douglas-Home clearly enjoyed and encouraged personal briefings from unofficial adventurers – even though they continued to circumvent and contradict intelligence provided by the JIC and the advice of cautious diplomats.[68]

The new prime minister hated Whitehall foot-dragging on action against Nasser. Bitter divisions within government were preventing a coherent strategy of countering Egyptian subversion in Aden or aiding the royalists against Egyptian-backed republicans in the Yemeni civil war. Civil servants were notably terrified of McLean – throughout this period they repeatedly begged ministers to stay away from someone who was 'closely associated with the conduct of mercenary operations inside the Yemen'.[69] Fed up with competing advice and assessments, Douglas-Home ordered a review of both the intelligence and the accordant policy in the spring of 1964. The prime minister had not been in office long, but he realised that the security situation on the ground in Yemen was rapidly deteriorating as Nasser increased his subversive efforts there. He demanded a fresh look at the situation, and ordered an up-to-date JIC assessment to be circulated amongst the most senior policymakers. Intelligence officials remained gloomy, and emphasised the dangers of arming the rebels directly.

MI6 was sceptical. Dick White dismissed McLean as a romantic and a wistful adventurer. More importantly, he knew that John F. Kennedy and his successor Lyndon Johnson had both opposed covert intervention in Yemen, and that American companies were even building roads for Nasser's forces there. He feared Anglo–American crossed wires.[70] Rab Butler, the foreign secretary, drew heavily on the new report to argue that indirect aid to the royalists was futile, and risked escalating the violence. He pressed the prime minister to limit covert aid to the frontier tribes rather than the Yemeni royalists. Yet the colonial secretary, Duncan Sandys, was a passionate supporter of the royalists and wanted more covert action. Douglas-Home was not 'yet convinced' by the JIC's review, and was inclined to back Sandys, not Butler.[71]

The prime minister sent an unhappy Butler off to Washington to meet McGeorge Bundy, President Johnson's national security advisor. Even before he arrived, the Americans knew the British were divided, and that Butler himself did not agree with 'Sandysism'. The Americans believed that the best way to deal with Nasser was 'to string him along, not give him a bloody nose', and so wanted to continue their aid programme.[72] A loyal Butler warned Bundy that Nasser was 'a major enemy' who sought to evict the British and Americans from their bases in the Middle East, adding that 'The British will not see the Royalists go down.' Bundy questioned the whole covert strategy, insisting that the royalist guerrillas did not have access to seaports, so he could not see the value of giving them money. Butler replied that 'The tribes were very venal and money would buy support as well as arms which could be brought over borders.' Bundy was not convinced, and explained that he did not want to 'annoy or antagonise Nasser' by withdrawing American aid, which would mean 'losing what little influence we have in Cairo'. Departing in disagreement, Butler underlined that 'what he had presented reflected Sir Alec Home's view', and warned that there were 'extremists in the cabinet' whose position was 'much more radical'.[73]

Washington was horrified. Bundy also ran the '303 Committee', which commanded all American covert action, and he now realised that the two allies were effectively backing opposite sides in a secret war. His advisers conceded that they 'could <u>bleed</u> Nasser indefinitely in the Yemen (as UK has been doing in fact for many months)', but thought that this approach would just keep him in the country and give the Arabs an anti-Western cause to unite around. More covert action, they insisted, would bring 'nothing but trouble', and would inflame anti-colonial feeling, merely to 'bail out a <u>lame duck cabinet</u> whose policy might get reversed come October'. They urged Bundy to raise the stakes and wheel out the president 'to take the case to Home'. President Johnson should now 'turn the UK off hard'.[74]

However, Douglas-Home pushed on, and attempted to inject more coherence into the campaign, instructing Butler to appoint someone to 'take grip' of the competing Foreign Office, Colonial Office and Ministry of Defence interests, and emphasising the need for deniable operations against Nasser.[75] At around the same time, he was proving to be a keen supporter of cabinet secretary Burke Trend's ongoing review of the cabinet committee system. Demanding increased efficiency within the Cabinet Office, Douglas-Home enjoyed the prime ministerial prerogative of being able to set up *ad hoc* and standing committees as well as to nominate their members and chairmen.[76] Together, he and Trend dissolved a number of superfluous committees. They also created an influential new one that has remained so secret that its name is almost never spoken.

An urgent desire to fix the Yemeni policy malaise, combined with a review of Whitehall machinery, allowed Douglas-Home and Trend to establish the 'Joint Action Committee' in July 1964.[77] Another committee imposed upon the Whitehall bureaucracy may, to the uninitiated, sound dry and uninspiring. On the contrary, the new body followed the tradition of using a bland name to mask interesting and provocative activity. The prime minister tasked it 'to co-ordinate interdepartmental plans for clandestine operations in areas or situations overseas in which there is likely to be intervention by United Kingdom forces'.[78] It became an influential body in the coordination of covert action from Whitehall, and was used repeatedly – including in Northern Ireland and Afghanistan – until being replaced in the mid-1990s.

The JAC met the prime minister's desire to accelerate action but to avoid 'rogue elephants'. He wanted action, but not operations that were unapproved. The JAC ensured that proposals for covert activity were efficiently and adequately discussed within Whitehall, and that it would be conducted in as responsible a manner as possible. It focused on larger-scale special operations, especially those involving the coordination of MI6 and special forces.[79] Demonstrating the scale of British covert action under Douglas-Home, the committee met surprisingly regularly – fortnightly, with extra *ad hoc* meetings as required.[80] One of its first papers advocated lying to Parliament and the United Nations in order to protect deniable operations.[81] This striking suggestion lies in stark contrast to the expressions of 'trust' on matters of domestic intelligence and counter-espionage that Douglas-Home had made before the House. While calling for greater openness about MI5, he was in fact somewhat economical with the truth when it came to the shadowy work of MI6. In July 1964 he brazenly informed Parliament that 'Our policy is one of non-involvement in the civil war in the Yemen.'[82] This was simply not true.

In fact, as early as the spring of that year, covert operations in Yemen included mine-laying, issuing arms and ammunition to tribesmen, as well as sabotage and subversion.[83] Twenty thousand British Lee Enfield rifles, much prized by the local tribesmen, had been purchased through a Jersey-based arms consultant who had previously worked with MI6. By March, there were clandestine night drops of arms and supplies, which even included former German automatic weapons purchased in the Eastern bloc.[84] This was in response to a direct written request from Billy McLean to Douglas-Home. His shopping list included not only the rifles, but also £250,000 in gold, anti-tank mines and plentiful ammunition. With a typical flourish, McLean signed himself 'Member of Parliament for Aden'.[85] Rab Butler discussed a list of potential further covert operations with the prime minister. These included offensive tactics such as 'non-retaliatory sabotage' deeper inside Yemen, and even 'the assassination of Egyptian intelligence officers'. Butler was horrified by some of the suggestions, and commented drily that certain options 'may involve more political risk' than others.[86] The prime minister sanctioned some, but vetoed others. He was reassured by the fact that there was now a machine in place that allowed him control in this delicate field.[87]

In the field of foreign intervention, all premiers grow in confidence over time. By the summer of 1964, Douglas-Home had agreed to intensify the covert action, and supported providing more assistance to the royalists.[88] Although shying away from an all-out war, he authorised a more aggressive line, so long as it was tightly controlled from the centre and directed against a particular target.[89] Dick White had now come on board after a visit from Dick Helms, deputy director of plans at the CIA. Helms had confided that he was horrified by Nasser's advances in the peninsula, and was keen to undermine the State Department's passive policy on Yemen. White delivered an assured, professional and 'brilliant performance' during two thirty-minute meetings in the Cabinet Room which convinced the prime minister to support a more clandestine approach, using support from Mossad, the Israeli secret service.[90] Under Douglas-Home, Britain launched what amounted to a covert proxy war against Nasser's forces in Yemen. Ministers were informed that 'friends in the area' had undertaken attacks on Egyptians across the frontier. 'Eight years after Suez,' concluded one historian, 'the British were still waging their war against Nasser, although prudently they were now doing so outside the glare of international publicity.'[91]

Douglas-Home also directed MI6 against Indonesia. Chairing the Defence and Overseas Policy Committee, he received a number of submissions on covert action at the start of 1964. Rab Butler, for example, agreed to raise (orally owing to issues of secrecy) the 'question of retaliating in kind' to the 'Indonesian campaign of subversion and guerrilla raids' as part of a broader strategy of attrition.[92] Peter Thorneycroft, the defence secretary, also pressed for covert action. Towards the end of January, Douglas-Home and his colleagues agreed that Dick White and MI6 should begin planning a campaign of covert action.[93] The government had a pre-prepared response should any details of covert action leak: 'Ignore, deny or refer to undemarcated nature of frontier, in that order of desirability.' For good measure, it also intended 'to draw on many earlier ludicrous Indonesia allegations so as to cast doubt on any future charges'.[94]

By the summer, Britain was working with the Malaysian government in 'giving some encouragement to the dissident elements involved' on various Indonesian islands.[95] The prime minister knew exactly the extent of British covert intervention: he was personally briefed by a senior Malaysian civil servant in London in July 1964, being told how the Malaysian government had 'received very valuable assistance in drawing up plans for subversive operations against Indonesia'. As with Yemen, despite supporting covert action, Douglas-Home continued to hold back from the most aggressive proposals. But the Malaysians sought to implement a maximum strategy and use covert action to break up Indonesia entirely.[96] For over a year Tunku Abdul Rahman and his secret service chiefs had been pressing for 'special political action', and the British feared that if they did not cooperate, the Malaysians would go ahead independently. 'This could be very dangerous,' noted one official.[97] Conscious of the parallels with debates surrounding Yemen, Douglas-Home wanted to keep local ambitions in check.

As with Yemen, the prime minister was conscious that one of his main enemies in all this subterranean work was the US State Department. In the early 1960s, a number of American diplomats, and indeed President Kennedy himself, had been keen to 'mend fences' with Nasser and Sukarno, much to the vexation of both Downing Street and the CIA. In January 1964, Douglas-Home met John McCone, head of the CIA. Oliver Wright, his principal private secretary, suggested to the prime minister, 'You may like to speak forcibly to him about Indonesia.' 'Ought I to have "C" with me?' Douglas-Home asked, wanting back-up.[98] Bernard Burrows, chair of the JIC, added, 'It may be desirable to give Mr McCone frankly our views on policy with regard to South East Asia,' for fear that the Americans were unsympathetic towards Britain's plight in Indonesia as a retaliation for British lack of support for American policy in South Vietnam.[99] When it came to the meeting, Douglas-Home seemingly did not speak particularly 'forcibly', but instead played the diplomat, telling McCone that he 'understood' the purpose of American manoeuvrings. The two men agreed that 'it was not an attractive prospect to fight for an unknown number of years against guerrillas infiltrating over a thousand-mile frontier'.[100] Nonetheless, the following month, Douglas-Home implored President Johnson to cease giving aid to Sukarno, explaining that Britain was effectively fighting an undeclared war against Indonesia. Johnson replied, rather unconvincingly, that he would love to help, but was being prevented by the State Department.[101]

In July 1964, the Joint Action Committee approved a number of defensive covert actions. Again, these would have been signed off by Douglas-Home. His government agreed to deniable operations to disrupt bands of Indonesian guerrillas within 3,000 yards of the border. British agents were not, though, authorised to engage in direct action against Indonesian forward bases, as these, according to Thorneycroft, 'could not be denied'. The long, diffuse and unidentifiable jungle border could, however, be exploited to increase the distance British agents could deniably penetrate. Moreover, British officers, most likely from MI6 and special forces, busily trained Malaysian instructors in subversive operations. These proved more difficult in Sumatra, which was under strict police control. Subversive operations saw more success in Celebes, where a stronger independence movement had developed.[102]

Indonesian complaints to the UN offer some clues about specific British operations – although these claims must be taken with a pinch of salt. In 1964, according to Indonesia, Britain had established a shadowy organisation in a town in north Borneo 'to promote smuggling and to provide rebel groups in Kalimantan with arms and money'. Some fifty Indonesians had apparently been trained in north Borneo in 'handling weapons, psychological warfare, and inciting people to revolt'. Meanwhile, in central Celebes, the Indonesians claimed to have discovered '573 Lee-Enfield rifles, six Bren guns, six mortars and tons of ammunition dropped in shallow waters', destined for a rebel group.[103] We do know that Thorneycroft had been pushing for covert attacks on Indonesian communications, while the prime minister sought a role for the SAS. The former, 'limited and deniable attacks on lateral communications ... in which the

Indonesians cannot prove the border has been crossed', had been approved by summer 1964.[104]

MI6 also launched deception and psychological action. Some ideas were bizarre, and bordered on farce. One former MI6 officer in the region remembers that at around this time officials planned to convince Indonesians that their territorial waters were haunted. Essentially, the idea was a reprise of the 'Q' boat system from the First World War. Ships were to be disguised as old steam or tug boats, and would sink Indonesian vessels from out of nowhere. Officials hoped that sinking four or five ships in this manner would act as a deterrent. It would also play on Indonesian superstitions about evil water spirits. The locals would supposedly believe that their ships were being shot down by ghosts in the Malacca Strait. Predictably, this plan was rejected as silly; some reasoned that it might simply put the Indonesians on heightened alert.[105]

Intelligence and covert action were now part of mainstream foreign policy, but problems of control remained. As early as March 1964, the chiefs of staff were reflecting on the 'defects' of the Counter-Subversion Committee, a key coordinating body for fighting communism in faraway places like Guinea and Zanzibar. One of the issues was simply the eye-watering secrecy of covert action. In a note that was itself marked 'very restricted circulation', they recorded 'the reluctance of the friends to have secret operations discussed in committee with an extensive membership'. 'The friends' was Whitehall slang for MI6.[106] Their proposed answers to the problem of 'Sino–Soviet penetration in Black Africa' were not particularly convincing. They suggested, for example, increasing the supply of primary-school teachers, and mused that the visit of a British football team to West Africa 'would be desirable for counter-subversion purposes'. Perhaps the coordination of these matters had become a little too broad and inclusive. The legacy of Attlee, the consummate committee man, who had sought to impose an integrated cross-Whitehall approach on secret affairs, had its limits. Ultimately, the prime minister and his inner circle remained the authority for the more dangerous work.[107]

Precisely because of prime ministers, covert action in both Yemen and Indonesia outlasted Douglas-Home's government. Despite their very different public personas, and their divergent ideologies, the occupants of Downing Street were privately consistent in this matter throughout the 1960s. Demonstrating that recourse to such operations is not determined by political affiliation, Harold Wilson continued using MI6 and special forces, collaborating with Mossad and the CIA respectively, until the end of the Indonesian Confrontation in 1966 and withdrawal from Yemen in 1967.

In October 1964, Douglas-Home's exit from Number 10 marked the end of over a decade of Conservative rule. Successive prime ministers had faced a series of intelligence challenges over that time, the most fearsome related to communist subversion, spy scandals and the upper echelons of British society. Each incumbent of Number 10 had highlighted the dangers of a police state at home and prompted a good deal of heart-searching. Like Churchill, each had been much less afraid to use covert action abroad, seeking to leverage the benefits of secret service. Like Attlee, each had also been keen to create efficient machinery to ensure close control by Downing Street. Now Labour had reclaimed power after a decade in opposition. Harold Wilson, a man who knew nothing of covert action, inherited this growing secret machine. He also had some tough decisions ahead.

PART FOUR

DÉTENTE
AND DISSENT

11

Harold Wilson
(1964–1970)

I was inevitably preoccupied with security questions.
But anyone who has held this responsibility knows
just what can be at stake.
HAROLD WILSON

October 1964 seemed to signal a fresh start for Britain. London's Carnaby Street was swinging and the music of the Beatles filled the airwaves. A new government was stepping forward, promising to harness the white heat of the technological revolution. Harold Wilson had already proved to be a brilliant leader of the opposition. Highly intelligent and articulate, he was able to shape the agenda in a way that had kept Harold Macmillan and Alec Douglas-Home, his sparring partners across the chamber, on the back foot. He easily outplayed a fading Macmillan, withering in the aftermath of the Profumo affair and de Gaulle's European veto. Douglas-Home fared somewhat better, but prior to his arrival at Number 10 the gentle, aristocratic ex-lord had not set foot in the House of Commons for over a decade. Despite his inner toughness, in the eyes of the public he had seemed notably ill-matched to the modern age.[1] Wilson could not wait to walk through the famous black door.[2]

Despite his publicly expressed interest in security matters, Wilson was surprisingly unprepared for dealing with the secret world. He had served in Attlee's cabinet as President of the Board of Trade, and had been shadow foreign secretary under Hugh Gaitskell until Gaitskell's death in January 1963. Yet, he remained oddly naïve about Britain's intelligence agencies. When, as leader of the opposition, he was briefed on Kim Philby in 1963, he claimed ignorance about the secret service. A surprised Harold Macmillan had to patiently explain about the leadership of MI6, and to offer some background on Sir Dick White, one of the most distinguished British spy chiefs of all time. Wilson's apparent insouciance about such matters contrasts starkly with successors such as Tony Blair, who lunched with the heads of both MI5 and MI6 while leader of the opposition.[3]

But Wilson learned about intelligence fast. Arriving in Downing Street on 16 October 1964, he faced, by his own admission, 'a stormy welcome'. The Chinese had exploded their first nuclear weapon the day before, extending the dangers of nuclear annihilation, while the day before that, Nikita Khrushchev had been overthrown as Soviet leader. Khrushchev's enforced retirement – a kinder fate than that of previous deposed Soviet leaders – raised questions about future Russian policy. Meanwhile, the 'Confrontation' with Indonesia was escalating.[4] Wilson knew that intelligence would be vital to understanding such issues, and he now had the perfect guide to the secret world. The previous year, the long-serving cabinet secretary Norman Brook, who had helped Attlee reshape Britain's intelligence machinery, had retired. His replacement was Burke Trend, who had looked after the intelligence budget at the Treasury and was already recognised across Whitehall as a quiet enthusiast for secret matters. He briefed Wilson on the intricacies of the JIC, espionage tradecraft, and the perils of hostile audio surveillance and bugging.[5]

Above all, Wilson wanted to avoid another Profumo. He had watched the press torment Macmillan during what one young reporter on the *Daily Express* recalls as 'a year of pure journalistic excitement'.[6] Wilson had also taken visible delight in baiting Macmillan at the despatch box, and now that he was in office he was determined to avoid the same fate. So his immediate focus was preventive security and personal protection, rather than matters of traditional espionage. Recognising that MPs were a possible weak link, he quickly found a role for his friend, the lover of secrets and self-styled security expert George Wigg, as his paymaster general. Wigg, together with Dick Crossman, had personally launched the Profumo affair in the House of Commons, and was regarded by Macmillan's inner circle as 'positively evil'.[7] He had also successfully managed Wilson's party leadership campaign, skilfully using a range of 'cajolery and threats' to ensure his man received the requisite votes. Wilson now intended to make further use of Wigg's loyalty and skills as an enforcer. With a roving brief to keep abreast of trouble across the whole security scene, he enjoyed direct access to the prime minister through his own private door into Downing Street. Wigg stalked the corridors of Westminster, keeping his long ears to the ground, and with his beaky nose sniffed out any juicy gossip about his parliamentary colleagues in order to discover if anyone was sharing call girls with Russian spies.[8]

Wigg's unofficial reports on the political and sexual activities of Labour ministers fascinated the prime minister. Roger Hollis of MI5 and Dick White of MI6 were more sceptical. Hollis in particular, used to reporting through the home secretary, complained about confusion over lines of ministerial accountability.[9] In truth, they hated an amateur encroaching on their patch and stirring things up. Burke Trend warned Wilson that Wigg 'should preferably be confined to security and should not extend to secret intelligence as well',[10] and suggested that he 'make it clear' to Wigg 'orally that he will not be concerned with M.I.6. or with intelligence matters',[11] reminding the prime minister of the need not to 'blur Ministerial responsibilities or to tread on Departmental corns!'[12]

Ministers hated what they called 'wiggery-pokery'. The defence secretary, Denis Healey, recalled how Wigg's 'interest in security made him both see and organise conspiracies everywhere', perhaps encouraging Wilson's predisposition to paranoia. Similarly, Roy Jenkins, the home secretary, described Wigg as 'half comic, half sinister', and a 'licensed rifler in Whitehall trash cans and interferer in security matters'.[13] Against such hostility, Trend felt the need to spell out to Wilson exactly why the home secretary, rather than somebody like Wigg, should have responsibility for MI5. Only the home secretary, Trend lectured, could issue warrants 'for the interception of communications'. He therefore needed 'full knowledge of the work of the Security Service'.[14]

Wigg would not be told. Within a month of taking up office, he demanded that ministers of state, parliamentary secretaries and parliamentary private secretaries in departments that dealt with foreign and defence policy should be positively vetted. Burke Trend and his team gasped with horror at the thought of probing the private lives of MPs. Even the Americans, Trend exclaimed, who 'have had occasion to look critically at our practices have never suggested for a moment that positive vetting ought to be applied to Ministers'. They sought to explain their objections to Wilson in delicate language, arguing that field enquiries by MI5 would result in a 'considerable body of intimate personal detail of a kind that it would hardly be suitable for officials to review where Ministers are concerned'. The result would be 'serious embarrassment' of a kind that might 'damage the government'. They were trying to tell Wilson that once this explosive information was gathered, it was likely to leak, creating exactly the kind of scandals he was so anxious to avoid. Wilson was soon persuaded to drop Wigg's idea.[15]

But Wigg continued to cause endless security trouble. In 1965 he tangled with the home secretary over a revised directive for the new director-general of MI5, Martin Furnival Jones.[16] This cued much verbose to-ing and fro-ing about when and under what circumstances the director-general should have direct access to the prime minister.[17] A year later, Wigg's name was at the centre of a 'parliamentary row' over the tapping of the phones of MPs. Wilson broke with precedent and addressed the Commons full on. He recalled:

> My answers made clear, first, that there *had* been tapping of MPs'
> telephones up to the time Labour came into office; second, that
> this had covered members of more than one party; third, that I
> peremptorily stopped it when I became prime minister. From
> that moment no member had his phone tapped so long as Labour
> remained in office.

Instead of being thanked for his remarkable candour, Wilson was accused of having 'smeared' his predecessors.[18] Wigg remained in place, and like an overexcited amateur detective he often became sidetracked by trivial matters and red herrings, such as the 'employment of foreign au pair girls'.[19] He contributed almost nothing to national security, yet Wilson met with him more frequently than with any other minister.

With Wigg watching the parliamentary rumour mill and the domestic security scene, Wilson felt that he himself could safely turn to foreign intelligence. At first, he remained somewhat ambivalent, showing only occasional interest in top-secret material on world affairs, published weekly in the highly classified JIC 'Red Book'. Wishing the Red Book to have more 'direct political interest', Wilson's private secretary, Michael Palliser, felt that 'some weeks it seems extremely long and boring'. Yet, Wilson boasted a penetrating intellect, and when he did engage with JIC intelligence he would 'often spark' on it and 'throw up comments', scribbling notes in a green ink normally reserved for 'C'. The intelligence assessors, in turn, were delighted to see prime ministerial enthusiasm for their work.[20] As world events required him to pay more attention to secret intelligence, Wilson became a surprisingly keen supporter of both espionage and covert action. He chose to continue both of Douglas-Home's secret wars, in Indonesia and Yemen, but his most intractable problems were in sub-Saharan Africa.[21]

On 24 February 1965, Kenneth Kaunda, the first elected president of Zambia, briefed Wilson about fast-moving events in Central Africa. Kaunda was fond of Britain, not least because Daphne Park, the local MI6 officer, had funnelled money into his election campaign on the basis that he was the 'least undesirable' of the many candidates.[22] A radical nationalist, he nevertheless thought of himself as Britain's critical friend, and proceeded to sketch out the volatile landscape of Central Africa for Britain's new prime minister. In the 'war-stricken' Congo, a motley band of Belgian security police and CIA-sponsored mercenaries had been fighting a confused civil war that had impacted on the whole region. Kaunda was keen to underline the dangers of American intervention in the region, which he feared would remain the 'target of intrigue in African polities'. He complained that the CIA's protégé in the Congo, Moïse Tshombe, had decamped with 'millions' from state funds, and 'with his team of gendarmes and mercenaries in Angola remained an ugly menace to a country he has now come to rule'. 'Mercenaries must go ... especially as they are mostly South Africans noted for their contempt for black men.' Kaunda urged Wilson to try to restrain the Americans and Belgians who were backing Tshombe. He also lamented the death of Patrice Lumumba, 'the inspiration of the Congolese people'. Lumumba's unpleasant murder was common knowledge, but Kaunda was a realist on this issue and wanted everyone to move on, saying that there should be no inquest or investigation 'because his skeleton is in too many cupboards'. Wilson thanked him politely for expressing himself so 'fully and frankly'.[23]

Kaunda's current obsession, however, was not the Congo but a new crisis in Rhodesia. On 11 November 1965, Prime Minister Ian Smith declared unilateral independence in an attempt to thwart majority black rule. It was, in effect, a local revolt. The entire Commonwealth, already sensitive on the issue of neighbouring apartheid South Africa, was incensed. Wilson recalled that Kaunda 'put us in the dock on charge after charge', contrasting Britain's inaction in southern Africa with its use of force in Cyprus, Kenya and Aden.[24] Kaunda himself mobilised the Zambian Rifles and confronted the Rhodesian Light Infantry across the Victoria Falls. Smith had instituted 'Operation Wizard', a top-secret contingency plan designed to forestall invasion by Commonwealth forces. But because of his vast military commitments against Indonesia, Wilson simply did not have the forces to carry this out, and instead he opted for sanctions.[25]

On Rhodesia, Wilson's overweening confidence in his own intellectual abilities allowed him to succumb to a well-known prime ministerial disease: regarding himself as a 'DIY intelligence analyst'. Taking personal charge, he firmly believed that economic sanctions would coerce Smith into changing his attitude.[26] Wilson should have been on home turf here, but as a former President of the Board of Trade and Oxford economist, he valued his own judgements too highly. Fascinated by economic warfare, he was 'positively thriving' on the crisis.[27] In one instance, armed with an MI6 report confirming Portuguese assistance to Rhodesia, Wilson demanded: 'Kick up hell with the Portuguese and frighten them.'[28] Rhodesia was, according to one cabinet minister, 'his Cuba'.[29]

Wilson boasted publicly that his sanctions would deliver results within 'a matter of weeks not months', and suffered ridicule when they failed. Sanctions proved hard to apply. Unsurprisingly, the Soviet bloc did its best to undermine Britain by supplying heavy machinery and accounting for over half of Rhodesia's illicit deals. But friendly countries also proved problematic; political and security alliances can flounder in the economic arena. The Americans continued to buy strategic materials from Rhodesia, especially chrome. Perhaps more crucially, Britain's own economic fortunes were linked to South Africa, which was determined to undermine the sanctions. Pliant companies in Austria, West Germany, Switzerland and Belgium arranged many of these transactions. By mid-February 1966, petrol was flowing across the border from South Africa, arranged by the 'Friends of Rhodesia Association'. Ian Smith was receiving 235,000 gallons of fuel a day purchased from BP, in which the British government held a majority stake. All that British intelligence agents could do was to watch the long lines of petrol tankers crossing the border.[30]

Wilson recognised that the economic campaign against Rhodesia was a mess, involving too many officials from too many departments, but his decision to put his erratic friend George Wigg in charge did not improve matters.[31] One observer commented that Wilson's sanctions had only resulted in a 'shortage of Angostura bitters and Marmite', while creating a bizarre underworld of black-market dealers and blockade-runners in which 'James Bond would be truly at home'.[32] After a year, the JIC warned Wilson that deliveries of oil from South Africa meant that Rhodesia could 'continue to exist indefinitely', albeit with its economy at a reduced level.[33] The Americans described Wilson's performance as a 'classic instance of the policy wish fathering the intelligence estimate'.[34] This was quite incorrect. The British intelligence community had not doctored material to conform to Wilson's world view. Rather, Wilson had spun the statistics and ignored his JIC assessments. But he eventually learned his lesson, and concluded that 'much greater importance should be given in future to economic intelligence' – especially on the non-communist world.[35]

Meanwhile, South Africa and Rhodesia launched intelligence operations in London. In 1965, a South African intelligence officer called John Fairer-Smith arrived in Britain, and was soon running a veritable army of spies. The main targets were African liberation movements and their contacts in frontline states such as Angola, Mozambique and Zambia. Their top agent was Norman Blackburn, a British national who had been recruited while serving in the Rhodesian army. He returned to Britain in 1966 to join a network that had now swelled to some seventy agents. In his turn, Blackburn recruited a twenty-one-year-old typist who had just begun work at Downing Street called Helen Keenan. Known as one of the 'garden girls' because she was part of a team that worked in a basement office that adjoined Number 10's pleasant inner garden, she handled the most secret correspondence, and handed over her shorthand notes about Rhodesia and South Africa for the princely sum of £10 a page. In 1967, Keenan and Blackburn were arrested by Special Branch, and received prison sentences.[36] The Security Commission focused on Keenan, who claimed that 'London life had gone to her head' after her arrival in the capital from Yorkshire. But it was the South African dimension that caught the eye of Wilson and Burke Trend.[37]

During 1965 and 1966, secret deals were explored by both sides. The role of MI6 during these complex negotiations remains mysterious. The first head of Central Intelligence in Rhodesia was a Cornishman called Ken Flower. Beginning his career with HM Customs and Excise, he rose through the ranks of the police in South Africa before heading up Rhodesian intelligence from 1963. Flower enjoyed a good relationship with Dick White of MI6, and came to London whenever he wished. A ruthless figure who planned many assassinations, he was nevertheless realistic, despising what he called the 'diehard' element in the Rhodesian cabinet and frustrated that Salisbury's politicians refused to make political concessions at opportune moments.[38] Remarkably, Flower met secretly with Wilson and Trend in early 1966 and urged negotiation on them, insisting that senior members of the Rhodesian armed forces were more 'reliable' than London thought.[39]

In March 1966, Wilson was considering the possibility of a soft coup by moderates in Rhodesia, while keeping the door open to secret talks.[40] In

late April, Wilson and President Johnson were discussing the latest
'Rhodesian feeler' and also pondering a confidential Rhodesian negotiating document that the CIA had just 'acquired'. 'You appear to be playing
this nibble just right,' Johnson enthused, 'although I agree the fish isn't
hooked or landed.'[41] Throughout the summer Wilson continued to toy with
the covert action option – instigating a coup d'état that would put more
liberal whites into power. But the Rhodesians were ahead of the game, and
discovered British paratroopers carrying out an exercise at Malta's Luqa
airport as a dry run for a strike on Salisbury airport.[42] In December, Wilson
coaxed Smith into talks on the Royal Navy cruiser HMS *Tiger*, and these
negotiations almost bore fruit. But there were always too many parties to
please. At Commonwealth summits, Kenneth Kaunda of Zambia asked
loudly why Britain had used force elsewhere to end revolts, but did not
bring Smith to heel. Wilson could not keep the leaders of the New
Commonwealth happy without military action or harsher general sanctions that would have hurt British economic interests in South Africa.[43]

At a more subterranean level, Wilson's caution connected to domestic
politics. In the summer of 1968, he recruited Max Aitken of Beaverbrook
newspapers and the lawyer Arnold Goodman, an experienced Wilson
'fixer', to revisit the possibility of a negotiated settlement. Before their
departure for Rhodesia, Wilson warned them sternly that Smith was not
only 'a liar and schizo: he is also an eternal optimist'. More darkly, he
hinted that Smith's strategic objective was to work with certain people in
Britain to get rid of the Labour government, believing Rhodesia could get
'a better deal from the Conservatives'. Worries about what Rhodesians and
South Africans were doing in London had already begun to loom large in
Wilson's mind.[44]

Wilson's hands were tied over Rhodesia because of the conflict with
Indonesia. Sukarno, its president, was now widening the war by attacking
Malaysia and its pro-British leader, Tunku Abdul Rahman. Wilson therefore deployed some 50,000 troops and a third of the Royal Navy to engage
in this secret war. British soldiers, including members of the special forces,
were being awarded the Victoria Cross for actions that could not be
publicly avowed. Wilson feared that if even a few more soldiers were
required, he would have to cancel the Trooping the Colour ceremony in
June – there were just no more military resources left.[45]

Whitehall's secret machinery was 'ready to examine any formula which
might make it possible for the Indonesians to abandon or at least modify

this policy'.[46] This included 'covert propaganda and clandestine operations' both to erode the will of the Indonesian military and to aid rebel groups inside Indonesia.[47] Wilson's officials even considered a rerun of wartime deception operations.[48] The MI6 effort against an increasingly pro-communist Indonesia was run by John Colvin. Previously involved in the last phase of the Malayan Emergency, he had worked out of the British high commission in Kuala Lumpur. Colvin was an intellectual, and combined his love of South-East Asian history and culture, especially ceramics, with counter-insurgency measures against the Indonesians. Returning to London in 1964, he became the architect of the more deniable aspects of an undeclared war.[49]

Fortunately, wider circumstances were moving in Wilson's favour. President Johnson was less well disposed towards Sukarno than his predecessor had been, and was escalating American involvement in the Vietnam War.[50] Demonstrating parallels with Churchill and Iran over a decade earlier, Wilson skilfully played on American fears about the Indonesian leader's increasing collaboration with the Communist Party of Indonesia, or 'PKI', and his growing links with Mao's regime in Peking.[51] There were also opportunities inside Indonesia. Over the last five years, with the gradual collapse of parliamentary politics and a series of internal rebellions, the country's politics had increasingly become a subtle competition between various army factions, ranging from the centre to the right, and the communist PKI on the left. The army also entertained increasing misgivings about the 'Confrontation' with Britain, which it felt was being badly misdirected by Sukarno. He had recently ordered seaborne and parachute landings on the Malaysian mainland by sabotage teams who had quickly been massacred. Senior army officers were so dismayed that they had begun to hold secret negotiations with Malaysia via their secret service in Bangkok, hoping to avoid escalation. Amid all this, each Indonesian faction feared a coup by the other.[52]

Wilson wanted American help in getting rid of Sukarno. In early 1965, he warned Johnson that Sukarno was 'crooked and irrational'. The PKI, he said, had strengthened recently, 'primarily due to Sukarno's support', adding that his ideas had moved 'steadily leftward for many years'. He then set out possible future scenarios: 'We do not believe that the PKI's position will look so strong if Sukarno dies or gives up within the next year or so.' If Sukarno fell, Wilson argued, then in any subsequent coalition, right-wingers in the army would eventually win the ensuing struggle for power. 'Although, therefore, Sukarno's death would probably not in itself put an end to confrontation', he thought there would be a very much better chance of a settlement. Conversely, Wilson insisted, if Sukarno remained in power, and was 'thus able to continue his policy of strengthening the PKI', the outcome would be a communist government in Indonesia.[53]

Wilson's views were not an invitation to liquidate the Indonesian leader. Instead, they reflected a whole new field of intelligence-gathering: the medical state of world leaders. The CIA had pioneered this field, obtaining and analysing the urine of King Farouk of Egypt in the early 1950s. In 1959, it had bribed an airline steward to recover a sample of Sukarno's urine after an international flight. Along with heart problems and the effects of a minor stroke, the Indonesian leader was also subject to a range of other ailments. As the CIA put it: 'Although his bedroom proclivities have almost become legend, Sukarno does have a serious health problem.'[54] Only three months after Wilson had entered Downing Street, MI6 circulated its own intelligence report showing that Sukarno was believed to be suffering from kidney stones and various urinary complications, and was being treated in Vienna by a specialist. MI6 later managed to obtain X-rays of the Indonesian leader. In early January 1965, the JIC had predicted that without an operation Sukarno might only live twelve months.[55]

In the spring and summer of 1965 Indonesia was convulsed by public talk of British plots. The trigger was the so-called 'Gilchrist letter'. On 1 April 1965, a communist youth group linked to the PKI had attacked the luxury villa of a gregarious American film distributor called Bill Palmer whom they suspected of being a CIA agent. In the ransacked building they claimed to have found a letter from the British ambassador Sir Andrew Gilchrist to London which mentioned future cooperation between the British and 'our local army friends'. Gilchrist was known to have an intelligence background – he had headed SOE in Bangkok during the war, as well as the JIC Far East during the mid-1950s. The letter fuelled existing fears of a right-wing army coup against the PKI and Sukarno.[56]

In late May, Sukarno ordered his intelligence agencies to conduct a forensic comparison of the Gilchrist letter with other documents and signatures by Gilchrist. Despite being told that the letter was a high-quality forgery, he publicly declared it genuine at a combative press conference in Cairo as he returned from a conference of non-aligned nations in Algeria.[57] By apparently thwarting Western plans and waging 'a glorious battle against imperialism', Sukarno's prestige in the Third World soared. But who had forged the Gilchrist letter? The CIA suspected that it was the work of either Sukarno's leftist associates, the PKI or the Chinese. In fact it was none of these. The Czech defector Ladislav Bittman later insisted that the forgery was the work of his own secret service, in cooperation with the Soviets, and part of a plot called 'Operation Palmer'. They had passed the forged letter to a leftist Indonesian ambassador in The Hague, who cooperated by planting it on other associates in Jakarta in return for 'an apartment and a steady stream of female companions'. Bittman also claimed that the rumours about the film distributor Bill Palmer working as a CIA agent were spread by Indonesian journalists working for Czech intelligence in South-East Asia.[58]

'Operation Palmer' signalled the beginning of a new wave of Soviet secret service activity called 'disinformation'. It fell on fertile ground, because Sukarno and his immediate circle were already paranoid about the CIA and MI6. In February 1965, Sukarno had told one of President Johnson's aides that the CIA was out of control in Indonesia. In June, when the American Ambassador Howard Jones left Indonesia at the end of his term, Sukarno assured him that the CIA was planning his assassination. Oddly, the Indonesian leader also believed that Professor George McTurnan Kahin, a leftist Asian scholar and anti-Vietnam War campaigner, was the CIA head of station in Jakarta. Ambassador Jones and Professor Kahin were good friends, united by many things including their dislike of the CIA, so they found all this extremely funny. But in the autumn of 1965 matters took a more serious turn.[59]

Sukarno's poor health now intervened. Intelligence derived from the Indonesian premier's urine was the subject of fierce competition between the secret services of East and West. The Chinese had the inside track. Sukarno was extremely superstitious, and had been told by a soothsayer that he would die during surgery. So, instead of undergoing the normal procedure for his ailments, an operation to remove his kidney stones, he preferred treatment by Chinese doctors with herbs and acupuncture. The Chinese were thus able to inspect his urine samples and X-rays in forensic detail. Like London, Peking knew that the prospects for the PKI were largely dependent on Sukarno – and he was clearly in rapid decline.[60]

Sukarno was not a communist, but the PKI knew its fortunes were intertwined with the faltering leader. It was therefore preparing, with Chinese military aid, a coup that would eliminate the right-wing army threat, while keeping the ailing Sukarno as a figurehead. On 28 September 1965, Sukarno was stricken with severe pain while making a speech, and had to leave the rostrum. Chinese doctors suggested he would live no more than a week, and this triggered the PKI coup. However, the Chinese were not yet ready to launch it, and the weapons destined for the PKI were still in their crates. On 30 September, an amateurish coup attempt went ahead, but Major General Suharto, who headed the army's strategic reserve, soon put down the rebels. Six leading Indonesian army generals were killed in the confused fighting, and the military, which had formerly been the soul of moderation, had now been provoked.[61]

Over the next year, the army carried out a remarkable anti-communist purge. Some scholars have suggested that more than 500,000 people were liquidated in the ensuing violence, and perhaps a further million were incarcerated. Harold Wilson was fed remarkable details on the complications of the coup and counter-coup, including the precise movements of Sukarno, based largely on sigint from GCHQ. Within a few months, the PKI ceased to exist as a serious political entity, and Suharto succeeded in taking power. Sukarno shrank away and, as a result of chronic kidney problems, died in June 1970. In the wake of Suharto's accession, the secret talks in Bangkok accelerated, 'Confrontation' gradually drew to an end, and the Southeast Asian Treaty Organization (SEATO), the regional collective defence alliance, was created, allowing Wilson to withdraw from burdensome and expensive military commitments east of Suez.[62]

Exactly how far Whitehall and Washington were involved in events in Indonesia remains a mystery. Britain had certainly worked hard to convince American military chiefs and the CIA that Sukarno should be removed. The US military had strong links with senior commanders in Jakarta, and had trained over a thousand officers. While the CIA has denied any involvement in the killings of October 1965, it has since transpired that the American government provided extensive name lists of communists to Indonesian death squads.[63] The British were clearly keen to accelerate the purge, and shortly after the coup launched a covert propaganda operation designed to 'surreptitiously blacken the PKI in the eyes of the army and the people of Indonesia'.[64] Gilchrist, the British ambassador, arranged for messages to be passed to the army high command assuring them that there would be no British attacks in Borneo while they were busy dealing with the PKI.[65] Several secret services had contributed to the dramatic events, but no one was in control. Ladislav Bittman, the Czech deception operative, reflected ruefully on the unexpected outcome. Operation Palmer was merely 'one of the customary backstairs skirmishes' between Eastern and Western intelligence services in which 'both sides tried to harass the opposition'. He added, with some understatement, that 'the operation outgrew its initial intention' and became an 'explosive' factor in Indonesian politics and the country's relations with the West.[66]

By the mid-1960s, Downing Street was worried about the increasing public profile of the CIA. The White House was also alarmed at the way in which the press was hinting at American covert action in locations ranging from India to Chile. In January 1965, John McCone, Johnson's CIA director, held a crisis session of his Executive Committee, berating his top team 'rather violently' about a range of leaks and security failures. McCone spoke 'very stonily' about fraternisation between CIA officials and the press, and ordered that this cease immediately. He warned them that President Johnson 'is determined to find out the source of the leaks to the press and … when he does, he will ride the culprit out of town'. But CIA officials ignored this, and continued to enjoy bibulous lunches with their press contacts.[67]

By contrast, the British were still bound by a culture of eye-watering secrecy. Historically, British officials had often used rather circumlocutory language to refer to intelligence work. One cabinet minister had earlier recalled that one of his senior officials 'could hardly bring himself to say "Secret Service"'. It was, he continued, 'like an old lady trying not to say "WC"'. Instead they called it, 'in a hushed voice', 'certain arrangements'.[68] Similarly, while British diplomats called MI6 'the friends', the CIA were 'the American friends'. Quaintly, the two services were sometimes referred to in the same breath as 'our friends and their friends'.[69] But such terminology did not always imply real friendship, and during the mid-1960s, when CIA covert action was at its height, British and American policy-makers did not see eye to eye in every region of the world.

Accordingly, during Wilson's first year in Downing Street, his officials were busy upgrading 'Guard' procedures. This was a special codename used to denote documents that were not, on any account, to be shown to the Americans. Its purpose was, as they put it delicately, to avoid any 'embarrassment of relations' between Britain and America. It was also used to safeguard 'Intelligence that was obtained unofficially from American sources'. This sensitive material, when communicated, was accorded 'special cipher security treatment', and guidelines laid down by the London Communications Security Agency were strictly followed.[70] There was clearly some anxiety about a codebreaking attack by the NSA – British officials were exhorted not to send 'Guard' material electronically at all if possible. If a wireless signal or a telegram was essential, then ideally it had to be sent using a laborious one-time pad, the most secure cipher available.[71] JIC papers were usually sent out under a 'UK Eyes Only' cover, with the Americans given a different product designed especially for them.[72]

What sorts of things were kept from American eyes? Remarkably, during the mid-1960s, GCHQ was reluctant to share diplomatic sigint on a whole range of areas, including the Gulf states of the Middle East because of oil issues.[73] Another area of concern was arms sales, where the British, French and Americans competed vigorously.[74] Yet another was that Washington might find out the limits of Britain's capability in the field of nuclear weapons. The chiefs of staff noted that the Americans were 'anxious to find out the extent of our knowledge and we should lose a significant bargaining counter if they were to do so'.[75] We shall probably never know whether the Americans did try to read British codes. But the desire was certainly there. In the immediate wake of the Second World War, even as the famous UKUSA sigint treaty was being negotiated between GCHQ and the USA, senior intelligence officials in Washington pondered the list of their post-war priority sigint targets. Remarkably, it ran as follows: Great Britain, Russia, France, the Netherlands, China and Argentina.[76]

Vietnam was another point of friction. One of Harold Wilson's major achievements was to keep Britain out of this conflict. By 1966, Johnson had committed hundreds of thousands of troops, and was desperate for British support. 'Lyndon Johnson is begging me even to send a bagpipe band to Vietnam,' said Wilson to his cabinet colleagues. But for much of the British Labour Party, opposition to the Vietnam War was a *cause célèbre*. Michael Stewart, who replaced George Brown as foreign secretary in March 1968, felt that Vietnam was 'the most agonizing of all the problems I had to face'. Wilson knew that the American bombing of North Vietnam was an especially sensitive domestic issue and wanted it to stop, yet he needed Johnson's support on a range of other thorny international issues.[77]

Wilson used intelligence assets in Asia to address this dilemma. He deployed these to give secret support to the Americans, knowing that it helped to placate the White House, while remaining below the radar of British public opinion. This clandestine aid took various forms. Britain sought to support and cover American specialist intelligence assets in Europe, such as signals intelligence monitoring flights, in order to release more US capacity for the air battle over South-East Asia. In Asia, GCHQ provided volumes of signals intelligence from its large monitoring stations at Little Sai Wan and Tai Mo Shan in Hong Kong. That colony was also host to America's largest CIA station in the region, which masqueraded as a 'consulate' and boasted hundreds of staff. Within North Vietnam itself, Britain's most significant contribution was the intelligence activities of its consulate-general in Hanoi.[78] At the height of the Vietnam War this obscure outpost was sequentially the home to at least six MI6 officers, including John Colvin, who arrived in 1965 fresh from directing Britain's secret efforts against Sukarno.[79]

John Colvin, then Brian Stewart and finally Daphne Park offered Harold Wilson first-hand reports on the gradual escalation of American bombing, from tactical strikes to heavy raids, known as 'Operation Rolling Thunder'. The North Vietnamese authorities had their suspicions, and tried to make life difficult for the MI6 officers by restricting supplies. Daphne Park recalls that when running short of petrol she sought permission to import a bicycle so she could meet her diplomatic visitors arriving by plane. The Hanoi authorities responded that it was 'unsafe for an honourable lady to be regularly cycling to the airport at night', so she requested a licence to import a tandem, but this was met with silence. After some months she suggested a trishaw, with a member of the North Vietnamese counter-intelligence bureau as pedaller – which was approved. However, her sense of mischief went too far: 'She turned up at the Soviet national day with a Union Jack on the handlebars. The trishaw was suddenly withdrawn.'[80]

These MI6 officers offered both Wilson and Johnson valuable insights into the effects of the air war over Hanoi. Their priceless material also went to Walt Rostow, US national security advisor, along with the CIA and its military equivalent, the Defense Intelligence Agency. Johnson was desperate to assess the impact of 'Rolling Thunder', an expression of his policy of 'gradualism' which was the subject of constant argument in the National Security Council. The White House puzzled over how to find an approach that would apply more pressure on the North Vietnamese, but without the risk of destroying targets that might jeopardise negotiations. Johnson certainly received impressive detail. In May 1967, he was given a first-hand account of a recent bombing raid. John Colvin was actually standing on the balcony of the consulate with his colleague Geoffrey Livesey as air-raid sirens sounded. Seven or eight F-105 Thunderchiefs shot across their vision at rooftop height, seeming 'so close we could almost touch them or call out to the pilots'.[81]

London used this remarkable intelligence direct from Hanoi to push the 'implacability thesis' – that war was now a way of life for the North, and that its people were resigned to a protracted struggle. Graduated bombing had not broken their will, but had merely assisted the communist propaganda machine. Wilson was keen to make sure that the flow of information from Britain underpinned his assertion that the air raids ran counter to Johnson's ultimate intended objective: a negotiated settlement. In 1966, he publicly criticised the bombing of Hanoi and Haiphong – much to Johnson's fury. Meanwhile, the Americans excluded Britain from their secret diplomatic peace effort known as 'Operation Marigold', details of which were uncovered by Colvin in Hanoi.[82] Wilson's MI6 contacts told him that the Americans were bungling the peace effort, describing it as 'a rather gloomy story of muddle, lack of confidence, and incompetence'.[83] Washington also undermined Wilson's own peace initiatives via Soviet premier Alexei Kosygin, of which he had not told Washington.[84] He had confided to Kosygin that Britain in effect had North Vietnamese 'representatives' in London masquerading as press reporters. Playing the socialist card, the prime minister kept in touch with them via his parliamentary private secretary, Ernest Fernyhough, who was 'an old friend of Ho Chi Minh's'. Kosygin observed that he thought this channel and the MI6 presence in Hanoi was 'a good thing'.[85]

When MI6 officers occasionally reported material that seemed to show that the bombing policy was on the right track, it was suppressed and not passed to Washington. Sir Arthur de la Mare, the senior official superintending Asia, noted on one despatch, 'You should not, repeat not, show Hanoi Despatch No.7 to the Americans.'[86]

Ironically, both Lyndon Johnson and Harold Wilson were finally outflanked by Richard Nixon. The Republican presidential candidate had already embarked on a career of illegality even before entering the White House. We now know about his amazingly devious efforts, by all accounts successful, to destroy the Paris peace talks of 1968. These took place in the closing weeks of the presidential campaign, after the British had persuaded Johnson to pause the bombing of North Vietnam in search of a settlement. Behind their backs, high-level emissaries for Nixon promised South Vietnamese President Nguyen Van Thieu that he would receive much better terms if Nixon was in power, but would fare badly if Hubert Humphrey, Johnson's vice president and the 1968 Democrat nominee, was in the White House. Thieu thought this argument had strength, and so boycotted the peace talks. Nixon's intervention probably cost thousands of

American lives by prolonging the war, and was almost certainly illegal. The road to Watergate and a White House culture of secrecy and corruption had already begun, with profound consequences for all of Britain's prime ministers in the 1970s.[87]

If Harold Wilson was ambivalent about America, the feeling was reciprocated. The CIA was taking a close interest in the prime minister, and sending some rather odd material to the White House. Prior to Wilson's first visit to Washington, Richard Helms, then deputy director for plans at the CIA, reported on 'rumours current in London' about Harold Wilson's supposed affair with his political secretary Marcia Williams, and on her 'impending divorce'. The intelligence was wrong on almost every point. In fact, Williams had divorced some time previously, and the assertion that her husband was 'a card carrying member of the British Communist Party' was untrue. But what this revealed was how active the CIA station in London was in watching Wilson. Helms spoke of a 'personal contact' of one of his officers 'on the editorial staff of the *Daily Herald*', Labour's most supportive newspaper, who had relayed recent discussions of the alleged affair at Labour Party headquarters. Another CIA officer had obtained information from 'prominent London lawyers'. Helms added that due to the sensitivity of the issue, the CIA was 'in no position to check back through our normal liaison with the British Security Service'.[88]

As we have seen, the CIA's Soviet defectors were a well-spring of security suspicions about Wilson, and these leads were passed to London. The new prime minister thus had the rather dubious honour of being the only occupant of Downing Street on whom MI5 kept a file. Dating back to 1945 and Wilson's first election as an MP, for Ormskirk, the file was so sensitive that its subject had to be disguised under a top-secret pseudonym: 'Norman John Worthington'.[89] The young Wilson had been on the MI5 watch list for a while. His time as President of the Board of Trade allowed him to visit Russia frequently, and he had continued to keep one or two dubious contacts there, raising eyebrows inside MI5. After a game of cricket by the River Moskva, he once claimed to be 'the only batsman ever to have been dropped at square leg by a member of the NKVD'.[90] Enjoying a wide range of company that included the far left, Wilson cannot have been surprised by MI5's interest in him. In fact, he was strangely proud of it, seeing it as 'evidence that he was taken seriously as a left winger'.[91] When Roger Hollis met the new prime minister for the first time in November

1964, he tried to alleviate any concerns about MI5 suspicions of the Labour Party by stressing that the service avoided 'Party political matters'.[92]

During the 1960s, the KGB defector Anatoliy Golitsyn was the main problem. After having impressively outed John Vassall at the Admiralty and offered firm evidence against Kim Philby, he was taken seriously. Yet he loved to weave conspiracy theories, suggesting not only that Harold Wilson was a Soviet spy, but also that Hugh Gaitskell, Wilson's predecessor as Labour leader, had been dramatically assassinated to make way for Wilson. During debriefing sessions in London in 1963, Golitsyn had said that a KGB chief of operations in northern Europe had talked of killing an opposition leader in the West. This may have been true, but it was not Gaitskell. In January 1963, Gaitskell died of lupus, which caused his joints to swell and his vital organs to fail. While rare, lupus could not have been caused deliberately. Arthur Martin, the diehard counter-intelligence officer who had left MI5 for MI6, spoke to Gaitskell's doctor, who thought the suggestion improbable. In any case, at the time George Brown, rather than Wilson, would have been the most likely beneficiary of Gaitskell's death. Nevertheless, MI5 now opened a file on the Gaitskell theory.[93]

Wilson was not a Soviet agent. The KGB had, however, also opened a file on him, as it did on almost any foreign politician who visited Moscow. Soviet intelligence hoped to target the young politician, codenamed 'Olding', as a long-term penetration agent. Unsurprisingly, the same issues that had caught MI5's attention had appealed to Moscow: Wilson's active promotion of East–West trade and regular contacts within the Soviet Union as well as with members of the far left in his own party. But while the KGB valued Wilson's loose-lipped political gossip, it never managed to recruit him.[94]

Spurred on by Golitsyn, the CIA *also* opened a file on the prime minister. Wilson had achieved a quite remarkable hat-trick, and become a personification of the Cold War paranoia spanning London, Washington and Moscow. This time he was codenamed 'Oatsheaf'. James Jesus Angleton, the chain-smoking head of CIA counter-intelligence, led the American charge. Obsessed with KGB moles, he pursued Golitsyn's rumours with evangelical vigour – the betrayal by his close friend Kim Philby perhaps increasing an already zealous fundamentalism in his counter-intelligence work.[95] A divisive figure regarded as a genius by some and as the leader of a witch-hunt by others, Angleton undoubtedly destroyed the careers of a number of innocent and loyal public servants. He was eventually fired in 1974.

Harold Wilson was not paranoid. Rather, he was the victim of a paranoia that gripped some of Britain's most accomplished and dedicated
counter-intelligence officers. Fuelled by Golitsyn and encouraged by
Angleton, a small hard-core of dedicated fanatics began to flourish inside
MI5 and MI6. Remarkably, at one point their growing list of suspects even
included the redoubtable Daphne Park. Once they were convinced of their
grand theology, recalled one rueful MI6 officer, they then 'dug for material
to fill out the case'.[96] London-based CIA officers were startled by the
'openly scurrilous and disloyal remarks' made by MI5 staff about the
prime minister.[97] In fact, Wilson was not their main target. They were busy
covertly filming Graham Mitchell, the deputy head of MI5, through
one-way glass in his own office by day and combing his wastepaper basket
by night. But because even Wilson was a suspect, no one was in charge,
and the madness was able to spiral out of control. Unlike Macmillan and
Kennedy, who had been briefed regularly on the Golitsyn revelations,
Wilson was only dimly aware of the fantastic things going on in buildings
only a few hundred yards from Downing Street. Perhaps it was just as
well.[98]

Remarkably, even while Wilson and senior security figures were under
suspicion, the prime minister relied heavily on MI5. This was most visible
during the National Union of Seamen's strike in the late spring of 1966.
He lapped up briefings at a rate of almost twice a day from Martin Furnival
Jones, MI5's director-general, and Dick Thistlethwaite, its head of counter-
subversion:[99] 'No previous Prime Minister had shown such enthusiasm
for regular up-to-the-minute Service reports during an industrial
dispute.'[100] Wilson was particularly delighted by the fact that MI5 had
comprehensively bugged the Communist Party's headquarters in Covent
Garden, and felt that the resulting intelligence allowed him to 'predict the
exact line the group would take at the next meeting, as well as the
approaches made to Communist sympathisers in unions whose support
the seamen were canvassing'.[101] The prime minister even repeated MI5
assessments verbatim inside the House of Commons in order to accuse
the communists of influencing the strike.[102] He named the Party's 'ruthless'
national industrial organiser Bert Ramelson as the figure behind a 'takeover bid' for the union, adding that the London docks provided his
'hunting ground'.[103]

Wilson had overplayed secret intelligence at the expense of other political factors. Even Dick Thistlethwaite worried that he would interpret
these problems through communist eyes 'as we were forced to do', thereby

taking insufficient account of non-communist influences which MI5's charter did not cover.[104] The prime minister should have taken MI5's advice about the wider context, but instead he sought to use secret intelligence narrowly to break the strike, desperate to protect his pay policy.[105] This emphasis on the communist role both exasperated and alienated the left wing of the Labour Party,[106] with Wilson maintaining that moderate members of the union executive were 'virtually terrorised by a small professional group of Communists or near-Communists'.[107] Oddly, he was more security-minded than MI5 on union politics and left-wing entryism.

Harold Wilson prided himself on his positive relations with the press, and his honeymoon period with the newspapers lasted longer than most. But in 1967, the 'D-Notice affair', which some have described as 'Britain's Watergate', obliterated all his previous efforts to charm the media.[108] The issue dominated Downing Street for weeks on end, and Wilson once again took personal charge and made some ill-judged decisions. Ruefully, he later remarked that the 'self-inflicted' saga was 'one of the costliest mistakes of our near six years in office'.[109]

On 22 February 1967, Wilson rose to his feet to answer a routine question in the House of Commons on D-Notices. Still in existence today as 'Defence and Security Media Advisory Notices', this mechanism provides a set of guidelines agreed between the government and the press when publishing on sensitive subjects like intelligence. It was, and remains, a voluntary system which informs editors of the types of information needed to be kept classified for reasons of national security. Available 365 days a year, the D-Notice secretary provided a friendly channel between the two sides, acting as a negotiator to ensure that compromises were reached. It was a challenging role, relying on charm and persuasion rather than power. Nonetheless, the system had worked fairly effectively for years.

But Wilson was in a foul mood. The previous day, the *Daily Express* had published a story by Chapman Pincher, its notorious defence correspondent. Known as the lone wolf of Fleet Street, Pincher had a unique flair for unearthing sensational intelligence stories, and was feared by the leaders of all parties. His favourite method involved using grouse-shooting sessions as a means of bonding with, and extracting leaks from, establishment figures. This *modus operandi*, combined with his many enemies, landed him in particularly hot water on one occasion, when his bloodstained car was found near a murder scene. He was, however, guilty only of shooting pheasants and stuffing them into his boot.[110]

Pincher had chosen to expose an especially sensitive target: GCHQ interception activity, the most secret part of the secret state. It is hard to imagine just how breathtakingly secret this matter was – at this time no one had even heard of Bletchley Park as a wartime codebreaking centre. Pincher's scoop did not mention GCHQ by name, but revealed the government's secret collection and copying of hundreds of international cables before they left the country. The process was known as 'cable vetting', but more so than today, simply to breathe words like 'signals intelligence' or 'interception' caused a neuralgic twinge in Whitehall.[111]

Despite Wilson having presented Pincher with a 'journalist of the decade' award just months before, he remained a thorn in the government's side,[112] having published an inaccurate story suggesting that the Labour leadership's 1961 hunt for crypto-communists amongst its backbenchers had sparked a major MI5 investigation of the party.[113] Sharing Harold Macmillan's frustration at Pincher's series of scoops, Wilson suspected that the journalist had become too friendly with the D-Notice secretary, Colonel Sammy Lohan. The two certainly knew each other well, and Wilson feared that Lohan was actually feeding stories to Pincher – he apparently authorised bugging Pincher's phone to try to prove it. The prime minister became obsessed with preventing damaging leaks, and even suggested installing a camera above the Downing Street photocopier.[114]

If the prime minister disliked Pincher, he loathed Sammy Lohan. The D-Notice secretary was a bowler-hat-wearing, mustachioed Whitehall character who could easily 'have been incorporated into the next James Bond film'.[115] To Wilson, Lohan was an incompetent and bibulous Tory sympathiser whom he suspected of tipping off the opposition with material for embarrassing parliamentary questions on defence, and maybe even of colluding with elements inside MI5 to undermine the government.[116] Following allegations about Lohan's rampant womanising and excessive drinking, MI5's director-general, Roger Hollis, had discreetly investigated him in the summer of 1965. Although Hollis could not find enough evidence to sack him, Martin Furnival Jones, Hollis's successor-in-waiting, did admit that Lohan was 'sometimes fuzzy with drink' in the afternoon.[117]

The prime minister also bore a specific grudge against the *Daily Express*. The paper had already launched what he felt was 'an ugly campaign' against his political secretary Marcia Williams, and Wilson's anger only intensified when he heard that it had apparently been repeatedly warned, firstly by

Lohan and then by George Brown, the foreign secretary, that Pincher's cable-vetting story breached the D-Notice guidelines.[118] He was therefore livid when he found out that the *Express* had decided to publish regardless.

Burke Trend warned Wilson not to overreact,[119] but when the angry prime minister rose to his feet in the House of Commons to answer a routine D-Notice question he added an emotional afterthought, accusing the *Daily Express* of undermining the 'confidence and trust' on which the entire D-Notice system depended. He then accused Pincher of writing a 'sensationalised and inaccurate story' which created the impression that 'under the Labour Government there was a "big brother" system of snooping into private affairs'.[120] Finally, he accused the paper of clearly breaching not one but two D-Notices, despite having been warned in advance.[121] Richard Crossman confided to his diary that the prime minister had acted 'rather abruptly and savagely'.[122]

Wilson had picked a fight with the press. To make matters worse, he had done so without being in possession of the full facts. The following day the *Daily Express* launched a predictable counter-attack. It argued that contrary to the prime minister's parliamentary statement, Lohan had in fact assured Pincher that the article would not breach a D-Notice – although he had advised against publication.[123] *The Times* and the *Telegraph* swiftly joined in the attack on Wilson, arguing that if the story was inaccurate, then surely it could not have breached a D-Notice in the first place.[124] Stubbornly, Wilson stood his ground: 'I must repeat that the story published that morning was a breach of the long-standing "D" Notice convention; and that this had been made clear to those concerned.'[125] He was wrong. Far from colluding with Pincher, Lohan had in fact tried to discourage him from publishing.[126] Unfortunately, messages had become mixed – not least because both Lohan and George Brown, who had spoken with Pincher's editor the night before publication, were under the influence of alcohol at crucial moments.

By his own admission, Wilson behaved heavy-handedly and failed to foresee the vicious press attack that awaited him.[127] The editor of the left-wing *Mirror* resigned from the Services, Press, and Broadcasting Committee in protest, stressing that 'the "D" Notice Committee is not an instrument of censorship but a voluntary body'.[128] Wilson had hoped in vain that the committee would carry out an inquiry into the affair; not giving up, he asked Lord Radcliffe, a senior judge, to conduct one instead.[129] The prime minister was dismayed by the resulting report, which concluded that Pincher's story had neither been inaccurate nor breached a D-Notice. In short, it showed that Wilson was wrong. Angrily, he summoned Radcliffe to Chequers and unsuccessfully attempted to persuade him to suppress his conclusions.[130] After then being told it was too late to include new and damning evidence against Lohan, Wilson asked Radcliffe to publish some of the secret evidence taken during the inquiry alongside the report, in the hope that it would damage Lohan. As Christopher Moran, Britain's leading historian of secrecy, observes, this was 'Wilson at his most scheming'.[131]

Egged on by George Wigg, Wilson foolishly decided to reject the Radcliffe report.[132] Bizarrely, he then grew obsessed with the publication of secret evidence and the idea of an alternative White Paper deviating from Radcliffe's conclusions, and spent hours consumed by what to include. Unsurprisingly, he asked the Foreign Office to remove all GCHQ material and references to signals intelligence from the published document, and asked Wigg to remove all politically embarrassing material too. But, revelling in the chance to attack Lohan, Wigg busily set to work removing statements that sympathised with the beleaguered D-Notice secretary.[133] Burke Trend had seen enough, and warned Wilson that his antics might unwittingly shed light on the secrets of GCHQ.[134] In return he received a stinging lecture on prime ministerial responsibility. Wilson stated that 'The last battle is fought under my direction', and 'I shall be somewhat intolerant of intervention by the official machine once we move into the political phase.'[135] He then proceeded to 'single-handedly and determinedly' rubbish Radcliffe's findings.[136] The prime minister's stubbornness permanently damaged his relationship with the cabinet secretary.[137]

In late June, Wilson gave his statement on Radcliffe in Parliament. He began well, giving the impression of a responsible leader rightly concerned with security.[138] But with the House seemingly under control, he suddenly went off script. Stating ominously, 'I want the House to hear this', he began a personal attack on Lohan. Against much shouting and the speaker's cries of 'Order!', Wilson emphasised the overly close relationship between Lohan and Pincher, alluded to Lohan's character defects, and stressed his lack of full positive vetting.[139] Having saved this emotional outburst until the end, the prime minister 'sat down to tumultuous cheers' from the Labour benches.[140] Not everyone was impressed. Dick Crossman deemed it a 'fatal mistake', and Barbara Castle felt that the 'last-minute rabbit out of the hat had a nasty taste about it'.[141]

The prime minister had ruined his relationship with the press, which had taken many years to develop.[142] Journalists responded by pursuing ever bigger stories concerning intelligence and security. The *Sunday Times* and the *Observer* both published exposés on Kim Philby. Meanwhile, the feud between Wilson, Wigg and Pincher became increasingly personal and petty.[143] In early September 1967, Pincher, ever the country sportsman, sent a fresh salmon he had just caught to Wigg as a peace offering. Sneeringly, Wigg told Pincher that the fish was 'slightly off', so he had fed it to his neighbour's cat. 'I much prefer my salmon served with a tin opener,' he added. 'Fish, like newspaper stories, are best when they have verifiable sources of origin and when they are quite fresh.'[144] Pincher did not see the funny side, and thought Wigg's response to his gift 'contemptuous'.[145] Wilson, however, enjoyed the exchange immensely, and cheekily asked, 'Does the Paymaster [Wigg] like to have his salmon positively vetted?'[146]

Wilson had blundered badly over the D-Notice saga. Desperate to seem competent in the sensitive field of security, he now appeared the very opposite. He had also offended his loyal cabinet secretary, Burke Trend. Yet, at exactly the same time, behind the scenes he joined with key ministers to help Trend carry out important reforms to the central intelligence machinery, many of which survived into the twenty-first century. Wilson served as a wartime official, and had then joined Attlee's cabinet during the late 1940s. He was thus the last direct link to the formative period of the British intelligence community under Churchill and Attlee. It was therefore entirely appropriate that he should have initiated the first major review of intelligence processes in Whitehall since his Labour predecessor almost two decades before.[147]

Back in 1950, the key question raised by Attlee was whether there should be an intelligence overlord. The consensus had been 'no', partly because there was a lack of obvious and capable candidates. At the urging of Trend, this decision was now reversed, and the post of coordinator of intelligence was created within the Cabinet Office. This was partly because there was now a superb candidate, Sir Dick White, who had served as both director-general of MI5 and chief of MI6. Wilson liked the affable White, who had also been Trend's schoolmaster in the 1930s. The importance of his arrival as intelligence coordinator has been somewhat downplayed.[148] It is correct to say that this was a part-time position, and that White was by no means an overall controller or director. Yet he exerted an important unifying influence, reconnecting GCHQ with important parts of Whitehall that looked at cipher machines and speech security. He was also keen to promote the application of computing across the whole intelligence community, and gave Teddy Poulden of GCHQ the task of exploring this issue.[149] But his most significant role was to serve as the intelligence community's main financial planner, working on behalf of Trend and his PSIS committee, which formulated future intelligence strategy.[150]

Given his position at the centre of government, Trend inevitably took a keen interest in the structure of the intelligence services. In a notably brief and slightly bizarre commentary on national security in Britain, Harold Wilson once wrote that Downing Street's 'responsibility is exercised through the secretary of the cabinet, who is the prime minister's link with the authorities concerned'. Trend had a deep personal interest in security matters, and was an avid reader of John le Carré. As a young Treasury official, he had looked after the 'secret vote' which determined the funding of the secret services. Wilson had great respect for Trend, and relied heavily on him for advice on intelligence, despite his departing from the script during the D-Notice affair.[151]

These important changes have rightly been called 'the Trend reforms', but they also owed something to Wilson, Defence Secretary Denis Healey and Foreign Secretary George Brown. In great secrecy, Wilson's government had begun an annual Whitehall 'Intelligence Methods' conference, attended by Trend and senior ministers, at which ideas about improvements were floated. Well aware of the impressive national intelligence estimates machinery that served President Johnson in the United States, they felt a need to catch up. At the third conference, in 1967, Healey praised the intelligence community but also expressed a strong desire to see the central machinery strengthened. Brown agreed, and there was a general sense that the sophisticated intelligence mechanisms in Washington and the Americans' use of computers warranted close attention.[152]

Wilson had recently launched the Fulton Committee inquiry into the future of the Civil Service, in response to widespread concern that economic, technical and scientific expertise was lacking in the higher echelons of government.[153] His own input can be seen most clearly in the attempt to connect intelligence to economics, science and technology. Mindful of the Rhodesian experience, he and Trend were keen to strengthen the JIC, and to widen its focus to include economic and technical matters. In April 1968, the JIC was bolstered with the creation of a new Assessments Staff in the Cabinet Office to support its writing of papers. It was also divided into two committees, one focused on security issues and the other on economic affairs, with the Treasury chairing the latter.[154]

Soon after his appointment as intelligence coordinator, Dick White was struck by Britain's failure to predict the Soviet invasion of Czechoslovakia and the crushing of the 'Prague Spring' in 1968. He discovered that lowly British Army intelligence units in Germany had forecast this accurately, 'while the FCO and the friends had been wrong'. In response, he boosted the role of the head of Defence Intelligence and increased his staff, to the dismay of the diplomats. His personal remit for this expanded unit was 'to tell those who won't listen all the things they don't want to know'.[155] Yet, neither Trend nor White addressed the growing struggle between the diplomats and defence officials for control of intelligence.[156] The very fact that White had moved from the post of 'C' at MI6 to that of cabinet intelligence coordinator triggered a further round in this turf war. The Ministry of Defence wished to see White's friend and colleague Maurice Oldfield appointed as his successor. But the Foreign Office, which controlled MI6, insisted on appointing a diplomat rather than a seasoned MI6 officer to this post. Its choice was Sir John Rennie – and his tenure as 'C' during the last two years of the Wilson government was not a success.[157]

The brutal crushing of the Czech government in August 1968 hardened Wilson's attitude to the Soviets. Parliament was recalled, and the prime minister was hurriedly flown from his holiday home on the Scilly Isles to London in an RAF helicopter of dubious reliability. MPs on all sides of the House were incensed by the Soviets' action, and he assured them that Britain was not 'powerless', adding that he would do more than deliver 'an impotent protest'.[158] Conferring with his new foreign secretary, Michael Stewart, he decided to turn the heat up on the Soviet embassy. Stewart observed that the number of Soviet officials in Britain had 'gone up very sharply in recent years'. So too had the number of spies – in total, MI5 had 'identified 137 Soviet officials in this country as having intelligence functions'. Wilson agreed with Stewart that the UK had 'tolerated this for too long', and that some sort of action had to be taken. Stewart was willing to expel a number of Soviet personnel, but felt that they should keep this option 'in reserve' until they had seen 'whether less drastic measures have some effect'. Instead, Wilson decided to give the Russians a warning, and to cap their diplomatic and non-diplomatic lists at the embassy 'to their present figures'.[159] On the afternoon of 11 November 1968, Paul Gore-

Booth, Britain's most senior diplomat, delivered a formal rebuke to the Soviet ambassador, Mikhail Smirnovsky.[160]

Wilson and Stewart knew that this would not be enough. Reminiscent of Stanley Baldwin's 'Arcos' raid back in 1927, Martin Furnival Jones at MI5 pointed out that no limit had been imposed on the separate Soviet trade delegation – still a potential hotbed of espionage and subversion.[161] Stewart urged that it be closely monitored, in case the Soviets 'started packing it with more intelligence officers in order to frustrate our purposes in freezing the levels of the Embassy staff'.[162] Furnival Jones also noted that not all Soviet intelligence personnel were based in the embassy or at the trade delegation, since the USSR had recently been allowed to open new consulates outside the capital.[163] Dick White was now giving personal attention to a plan to counter the swarms of Soviet spies in London.

White's central work as coordinator was continuing the British tradition of building a joined-up intelligence community. Symptomatic of this was the creation of some of the first joint sections between MI5 and MI6. One of the most important of these new units worked on the problem of Soviet intelligence activities in London, and was led by a formidably brave former SOE officer, Tony Brooks. Called 'the London Station', this innovation would eventually bear fruit with the spectacular recruitment of KGB officers in the 1970s, beginning in the capital. Over the next few years, Brooks and his team patiently played their game against the Soviet opposition, and even as Harold Wilson's successor arrived in Downing Street, they were preparing for action.[164]

12

Edward Heath
(1970–1974)

Well over 100 of the 500 staff at the Soviet embassy
were intelligence officers ... firm and carefully
prepared action had to be taken.
EDWARD HEATH[1]

Edward Heath liked secret service. Increasingly obsessed with subversion, he thought the secret world had an invaluable role to play in the growing battle with his domestic enemies. The early 1970s heralded a period of change in Britain's security landscape, as Cold War intrigue slowly gave way to industrial unrest, political violence in Northern Ireland and the ominous rise of international terrorism. New groups were emerging, and this required a refocusing of the intelligence effort. MI6, for example, had spent years penetrating the official Communist Parties in Western Europe. But, as one MI6 officer who was regional controller for Europe recalls, 'Now there was the radical "New Left" – about which we knew nothing!'[2] The world of subversion and conspiracy hit much closer to home, too. It touched Heath personally. On 4 May 1971, crude home-made bombs were found near Sidcup and Chislehurst Grammar School in his parliamentary constituency, where he had just received the freedom of Bexley. On the same day an unexploded bomb was found attached to the underside of Lady Beaverbrook's car. The authorities suspected a range of different organisations. Even the leafy Home Counties now seemed to be seething with assassins. Death might lurk around every corner.[3] It is hardly surprising that the prime minister saw himself at war with revolutionaries.

In his dealings with intelligence, Heath was well advised, both officially and unofficially. The new prime minister inherited Burke Trend, a consistent enthusiast for the intelligence community, as cabinet secretary. Trend was assisted by the affable and hugely experienced Dick White, the first cabinet intelligence coordinator. Heath had been 'much impressed' by White ever since their paths first crossed in the early 1960s when Heath was Lord Privy Seal.[4] White charmed both Wilson and Heath with his unfailing good humour and sense of proportion. One of his MI6 colleagues recalls that secret service creates 'some curious human types', while its operations can generate paranoia or limit understanding. By contrast, White remained a rational man at ease in the real world, and so won the trust of successive prime ministers.[5]

But Heath also had a fondness for unofficial advisers and special units. Accordingly, he created a Central Policy Review Staff under Lord Rothschild, which later became the Downing Street Policy Unit. Rothschild had served in MI5 during the war, running its anti-sabotage operations in Paris just after liberation, and remained close to many of the senior figures within the intelligence community. Heath used him as an informal secret service adviser.[6] Rothschild was more experienced and better-connected than Harold Wilson's equivalent, George Wigg, but Trend still did not appreciate this additional channel. The hospitality of Rothschild's office was legendary – a constant supply of smoked-salmon sandwiches and cider cup consisting almost entirely of brandy.[7] Nevertheless, Trend despaired at Rothschild's meddling in everything from computer policy to mole-hunting.[8]

The new prime minister was relatively experienced in dealing with the secret world. His predecessor, Wilson, had believed in cross-party consultation on intelligence, so as leader of the opposition Heath had met with MI6 before he entered Number 10. For example, in October 1966, Wilson and his foreign secretary, George Brown, invited Heath and Alec Douglas-Home, then shadow foreign secretary, to join them in Wilson's room at the House of Commons, where Dick White, then chief of MI6, briefed them on George Blake's escape from Wormwood Scrubs prison, his subsequent recapture and interrogation.[9] Similarly, Wilson consulted Heath closely in March 1970 over plans to commission an official history of British intelligence during the Second World War. The intention, Wilson explained, was a deliberate counterblast to Kim Philby's delightfully sardonic memoir, which had portrayed British intelligence as full of incompetent buffoons.[10] In the end, with Wilson losing the June 1970 election, the decision fell to Heath. On the advice of Dick White and under pressure from Trend, the incoming prime minister reluctantly agreed to commission the work.[11] The secrets of Bletchley Park, they warned, were going to come out anyway, and the government might as well stay in control.[12]

Heath may have had a reputation for U-turns, but he was a bold intelligence consumer. He knew his own mind, and his premiership is widely perceived as an intelligence success. He approved 'Operation Foot', the mass expulsion of almost a hundred Soviet agents, which crippled KGB spying operations in Britain for a decade. He made important intelligence interventions in Northern Ireland, especially banning torture despite some officials arguing its case. And he personally led the drive to enhance intelligence on subversion and industrial unrest, in the face of resistance from MI5. He may have been one of the first prime ministers with no direct experience of the Churchill/Attlee school of secret service, but by this time the intelligence community was firmly embedded within Number 10. Heath, like his predecessor, understood its power.

Edward Heath's premiership coincided with an upsurge of terrorism in the UK. Although this era is predominantly associated with IRA violence, in reality London was alive with all sorts of dangerous groups. Heath's first terrorism challenge emerged from the decade of counterculture. Between 1968 and 1971, a curious group that eventually called itself 'the Angry Brigade' carried out some two dozen bomb attacks in Britain. Influenced by Germany's Baader-Meinhof gang, they were convinced that everything about the establishment was wrong. Their targets ranged wildly, from MPs' homes to the Miss World contest, and from army barracks to the Biba fashion store in Kensington. In August 1969, one of their first acts was to set fire to the home of Duncan Sandys, Winston Churchill's son-in-law and former defence minister. But a year later, when they planted a bomb at the home of Metropolitan Police Commissioner Sir John Waldron, no one really knew who they were, since they signed their communiqués 'Butch Cassidy and the Sundance Kid', or 'The Wild Bunch'.

Heath began to take a personal interest when they targeted Robert Carr, secretary of state for employment. On the evening of 12 January 1971, a powerful bomb blew in the windows of his home as he sat down to open his ministerial boxes. A carefully timed second bomb then knocked police officers off their feet as they arrived on the scene. Miraculously, Carr and his family escaped serious injury. Heath had inherited Wilson's union troubles, and Carr was at the centre of controversial new employment legislation designed to restrict union power – the Department of Employment had been targeted the previous month. This time the mysterious perpetrators used a children's printing set to stamp the words 'The Angry Brigade' on their communiqué, and they would keep that name for all further attacks. On 23 March, they bombed the offices of the Ford motor company at Brentwood in Essex, just a week after Heath had met with the management. In June, the Angry Brigade upped the stakes, writing to *The Times* claiming that they planned to assassinate Edward Heath. The prime minister was unsurprisingly incensed, and not a little concerned. He demanded that the group be 'smashed'.

Heath set up a special bomb squad to catch them. A breakthrough came when Roy Habershon, a Special Branch officer who had previously been with the Fraud Squad, took an interest in forged cheques that were supporting the lifestyle of a number of communes associated with the group.[13] On 20 August 1971, police swooped on a flat at 359 Amhurst Road in Stoke Newington, north London. They uncovered two Beretta sub-machine guns, gelignite, detonators, counterfeit US dollars, and a long list of future targets. The signature child's printing kit lay amongst the vast and disorganised inventory. Police swiftly rounded up the leaders. They proved to be a group of young student militants, led by Ian Purdie and Jake Prescott, who were inspired by the Paris uprising in 1968. Both had run away from their sociology studies at Essex and Cambridge respectively – literally ripping up their finals papers in the exam room – to join communes. Eight people were eventually charged, and the trial judge, Mr Justice James, attributed the problem to campus Marxism, asserting: 'Undoubtedly, a warped understanding of sociology has brought you to the state that you are.'[14]

The Angry Brigade *were* rather odd. Although inspired by the Baader-Meinhof gang, they were more interested in smoking dope and writing for underground newspapers than in actual violence. They never managed to kill anyone, and have been described as a 'quaint Pythonesque version' of their more lethal German counterparts. Yet, they were important in creating a climate of social crisis at the beginning of the Heath government, and convincing the new prime minister that sinister revolutionary forces were at work.[15]

The Angry Brigade formed just one source of violence on the increasingly crowded British streets. The month before Heath became prime minister, two Molotov cocktails were thrown at the US embassy in Grosvenor Square. Four days later a firebomb was found and defused on a plane bound for Spain from Heathrow. In October 1970, two parcels containing grenades addressed to the Israeli embassy and the Israeli airline El Al's office in London were found in BOAC's London headquarters.[16] Just over a year later, on 15 December 1971, as the Jordanian ambassador's car passed down Holland Street in Kensington it was raked with sub-machine-gun fire, a member of Black September firing forty rounds from a Sten gun hidden under his coat. Few VIPs had bulletproof cars at this time, and the ambassador, Zaid al-Rifai, only survived by crouching in the footwell.[17] His sister told Heath that he had only been shot in the hand, and it had been 'a miraculous escape'.[18] MI5 concluded from evidence at the scene that the attack had been very easy to perpetrate.[19] Having read the latest JIC report about Black September with interest, Heath asked the obvious question: 'Why were greater precautions not taken to ensure the safety of the Jordanian ambassador?'[20] Intelligence officials thought he had been 'misled' by the reading of a previous JIC assessment on Black September. There had been no indication of an attack under preparation in the UK, and the attack had been planned and launched from Beirut. Frazeh Khelfa, the assailant, had arrived in Britain from France on 9 December, and left the country on a ferry from Folkestone four hours after the shooting. The ambassador had not thought he was a target, and so had not asked for protection. More embarrassing was the fact that the sub-machine gun was a British one recently sold to Libya.[21]

The horrific Black September attack on the Munich Olympics on 5 September 1972, followed by the disastrous failure of the German hostage-rescue attempt, further focused Heath's attention. In 1973, he suggested covertly posting members of the SAS on board the *Queen Elizabeth II* cruise liner after threats by Palestinian terrorists to attack it with planes as it carried 1,400 mainly Jewish passengers from Southampton to Israel.[22] Against this backdrop, Heath ordered a full-scale review of UK counter-terrorism, covering the military, the police and the security agencies. As part of this, he created a Cabinet Office official committee on counter-terrorism, and working groups that ordered joint exercises between the police, the military and MI5. The committee's brief was to create a cross-governmental strategy for dealing with terrorist incidents in the UK. Chaired by the Home Office, it included diplomats, the Ministry of Defence, MI5, the Department of Trade, and both the Metropolitan and Essex police forces, which respectively oversaw security at Heathrow and Stansted airports. The JIC pressed MI5 to conduct more counter-terrorism work, but there was little enthusiasm. Over half its effort remained devoted to counter-espionage while counter-subversion took up another third of its time.[23] Progress was slow, and even two years after the massacre at the Munich Olympics, only 3 per cent of MI5's time was devoted to international terrorism.[24]

Instead, the SAS took the lead. Shortly after Munich, the commanding officer of 22 SAS Regiment, Lieutenant Colonel Peter de la Billière, received an enquiry originating from Heath about the army's options for counter-terrorism. De la Billière and his adjutant had already proposed that 22 SAS Regiment create a specialist hostage-rescue unit codenamed 'Pagoda'. It was becoming clear that the reason the Black September gunmen at Munich were able to kill so many hostages was because the Bavarian police were untrained. Pagoda was linked to new terrorist-alert procedure exercises held in the Cabinet Briefing Room, or 'Cobra', which began in February 1973. Scenarios in which the new team would be called into action were given the codename 'Snowdrop'.[25]

The Angry Brigade may have been a curious coterie of disillusioned sociologists, and Palestinian attacks seemed like the reverberations of problems far away. But the work against international terror was gradually taking shape. By the early 1970s, MI6 had recruited at least one agent inside Black September. More remarkably, it had recruited one of its chief arms suppliers, a former SAS soldier turned gun-runner called Leslie Aspin. Codenamed 'Agent Kovacs', he supported Colonel Muammar Gaddafi's training school for Black September in north-west Libya. He also arranged for four arms shipments from Libya to the IRA in the early 1970s, and facilitated the transport of IRA terrorists to Libya for instruction. Nasty incidents that had hitherto taken place reassuringly far away began to connect with the more local and persistent problem emanating from Northern Ireland. By the early 1970s, the Irish too had begun attacking the UK mainland.[26]

Northern Ireland was Heath's biggest challenge. The failure of the Civil Rights movement to deliver adequate social change forced frustrated nationalists to turn to political violence. The dramatic upsurge in terrorism in the Six Counties between 1970 and 1972 caught Heath's government unawares. It peaked in 1972, when some 479 people died, mostly as the result of a wave of bombings. Crude security measures that had been blindly imported by the army from colonial counter-insurgencies in such far-flung places as Cyprus, Kenya and Malaya proved counter-productive.[27] A curfew imposed in the nationalist Lower Falls area of Belfast was but one example.

Heath sought a propaganda counter-attack against the IRA, particularly in the Catholic areas of Belfast and Derry's Bogside and Creggan districts.[28] In August 1972, he requested that Northern Ireland be 'flooded' with Whitehall staff 'experienced in psychological warfare'.[29] He was well aware that propagandists from the Foreign Office's Information Research Department were operating in the Province, and had been informed that senior officials such as Dick White and Norman Reddaway were devising means to place anti-IRA propaganda in the British press.[30] Trend also told Heath that MI6 and the Information Research Department were engaged in collecting material which could be used 'overtly and covertly, to blacken the IRA'.[31] Spurred on by the prime minister's enthusiasm, Heath's principal private secretary, Robert Armstrong, instructed that the 'counterattack should not be limited to the refutation of IRA allegations, but should also seek thoroughly to discredit both wings of the IRA. It requires an immediate, sustained, and continuing effort every day'.[32] This would involve 'using money freely' to gain information, win friends and influence people.[33] Such instructions look very much like a licence to bribe, handed down from the prime minister himself.

More dramatic was Heath's decision to opt for 'internment without trial'. Just weeks earlier, Trend had warned him to be 'wary' of adopting internment before it was absolutely necessary. Senior military advisers also warned of the dangers, and even Heath himself recognised that the move might have international implications, and draw the scrutiny of the United Nations. However, he felt he had little choice. For him, the only alternative was direct rule.[34] Unsurprisingly, internment was a disaster. Beginning on 9 August 1971, British troops rounded up scores of innocent Catholics. A propaganda victory for the IRA, it fuelled nationalist hostility towards the British for years to come. Heath later placed the blame on 'hopelessly out of date' intelligence. Indeed, the majority of those interned were not current republican activists, and many important figures had fled south.[35]

Heath also faced a new Irish organisation: the Provisional Irish Republican Army, or 'PIRA'. Created at the end of 1969, PIRA emerged from a split in the nationalist movement. It conducted over 1,300 bombings in two years, often targeting businesses and commercial premises. On 21 July 1972, no fewer than twenty-two bombs were detonated in Belfast city centre. Meanwhile, loyalist paramilitaries, such as the Ulster Volunteer Force and the Ulster Defence Association, accelerated their campaign of sectarian killings. Both Catholics and Protestants fled from mixed residential areas, as a result of either intimidation or well-founded anxieties. The security forces felt that they now confronted an emergency.

British interrogation methods were imported from the colonies. During the First World War, the British were famous for innovative questioning. Intelligence officers working in the Middle East, for example, would question prisoners on an 'electric carpet' – a large Persian rug with electrodes hidden underneath.[36] Reluctance to answer questions resulted in a series of shocks. If this did not work, they would suspend the hapless individual upside down and urinate into his nostrils. The effect was not dissimilar to modern waterboarding.[37]

By 1965, Britain could claim to have developed a more sophisticated interrogation doctrine. And with military interrogation teams providing assistance to internal security operations as far apart as Aden, British Guiana and Indonesia, a doctrine was certainly needed. It advocated high standards of behaviour on grounds of both morality and effectiveness. The JIC issued the guidelines in February 1965, and its tone was unambiguous: 'Apart from legal and moral considerations, torture and physical cruelty of all kinds are professionally unrewarding since a subject so treated may be persuaded to talk, but not to tell the truth.' Among the activities prohibited were 'cruel treatment and torture' together with 'humiliating and degrading treatment'. Commendably clear about achieving success through empathy, the JIC directive was referred to as 'the Interrogator's Bible'.[38]

Interrogators in Ireland paid little attention. Trying to capitalise on internment, the Royal Ulster Constabulary deployed an approach termed 'highly coercive interrogation', more commonly called 'interrogation in depth', against suspected PIRA members. This was usually applied by RUC interrogators working under the guidance of the Army Intelligence Corps. They made full use of five notorious techniques to wear down their subjects: wall-standing, hooding, subjection to noise, sleep deprivation, and deprivation of food and drink. Detainees would be subjected to a combination of these techniques over the course of about a week. It was a far cry from the 'kindness and cups of tea' doctrine set out in 'the Bible'.[39]

The introduction of internment was seen as a potential intelligence bonanza. It would, authorities hoped, lead to the detention of myriad IRA members who could then be softened up and questioned, generating a wealth of actionable information. And the security forces did manage to acquire some useful intelligence relating to safe houses and the IRA Order of Battle, while also uncovering an arms cache.[40] Most of those interned were innocent, and had been involved only in the earlier campaigns of the 1920s or 1950s. They had no information to offer. To make matters worse for the prime minister, rumours about the 'five techniques' used during 'deep interrogation' soon leaked, and were splashed across the front pages of Britain's newspapers.

The scandal forced Heath's government to order an inquiry into interrogation in the autumn of 1971. It suffered from serious weaknesses. Not only was Edmund Compton, the judge who led it, close to the unionists, but for security reasons he agreed to 'say nothing of the interrogation process itself'. This odd decision seemed to cut across the very remit of his inquiry.[41] A febrile atmosphere developed as the press continued to apply pressure. The *Sunday Times*, for example, highlighted the use of 'white noise', an interrogation technique which 'literally drove [people] out of their minds'. Emphasising the sinister connotations, journalists asserted that it was founded on 'Russian brain-washing techniques', refined for British use by an RAF wing commander who had later committed suicide.[42] Memories of the iconic 1965 film *The Ipcress File*, in which Michael Caine's character was subjected to mind-bending sound techniques, loomed prominently. The public felt that something nasty must be going on. Parliament also took a strong interest, with MPs referring to a 'noise torture machine'. Anxious civil servants began investigations, and insisted that the volume of sound to which prisoners were subjected was eighty-seven decibels, slightly less than that encountered in a tube train with its windows open. The noise was likened to an untuned radio or a railway engine letting off steam. There was no discussion of the effects of prolonged exposure, which often disturbed people greatly.[43]

When Compton delivered his report in November, the prime minister was furious. He had hoped for 'a clean bill of health' for the security forces, but instead Compton was critical of their behaviour. 'It seems to me one of the most unbalanced, ill-judged reports I have read,' Heath fumed. On the matter of interrogation, he bitterly lamented that Compton had gone to 'endless lengths to show that anyone not given 3-star hotel facilities suffered hardship and ill-treatment'. What troubled him most was that Compton had seemingly given media sources the same weight as official evidence.[44]

Publication of the report created a furore. This was not unexpected – as soon as the cabinet had seen the report, they had realised that there was likely to be a public outcry over deep interrogation. Republicans inevitably argued that it was a whitewash, while others maintained it proved that the RUC and the army were much too restrained. In the *Daily Express*, Chapman Pincher accused Compton of being 'rather squeamish'. Pincher insisted that 'This intelligence can't be obtained by just giving people cups of tea. The people have got to be frightened into giving information.'[45] To complicate matters further, many competing investigations swirled around interrogation techniques. In addition to Compton and press attention, Amnesty International ramped up the pressure, while the Irish government brought the detainees' cases to the European Court. Meanwhile, Members of Parliament constantly pressed for more details.

Heath had used Downing Street's intelligence machine in an attempt to pre-empt the furore. A fortnight before the report was published, the government decided to invite the intelligence coordinator, Dick White, to reassess methods of interrogation in Northern Ireland.[46] Somewhat anticipating this, a few weeks earlier Brian Stewart, an MI6 officer who was serving as secretary of the JIC, had visited the Province. Stewart, a fan of the five techniques, argued that limited hooding was genuinely necessary to prevent individuals from seeing and being seen, in the interests of both their own security and that of others, and claimed that limited wall-standing was necessary to secure discipline when in transit. For Stewart, 'white sound' at a non-offensive level was 'essential' to prevent prisoners overhearing or being overheard. However, he admitted that these techniques were also being used to wear people down.[47] When Dick White visited the Six Counties he took much the same line.[48] By December 1971, even White had realised that the main priority was 'to clarify our rules'. It was important 'to remove all possibilities of charges that we are engaged in "brain-washing" and "mind-bending"'.[49]

With Amnesty and the European Court conducting inquiries, Heath began to feel the heat. After talking to Harold Wilson, he felt he had little choice but to set up a new committee of three privy councillors under Lord Parker to press more deeply into interrogation methods.[50] Its report, which Heath felt lacked direction, did little to soothe the prime minister's anger. Alec Douglas-Home captured the cabinet's dilemma neatly. 'I find this insoluble,' he mused. 'Interrogation undoubtedly saves lives and on the evidence the interrogated does not suffer permanent harm. I will leave it to the lawyers at home.' This was an understatement. The lawyers were doing a roaring trade, and all eyes remained cast towards the impending cases in the European Court. Predictably, perhaps, with this alarming ball bouncing into their court, ministers decided to ban the five techniques outright.

In March 1972, Heath ordered the JIC to rewrite its directive on interrogation. Aware of the political importance, Trend asked its new secretary, Michael Herman, to accelerate the work.[51] In fact, the JIC was already at an advanced stage in rewriting 'the Bible'. The new rules were robust. Interrogation was now to be a matter for the civil authorities, and the participation of military personnel required ministerial permission. The new directive put strong emphasis on both international and domestic law. It stressed full compliance with the Geneva Convention, unequivocally asserting that it was 'of paramount importance' that interrogators 'should not act unlawfully in any circumstances'. It also forbade the five techniques, including the use of noise equipment.[52] Herman wisely advised Trend that, while the document was secret for now, at some unforeseen point in the future it might well have to be published, and so should be drafted with public inspection in mind.[53]

Privately, British officials remained divided. The general officer commanding Northern Ireland, General Frank King, wrote to the secretary of state for Northern Ireland lamenting the effects of the new restrictions – he was 'increasingly disturbed by the lack of intelligence forthcoming from the questioning of many terrorists that we have arrested'. The new regulations, he continued, made no sense 'in current insurgency conditions'.[54] But with cases making their way to the European Court in Strasbourg, British diplomats were taking a 'low profile defensive approach' as they confronted the attendant publicity. J.B. Donnelly of the Ireland Department predicted that the court settlements would have propaganda value for the IRA, and would also be used widely by human rights bodies in international organisations. 'These cases constitute a skeleton in our cupboard,' he added, and unfortunately 'the cupboard door is likely to be opened at regular intervals over the coming months as more of these cases are settled'.[55]

Heath had been robust on intelligence in Northern Ireland. One hundred and nine soldiers were killed in Ireland in 1972, along with twenty members of the Ulster Defence Regiment. This was more people than were killed in any one year during the recent fighting in Iraq or Afghanistan. Although he outlawed the notorious five techniques, under Heath the army developed a whole new intelligence and covert action arm that undertook dangerous operations, derived from its experience in Kenya. The full story of this lethal battle is only just emerging. Heath's gains against the IRA came at the cost of alienating the nationalist community.[56] The Troubles would last another generation.

For MI5, Soviet counter-espionage still formed the greatest threat. The service's leaders had long sought to act against the large numbers of Soviet spies based in London under official cover. But under Wilson, both Downing Street and the Foreign Office had feared that this would upset détente, and repeatedly shied away from action.[57] In 1968, after a number of provocations, including the recruitment of the British ambassador in Moscow by an attractive female house servant working for the KGB, Whitehall did place a limit on staff at the Soviet embassy in London. As we have seen, Moscow easily evaded this by expanding its trade mission. With impending recognition of East Germany and the likely influx of yet more Eastern bloc diplomats with new embassies, things were going from bad to worse.[58]

The arrival of Heath in Downing Street represented an opportunity for the intelligence community. Less interested in détente than Wilson, he was not afraid to upset the Russians, and later lambasted the vast programme of KGB activities for being 'as blatant as it was widespread', and constituting a 'real threat to our national security'.[59] Fortunately for Heath, an operation run by the experimental joint MI5/MI6 'London Station' had acquired an inside man. This was Oleg Lyalin, a KGB officer charged with planning special operations designed to spread turmoil in Britain on the outbreak of war. These included attacks on the early-warning facility at Fylingdales in Yorkshire, plans to use bombs to flood the London tube network, and, most drastically, the distribution of poison-gas capsules in the tunnels beneath Whitehall. Under cover as a Midlands-based textile buyer, Lyalin was one of many spies attached to the trade mission.[60]

Tony Brooks of MI6 and Harry Wharton of MI5 confronted Lyalin with compromising evidence that he had been conducting an illicit affair with his secretary, and persuaded him to become a British agent in return for eventual resettlement for himself and his girlfriend.[61] Codenamed 'Goldfinch', Lyalin was extensively debriefed; his information eventually ran to five volumes of material, crucially including a complete list of the Soviet intelligence officers based in London.[62]

But Lyalin's tempestuous love life made him a hard agent to run. By the late spring of 1971, he had embarked upon another affair, this time with a married Englishwoman. Predictably, relations with his wife were volatile, and he was reproved by his KGB managers in London. A snappy dresser with sharp suits and sideburns that would not have disgraced a pop star, Lyalin hardly fitted the image of a Soviet trade official buying woollen cloth and knitwear. He wanted MI5 to arrange for him to be expelled and sent back to Moscow, where his private life would stabilise and he could act as an agent for the British. But MI5 knew that if this happened he would soon be uncovered, and killed. Instead, to restore the reputation of the well-groomed lothario, they arranged for him to recruit an 'agent' in the Ministry of Defence, and deliberately supplied him with classified material so as to improve his standing with Moscow.[63]

The information supplied by Lyalin was alarming. On 25 May, Martin Furnival Jones, director-general of MI5, and John Rennie, chief of MI6, arrived at the Foreign Office for a meeting with Sir Denis Greenhill, its senior official. Furnival Jones reported that Soviet spies had penetrated the Foreign Office, the Ministry of Defence, the army, navy and air force, the Labour Party and the Board of Trade. They were also swamping MI5's 'watchers' who tried to track them. With 189 people in the embassy, 144 in the trade delegation and on contract work, and 134 working for the TASS news agency and Aeroflot, together with what the Soviets called 'working wives', there were almost a thousand Russians milling around London, of whom MI5 thought a quarter were involved in some kind of subterranean activity. This was an absurd number, far above that for any other European capital. Rennie added that scientific and industrial secrets formed a major target, with potentially serious costs to Western defence. On 30 July, Alec Douglas-Home joined with the home secretary to press for action.[64]

Heath recalls that this began with polite but firm requests to cut down on espionage which were relayed to the Soviet foreign minister Andrei Gromyko when he visited Britain. Their guest replied with an impressively straight face, 'The Soviet Union does not have spies.'[65] Undeterred, Douglas-Home then wrote to Gromyko over the summer of 1971, hoping to achieve a quiet withdrawal of at least some KGB officers. On 4 August, he sent a final warning. Gromyko did not reply – the ultimate insult to a gentleman like Douglas-Home.[66] In reality, Gromyko probably lacked either the power or the personality to curb the KGB, which was now run by the powerful Yuri Andropov. Burke Trend captured Gromyko perfectly. He was, according to the cabinet secretary, 'one of nature's henchmen', and 'temperamentally afraid' of taking responsibility.[67] A confrontation was now inevitable – but the timing was determined by chance.

On 30 August Oleg Lyalin was arrested for driving drunk down the Tottenham Court Road. He asserted his diplomatic immunity to the police by dramatically protesting, 'I am a KGB officer.' In police custody, and knowing that he would now be sent back to Moscow immediately, Lyalin decided to defect. He contacted his MI5 handlers, who sent a support team equipped with antitoxins in case the Russians tried to poison him. He was resettled with his girlfriend, but the Russians were looking for him. More importantly, Britain had lost its key agent inside the KGB. On the very day that Lyalin was arrested, a Royal Navy officer, David Bingham, confessed to passing secrets to the Russians, underlining the constant threat of the large community of Russian spies.[68]

On 21 September, Heath assembled a group of trusted senior ministers and officials inside Number 10 to take a final decision. It is perhaps surprising that on a matter which relied so heavily on secret intelligence, and which was actually *about* secret intelligence, there were no represent-atives from the intelligence services present. Although KGB spies were not a priority for him, the prime minister was well aware of the stakes. The move risked a possible complete cessation of Anglo–Soviet relations, as had happened in 1927 at the time of the 'Arcos' raid. But he also under-stood the security and political implications of the swarm of Soviet spies on British shores. He hoped to restore the reputation of British intelli-gence, and privately grumbled about Wilson's perceived unwillingness to tackle the issue.

Next to Heath, the most important person at the table was Douglas-Home, an experienced and tough elder statesman with long experience of dealing with Moscow. Heath was cautious, and sought reassurance from his colleague. Douglas-Home explained that they had already tried a quiet approach, pressing the Soviets to remove their spies discreetly. But the Soviets had only responded by expelling two Britons. Reginald Maudling, the home secretary, was also in favour of expulsions, and worried that the government would be criticised for having allowed so many Soviet spies to roam the streets of London for so long. The only dissenting voice was that of John Davies, minister for trade and industry, who was anxious about the loss of exports. Heath decided on sudden and public expulsion.[69]

The prime minister remained nervous the following day, and asked Douglas-Home to reassure him that 'our case is fully prepared to defend the steps we are taking against those who will criticise them on political grounds'. He wanted to know that Britain could 'show that there was no satisfactory alternative way of handling the situation'. About to fly off to the United Nations, the foreign secretary assured him that he was 'completely satisfied'.[70] The final decision, according to Heath's biographer, was the prime minister's 'personal ruling'. He then had to reassure cabinet as to why they had not been consulted in advance.[71]

With the prime minister's personal backing, Denis Greenhill summoned Ivan Ippolitov, the Soviet chargé d'affaires, to the Foreign Office, and handed over a list of expellees that went on for several pages. Ninety people were expelled, and a further fifteen who were presently out of the country were debarred from returning. Ippolitov was clearly shocked, but replied in a husky voice, 'All is clear. Very drastic measures, Sir Greenhill, very drastic!' Perhaps he allowed himself an ironic smile, given that he himself was a KGB officer running under diplomatic cover, and was not on the list. The Foreign Office had already briefed the newspapers with some choice morsels about Lyalin to justify its actions, so even as Ippolitov was being chauffeured back through the London streets towards the Soviet embassy, the billboards for the *Evening Standard* already announced 'KGB OUT!'[72] The British government released a remarkable amount of detail to the press after Lyalin's defection, and worked with a BBC director, Graham Carr, to produce an hour-long documentary which included MI5 footage of KGB agents collecting intelligence from a dead-drop in a London park. 'Public opinion in this country,' Heath proudly told the cabinet, 'has in general shown a ready understanding of the Government's action.'[73]

For the next fourteen years, the KGB 'found it more difficult to collect high-grade intelligence in London than in any other Western capital'.[74] The reverberations of 'Operation Foot' went wider still. The Soviet leader Leonid Brezhnev abandoned a tour of Eastern Europe to return to Moscow for an emergency meeting, and the Soviets withdrew most of the sabotage officers from Lyalin's department across Europe, on the assumption that they had all been compromised. No attempt was made to resume their work. The KGB explained the disaster in terms of Lyalin's prodigious seduction of other officials' wives. Most remarkably, Yuri Voronin, the previous head of the KGB in London, was identified as the main culprit in the cover-up of Lyalin's romantic activities. A rising star as head of the Third Department of foreign intelligence, he was nevertheless dismissed from the service and retired in disgrace.[75]

MI5 hosted a marvellous party to celebrate. The organisation was a rather bibulous place in the 1970s, and officers now opened a vast safe to reveal an impressive range of alcohol hidden inside.[76] Heath took equal pride in Operation Foot. It had proved a brave decision. To him, it was 'the most important security action ever taken by any Western government. Moreover, it completely destroyed the large Soviet intelligence network which had previously been conducted from London.'[77] The British had won the counter-espionage war against the KGB perhaps more decisively than anyone understood at the time. Although Heath happily celebrated an important victory over the Soviets, his real concern came from industrial subversion. In contrast to his action against the USSR, this soon brought him into conflict with MI5.

Heath increasingly fretted over secrecy and subversion. He had not enjoyed amiable relations with Martin Furnival Jones. Rank-and-file staff at MI5 considered the director-general rather aloof. His limited contacts with Heath did not make a favourable impression, and almost uniquely for a prime minister, Heath went out of his way to underline his disdain for Furnival Jones in his memoirs. According to Heath, he was 'unconvincing', and unaware of the best way to spend the prime minister's time.[78] This discord was partly about personality, but also about policy, indeed even principle. From the outset, Heath pressed both Burke Trend and MI5 for stronger action on what he saw as industrial subversion. Confronted with a dock strike at the beginning of his administration, to which the government capitulated quickly, he demanded that MI5 provide more advanced warning of such events. MI5 replied that this was impossible.

The prime minister did enjoy some successes. He approved a warrant for the monitoring of Jack Jones, leader of the Transport and General Workers' Union, including postal and telephone interception. This was done against the advice of Maudling, and after much argument MI5 eventually justified it on the grounds that it could lead to evidence of Russian influence in the union. It added that in any case, the operation would produce general intelligence 'of great value in particular to the Department of Employment and to the Government generally in the field of industrial disputes'. Civil servants shifted uncomfortably, as Heath's persistent requests seemed political, representing awkward territory for the secret service.[79]

In December 1970, Heath's government had published a controversial Industrial Relations Bill designed to force unions to hold proper ballots before calling strike action. A week later, the power stations began a work-to-rule. Perceiving this as a left-wing conspiracy to take over the country by undemocratic means, Heath deemed it 'subversion', and personally demanded that MI5 place an electronic listening device in the room in which the unions were holding a key meeting to direct the dispute. Again, MI5 felt uneasy. Its deputy director, Anthony Simkins, feared that 'an eavesdropping attack against this target would take us right outside the field in which the security service had operated throughout my twenty-five years with it'. There followed an anxious debate about whether Heath's request was for partisan intelligence supporting a political party against a trade union genuinely seeking to improve wages for its members, or legitimate security intelligence to resist an attempt by militants seeking to undermine democracy, possibly even supported by an external power. No one knew the answer. In the event, and against Heath's wishes, Burke Trend made sure the bugging of the union meeting did not go ahead.[80]

In January 1972, a major strike by the National Union of Mineworkers took Heath by surprise. The use of flying pickets, advocated by Arthur Scargill, the youngest member of the NUM executive, proved an effective tactic and presented the government with the prospect of national chaos, including the breakdown of communications, food, power and sewerage, and perhaps even law and order. The government soon surrendered. MI5 monitored the links between the miners and the Communist Party of Great Britain, whose headquarters it had bugged, but insisted that they were limited. By contrast, Heath was convinced that the strike was evidence of subversion, and demanded a major review of intelligence. MI5's response disappointed him and his cabinet, as it focused narrowly on the CPGB, and stated that the communists had influence but not control. It ignored the 'New Left', which was much more amorphous. Trend told MI5 that Heath believed the current unrest was the work of 'a number of evil minded men particularly in the unions', and that some of them must be 'done'. He attempted to restrain the prime minister, but in this heated atmosphere his only supporter in the cabinet was Reginald Maudling.[81]

Amazingly, we now know that Joe Gormley, president of the NUM, agreed with Heath. The moderates in the miners' union were so anxious about the determination of extremists to implement industrial sabotage that some actually began to spy for the government. Gormley himself was a Special Branch informant during the 1970s, and passed on details of Arthur Scargill's and other miners' plans for industrial action. Despite this remarkable stream of intelligence, the government failed to head off the 1972 strike. Scargill, who later replaced Gormley, took deliberate steps to avoid surveillance, and remarked that the union movement was 'littered with people in leadership positions who were either connected with Special Branch or connected with the State'.[82]

Heath, his government and top industrialists were terrified of the militants. According to Special Branch officers, the Ford motor company only agreed to build a new car-manufacturing plant on Merseyside because of the promised support of MI5 and Special Branch. Tony Robinson, a former Special Branch officer, asserts that job applicants – and indeed the entire workforce – were routinely vetted and 'kept clean of subversives'.[83] The majority of large corporations worked either with Special Branch or with private security companies, which performed much the same task.[84] The historical reluctance of MI5 to step into the fray of industrial strife had left a vacuum which was increasingly filled by privateers, including the 'Economic League', a long-standing group of anti-communist enthusiasts which was now expanded rapidly. During 1972, its big backers, including British-American Tobacco, Shell and Imperial Tobacco, all increased their contributions substantially at the urging of its leader Sir David Barran. The company secretary of British-American Tobacco explained: 'The League does very good work in disseminating information about economic and industrial problems and in combating extreme left-wing propaganda.'[85] Various groups of privateers had more freedom of action than MI5 and went from strength to strength, emerging as an entirely separate intelligence entity under Margaret Thatcher during the 1980s.

The summer of 1972 saw a changing of the guard at MI5. Furnival Jones was retiring. Reginald Maudling and the civil servants had wanted him replaced by an official from the Home Office rather than a serving MI5 officer. When he found out, Furnival Jones was appalled. He knew that the last time this had happened it had been 'pretty disastrous'. Victor Rothschild also warned Heath that appointing an outside candidate would destroy morale. To Furnival Jones's relief, Heath met the outside candidate, but found him too cautious. Instead, he plumped for MI5's own candidate, the then deputy director Michael Hanley, a burly man of action. Hanley recalled, 'I hit it off with him, I always did.'[86] Shortly afterwards, Heath removed the mild-mannered Reginald Maudling from his post as home secretary and replaced him with the tougher Robert Carr, promoted from Employment. Carr had been at the forefront of the battle with the unions and had a personal history of confrontation with the Angry Brigade, which had tried to bomb him. Heath clearly wanted a tough new approach from MI5.

The appointment of Hanley was symbolic of a wider change. The intelligence community was gradually shifting its focus from counter-espionage to counter-subversion and counter-terrorism. Hanley rather welcomed Heath's obsession with subversion, since it allowed him to concentrate more on home-grown domestic targets, especially the extreme left. Meanwhile, there was the enormous challenge of Irish terrorism, and further violent incidents in London related to the Middle East conflict.[87] When Hanley was appointed in 1972, MI5's morale was low. But the new director-general addressed these new targets, raised MI5's profile and met regularly with the home secretary, something his predecessors had not done.[88]

Action was now taken. In the summer of 1972, a new committee was established under the Home Office to assess the whole internal security situation in the UK. Hanley intended to create something like the JIC, but for internal security. He loathed the JIC, which he regarded as a creature of the diplomats that was 'packed by the FCO' and had 'bugger all' to offer on the domestic scene. Burke Trend knew that he had lost the battle with Heath over anti-subversion, and at the group's first meeting on 31 July 1972 he explained that the prime minister wanted more to be done to expose the 'hidden hand' of the communists. MI5, he reported, had to take a closer interest in industrial unrest. This included technical surveillance of the leaders in the ongoing dock dispute. Later in the year, Heath wanted the whole charter on which MI5 activity was based to be revisited, and its mandate expanded to address what he saw as leftist conspiracies.[89]

During early 1973, Heath put renewed pressure on MI5 to reveal intelligence about subversives to industry. Tim Powell, the head of the tractor manufacturers Massey Ferguson, complained of having no way of knowing if he was recruiting 'troublemakers', and requested a list of people to 'watch out for'. Instead of automatically referring Powell to the Economic League, this time Heath sanctioned an oral briefing by security officials. In doing so, he overruled the cabinet secretary's objections that the government could be accused of interfering with the employment field.[90]

Heath knew he was playing with fire. In the United States, Richard Nixon was being publicly crucified precisely because of revelations about bugging his political opponents. On Friday, 17 August, with Parliament in recess, Heath had a quiet lunch with Trend to discuss 'the present attempts to create a Watergate atmosphere in this country'. A few days later they spoke again, and the focus was on what Heath called 'our industrial intelligence and the methods used by those responsible for it'. He tasked Trend to review current operations and their dangers. Trend discussed the matter with Michael Hanley, officials in the Home Office and also, conscious that he was a month from retirement, his successor John Hunt.[91]

Trend offered Heath reassurance. He thought the number of warrants was relatively small, and that they were solidly justified by 'genuine subver-

sive risk' rather than 'a risk of purely industrial trouble'. Heath was also
promised that 'the operations involved are carried out with very great care',
suggesting that in some cases they involved physical intrusion rather than
just telephone intercepts and mail opening. Trend felt that it was safe to
leave things as they were 'without running into too much danger'. But he
was also aware that Heath was heading towards another confrontation
with the National Union of Mineworkers, and as a result the subject would
become 'increasingly sensitive', and 'Any exposure of our activities would
be proportionately damaging.' He advised Heath to have a personal chat
with Hanley to ensure that projected activities in the future would be
'neither too few for usefulness nor too many for safety'.[92]

A month later, Heath and his inner circle were asking Hanley if MI5
could provide forewarning of strikes. But the Industrial Assessments
Group, or IAG, which was the main potential source of such warnings, was
wary, pointing out that even 'covert sources' could contribute only slightly
to these sort of general assessments. Even union leaders themselves did
not know what would happen a week ahead, since the 'situation is so fast
moving' and one event interacted with another in ways that no one could
predict. The IAG feared 'getting into the realm of pure speculation'.
Nevertheless, it agreed to make an effort to open its weekly reports to
Heath with 'a general assessment of the immediate future across the industrial front'.[93]

Heath paid close attention to the IAG's weekly reports. On 17 December
1973, with another miners' strike looming, he abandoned the caution he
had displayed over the summer. Wanting to use the IAG intelligence to
attack the miners, he asked if information contained in particular paragraphs 'could in some way be got out in public'.[94] Hunt reminded him that
Sir Patrick Dean, who when at the Foreign Office back in the 1950s had
been closely involved in intelligence, presided over a small interdepartmental group of officials that met in the Home Office to monitor subversive activity, and pointed out that this group already had a remit to counter
subversion that included publicity and 'exposure'.

Hunt and Heath's principal private secretary Robert Armstrong went
along to investigate 'how far the methods' might be applied to the impending miners' strike. Hunt pointed out that the close relationship between
the NUM and the CPGB was already a matter of public record, and that
the problem was that 'the public quickly forgets these points'. Most of what
Heath wanted to get out into the public domain could be released 'without
reliance on covert sources'. Hunt knew he was on delicate ground here,

advising Heath against setting up 'a mini-ministry of information' or involving civil servants in 'party political activity'. But equally he felt that where there was open evidence that militants were trying to 'destroy the democratic system', then action had to be taken. Both he and Dean recommended a 'small operational team', including some members of the secret services, which could react quickly and get material out into the media.[95]

As an increasingly angry Heath entered his last fraught months in office, he actually wanted to use the intelligence material himself. On 8 January 1974, as Britain began a three-day working week, he prepared to give a speech on 'subversion' using material that had been agreed with officials in MI5 and the Department of Employment. Hunt was confident that no covert sources would be betrayed, but cautioned, 'Whether it is wise to use it in this particular debate is a matter of political judgement.'[96]

Heath now believed that he was fighting a conspiracy, and to some extent he was. By this point a more aggressive MI5 was closely monitoring Mick McGahey, the communist leader of the Scottish miners, and Arthur Scargill. They found increasing evidence that some of the NUM executive were coordinating strategy with Bert Ramelson, the highly effective industrial organiser of the British Communists, with a wider aim of overthrowing the government. In early 1974, armed with this new stream of intelligence, Heath decided to go to the country on the issue of 'Who governs Britain?'[97] To his surprise he lost the 28 February election, and handed over to Harold Wilson. With MI5 taking an increased role in counter-subversion, further intelligence storms were brewing. Engulfed in an astonishingly febrile climate, in plots and paranoia, Wilson would soon be asked the same question: Who governs Britain? Unlike Heath, his answer lay closer to the establishment.

13

Harold Wilson
(1974–1976)

If a policeman is firm or polite he may well look forward to
promotion. If he is both, he will apply to join the Special
Branch. And if neither he will join the Security Service.
HAROLD WILSON[1]

Most prime ministers reveal little about intelligence matters. When in
office and even in retirement, the secret world remains just that: secret.
Harold Wilson was not like most prime ministers. Shortly after his
surprise resignation in March 1976 the ailing Yorkshireman summoned
two rookie reporters to his home and handed them what could have been
the scoop of their lives. A remarkable story of international intrigue, plotting, subversion and attempted coups, it might have been the British
Watergate.

Famously, Wilson offered his narrative in fantastical terms. 'I see myself
as the big fat spider in the corner of the room,' the recently retired prime
minister gabbled. 'Sometimes I speak when I'm asleep. You should both
listen. Occasionally when we meet, I might tell you to go to the Charing
Cross Road and kick a blind man standing on the corner. That blind man
may tell you something, lead you somewhere.'[2] Obsessed with the ways
and whisperings of the secret world, Wilson left office convinced of a
conspiracy against him; a conspiracy involving not only British intelligence but the CIA and the South African secret service too.

The 'spider' episode has been revisited countless times, and to a precise
purpose. Harold Wilson has routinely been portrayed as paranoid – even
mad. In retrospect, Wilson, a highly intelligent man, was simply asking the
right questions. Every day, remarkable revelations from the post-Watergate inquiries were spilling out of the United States. During the 1975
Labour Party annual conference at Blackpool, one minister noted that the

FBI had just admitted to 250 domestic burglaries, while the CIA was revealed as funding West European socialist parties. Washington also learned that while he was in the White House, President Nixon had apparently arranged to have 'the most salacious bugging reports gathered by the FBI and the CIA put before him every night to read in bed'.[3] Quite naturally, Labour ministers wondered what on earth was going on in Britain.

In fact, it was the British intelligence services, rather than the prime minister, that were in the grip of real paranoia. A group of counter-intelligence officers were still harbouring an 'obsession' with moles, an obsession which some of their MI5 colleagues regarded, in their own words, as 'quite mad and certainly dangerous'. Ironically, by the 1970s the mole-hunters were causing almost as much trouble as the real Soviet moles of the previous decades. To a degree, Wilson and his colleagues were subverted by this climate of continued suspicion.[4]

Harold Wilson squeezed back into Downing Street in March 1974 at the head of a minority government. The subsequent October election saw him gain a majority of just three. This, together with a continuous flow of stories about Watergate, lent the entire political landscape a sense of febrile unease. But Wilson's relationship with intelligence has been misunderstood. Often represented as one of fear and loathing, in fact, the prime minister had a complex 'love–hate' relationship with the secret world, and was even to some extent part of it. MI5 judged its relations with the returning prime minister as 'perfectly friendly'.[5] In return, Wilson did not entirely trust it, but nevertheless used intelligence extensively, not least against the unions.[6] Overall, his relationship with serving intelligence officers was far more warm and positive than is commonly acknowledged.

Wilson also loved secret channels of communication, and shamelessly played the socialist card to engage with revolutionary groups. During his first administration, as we have seen, he bypassed the Americans to seek his own peaceful resolution of the Vietnam conflict. As leader of the opposition, he even established secret communications with the IRA. It was an unorthodox move, but with Edward Heath's consent Wilson appeared a suitable candidate for such a role. Heath had refused to allow his government to talk to the IRA directly, while Wilson had publicly backed a united Ireland, thereby perhaps giving him greater traction with the rebels.[7] In March 1972, Wilson quietly travelled to an anonymous house on Dublin's Phoenix Park estate. Inside, he met three Provisional IRA leaders – but refused to shake hands. These were Dáithí Ó'Connaill, a leading political strategist on the IRA's Army Council; Joe Cahill, the IRA's Belfast commander; and John Kelly, serving on the IRA's General Headquarters Staff.[8] It was an unprecedented meeting, the first time the IRA had ever met with British politicians.

Wilson sat across from the IRA men and puffed on his pipe. Smoke filled the room, adding a thick layer to an atmosphere already dense with intrigue. He probed IRA intentions about a potential bombing campaign on the mainland, but received no more than a noncommittal reply. Sitting back in his chair, he changed tack and unsuccessfully tried to persuade the rebel leaders that their violence was not going to work. After another puff on his pipe, Wilson sounded them out on their trust of Northern Ireland's existing nationalist politicians. This was unwise. The senior Provos had no intention of being patronised or working through nationalist middlemen. Little progress had been made by the time the clock struck midnight. 'Well that's it then,' Wilson said with an air of resignation. 'Off we go.' A seventy-two-hour ceasefire ended just an hour later.[9]

To his credit, Wilson did not give up. A few months later he secretly met a small group of second-tier IRA leaders at his Buckinghamshire cottage close to Chequers.[10] This meeting made as little progress as the first, and was dominated by a verbose Irish lecture on British oppression dating back to 1610.[11] But Wilson sought to hear the authentic voice of the opposition, and like Churchill, wanted intelligence in its rawest and most immediate form. This played to the sense of self-belief that all premiers must have to some extent; as someone who could make deals and even shape history. Wilson was thoroughly enjoying his role as secret interlocutor, a mac-wearing international man of mystery.

In November 1974, having returned to Downing Street with a small majority, Wilson approved the opening of a permanent secret back channel between MI6 and the Provos – the first direct, if informal, meeting since Wilson's own private forays.[12] The back channel connected Michael Oatley, a subtle and independent-minded MI6 officer, with leading republican Ruairí Ó'Brádaigh, a man mockingly nicknamed 'Rory O'Bloodbath' by *Private Eye*.[13] The real hero was 'the contact' linking these two men – two men who wanted very different things, and who shared only a need to operate covertly. This was Brendan Duddy, a brave and selfless Derry businessman who knew he could easily be killed for his commitment to the peace process. He was a nationalist, but also a pacifist and keen on dialogue. The back channel proved fruitful: Duddy went on to act as a go-between during the 1981 hunger strikes, and as we shall see, became a key player in the peace process during the 1990s.

Like Heath before him, Wilson insisted that the dialogue remain clandestine. Britain simply could not be seen talking to terrorists. In fact, he treated the negotiations with such secrecy that he kept all of his cabinet colleagues, except for Merlyn Rees, the secretary of state for Northern Ireland, ignorant of them – and even Rees was initially kept in the dark about Duddy's identity.[14] Michael Oatley informed Frank Cooper, the senior British official at the Northern Ireland Office, about 'the contact'. Cooper then consulted with John Hunt, the cabinet secretary, and Wilson. Everything was held within this small, tight circle.[15] The back channel allowed intelligence about IRA attitudes to ceasefires and other political intentions to be carried directly to the prime minister.[16]

Wilson took a personal interest in IRA intelligence. Bypassing the home secretary, Roy Jenkins, he periodically summoned Michael Hanley, the MI5 director-general, to Number 10 on a Thursday morning for detailed briefings on the IRA during the 1975 ceasefire.[17] In theory, MI5 was responsible to the home secretary, but Wilson liked being centre stage. Towards the end of the year, he even played at being a DIY intelligence analyst. Displaying a Churchillian passion for raw material, the prime minister requested a personal copy of a 'death list' found inside an IRA safe house. Targets ranged from the Queen's art gallery to Madame Tussauds, from the Post Office Tower to the London Stock Exchange. Individuals marked for death included MPs, lords, police officers and military personnel. Although the Home Office agreed to Wilson's request, officials worried about the prime minister's excitable and obsessive streak, politely reminding him not to get carried away. 'The list,' one wrote, 'is not a "death list", and it would be wrong to talk of it as such.' Nonetheless, Wilson, like his wartime predecessor, could not resist getting involved, and liked to be close to the action. He scribbled his own personal assessment on the top: 'Obviously this is scrappy', and 'some of it seems to be out of date'. He then enjoyed playing the forensic analyst, and made some suggestions to the investigating intelligence officers about the named targets: 'No doubt they will check to see how many are [already] dead or changed jobs or address – as a guide to age each piece of paper.'[18]

Wilson was not unique in his prime ministerial love of intelligence. However, he was unusual in his anxiety about communications security and the threat of bugging. Again, this has sometimes been misrepresented as paranoia. In fact, he knew that even some of the most secret discussions about Ireland, when held in Downing Street, had leaked. For example, during a brainstorming meeting about the Troubles, Wilson briefly toyed with the idea of reunification with the South. Within hours, Dublin rang Downing Street quite unbidden to say privately and firmly that it did not want any part of the North and its problems, under any circumstances. Wilson was shaken.[19] On hearing about the capture of another important Provo document, he summoned Joe Hooper, the intelligence coordinator and a former director of GCHQ, to a meeting at Chequers. The prime minister feared that Downing Street was both leaky and bugged, and so insisted on using the Buckinghamshire retreat as a safer alternative. Hooper rang the doorbell, and to his surprise the eager prime minister answered the door himself. Wilson promptly sat him down and began enquiring about the new intelligence.[20]

Harold Wilson was also a fan of covert action. He was unafraid of using unorthodox measures and secret organisations to get a job done. For example, he continued Edward Heath's policy of covert British involvement in Oman, where the sultan had been waging a counter-insurgency campaign to quell a regional uprising since the late 1960s. Despite claiming publicly that no British personnel were actively involved, Wilson sanctioned secret, but deniable, SAS participation. Until at least January 1975, he approved daring cross-border raids into Yemen by tribesmen who had been secretly trained by the SAS. Only the prime minister, the foreign secretary and the defence secretary knew the truth about the extent of SAS involvement.[21] In this sense, Wilson deliberately continued a secret war instigated by a Conservative predecessor – just as he had done in Yemen and Indonesia after entering Downing Street for the first time in 1964.

Wilson's use of the SAS extended to Northern Ireland. This time the prime minister broke with tradition. Rising to his feet at the despatch box, he publicly declared SAS involvement in the conflict. At Heath's request, the SAS had developed an anti-terrorism function, in the form of a counter-revolutionary-warfare unit, in the aftermath of the Munich Olympics terror attack. The new function, however, was kept quiet. Yet, by the summer of 1975, Ministry of Defence officials pressed Wilson to publicly acknowledge SAS capabilities in this growing field. Silence was counter-productive. They argued that 'In our view there is little to be gained from refusing to admit SAS involvement in anti-terrorist operations and there might be advantages in adopting a more open policy.' The military worried that 'to persist in our present refusal to come into the open could easily create the impression that there is something sinister about SAS involvement'.[22] This was certainly a valid concern, given the swirling rumours around nefarious SAS activity and perceptions of the regiment as some sort of covert hit squad. Wilson agreed that acknowledging SAS operations on UK soil might have a useful deterrence value, and in any case he relished sounding tough.[23]

This new approach was triggered by atrocity. In the late afternoon of 5 January 1976, a man in British Army uniform flashed a torch to pull over a red minibus carrying textile workers back from work in Armagh. He was soon joined by gunmen with blackened faces who had been hiding in the hedges. They weeded out the one Catholic among the passengers, lined up the Protestants, and shot them at close range. Ten people died. With violence escalating, unionist leaders called for firm government action. In an unprecedented move, Wilson informed Parliament that 'troops of the Special Air Service' would be sent to County Armagh. 'They will be used for patrolling and surveillance, tasks for which they are particularly suited and trained.' 'They will operate,' Wilson continued, 'wherever they are required throughout the country.'[24] Although Wilson had informed the Chief of the General Staff and the General Officer Commanding of his intentions the previous day,[25] the decision may have taken the SAS itself by surprise. The regiment had lobbied for roles in Oman, Aden and Borneo, but the deployment to Ireland was apparently 'imposed by the prime minister without warning and without reference to the Ministry of Defence'.[26]

Wilson's announcement proved something of a double-edged sword. It certainly had political benefits, insofar as public knowledge reassured the Ulster Protestant community about London's commitment to countering violence. It also risked sensationalising the SAS's fairly routine intelligence role, and raised questions about what else these trained killers might be getting up to.[27] Wilson claimed that the House knew full well that the SAS would be undercover.[28] This was probably the case, but the regiment's covert nature bred rumours of underhand activity. Gerry Fitt, leader of the Social Democratic and Labour Party and MP for Belfast West, challenged Wilson in Parliament: 'Is the Prime Minister aware that there is a good deal of suspicion – some people would say mythology – about the SAS Regiment?' Fitt accordingly called for the SAS to operate under strict military discipline.[29] Unsurprisingly, Wilson responded by reassuring the House that there had been 'some misunderstanding about its role, its nature, its training, its purpose in life, and all the rest of it'. Of course the

SAS were not bogeymen, and they would be 'employed and deployed solely under the control of the GOC as soldiers aiding the other soldiers in dealing with all the problems of terrorism in the area'.[30]

Oddly, the prime minister chose the CIA as his point of reference. Despite not being asked about the Americans, he declared that 'I see nothing at all comparable between the SAS and the CIA. In as much as I understand what the CIA does – and I find it more difficult every day – I think its official role in most cases is the collection of overseas intelligence. This is not, may I say, the basis of the SAS'.[31] While correct, this was a slightly odd comment, given that Wilson had just stressed the SAS's surveillance role. More importantly, it underlines how all discussion of intelligence activities was framed by the stream of sensational revelations about the CIA emanating from the post-Watergate inquiries on Capitol Hill. Here Wilson was caught by his own ambiguities, since he wanted the deployment of the SAS to look like tough action. A few days later, he was 'very agitated' when the *Daily Express* revealed that only twenty SAS men were actually being sent to Ireland, despite all the publicity about his 'big special measure'.[32]

Like so many prime ministers discussing intelligence matters at the despatch box, Wilson's parliamentary performance contained a range of half-truths. The SAS had in fact already been deployed to Northern Ireland. The regiment was first sent there in 1969, at the outbreak of the Troubles, and again in 1974 – both times on Wilson's watch. His 1976 announcement was therefore very much a political act.[33] Moreover, despite his emphasis on its surveillance role, the SAS did bring 'mature, aggressive soldiers who were quite prepared to use weapons' into the conflict.[34] They went on to be more active than Wilson had implied in his announcement, and to serve in even more covert units.

In private, Wilson was unafraid of calling for the ultimate sanction: assassination. In 1974, the returning prime minister sat alone in his Downing Street study brooding on the ongoing bloodshed in Uganda at the hands of brutal dictator Idi Amin. He asked Joe Haines, his press secretary, to come upstairs and join him. Haines recalls that Wilson was 'so shocked by the mass slaughter – thousands every week – taking place in Uganda that he consulted me about the desirability of having Amin assassinated'. Wilson was a lifelong opponent of capital punishment, but he believed that an exception could be made for Amin. The prime minister was less unhinged than Eden, and was deadly serious. As Haines logically put it, 'It was a rare opportunity to save thousands of lives by eliminating one man.' Haines later recalled that 'Harold did no more than Eden. They might have come from different eras, but Eden would have done that, and Harold did too.'[35]

Wilson achieved even less than Eden. He approached the Foreign Office to see what could be done, but his unorthodox request sent the mandarins into a panic: they were 'almost frightened out of their diplomatic strait-jackets', seeing assassination as somehow akin to cheating in the gentle-manly game of international diplomacy. They warned of the risks of Ugandan retaliation and of an escalating war of dirty tricks. Assassination, they argued, constituted a slippery slope for any country. Wilson was unconvinced, and after much prevarication by the Foreign Office, pressed for a firm answer. 'We don't have anyone to do that kind of thing,' came the curt reply. With that, the prime minister was forced to drop it.[36]

This was probably the truth. MI6 was a very different place in the mid-1970s from what it had been twenty years earlier. The glory days of the mavericks such as George Young were long gone, and in 1973 Maurice Oldfield, the chief, had issued a memorandum assuring his staff that MI6 never resorted to assassination.[37]

Idi Amin may have escaped from Wilson's crosshairs, but the successor Labour government returned to the issue just a few years later. As foreign secretary under James Callaghan in the late 1970s, David Owen also raised the possibility of Amin's assassination. Again, Owen felt such an action logical and proportionate, given Amin's 'appalling atrocities'. He put his request to MI6, but was 'rather haughtily' told that the agency 'would not contemplate arranging such a thing'. Instead, Britain decided to rapidly increase the Tanzanian aid budget, in the full knowledge that this would provide resources for President Julius Nyerere to authorise a military attack on Uganda and oust Amin.[38]

Wilson's final years as prime minister were not about descent into para-noia. As we have seen, he used intelligence creatively, valued the role of special forces and initially enjoyed cordial relations with MI5. This cordi-ality proved short-lived in the realm of domestic security. One of the turn-ing points came when Wilson discovered that MI5 had failed to tell him about the investigation into former director-general Roger Hollis. 'Very disturbing stuff,' he scribbled when he finally saw the review.[39] In fact, mid-ranking MI5 officers had wanted to speak to Wilson directly, but had been diverted into seeing John Hunt, the cabinet secretary, instead.[40] What

MI5 could not tell him was that back in 1962, the same defector who had pointed to a mole in its own organisation had also pointed to Wilson himself.

By the summer of 1975, relations had become so strained that Michael Hanley, MI5's forthright director-general, 'a large, gruff, red-faced man who had a reputation for being abrupt and having a fierce temper',[41] met the prime minister for talks to clear the air. Far from this alleviating the problem, a terrible row broke out between them. The director-general protested in vain that he was being asked unreasonable questions, but Wilson allegedly ended the meeting by swearing at Hanley, who in his own words simply 'could not get off the hook'.[42]

The prime minister later confided in John Hunt. He worried that MI5 was 'conducting some sort of vendetta against him', and that he was 'being watched or monitored, observed by both hostile and some friendly intelligence services'.[43] Wilson ended the year convinced that rogue elements from MI5, together with the CIA and the sinister South African Bureau of State Security, known as BOSS, were all out to destroy him. He even grew obsessed with the idea that the South Africans sought to frame the beleaguered Liberal leader Jeremy Thorpe with false charges of homosexuality. On this, the prime minister was wrong. Thorpe had repeatedly lied about his sexuality, and was later arrested and then acquitted for conspiracy to murder his former male lover. Nonetheless, Wilson requested a report on South African intelligence activities, and later lambasted Joe Hooper, the cabinet intelligence coordinator, insisting that MI5 was not taking the threat they posed seriously enough.[44] Wilson also asked Hunt for a report on the activities of the CIA, as well as intelligence agents from Russia and South Africa. Hunt appeared to comply, but eventually 'produced a report on just the Russians'.[45]

The KGB also captured Wilson's attention. He feared that Soviet intelligence ships disguised as trawlers were spying on him during his annual holidays on his beloved Scilly Isles.[46] Never one to keep his suspicions to himself, he pressed the Ministry of Defence on Soviet activity in the area, and probably felt vindicated to learn that a Soviet electronic intelligence vessel did indeed pass just thirty miles off St Mary's while he was staying there. It was disguised as a trawler – just as he had suspected. As the Ministry of Defence tried to stress, this was neither a new nor an exceptional occurrence, for spy boats could often be seen off the coast of Plymouth and Portsmouth. They insisted that there was no direct evidence of the Soviets trying to intercept Wilson's communications when he was on holiday.[47]

These assurances were misplaced. The greatest threat to Wilson's communications security came from Soviet interception of walkie-talkie devices and telephone calls carried by microwave.[48] The British and Americans had begun to collect these sorts of signals inside the Soviet Union themselves, and they were providing an intelligence bonanza in the early 1970s. But all this clearly struck a nerve with the Cabinet Office security team, who were convinced that Russian 'trawlers' bristling with aerials patrolled the seas around the Scilly Isles hoping to pick up snippets of prime ministerial gossip in the same way.[49] Wilson's ever-present Special Branch detectives joked that they had no need to worry if he got in trouble while swimming, since he would immediately be 'rescued by the Russian spy ship – sprouting aerials'.[50]

One of the tasks of Wilson's Special Branch team was to patrol the beaches looking for areas of good reception so he could communicate with his private secretary, Robin Butler, about urgent Treasury matters. One day, focused intently on important policy, and with radio-phone reception fading in and out, Wilson 'suffered an audible attack of Gale Force Ten flatulence' within inches of Marcia Williams. The policemen retreated to a safe distance as Williams responded with a stream of invective.[51] Williams had replaced George Wigg as Wilson's political enforcer, and as with her predecessor, they met constantly. Downing Street insiders described her as 'a one-woman intelligence service, watching and reporting every significant move by members of the Parliamentary Labour Party'. As a result Williams acquired enormous importance at Wilson's side, and was used for the most sensitive tasks, including go-between missions to the Israeli embassy.[52]

Wilson's entourage may have enjoyed their jokes about his seaborne Russian listeners, but speech security also had its serious side. It was under Wilson's second government that spending on an absurdly expensive system for providing encrypted secure speech spiralled out of control. Some 4,000 state-of-the-art scrambler telephones were to connect MI5, MI6, GCHQ, the weapons research centres at Aldermaston and Porton Down, the early-warning facility at Fylingdales, Buckingham Palace, Downing Street, and of course Wilson's holiday home on the Scilly Isles. Even more technical effort was directed to encrypting phone calls between Downing Street and the White House.[53]

Oddly, the weak spot in these elaborate defences was Downing Street itself. Huge effort had been expended over decades on speech security. Yet there was not enough space in Number 10 for the complex crypto equipment associated with the secure telephone line that connected the prime minister and the president. It was thus housed in 'Room 219', the Communications Centre of the Cabinet Office that served the JIC. The vulnerable spot was a plain voice and text line that connected this highly secure centre and Downing Street, passing along a double-screened duct on the roof. Because this line had no encryption, it was inspected regularly for 'eavesdropping devices and signs of tampering' by engineers from GCHQ. It was also patrolled by police at night. Everyone knew this was the 'prime target' for hostile intelligence services.[54]

As Wilson's final term progressed, there is no doubt that his health and his mental capacities declined. He drank too much brandy, grew more insecure and acted in a seemingly paranoid manner, becoming convinced that Downing Street had been bugged by scheming intelligence agencies. Famously, on one occasion he stood in the toilets in Number 10 with a colleague, pointed up at the electric light fitting, and pressed his finger to his lips. The implication was clear: someone was listening to them. On another occasion he turned on all of the taps in the toilets before speaking, in the hope that the gushing water would frustrate the apparently ubiquitous bugs.[55] Avoiding the listening devices became an everyday aspect of government business. Bernard Donoughue, one of his closest policy advisers, recalled a comic moment. Wilson, he noted, 'calls me into the lavatory with him. Discuss the Budget and this week's cabinet over a pee. Relaxed and totally without side. Presumably there are not listening devices in the lavatory!'[56] Elsewhere in Downing Street, Wilson would point to a mysterious hole in the wall behind a portrait of William Gladstone in the Cabinet Room, convinced it contained some sort of listening device.[57] As late as February 1976, he arranged for a private security expert to sweep his Downing Street study for bugs,[58] and his own security staff patrolled day and night looking for the devices of hostile services. Wilson's bug-dodging behaviour may have appeared paranoid, but as we now know, he was right to be worried. Harold Macmillan and Alec Douglas-Home had wired Number 10, and these microphones were only removed by James Callaghan after Wilson had left office.

Wilson expressed his concerns widely. In February 1976 he met US Senator Frank Church. The crusading senator had spent the past year leading an inquiry on Capitol Hill that was investigating intelligence activities and exposing CIA abuses of law and power, including numerous assassination attempts. His investigation was the main source of the lurid CIA stories that had filled British newspapers, and Britain's intelligence agencies had been worried that their own secrets would be dragged through the American media and congressional circus – the CIA torched its records of the Anglo–American coup in Iran precisely out of fear that this would happen.[59] Wilson, however, had a slightly different perspective. Unlike many of his colleagues, the prime minister appeared to rather enjoy the Church committee revelations, morbidly intrigued by the tales of coups and Sicilian hitmen. When the two met, Wilson thought he had found a sympathetic ear. He told Church that he had 'always been assured that the CIA were not engaged in covert operations in this country' – but added that this was probably only 98 per cent true. Church agreed. The prime minister then expressed his concerns about the underhand activities of the CIA and BOSS, and their supposed illegal operations in London. Specifically, he was worried about South African and CIA money being used to fund the recruitment of British mercenaries to fight in the Angolan civil war. Given his fears about private right-wing armies launching a coup in Britain, the recruitment of mercenaries reverberated with the prime minister.[60]

Church conveyed Wilson's concerns to American officials. The following month George Bush, then director of the CIA, flew to London to re-assure Britain's intelligence leaders that their secrets were safe despite Church's marauding through recent CIA history. James Callaghan, the foreign secretary, was offered a chance to meet him, but 'on balance' politely declined. There were certainly no plans for the prime minister to busy himself meeting the CIA director. Instead, Bush's schedule involved lunching with 'C', dining with the Joint Intelligence Committee, and meet-ing privately with John Hunt and MI5 leaders.

Unsurprisingly, this plan did not last long. Being Harold Wilson, the prime minister could not let the opportunity for talks with the upper eche-lons of the secret world slip by, and requested drinks with Bush at his friend George Weidenfeld's flat (again, perhaps fearing that Downing Street was bugged). Officials convinced Wilson that Number 10 would be more appropriate, and hastily arranged a forty-five-minute meeting. Briefing the prime minister, Hunt advised Wilson to focus on the impor-tant matter of the Anglo–American intelligence relationship, suggesting that he stress the value of the intimate transatlantic alliance and soothe any American concerns about cuts to British security and defence expenditure.[61]

Wilson did not stick to the script. Instead he pursued a rather more personal agenda, pressing Bush on whether any CIA money had been used to arm British mercenaries in Angola. Bush conceded that it had.[62] There had also been reports of joint CIA and MI6 work with mercenaries in southern Sudan.[63] All this troubled Wilson. The recruitment of British mercenaries, whom he described as 'small-time crooks', served only to fuel his suspicions of South African espionage inside the UK, to which MI5 supposedly turned a blind eye.[64] Developing his theme, Wilson pressed Bush on other nefarious South African activities in London, especially links to a series of burglaries.[65] One can only imagine the stifled exasperation on the face of poor John Hunt as the prime minister veered towards conspiracy. Taken aback, the CIA director emerged from the meeting asking, 'Is that man mad? He did nothing but complain about being spied on!'[66] Nonetheless, Bush later wrote to Wilson thanking him for his hospitality and praising the professionalism of British intelligence. Wilson took the note home with him, leaving only a photocopy in the official record.[67]

Despite his protestations, Wilson himself was actively encouraging surveillance activity in other fields. He had troublesome trade unions placed under electronic observation. Meanwhile, right-wing trade unionists worked with MI5 against communist infiltrators, probably with Wilson's knowledge. Sir Harry Crane, a leading light in the General and Municipal Workers' Union, who also ran the planning for the Labour Party annual conference, was deeply involved in this. Crane confided to one cabinet minister that left-wing subversion was problematic: 'I used to have regular contact with the Security Services and whenever I got information about anybody from them, I would pass it on to Sara Barker.' Sara Barker was the national agent of the Labour Party, and had the power to expel members. He added: 'You have got to watch the Communist Party all the time.' Such private relationships between right-wingers in the Labour Party and MI5 were held close, and nothing was written down.[68]

By the time of his retirement, Wilson firmly believed that MI5 had kept things from him: 'I am not certain for the last eight months when I was prime minister I knew what was happening, fully, in security.' He accused certain people inside MI5 of being 'very right wing', and could not rule out the possibility that individuals in both MI5 and MI6 had been involved in smearing him with talk of a communist cell inside Number 10. He even claimed that Maurice Oldfield, chief of MI6, had confirmed that there was indeed an 'unreliable section' within MI5. Oldfield apparently promised to help the prime minister deal with it, but had never reported back.[69]

By 1976, Wilson was increasingly convinced of plots against him. The crucial question is whether or not he was correct. MI5's authorised historian Christopher Andrew categorically rules out any so-called 'Wilson plot'. He makes it very clear that there are no MI5 records that point to orchestrated malevolence, and multiple interviewees have confirmed this. Nonetheless, subsequent director-generals of MI5 took the view that this story had become an urban legend, and that it was in the interest of the service that it be confronted. Stella Rimington, who joined MI5 in 1969 and rose to be director-general, eventually organised a meeting with senior Labour Party grandees to try to put the 'Wilson plot' to rest, but her well-intentioned efforts simply prompted more conspiracy theories.[70] James Callaghan eventually concluded that through ill-discipline and internal factional disputes, one or two bad eggs in the security services were 'out of control'. 'It was a great misfortune,' he added, 'that those who were concerned at the time were not absolutely candid with Ministers when asked about such matters.'[71]

Home secretaries from the 1970s have, in retirement, confessed to 'the most acute suspicions about what was going on'.[72] Looking back over his early career, Roy Jenkins, one of Britain's most distinguished cabinet ministers, even blamed political surveillance for his initial entry into politics, insisting that it had blighted his attempts to develop a career in the media. In 1993, he finally revealed his experiences, and explained to the House of Lords how they had shaped his career:

When I became involved later with the CND I soon discovered that they were on my track again, but I cannot be sure whether it was MI5 or MI6. My telephone was being intercepted. My flat in Putney was eventually burgled. Nothing was taken, but papers and documents were spread all over the place ... I tried to join the BBC. I was accepted, but a curtain came down after a while. I tried another department. I was accepted again. The curtain came down when I filled out the application form. So I gave up being a broadcaster and decided to become a trade union official. I drifted into politics and eventually finished up in Your Lordships' House. Your Lordships have MI5 or MI6 to thank, or blame, for my presence here.[73]

Jenkins' personal experiences as a subject of surveillance and vetting, together with his time as home secretary, inclined him to the view that MI5 was unsuited to the political surveillance role. He argued that it involved a fine judgement between what is subversion and what is legitimate dissent, which he thought unlikely to be found 'in those who live in the distorting and *Alice-Through-the-Looking-Glass* world in which falsehood becomes truth, fact becomes fiction and fantasy becomes reality'.

Roy Jenkins complained of an 'ingrowing mono-culture' in MI5, and a 'tendency to engage in the most devastating internal feuds'.[74] He also asserted that MI5 had used secrecy to run rings around ministers, and thought that 'living in a spy-bound world' in which they were frantically searching for moles in high places gave them 'a distorted view of life'. However, Rimington is right to observe that much of the problem was the fault of the cabinet, and lay in deliberate compartmentalisation. Ministers and senior officials did not actually want to know too much about what was going on. Although Jenkins was not impressed by the way MI5 discharged its duties, he deliberately did not probe such matters.[75]

MI5 in the 1970s was in fact outmoded and underperforming rather than malicious. The organisation certainly contained some dullards, and its officers were often figures of fun. Rimington recalls how their social attitudes were trapped in a time-warp. Many of the officers undertaking positive vetting across Whitehall were former colonial policemen who defined themselves as 'the Malayan Mafia', or 'the Sudan Souls'. Morning drinking and long afternoon naps were common – one senior counter-intelligence officer 'collapsed in a lift after one of these sorties and was not seen again'.[76] Rimington's unedifying picture is confirmed by her colleague Stephen Lander: 'Yes, there was a lot of drinking and laziness'.[77]

These were refugees from another era, and their political antennae were simply out of tune with modern Britain. They certainly lacked political awareness of the diverse categories of the new left that had begun to appear. Bernard Donoughue was on the receiving end in Downing Street. 'An intelligence man came in to discuss the positive vetting of one of my staff. These people are incredible. Generally dim with little political sense. He was worried that my housing man had a beard.' MI5's suspicion of men with beards may have been unwarranted, but was really no more sinister than that.[78]

Wilson, an adept self-publicist, enjoyed the sense of melodrama that all this created. One could even ask whether the 'Wilson plot' was precisely that – a plot developed by Wilson himself. Serious historians, though, remain certain that some dirty work was afoot, and there is clear evidence pointing to smear campaigns against the prime minister.[79] The emerging truth is that there was not one plot but a series of mini-plots, some incompetent and even farcical. Most lay outside MI5, and rather than a deliberate attempt to subvert democracy, they formed a 'loosely connected series of unlawful manoeuvres'.[80]

The context is crucial. Paranoia had seeped into the whole British establishment by the middle of the 1970s. And there was plenty to be paranoid about. The entire left wing was gripped by the Watergate scandal and Senator Church's startling CIA revelations, all of which seemed to be confirmed by right-wing military coups in Chile and Greece. Anxiety about plots knew no political boundaries, and infected the right wing too. Oil prices, union militancy, a leftist coup in Portugal, grisly leftist guerrillas in Mozambique and Angola, and rising Palestinian terrorism on the streets of Europe all pointed to a crisis of Western liberal democracy. In Germany, civil servants and lawyers were hiding members of the Baader-Meinhof gang in their basements. The entire fabric of the state seemed under threat.[81] MI5 officers were highly sensitive to the dangers of communist and left-wing subversion. Having been betrayed by the likes of Philby, they genuinely feared deep Soviet infiltration of the British establishment.[82] Wilson's claims may have appeared ridiculous, but many were making such claims, and set in their context, they become less far-fetched.

Paranoia was at its worst inside MI5. Stella Rimington explains that over the previous decade, MI5 had 'almost torn itself apart' because of a fear of high-level Soviet infiltration. The same anxieties that had led Harold Macmillan to organise the extensive bugging of Downing Street had prompted an orgy of self-doubt within the secret services themselves. One faction in MI5, led by a senior mole-hunter called Peter Wright, had nearly brought the service to a standstill because of their conviction that there was a KGB presence 'at both the high and middle levels of the Service'. Several directors and deputy directors had come under suspicion, including Roger Hollis and Michael Hanley, the irascible figure who led the organisation under Wilson. Wright worked with James Angleton of the CIA, and they 'fuelled each other's paranoia', reinforced by defectors from the Soviet Union who enhanced their status by retrospectively remembering further penetrations.[83]

The two most famous accounts of plots came from Peter Wright himself and from Colin Wallace, an army information officer in Northern Ireland.

Both are deeply flawed. Convinced that Harold Wilson was a security risk, Wright claimed that a group of around thirty MI5 officers had secretly plotted to destabilise or even overthrow his government. Using the press to smear the prime minister, it was supposedly a 'carbon copy of the Zinoviev letter, which had done so much to destroy the first Ramsay MacDonald Government'.[84] Wright, however, was a far from reliable source, given that he had left MI5 acrimoniously, feeling cheated out of his pension. His 1987 memoir, *Spycatcher*, was ghostwritten to a large degree, and was riddled with errors.[85] When pressed, he publicly admitted exaggerating the so-called rebel MI5 faction, but by then the damage was done.

Wright was unquestionably a senior MI5 officer who harboured deep suspicions about Wilson. But, by the 1970s, he was regarded as a maverick, and found himself increasingly marginalised.[86] Importantly, though, some of his accusations have since been confirmed by John Hunt, Wilson's cabinet secretary, a manifestly trustworthy source who conducted an inquiry into the matter. Hunt later recalled how the small MI5 cadre involved followed a logical train of thought which was quite natural in the paranoid Cold War climate: the Russians sought to entrap or recruit everybody of interest; this of course included Wilson, who had some suspicious friends; the Russians had been successful in the past. There was therefore a possibility that they had been so with Wilson. 'There is absolutely no doubt at all,' Hunt remembers, 'that a few, a very few, malcontents in MI5 … a lot of them like Peter Wright who were right-wing, malicious and had serious personal grudges – gave vent to these and spread damaging malicious stories about the Labour government.'[87]

The army information officer Colin Wallace also alleged that an intelligence plot existed to 'discredit Harold Wilson'. His evidence relates to activity in Northern Ireland between the two 1974 elections, when Wilson's position was at its most precarious. This time the plot formed part of a psychological warfare operation codenamed 'Clockwork Orange'. Spreading disinformation, intelligence officers apparently smeared the prime minister by presenting him as an ally or agent of the pro-IRA Soviet Union. Themes supposedly leaked anonymously to the press included Wilson's alleged financial, sexual and political misbehaviour, supposed Soviet influence over the Labour Party, and even the idea that Wilson was being run by the Communist Party.[88] Unsurprisingly, successive British governments have since vigorously denied the claim that intelligence officers in Ulster conspired to smear Wilson.[89] But Merlyn Rees, Wilson's own Northern Ireland secretary, belatedly admitted that such activities were carried out against other people:

> With regard to Northern Ireland, I discovered that the 'dirty tricks' campaign in Northern Ireland ... included a list of politicians in all parties. They are listed under the headings of sex, politics and finance. It is the most illiterate rubbish that I have ever read, even worse than that found in some of our national newspapers. It was quite extraordinary. A psych-ops operation was run against politicians in the south and politicians in Northern Ireland. It is no way to win the battle of Northern Ireland, let alone to get involved in politics here.[90]

Like that of Peter Wright, the evidence from Wallace has been partly discredited. He was forced out of the Ministry of Defence in 1975, and later imprisoned for the manslaughter of a colleague's husband. Although the conviction was quashed, leading to rumours that Wallace was framed, his reputation never recovered.[91] Nonetheless, certain claims made independently by Wallace and Wright, and belatedly by Rees, do corroborate each other.[92] A third source also adds weight to Wilson's suspicions. Anthony Cavendish, a former senior intelligence officer with MI6, later recalled that smears targeted anyone 'of consequence' who appeared to be pro-Catholic or to want to radically change the existing North–South relationship.[93] On these grounds the prime minister would have been a prime target, since he had contemplated a radical solution to the Irish problem on more than one occasion.[94]

Wilson was not alone in sensing a smear campaign. His friends and a range of policy advisers also held suspicions. The publisher George Weidenfeld, for example, was present at a dinner party one night when conversation turned to rumours of a communist cell inside Downing Street. Although absurd, the rumour was dangerously persistent. It reverberated around the clubs and drawing rooms of the London elite, no doubt growing more embellished as it quietly seeped through the establishment. Weidenfeld recalled, 'It did look as if there was an orchestrated effort to denigrate and smear [Wilson] and cut him down to size.'[95]

A string of political burglaries remains unexplained. Throughout Wilson's second period in Number 10, he and his closest advisers suffered a startlingly large number of domestic break-ins. In the spring of 1974, somebody stole personal tax papers from Wilson's house in Lord North

Street, while his secondary offices on Buckingham Palace Road were raided only a few weeks later. His lawyer's offices were burgled twice in just a few months, while burglars also targeted Michael Halls, his principal private secretary; Bernard Donoughue, his press secretary; and Anthony Crosland, a senior ministerial colleague. Marcia Williams, perhaps Wilson's closest adviser and confidante, had two houses – in London and the country – targeted. Somebody also burgled her brother, Tony Field.[96] Surely such activity lies beyond the realms of coincidence.

Finally, coup plans were discussed in high places. These dated back to a quiet meeting between Cecil King, the media magnate with delusions of grandeur, and Lord Mountbatten, cousin of the Queen and former Chief of the Defence Staff, during Wilson's first tenure as prime minister. Late one afternoon in August 1968 the two met, together with Hugh Cudlipp, a newspaper publisher, and Solly Zuckerman, the government's long-time chief scientific adviser, at Mountbatten's small London flat, just behind Buckingham Palace's gardens. King, who was also a long-term MI5 agent, opened the proceedings.[97] He extolled Wilson's failings in apocalyptic language and pressed for action, warning of bloodshed, chaos and civil violence. In the process, he apparently hinted that Mountbatten should head a government of national unity following a coup against Wilson. Mountbatten would have been a credible candidate. He was an impressive figure with royal authority who had served with distinction in both world wars, reconquered Burma, oversaw the Japanese surrender in Singapore, and then become viceroy of India.[98] Cudlipp recalls that Mountbatten's face darkened as King spoke. Mountbatten turned to his old friend Zuckerman and asked his thoughts. 'This is rank treachery', Zuckerman replied. 'All this talk of machine guns at street corners is appalling. I am a public servant and will have nothing to do with it. Nor should you, Dickie.' Having risen to his feet, Zuckerman promptly stormed out of the flat. Courteously but firmly, Mountbatten told King that all this was 'simply not on'.[99]

Unsurprisingly, King's account differs. He claims that Mountbatten expressed the Queen's concerns about the state of the nation, and said nothing to indicate that he found his proposed role in a new government unattractive.[100] Mountbatten of course denied ever having been interested, but given his experience and his character, it is possible that he privately daydreamed of restoring the country to its former glory.[101] The full truth is unlikely ever to be known, but of the two accounts, Cudlipp's is more likely. Firstly, Mountbatten was himself a left-winger and a free-thinker whose wartime male lover had been a communist. He respected Wilson, and was pleased when the Queen knighted him. Secondly, as a stickler for political legitimacy, and having presided over many formal transfers of power in the Empire–Commonwealth, Mountbatten was the last person to contemplate unconstitutional action. He loved strong leadership, but would only have taken charge if the Queen and political leaders unanimously asked him to do so.[102] Whatever the truth, Wilson found out about the meeting. He was furious, and confronted poor Zuckerman at a Buckingham Palace party. Pressing Zuckerman, a short and stocky man, up against the buffet table, Wilson breathed whisky all over him and ranted about MI5 plots.[103]

King's plot was not a one-off. In 1974, Val Duncan, the influential chairman of a mining conglomerate, invited senior journalists to a dinner. After a few bottles of wine, he encouraged his guests to participate in a coup along with the retired generals and other captains of industry also sitting around the table. Rousing his potential fellow revolutionaries, Duncan exhorted them: 'It's time to tighten our belts, the country is becoming ungovernable and is on the verge of anarchy. We,' he continued, 'are going to have to step in very soon and take over.'[104] Once more, it amounted to little more than dinner-table talk.

Simultaneously, Frank Kitson, a senior military theorist on low-intensity operations and closely associated with dirty tricks in Northern Ireland, had been espousing the need for military intervention to defeat domestic subversion. His idea essentially involved using troops to defeat militant unions. This view attracted sympathy among the army's upper echelons, and Kitson, long a controversial figure, was later forced to deny that his ideas represented involvement in coup plotting.[105] In 1975, the eminent military historian John Keegan heard Cecil King talk at Sandhurst about the need for the army to save the country. This time, Keegan was in no doubt that it formed 'a treasonable attempt to suborn the loyalty of the Queen's officers'.[106]

A few retired military leaders went further than disloyal dinner-party talk. General Sir Walter Walker gallantly 'stepped forward as Britain's Pinochet'.[107] Having previously overseen the secret war in Borneo and been Commander-in-Chief of NATO forces in Northern Europe, Walker had had an illustrious military career. In 1974, he founded a right-wing group known as Civil Assistance, which promised to step in when the inevitable political crisis arrived. Deluded with a sense of his own importance, Walker rather extravagantly claimed that its membership neared three million people. And yet he was far from alone in his endeavours. Former MI6 deputy director and all-round far-right-wing maverick George Young had set up a similar group called Unison in 1973 (from which Walker's Civil Assistance evolved). Young conceived of Unison as a domestic equivalent of the Special Operations Executive, a 'formidable vigilante group to help protect the nation against a Communist takeover'. He even claimed to have been 'taking note of disloyal groups and subversive elements' in preparation.[108]

David Stirling established yet another group: GB75. The maverick founder of the SAS and a regular participant in many of MI6's most daring post-war covert operations, Stirling had experience and authority which could not be easily dismissed. Indeed, many of these private right-wing groups seemed to be linked to individuals with senior intelligence, security or military connections. With this in mind, and with the streets seemingly crawling with secret organisations, the idea of a conspiracy becomes less ridiculous.[109] Troop manoeuvres at Heathrow, billed as a routine exercise but about which Wilson was never informed, were interpreted by some as a pre-coup show of strength.[110]

Only Walker's organisation had any substance. But rumours swirled, and there was frequent talk of chaos and public disorder. Roy Mason, the defence secretary, assured Wilson that there was no evidence that any of these groups actually sought a coup, and that none could yet be described as subversive. He was, however, slightly concerned about potential dissidence amongst the armed forces. Unsurprisingly, Wilson requested a meeting to discuss the issue further.[111] After Wilson won his second election in 1974, the various right-wing groups became less active. Nonetheless, as late as 1976, Wilson's own officials described him as 'genuinely petrified of a right-wing coup in Britain using ex-servicemen as shock troops'. It is unsurprising that he was so strongly opposed to the recruitment of British mercenaries and the idea of private armies.[112]

Wilson has increasingly become a figure of fun, and few historians have failed to laugh at the self-professed 'big fat spider'. By 1976, some had written him off as overtaken by psychological pressures and unfit to hold office. He was certainly a man 'who relished mystery', a 'romantic who loved to arrive late at a cabinet meeting with stories about secret conversations with the White House or the Kremlin'.[113] After an investigation in 1987, Margaret Thatcher told the House of Commons that there had, after all, been no plot.[114] This is probably true, and there is certainly no evidence confirming that an organised MI5 conspiracy against Wilson existed.

But Wilson was correct to sense that something was wrong at the heart of Britain's secret state. Peter Wright should have been fired by Michael Hanley, but instead he was tolerated and continued his troublemaking. Callaghan and Thatcher each detected the same dysfunctional culture when they became prime minister, and both brought in outsiders who had not served in MI5 to try to sort the problems out. As Stella Rimington recalls, there was a curtain of secrecy and a stifling wartime Britishness, even between parts of these organisations, which prevented them being addressed. 'No one thought it appropriate to comment.'[115] It was not until the late 1980s, under the diplomat Antony Duff, that MI5 at last turned the corner and modernised.

Downing Street felt the reverberations. Bernard Donoughue, Wilson's press adviser, initially thought his boss was mad, but by 1976, he had come to agree that some very odd things were going on: 'I believe my room is bugged. Certainly my phone is tapped.' Other officials in Downing Street had warned him that his room was bugged, but initially he had dismissed this out of hand, deliberately trying to 'resist the kind of paranoia' that he felt swirled around Wilson and Marcia Williams. But the evidence was unmistakable, and over time he noticed that others knew things that he had confided only to one or two people. In the end, he simply came to regard surveillance as a natural state of affairs, observing rather phlegmatically, 'The Cabinet Office is of course the centre of intelligence activities.'[116] It now fell to James Callaghan to wrestle back prime ministerial authority.

14

James Callaghan
(1976–1979)

And your telephone isn't tapped ... Not even all
the foreign embassies are tapped.
JAMES CALLAGHAN[1]

James Callaghan understood the secret world. He had served as a naval intelligence officer during the war, and by 1950 had become a junior minister in the Admiralty working on European defence issues. In Harold Wilson's first government, Callaghan had enjoyed control of MI5 as home secretary, and had also come to understand the workings of Special Branch. As foreign secretary in the mid-1970s he oversaw both MI6 and GCHQ. Combined with his stint as chancellor of the exchequer, Callaghan had an unrivalled depth of cabinet experience. This made him more level-headed and confident than his predecessor when handling intelligence matters.[2]

Yet for all his confidence, Callaghan's government moved in the deepening shadow of Watergate. Although Richard Nixon, the disgraced American president, had departed in the summer of 1974, the aftermath stretched on for several years. The full revelations were only now emerging as separate hearings into Nixon's excesses and the misdeeds of the CIA continued into 1976. Sensational details emerged of attempted assassinations of foreign leaders.[3] Remarkable material had been captured on the White House recording system. The moment that sheds most light on Nixon's character is his direct and repeated request for a break-in at the Brookings Institution, a leading Washington think-tank, early in his presidency. 'You remember Huston's plan?' he asked. 'I want it implemented on a thievery basis.' The safe there was thought to contain information about Vietnam, Nixon's political enemies and Nixon himself. 'Blow the safe and get it,' he insisted. Tom Huston was Nixon's most adventurous operative, but there were things that even he refused to do. Beset by the multiple reverses of Watergate, the oil crisis and defeat in Vietnam, America now embraced what some have called 'the paranoid style'.[4]

This paranoia was infectious. British journalists, scanning the headlines of the *New York Times* in amazement each morning, naturally wondered what was happening at a subterranean level in Britain. Whitehall officials also worried that almost any aspect of British intelligence or special operations would be seen by press commentators through the prism of the so-called 'nefarious activities of the CIA', which, they added, were now 'under constant attack'.[5] As a result, Callaghan's more left-wing cabinet colleagues such as Tony Benn asked increasingly awkward questions about the accountability of the security agencies. Initially, the prime minister found this irritating, but Benn proved to be ahead of his time in suggesting some sort of parliamentary oversight committee. Eventually, even the sensible Callaghan found himself asking some probing questions – and uncovering one or two surprising answers.

Callaghan disliked any public discussion of intelligence. Perhaps he took this a little too far in his first year of office when he turned down an invitation to open the vast new 007 sound stage at Pinewood Studios, where the latest Bond extravaganza, *The Spy Who Loved Me*, was being filmed. Somewhat chagrined, the studio turned to his recently retired predecessor Harold Wilson, who accepted with alacrity. On 5 December 1976, Roger Moore acted as master of ceremonies after arriving dramatically with his co-star Barbara Bach on a Bond-villain monorail. Wilson gave a stirring speech to the world's press in front of three full-sized replica Soviet nuclear submarines. His chosen theme was suitably Bondian: he used the impressive new sound stage as a metaphor for Britain's continued ability to think 'big' and to maintain a leading role in the world.[6]

Even as he stood on the stage, Wilson was unleashing his own espionage drama. As we have seen, upon leaving Downing Street he had told two reporters about the supposed plots to undermine him. Their resulting book, *The Pencourt File* – its title an amalgamation of the authors' names, Barrie Penrose and Roger Courtiour – was serialised by the *Observer* and launched with enormous publicity in the summer of 1977.[7] Consequently, Callaghan's period in office was dogged from the start by a torrent of stories about conspiracy and surveillance that focused on Downing Street under his predecessor. Bernard Donoughue, head of Callaghan's Downing Street Policy Unit, found the whole saga 'incredible', especially 'the paranoia it revealed ... about the CIA etc'. The press began to explain Wilson's resignation, in reality motivated by increasing ill-health, in terms of dirty tricks by a kaleidoscopic range of possible perpetrators, from the CIA to Mossad and onwards through the KGB and BOSS. Donoughue suspected that Wilson had started certain rumours himself as deliberate mischief.[8] Other ministerial aides thought Wilson's worries reflected his own Nixon-like misdeeds, one of them observing that 'Harold was afraid the security services would reveal that he himself had ordered the bugging of Denis Healey and Jim Callaghan and everyone else.' Benn wondered if the Pencourt book was itself a plot, and the journalists had played on the South African issue to inveigle Wilson into saying wild things he now regretted. 'They might well have been working for the security services all along.'[9]

Callaghan took the 'Wilson plot' seriously. Both he and Merlyn Rees, his home secretary, were troubled by the fact that Wilson insisted that Michael Hanley, the director-general of MI5, had admitted to him the existence of disaffected right-wing factions within his service. Although Hanley assured them both that Wilson's account of their meeting was not correct, some of the minor elements of Wilson's stories were true, at least to the extent that not everything reported in the *Observer* could be officially denied. Callaghan therefore felt he could issue only a general statement asserting confidence in the integrity of MI5. He did not wish to offend Wilson, fearing that his predecessor might escalate matters by publicising the security inquiries into Roger Hollis and Graham Mitchell as possible Soviet agents. Quite correctly, Callaghan realised that Wilson was capable of generating an even bigger scandal if he wished.[10]

The new Conservative leader, Margaret Thatcher, was also unsettled. Anxiety extended to plots on the right as well as the left. Prompted by Callaghan, the cabinet secretary John Hunt held discussions with her at Scotney Castle on 9 August 1977 and again in Chelsea two days later. Thatcher's main concern was not the bugging of Downing Street, a story which she did not believe. Instead, she was anxious about Wilson's political reliability. Like MI5's initial suspicions, this stemmed from his visits to Russia and some of his personal friends, including the journalist Geoffrey Goodman and the businessman Joe Kagan, both of whom had been in contact with Eastern bloc security agencies. On 23 August, partly in response to Thatcher's concerns, Callaghan issued a public statement asserting that there had been no bugging of Downing Street under Wilson and also, in polite language that had taken much drafting, confirming Wilson's loyalty.[11]

Callaghan was already probing these matters personally, and had himself previously asked Hanley about the identity of the mysterious 'Fourth Man'. Hanley replied rather vaguely that there were many theories.[12] Although an intensely secret inquiry by Burke Trend had put the fears about Hollis to rest, the press now smelled a new story about other agents associated with Philby, Burgess and Maclean. The Anthony Blunt 'time-bomb' remained inert for the time being, but Downing Street knew that journalists were working feverishly to explode it. They would eventually succeed during the first months of Margaret Thatcher's administration – much to her embarrassment.[13]

Inspired by events in America and by Wilson's allegations, more and more investigative journalists now turned surveillance back upon the state. In 1977, Britain's most closely guarded secrets, many of them concerning GCHQ and its American partner the National Security Agency, were spilled in a series of press stories, and horrified authorities reached for the courts. Foreign Secretary David Owen and the attorney general were in the vanguard of those pressing for legal action. The following year, the crown prosecuted three individuals, including two journalists, under the Official Secrets Act. They included Duncan Campbell, who over the next ten years would rise to the status of Britain's top investigative journalist probing intelligence matters. With the National Union of Journalists and the National Council for Civil Liberties prominent in their defence, the case became a *cause célèbre*. The trial itself was an elaborate charade, with one of the government witnesses, a Colonel O'Connor, given the codename 'Colonel A' and brought to court hidden in a horsebox amid pantomime secrecy. Callaghan's advisers were indignant, and called the trial 'a ludicrous farce and a waste of money'.[14]

In retrospect, the trial was a spectacular own-goal. Even before it began, Joe Hooper, previously one of GCHQ's most experienced sigint veterans, had warned the cabinet secretary that any revelations arising from it would be 'politically embarrassing' rather than technically or operationally damaging to sigint. Hooper was right. Moreover, the court case opened several cans of worms: it raised enormous questions about the avowal of peacetime sigint, the future of the Official Secrets Act, and how the secret state should address a growing army of specialist journalists determined to uncover more secrets. The judge had deemed the use of the Official Secrets Act in this case 'oppressive', and leading Labour MPs were now pressing for its reform. John Hunt, the cabinet secretary, had also expressed reservations, warning that 'The police should be very sure of their ground before blundering into something which could well backfire.' He added ruefully, 'And what a backfire it had been.'[15] The prime minister himself did not comment publicly, but in private explained to Margaret Thatcher that security breaches involved in the case were too trivial for them to be referred to the Security Commission.[16] Only Thatcher wanted to press on.[17]

To Callaghan's dismay, the trial prompted both backbench MPs and cabinet ministers to ask more questions about surveillance. The most persistent was Tony Benn, secretary of state for energy. Benn had been shocked by what he read in the newspapers about CIA dirty tricks in America, but reasoned that at least in Washington the laundry was being washed in public and new oversight mechanisms were being created. He wondered what was going on in Britain, a much more opaque country. As the leading light of the Labour left wing, state surveillance had always been a matter of fascination for him, but even now as a cabinet minister the answers to his questions always seemed just out of reach. His own department looked after the safety of nuclear materials, so he sat on cabinet counter-terrorism committees. Yet, when he asked questions about security he received obfuscating answers from civil servants.

Benn had to use his own contacts to probe security matters. One Christmas Eve he had late-night drinks with Mark Arnold-Forster, an old friend who was then diplomatic editor of the *Observer*.[18] Benn expressed concern that the security services were extending their surveillance over all of British public life, but was not sure which particular secret service was to blame. The whisky was perhaps taking its effect on Arnold-Forster, who responded wrongly that 'MI5 is espionage and MI6 is counter-espionage.' Benn readily agreed. As he was famously teetotal, his ignorance indicated his deliberate exclusion from secret circles rather than drink-induced fuzziness. Nonetheless, he was dubious about assurances that telephones could not be tapped without a Home Office warrant. He knew that certain audio bugs which did not use telephone lines did not require warrants, and even suspected that his own house had been bugged. He also said that he had been at a CBI dinner in 1971 at which, much to his concern, Harold Wilson had boasted to industry figures about the extent to which trade union leaders were 'tapped or bugged'.[19]

Arnold-Forster then swore Benn to secrecy, and confessed to having worked for MI6 himself since the end of the war. This reassured Benn, given that his friend had always emphasised that the British security services were relatively clean, claiming that by contrast one of the tasks of their French counterparts was to vet the president's mistresses. Yet here was one of the more senior editors on the left-leaning *Guardian* and then the *Observer* working simultaneously for MI6. Benn expressed his worries that the CIA might 'destabilise' Britain under a Labour government, but Arnold-Forster again sought to calm his friend by arguing that the trans-atlantic links were simply too close for that to be allowed to happen.[20]

Many sensible people in wider public life had told Benn of strange experiences with bugging and telephone-tapping during this period. The union leader Clive Jenkins, who later became chairman of the TUC, said to Benn that he knew his own phone was bugged. Occasionally, when he had been on the line, the voice of the person listening in had actually broken into the conversation and warned him. Jenkins assumed that this was the action of a dissident surveillance officer.[21]

In late July 1977, with the 'Wilson plot' saga at its height, Benn infor-mally raised the matter of bugging over drinks at Downing Street with David Owen and Merlyn Rees. Both were adamant that they 'control the security services completely', and they added, 'You would be surprised about how good and decent they are.' Discussing specific cases, however, Rees conceded that 'At some periods in industrial disputes it does happen', and was horrified to hear that Wilson had boasted about the practice. Owen added that he thought bugging had taken place during the seamen's strike in 1966. The exchange was friendly, but Benn left unconvinced that Owen or Rees enjoyed the 'very tight control' that they claimed over their agencies.[22]

Callaghan was indeed watching the unions. He feared militancy as a threat to his economic strategy. The sterling crisis forced him to seek a bailout from the International Monetary Fund shortly after taking office. Inflation was running at 16 per cent a year, and the prime minister had little choice but to implement savage spending cuts. He needed union support, but although the core of the TUC was on-side, its highly organ-ised left wing threatened to pull the unions away. Callaghan feared subver-sion, and MI5 had suspicions of KGB influence.[23] He thus revived a secret group in the Home Office that kept an interdepartmental watch on subver-sion in public life. But the whole idea of 'subversion' was difficult and slippery. Unlike other issues that MI5 was supposed to watch, it was not a criminal offence. John Jones, the deputy director of MI5, was anxious that both ministers and senior officials might come to 'equate subversion with activity that threatens a government's policies'.[24]

Callaghan was equally anxious about Trotskyists within the Labour Party. Many groups existed, but the most alarming, 'Militant Tendency', was led by Ted Grant, a South African-born Trotskyist. This highly secretive Marxist group took control of the Labour Party Young Socialists in the early 1970s, and had also infiltrated local constituency Labour parties. Although the party's national organiser, Reg Underhill, had conducted a probe into Militant Tendency in 1975, the extreme left had enough support on Labour's National Executive Committee to bury it amid claims from Grant that documents obtained by the inquiry were 'CIA forgeries'.[25] In May 1977, the NEC conducted another review, but others accused Underhill of being in league with MI5. Many cabinet ministers were running scared of extremists in their constituency organisations.[26]

Publicly, the prime minister remained aloof from the Militant issue. Privately, he saw Militant Tendency as a subversive threat to democracy, and subjected it to a substantial programme of telephone-tapping, audio surveillance and agent penetration by MI5. Run by a security-conscious inner group of thirty, Militant Tendency presented a tough target. Nonetheless, MI5 managed to penetrate it. In August 1977, Merlyn Rees and Robert Armstrong, the senior official at the Home Office, visited MI5 headquarters for an extensive briefing by the director-general. It was now thought that Militant Tendency had a foothold in as many as eighty local Labour Party branches.[27] The Labour National Executive Committee formed the key battleground, and Callaghan's advisers recall a convoluted 'plot' in 1977 to get rid of two female members, whom Downing Street referred to as 'Stalin's grannies', and replace them with right-wingers.[28]

Despite this subversive threat, Tony Benn's fears about oversight still stood. In late 1977, he met with Tom Farmer, an old American acquaintance from his student days at Oxford. Farmer had served in the CIA during the early 1950s under Allen Dulles, and for the last six months had chaired President Jimmy Carter's new intelligence oversight panel.[29] He told Benn that the current CIA director, Stansfield Turner, was committed to reform, and that together 'they were trying to sort things out'. He added that he had come to London to discuss all this with Joe Hooper, the Cabinet Office intelligence coordinator. Benn observed that it was 'absolutely typical' of Whitehall that despite being a cabinet minister involved in counter-terrorism, he had never heard of Hooper.[30]

Benn's enquiries had a purpose. He wished to propose an American-style oversight system for the British security agencies, but Callaghan simply ignored him. In October 1978, Benn decided to catch Callaghan's attention by writing formally and directly to Merlyn Rees to ask if his phone had ever been tapped. No reply came for weeks, so Benn wrote again. Eventually, he was told that Callaghan wanted to see him, and noted with delight, 'That means I have hooked the big fish.' Late on the afternoon of Wednesday, 25 October he went to see Callaghan in the Cabinet Room at Downing Street, and after some beating around the bush they got down to business. 'We hardly bug anybody,' Callaghan assured him, and it was 'all under ministerial control'. He added, 'Incidentally, your phone isn't tapped.' Benn countered that no one really knew for sure, and that the number of ministers and officials who had oversight was too small to check. Callaghan estimated that only 139 phones were tapped, and insisted that each warrant had to be reviewed by the home secretary every three months. Benn replied that as postmaster general he had been close to the Post Office workers' union, which had estimated that 'between 1000 and 2000 phones in London alone are tapped'. Inevitably, the conversation turned to Wilson. 'Harold is just Walter Mitty,' insisted Callaghan, and then recounted his own Wilson story. 'Once, in his study upstairs, he turned round the picture of Gladstone and there was a hole in the wall … He put his hands to his lips and said "Shhh!", pointing to the hole.'[31]

The debate about bugs was merely a preliminary. Benn now had concrete proposals for reform that borrowed from President Carter's new oversight mechanisms in Washington. Although he had suffered a slight demotion as secretary of state for energy, he still enjoyed a strong power-base on the Labour Party National Executive Committee.[32] He now used this to propose an inquiry by its Home Policy Committee into ways in which 'greater public accountability by the Security Service could be achieved, without endangering national security'. His paper proposed regular publication of budgets and staff numbers, the creation of an over-sight committee consisting entirely of privy councillors, and an appeals procedure relating to personal records held on individuals. All this would be underpinned by an annual Security Services Act, putting the agencies on the statute book for the first time and giving them an avowed legal identity. Benn's proposals, which seemed radical in 1978, were in fact largely what the British government would enact between 1989 and 1994.[33]

The American intelligence system was respected in Whitehall, so Callaghan took Benn's suggestions seriously, asking John Hunt to discuss them with Robert Armstrong and Sir Antony Duff, chair of the Joint Intelligence Committee, and report back. In the British system, cabinet ministers approved domestic surveillance and overseas intelligence operations, while the strategic direction and financial control of the agencies was handled by the PSIS committee of permanent secretaries, which dated back to Attlee's premiership. Although the present system 'has served us well', Hunt conceded that 'it depends for the avoidance of abuse essentially on trust'. Nevertheless, he argued that the new American system of congressional oversight committees, so admired by Benn, had 'disadvantages'. Germany used a similar system, but there had been 'a succession of leaks' that had damaged security and reduced effectiveness. He thought a better option would be a ministerial committee on intelligence, but feared it could become a 'cosmetic device'. Canada employed this system, but he observed that it merely 'rubber stamps' existing decisions.[34] Benn himself did not expect much movement, but found himself appointed to a new cabinet committee on freedom of information, and so was delighted.[35]

Behind the scenes, Callaghan worked with Merlyn Rees and David Owen to stall Benn's efforts to take this issue further in Labour Party policy circles. Rees, accompanied by one of Callaghan's special advisers, David Lipsey, was sent to the next Labour Party National Executive Committee meeting, at which Benn's proposals were tabled. The meeting went on interminably, with all sorts of suggestions for increased oversight being made. 'Rees sat with his head in hand, mumbling incoherently about how difficult it all was.' As proceedings finally drew to a close, Lipsey had no idea how to draft the minutes of this vast, rambling discussion, and plucked up the courage to ask what exactly had been decided: 'Rees's mumbling recommenced until I just gave up.' The meeting then adjourned and people went their separate ways.

> I shepherded Rees to the lift, still clutching his head as if it might
> fall off with the stress. We got in and the lift doors closed. Rees
> lifted his head, looked around him to check there was no one to
> hear, smiled broadly, and said: 'That went well, didn't it, David? We
> didn't agree to anything, did we?'

Lipsey suddenly realised that Rees did indeed have 'something of the "Merlin" about him', and had worked a piece of magic. This was 'indeed a triumph' for Callaghan, although not one that made Lipsey's job as minute-taker any easier.[36]

Callaghan did not like Benn's proposed reforms, partly because he had his own in mind. Rather than widening ministerial engagement with intelligence, his instinct was to narrow it to a committee of one. He considered taking all three agencies away from the Foreign Office and the Home Office and placing them under the prime minister, with the possibility of their merger into one entity being discussed in the same breath.[37] By the end of 1978, David Owen was anxious about losing control of MI6 and GCHQ to Callaghan. His fears were not entirely unfounded, given Callaghan's decision to work independently with MI6 over issues like the Falkland Islands.[38] In the event, a range of crises, including the 'Winter of Discontent' and waves of IRA attacks, distracted Callaghan's attention in his last year of office.[39]

Callaghan's own limited attempts at liberalisation came to nothing. He wished to end the farce of pretending that MI6 did not exist, but David Owen backed MI6 in arguing that the time-honoured tradition of saying nothing had served its purposes best.[40] Callaghan also failed to instigate a culture change at MI5. When Michael Hanley came to retire in 1978, the prime minister decided that the service needed a breath of fresh air. While the conventional decision would have been to promote the existing deputy director, John Jones, Callaghan instead insisted on an outside appointment. This was an unusual step, especially given that the last attempt to appoint an agency head from outside had not been a success. Callaghan decided to plump for Sir Howard Smith, until recently the British ambassador in Moscow, whom he knew quite well.[41] Smith was no stranger to intelligence, having worked at Bletchley Park during the war and studied the Soviets at close quarters since.[42] Still, his appointment was rather risky, given that the KGB had long targeted Western embassies in Moscow. A honeytrap – or 'swallow' in KGB parlance – operation had successfully recruited Britain's Moscow ambassador back in the 1960s. While no one has suggested that Smith had been suborned by the Soviets, Callaghan's decision was still a remarkable one, given the recent anxieties about Roger Hollis.[43] On his appointment, the prime minister wrote to Smith personally in Moscow: 'Say goodbye to Gromyko – tell him you're coming back to take charge of MI5.'[44]

The Home Office hid the news of Smith's forthcoming appointment from MI5, knowing it would be controversial. When it was finally announced, Hanley took it very badly indeed, and burst into Merlyn Rees's office shouting, 'It's a fucking disgrace!' Known for his temper, Hanley would doubtless have given Callaghan the same robust treatment had he been able to gain access to the prime minister. His formal objection related to Smith being too soft on the Soviets, but the choice of someone from outside the service was also a slap in the face for MI5. Hanley's rift with the prime minister intensified. Before he departed he impeded Callaghan's attempts to reform MI5's recruitment intake by appointing new people to senior posts immediately. He also took the unprecedented step of seeing opposition leader Margaret Thatcher and giving full vent to his feelings. Callaghan responded by appointing Lord Crowham to lead an inquiry into MI5. Crowham's report was generally complimentary, but confirmed the need to broaden recruitment, moving away from the intake of former colonial policemen. Sadly, Smith was a personal disaster and failed to bring change. Lacking charisma and warmth, he often seemed to disapprove of much of MI5's work.[45]

Callaghan did insist on the publication of Harry Hinsley's long-running history of wartime intelligence, initiated by Dick White and Burke Trend a decade before. Ironically, the strongest opponent was Maurice Oldfield, who had been White's deputy and protégé. Oldfield, now chief of MI6, urged that they should strive 'to keep whatever threadbare secrecy can be kept'. It was not just a matter of protecting 'our agents, our operations and liaisons', but also of 'shielding future governments from potentially explosive embarrassments'. Oldfield pointed to 'the continuing aftermath of the Zinoviev letter and the Crabb case'.[46] Bill Bonsall, the director of GCHQ, also preferred that 'nothing be published at all'.[47] Margaret Thatcher was especially anxious that the book should not appear, advising Callaghan that as a law student she had learned the important lesson 'Never admit anything unless you have to'. Wisely, Callaghan overruled them all and allowed the publication of the Hinsley history, to great public acclaim.[48]

Callaghan was the first prime minister to work closely with the SAS. Although his predecessors had attempted to look tough on Northern Ireland by boasting about sending in the regiment, it was Callaghan who decided to use it more widely in the Six Counties.[49] The conflict also saw increased use of other covert outfits, including the Special Reconnaissance Unit, all of which attracted press interest and speculation.[50] Unsurprisingly, Callaghan's private secretaries grew anxious that at any moment the prime minister might be quizzed by the media about 'assassination squads'.[51] In reality, the biggest problem came from the SAS simply getting lost south of the border. Members of the regiment had recently crossed into the Irish Republic on kidnap missions,[52] but in May 1976, no fewer than eight SAS men, carrying sub-machine guns and a shotgun with 222 rounds of ammunition, were arrested by the Dublin government. They refused to discuss their mission.[53] Callaghan and his cabinet could not agree on how to handle the issue. Roy Mason, the Northern Ireland secretary, insisted that the SAS men had to appear in court in Dublin in order to prevent the collapse of cross-border cooperation. He hoped the Irish president would simply pardon them and send them back. Others warned that if they were sent to an Irish jail, the IRA would assassinate them within days. In the end, Callaghan had secret talks with Garret FitzGerald, the Irish minister for foreign affairs, and resolved the matter quietly. Personal diplomacy was Callaghan's strength – he explained to FitzGerald, 'I have Irish blood in my veins.'[54]

Elsewhere, the SAS was winning friends for Callaghan in Europe. Since the late 1960s, the regiment had been studying how to address terrorist hijacking and hostage-taking. After the Palestinian attack on the Munich Olympics in 1972 it created a Special Projects Team, and carried out many exercises and experiments. Drawing on this experience, in May 1977 Callaghan authorised the SAS to assist the Dutch security agencies in dealing with a train hijacked by terrorists from South Molucca. The siege was brought to an end successfully, and the SAS continued to hone their skills. In September, the regiment carried out a full-scale exercise on the Hereford to Worcester railway line with the support of British Rail and the local Special Branch, followed by extensive exercises at Heathrow airport. There were also secret exchanges of expertise with the Israelis, who had recently carried out a spectacular hostage release raid at Entebbe airport in Uganda.[55]

A month later, the West German Chancellor Helmut Schmidt called Callaghan, asking for urgent SAS assistance with another hijacking. On 13 October 1977, Lufthansa Flight 181 had left Majorca for Frankfurt, carrying ninety-one holidaymakers home. Four terrorists had also managed to board the plane. Armed with guns, grenades and explosives, they took over the flightdeck and instructed the pilot to head for Rome. Their demands included the release of eleven Baader-Meinhof members from prisons in West Germany and £10 million in cash. Flight 181 refuelled at Rome, then flew on to Cyprus, Bahrain and Dubai, where the hijackers bargained unsuccessfully on the airport tarmac with the German ambassador.[56]

Late on Friday, 14 October, the heads of GSG-9, an elite German commando unit, flew to London. Arriving at Downing Street, they joined a meeting with SAS personnel and four cabinet ministers. The British offered their German counterparts advice on weapons and tactics, together with a full rundown on the geography of Dubai airport.[57] Sergeant Barry

Davies and Major Alastair Morrison were among those from the SAS who had been summoned to Downing Street. Davies, the lead specialist in anti-terrorism technology, had been bundled into a helicopter at regimental headquarters in Hereford at very short notice. He arrived at Battersea heliport still 'clutching my bag of dirty washing', and told the police officer, 'Take us to Number 10 Downing Street.' The policeman looked incredulous, but complied, and ten minutes later Davies joined Major Morrison on the pavement outside for a 'swift, huddled briefing' before going in.[58]

Inside Number 10, Davies was greeted by 'a short gentleman in a penguin suit' who gave him the largest gin and tonic he had ever seen. 'I took a sip and nearly choked – it must have contained nearly half a pint of neat gin.' Suitably stiffened, he sat at the cabinet table and took the lead in explaining to the assembled ministers that the best chance of liberating those on board the plane was to use a newly developed stun grenade called the G-60. This produced 160 decibels of noise and a flash of 300,000 candlepower, but little blast, and immobilised people for three to five seconds. He recounted the latest exercises the SAS had carried out at Heathrow, and what they had learned. The SAS also proved important in terms of local diplomacy, since the presidential guard in Dubai was run by ex-SAS men. In Dubai, the head of the GSG-9 team and his advance party were initially treated as hostile entities and marched about under guard until the SAS intervened.[59] During several lengthy telephone calls, 'Callaghan advised Schmidt not to give way under any circumstances.'[60]

Meanwhile, the hijacked Boeing 737 was moving on. Trying to land in Oman's Dhofar province but finding the runway blocked, it headed on to Aden. There the pilot, Captain Jürgen Schumann, deliberately made a heavy landing and then pretended to inspect the undercarriage. He bravely used the opportunity to run over to the control tower and brief officials on the explosives and weapons on board, and the hostages' situation, but the hijackers compelled his return by threatening to blow up the aircraft. After taking off again, Schumann was marched into the passenger cabin and shot in the back of the head in front of the passengers while the co-pilot flew on towards Mogadishu in Somalia. There Schumann's body was thrown out onto the tarmac, prompting GSG-9 to decide on speedy action. Germany had sent out a team of thirty commandos. Callaghan agreed that the SAS could join the operation, and Major Morrison and Sergeant Davies flew out immediately, carrying a supply of SAS stun grenades.[61]

Just after midnight on 18 October, the rescue teams silently approached the aircraft. Different squads, each carrying lightweight ladders, were assigned to each door. They forced the doors open and threw in the stun grenades, blinding and deafening all inside – the two SAS advisers insisted on throwing some of the grenades themselves. The terrorists were taken by surprise. The commandos quickly identified and shot all four, killing two of them and wounding the other two. Although one dying terrorist managed to throw his explosives into the passenger cabin, the operation resulted in no serious injuries among the hostages. It was a triumph, and the same day Callaghan flew to West Germany where he shared in quiet celebrations.[62] Unlike the security services, the SAS had enthusiastic and unqualified support in all quarters. The Ministerial Committee on Terrorism knew that the regiment now had a team ready to be flown anywhere in the country to deal with terrorism, including the new, and potentially vulnerable, oil rigs in the North Sea. It wanted the SAS expanded, as Britain's oil production was worth £7 billion a year, and any insurance premium to cover that sort of risk would cost far more than having the SAS on constant standby.[63]

Yet, even as they spoke, a murkier SAS story unfolded. In mid-October 1977 John Hunt informed Callaghan that MI5 and the SAS had discovered that 'a plot, involving ex-members of the SAS, was being worked up, with the objective of assassinating an African president'. The evidence, Hunt added, 'pointed to a plot to assassinate the president of Togo'. Sir Antony Duff called an emergency meeting at Downing Street that included MI5, MI6 and the SAS along with Special Branch, the Ministry of Defence and the Home Office. He concluded that 'there was no doubt that the operation was being planned and that various ex-members of the SAS had been recruited for it'. Surprisingly, there were no statutes under which the men could be prosecuted, but Callaghan was assured that SAS headquarters and Special Branch were working together to find the men and tell them 'the plot had been blown'. They also considered 'conveying a warning to the target'.[64]

Over the weekend, 'the SAS saw their ex-members', and felt certain that the team had been 'broken up'. But to Callaghan's dismay, MI5 now uncovered a second team, led by a Canadian soldier of fortune, which consisted mostly of foreigners but also included two ex-SAS soldiers. This team had also been warned off, but unlike the first, it had 'not yet agreed to drop out'. The reason for two hit teams seems to have been that the president of Togo's deputy was also marked for assassination, in order to 'pave the way for a third man'. Tying the plot to Britain, MI5 had intelligence that the hit squads intended to leave by light aircraft from Sussex. Callaghan was incensed, and demanded that criminal charges be brought, but the police remained emphatic that no evidence existed that would allow any of them to be charged. The Canadian leading the second team, who was already a wanted man in his home country, now vanished on a plane to Switzerland.[65]

The SAS was part of a vast network of regime security that protected many foreign leaders. The CIA and the KGB also had their protégés around the world, whose safety they jealously guarded. In the late 1970s, no premier was more important to London or Washington than the shah of Iran – and so his toppling by Ayatollah Khomeini in January 1979 was, in the words of David Owen, 'a geopolitical disaster'. Britain was not directly responsible for the shah's personal security, since this was looked after by what Owen called 'the loathsome SAVAK', a fierce secret police force with a propensity for torture. But Owen did feel that Iran was an intelligence failure, and moreover that the fall of the shah contributed to further disasters – the Soviet invasion of Afghanistan, the Iran–Iraq War and the rise of Islamic fundamentalism in the region.[66]

After the fall of the shah, Owen ordered a 'post mortem' to look for mistakes. He recalled that Britain was agonising over whether the shah would survive as early as August 1977. Rather than any 'intelligence failure', the problem had been the incompetent British 'handling of the shah', who was proving to be a difficult puppet, weak and cowardly, but at the same time too arrogant to accept advice. Britain failed to infuse him with the required 'ruthlessness' to face down the Islamic revolution, while he was too pompous to be guided towards an alternative and more stable form of government. Owen believed that the West should, in effect, have carried out its own soft democratic coup, replacing the shah with his son Reza and a more constitutional regime well ahead of the fundamentalist revolution.[67]

Perversely, the Iranian revolution had its origins in precisely this sort of Western meddling. During the mid-1970s, human rights in the country had become a *cause célèbre*, with newspapers like the *Sunday Times* running veritable campaigns about 'Torture in Iran'. Amnesty International singled out Iran as having the highest rate of death penalties in the world, no civilian courts and an extraordinary history of torture. The American Congress also took an interest, and once in power, Jimmy Carter put pressure on Tehran to introduce reforms. The shah instructed SAVAK to cease torture, which it largely did, and allowed a Red Cross inspection of the prisons. He kept the communists in prison, since the West regarded them as dangerous, but released 280 religious fundamentalists, including some who had been involved in the assassination of Prime Minister Hasan Ali Mansur in 1965.[68]

Parviz Radji, the Iranian ambassador in London, bore the brunt of the press assault on SAVAK, which was led by *Private Eye* and the Persian section of the BBC World Service. The shah seemed to take a particular dislike to *Private Eye*, and when Radji visited Tehran in July they discussed taking secret action against the magazine. The shah was warned that 'To try to "buy" them would be disastrous,' as the *Eye* would be likely to report the effort gleefully.[69] Later, when a BBC correspondent was expelled from Tehran, Radji counselled that it would be more effective to conduct covert action against the BBC's transmitters at Masirah island, off the coast of Oman. 'There are teams of Iranian frogmen who are probably overpaid and underworked,' and they could create what he politely called an 'improvised storm' that would take down the transmitters. This, he remarked, was the best way of 'silencing the Persian Service'. Radji was genuinely indignant at the failure of the Western media to appreciate how much the shah's regime had reformed Iran. Charting an uncomfortable course between a histrionic ruler in Tehran and his press persecutors in London, the miserable Radji was aware that his telephone calls were tapped at both ends, by MI6 in London and by elements hostile to his own faction in Iran.[70]

On Thursday, 14 September 1978, Callaghan explained to his cabinet that 'We must continue to support the Shah against the mad mullahs and the Soviet agents who are opposing him.'[71] What he could not tell them was that a member of the KGB station in Tehran, Vladimir Kuzichkin, had recently begun working as an agent of MI6. Kuzichkin was able to assure the British that KGB operations in Iran were ineffective and incompetent. The Soviets were losing the battle against what he described as the 'rabid' security officers of SAVAK, who had uncovered Moscow's best agent – he was publicly executed at the end of 1978. Confident of prevailing in the Cold War struggle for Iran, Callaghan nevertheless remained anxious about the general stability of the shah's regime and what this meant for Britain's overseas oil revenues and defence sales.[72]

The prime minister's biggest problem was not Cold War competition in Iran, but the shah's fear of British conspiracies propagated by the BBC World Service. By 1978, this was the only outlet in Iran through which the voice of the opposition could be heard, and it had become immensely popular, prompting the shah to describe it as his 'number one enemy'.

Lurking behind the BBC, he believed, was the all-powerful hand of MI6. Princess Ashraf, the shah's sister and the most powerful member of his circle, came to visit Callaghan. Her main purpose was to complain vehemently about the activities of the British press, and especially the BBC Persian Service. A pliant Callaghan agreed that the Persian Service was 'deplorable', but said there was nothing he could do about it. The princess pointedly observed that the British government funded the BBC. Shortly afterwards, the Foreign Office considered abolishing the BBC Persian Service.[73]

Both Britain and America had a curious 'no-spy' rule concerning their protégé in Iran. Britain's MI6 was respected by the shah, since it had helped to put him in place; indeed, Owen recalls that most Iranians were 'ready to ascribe almost magical power to the British Secret Service'.[74] MI6 had a liaison man talking to Iranian intelligence in Tehran, but it did not maintain a normal MI6 station there, nor did it spy on the Iranians with human agents. The Americans pursued largely the same policy, and while the CIA had a big station in Iran, it was used as a platform for spying on the neighbouring Soviet Union, and kept out of internal politics. A minority of CIA officers who did want to watch the domestic scene in Iran and talk to the opposition were vetoed, and in any case almost none of them spoke Farsi. GCHQ had bases in northern Iran, but there too its electronic ears were directed northwards towards Soviet missile test sites near the Caspian Sea.[75]

The lack of intelligence coverage in Iran was remarkable given its importance to Britain. British Petroleum obtained about half its total supplies from this country under agreements negotiated in the wake of the 1953 coup. Iran also kept the British defence industry afloat almost single-handed, purchasing over a thousand tanks of different kinds during the mid-1970s, albeit the Iranian army failed to maintain them. Economically, Britain was struggling, and both military and civilian exports to the Gulf were nothing less than essential in offsetting the oil-price shock. Regionally, as Britain continued its closure of naval bases, Iran's Imperial Navy pretty much dominated the Gulf. Britain was locked into an ever tighter relationship with the Peacock Throne.

In the absence of intelligence on the opposition, London depended on diplomatic reportage. Anthony Parsons, Britain's long-serving ambassador in Tehran, backed the shah right up until the eve of the Iranian revolution. Focused on the regime with its many palaces, he failed to understand the growing tensions on the streets. The whole of the last twelve months of the shah's rule was racked by dissension, beginning with rioting in the religious centre of Qom and calls for the return of the exiled religious leader Ayatollah Khomeini, who was masterminding widespread agitation from Paris and who had captured the support of most of Iran's students. Yet Parsons remained optimistic, and thought the shah's fearsome internal security service, together with the army's loyalty, would carry him through. In the summer of 1978, he noted cheerfully: 'I do not foresee any serious trouble in the near future. There will be ups and downs, but in the short term I think the Shah … is at present, without any genuinely dangerous opposition from any quarter.'[76]

The CIA was also wide of the mark. Zbigniew Brzezinski, the national security advisor, told President Carter, 'Good news! According to a CIA assessment, issued in August, Iran is not in a revolutionary or even a pre-revolutionary situation. There is dissatisfaction with the Shah's tight control of the political process, but this does not at present threaten the government.'[77] By October 1978, Tehran looked much more unstable, but Parsons urged London to stay with the shah, insisting that the situation could still be saved. Any effort at 're-insuring' by exploring alternative leaders, he warned, would only undermine the regime further. James Callaghan was less optimistic, and on 30 October wrote on Parsons' latest report: 'On the basis of this I wouldn't give much for the Shah's chances. I think Dr Owen should start re-insuring!' Attacks by mobs on foreign embassies had already begun, and the British embassy was overrun a few days later.[78]

In retrospect, David Owen lamented that GCHQ should have spent more time listening to the Iranians and not the Russians. He also observed that the British should have spoken to Mossad, but relations with the Israeli secret service were still poor in the wake of Heath's neutrality during the 1973 Yom Kippur War. Most of the Mossad personnel serving in Iran were Jews who had grown up in Tehran and were immensely well networked. As early as August 1978, as Parsons advised Owen that the shah would survive, the Israelis were already evacuating their personnel, knowing full well that a hurricane was coming.[79]

Unfortunately, the shah was the worst kind of dictator. An incompetent reformer and moderniser, he had allowed enough space for the religious opposition to mobilise.[80] This tendency was encouraged by the West, which wanted his export market, but squirmed impotently at press reports describing the nefarious doings of his secret police. Once faced with determined opposition the shah proved to be autocratic only in style, displaying his 'neurotic and indecisive personality'. MI6 relied on SAVAK for its reporting on Iranian politics, and drew back from any contact with Iranian opposition leaders or the leading mullahs for fear of offending the shah. In the last year of the shah's rule, Britain's senior MI6 officer was Desmond Harney, working undercover as an adviser to the bankers Morgan Stanley.[81] Despite having learned his trade at the feet of Professor Ann Lambton at the School of Oriental and African Studies in London, he was no less surprised by the onset of revolution.[82]

Britain's biggest problem was American indecision. Carter had pressed the shah strongly on the issue of human rights, and had refused to supply his armed forces with CS gas for riot control. Even as the shah fell, the US president's advisers were deeply divided as to whether they should encourage a military coup to fill the resulting vacuum. Brzezinski wanted immediate military action, but Cyrus Vance, the secretary of state, was adamant that a civilian government should be given a chance. Carter despatched a senior air force general, Robert Huyser, to Tehran on 7 January 1979 to talk to the Iranian military. A week later, as the shah fled the chaos, Huyser held a crucial meeting with General Amir Hossein Rabii, commander of the Imperial Iranian Air Force. Rabii told him that the Iranian generals all wanted a military coup as soon as the shah's plane left the ground, explaining that the military would 'come apart rapidly otherwise'. They looked to Washington for a green light, but instead Huyser told them they should give a civilian administration a chance. In fact, the civilians were swept aside within days by the Islamic revolutionaries, and Rabii paid with his life for American hesitation.[83]

Britain had provided an expert in riot control during the mounting trouble of 1978, together with ample supplies of CS gas. Callaghan and Owen had worried about doing this, but believed the only alternative was the likely use of the British tanks on Tehran's streets. MI6 decided not to have any contact with Khomeini's staff in Paris. After the shah's departure, the CIA 'tried to establish a deal with Khomeini' when he returned to Tehran on 1 February 1979, but was abruptly rebuffed. In the final days of the shah's rule, the Iranian military, which had especially close links with Mossad, asked the Israelis to assassinate Khomeini on their behalf, but they refused. With the shah safely out of the country, his former prime minister Medhi Bazargan was captured, sentenced to death and 'in a matter of minutes' shot in his prison cell.

In January 1979, Western leaders met for a summit at Guadeloupe. Callaghan admitted that the shah had been unmanageable, effete and paranoid: 'Everybody is of the same opinion ... very weak.' He added, 'Nobody has been willing to tell the shah the truth. We haven't told him the truth about the disintegrating situation in ten years.'[84] The shah had been offered exile in the United States, but Carter withdrew the offer as the hostage crisis unfolded. He owned a palatial house in Surrey, but was not welcome there either – Downing Street accepted the advice of officials that if he came to Britain, Tehran would assume that MI6 was plotting to restore him. Remarkably, neither MI6 nor even Mossad knew that the shah was suffering from cancer, and did not have long to live. In the event, the ailing and unwanted former ally shuttled between Morocco, the Bahamas and Mexico, eventually dying in Egypt in July 1980.[85]

When Robert Armstrong, the senior official at the Home Office, first heard media stories about BOSS agents in Britain, he had scoffed that the BBC 'all look fools' because it had joined Harold Wilson in his 'mad pursuit of South African spies'.[86] But by 1979, uncomfortable evidence was piling up, and Armstrong's department had no option but to investigate. This realisation was symptomatic of a wider and more worrying shift during the 1970s. Prior to Heath's famous expulsion of KGB officers in 1971, the streets of London had been overwhelmed with Soviet spies. Now there was growing concern about all sorts of exotic secret services, including Middle East operatives engaged in assassination and working hand in glove with terrorists.

Callaghan was well aware of all this. In 1978, two Labour MPs had complained to him about undercover agents they had spotted at anti-apartheid meetings, and assumed they were under MI5 surveillance. The prime minister assured them that this was not the case. The agents, he explained, were there 'to keep an eye on BOSS – the South African secret service, and to find out what meetings they were attending'.[87] MPs began to ask probing questions. Why had these South African agents not been ejected, given that Britain had expelled nearly a hundred KGB officers a decade before? Officials were in a pickle. They noted that the South African intelligence officers in London were 'primarily concerned with groups opposed to the present regime', rather than working directly to undermine UK national security, as had been the case of the Russians. Moreover, they added, they could not 'allow it to be known' that there had been South African intelligence officers present in Britain with the knowledge and consent of the Callaghan government. Senior officials muttered, 'The less said, the better.'[88]

South Africa's most active agent in Britain had been Gordon Winter. Employed as a journalist in London, he illustrated the strange way in which the worlds of secrecy and publicity seemed to be converging. By the late 1970s, Winter was disturbed that the British press had begun to uncover his activities. His managers assured him that there was no danger of him being outed by the British government, because they had leverage in the form of a full dossier on a top-level sex scandal that 'would make the Christine Keeler business look trivial'. This episode involved a female CIA operative who had been seconded to Whitehall and who had slept with several MPs in order to gather intelligence for Washington.

> At least three of these MPs had also been involved in sex orgies in a London house and BOSS had various photographs taken in a first floor bedroom of that house, including snippets of a movie film showing two of these MPs together on a bed with two naked women ... What pleased BOSS most was that the father of the woman who owned the house worked at the Soviet Embassy in London.

Winter and his friends were sitting on a world of secrets that would discomfort Whitehall. He had acquired them through his close association with the MI6 agent and gun-runner Leslie Aspin and his friendly relations with the Metropolitan Police Special Branch. BOSS managed to suppress much of this during the late 1970s, only for Winter to embrace the anti-apartheid cause and flee to Ireland, where he published a remarkable tell-all account a few years later.[89]

MI5 had many other miscreants to watch. In July 1978, the assassination of former Iraqi prime minister Said al-Naif, on the orders of Saddam Hussein, became the third major terrorist incident involving Arabs in London that year. In January, Said Hammani, the PLO's London representative, had been murdered, and four days previously two Syrian embassy officials had been blown up in their cars. In 1977, three people, including a former North Yemeni prime minister, had been killed in London, and General al-Naif had himself escaped a previous assassination attack. The streets of the British capital had become a dangerous playground for the gunmen of foreign intelligence agencies. MI5 argued that Libyan, Iraqi and Yemeni intelligence services 'engaged on a significant scale' in the 'location, monitoring of and, if necessary, assassination of dissidents' in Britain, and also the support of terrorism. Both MI5 and the Home Office stressed the need to 'clamp down' on these gangs of 'criminal thugs'. Recent European agreements on counter-terrorism cooperation meant Britain now had a wider responsibility to bring these rogue secret services to order.[90]

For Callaghan, the most troubling political violence came from a surge in IRA attacks. In a single day at the end of November 1978, the IRA bombed sixteen towns in Northern Ireland. On 17 and 18 December, they planted some thirteen bombs in London and Liverpool. Although the security services managed to defuse many of the bombs and there were no fatalities, the IRA had successfully attacked the oil refinery at Canvey Island and the Blackwall Tunnel. The IRA campaign in England then began to diminish, partly because of poor operational preparations, and also because of increasingly successful penetration by agents for the Irish Joint Section, run by MI5 and MI6 together. IRA operations on the Continent proved more successful. During August 1978, they succeeded in planting a number of bombs at British Army barracks across Germany. Although there were no fatalities, the IRA had found a weak link: the numerous and greatly dispersed British targets in Europe. They began serious reconnaissance.[91]

Late in the afternoon of Thursday, 25 January 1979, Roy Jenkins, president of the European Commission, had a visit from the head of his protection service, accompanied by a British security officer 'in great agitation and secrecy'. 'British sources' had informed them that 'there was a serious IRA plot to assassinate in the fairly near future a senior British representative' in Brussels. They had narrowed the list down to Jenkins, the diplomats Christopher Tugendhat and Crispin Tickell, and two generals. British intelligence had obtained remarkable detail about the plot. Jenkins was told that the IRA had 'set up some sort of watching/firing post quite some time previous outside the house of the person who was the target', and were finding him quite annoying as his habits and movements were 'somewhat irregular'. Jenkins recorded in his diary with obvious relief, 'not true of mine'. They had been told that the assassination would happen 'in the next few weeks'. Nervously, Jenkins walked home, 'rushing across the pavement' as he realised how 'incredibly exposed' someone in this position is, and how little they can do.[92] Five days later, there were three bomb attacks on British diplomatic premises in France. As late as 19 February 1979, an MI5 report on the assassination threat in Brussels was being discussed in Downing Street.[93]

Increased security measures proved only partly effective. On 22 March, Sir Richard Sykes, British ambassador in The Hague, and his valet Karel Straub were fatally shot at short range by two men who fired a total of eight rounds. Sykes was targeted because he had been head of the Foreign Office department dealing with Ireland. His valet may have been mistaken for the chief of MI6, Dickie Franks, who had met Sykes the previous day, having changed the date of his visit at the last moment as a security precaution.[94] On the same day André Michaux, a Belgian financier, was shot and killed as he came out of his house in Brussels. Paul Holmer, a senior member of the British delegation to NATO who lived across the street, was almost certainly the intended target. Roy Jenkins noted that this tied up with intelligence the British had received six weeks before, but he had 'typically forgotten about in the meantime'.[95]

Callaghan was horrified, and ordered a crackdown. Heads of mission were issued with bulletproof cars, and an SAS team was sent out to inspect vulnerabilities in Paris, where the ambassador, Sir Reginald Hibbert, looked like the next target. Unfortunately, there were not enough bullet-proof cars to go around, and the next person to be shot at in Europe was Christopher Tugendhat in Brussels, whom the would-be assassin 'narrowly missed'.[96] The response was an extensive collaborative effort between the intelligence and security agencies of Holland, West Germany and Britain, although the Dutch were hampered by the fact that warrants for the bugging and telephone interception of IRA sympathisers were almost impossible to obtain from their government.[97] On the British side, MI6 took the lead, assisted by the intelligence and security arms of the British Army of the Rhine. With the West German and Dutch security services, a number of highly successful penetration operations were carried out against the IRA, eventually forcing it to fold its Continental activities.[98]

However, on 30 March 1979, the IRA assassinated the British MP Airey Neave in London. Few assassinations in British political history have been more significant. In terms of internal party politics, it was Neave who persuaded Thatcher to stand for the leadership of the Conservative Party, and had then masterminded her campaign with what Jim Prior describes as a mixture of 'persistence and almost obsessive scheming'.[99] Neave was vital to Thatcher, who was still not fully accepted by the majority of her shadow cabinet.[100] Having headed up MI9, the British escape and evasion service, during the war, Neave was also close to MI5's main expert on left-wing subversion, Charles Elwell.[101] There are suggestions that Thatcher had planned to appoint him to a new government position to oversee the security and intelligence community.

Assassination and turmoil on the streets of London were not the only thing to concern Margaret Thatcher as she made her bid for Number 10.

Britain was simultaneously paralysed by strikes. Callaghan had initially convinced union leaders that, with an election looming, any strikes would favour Thatcher. They therefore had a strong incentive to maintain consensus around containment of inflation. But a wave of discontent grew as wages slipped further behind prices, and union leaders preferred to fight the government than to take on their angry members. This led to massive industrial action, especially in the public sector. Callaghan's adviser David Lipsey recalls: 'In Liverpool the dead lay unburied as the municipal workers struck. In Leicester Square a few hundred yards away from the centre of government, stinking rubbish was piled high in the streets. We felt we had lost control. Indeed we had lost control.' The strikes were a genuine upsurge from below, and were not the work of militants or communists.[102] Regardless, Margaret Thatcher perceived them as evidence of a plot. Alongside domestic terrorism and apparent subversion, as well as the various crises precipitated by the fall of the shah in Iran, Margaret Thatcher's first few months brought some momentous events. Once inside Number 10, she was determined to take personal charge.

15

Margaret Thatcher
(1979–1990)

I am very well aware of the
disinformation practices of the KGB.
MARGARET THATCHER[1]

Margaret Thatcher adored intelligence. Nigel Lawson, her chancellor, observed: 'Most prime ministers have a soft spot for the security services, for which they have a special responsibility. But Margaret … was positively besotted by them.'[2] With a notorious appetite for late-night paperwork and a gimlet eye for detail, she paid more attention to incoming intelligence than any prime minister since Winston Churchill. Like her wartime predecessor, Thatcher's view of intelligence was incurably romantic, fuelled, according to Lawson, by the fact that she was 'an avid reader of the works of Frederick Forsyth'. On Friday, 29 February 1980, still in her first year of office, she became the first prime minister to attend a meeting of the Joint Intelligence Committee. Afterwards she told its chairman, Antony Acland, that she thought sitting with them had allowed her to understand intelligence in its proper context. More importantly, she had found the experience 'thoroughly enjoyable in its own right'.[3]

'She was difficult to deal with,' recalls Acland. 'She was very confrontational and you had to be pretty tough and sometimes quite rude to her.' He added that quite a lot of people always thought that Margaret Thatcher had been up at five o'clock, had read the brief, had made up her mind and that the buck stopped with her, so 'there was no point in arguing'. Actually, she enjoyed being challenged, and 'occasionally, she would change her mind'. 'But you had to be pretty rough.' In order to gain her attention, Acland would later threaten to resign.[4] Few prime ministers spent so much time poring over the JIC's famous 'Red Book' of weekly intelligence highlights. As well as the Red Book, GCHQ also produced the 'Blue Book', full of its best sigint, while MI6 produced the 'CX Book', which contained its top human agent reports. Thatcher devoured these, and often took them to Chequers on the weekend to read at her leisure. Charles Powell, her private secretary, would mark things up for her attention, and they would come back on Monday covered in scribbled annotations demanding action or more information.[5]

Thatcher was also a risk-taker. No less than Ronald Reagan, she wished to accelerate the Cold War against Moscow. Elected a full twenty months before Reagan, it was Thatcher and her ministers who set the pace and wanted to unleash both MI6 and the CIA to engage in covert action. While Britain secretly fought the Soviets in Afghanistan, Thatcher's policy advisers pressed for a new Cold War using resistance groups, secret radio stations and subversion all around Moscow's borderlands. Controversially, she was also happy to assume the offensive on the home front, hounding what she called 'the enemies within' with her own band of privatised secret agents, who alarmed and indeed competed with the sober sentinels of MI5.

As prime minister, Thatcher was personally close to a number of intelligence figures. She admired Sir Maurice Oldfield, who had been head of MI6 between 1973 and 1978. Shortly after arriving in office, she sent him to Northern Ireland to coordinate a badly fragmented intelligence effort between the police, the army, MI5 and MI6.[6] She was intensely loyal to her friends, and when the controversial subject of Oldfield's homosexuality surfaced, she gave a full and supportive statement to the press.[7]

Despite her portrayal as 'the Iron Lady', Thatcher had a sentimental side when it came to intelligence personnel. She shared their love of action, admired their risk-taking and sympathised with the personal torments of spies when things went wrong. She also valued loyalty, service and friendship, often showing kindness to those around her. She expressed concern for Roger Hollis, the former director-general of MI5, when he was accused of being a Russian agent. Clearly disbelieving the allegations, which lingered during the first half of her premiership, Thatcher lamented, 'It's awful for his family, being persecuted after all this time and having his reputation attacked in this cruel way.'[8]

Thatcher's relationship with the secret world is often misunderstood. All prime ministers are intrigued by the secret world of intelligence, but as we have seen, in the 1970s markedly different styles had been displayed at the top. Edward Heath and James Callaghan had worn the duties of intelligence oversight lightly. Harold Wilson was preoccupied by intelligence in his second administration, but this cast a dark shadow, since he feared that he himself was a victim of plots and conspiracies. Margaret Thatcher has been rightly portrayed as a boundless enthusiast for intelligence, but she did not trust Britain's intelligence services.[9] Just as she suspected the Foreign Office of being asleep on the job of looking after British interests, so she suspected MI5 and MI6 of being inactive against the Soviet Union. Urged on by a number of secretive private advisers, she wanted to go further in the struggle against the enemy: global communism.

Thatcher nurtured a curious band of self-appointed private Cold Warriors during her time in office. But more importantly, these shadowy figures shaped her mind-set in the years immediately before her premiership. They included Airey Neave, Maurice Oldfield and the former *Economist* journalist Brian Crozier. Regular meetings encouraged a view of world politics that was not only Manichean but also deeply conspiratorial. Indeed, one might say that the security style of the future Thatcher administration was shaped by an ongoing secret conversation with retired hardliners from the intelligence world. These figures moved unseen while Thatcher was in opposition, but once she was in office senior Foreign Office officials became alarmed by the way in which 'all sorts of strange people' were advising her, and saw some of these characters as 'cronies' and 'crooks'.[10]

Each of these individuals was, in the words of one of them, 'a fanatical, zealot anti-communist'.[11] Perhaps the most remarkable was Brian Crozier, who worked closely with the CIA and with recently retired senior MI6 officers including George Young and Nicholas Elliott. In the 1960s, Crozier created the British-based news agency Forum World Features, with secret American support, and in the 1970s he founded a right-wing think-tank called the Institute for the Study of Conflict.[12] His first meeting with Thatcher was at a formal dinner on Tuesday, 9 March 1976, at which he expounded on the theme of 'Soviet subversion in the United Kingdom and worldwide'. To his surprise, she produced a notebook and scribbled away: 'I soon learned that her appetite for facts and views was inexhaustible.' Crozier worked with Nicholas Elliott to prepare briefs for her. Crozier was soon hosting meetings attended by Thatcher, Keith Joseph, Willie Whitelaw and Lord Carrington.[13] Elliott would also report on sensitive issues such as Rhodesia, where he advised bolstering the Smith regime.[14]

During this formative period before Thatcher's election, Crozier and his associates sketched out a 'full counter-subversion programme' against the far left. His idea was to employ Soviet-style tactics of entryism and subversion – what he called the enemy's own methods. Crozier was especially important in connecting this activity with various transatlantic supporters, including the Heritage Foundation and later the CIA.[15] It is important to appreciate that the 1970s was a time of immense political uncertainty, with coups, plots and revolutions in countries such as Portugal, Spain, Turkey and Greece. Across Europe the response from the right was the creation of the 'Pinay Cercle', named after its founder Antoine Pinay, who had been premier of France in the early 1950s.[16] The Cercle was described by one of Thatcher's ministers as a right-wing think-tank 'funded by the CIA' and run by a group that included Julian Amery, whom even his close friends regarded as 'obsessively, dottily, anti-Soviet'.[17]

The Cercle constituted an 'invisible' network that sought to shift the political climate of Europe to the right. It also sought to create a private intelligence service that would bolster the existing security services of the West, and go where officials feared to tread. In each European country there was an action group; in Britain this operational arm was known as 'the 61', and it was instrumental in developing many of Thatcher's security ideas while she was leader of the opposition in the late 1970s. Crozier's picture of Thatcher at this time is somewhat surprising. He describes her as highly intelligent, but also naïve and lacking in confidence. But she was a quick learner, and soon absorbed the ideas of the 61, eventually coming to regard them as her own.[18]

By May 1979, when her premiership began, Thatcher and her key ministers were already obsessed with subversion and 'wreckers'. Immediately on her accession she called a meeting with the director-general of MI5, together with her adviser Lord Rothschild and the cabinet secretary, to demand 'solutions'. The cabinet secretary resisted, telling her that MI5's mandates covered subversives but not industrial wreckers. Nevertheless, by October, the Cabinet Office boasted a new unit designed to forestall industrial disruption, headed by a high-flying MI5 officer, John Deverell, who was close to the prime minister's informal network.[19] Other private groups such as the Economic League were also on the rise.[20]

The security services were alarmed by Thatcher's focus on conspiracy, and were aware that she believed the KGB was deeply connected to the peace movement. Joan Ruddock, the chair of CND, had indeed unwittingly held meetings with Soviet officials who were in reality KGB officers. The KGB itself had made exaggerated claims about this, and the security services had 'fears' that if these claims were reported to Thatcher she would take them 'too literally'.[21] MI5 did not trust Thatcher on this issue, and Thatcher did not trust MI5. Instead, private organisations such as the Coalition for Peace Through Security were conjured into existence as counter-movements. These bodies infiltrated CND in the hope of gathering evidence of manipulation by the far left and the hidden hand of Soviet intelligence or special forces. Bizarre stories soon circulated, involving female Soviet commandos mingling with women in the peace camp outside RAF Greenham Common. While MI5 certainly monitored contacts between CND and the extreme left, officials were outpaced by Thatcher's private security effort. Indeed, they were amazed by the scale and audacity of the operations launched by the privateers, which included stealing documents from CND's headquarters – nothing moved in the offices of CND without the knowledge of this band of secret watchers.[22] Ministers played their part, and Douglas Hurd, a former home and foreign secretary, is one of the few senior government figures to have referred openly to the Thatcher government's 'successful campaign against CND'.[23]

Bernard Ingham, Thatcher's bulldog press secretary, often complained about the way journalists wove conspiracy theories around Number 10. Speaking before the Media Society in November 1985, he drew on a fictitious work of reference, *Black's Compendium of Journalists' Diseases*, to identify what he called 'le Carré syndrome': the conviction that government is inevitably, irrevocably and chronically up to no good, not to be trusted and conspiratorial. This, he continued, could be made worse by 'Conan Doyle complication'. No journalist suffering from this condition would go for the simple explanation when an alternate theory of fantastic complexity could be constructed. He traced the beginnings of this conspiracy-mania back to Watergate, noting that the Nixon government had 'a lot to answer for'. But we now know that truth was stranger than fiction. Some of Thatcher's closest advisers were completely fascinated by the idea of plots and counter-plots.[24]

The Soviet invasion of Afghanistan on Christmas Day 1979 was not a surprise. Western intelligence performed well, and top-level intelligence reports on Soviet mobilisation had been shared by 10 Downing Street and the White House for some weeks before the invasion. GCHQ and its American equivalent organisation, the NSA, had been watching a strange black armoured train deep inside the Soviet Union. This was the secretive mobile headquarters for the Soviet armed forces, and as it sped from one underground tunnel to another, the West was monitoring its movements and communications. Whenever the train was moving, something was happening.[25]

There have been suggestions that the ability to read high-level Soviet communications, which the West enjoyed only briefly, allowed some manipulation of Moscow on this issue. London and Washington knew that the Russians were highly suspicious of the current Afghan premier, Hafizullah Amin, since he had studied at Columbia University in New York, and had even run an American-financed student group in Kabul. The KGB station was convinced that he was an American agent and would try to turn his country to the West, as Anwar Sadat had recently done in Egypt. In the summer of 1979, Jimmy Carter had signed a presidential 'finding' to approve covert action operations designed to aid Islamic fighters, which increased this anxiety. Yuri Andropov, the head of the KGB in Moscow, pressed the Politburo and an ailing Leonid Brezhnev to invade Afghanistan, against the advice of the Russian military, who knew it would be a quagmire.[26]

Thatcher had a meeting with Carter a week before the invasion, at which Carter showed her photographs from America's powerful satellites which indicated that troop levels were rising – two divisions that had vanished from the Soviet border area were thought to have moved into Afghanistan. Four battalions had been stationed near the airstrip at Kabul, and Carter thought the Soviets 'were increasingly prepared to act militarily in Afghanistan'. He had already expressed his concern publicly, and asked if Thatcher could do the same 'on the BBC'. He also asked if she 'would like to receive regular reports through the CIA' on the situation in Afghanistan. Unsurprisingly, Thatcher responded that she 'would indeed'.[27]

On Christmas Day, the KGB, assisted by special forces, closed in on the Darul Aman Palace on the outskirts of Kabul. They fought their way into the palace complex, and after a fierce exchange of fire in which a KGB general was killed, took control. The American-educated President Hafizullah Amin and his supporters were put up against a wall and shot. Earlier, the KGB had managed to infiltrate an agent into the palace with instructions to poison Amin's food, but the president survived. All these operations had been personally approved by Brezhnev.

Thatcher recalled the invasion of Afghanistan as one of those 'genuine watersheds' which are so often predicted but which rarely occur. She wanted to punish the Soviets for their aggression, and saw covert action as the way forward. Speaking with her on the telephone three days after Christmas, Carter asserted, 'I don't think we can afford to let them get away with this.'

Thatcher agreed: 'I think when something like this happens the important thing is to act right at the beginning.'[28] While we tend to associate the Thatcher era with Ronald Reagan, in fact Reagan did not arrive at the White House until January 1981; Thatcher's first collaborator on Afghanistan was Jimmy Carter. Carter found Thatcher to be highly opinionated, and felt that she 'cannot admit that she does not know something'. She for her part considered him soft on communism. But their views were aligning, not least because Carter had been growing increasingly impatient with Soviet foot-dragging over arms control. Afghanistan was the last straw.[29]

Thatcher's colleagues were also keen on action. The foreign secretary, Lord Carrington, thought the invasion was a most serious challenge, because it might well be repeated. A similar Soviet incursion into Yugoslavia would give it a major presence in the Mediterranean, which would be potentially disastrous. But he was also clear that there were opportunities for the West. On 2 January 1980, he predicted that the Soviets were likely to be drawn into a long and difficult counter-insurgency campaign in Afghanistan.[30] In mid-January, Carter wrote to Thatcher that they should make it clear that the Soviets could not do this sort of thing without 'the most serious penalties'.[31] A few days later, Thatcher responded, assuring him that 'We are also looking at a variety of possibilities for covert action.'[32]

On a tour of the region, Carrington found the Gulf states in disarray, but was pleased to find that Saudi Arabia was working with Pakistan to mobilise Muslim opinion against Soviet action. He was especially worried about the Pakistanis, who felt squeezed between the Russian troops in Afghanistan and India on their eastern border. Pakistan feared Soviet raids into their territory. Nevertheless, Carrington wanted a widespread campaign of covert action: 'We should consider the practicability of promoting insurgency in Soviet-dominated areas such as the PDRY [Yemen], Ethiopia and Afghanistan itself.' He also wanted to improve the flow of intelligence assessments to friendly states in the Gulf and to Pakistan, as well as assisting them with counter-subversion.[33] Meanwhile, Robert Armstrong, the cabinet secretary, had been to Paris to talk to Britain's European allies. The French, always enthusiasts for covert action, were advocating sending weapons via Iraq, but the West Germans were horrified by the idea of secret warfare.[34]

By the end of the month Carrington had concrete proposals for covert action, and outlined 'what further action we need to set in train':

Two ideas are already being pursued. The first is support for patriots inside Afghanistan through the covert supply of arms and training, amongst other things. French officials favour this; the Chinese are also interested; and the US are already active in this respect. Moslem money is already flowing, and may be sufficient. There is a risk that the Russians would see this as a pretext for raiding over the Afghan border. The Pakistanis are understandably nervous.

The second idea was to persuade the various Afghan patriotic organisations to overcome their 'chronic disunity'. This could best be done by encouraging the Islamic countries to support a united 'Afghan Liberation Organisation'. The purpose of covert action, Carrington explained to Thatcher, was to maintain military pressure in Afghanistan and to show the world that the Russians were 'not having things all their way'. He accepted that the war would be long, and that the prospect of Russian departure in the short term was 'remote'.[35]

Pakistan gained confidence, and as a result, British involvement in covert action accelerated towards the end of 1980. On 15 October, President Zia-ul-Haq of Pakistan visited Carter in Washington, and raised 'the very sensitive question of external aid to the Afghan national resistance movement'. Zia wanted more external aid, and particularly to stress that he would be receptive to British initiatives in this area. On the same day, Carter asked Thatcher to increase the pace, noting that the Americans were 'already active'. He said that Zia had asked for 'a positive expression of support from you in this regard', and that he hoped Thatcher's reply could be 'channelled to him very directly'. He added, 'I am asking the Director of the Central Intelligence Agency to be in touch with his appropriate counterpart in Britain to pursue this matter on a more active and tangible basis, subject of course to your political decision.'[36] This was one of Carter's last substantive messages to Thatcher prior to the end of his administration. Ronald Reagan was already preparing to move into the White House.

The CIA and the British prime minister were moving closer together. On 28 February 1981, a few weeks after President Reagan's inauguration, Margaret Thatcher was awarded the Donovan Medal by the Office of Strategic Services veterans' association. The OSS was the forerunner of the CIA, and had constituted America's intelligence and special operations service during World War II. The same award had been given to Allen

Dulles, Richard Helms, David Bruce, John McCone and Sir William Stephenson.[37] After a dinner at the Waldorf Hotel in New York, Thatcher was introduced to the assembled veterans of America's secret world by Bill Casey, Reagan's new director of central intelligence. In her speech she reeled off the names of those who had served in what she called General Donovan's 'University for Courage': David Bruce, Carleton Coon, William Langer and Arthur Schlesinger. She then turned to Casey and added, 'What could be more heartening for us in Britain than to have as the new director of the CIA a man who ran the Secret Intelligence Section of OSS in London during the last war?' She went on to denounce the dangers of Soviet expansionism, singling out Afghanistan for particular mention.[38] Thatcher loved addressing an audience of veteran secret warriors, and was at her rhetorical best, drawing deafening applause and remaining in a state of 'euphoria' for hours afterwards.[39]

MI6 enjoyed a high reputation at the start of the Afghan War. It boasted the best relations with Ahmad Shah Massoud, one of the key warlords in Afghanistan – 'We think he has all the makings of a second Tito,' claimed one senior MI6 officer. Moreover, Massoud controlled the area of Afghanistan through which much of the Soviet logistics had to travel.[40] MI6 also enjoyed the enviable advantage that its personnel were allowed to enter Afghanistan, while CIA officers were forbidden, hovering timorously on the border. MI6's day-to-day contact with the guerrillas was maintained by three SAS operatives who spent weeks at a time in country. Their experiences – which included lying awake at night listening to the terrible sounds of Massoud's men torturing a Soviet prisoner – were raw, and the SAS had little regard for those back in Whitehall directing their activities, habitually referring to Foreign Office diplomats as 'the gay graduates' and to MI6 officers as 'the wankers'.[41]

The CIA was keen to boost British participation for three reasons. First, Britain had a historical familiarity with the region. Second, the framework of legal restrictions governing its action was suddenly looser, especially in the realm of assassination. The CIA had found itself in a great deal of trouble over this issue in 1975, when the US Congress chose to probe the matter of the agency's efforts to eliminate several premiers. Finally, as the CIA put it, Britain had a prime minister who was 'somewhere to the right of Attila the Hun'. By contrast, the CIA was labouring under a mountain of new restrictions placed upon it following the post-Watergate investigations. However, most of the aid from different countries was channelled through the Pakistani leader General Zia, who controlled everything.

Hugh Tovar, one of America's most distinguished secret operatives, who had spent a lifetime in the OSS and then the CIA, recalled that only recently covert action had been 'a dying art form'. They were now relearning the trade.[42] The Thatcher period offered them new opportunities, and Gust Avrakotos, a CIA officer serving in Afghanistan, recalled: 'The Brits were eventually able to buy things that we couldn't because it infringed on murder, assassination and indiscriminate bombings.' He added: 'They could issue guns with silencers. We couldn't do that because a silencer immediately implied assassination – and heaven forbid car bombs! No way I could even suggest it.'[43]

MI6 used ex-SAS personnel supplied by a company called Keeny Meeny Services. Initially specialising in close protection, it now ran training schools for Afghan guerrillas at bases in Saudi Arabia and Oman. By 1983 it was operating such an establishment in Scotland for junior Afghan commanders, who came for three weeks and were taught how to plan complex operations and coordinate groups on the battlefield, and were trained in explosives, ambushes and attacking airbases. Somewhat implausibly, they were told they were in Norway.[44]

In 1984, General Zia asked Margaret Thatcher for more media coverage of the secret war. Assistance to the Afghan guerrillas was an open secret in the West, but open secrecy was not Thatcher's style. Nevertheless, MI6 turned to the veteran ITV reporter Sandy Gall, who had already made one film about the guerrillas, and conveyed Zia's offer of support if he made another visit to the country. On arrival, he discovered that Pakistani special forces would accompany him into Afghanistan, and suggested they take some Soviet-made SAM-7 anti-aircraft missiles with them: 'It would make a brilliant picture if we filmed a Russian helicopter being shot down by a Russian missile.' Zia agreed, but although the delivery was made, no helicopters were shot down. On his return to Britain, Gall was treated to lunch by 'C', Sir Colin Figures, at MI6 headquarters in Century House.[45]

British influence in the secret war declined over the next five years, while the efforts of the Saudis, Pakistanis, Chinese and Americans accelerated. Urged on by Congress, by the mid-1980s the CIA was spending $700,000 a year on the war in Afghanistan, more than the entire budget of MI6. In addition, the equipment provided by Britain was suspect. Its 'Blowpipe' missiles, supplied by the hundred, failed to shoot down a single aircraft, and the guerrillas turned instead to the effective American 'Stinger' missile. Britain was a welcome source of .303 ammunition for the anti-Soviet mujahideen rebels' antique rifles, but the Ministry of Defence only provided 500,000 rounds – the Americans were in the market for five hundred million.[46]

Sandy Gall was critical of Britain's poor showing. As the war dragged on, Massoud, MI6's protégé, received fewer and fewer supplies. Meanwhile the CIA backed a more political figure, Gulbuddin Hekmatyar. When one of the team that had accompanied Gall into Afghanistan, a former SAS soldier, was murdered en route to see Massoud, Hekmatyar was thought to be the culprit.[47] Just as in wartime Yugoslavia, there was vicious factional fighting between the different groups, some secretly provoked by the KGB's skilful use of proxy forces. By early 1983, the Soviets had trained some eighty Afghan guerrilla units that posed as CIA-supported muja-hideen to create confusion. To the exasperation of MI6, the CIA later conceded that it had been backing the wrong man.[48] Hekmatyar and Massoud would fight a brutal civil war in the early 1990s, after the Soviets had departed.

Margaret Thatcher was not averse to using covert action outside Afghanistan either. Demonstrating her hatred of civil servants, espe-cially Foreign Office diplomats, she brought in special advisers, thinkers and planners who were ideologically more to her taste.[49] This was particularly true of foreign policy, where a raft of new thinkers arrived determined to make the Cold War hotter. One of the issues that had dismayed them most was the way in which Callaghan's government had shut down the Information Research Department, a unit that conducted propaganda and political warfare. They were determined that it would be revived, and more importantly that they – not the civil servants – would control it.[50]

Thatcher was interested in ideas, and attracted ideologues. She was the Western leader most influenced by the dissident novelist Alexander Solzhenitsyn and his writings about the true nature of the Soviet regime.[51] George Urban was typical of her new Cold Warriors. In February 1981, he was busy writing a paper for Thatcher on the subject of reviving the Information Research Department and calling for an information war with the Soviet Union. Urban noted gleefully in his diary that 'It will certainly strike the Foreign Office crew if they are ever shown it – as wildly out of tune with the ways of sedate government.' But this would be a bonus, since the prime minister was, he noted, 'suspicious of Foreign Office advice'.[52]

Urban was setting out nothing less than a Western ideological coun-ter-offensive vis-à-vis the Soviet Union. He lamented Western defeatism in the face of a seemingly unstoppable adversary, which, he noted, enjoyed in its information policy all the advantages of a totalitarian power at war. By contrast, 'We suffer from all the restrictions of a parliamentary democratic order at peace.' But, he added, 'We can shoot back.' Urban called for a 'combination of overt and covert action'. This new programme would include 'free radios', akin to the CIA's Radio Free Europe, but broadcasting to countries like Angola, Eritrea and Afghanistan. He advocated clandestine broadcasting by black stations with hidden identities to places like Ukraine, the Baltic states and Soviet Central Asia, together with 'intelligence and financial support' for resistance groups in these areas. Britain, he insisted, and not America, should take the lead in this new secret struggle, for although Ronald Reagan was a welcome sign of an American revival, Washington had not yet emerged from the 'trauma and self-mortification of Watergate and Vietnam'.[53]

Julian Amery, a long-term devotee of special warfare, was one of Thatcher's most important emissaries in this secret work, and served as her private ambassador to the Pinay Cercle.[54] Throughout the 1970s, Amery had kept alive his dream 'to roll back the Iron Curtain', and now, with a 'supporting cast of tight-mouthed, hawk-eyed ladies', he found he had influence. Foreign Office officials who had nurtured détente for decades found all this talk unrealistic, and were resigned to Britain's declining position in the world. To them, Amery, with his fantastic games of 'world strategy', seemed just one of a number of 'escapologists from reality'. But in fact, the privateers had spotted that the Soviet edifice was cracking, and they had the ear of Number 10.[55]

Remarkably, Thatcher put the idea of 'liberation' into action. MI6 and the CIA worked together to support the Solidarity movement in Poland, channelling secret funds. In a prescient observation, the journalist Timothy Garton Ash commented that if Solidarity could happen inside the Soviet bloc without triggering a 1968-style invasion by the Red Army, then communism was effectively finished. He was right, and was perhaps the first high-profile public commentator to anticipate the fall of the Soviet Union.[56] Thatcher launched her own personal efforts to pull away the countries of Central and Eastern Europe with a visit to Hungary in May 1984. Here she used the classic language of liberation – speaking of 'the captive nations of Eastern Europe'.[57]

Thatcher's love of secrets was mirrored by an intense loathing for public revelations. Most of all, she hated public talk about espionage, and her period as prime minister was punctuated by noisy confrontations over official secrecy with writers, journalists and ex-intelligence-officers-turned-memoir-writers. Advocates of open government, however, could have been forgiven for a bout of optimism at the start of her premiership. In November 1979, Andrew Boyle, a radio journalist and creator of the BBC Radio 4 current-affairs programme *The World at One*, published *Climate of Treason*. It pointed squarely to Anthony Blunt as the Fourth Man, dwelling at length on his association with the more flamboyant Guy Burgess – although it did not name him because of libel laws. A respected knight of the realm and personal adviser on art to the Queen, Blunt was now exposed as a key member of the traitorous Cambridge spy ring alongside Philby, Maclean and Burgess. The embarrassment was social as much as political; and delightfully English – the intelligence establishment squirmed once more.[58]

Blunt was a fizzing time-bomb that five of Thatcher's predecessors had managed to avoid. She was now called on to explain why the government of a previous Conservative prime minister, Alec Douglas-Home, had approved a secret deal to protect Blunt from prosecution in 1964. In a lengthy statement to the Commons in November 1979, Thatcher broke with tradition. Historically, prime ministers had strained every sinew to say as little as possible about intelligence. Going against her own instincts and the advice of her cabinet secretary, she revealed a great deal about Blunt, believing that a full account would draw a line under things and shut the subject down.[59] With the House of Commons full and the prime minister leaning forward in what Ian Gow called 'the Blue Peter position', she answered the many questions in ever-expanding detail.[60]

This merely encouraged a growing mole-mania amongst the press. In March 1981, to Thatcher's visible dismay, she was again forced to make a full statement in the House on KGB moles. This time it was after the publication of a book by Chapman Pincher, which wrongly and sensationally accused the former director-general of MI5, Roger Hollis, of having been a Soviet spy from the 1940s until his retirement in 1965.[61] Burke Trend, the previous cabinet secretary, had been called out of retirement to conduct an inquiry. Thatcher publicly asserted that Hollis had been cleared; but Pincher insisted that a year later, Britain's closest allies were being urged to conduct damage assessments. By 1982, it appeared that an uncomfortable statement to the House on security matters had become an annual ritual when she addressed the subject of Geoffrey Prime, a GCHQ mole, at some length.[62]

These episodes did not prove to be the dawn of a new era of government candour about MI5 and MI6. Quite the contrary – Thatcher was a keen protector of secrets, and consistently sought to stifle public debate about intelligence matters: her nine-hundred-page memoir barely mentions the subject at all.[63] Not only did she veto the publication of two official histories of wartime intelligence, she also frequently wielded the 1909 Official Secrets Act to bludgeon those who leaked.[64] Whitehall had been considering reforming the antiquated Act before Thatcher came to power, yet during the first five years of her administration she deployed it once every eighteen weeks. This is quite staggering, given that throughout the first seven decades of the Act's existence it had been used on average only once every two years. Eleven civil servants were prosecuted under Margaret Thatcher.[65]

Thatcher's obsession with secrecy was legendary. The most famous episode in her ten-year effort to suppress secrets emanated from an unlikely source. In 1984, Peter Wright, a former assistant director of MI5, decided to write his memoirs from the safety of retirement on a Tasmanian stud farm. His powers failing, they were completed and expanded by Paul Greengrass, a producer on Granada Television's *World in Action* series, and subsequently the director of the Jason Bourne film trilogy. The book was to be published by Heinemann, from the safety of its Sydney office. In July 1984, Wright appeared in a *World in Action* documentary, sparking panic across Whitehall and a frantic debate about how to shut him up, given that he lay beyond British jurisdiction. Wright had been MI5's mole-hunter extraordinaire, working with an elite team of counter-intelligence officers from the United States, Canada and Australia on projects so secret that most of the Western intelligence community knew nothing about them.[66]

Wright's imperfect memoir, *Spycatcher*, was reviled by Downing Street for several reasons. First, although it was ostensibly about MI5, some of its most sensitive secrets concerned GCHQ, the successor to the Bletchley Park codebreakers. GCHQ was perhaps the last really secret aspect of British government. During Thatcher's era, its true size – more than twice that of MI5 and MI6 combined – was kept hidden even from the British cabinet.[67] Second, it broke the convention that secret servants should not write memoirs, and so threatened a flood of emulators. Third, it revived the damaging accusations against Roger Hollis, which Thatcher had tried to quash when they were published by Chapman Pincher three years earlier – in fact, Wright had been the main source for Pincher's repetitious stream of publications on moles. Fourth, it set off a new wave of rumours about other moles, including some in Thatcher's immediate circle, such as Victor Rothschild.[68]

Thatcher despatched her cabinet secretary, Robert Armstrong, to give evidence in the Supreme Court of New South Wales. This was unprecedented, and an altogether rather odd thing for a cabinet secretary to be asked to do. Armstrong, whose relationship with Thatcher was already strained, was clearly stressed. At Heathrow airport, on being questioned closely by the press he actually 'lashed out with his briefcase at photographers and pushed one of them against a wall'. Later, under the withering fire of sharp Australian lawyers, he disintegrated. He denied the existence of MI6, and then discussed the role of Dick White as head of the same service. He admitted that the government had secretly obtained copies of Wright's book before it was published, and conceded that the government had been 'economical with the truth'. Thereafter, he was subjected to ridicule by the judge, the press and the wider public.[69]

Parliament was in uproar. David Steel, leader of the Liberal Party, described Armstrong as a 'garbage operator' for the government, engaged on an overtly ideological mission that compromised his political neutrality; as such he was now 'damaged goods'.[70] The trial cost the British taxpayer more than £3 million. Amazingly, Thatcher ignored the press commentary and told her inner circle that Armstrong was 'doing well'. Regardless of whether she won or lost, she deemed it of 'great importance' to have brought the case at all – perhaps as an expression of the ideology of secrecy. The main purpose was to deter former secret service members from 'pursuing their own quarrels' in the public sphere or seeking 'to make money out of them'.[71]

Ironically, banning the book made Peter Wright millions. Topping the New York Times bestseller list, it remained banned in Britain, with newspapers under a gagging order that forbade them to report its contents. In the marketplace in Cambridge, an enterprising stallholder gave away free copies of Spycatcher if people bought a postcard for £10. Bemused police constables looked on, but decided that this was legal. These rich absurdities made the law an ass, and ensured an unending stream of publicity for a book that for the most part repeated old stories and some inaccuracies. In October 1988, the law lords finally ruled that overseas publication had made the injunction pointless. But Thatcher had not given up, and the following year introduced a draconian new Official Secrets Act which explicitly forbade former or present members of the intelligence and security services from claiming public interest when making disclosures.[72]

In early March 1982, a comic episode was under way in the South Atlantic. It concerned South Georgia, a dependency of the Falkland Islands. This was a small colony of a colony, and the island from which Ernest Shackleton had departed on his Antarctic explorations. Argentina claimed both South Georgia and the Falkland Islands, and some Argentinean scrap-metal merchants had shown up on South Georgia, raised the Argentinean flag and were making a nuisance of themselves. Journalists in Fleet Street found the whole episode laughable, and referred to the amateur invaders as 'Latin Steptoes'.[73]

There may have been laughter in London, but there was panic in Buenos Aires. For months, the fascist Argentinean junta had been secretly planning a surprise attack on the Falklands, with a launch date of the autumn of 1982. But now, fearing exposure, they crashed the gears. On 23 March, the military were told that they no longer had six months to prepare – instead they had six days. The senior officer who was to run the new Argentinean administration on the 'Islas Malvinas', was only told of his role a day before the operation was launched. Remarkably, the attack on the Falklands was not only a surprise to the British, but also to most of the senior Argentinean officers who participated in it. This helps to explain why British intelligence failed to notice the invasion preparations, since there were very few to see.

Nevertheless, the British intelligence machine had failed. Having been asked about the possibility of such an invasion every six months for as long as they could remember, intelligence assessors had come to believe that it was intrinsically unlikely. They had also developed a fixed model of how any war over the Falklands would break out, based on gradually escalating tension. Over the weekend of 27–28 March, the British ambassador in Buenos Aires was told by the Argentines that South Georgia was now a 'closed issue', and would not be discussed further. This ominous sign was accompanied by general instructions to Argentinean embassies around the world to cancel all leave. All this activity was monitored by GCHQ, yet the JIC still did not think the crisis over South Georgia would have immediate implications for the Falklands.[74]

Margaret Thatcher proved to be a better intelligence analyst. As we have seen, both MI6 and GCHQ maintained their long-established practice of selecting choice items of raw intelligence for Downing Street. This allowed Thatcher to engage in some Churchill-style 'DIY analysis'. When she and her foreign secretary Lord Carrington saw the raw intercepts on South Georgia, their gut instincts told them that this meant trouble. Discussing the matter over a secure scrambler phone on the evening of Sunday, 28 March, they resolved to send three nuclear submarines south immediately. To their credit, these were sailing within perhaps three days of the moment at which the junta had suddenly decided to invade the Falklands.

On Wednesday, 31 March, GCHQ finally picked up clear signs of an impending attack. The Argentine submarine *Santa Fe* was landing a commando reconnaissance team on the beach at Mullet Creek on the Falklands. This could mean only one thing – invasion was close. The intelligence was flashed to the Cabinet Office. GCHQ also detected a rapid rise in radio traffic, suggesting that an invasion fleet was mustering off the Falklands. Late on Wednesday afternoon, a team from the Defence Intelligence Staff arrived at the House of Commons office of the defence secretary, John Nott, to give him a briefing. Reviewing a range of intercepted messages, it was now very clear that an invasion was planned for the morning of Friday, 2 April. Nott asked to see the prime minister immediately, and an informal meeting of ministers and permanent under-secretaries gathered in her room to discuss initial reactions. Thatcher recalled that the material from GCHQ was compelling, and there was 'no ground to question the intelligence'.[75]

Towards the end of the meeting Henry Leach, the First Sea Lord, arrived in full-dress uniform. Thatcher recalls it as a moment of 'comedy' in an otherwise dark episode. With 'supreme self-confidence and assertiveness' Leach reported that much of the British fleet just happened to be exercising off Gibraltar. It would be possible to send a large task force to the South Atlantic within a week, and he predicted that the Argentines would flee at the sight of the White Ensign. Could he have permission? Thatcher agreed immediately, and with visible relief. She knew that her government was in very serious trouble, and the performance of her ministers in the ensuing emergency debates did nothing to dispel the general air of incompetence. Many have concluded that if the risky decision to send the task force had not been taken, the Thatcher government would not have survived.[76]

On the same day, Thatcher fired off a message to Ronald Reagan, asking whether he had received the same sort of intelligence from America's NSA. Lurking underneath this apparently innocent enquiry was a worry in Whitehall that someone in one of the many American agencies might have had an inkling of the attack and not told the British. Antony Duff, Margaret Thatcher's intelligence coordinator in the Cabinet Office, found it 'infuriating' that he had to spend time fending off such suggestions, some from experienced senior intelligence officers who could not believe that America's enormous fleet of surveillance satellites would not have picked up the invasion force as it mustered. Bobby Ray Inman, the deputy director of the CIA, issued a public denial of this a month after the invasion.[77]

On Thursday, 1 April, Lord Carrington arrived at Number 10 to see Thatcher. As he walked towards her office he signalled his wish to resign by giving a 'thumbs down' signal to Bernard Ingham, her press secretary.[78] Carrington felt he had to go partly because of the intelligence failure, since the Foreign Office chaired the JIC and also commanded Britain's two external intelligence agencies, GCHQ and MI6. On 5 April, he finally departed after his rough reception at the hands of backbenchers at the 1922 Committee, when he encountered what Jim Prior described as little short of 'sheer hatred'.[79] This had left him 'very upset'. Carrington was a superb foreign secretary, but because he was not an MP he was almost unknown in the Commons. Thatcher pondered replacing him with the buccaneering Julian Amery, but opted instead for Francis Pym.[80]

Telephone calls early on the morning of 2 April summoned cabinet ministers to a special meeting at Number 10. Most had no idea what was going on, and were 'caught by surprise' – one arrived in the family Metro, another by bicycle.[81] Kenneth Baker, then a junior minister, recalls: 'There was no sense of crisis at Number 10 and Margaret was very cool.' Baker had arranged a lunch in Downing Street for that day at which the prime minister would meet four industrialists and four academics to discuss the training of technologists. He expected it to be cancelled, but it went ahead. However, she asked if they minded her leaving a little early, remarking as she rose from her place, 'I must sort out rumour from fact.'[82] By 3 April, it was clear that the Argentine force was firmly established on the Falklands, in some numbers.[83]

An anxious American delegation, led by secretary of state Al Haig, was soon propelling itself through the famous black door of Number 10. Like many others, Haig confessed to 'astonishment' that America's electronic eyes and ears had not picked up signs of the invasion beforehand. Although Washington's initial position was one of neutrality, with Haig attempting Kissinger-like shuttle diplomacy, behind the scenes the US intelligence community had already declared for Britain. When Jeane Kirkpatrick, the US ambassador to the United Nations, told the US National Security Council that backing Argentina was crucial to American security, it was Bobby Ray Inman from the CIA who responded that she was talking rubbish – a stand-up row in front of Reagan followed. A week later, when senior MI6 officers visited the CIA headquarters at Langley in Virginia, they found the corridors decorated with Union Jack bunting, a moment that brought tears to their eyes.[84]

Almost exactly a month later, the most controversial action of the war occurred. On 2 May, the Argentine cruiser *General Belgrano* was sunk by a British nuclear-powered attack submarine, HMS *Conqueror*, while outside the exclusion zone that the British had declared around the Falklands. The *Belgrano*'s main threat was her powerful radar, while the destroyers that were accompanying her carried deadly Exocet missiles, which posed a serious danger to the British task force. The group was being shadowed by HMS *Conqueror*, under Commander Christopher Wreford-Brown, and the Admiralty asked for a change to the rules of engagement to allow an attack on the cruiser while she was outside the exclusion zone. After some debate, the war cabinet gave its approval at ten o'clock in the morning. It was Willie Whitelaw, the deputy prime minister, who asked the key question: if the *Conqueror* was asked merely to shadow the *Belgrano* group for the time being, could she be certain to maintain contact? Due to bad weather, the answer was an emphatic 'no'. Even while this fraught discussion was going on, and unbeknown to the cabinet, the *Belgrano* group changed course and, gently zig-zagging, began heading away from the Falklands. At 1.30 in the afternoon the *Conqueror* rose to the surface and accessed a satellite signal which gave her permission to attack.[85]

Choosing Mark 8 torpedoes of Second World War vintage, Wreford-Brown gradually moved to within two miles of the *Belgrano*. At the last moment he thought he had misjudged his approach, but after a few seconds' hesitation he fired three torpedoes. Less than a minute later, the first of them hit the *Belgrano* just ahead of the front gun turret. A massive flash lit up the sky, and the explosion nearly blew the entire bow of the ship off. The *Belgrano* was already doomed when the second torpedo slammed home. The third also found its mark, but failed to explode. The *Belgrano* was sunk thirty miles outside the exclusion zone, and 386 Argentine sailors perished. By the following day, all Argentinean naval vessels had been recalled to within a few miles of the coast.

The *Belgrano* story is all about signals and real-time intelligence. The officers on board the *Conqueror* were delighted with the flow of secret material from GCHQ. 'We are evidently able to intercept much, if not all the enemies' signals traffic,' noted one of them in his diary, adding: 'The boys at Cheltenham know their stuff.' But at the same time, they believed that the Soviets might well be passing sigint and imagery intelligence to the Argentines. So, to avoid detection, they could only rise to the surface to receive signals from London in the periods between the passing over-head of Soviet satellites. To make things worse, the *Conqueror* was having problems with one of her communications masts, and so was routing her messages through New Zealand rather than direct to London. All this had an impact on the chain of events.[86]

Margaret Thatcher was severely criticised for permitting the attack outside the exclusion zone. However, it now seems that the key signals intelligence concerning this controversial action reached London before the *Belgrano* group had changed course. Events turned largely upon a sequence of Argentine navy signals that were intercepted and read by GCHQ. On 1 May, the Argentine navy was told to locate the British task force and launch a 'massive attack'. The *Belgrano* was ordered south, and into the exclusion zone. This alarming signal was intercepted by GCHQ, and shaped the government's deliberations. Shortly afterwards, the war cabinet met at Chequers and authorised the controversial attack on the *Belgrano*. Although at this moment she still lay outside the exclusion zone, she clearly constituted a serious threat. Later, a new batch of intercepted signals revealed that the Argentinean military chiefs had changed their minds and ordered the *Belgrano* to reverse course. But the new intelligence was not processed and distributed to London until the following day. Nor could there be immediate contact with the submarine. Many asserted that Thatcher had pursued this action in order to 'torpedo' an American-backed Peruvian peace plan, but it now seems clear that the *Belgrano* was sunk for operational rather than political reasons.[87]

With Argentina's navy on the run, the biggest threat to the task force became its air force. Equipped with extremely effective French-made Exocet missiles, the Argentinean pilots had a good chance of destroying the task force, and the British strained every muscle to reduce the impact of this threat. An SAS reconnaissance team was sent into Argentina to watch the runways and send a warning signal whenever enemy aircraft took off, while, the French were persuaded to hand over the technical details of the Exocets. Most importantly, MI6 launched several operations to prevent more missiles being bought on the open market, since the French had sold over a hundred to various governments around the world.

The latest intelligence suggested that the Argentines had 'only two or three Exocets still operational'. However, the game-changer was external sources. It was thought that 'deliveries' might raise this total to as many as ten within three of four weeks.[88] The biggest worry was a shipment of Exocets that was due to leave France for Peru, an ally of Argentina. Thatcher warned François Mitterrand, the French president, that they were likely to be passed to Argentina, adding that this would have 'a devastating effect on the relationship between our two countries. Indeed, it would have a disastrous effect on the alliance as a whole.' Mitterrand assured her that they would not reach Peru.

On 4 May, two days after the sinking of the *Belgrano*, the British destroyer HMS *Sheffield* was lost to an Exocet strike. The anxiety about additional Exocets now turned to panic. The French had supplied this missile to many countries, and arms dealers knew they were now at a premium. MI6 and special forces around the world were ordered to find further shipments which were believed to be moving through Israel, South Africa and Libya – all countries which were suspected of helping Argentina. Drastic action was now being contemplated, and the legal position had to be considered. Michael Havers, the attorney general, advised: 'The risk of re-supply to the Argentineans of further air-to-sea missiles justifies consideration of all options to prevent this – even the most way-out – which may be thought more appropriate to a James Bond movie!' He suggested that British agents could possibly hijack any cargo aircraft en route. Havers conceded that it was a 'dirty business', but felt it was a price Britain might have to pay to save the task force. Intelligence reports soon flooded in about possible sales by both Iran and Libya to Argentina via Brazil. The British air attaché came within four metres of a suspicious Boeing 707 at the Brazilian city of Recife which was carrying Exocet-shaped containers. Britain agonised about the costs of a sneak attack on an aircraft on Brazilian soil, but decided the risks to future relations with Brazil were too high, and decided to leak the information in order that media pressure would be applied instead.[89]

The secret war against the Exocet would eventually be won, partly thanks to an MI6 sting operation undertaken by the Hamburg-based agent Anthony Divall. Posing as an arms dealer and equipped with a £16 million bank facility, he fooled Argentinean arms buyers into believing he could provide thirty Exocets. They were still undelivered when the

Union flag was hoisted over Port Stanley on 14 June 1982.[90] Despite the personal assurances from Mitterrand, London remained suspicious of French motives. There were reports that civilian technicians from the French aviation company Dassault were in Argentina helping with missile-launch protocols. In fact, DGSE, the French secret service, which has a particular reputation for brutality, was busily acting in the interests of the British. Several European arms dealers working on behalf of Argentina were liquidated by French agents, who had a long history of eliminating troublesome arms suppliers that stretched back to the Algerian war. MI6 officers based in Paris were amazed, and recalled it as the best moment of their career – the only time when they literally had a licence to kill.[91]

Margaret Thatcher was as good as her word. She had informed Mitterrand that the future of the Anglo–French relationship stood or fell on this issue, and the French had delivered. Her views on France had been transformed. In 1984, she approved the construction of the Channel Tunnel, which she had hitherto resisted. To her fury, the Americans had initially tried to play the honest broker, seeking a compromise over the islands. By contrast, the French had come to Britain's aid immediately. Loyalty was the quality that Thatcher prized above all else, and to her considerable surprise Mitterrand had proved to be 'one of us'.[92]

In late 1985, an RAF helicopter swooped low over Fort Monckton, the Napoleonic fortification near Gosport on England's south coast that was now MI6's training establishment. The helicopter carried Bill Casey, director of the CIA, and waiting for it below was the chief of MI6, Christopher Curwen, who had invited him to lunch. The guest of honour at this memorable gathering was not Casey but a KGB intelligence officer called Oleg Gordievsky, who was perhaps the most important agent British intelligence had ever recruited.[93] The meeting was all the more remarkable because Gordievsky had only recently cheated death by escaping from the clutches of the KGB. A perilous MI6 operation, personally approved by Margaret Thatcher, had saved him from interrogation in Moscow and almost certain death at the hands of a KGB firing squad.[94]

With a major summit meeting in Geneva approaching, Gordievsky gave Casey wonderful insights into Soviet thinking. He told him that the Soviet leader Mikhail Gorbachev was so terrified of America's anti-missile 'Star Wars' technology that in order to stop its development Moscow was willing to offer deep cuts in its weapons stocks. Gordievsky also showed

Casey hundreds of pages of Soviet documents he had procured. This intelligence material would inform the position of Reagan and his secretary of state, George Shultz, at the summit. It also bolstered the prestige of British intelligence, and by association Britain's prime minister, in the eyes of the Americans, who were amazed at what they had achieved.[95]

The 1980s was a decade of top spies. The CIA had recruited a senior officer on the Soviet general staff who was giving them excellent material on the Soviet leadership, while Ryszard Kukliński, a Polish diplomat, was providing the inside track on the Solidarity crisis. The KGB had not penetrated Reagan's inner circle, but it had recruited agents who gave it access to US naval communications and operations.[96] It had also recruited Aldrich Ames, who ran CIA operations inside Russia, and Robert Hanssen, a senior FBI counter-intelligence officer who gave top-level American intelligence assessments of Gorbachev. This allowed the Soviets to protect their own spies, and also to close down many Western espionage operations inside the Soviet bloc.[97]

However, the most important agent of the 1980s was run by MI6. Oleg Gordievsky had joined the KGB in 1963, and was later posted to Denmark. Disillusioned by the Soviet invasion of Czechoslovakia in 1968, he was recruited by Robert Browning, the MI6 head of station in Copenhagen, after a chance encounter at a local squash club. Gordievsky was already a star MI6 recruit in the 1970s, but his value became inestimable when, in 1982, he became a senior KGB officer in London, presiding over dozens of Soviet agents and their operations. Expulsions of key Soviet intelligence personnel in London, including the chief of military intelligence, followed. During 1983, over a hundred Soviet intelligence officers were declared *persona non grata* in Western countries around the world, many of them identified by Gordievksy. The KGB was frantically searching for its mole.

Gordievsky explained how the Soviet Union's innermost circles worked, not only providing fabulous documents but also interpreting them by decoding the curious Kremlin-speak in which they were written.[98] His most notable contribution was averting a potential nuclear confrontation by alerting the West to the KGB's 'Operation Ryan', an activity so bizarre that, at first, his MI6 contacts did not know what to make of it. Operation Ryan had its origin in May 1981, when Leonid Brezhnev met with the leaders of the KGB, including Yuri Andropov. They were deeply alarmed by the election of Ronald Reagan, feared his accelerated nuclear programme, and agreed to launch Operation Ryan to collect intelligence on what they saw as his planned nuclear-missile offensive. Many KGB officers in the field regarded these fears as exaggerated, but nevertheless joined the intelligence collection effort with vigour.

In May 1982, Andropov left the KGB for the Politburo, and Operation Ryan slowed down. But after Andropov was elected to succeed Brezhnev as Soviet leader in November 1982 it gathered pace again, with East European intelligence services being recruited into the effort. The US decision to deploy Pershing II missiles in Europe, with their very short flight times, did nothing to reassure Moscow. For several years during the early 1980s, KGB intelligence chiefs were ordered to find evidence of an impending American first strike. This arrived in the autumn of 1983, in the form of NATO's 'Able Archer' exercise, which caused panic in Moscow. Russian consternation was no bluff: the world was closer to nuclear disaster than it had been at any time since the Cuban missile crisis. Reagan found the events 'really scary'.[99]

'Able Archer', a routine annual NATO command-post exercise in West Germany, passed off without incident – or so it seemed. Margaret Thatcher was told a few months later that it had actually almost triggered a nuclear first strike by a paranoid Soviet Union. Over several decades Moscow's leaders had become increasingly anxious about a sneak nuclear attack by the West. They had introduced elaborate warning measures, including primitive computer models, which were so baroque that they had gradually come to believe their own theories. Andropov, as a former KGB officer, believed that 'Able Archer' might well be a cover for a Western attack. The main source of this frightening intelligence about Moscow's state of mind was Oleg Gordievsky.[100]

In the Cabinet Office, the Assessments Staff realised that during this crisis Soviet nuclear-capable bombers had actually been ready for take-off on a runway in East Germany. Harry Burke, a fifty-seven-year-old veteran Soviet analyst at GCHQ, was the first to notice that something distinctly odd was going on within Moscow's command and control network. After three decades of watching the behaviour of the Soviet military, Burke knew something was not quite right. But it was the verbatim testimony of Gordievsky that alerted Margaret Thatcher to the true seriousness of the situation.[101] His intelligence persuaded her to try to influence the Americans to put the brakes on their 'Star Wars' programme, which had placed tremendous pressure on the whole Eastern bloc. It eventually helped to convince Reagan to accelerate strategic arms limitation, against the advice of the hawks in his administration. Thatcher recalled that she resolved to keep 'tight personal control' over these matters, adding that 'ministerial muddlers ... could not be relied on'.[102]

This episode also changed London's strategic thinking. For Thatcher, it confirmed that Britain had to take the lead. While she thought Reagan's instincts were right, his footwork was deemed clumsy, even dangerous – before one key meeting with Gorbachev he even suggested Thatcher read *Red Storm Rising*, a thriller by Tom Clancy, to give insight into Russian thinking.[103] The West had to move beyond the rhetoric about the 'Evil Empire' and find a way to communicate with a new generation of Soviet leaders. Again, Gordievsky was crucial, personally assisting Thatcher during the rise of Mikhail Gorbachev. His intelligence informed her trip to Moscow on 9 February 1984 to attend the funeral of Andropov. She was not impressed by his elderly and infirm successor Konstantin Chernenko, but warmed to Gorbachev, and invited him to London: 'I spotted him because I was searching for someone like him.' She added that he was 'clearly the best-educated member of the Politburo', and 'began to take special notice when his name was mentioned in reports on the Soviet Union'.[104] At subsequent meetings Thatcher was always informed by crib notes prepared by Gordievsky, whom she met personally four times.[105] For a brief period he was in the odd position of preparing briefing notes for both Gorbachev and Thatcher before they met.[106]

Operation Ryan underlines the importance of secret intelligence as a window on reality for heads of government. In late 1982, some Soviet officials had been so worried about the paranoid activities of their leaders that they had privately sought to warn the West. George Walden, then head of the Foreign Office planning staff and a Soviet specialist with excellent Russian, had visited Moscow and fallen into conversation with Dr Georgi Arbatov, director of the Institute of US Affairs there. Arbatov was at pains to convince Walden that Moscow was deeply frightened by the tone of Reagan's rhetoric, 'and that the risk of destabilization was becoming serious'. Walden noted, 'he seemed anxious to make himself believed'. But he regarded Arbatov as 'a slob of a man', an 'indefatigable propagandist and disinformationist', and so took little notice. Arbatov pleaded for his message to be passed to Carrington and Thatcher, but Walden 'thought no more about it, and did nothing'. The level of cynicism had become so great that simple diplomatic communication was impossible, and only the best intelligence could pierce the veil.[107]

On 22 May 1985, Gordievsky was suddenly ordered back to Moscow. Confined to a KGB compound outside the city, he was drugged and questioned by a Soviet security team. Although interrogated for about five hours, he admitted nothing. The KGB clearly had relatively little information to go on, and was uncertain of its case. Gordievsky was released, but was told that he was under a cloud of suspicion, and would never work abroad again. Hoping that he would now make a false move, the KGB kept him under surveillance, but Gordievsky managed to send a signal to MI6 about his perilous situation.

Margaret Thatcher was then at Balmoral, staying with the Queen. Christopher Curwen, the chief of MI6, was most insistent about mounting a rescue effort, and Charles Powell, the prime minister's foreign affairs adviser, flew to Scotland to seek her permission. Thatcher was very clear: 'We have an obligation and we will not let him down.'[108] This was a difficult decision to take. Although Gordievsky was not being held in a secure building and was at large, extracting him from Russia would be a risky business. Thatcher hesitated, but knew that Curwen would resign if no attempt was made to rescue Gordievsky. The British ambassador in Moscow was horrified by the idea, but was overruled. On 19 July, Gordievsky went for his daily run. Dodging his KGB surveillance, he took a train to Leningrad, from where two MI6 officers, together with their wives and small children, smuggled him over the Finnish border in a car. He was then flown to England via Norway, and debriefed for a period of three months.[109]

The MI6 team had resorted to every ruse to get Gordievsky over the border. Travelling as a family, they had thrown soiled nappies from the car when they were approached by border guards with dogs, laying down a powerful alternative scent trail. When the KGB finally worked out how the extraction had been accomplished, it called in the new British ambassador, Brian Cartledge, and fingered the two MI6 officers in a photograph, before expelling them. Further rounds of expulsions followed. In a message that went to Thatcher, Cartledge advised against counter-expulsions from the Soviet embassy in London, adding: 'Never get into a pissing match with a skunk.' But Thatcher went for further retaliatory rounds of expulsion, and as Cartledge ruefully reflected, soon 'we'd lost half our embassy'.[110]

Who had betrayed Gordievsky? In London, his identity had been tightly held. In the corner of the office of the permanent secretary at the Foreign Office was a huge safe, 'the size of a washing machine', in which papers that were too sensitive for the main archive were kept. Its contents were 'explosive', and included files on possible Soviet moles in MI6 and details about 'the misbehaviour of members of the royal family' overseas, along with 'secret subventions' to deposed foreign rulers who had been helpful to Britain. But Gordievsky's identity was even more secret than any of this. Instead, Peter Wallis, the liaison between MI6 and the permanent secretary, would come from MI6 headquarters at Century House with an anonymous locked briefcase. After the two men had met, the excruciatingly secret material would be taken away again. No one else was allowed to see it, and no one ever asked what it was.[111]

However, MI6 had shared Gordievsky's priceless intelligence with Washington, although it had not revealed his name to the Americans. The CIA could not control its curiosity, and tasked its senior Soviet operations officer, Aldrich Ames, with identifying London's wonderful source – which he soon did. Unbeknown to his colleagues, Ames was a high-level KGB agent, and in some ways the mirror image of Gordievsky. It is often assumed that it was he who betrayed Gordievsky, who was recalled to Moscow in mid-May 1985, at about the same time Ames made his first offer to work for the KGB. But, in fact, Ames only gave the Soviets his list of Western agents – which included Gordievsky – the following month. Someone else had compromised Gordievsky's identity. Remarkably, the KGB's Colonel Victor Cherkashin claims that it was a British writer based in Washington, who had a long track record of assisting the KGB.[112]

Thatcher's last brush with espionage would be notably personal. She was greatly attached to Gordievsky, and regarded him as a man of exceptional bravery. She later sent him a photo of the two of them together, with an inscription in which she described him as 'a true hero'. He was also received warmly by both Ronald Reagan and his successor George Bush.[113] Thatcher persistently sought to have his family released from Russia. In Moscow in December 1987, she broached the subject once again with Gorbachev. She chose her moment carefully. Gorbachev's wife Raisa had taken some of Thatcher's retinue to watch a nativity play at a local school, and Thatcher was chatting to Gorbachev, who had just recited for her a Russian folk song in front of a Christmas tree. The atmosphere was festive and friendly, moreover the Soviet interpreter was momentarily out of earshot: 'I asked Mr Gorbachev … whether he would let Oleg Gordievsky's family out of the Soviet Union to join him in Britain. He pursed his lips and said nothing: the answer was all too clear.'[114]

Margaret Thatcher's most difficult intelligence issues were not concerned with Mikhail Gorbachev, but with Ronald Reagan. On 28 May 1986, John Poindexter, Reagan's new national security advisor, assured a senior British diplomat that the United States stood firm on its policy of not making deals for hostages. On the very same day, his predecessor, Bud McFarlane, arrived in Tehran with a plane loaded with weapons, expecting American hostages being held in Lebanon to be released as a result. McFarlane was accompanied by Major General Richard Secord and Colonel Oliver North of the National Security Council Staff, and also by George Cave, a retired CIA station chief who spoke fluent Farsi and had served in both Iran and Saudi Arabia. McFarlane delivered the goods, but the hostages were not released. Furious, he accused the Iranians of 'extreme bad faith'. In fact, the various factions in Tehran were fighting amongst themselves over how to respond.[115]

North and McFarlane were trying to kill two birds with one stone. Hezbollah, a radical group in Lebanon controlled by the Iranians, had taken a number of hostages, including the CIA's Beirut station chief, Bill Buckley. Incredibly, a Mossad agent inside Hezbollah had warned of Buckley's impending kidnap, at grave risk to his own life, but senior intelligence officials in Israel failed to pass the warning on to the Americans.[116] On 16 March 1984, Buckley was snatched on his way to work, and the Americans were desperate to retrieve him. Bill Casey, who had personally pressed Buckley to take on the assignment, was willing to go 'to the ends of the earth' to find a way to retrieve him. On the other side of the world, Congress had imposed a ban on American assistance to the Contra rebels in Nicaragua, citing human rights abuses and bringing the CIA's secret war against Nicaragua's left-wing government to a screeching halt. Reagan's officials planned to sell arms to the Iranians via Israel to assist in their war against Iraq, which they were also arming, in return for the release of the hostages. By selling rather than giving the arms to Iran, they planned to create a pool of untraceable cash that they could then funnel to the Contras. Reagan signed a directive that launched 'Iran–Contra' three weeks after the kidnap of Bill Buckley.[117]

Buckley was already dead by the time the first arms were delivered. Casey had been sent three tapes of his screams as he was tortured by both Lebanese and Iranian interrogators; each recording was more harrowing than the last. But with a dozen other Americans held captive, they persevered.[118] The British had a particular interest in this operation. Thatcher had mostly stood firm on hostage situations. Earlier in her administration, when terrorists took over the Iranian embassy in Kensington, taking twenty-six hostages, she had refused to give in to their demands. With the SAS en route from Hereford to London she convened an emergency meeting in Cobra at which she 'bustled about trying to organise everybody until she was gently and politely escorted to the door' – but she left those involved in little doubt that the streets of London could not be seen as a stage for hostage-taking. One SAS officer even alleges that she verbally passed a top-secret communication to the regiment which implied that no terrorists should be left alive.[119] Either way, five of the six hostage-takers were killed in a dramatic SAS raid on the embassy that played out live on television.

In 1986, Thatcher also refused to negotiate with the Libyans for the release of two hostages in Lebanon. The previous month she had allowed Reagan to use UK bases to bomb Libya in retaliation for a terrorist attack on a disco used by US servicemen in Berlin. NSA intercepts of Libyan communications proved Gaddafi's involvement beyond doubt, and to the consternation of both the NSA and GCHQ, Reagan made them public. The raid took place on 15 April 1986, and in retaliation two Britons and one American were executed by the regime in Tripoli.[120] Julian Amery, one of Thatcher's inner circle, could not resist making the comparison between Libya's Muammar Gaddafi and Nasser, and offered the advice that such leaders should be admired from a distance or killed, but not provoked or prodded. Asked if he was advocating assassination, he replied, 'I would not be too squeamish about taking such action.' He also observed that Suez had taught that the Americans could not entirely be trusted.[121]

Thatcher already knew she was being lied to by the Americans about Iran–Contra. Late the previous year, shortly after leaving his post as national security advisor, Bud McFarlane had flown to London as a private citizen to attend a secret rendezvous with Oliver North and an Iranian arms dealer, Manucher Ghorbanifar. They held an uneasy meeting at the Hilton hotel near Heathrow airport. Because McFarlane was no longer a US government representative, MI5 had no hesitation in placing him under technical surveillance, and they were amazed by what they heard. Afterwards, a highly classified report of the bugging was circulated to Thatcher and a small circle of ministers and security officials. A few weeks later she despatched Antony Acland, now head of the Foreign Office, and JIC chairman Percy Cradock to Washington to interrogate Poindexter, McFarlane's successor and the new mastermind of Iran–Contra. 'Are you doing a secret deal with the nasties?' Poindexter was asked. He refused to confirm or deny. For Cradock this was 'as good as a yes'.[122]

Other intelligence was coming Thatcher's way. One of the middlemen involved in these multiple transactions was Leslie Aspin, the former SAS operative turned arms dealer who reported intermittently to MI6.[123] Moreover, Israeli intelligence and Adnan Khashoggi, a Saudi Arabian tycoon, had asked a well-known British businessman, 'Tiny' Rowland, the owner of Lonrho, to use his company to help deliver arms to Iran. Lonrho had worked with other American covert operations, including supplying the Angolan rebels under Jonas Savimbi, and had conducted sanctions-busting operations in support of Rhodesia. He was assured that this secret operation was backed by the White House. Incredulous, he contacted the State Department, which insisted it knew nothing about it, as was indeed correct.[124] But Thatcher's famous moral compass went into a spin when arms deals or intelligence were involved, so Downing Street said nothing.

Thatcher's ministers hated the various Middle East hostages and their would-be liberators as much as the hostage-takers. The Foreign Office told people not to travel to Lebanon, but this advice was blatantly ignored. Officials then spent thousands of hours trying to free these 'brave travellers' from predictable captivity. One of these was Terry Waite, the Archbishop of Canterbury's envoy, who met Oliver North at least a dozen times and travelled to Beirut on special forces helicopters, although he reportedly refused to wear a CIA tracking device designed to be hidden in his voluminous beard.[125] William Waldegrave, one of the ministers who dealt with this sorry business, recalls: 'Terry Waite, a man not given to taking advice, suffered terribly for attempting to conduct a sort of one-man foreign policy not entirely separate from the dangerous people in the illegal Iran–Contra deals run by mavericks in the US government.'[126]

Dramatically, Thatcher was in Washington when the Iran–Contra 'mavericks' were finally exposed. During the last week of November 1986, as the press went into a frenzy, Oliver North and his secretary Fawn Hall destroyed so many documents that the shredders jammed. Desperate to hide the evidence as investigators closed in, Hall smuggled more documents out of the office under her dress and in her boots. John Poindexter destroyed what many believe to have been the only signed copy of a presidential covert action finding that allowed CIA participation in the shipment of missiles to Iran. Thatcher was in Washington when Poindexter resigned and Oliver North was fired by Reagan. The White House sought to lay the blame at the door of Israel's Mossad.[127]

Publicly, Thatcher was extremely supportive when asked about Iran–Contra, asserting her firm belief in the president's 'total integrity on that subject'. Later, she met Reagan alone at Camp David without note-takers, and we can only speculate about what was said. In private, Thatcher did not hesitate to upbraid Reagan, but in public she was an unqualified supporter, and the president was notably grateful.[128] Six months later, the truth about Britain's own involvement in the affair began to seep out. North's frenzy of shredding had been incomplete, and a chart found in National Security Council files revealed that Keeny Meeny Services, the company staffed mostly by SAS veterans which had previously undertaken contract work for the Foreign Office, was part of the private network that assisted Nicaraguan insurgents during Iran–Contra, including the recruitment of Rhodesian pilots to fly aid to the insurgents.[129] On 26 November 1986, Senator John Tower was appointed to conduct a congressional investigation into Iran–Contra. Bill Casey died in May 1987. At the beginning of the decade it was Casey who as director of the CIA had presented Thatcher with the OSS's Donovan Medal. The proud British holder of this award, although vexed by affairs like Iran–Contra, had nevertheless followed the cause of freedom.

Intelligence was a deadly serious business throughout the 1980s. In 1982, intelligence failure over the Falklands had come within a whisker of ending Thatcher's administration. A year later, the possibility of nuclear war with paranoid Kremlin leaders was averted by an extraordinary intelligence success, the MI6 recruitment of a star agent who rose to become the KGB head of station in London. The most troublesome issue was hostages, two of whom had been executed by the Libyans after the US strike on Tripoli. Meanwhile, there was the constant shadow of a very personal secret war with the IRA. Thatcher's arrival in office had been preceded by the assassination of her close adviser Airey Neave, and her departure followed shortly after the killing of the Conservative MP Ian Gow, expressly because he had been involved in Northern Ireland policy and was close to the prime minister, indeed perhaps her closest personal confidant.[130] Thatcher herself had escaped death only by a whisker at the hands of the IRA in the Brighton hotel bombing in October 1984. Further close shaves awaited her successor, John Major.[131]

PART FIVE

TURBULENT TIMES

16

John Major
(1990–1997)

Overnight, security moved in … Electronic devices invaded
the house and garden like unwanted Daleks.
JOHN MAJOR[1]

John Major took office at a time of momentous flux. The Brandenburg Gate in Berlin had reopened just before Christmas 1989, and Germany was reunited in October 1990. Major arrived in Downing Street a month later, on 28 November. By the end of the year the only communist leader left in what was once the formidable Eastern bloc was Mikhail Gorbachev. Oddly, only Gorbachev seemed to believe that the Cold War was not quite over, and thought he could sustain the Soviet empire by the force of his own personality. Just like previous Moscow leaders, he welcomed KGB intelligence when it confirmed his views. But when 'policy and reality began to diverge', recalled one senior KGB officer, 'Gorbachev did not want to know'.[2]

Although the JIC failed to predict the unravelling of the Soviet bloc,[3] the committee did forecast that Gorbachev would soon be replaced by Boris Yeltsin, a charismatic figure less tainted by the past. Intelligence also spotted, through a combination of intercepts and human sources, the beginnings of a KGB counter-coup.[4] Major had only been in office for a matter of months when he received advance notice of this from Percy Cradock, the legendary JIC chair. Such was the urgency that the prime minister and Cradock authorised an immediate warning to be sent to Yeltsin over an open phone line by the British ambassador in Moscow, Rodric Braithwaite. The KGB counter-coup was incompetent and remarkably indiscreet. Its failure also settled an acrimonious debate that had been running for over eighteen months, involving every intelligence analyst in Whitehall, about whether this really was the end of the Soviet Union, or some elaborate deception.[5] On 22 August 1991, Cradock dispensed cham-

pagne to the Assessments Staff in the Cabinet Office and invited everyone
to toast 'the demise of Soviet Communism'.[6]

Major was now asked to approve a series of bizarre MI6 shopping trips.
Across the former Soviet bloc, secret services with which the British had
battled for years were unravelling. Once-elusive KGB officers, carrying
armfuls of secrets, now offered to defect to the West. The files that the East
German Stasi had kept on British citizens started to become available, and
in Prague protesters made their way into the archives of the Czech overseas secret service and obtained the names of their country's agents serving in locations as far away as China and Iran. There were reverberations
in the West, too. The Dutch government wound up its overseas secret
service, declaring its networks of agents redundant. Opportunity beck-
oned, and MI6 sat like a hungry bear bewildered by a stream teeming with
more fat salmon than it could possibly eat. It set out to purchase the best
agents in what was a frenzied buyers' market. In the chaos, not everything
went well. Some Czech agents around the world, whose names had become
public knowledge, were rounded up and shot. In The Hague, the MI6 head
of station, who had been successfully buying up the best Dutch intelli-
gence-agent networks ahead of the American competition, was declared
'persona non grata' and expelled from the country.[7] These were turbulent
times.

Some nasty secrets were coming westward. One of the first important
Russians to defect to Britain at the end of the Cold War was Vladimir
Pasechnik, a microbiologist whose haul of intelligence showed that
Moscow's biological warfare programme was ten times larger than MI6
had previously thought. The West had known for many years that the
Russians were breaking arms-control treaties that forbade offensive
biological warfare programmes, but it had no idea of the scale. Gorbachev
had been asked about it, but told barefaced lies.[8] In 1992, Pasechnik's
intelligence was confirmed by a second defector, Ken Alibek, who claimed
that development of horrific new strains of genetically-engineered super-
weapons was continuing. These included enhanced and weaponised
versions of anthrax, ebola, plague and smallpox. By 1995, the JIC was
reflecting on the use of nerve gas on the Tokyo subway by an obscure
Japanese terrorist group called Aum Shinrikyo. During Major's first years,
fears of nuclear obliteration were replaced almost seamlessly by the new
perils of proliferation and weapons of mass destruction, albeit for now
these worries circulated only quietly within Downing Street.[9]

John Major was not a fan of intelligence. Unlike Margaret Thatcher, and indeed Winston Churchill, for whom it exercised a special fascination, he was more interested in domestic affairs and economics than foreign policy: he has admitted that his heart sank when Thatcher asked him in 1989 to become foreign secretary for what proved to be a short and rather overwhelming period. He did not get to know the intelligence chiefs, and remained inexperienced in diplomacy and defence.[10]

As prime minister, he met his intelligence chiefs every couple of months.[11] On one occasion, Stella Rimington, director-general of MI5, showed him the number of people for whom she had warrants to keep under surveillance. Major responded by asking how many people MI5 monitored without warrants. Rimington was aghast, wondering what on earth the prime minister thought MI5 did. It fell to one of his private secretaries, after he had left the room, to apologetically explain away Major's question as innocence.[12] As he settled into his role, Major paid diligent attention to intelligence in times of war and crisis, especially regarding the break-up of Yugoslavia, but otherwise left the secret world to senior officials. He was a sensible man, and did not prioritise secret material over non-secret. In contrast to his predecessor, his JIC chair therefore rarely needed to track him down and contextualise intelligence provided directly by the agency heads in order to prevent him getting carried away.[13]

This reflected a very different personal style from that of Thatcher. Major was good at diplomacy, but less keen to stay up until four in the morning reading briefs. Percy Cradock recalled that although Major 'read less and was lazier' than Thatcher, he greatly admired the prime minister's negotiating skills and his ability to create consensus.[14] Major was more collegiate, and disinclined to deal with secret matters by creating small and informal groups of trusted ministers and officials. Thatcher had wanted to own intelligence personally within her private office, and gradually came to dislike the central analytical machinery of the JIC, an alarming trait that would also be shown by Tony Blair a decade later. By contrast, Major was more inclusive, and eventually created a cabinet committee to allow ministerial oversight of the intelligence services.[15]

History will be kind to John Major, and observers are already revising his stature upwards. His greatest achievement was to reserve Britain's position indefinitely on European Monetary Union, a complex negotiation in which his skilful use of secret intelligence played no little part. In retrospect, viewed through the prism of the financial euro-miseries endured from Dublin to Athens and from Rome to Madrid over the past two decades, this was a titanic achievement. Despite a slim parliamentary majority, he also managed to keep the Conservative administration in power for seven years beyond its natural life. Dogged by dissent in his own party and disarray in world politics, he was nevertheless a steady captain who was able to radiate genuine trust and warmth, especially on a one-to-one basis. As one backbencher acutely observed, John Major's body language said, 'Trust me, I like you,' whereas Tony Blair's said, 'Trust me, you like me.'[16]

The end of the Cold War profoundly shocked the British intelligence community. Although not as myopically focused upon Moscow as its American counterpart, much of the British machine had fixed its gaze upon a frozen frontier that had demarcated East from West for more than forty years. With the main threat gone, Parliament soon called for budget cuts. In the previous decade, Thatcher's love affair with secret service meant that, in the words of one of her chancellors, 'Their establishments and their hardware were one of the very few areas untouched by the economic rigours of the 1980s.'[17] But now Major's government launched spending reviews, and made brutal cuts across all three intelligence agencies. Although losing some £200 million a year, GCHQ remained the big spender – dwarfing the so-called 'tiddlers', MI5 and MI6.[18]

And yet, in reality, intelligence chiefs now needed more money than ever. Technology was changing fast, and security problems in the world moved to unpredictable places, requiring new language skills. They faced a fundamental reappraisal of threats and priorities. New intelligence challenges included narcotics, money-laundering, people-trafficking, terrorism, nuclear proliferation and the illegal light-weapons trade, but most seemed smaller in scale than the preceding Cold War. There was also much more talk of economic intelligence.[19] All three services had spectacular success against organised crime in the 1990s, but still viewed this activity as less prestigious than their Cold War anti-Soviet activities. Lurking on the horizon was the possibility of merger.[20] By the middle of the decade, however, Major had publicly praised the intelligence community for responding rapidly and with flexibility to the changing security landscape.[21]

Major now oversaw a period of cultural change. Hitherto the 'secret services' had hoped to escape notice. Under Major they were allowed more freedom to undertake public engagement. Alongside William Waldegrave, then Chancellor of the Duchy of Lancaster, the prime minister was a driving force behind the openness agenda.[22] The oppressive secrecy that had dogged Thatcher's last days had now lifted.[23] A new generation of modernising chiefs, operating out of highly visible headquarters, sought to reshape their services with a legal identity. Stella Rimington, the director-general of MI5, was for example determined to change the image of the agencies. 'Our detractors who accuse us of being conservative, old-fashioned Cold Warriors are a very long way from the truth,' she asserted. 'We would like to see these myths blown away.'[24] Similarly, Stephen Lander, her successor from 1996, was 'open, relaxed, frank, at ease with the democratic process, which could not be said of all his predecessors'. One parliamentarian noted: 'Did you ever dream you might hear the Director General of the Security Service bandying around articles of the European Charter of Human Rights with such fluency?'[25] In the new climate, Major's spy chiefs had less to fear from exposure. All they had to do now was show that their activities were proportionate. Civil rights campaigners found this a continual source of disappointment. Having presumed that more regulation would mean more restrictions on the secret state, they soon discovered that this was permissive legislation: it allowed more freedom of action. Paradoxically, being 'legit' often meant more operations.[26]

With openness came oversight. Over the previous ten years, both Britain and Sweden had been criticised by the European Court because their agencies had no legal existence and limited oversight. There followed a headlong rush towards regulation right across Europe. Senior mandarins such as Percy Cradock were wary: 'The idea of openly accountable services remains a contradiction in terms.'[27] Nevertheless, Britain had put MI5 on the statute book in 1989, and under Major it admitted to having foreign intelligence organisations. The Intelligence Services Act of 1994 placed MI6 and GCHQ on a legal basis alongside MI5.

The 1994 Act also created a new oversight body, composed of parliamentarians, called the Intelligence and Security Committee. Although this looked like a parliamentary select committee, it was in fact responsible to the prime minister, and lacked many of the powers normally associated with select committees. Meanwhile, the real parliamentary select committees with a legitimate interest in intelligence, such as Defence and Foreign Affairs, were finding that the government tended to resist their efforts to probe secret matters. Instead, they were told that intelligence was now the province of the Intelligence and Security Committee. Some have argued that John Major's experiment with openness was really about reaffirming secrecy and reasserting control.[28]

Major inherited an ongoing war. He may have been inexperienced in defence, diplomacy and intelligence, but the new prime minister had to learn fast. In August 1990, Iraq had invaded Kuwait. Intelligence had performed reasonably well, and GCHQ successfully picked up the movements of Iraqi armoured divisions as early as 24 July. Two days later, and five days before Iraq's attack on Kuwait, the JIC gave a clear warning that aggression was likely. In addition to this appearing in the prime minister's Red Book, Percy Cradock had personally warned Margaret Thatcher of his conviction that the Iraqis would soon attack, but was uncertain of the exact timing. Warning signals continued to appear, and three days later Iraq's Soviet-built long-range radar units, codenamed 'Tall King', became very active, having been silent for some months. Spy satellites monitored closely. Amazingly, Downing Street and the White House ignored all of this, and Saddam Hussein's attack achieved surprise despite the JIC's warning.[29]

The attention of world leaders was elsewhere. President Bush was entirely focused on a terrifying nuclear stand-off between India and Pakistan over Kashmir, which was unexpected. At the same time, Thatcher was dealing with a personal tragedy. Ian Gow, one of her closest personal confidants, had just been assassinated by the IRA. Egyptian and Saudi diplomats assured the West that Saddam was committed to a negotiated solution over Kuwait, causing Thatcher to reject the advice of her notoriously gloomy intelligence adviser. Choosing to conclude that Iraqi military movements were mere sabre-rattling, she headed for an economic conference at the Colorado ski resort of Aspen.[30] Mossad came to the same conclusion, and insisted that Saddam was bluffing.[31] Douglas Hurd, the foreign secretary, was also taken by surprise. On 1 August he was looking forward to a well-earned summer holiday. Virtually the last thing he did in the office was to see the heads of MI6 and GCHQ, who had little to report, before taking his children to the circus. When he awoke the next morning, he recalled, 'I turned on the radio. Iraq had invaded Kuwait.'[32]

With the UN demanding that Saddam withdraw or face military action, John Major found himself preparing for war within days of arriving in Downing Street. He inherited a chaotic ministerial group which doubled as a quasi-war cabinet, officially known as Overseas Defence (Gulf), which excluded the cabinet secretary and other senior officials. Major swiftly rectified this.[33] He also inherited Percy Cradock, as both foreign policy adviser and chair of the JIC, who had served in that position since 1985.

Major, quite rightly, thought the combination of these two roles unorthodox and perhaps even unhealthy. He recalls Cradock as an 'intriguing character' who thrived on dry intellectual rigour and contempt for sentiment. Inclined to be abrupt, Cradock believed that politicians were made of inferior stuff to diplomats, and offered his acerbic advice to Major in 'full and generous measure'.[34]

Major had two questions for Cradock and his intelligence assessment teams. Firstly, he needed to know exactly how good Iraq's armed forces were. Saddam's military was huge and well-equipped, as he had purchased some $13 billion worth of new equipment from Moscow, mostly on credit. It was also battle-hardened, having fought a vast and deadly conflict with Iran that had ended only two years before. In his response to the prime minister, Cradock 'never tired' of speculating how outstanding Iraq's elite Republican Guard might be. The second question was whether Saddam would dare to use chemical or biological weapons on the battlefield – or indeed against population centres in the UK or the USA. Western embassies were no longer functioning in Baghdad, but private avenues of communication provided by the intelligence services communicated a warning to Saddam about the dire consequences of doing so.[35]

Just before Christmas, Major was briefed on the plan of attack. Such operational plans are among the most secret and highly sensitive of documents. Amazingly, that very evening, the same attack plans used to brief Major, including a crucial deception operation designed to cover the advance, were stolen from a Vauxhall car heading from Whitehall to Strike Command at High Wycombe. Wing Commander David Farquhar, aide to Air Chief Marshal Sir Patrick Hine, commander-in-chief of British Forces Middle East, had decided to stop and look in a Land Rover showroom on the way, and had left his briefcase on the back seat. A thief swooped. Police retrieved the papers, which were of no monetary value, but a laptop containing the same information remained elusive. John Major decided that the United States should not be informed, but on 29 December the *Mail on Sunday* revealed all – to the extreme embarrassment of the British. We 'look stupid', fumed General Peter de la Billière, the commander in the Gulf. A few days later a character called 'Edward', describing himself as a 'patriotic thief', returned the laptop. The compromised plans remained in place up until two days prior to the war starting. Then an entirely new plan was introduced. Farquhar was later found guilty of negligence by a court martial, but Pentagon officials felt 'He should be shot'.[36]

Because of this incident, only a handful of people in London had advance notice of the Western allies' operation to retake Kuwait, code-named 'Desert Storm'. It began on 17 January 1991, with a wave of air attacks. Downing Street was on a war footing. The Middle East Current Intelligence Group met through the night.[37] Every morning in the Cabinet Office, the Assessments Staff met at 4 a.m. to pull together intelligence from myriad sources. The JIC sat at 6 a.m. to overview their product. This was placed before senior officials at 8.30 a.m., and finally before ministers at 10 a.m. Each morning similar patterns of activity were replicated in operational headquarters at different levels.[38]

Despite the mishap with the laptop, the operation achieved surprise. British forces conducted a classic operational deception, superintended by a unit codenamed 'Rhino Force'. During several field exercises by Britain's First Armoured Division, the units transmitted on low power to avoid interception by Iraqi signals intelligence units. In the actual ground attack, on 23 January, 14 Signals Regiment played back recordings of these earlier transmissions at full power. The Iraqis heard them clearly. The idea was to 'convince the Iraqis that the British Division had moved back to its original position by the sea'. In fact, most of the British forces had moved about 125 miles to the west to link up with the main US Seventh Army Corps. Signals intelligence showed that the Iraqis had bought this deception in its entirety. Meanwhile, an MI6 radio station based in Saudi Arabia pretended to be 'Radio Kuwait', and broadcast the false news that Kuwait City had already fallen, causing several Iraqi units to flee in panic.[39]

In London, wild rumours circulated amongst backbench MPs about the secret war. Edwina Currie, one of Major's cabinet colleagues, noted in her diary: 'Apparently the SAS engaged in "direct action" to assassinate a lot of top officers so that the Iraqi army would be demoralised ... One bunch ... brought back key Iraqi officers for interrogation. It is probably wisest not to ask how they got the information needed, or whether the men are still alive.'[40] British special operations and covert action were not, however, especially successful. An experienced MI6 officer was sent out to Riyadh to head up an operation to train Kuwaiti exiles as a resistance force. There were hopes that they could carry out sabotage inside Kuwait, and also locate British hostages who had fallen into Iraqi hands during the initial invasion. Armed with Heckler & Koch sub-machine guns and trained jointly with the SAS, they achieved little. SAS efforts to hunt for SCUD missiles were also ineffective. Major came up with the idea of a no-fly zone in northern Iraq to protect Kurdish refugees from Saddam Hussein's attacks, an imaginative move which boosted resistance and earned him hero status in the eyes of many Kurds.[41] It is perhaps unsurprising then that Iraqi breaches of the no-fly zone stoked Major's appetite for intelligence. Abandoning his usual practice of rarely summoning the JIC chair, the prime minister grilled his intelligence advisers on the implications, and whether Saddam planned more breaches.[42]

MI6 also sponsored an exile group in London called the Iraq National Accord, whose membership consisted largely of military and security personnel who had defected from the Iraqi army. Among its leaders was General Adnan Nuri, a former brigade commander in Saddam's special forces. It also gained support within the CIA's London station, as Bush administration officials looked for a way to get rid of the Iraqi leader. Downing Street and the White House both backed failed popular insurrections in Iraq, some of which were launched from Accord's expensive new offices in Jordan.[43]

Once the military operations began, there was real fear about Iraqi subterranean operations in Britain. The security agencies had long experience of this. African states had periodically kidnapped and murdered people in London, as had Israel's unruly secret service, Mossad. Gaddafi's regime had been especially outrageous in abusing the diplomatic privileges afforded to its London embassy and attacking dissident students on British university campuses during the 1980s. But now the fear was even greater, and the JIC warned ministers of sabotage and assassination attempts by Iraqi intelligence agents operating in London. There were anxieties about a range of militant factions sympathetic to Baghdad. Most of all there were worries that the Iraqis might have smuggled chemical or biological weapons into their embassy in the heart of London. Percy Cradock, nettled by the fact that his warning of the Iraqi invasion had been ignored, enjoyed circulating blood-curdling tip-offs about possible attacks on ministers. All the Iraqi embassy personnel thought to be intelligence officers were expelled, together with about sixty other Iraqi nationals. In addition, Whitehall mounted a covert operation to establish if any weapons were lurking in the embassy, but nothing was found. Officials kept a squadron of SAS on standby in case of hostage-taking or assassination attempts.[44]

An attack was not long in coming. On Thursday, 7 February 1991, Percy Cradock was sitting in on a war cabinet meeting discussing the likely cost of the reconstruction of Kuwait once it had been liberated. The Treasury chief secretary, David Mellor, was delivering an inordinately long presentation. Cradock had been quietly praying for an interruption when an explosion went off in the garden of Number 10, answering his prayer.[45] Tom King, previously Northern Ireland secretary, recognised the distinctive sound, and shouted, 'It's a mortar!' Thinking quickly, Charles Powell, Major's private secretary, pushed the prime minister under the table. Two further explosions followed. A special iron-mesh curtain designed to catch flying glass and installed at the suggestion of MI5 prevented many injuries. It was a near-miss, and Major recalls that 'If it had been ten feet closer half the cabinet could have been killed.' He suggested they start the meeting again somewhere else, and the war cabinet trooped stoically off towards Cobra, the secure underground meeting room below Downing Street.[46] It soon became clear that the attackers were not Iraqi commandos, but members of the IRA.

Major was one of a long line of British prime ministers targeted by Irish nationalists. His predecessor escaped the Brighton bomb only by luck – one of her ministers likened it to 'von Stauffenberg's briefcase', adding that the attack was a huge 'coup' for the IRA.[47] By contrast, Major's escape was not a fluke. Continual assassination attempts, including the killing of Ian Gow in 1990, triggered constant improvements in physical and personal security.[48] Before leaving office Thatcher had controversially installed imposing black gates preventing public access to Downing Street altogether. Major's chancellor of the exchequer Norman Lamont had been intending to have the security curtains removed from Number 11, because they 'spoiled the view of Horse Guards Parade', but on the day of the bombing they saved his family and staff from hideous injury. After the 1991 attack a further round of reinforcement began at Downing Street.[49] Cabinet ministers became used to living alongside protection squads with increasingly fearsome weaponry in their family homes. William Waldegrave recalls: 'We tried to get the police to use their Uzi submachine guns to exterminate the grey squirrels that were destroying the beech trees around our cottage in Somerset, but they would never oblige.'[50]

During the 1990s, the IRA grew closer to military victory than at any time in the previous fifty years. They abandoned their strategy of attacking British forces in Europe, and concentrated on London. In the 1980s, there had been only a dozen bomb attacks in the capital. Between 1990 and 1994 there were over a hundred, and their increasing focus on economic targets proved very effective. In April 1992, the IRA bombed the Baltic Exchange in the City of London, using a large white truck packed with fertiliser. It caused £800 million worth of damage, more than the total damage costs from all 10,000 previous IRA explosions. The next day a large bomb exploded underneath the flyover at Staples Corner, near the start of the M1 motorway, paralysing the transport system. In April the following year the IRA again bombed the City of London, this time in Bishopsgate, causing £1 billion worth of damage. The insurance costs were so large that Lloyd's of London almost went bankrupt. In December 1993, coded bomb warnings closed dozens of railway and underground stations, costing London's economy an estimated £34 million. A few months later, mortar attacks closed Heathrow airport. In 1996, the IRA bombed both Canary Wharf, causing an estimated £100 million worth of damage, and Manchester city centre, causing £700 million worth of damage.

Perversely, all this was taking place at a time when the IRA had decided to abandon the armed struggle. At the end of a rainy February afternoon in 1993, John Major was sitting alone in the cabinet room. Interrupting his thoughts, a private secretary, probably Stephen Wall, brought the prime minister a remarkable message. It had come, via an MI5 conduit, from the republican leader Martin McGuinness, and stated: 'The conflict is over but we need your advice on how to bring it to a close.' It offered an IRA ceasefire and the prospect of negotiation, as long as this was not publicly presented as surrender. Taken aback, Major was unsure whether to believe the message, and checked its authenticity with MI5. Believing the IRA to be 'steeped in bigotry and utterly ruthless', he feared that this was merely a ploy in which the government would be confronted with unreasonable demands and then blamed for the renewal of violence. He also worried about the political ramifications if attacks continued after he had opened negotiations. No prime minister wants to be seen as soft on terrorism. Even if the IRA was serious, Major wondered how the vicious loyalist paramilitaries would respond. MI5 assured the prime minister that the message was genuine. And Major took it very seriously indeed.[51]

Intelligence penetration of republican ranks had been increasing for some time. Major oversaw a transfer of overall responsibility for the IRA from the Metropolitan Police Special Branch to MI5, resulting in the more aggressive running of agents. Under Patrick Walker, MI5 had developed a well-organised campaign to persuade the Whitehall securicrats, including Percy Cradock and Robin Butler, the cabinet secretary, to give them this new turf.[52] Impressed, Butler had informed the prime minister that the Met's strengths lay in operational policing and post-incident investigation. It simply could not compete with MI5's superior intelligence skills. In

November 1991, Major agreed that there was an 'a priori case for the Security Service to take over intelligence operations against republican targets on the mainland'. Given the complexities involved, he requested a more detailed report, and did not finally approve the change until six months later.[53] At a time when Cold War subversion targets were shrinking, domestic counter-terrorism was welcome new work for MI5. The service performed admirably, placing pressure on the IRA and earning the prime minister's personal congratulations.[54]

MI6 continued to help pave the way for the peace process through a back channel of secret contacts with the IRA that lasted from the early 1970s to the late 1980s. As we have seen, much of the contact had been between the Derry businessman Brendan Duddy and MI6's Michael Oatley. In 1991, Duddy recontacted his old friend, who was about to retire, having risen to the position of controller Europe, and invited him to dinner. To Oatley's surprise, Martin McGuinness joined them afterwards. Oatley thought him reasonable and a good interlocutor, likening him to a middle-ranking officer in the Parachute Regiment or the SAS. A week later, the IRA launched its mortar attack on 10 Downing Street, underlining its determination to keep fighting while talking. This did not surprise Major and his colleagues, who expected the IRA to negotiate from a position of strength.[55] Because MI5 now had the lead on Irish terrorism, its counter-terrorism branch and John Deverell, its director and coordinator of intelligence in Northern Ireland, took over the back channel, as Stella Rimington was 'vehemently opposed' to MI6 operating on MI5's turf.[56] As a result, MI5 held fortnightly meetings with Martin McGuinness.[57] Major had personally approved the secret links, and an MI5 officer briefed him that Duddy was 'a remarkable man who is devoted to achieving peace in Northern Ireland despite the high risk to himself'.[58]

Because of the fragmented nature of the republican movement, the violence continued. Nonetheless, all of the intelligence chiefs advised Major that their best information confirmed that at least some of the IRA leadership were genuinely rethinking their approach. But in March 1993, just as the IRA and Downing Street began to consider structured talks, the IRA struck again, when a bomb in the centre of Warrington killed two young boys. This was followed by the massive bomb which destroyed much of Bishopsgate. British intelligence officers continued to visit McGuinness at his mother's house despite these terrible events. Then another major bomb in Belfast brought the process to a grinding halt, and Major's inner circle decided that they could not continue to negotiate until violence stopped. The government informed Gerry Adams and McGuinness, Sinn Féin's top brass, via the usual back channels, but later that month the intelligence link was revealed in the *Observer*. Major was incensed about the leak but, despite an inquiry he never found the source.[59]

Parliament greeted the revelations with dismay. They came against a backdrop of lethal IRA violence, and to make matters worse, Major had earlier told MPs that face-to-face contact with the IRA would 'turn [his] stomach'. 'We will not do it,' he had publicly and defiantly stated.[60] The secret talks were ruined. Major later expressed how he 'regretted the loss of the back channel. It gave us some difficult moments, but it played its part.' 'Making peace,' he lamented with characteristic understatement, 'is a tricky business.'[61] Like many others who have resided in Number 10, Major became starkly aware of the need to lie publicly about talking to terrorists – and the damage caused if the public found out.

The prime minister now lost his political nerve. After consulting Patrick Mayhew, the Northern Ireland secretary, he decided to publish the exchanges with the IRA to show that the government had 'not struck any secret deals'. Mayhew unfortunately bungled the transcription of some of the documents, while certain government denials had to be retracted after it transpired that an intelligence intermediary had held 'an unauthorised face-to-face meeting' with McGuinness. Both damaged the credibility of the government's account.[62]

The republicans also scampered for cover, accusing Downing Street of forging messages. Martin McGuinness claimed that he had never sent the original message to Major, and insisted that 'it had been invented by the British government to get him killed by other republicans'.[63] 'Slander which beggars belief', Major later called this. Dublin stepped in to try to keep the momentum going, and helped to achieve 'the Downing Street Declaration' of December 1993, but progress stalled as Gerry Adams failed to carry the rest of the republican movement with him.

Long after the Downing Street attack, the threat of assassination contin-ued to hover over the prime minister and the cabinet. One tabloid editor went to visit Michael Howard, the home secretary, at his home in Eaton Place. He was curious to see how a home secretary 'lives in the permanent shadow of an IRA attack'. 'Pretty grimly,' was the answer. From the moment he arrived at the door there were armed policemen everywhere, inside and outside the house – 'Some actually live downstairs all the time.'[64] Howard was not alone. After the names of members of Major's intelligence and security team who had debated the nature of the McGuinness letter were leaked, elaborate security systems were set up in their homes, although a series of false alarms meant that they did not always last long.[65]

Despite this climate of insecurity and uncertainty, intelligence revealed that the IRA was moving towards a ceasefire. On his return from his summer holiday in 1994, officials informed Major that a ceasefire was now imminent. The intelligence was correct, and six days later the provisionals declared a 'cessation of hostilities'.[66] The prime minister was unconvinced that this ceasefire would hold long, and the intelligence and security community had to reassure him that it was genuine.[67] Eventually, after headway was made by MI5, and following some pressure from President Clinton in the United States, the IRA declared a cessation of military operations in 1994. Talks dragged on with painful slowness, but 1995 was the first year without terrorist killings for a quarter of a century.[68] The path to the April 1998 'Good Friday Agreement' had begun, and with the exception of the sceptical chancellor Ken Clarke, Major's cabinet were convinced that there was now the possibility of progress towards a lasting peace.[69] The prime minister, who faced greater political risk than his successor Tony Blair, given inherent Conservative antipathy towards nationalism, had helped lay the foundations.

Intelligence had broadened in the post-Cold War world. With former targets fading fast and even the IRA stumbling awkwardly towards an accommodation, by the mid-1990s 'economic well-being' became ever more important – and was explicitly mandated in the Intelligence Services Act.[70] Economic strength rather than military might became an indicator of state power, and economic security grew increasingly linked to state security. This involved spying on allies. Even where political and military alliances are strong, economic competition will still exist.[71]

Cognoscenti in Whitehall and Westminster who had responsibility for economics, trade or negotiations fully appreciated the need for intelligence. Indeed, it was often those with dull-sounding jobs who caught sight of the most fascinating material. Chris Mullin, parliamentary under-secretary of state at the Department for the Environment, Transport and the Regions, for example, recalls reading fascinating top-secret signals intelligence material – but only ever in the presence of two gloomy GCHQ officers in grey suits, whom he nicknamed 'the undertakers'. The material drew on intelligence gathered on economic competitor countries that most people would have regarded as neutrals or friends. Only America, New Zealand, Australia and Canada were off-limits for purposes of spying.[72]

European countries were fair game. John Major once observed that Britain belongs to more 'summit-holding clubs' than almost any other nation. Alongside the European Union, which holds between two and four top-level meetings a year, Britain is also a member of the G7, the G20, NATO, the Commonwealth, the Organisation for Security and Cooperation in Europe, and strange organisations such as ASEM, the Asia–Europe Meeting, which promotes cooperation between South-East Asia and Europe. Not to attend looks like a deliberate snub, but summitry had 'exploded' during Major's period in office, and he thought the currency of these meetings 'has been debased in proportion to their alarming proliferation'. Nevertheless, some meetings were important, and none mattered more to Major than those surrounding the Maastricht Treaty in 1991 and 1992 that turned the European Community into the European Union. Major believed Britain's future lay in Europe, but he had reservations about issues such as monetary union.[73] Negotiations therefore needed to be carefully handled. British intelligence had invested heavily in a support team for international negotiations and summits. This now paid substantial dividends.

The British intelligence and security agencies had long been engaged in bitter territorial competition and rivalry, including in Northern Ireland. Negotiations, however, proved an exception, in that Britain possessed an inter-agency team drawn from all the services. In the 1980s, the state of the art involved bugs in doors with long strings of batteries, and spike mikes through walls. By the 1990s, these had been supplemented by an army of 'cleaners' who busily inserted special USB sticks into any and every unprotected laptop and desktop computer they could access. Computer security was weak, and the British had a field day.[74]

The end of the Cold War impacted on Western Europe no less than the East. Germany was determined to reunify, and many countries, especially France, did not like the idea of a resurgent Teutonic leviathan. Germany responded by using the European Community to reassure its neighbours. Its answer to French paranoia involved deeper integration, including a European Union with universal citizenship, free movement of populations, and the creation of a European currency, the 'Euro'. But this horrified the Conservative Party, whose rank and file detested European federalism. Major faced a civil war within his party, and his very political survival depended on the texture of the negotiations over the new European Union. He sought to secure a series of 'opt-outs' on the single currency and social legislation. In short, the looming negotiations in late 1991 were a matter of political life or death for Major.

Major needed all his wits about him. He recalls that European Council meetings always began with an informal lunch, 'with excellent food and exceptionally fine wine'. During these lunches, Jacques Delors, the long-serving and wily French president of the European Commission, could be formidable and 'dangerous'. As the meal progressed, the chairman would urge people to raise pertinent matters, and Delors often 'took full advantage'. His accent deliberately thickening, he would spiral off into vague generalities on subjects the British might find unappealing. Major decided not to touch the wine: 'I did not fancy telling the Commons that some dreadful proposal had slipped past me as I savoured an excellent glass of Puligny Montrachet.'[75] In truth, his strategy relied more on excellent intelligence than sobriety and concentration. One source of information was John Kerr, Britain's ambassador to the EU. During a particularly critical round of negotiations, from which advisers were banned and only heads of state were permitted, Kerr hid under the table, from where he discreetly passed notes up to the grateful prime minister.[76]

Richard Tomlinson, an MI6 officer during the 1990s, recalls his colleagues asking the chief, Colin McColl, whether the agency spied on other European countries. McColl replied, 'Yes, we do. There are always important requirements for intelligence on the economic intentions of our European partners, particularly regarding their negotiating positions on the Maastricht Treaty.' French communications were an open book, partly because of their poor communications security discipline, and partly because of assistance provided to GCHQ by the American NSA. German and Dutch communications were more challenging, and necessitated the use of human agents. Britain therefore ran a high-ranking official in German government finance circles from the mid-1980s. Providing not only internal knowledge of the Bundesbank but also predictions of interest-rate movements and Maastricht negotiating positions, this was perhaps MI6's most important recruitment, certainly as significant as Oleg Gordievsky. In government circles this single 'star recruitment' was said to justify the entire MI6 annual budget.[77]

'We knew the stakes were high,' recalls Major. With some trepidation, his team flew out to Maastricht on 5 December 1991. It included some of Whitehall's best brains, among them Nigel Wicks from the Treasury, responsible for drafting the euro opt-out; Michael Jay from the Foreign Office; and John Kerr, who according to Major was an expert in the

European game of 'twelve-dimensional chess'. In the shadows, Major and his team also brought a close-range collection unit from MI6 and GCHQ who had new devices for getting intelligence to their masters. Major's main tactic was to wait until the European heads of government began to fear stalemate, and then present his euro opt-out request. British intelligence targeted François Mitterrand, Major's main opponent, and fortunately French communications were porous. Major and his team also worked from their own highly sensitive document: a summary setting out their sticking points on every key clause. This was heavily annotated in Major's handwriting. At a break in the proceedings he asked to see it, and to his horror 'It was gone.' The British team feared that it had 'fallen into the hands of another delegation', and if so, 'all our bottom-line positions would have been revealed'. For a few moments there was sheer panic; one diplomat called it 'the worst moment of my professional career'.[78] But eventually it turned up in a jumble of Norman Lamont's papers.

That the British were monitoring other people's communications was an open secret. In fact, it was often obvious: their responses to European suggestions were simply too excellent and timely. Germany's chancellor, Helmut Kohl, a great fan of Winston Churchill and also a 'sharp and shrewd' negotiator, enjoyed teasing John Major about this. Kohl's banter focused on the prime ministerial red box carried by Major's private secretary. 'Yes that's it!' he would laugh loudly. 'All the British government's secrets. How to overcome Europe in one box.' For Kohl and Major this became a running joke, often elaborated on at some length over lunch. Major enjoyed the pantomime secrecy so much that he eventually had a replica red box made for his German counterpart. It looked like a British prime ministerial red box, but as Major explained to him, 'This one is different. It's full of German secrets,' turning it round to reveal a German eagle and Kohl's name 'embossed in gold'. Kohl was delighted, and Major could not resist extending the joke by adding that the following year 'you can have the key'.[79]

On a quiet evening in March 1990, a maverick artillery expert called Gerald Bull strolled out of his apartment in an elegant suburb of Brussels carrying a briefcase. Lurking in the shadows, an assassin waited silently. Two rounds were fired at close range into the back of Bull's skull. He died instantly. There was $20,000 in Bull's briefcase, but the assailant ignored it and left the money on the pavement. A few days later British Customs would seize eight huge steel tubes, each a metre across, designed to constitute a massive gun barrel sixty metres long. Exported under the heading 'petroleum pipes', they had been manufactured by Sheffield Forgemasters, and were waiting alongside a freighter bound for Iraq. Officials then found more components in five other European countries. Bull had wanted to work for the West, but when his experiments were not supported he sold his services to Iraq. Hundreds of his modified 155mm guns had given Iraq the edge in its long war with Iran, and this 'Super-Gun' was intended to be the apogee of his career. Codenamed 'Project Babylon', the Super-Gun was a massive Iraqi operation costing millions of dollars, but it never came to fruition.[80]

'Project Babylon' was an extraordinary story, so improbable that many British officials simply did not believe it. Ian Lang, the cabinet minister responsible for the Department of Trade and Industry at the time, recalls it as 'a James Bond-like tale' that involved 'spying, murder and an international plot to build for Saddam Hussein the world's biggest gun'. The Super-Gun was designed to fire special shells over a very long range. 'Mossad and MI6 were involved,' Lang continued, 'so too were Midlands engineering companies – and, inevitably, a government minister, Alan Clark.' Britain's role involved the manufacture of the high-quality steel tubes that formed part of the gun, which were 'seized at the last minute'. Lang observed that MI6 had been slow to investigate, despite being alerted by the manufacturers, and ministers were inadequately briefed. But this conclusion is hardly the whole story.[81]

Premiers often have to confront skeletons rattling in the secret service cupboard of their immediate predecessor. Margaret Thatcher was haunted by Anthony Blunt and mole-mania, while James Callaghan before her endured the torments of the 'Wilson plot'. But no skeletons were as noisy or as dangerous as the 'Arms to Iraq' episode, which for a time made it look as if John Major's administration would be terminated prematurely by an intelligence-related scandal. Major knew that Britain was heavily involved in many of the CIA's secret wars during the 1980s, from the labyrinthine secret struggles in Lebanon to the clandestine armies that supported the Contras in Nicaragua. Another war that the CIA joined was the long and bloody conflict fought between Iran and Iraq from 1980 to 1988. As the war reached its height, the British Parliament chose to support the United Nations arms embargo against both sides, and banned further arms exports to the troubled region. But because the West saw Iran as the bigger threat, ministers quietly 'reinterpreted' the guidelines to allow some exports to Saddam Hussein towards the end of the conflict. The government deliberately 'spun down' intelligence to fit the preferred policy of arms sales, by interpreting Iraq's intended use as civilian rather than military.[82]

Iraq had vast oil wealth, and it has been estimated that Saddam spent some £50 billion on weapons in the 1980s. Many countries, including France, Russia, Brazil and Chile, were indiscriminate in what they sold him. Faced with this free-for-all, Alan Clark at the Department of Trade and Lord Trefgarne, who looked after arms sales at the Ministry of Defence, lobbied hard to have restrictions eased. Major claimed that he had not been briefed on any policy changes, either as foreign secretary (despite participating in discussions on the sale of Hawk aircraft to Iraq) or prime minister. He also said that it was impossible for him to read all the available intelligence. Forty thousand pieces of intelligence came from GCHQ and MI6 each year, he claimed, and it was 'clearly absurd' that ministers should read them all. A filtering process was necessary.[83] As shadow foreign secretary Robin Cook put it powerfully (and sceptically) in the House of Commons: 'The prime minister's defence is well known. It is simple, if inelegant: nobody told him.'[84]

There were secret reasons for relaxing sanctions too. Some limited exports of ambiguous 'dual use' technology allowed insight into Saddam's weapons programme, especially his drive for chemical and nuclear weapons. British firms in the Midlands that produced high-quality machine tools, including lathes, were of special interest: MI5 recruited the export sales manager of a firm called Matrix Churchill, while MI6 reactivated a long-standing relationship with Paul Henderson, its managing director. Special Branch ran other agents, including John Grecian, the managing director of Ordtec, a company that made fuses. Accordingly, William Waldegrave, then at the Foreign Office, approved the request for more relaxed guidelines. All this took place against the background of the *fatwa* placed on the novelist Salman Rushdie by Tehran, an episode that refocused attention on Iran as the main enemy.[85]

Yet UK Customs and Excise was unaware of the secret activity. In 1991, Paul Henderson found himself in the dock, charged with breaching the UN embargo. His defence argued that the government knew and approved of his company's activities. Working with the full knowledge of MI6 to spy on Iraqi weapons programmes, cabinet ministers, including Geoffrey Howe, signed Public Interest Immunity Certificates to cover the government's tracks, risking the possibility that innocent men would go to jail. At best, the government acted hypocritically. At worst, it engaged in criminal conspiracy.[86] Either way, there was certainly a divergence between the actual policy and public government statements.[87]

Alan Clark, who had been involved in relaxing the guidelines, effectively collapsed the trial of Henderson. He admitted that his account of meetings with the managers had been 'economical' with the truth (or 'the *actualité*', as he put it), a phrase that deliberately recalled Margaret Thatcher's *Spycatcher* fiasco in the Australian courts. Similarly, Ian McDonald, head of defence sales, famously told the court that 'Truth is a difficult concept.' Thereafter the newspapers had a field day.

Major demanded to know what was going on. Percy Cradock put some pointed questions to Colin McColl, chief of MI6. McColl replied rather disingenuously that the reports MI6 had received referred either to traditional 155mm artillery or to tubes so large that they were 'not recognised as artillery'. Again, this perhaps demonstrated a deliberate 'spinning down' of intelligence to fit the policy of civilian use. The subsequent inquiry by Justice Richard Scott saw the internal MI6 briefing notes for McColl, and concluded that there had been no confusion. In other words, Scott thought McColl had deliberately tried to mislead Downing Street and to cover intelligence tracks in the Super-Gun affair.[88]

John Major felt he had been lied to by many people. When the affair first erupted, the prime minister, who had only been in office a matter of days, summoned Alan Clark to the cabinet room and asked if he had deliberately advised the companies on how to conceal the military use of their exports. Clark soberly assured him and the cabinet secretary, Robin Butler, that this was not the case. He did, however, then amend Butler's note of the meeting to downplay his advice.[89] Nonetheless, on this basis the government rejected the press assertions against Clark in the House of Commons. But when the Matrix Churchill case came to trial in November 1992, Clark changed his story. Major felt betrayed. Other prosecutions were dropped, and four executives of Ordtec, a subsidiary company, who had already pleaded guilty to exporting a fuse assembly line, successfully appealed against their sentences. It now looked as if Britain and America had been secretly arming Iraq in a programme managed by MI6 and the CIA.[90]

John Major found himself being asked questions he did not wish to answer. Some concerned a shadowy figure called Stephan Kock, a former member of the Rhodesian SAS who seemed to have directed many of the arms companies involved in the Arms to Iraq affair. Pressed on his precise duties by Labour MP Michael Meacher, Major replied stonily, 'It remains the Government's policy not to comment on contacts which an individual may or may not have had with the security and intelligence services.'[91]

Although Parliament got no further with the mysterious Kock, it scented scandal, and pointed the finger at many of Major's ministers. He had no choice but to opt for an independent inquiry by a senior judge, in the hope of avoiding accusations of whitewash.[92]

Major swiftly appointed Lord Justice Scott, who enjoyed his inquiry immensely. At first glance this suited Major, since the inquiry, expected to report in six months, took three years to conclude. But the terms had been drawn very widely, allowing Scott to investigate all manner of interesting things, including MI6 and its relationship with the arms trade.[93] He called Margaret Thatcher to give evidence. She described how she received weekly intelligence material on the subject 'which comes round in the red book ... I would have that in my box every weekend and also there would probably be a note accompanying it giving me an effective summary and directing my attention to things which were extremely important to know.' But beyond declaring that chemical weapons were 'absolutely horrific', and adding, 'We knew they [the Iraqis] had used chemical weapons,' she claimed that she could recall nothing of detail.[94]

One of the reasons Major was anxious about the Scott Report was worries about the personal involvement of Thatcher and other people at the top. Prime ministers hate inquiring into their predecessors' possible misdeeds, and everyone knew that Thatcher and her immediate circle took a close personal interest in promoting British arms sales. In 1985, she had been visited in Downing Street by Caspar Weinberger, the US defense secretary, a staunch friend during the recent Falklands War. But instead of greeting him warmly, she berated him. The Pentagon had just chosen to spend $4 billion buying a top-secret encrypted communication system from the French called 'Rita', rejecting the equivalent British system, 'Ptarmigan'. This episode connected several of Thatcher's passions: secrets, conspiracy and commercial interests. Insisting that there had been 'dirty work at the crossroads', she complained, 'We have been cheated. Do you hear me? Cheated. And don't try and tell me otherwise.' General Colin Powell, who accompanied Weinberger, found the performance 'fascinating'. Margaret Thatcher's reputation was formidable, and now he had seen her 'swing her famous verbal handbag right at Weinberger's head'.[95]

Helmut Kohl once remarked that Thatcher was 'ice-cold in pursuit of British interests'.[96] But now, a decade later, many were wondering just what had been done in the rush to arm Iraq against Iran, and who was implicated in what. This was especially the case given that Thatcher had also performed a quiet U-turn on efforts to prevent Saddam Hussein acquiring chemical weapons after it emerged from American intelligence that British-made pumps were being used to manufacture mustard gas. Because of this, and because 'our own trade in CS gas has not escaped criticism (the Russians claim that our use of CW [chemical weapons] in Northern Ireland contravened the Geneva Protocol)', one diplomat warned, 'our own position on CW exports is not invulnerable'.[97]

As Scott was reporting in early 1996, a plot aided by MI6 to topple Saddam Hussein collapsed, triggering widespread retribution by his security forces. The CIA and MI6 were working through the Iraqi National Accord in London, led by Dr Iyad Allawi, a former member of Iraq's ruling Ba'ath Party who had lived in Britain since 1971. A regional outpost was created in Jordan in early 1996, which then tried to recruit serving Iraqi officers to topple Saddam. But many viewed the Iraqi National Accord as teeming with double agents working for Baghdad, so the conspiracy was rounded up quickly. Later that year, some eighty senior officers were arrested and executed. Local CIA officers ran a second operation out of the three Kurdish provinces from which the Iraqi army had withdrawn, but this unauthorised operation was also unsuccessful.[98]

Whitehall officials referred to the Scott Report as 'the poison chalice', knowing that the fate of several ministers, perhaps of the government itself, was at stake.[99] After three long years of investigation, it was placed before Parliament on 15 February 1996. William Waldegrave and Attorney General Nicholas Lyell sat on the front bench 'looking unhappy', and were perhaps most at risk.[100] Lyell told ministers that they had a duty to claim public-interest immunity for documents relating to MI6 that would have been central to the defence in the Matrix Churchill case. He could also have briefed Lord Justice Scott about the mounting panic among ministers, but failed to do so.[101] In the end, despite the fact that its release was carefully managed, Scott's report, which found that the government had failed to inform Parliament of the more relaxed policy, nearly brought down John Major's government. Ministers at the centre of the scandal were given advance sight of the report and coached about how to rebut Scott's criticisms, while the shadow foreign secretary, Robin Cook, was allowed just three hours to read a report of over a million words. Major whipped his party by asserting that a vote against his government would be regarded as a vote of no confidence. Cook performed brilliantly, and Major, who did not speak in the debate, escaped by a hair's breadth. As he recalls, 'We had crawled home by one vote, 320 to 319.'[102] Major only just survived his prime ministerial brush with an intelligence scandal in what was his last year of office. His successor Tony Blair, already waiting in the wings, had little idea of the way in which he too would almost be unseated by secret service controversy.

17

Tony Blair
(1997–2007)

It is more than my life's worth to start mucking around
with stuff from the Joint Intelligence Committee.
TONY BLAIR[1]

Controversy over intelligence defines Tony Blair's government. Like
Churchill and Thatcher before him, Blair was already fascinated by intelligence before taking office. But unlike Churchill and Thatcher, he had
never held ministerial office before entering Downing Street, and so
understood it poorly. Aside from the odd lunch with 'C' and a long-standing promise to allow GCHQ workers to unionise,[2] Blair had had very few
dealings with the secret world. In opposition, it had been Labour policy to
make oversight of the intelligence and security services the responsibility
of Parliament. But once in office, Blair decided to keep them under the
control of the prime minister – a sign of things to come.[3]

Immediately upon taking office, however, his initial experiences with
intelligence were reasonably successful, and gave little indication of the
impending storm. He inherited Major's negotiation efforts, supported by
an intense intelligence programme, to achieve peace in Northern Ireland,
while successful military interventions in Kosovo and Sierra
Leone, together with the four-day bombing of Iraqi weapons of mass
destruction (WMD) sites in late 1998, seemed to suggest that intelligence
could support effective military action. Similarly, the interventions in
Bosnia and Kosovo demonstrated the value of special forces to the new
prime minister.[4] There was the odd hiccup, though. When faced with the
foot-and-mouth outbreak and protesting farmers, a panicked Downing
Street asked the director-general of MI5, Stephen Lander, 'Why aren't
you doing the farmers for us like you did the miners for Margaret
Thatcher?'[5]

Blair revelled in the possibilities of intelligence. It was a new experience for him – a new toy – as he bounded exuberantly around Whitehall in his early days in office.[6] Enthused, he quickly began to reverse the cuts imposed on intelligence at the end of the Cold War. A pugnacious liberal who believed in exporting democracy, the new prime minister needed intelligence to support his military interventions. He also saw secret disruption as the answer to many of the insidious threats that accompanied accelerating globalisation, including drugs, organised crime and people-trafficking. In an early phone call with American President Bill Clinton, the two leaders discussed the rise and the dangers of stateless terrorism and organised crime. Clinton stated that groups across Africa and the Middle East, 'not associated with or funded by governments', were 'like in those old James Bond movies with SPECTRE and Dr. No', and predicted a 'twenty-first-century version of those'.[7] Perhaps a resurrection of James Bond skills would be needed to counter them.

In 1999, Lander and Francis Richards from GCHQ joined the new chief of MI6, Richard Dearlove, in an extended 'crime summit' at Downing Street that covered the threats from the Russian mafia and Latin American drug barons. They briefed Blair about the work of joint MI6, GCHQ and SAS teams in Colombia helping to hunt down and liquidate key targets. Blair was impressed, and requested more of the same. Emphasising the link between intelligence and crime, he asked all three agencies to work more closely with the National Criminal Intelligence Service.[8] Stepping through the famous black door clearly reshapes a politician's views: as shadow home secretary, Blair had previously been critical of using MI5 to counter crime.[9]

Although intelligence was expanding under Blair, the young prime minister failed to understand it. And the agencies found some of his thinking repellent. Early on, his government tried to resurrect the bizarre idea of an internal market for intelligence, in which the Foreign Office, the Ministry of Defence, the Cabinet Office and other government departments would pay for intelligence like water, gas or electricity. Richard Wilson, who was then cabinet secretary, explained that Gordon Brown, the chancellor of the exchequer, was 'trying to introduce a customer relationship between the agencies and their departments'. Wilson knew that this would be the end of objective intelligence reporting, and 'fought a furious battle to resist' the reform. 'I am pleased to say,' he later said, 'I won.' Ruefully, he recalls that he 'asked Number 10 for help on this', but 'they had other priorities'. Placating the irascible Brown was more important than protecting Britain's precious central intelligence machinery.[10]

Other things were going badly wrong with the central machine. In MI6, the separate line-management chain for overseeing the evaluation and circulation of intelligence was lost, resulting in a reduction in internal challenge and quality control.[11] At a higher level, ministers supposedly sitting on the Committee on Security and Intelligence, a senior body chaired by the prime minister to provide high-level oversight of the secret services, grew frustrated at its lack of activity. They repeatedly urged Blair to convene meetings, but he refused. In fact, largely because of his desire to personally own this area, the committee never met at all.

Eventually the prime minister began to ignore JIC papers too. Jonathan Powell, his chief of staff, later dismissed the JIC as producing 'lowest-common-denominator-type reports, hedging their bets and failing to give a clear steer in any direction'.[12] Instead, Blair preferred to receive 'stocktaking papers' from people he knew inside MI6, which had been 'sent to No 10 directly'. Senior MI6 officers later explained that this was because their 'relationships with Number 10 had become quite personalised', indeed 'too personalised'.[13] Blair's informal approach to government extended to the secret world.[14]

Finally, Blair preferred his information to have a point of view. He even toyed with the idea of abolishing the long-held and much-admired distinction between intelligence and policy advice. While one former home secretary has praised Blair's approach to intelligence for drawing on his legal training and not taking material at face value, those from the intelligence world have accused him of being uninterested in intelligence unless it conformed to his world view.[15]

The al-Qaeda terrorist attacks in America in September 2001 fundamentally altered Blair's personal relationship with the intelligence services. Prior to 9/11, Richard Wilson attempted to set up meetings between Blair and the intelligence chiefs to try to build a relationship, but the prime minister saw them infrequently. This changed overnight. Now the spy chiefs, and senior officers from MI6 in particular, joined him on the famous sofa at the heart of government. The prime minister would henceforth always turn to them first.[16] Blair and his closest advisers enjoyed the company of MI6 personnel. Alastair Campbell, Blair's director of communications and close confidant, certainly shared the prime minister's enthusiasm. The JIC chairman, Colin Budd, gave Campbell a personal briefing on the role of the JIC shortly after Blair's first ever cabinet meeting.

Although Campbell asked sensible questions, Budd remained cautiously aware of his relationship with the media. It was instantly clear that Campbell was central to Blair's government.[17]

Dearlove hoped that Downing Street and MI6 could 'increase and improve co-operation' on media activities, and in July 1999 suggested that Campbell visit MI6 headquarters and meet 'all his key people'. Campbell judged Dearlove to be 'pretty media savvy', and MI6 began ringing the spin-doctor for advice on whether to release certain pieces of intelligence to the press when it was in both their interests to do so.[18] Campbell did not object, and also pressed Richard Wilson to 'bring MI5 and MI6 media operations more into the centre'.[19] A few months later Campbell visited the new MI6 building, where 'they laid on a presentation about some of their information operations'.[20]

Blair and his aides enjoyed a respectful but more distant relationship with MI5 and GCHQ. Campbell also visited MI5, where Stephen Lander told him that the CIA's press operation cost more than his own agency's entire budget.[21] Fearful of the impact of GCHQ's expansion on MI5's funding, Lander worried that Blair had only limited interest in MI5 apart from on the Northern Ireland issue.[22] Again, however, 9/11 transformed relations between Blair and MI5. As Christopher Andrew puts it, they moved from 'distant to warm', and Blair publicly praised the work of MI5 more than any previous prime minister had. Lander was the first head of MI5 to be invited to a cabinet meeting specifically to be congratulated by the prime minister – this was for his role in a particularly large counter-terrorist operation which had prevented numerous attacks in Britain.[23] By contrast, although intensely interested in WMD, the prime minister seems to have been unaware that the UK's largest analytical centre on this was the Defence Intelligence Staff, just a few hundred yards from Downing Street. And it was analysis of this very issue that would define his administration.

Blair enjoyed some early intelligence successes. Secret intelligence proved central to supporting the developing dialogue with the republicans in Northern Ireland. Although MI5 initially feared that the new prime minister lacked interest in their work, he always paid close attention to intelligence reports on Northern Ireland.[24] Influenced by his training as a barrister, he read intelligence reports rationally and carefully before cross-questioning 'witnesses'. He saw intelligence as a vital part of government machinery, although he had not yet begun advancing elaborate policies which needed intelligence to back them up.[25]

By October 1997, Lander was able to tell the prime minister directly that intelligence on IRA thinking had improved.[26] This could only help the peace process, as Blair and his negotiators sought to get inside the minds of the protagonists. In the same month, the new prime minister met Gerry Adams and Martin McGuinness at Stormont for the first time. Indeed, it was the first time a prime minister had met openly with republican leaders for eighty years.[27] Intelligence proved central to the British approach, inherited by Blair, which sought to keep up the pressure on the IRA through vigorous penetrations by 'moles', while encouraging Sinn Féin down the political road. Intelligence helped him to confront this puzzling dual identity of the republican movement. For example, he repeatedly asked to talk to the high command of the IRA, but was never granted an audience. Yet from highly sensitive briefings, often for his ears only, he now knew which Sinn Féin leaders were in fact IRA commanders.[28]

Blair had been fortunate to inherit an increasingly effective intelligence set-up on Northern Ireland, including the various back channels resurrected under Major. Progress was such that on 11 December 1997 Adams and McGuinness visited Downing Street. Jonathan Powell recalls a great sense of history. Never one to miss a jibe, McGuinness observed, 'So this is where all the damage was done.' Powell replied, 'Yes, the mortars landed in the garden behind you. The Gulf War cabinet ... dived under the table, before retreating to the garden rooms below. The windows came in but no one was injured.' McGuinness was in fact referring to the fact that Downing Street was where Michael Collins signed the Irish Treaty back in 1921.[29] The exchange underlined the IRA's profound sense of history.

Gerry Adams was understandably sensitive to surveillance. He 'went without a mobile ... because he knew he could be tracked on it'.[30] The IRA leadership understood intelligence instinctively, since the whole of Northern Ireland had been monitored for decades; so much so that it almost verged on being an open prison. GCHQ had also been intercepting most of the telephone calls to and from Ireland in a large-scale operation only halted in 1998 at the insistence of Dublin.[31] Other protagonists feared surveillance too – if not always by the Brits. David Trimble, leader of the Ulster Unionists, for example, called Blair in September 1997 convinced that the IRA had bugged his phone – a 'slightly odd notion of the IRA's capabilities', Powell later mused.[32]

By contrast, Mo Mowlam, Blair's secretary of state for Northern Ireland, struggled to deal with the intricacies of using intercepts. Remarkably, she discussed her personal battle to stop the prime minister firing her with

Martin McGuinness in places where she was recorded by British bugging. More alarmingly, she sometimes introduced details into her conversations with Adams and McGuinness that the republicans knew could only have come from technical collection. Based on conversations with the loose-lipped Mowlam, the republicans were able to uncover listening devices in one of their key safe houses. In May 1998, Mowlam 'blew' a listening operation that had been mounted against Gerry Kelly, a leading Sinn Féin official living in Belfast. The bugging device, hidden in a wooden rafter in a country-style kitchen that had been hollowed out and packed full of listening equipment, had been providing good intelligence for three years.[33] Mo Mowlam may have been good at befriending nationalist leaders, but she was not a favourite with Britain's intelligence agencies.

During the peace process, Adams and McGuinness continually raised the spectre of dissident splits whenever the IRA was pushed to deliver progress. Again, intelligence played a role in countering this tactic. Blair was able to see through it, because intelligence showed Adams to be in 'uncontested control' of the republican movement.[34] A combination of long-term back channels, groundwork conducted under Major's government, and the use of moles and signals intelligence ensured that intelligence played an important role in the peace process. Nonetheless, intelligence can only carry negotiations so far. Blair's strength lay in his charm, leadership and diplomacy skills, described by Powell as 'fox-like'. He successfully built up personal relationships with both sides, bonding with the hardline Democratic Unionist Party leader Ian Paisley over scripture while convincing Adams and McGuinness to risk their careers (and their lives) by carrying the IRA to the negotiating table.[35]

By January 1998, peace was on the horizon. The Good Friday Agreement stated that Northern Ireland would remain part of the United Kingdom so long as this was supported by the majority of its people, and that the unionists would enter a power-sharing government with Sinn Féin. Shortly before the referendum on the agreement, MI5 reported that 'Whilst many members of PIRA [Provisional IRA] were initially sceptical about the Agreement, the long-held assumption by volunteers that PIRA would return to violence in May appears to have diminished.'[36] The historic agreement was signed on 10 April 1998. By the end of the year, a 'diminishing' amount of MI5 resources were taken up by Ireland. 'Islamic terror', observed Stephen Lander, was now 'the big growth area'.[37]

Asked what was Britain's primary source of danger, Lander replied without hesitation: 'France.' He was referring to Islamic radicals focused on

North Africa, many of whom had taken refuge in London.[38] But there was another network, al-Qaeda, which had been establishing itself more globally. Its founder Osama bin Laden, based in Afghanistan, had been building up regional offices which he called using a newly purchased satellite phone. By 1997, the NSA was monitoring his traffic – typically, not sharing the product with the CIA's bin Laden tracking unit. The numbers painted an interesting picture: there were six calls to the United States, fifty-seven to Saudi Arabia, fifty-nine to Pakistan, 131 to Sudan, and 260 to London.[39]

A few years later, on Sunday, 21 October 2001, Gerry Adams called on the IRA to disarm. Downing Street remembers this as a 'big moment'. For Blair it should have been the biggest moment of his premiership – the potential end of Britain's longest conflict of modern times. But the historic announcement was almost completely overshadowed by the 9/11 attacks on America a month before.[40] The terrorist scene had changed. Lander warned the prime minister, almost with a whiff of nostalgia, that al-Qaeda was different: 'We're not talking about the IRA, who wanted to go off and have a Guinness after they'd let off their bombs.'[41]

On 11 September 2001, international terrorists struck the United States. Simultaneous attacks killed 3,000 people in New York and Washington, DC. Across the Atlantic, Tony Blair was at the annual Trades Union Congress conference in Brighton when he heard the news. He rushed back to London by train, with his Special Branch protection unit using crime-scene tape to seal off part of the carriage for him.[42] As soon as he arrived in Downing Street, he was briefed by John Scarlett, chairman of the JIC, and Stephen Lander.

Uncertainty reigned. Both intelligence leaders were confident that the attack was the work of al-Qaeda. No other organisation had the capability to mount such a sophisticated multiple operation. Both felt that no governments were involved. Blair apparently 'looked fuzzy' at the mention of al-Qaeda, and asked Lander if he knew about them. Lander replied frankly that the JIC 'has been reporting about this. It was in the Red Book' – the weekly briefing of current intelligence. 'Perhaps you haven't read them,' he added. 'Fair enough,' Blair shrugged. With his quick intellect and lawyer's brain, the prime minister soon got up to speed, and by the evening he was firing questions about Osama bin Laden at his intelligence chiefs as though he was a long-time expert.[43]

This personal interest was unsurprising. From then on, the danger that al-Qaeda might assassinate Blair became a mounting intelligence concern.

Every day, David Blunkett, the home secretary, received intelligence reports stating that Blair was 'the second biggest target after [President George W.] Bush in the world'.[44] Blair's security was stepped up to the extent that moving him around London began to resemble a major military operation. Motorcycle outriders went ahead to stop the traffic with sirens wailing, while the prime minister was carried in an armoured Jaguar that had been fitted with a new system to protect its occupants from poison gas. On entering 10 Downing Street, even visiting MPs passed through an airport security scanner, only to be greeted by a policeman cradling a sub-machine gun.[45] At one point, Downing Street's core team toured a secret facility called 'Project Pindar', a three-storey underground bunker below the Ministry of Defence, to which they might retreat in the event of an emergency. A grim relic of the Cold War, it had bunk beds and its own television broadcast station.[46] Suddenly the prospect of occupying this emergency site seemed very real. Downing Street staff were divided into four groups – Red, Blue, Green and Orange – with only the former allocated places in the bunker. Cherie Blair was allocated a space, but Alastair's Campbell's wife Fiona Millar, who worked in much the same capacity for Cherie that he did for the prime minister, was not. Cherie pronounced the bunker to be 'totally underground and really spooky', and eventually ordered an expensive upgrade to the décor, to the vexation of ministers whose budgets were plundered to pay for it.[47]

In the immediate aftermath of 9/11, Lander, Scarlett and Blair worried about the American response. They feared that Bush would be under pressure to do something immediate and 'irresponsible'. This worry was not misplaced. Richard Clarke, Bush's counter-terrorism chief, recalls discussions about attacking Iraq on the very morning after 9/11, and was 'incredulous that we were talking about anything other than getting al-Qaeda'. A few days later Donald Rumsfeld, the secretary of defense, suggested bombing Iraq. 'At first I thought Rumsfeld was joking. But he was serious.'[48] British intelligence therefore focused on the hunt for bin Laden, hoping that his swift capture would temper the American thirst for revenge. Richard Dearlove reported that there was a large joint operation ongoing with the CIA to uncover the network behind the attack. By the end of the week, Francis Richards from GCHQ confirmed that everything pointed to bin Laden, training camps in Afghanistan and possibly some direct help from the Taliban, the hardline Islamist regime then ruling the country. But because some of the evidence came from sigint, 'it would not be possible to publish much of it'.[49]

The Taliban refused to hand over bin Laden, so Britain and America launched 'Operation Enduring Freedom', led by special forces, in early October 2001. Although the military focus was Afghanistan, Blair was keenly aware of an accelerating global conflict with many players. In Russia, President Vladimir Putin 'wanted to use it to go after Chechnya even harder'. Ariel Sharon, the Israeli prime minister, sought to exploit the emerging conflict to hammer the Palestinian leader Yasser Arafat. Similarly, India saw it as an excuse to get tougher on the covert war against Pakistan in Kashmir.[50] Tony Blair was clear that he needed to embark on a world counter-terrorism tour to manage the rather uneven global response.

Blair saw more of his intelligence chiefs in the four weeks following the 9/11 attacks than he had done in the previous four years of his administration.[51] Dearlove in particular often found himself on board the prime ministerial plane. He joined Blair on visits to Russia, Pakistan and India – and intelligence remained a constant theme throughout. Flying over the 'Stans', Blair and Dearlove bonded. Despite supposedly reporting to the foreign secretary, Dearlove became much closer to the prime minister. One member of the entourage described the spy chief as a 'fantastically comforting presence for the prime minister'.[52] Campbell recalls that on one trip he enjoyed 'a great laugh' with Dearlove about the name of the Indian secret service, which was the Research and Analysis Wing, or 'RAW'. They joked about renaming the Downing Street Research and Information Unit 'RAW', while 'the really secret stuff would be handled by a tiny elite team called RAW Hide'. At around this time, Campbell noticed that Dearlove was deliberately developing his personal relationship with Blair. It is, of course, impossible for any intelligence chief to reach the most senior levels without an astute sense of politics. As a public relations professional, Campbell admired the way in which Dearlove 'got himself close to Tony Blair and used that to generate support at the top for the service as a whole'. Dearlove struck Campbell as 'astutely political', and seemed to have a decent sense of the issues on which Blair sought to focus.[53]

In the second week of October, the Blair roadshow rolled on through Oman, Saudi Arabia and then Egypt. An intelligence cell travelled with them to provide the prime minister with up-to-date material, keeping him abreast of the effort against bin Laden on the ground in Afghanistan. As he travelled, Blair grew worried that the Americans were doing too much bombing of Afghanistan and not using enough ground forces to capture bin Laden. He was alarmed to be told that the Iraqis had just shot down an unmanned Predator surveillance drone, as he was also 'concerned that the CIA was actively looking for reasons to widen and hit Iraq'. He was so concerned that he went to Washington the following week and met George Tenet, the director of the CIA. At this point, Blair clearly thought war on Iraq was a bad idea, not least because several Middle East leaders had warned him that it would cause the international coalition against bin Laden to peel away.[54] In late 2001, Blair's inner circle saw it as their job to 'restrain Bush from attacking Iraq'. MI6 agreed.[55]

At four o'clock in the afternoon of 3 December, David Manning, Blair's foreign affairs adviser, asked MI6 for its latest views on Iraq. American plans for an invasion were 'building up apace'. Dearlove's top Middle East expert, Mark Allen, set to work feverishly, and two hours later he produced a vigorous argument against invasion.[56] He warned that action against Iraq would be seen as a change of agenda from the war on terror, which most Arab regimes supported, and so would 'undermine today's unity of purpose'. Everyday Arabs on the street would sympathise with the Iraqis, and this would threaten friendly Arab regimes, which moreover would 'see action against WMD as a trailer for action against themselves'. Attacking Iraq would mean lining up with the Shia Muslims and the Kurds, whom Allen considered to be 'unstable allies and a red rag to the neighbours'. 'Fundamentalism' would be boosted, and overall it would destabilise the region, since the governments of Jordan, Syria, Kuwait and Saudi Arabia were all fragile. Assessing the risks and costs, Allen's very last words were: 'Possible refugee/humanitarian crisis.' MI6 has rarely produced a more perceptive and accurate prediction.[57]

However, Blair liked military action, and so far everything had gone well. In Afghanistan, his entourage had been impressed by what a small number of intrepid pathfinders had achieved. As a British diplomatic presence and a United Nations office opened in Kabul, Alastair Campbell sensed a public relations coup, and hoped to publicise MI6 successes. He felt that there was 'a fantastic story to be told about the role played by a small number of our spooks and special forces' if Dearlove was 'up for it'.[58] Campbell was always aware of the potential role of MI6 in propaganda and information warfare.

After Christmas, Blair went out to visit Afghanistan. A convoy of armoured vehicles took him to visit Hamid Karzai, the new Afghan president, and his immediate circle – a 'pretty aggressive bunch'. They then moved on, slowly and cautiously, to the special forces HQ, where they were told about the war as seen by the SAS and the SBS. Blair had developed a personal interest in, and gratitude for, the SAS, and had summoned the director of special forces, Graeme Lamb, to Chequers shortly after 9/11. Lamb's briefing matched the slogan on the Bart Simpson socks he wore to the meeting: 'No problemo.'[59] Blair, like many prime ministers, saw special forces as a useful means to manage unmanageable problems, and was naturally (and excitably) drawn to the space in which the SAS operated. It fell to directors of special forces to downplay and manage this inclination, which often combined with rampant short-termism.[60] The first member of the special forces to speak to Blair in Afghanistan was a member of a four-man group that had been chasing bin Laden, and had received a tip-off that he was in a particular cave. Without supplies, they made do with what they found, including a thirty-hour period in which their only sustenance was a small bottle of water and leaves from the nearby trees. They engaged in hand-to-hand fighting with some of those guarding bin Laden, but frustratingly 'he had gone by the time they got there'.[61] In the weeks after 9/11, Blair was clearly developing close relations with the intelligence community. Unfortunately, this was soon the focus of intense controversy as attentions turned more closely to Iraq.

In March 2002, the prime minister held a full cabinet meeting, 'mainly about Iraq' and its weapons of mass destruction. Blair now wanted to act. Although there was deep concern and division about the idea of a full-scale 'military assault on Baghdad', most around the table felt that some sort of action would be acceptable with the support of the UN. Remarkably, Robin Cook, the foreign secretary, was one of the most supportive. Saddam, he said, was a psychopath – a psychopath who had resolved his problem of prison overcrowding by shooting the 15,000 inmates with the longest sentences. He had also, as Cook reminded his colleagues, 'gassed the Kurds'. Cook argued for regime change, insisting that it would only be worth taking military action if it was robust enough to get rid of Saddam completely. Blair chimed in by recounting his recent discussion with Hosni Mubarak, the Egyptian leader, who described Saddam as the most dangerous person he had ever come across, and had confided to Blair that removing Saddam would make 'a huge difference across the whole region'. Nothing was decided, but many around the cabinet table wanted to get rid of Saddam – so long as there was United Nations support.[62]

The strongest opposition to war came from the British military. On 2 April, Blair held a top-level meeting at Chequers to prepare for a visit to George W. Bush at his ranch in Texas. The prime minister opened by

Anthony Eden's failed MI6 men from Cairo: John Thornton Stanley and Charles Pittuck after being released from prison by Egypt's President Nasser in the wake of the Suez fiasco.

Castro and Nasser, twin survivors of assassination plots by Eisenhower and Eden.

Julian Amery (*centre*) and Archbishop Makarios discuss the GCHQ bases near Famagusta in Cyprus. Amery became Britain's unofficial 'minister for covert action'.

The watchmen. A Special Branch officer keeps an eye from the rooftops on the 1956 visit to London by Soviet leaders Nikita Khrushchev and Nikolai Bulganin – the first time the British secret services used portable radios for such duties.

Margaret Thatcher accepting the Donovan Medal from Bill Casey, director of the CIA.

The 'Super-Gun', one of the many Iraq episodes that swirled around John Major and his successors.

Tony Blair and US Defense Secretary Donald Rumsfeld in Downing Street. Jonathan Powell, Blair's chief of staff, joked to colleagues, 'I wonder where we're going to put the statue of Donald Rumsfeld.'

saying that it would be beneficial to remove Saddam if it could be done without terrible unforeseen circumstances. But the chief of the defence staff, Admiral Michael Boyce, was horrified, and tried to shape the meeting towards inaction. He also sketched out the sensitive problem of gathering intelligence on the core of American national strategy. Boyce acknowledged that Blair would be able to speak to President Bush and his national security advisor Condoleezza Rice, but questioned whether they really knew what was going on. Defending his position, Blair asserted that it was Bush who would take the final decision. Again, Boyce challenged the prime minister, arguing that the president merely followed the advice of Donald Rumsfeld, the defense secretary, adding that 'apart from Rumsfeld, there were only four or five people who were really on the inside track'. These included Vice President Dick Cheney, Rumsfeld's deputy Paul Wolfowitz, and Douglas Feith, the under-secretary of defense for policy.

Blair needed to know what this small in-group was thinking. Consequently, British officials embedded in hundreds of liaison posts around Washington's Beltway, including within the CIA and the NSA, were straining their ears for any news of Pentagon planning. The conundrum soon became clear: whether to go to war alongside the Americans and have some influence, or to step aside and have none. Before his departure for Texas, Blair was already leaning towards the former option.[63] The day before he left, MI6 made plain to him that Libya in fact posed a greater WMD threat than Iraq. According to Richard Dearlove, the prime minister 'understood the risk, therefore, of focusing on WMD in relation to Iraq'. According to one senior MI6 officer, Iraqi nuclear efforts were largely theoretical, existing 'in the cranium of just a few scientists'. Nonetheless, the prime minister headed for Crawford on 6 April 2002 favouring staying onside with the Americans. Although senior MI6 officers insist that he was 'a changed man' on his return, Blair had largely decided his strategy before his departure.[64]

Some of Blair's critics have focused on 'poodle-ology',[65] suggesting that Blair used intelligence to provide the US with a 'political figleaf' in making the case for war. This is incorrect. Bush certainly decided on 'regime change' first – remarkably, the British ambassador to Washington, Sir Christopher Meyer, dates this as early as 20 September 2001.[66] The conventional story is that the following spring, having been closeted with Bush for some days, a hypnotised Blair emerged blinking into the sunlight as an ardent supporter of invasion. His rhetoric in Texas was certainly evangelical. In a speech at the Bush Library on 7 April, Blair affirmed:

... when America is fighting for those values, then, however tough, we fight with her. No grandstanding, no offering implausible but impractical advice from the comfort of the touchline, no wishing away the hard not the easy choices on terrorism and WMD, or making peace in the Middle East, but working together, side by side ... If the world makes the right choices now – at this time of destiny – we will get there. And Britain will be at America's side in doing it.[67]

In fact, Blair, together with a rather reluctant British cabinet, had taken the decision a week before. Despite the prime minister publicly claiming to still be weighing up his options, Colin Powell, the American secretary of state, had assured Bush a week before the Crawford meeting that Blair 'will be with us should military operations be necessary'. Blair, Powell wrote, would use the meeting to present 'the strategic, tactical and public affairs lines that he believes will strengthen global support for our common cause'. Indeed, Blair had the skills and charisma to 'make a credible public case on current Iraqi threats to international peace' and to 'handle calls' for UN Security Council blessing.[68] For the prime minister, it was clearly better to join the USA in the driving seat than to stand on the pavement and watch.

MI6 officers soon noticed a change in requirements flowing from Downing Street, with regular requests for more material on Iraq.[69] In early September 2002, the Americans pressed the button. War was coming. For a long time Blair had planned to publish a dossier on Iraqi WMD, drawing on JIC intelligence, but not 'until we had taken the key decisions'. Now he changed his mind and asked for it to be published 'within the next few weeks', in the hope of influencing public opinion. Blair had grown concerned about public debate, especially given that the media was presenting military action as imminent, and parliamentarians and the public alike sought answers as to why Britain was seemingly planning to invade Iraq. A disorganised rush ensued. Alastair Campbell thought that turning around public sentiment would be 'very tough indeed'. He knew what the hardest questions would be: 'Why now? What was it that we knew now that we didn't before that made us believe we had to do it now?' He was also doubtful that there was much new evidence. Forlornly, he noted that there were now 'massive expectations' around the dossier.[70]

He was right. The problem was the need for newness. On Thursday, 5 September, prior to the recall of Parliament, Campbell met John Scarlett,

Julian Miller, from the Assessments Staff, and a number of officials from the Ministry of Defence and the Foreign Office, to go over the dossier. He noted that it 'had to be revelatory', but Scarlett warned that there was 'very little' on the nuclear weapons front. Afterwards, Scarlett met Dearlove, who 'agreed to go through all the relevant material'. Internal Whitehall politics was already at work, and the following Monday, Campbell and Scarlett met three MI6 officers, who were 'all pissed off' at reports that they had cold feet about the dossier, and believed the Foreign Office was setting them up for the blame if things went wrong.[71]

In formal terms Scarlett, as JIC chairman, controlled the dossier. Campbell was not in charge. He did, however, have strong input, meeting his 'mate' Scarlett some twenty times in a month on the subject. Both Scarlett and Dearlove have since been accused of becoming intoxicated by their proximity to the charismatic prime minister, and failing to rein him in.[72] Former JIC chairs have argued that the committee entered the prime minister's 'magic circle' and was 'engulfed by the heady atmosphere, failing to keep its distance and objectivity'.[73] Lines were certainly blurred, and Julian Miller recalls that the much-vexed 'forty-five-minute claim' about Iraq's preparedness to launch chemical weapons first appeared in a 10 or 11 September draft, and drew on a JIC briefing a day or two before.[74] As for Blair, he allegedly requested that the material be presented in a more digestible and convincing manner.[75]

On 12 September, the last substantial meeting on the dossier was held between Blair, Jonathan Powell, David Manning and Dearlove together with another MI6 colleague. Despite the recognition that Saddam needed to claim to have WMD 'for reasons of regional power', they discounted the idea that this was a deception. 'This stuff is real,' they concluded. The following day, Friday the 13th, Campbell met Julian Miller to go through a 'new structure' for the dossier. Meanwhile, Scarlett rushed off to Washington, partly because he had been told that the Americans were going to publish their own dossier, 'and we worried it could undercut ours'. Five days later Jo Nadin, a Downing Street speechwriter (whose specialism was teen fiction), gave the dossier a last read–through, and thought it 'very convincing' – other than on nuclear weapons. Blair's foreword, the most assertive element, was signed off with little discussion.[76] Tuesday, 24 September was 'dossier day', and over the next week, Downing Street was delighted by the press coverage, with its material leading every news bulletin.[77]

In retrospect, the Downing Street dossier looms disproportionately large in the Iraq story. It offered little that was new. The real intelligence fight was focused on getting a tough UN resolution and keeping Bush on a multilateral path – British sources in Washington revealed that the Rumsfeld clique was pushing the president into a corner. More importantly, intercepts from French communications, notably President Jacques Chirac's mobile phone, suggested that Chirac might veto any such UN Security Council resolution. The French intelligence services, like those of Germany, were convinced that Saddam had WMD. But Chirac thought his own intelligence services were wrong. Unlike Blair, he understood how much the different national intelligence services shared on this subject, and that this could lead to a kind of multinational intelligence 'groupthink'. Chirac put it rather well, arguing that the various intelligence agencies tended to 'intoxicate each other'.[78]

In early November 2002, the UN Security Council passed Resolution 1441. This asserted that Iraq remained in material breach of its obligations under various United Nations resolutions on WMD, and gave Saddam a final opportunity to comply with its disarmament commitments. At the end of the month, UN weapons inspectors moved back into Iraq after an absence of almost four years. They were heavily steered by undercover advice from a dozen intelligence agencies around the world. Yet by December, chief inspector Hans Blix conceded that they had found no smoking guns.[79]

British intelligence was now in the spotlight. On 28 January 2003, President Bush gave his State of the Union address, and it focused on the Iraqi WMD threat, surprisingly suggesting that Iraq was trying to develop nuclear weapons. Even more surprisingly, Bush pointed to evidence from British intelligence: 'The British government has learned that Saddam Hussein recently sought significant quantities of uranium from Africa.' One of the few pieces of fresh intelligence contained in the British dossier was the assertion that Iraq had been discovered attempting to buy milled uranium ore, known as 'yellow cake', from the African state of Niger.[80] Unfortunately, this 'intelligence' turned out to be poor-quality forgeries – much to Britain's embarrassment.[81]

A season of dirty tricks began. During February 2003, intelligence focused on diplomatic manoeuvrings in the United Nations, where Blair desperately hoped for a second resolution underpinning war. The crux of this was the 'Middle Six', the so-called swing voters among the non-permanent members of the Security Council: Angola, Guinea, Cameroon, Mexico, Chile and Pakistan. Blair wished to persuade them to support the new resolution. One American diplomat remarked that the six countries 'are really feeling the heat, and they're going to be feeling even more heat in coming days'. A UN Security Council resolution required nine votes, and the United States and Britain were only certain that they had Bulgaria and Spain on their side. They also hoped that enough support from the swing voters would dissuade Russia, France and China from using their veto. London and Washington now deployed all their intelligence power.[82]

In February, Blair telephoned Ricardo Lagos, president of the 'Middle Six' member Chile. 'I want to send two people to meet with you,' he said, explaining that they were his top experts on Britain's Iraq intelligence. They arrived in Santiago on 24 February, and were taken to a secure facility where they could speak freely. The two 'secret envoys' were David Manning, Blair's foreign policy adviser, and John Scarlett. Manning started the presentation, followed by Scarlett, who Lagos recalled 'was meant to show me the smoking gun on Iraq's WMDs'. Several times during the presentation Lagos interrupted his British guests and asked, 'I want to ask you straight: do you know where the weapons are?' They merely 'mumbled' in reply, 'Mr President, that's a secret: we really can't answer that question.' Privately, Lagos was comparing notes with a rival intelligence briefing he had received from the French the previous week, which argued the opposite case. He knew that Manning and Scarlett were on 'something of a tour', and were moving on to brief President Vicente Fox of Mexico. Later he rang Fox to discuss the British presentation, and they both judged it an 'utter failure'.[83]

During the same month, the *Observer* revealed a secret message from the US National Security Agency to GCHQ. It showed that the NSA was stepping up a sensitive operation to listen in on the telephone and email communications of the Middle Six at the UN, attacking not only their offices but also their representatives' homes. The NSA asked for GCHQ's help in 'mounting a surge' to reveal their attitudes on the second resolution on Iraq, as well as their 'negotiating positions' and what it called any 'dependencies' that would allow pressure to be applied. The leaked memo pointed to manipulation, and did a great deal of diplomatic damage to the British and American positions.[84] In Chile, the public had long been sensitive to reports of 'dirty tricks' by intelligence agencies dating back to the coup of 1973, allegedly sponsored by the CIA, that overthrew the democratically elected President Salvador Allende and replaced him with the dictator General Augusto Pinochet.[85] President Lagos telephoned Blair on Sunday, 2 March, within hours of the story appearing, and then twice again the following Wednesday, expressing himself very bluntly indeed. Meanwhile, Chile's foreign minister, Soledad Alvear, fired a series of awkward questions about GCHQ at her British opposite number, Jack Straw.[86]

Bugging and manipulating the United Nations looked bad. Clare Short, secretary of state for international development, publicly confirmed that she had seen intercepts of Kofi Annan's communications, and added that on 26 February Blair's cabinet secretary, Andrew Turnbull, had written to her threatening unspecified 'further action' if she continued talking about the matter. Short retaliated by brandishing Turnbull's letter on TV.[87] Jack Straw's special adviser Michael Williams admitted to a friend that 'just about every phone in the UN building was bugged' as part of a joint operation led by the Americans. The fallout from the whole episode was 'disastrous', and Williams warned that the bugging issue would continue to 'reverberate' on foreign relations for months, adding mournfully that it 'sticks like shit to your shoes'.[88]

The worst intelligence embarrassment, however, was an own-goal. As well as the Downing Street press office, Campbell also commanded the Coalition Information Centre. Based in the Foreign Office, this included an odd mixture of civil servants, diplomats and advisers from the Labour Party, all seconded from their normal jobs. Campbell ordered them to produce a second dossier. Superficially this was to emphasise Saddam's 'infrastructure of concealment', but it was also intended to demonstrate that Saddam was a nasty man by detailing Iraq's secret police state. Released on 3 February 2003, with a fanfare as being based partly on intelligence, much of it was in fact plagiarised from an article by a graduate student in California called Ibrahim al-Marashi. Not content with stealing his work unacknowledged, they manipulated it to suit their purposes. Phrases like 'aiding opposition groups in hostile regimes' became 'supporting terrorist organisations in hostile regimes'. Once the story broke, al-Marashi worried that the link between his work and a document supporting British policy could have 'a disastrous effect on my family back home' in Iraq. He added, 'I have already lost two relatives to the Saddam regime.'[89]

Blair referred to the document on the floor of the House of Commons as 'further intelligence'. When its real source came to light a few days later there was panic in Downing Street.[90] Campbell was horrified, noting that 'whole chunks were lifted off the internet'. He recorded that Downing Street suffered 'a lot of embarrassment', and while John Scarlett was 'very nice about it', it was 'a bad own goal'. Channel Four dubbed the document the 'dodgy dossier' – an epithet that stuck. Campbell wrote ruefully: 'Definitely no more dossiers for a while.'[91] Liberal Democrat MP Alan Beith from the Intelligence and Security Committee noted that 'the spooks were livid' about what they called a sixth-form essay, and were particularly infuriated by the implication that they had contributed to it. 'Needless to say, they weren't even consulted.'[92] At an 'inquest' the following week, Scarlett and Nigel Inkster, a senior MI6 officer, reported 'dismay' amongst their MI6 colleagues. David Omand, the new security and intelligence coordinator, sent round some new rules on the handling of intelligence in 'an obvious attempt to retrench.'[93]

By mid-March, there was an increasing sense that immediate events were in the hands of the Pentagon. As a Downing Street people-carrier took Number 10 staff along one of the circuitous security-approved routes around central London, Jonathan Powell cheerily joked, 'I wonder where we're going to put the statue of Donald Rumsfeld.'[94] On 20 March, the Americans told Blair that they had gone to war. Intelligence collected by the NSA and GCHQ had offered the chance of a decapitation shot at Saddam, and Washington had acted quickly, without initially telling Downing Street. After the invasion, one MI6 officer suggested that there was 'a sort of recognition that the WMD thing had served its purpose; we had got in, we had done the war.'[95]

Even before the war began, the press smelled a rat. Two days after the release of the 'dodgy dossier', Alastair Campbell was alarmed to discover that a BBC reporter, Andrew Gilligan, had obtained a secret Defence Intelligence Staff paper suggesting that there was in fact no real link between al-Qaeda and Iraq.[96] Even worse, as early as 10 April, Campbell confided to his diary: 'major problems ... where were the WMD?' On 29 April, John Scarlett called Campbell and asked, 'How big a problem would it be if we didn't find any?' Campbell's reply was concise and to the point: a 'big problem'. On the same day, a mischievous Vladimir Putin enjoyed tormenting Blair in public at a press conference about the missing weapons. David Manning was visibly squirming.[97] After an impressive campaign of 'shock and awe' had rapidly defeated Saddam's forces, combat operations ceased two days later. The Pentagon announced the formation of the Iraq Survey Group to search for the missing WMD. In fact, the CIA and MI6 had been frantically hunting for them for over a month, but had found virtually nothing. Privately, they knew another intelligence storm was brewing.

It broke just after six in the morning of Thursday, 29 May. In an interview with John Humphrys on the BBC *Today* programme, Gilligan
launched his claim that Downing Street 'sexed up' the September dossier,
focusing on the assertion that Iraq could use WMD at forty-five minutes'
notice. Gilligan insisted that the government 'probably knew that that
forty-five-minute figure was wrong even before it decided to put it in'.[98]
Interviewed again an hour later, he asserted that the dossier was 'transformed the week before it was published, to make it sexier'. In doing so, he
was effectively acting as the voice of the Defence Intelligence Staff, the real
WMD experts, who felt that they had been outflanked by MI6 in the
assessments process prior to war and in the development of the dossier.[99]
In particular, Defence Intelligence felt that MI6 had almost no WMD
expertise. Despite the fact that nuclear proliferation had been a big issue
for decades, the agency continued to recruit officers with degrees in
Classics from Oxbridge, when what it needed was people with a scientific
background: in 2001, the number of its staff with in-depth WMD expertise consisted of a single person poached from the Defence Intelligence
Staff.[100] Although Scarlett suspected that dissident anti-war MI6 officers
may have been to blame for briefing Gilligan,[101] Omand was more on-
target, being convinced that the Defence Intelligence Staff was responsible.[102] Some of Gilligan's claims were wide of the mark, but against the
background of the missing WMD there was now an explosion of press
coverage about the politicisation of intelligence.

Early the next morning, Campbell noted that the 'WMD Firestorm
was getting worse'. Waking Blair, he warned him that the papers were
'pretty grim'. The prime minister was 'worried that the spooks would
be pissed off with us', but Campbell reassured him that the September
dossier was 'the work of the agencies', adding that the idea that 'we would
make these things up was absurd'.[103] John Scarlett stopped short of agreeing to write a letter confirming this. The reality was that intelligence,
advice and public relations had been hopelessly intertwined on the sofas
of Downing Street, and no one could quite remember who had written
what.

On Sunday, 1 June, Gilligan attacked Campbell personally in a story
about the 'sexing up' of the dossier for the *Mail on Sunday*. This, Blair
remembers, started the war between Number 10 – or Campbell to be more
precise – and the BBC. The article 'really put booster rockets on it'.[104]
Travelling back from Poland, Blair was stunned by the Sunday papers. His
entourage felt the headlines were 'even worse' than they had been warned,

and Campbell realised that 'The WMD issue was really digging into us ... it was grim ... with huge stuff about trust.'[105]

Gilligan's sloppy charges ultimately played into Blair's hands. They allowed him to bullishly tell the House of Commons that 'The allegation that I or anyone else lied to the House or deliberately misled the country by falsifying intelligence of weapons of mass destruction is itself the real lie.'[106] His words were rather carefully chosen.

Despite Blair's defence, the Labour Party's historic anxieties about the secret world resurfaced. On 4 June, Dr John Reid, leader of the House of Commons and a cabinet minister with a great deal of government experience, told the media that 'rogue elements' in the security services were out to get the government. This was 'plastered all over' the front page of *The Times*, and triggered further panic in Downing Street.[107] Hilary Armstrong, the Labour chief whip, made similar allegations in briefings to journalists.[108] Even inside Number 10 there were fears that MI6 was trying to pass the blame to the government. Blair's long-time adviser Sally Morgan pointedly asked, 'Since when did the intelligence services ever support a Labour government?'[109]

Dossier dissection had become a national obsession. An enterprising journalist discovered that the second dossier, released as a Word file, revealed who had drafted each sentence. One of the contributors gloried in the official, but suspicious, title of 'head of story development'.[110] Despite having rushed his Downing Street team into producing this material at speed, Blair now held Campbell responsible, and personal relations with his most trusted aide deteriorated.[111] By 7 June, two sets of parliamentarians, the Foreign Affairs Committee and the Intelligence and Security Committee, had launched rival inquiries into Iraq, the dossiers and the missing WMD. Blair put on a brave face, insisting the missing weapons would soon be found, but one minister noted: 'We badly need to find a stash of nerve gas.'[112]

Like Blair, MI6 remained robust. Throughout the autumn of 2003 it insisted that once Iraqi scientists knew they were safe and were offered immunity from prosecution, 'something would turn up'. Similarly, during the war, Richard Dearlove would reassure Blair that 'Tomorrow we'll find them at this location or that location.' Blair would reply, 'Okay, good – they'd better be there.'[113] In an astonishing articulation of their relationship, Blair once admitted to Dearlove, 'Richard, my fate is in your hands.'[114] Unfortunately for the prime minister, Christopher Meyer reported the opposite from Washington. Many captured Iraqi scientists were already talking to the CIA, and 'were all singing the same tune': that Saddam disposed of his remaining chemical and biological weapons after his sons-in-law defected in August 1995, and 'has had nothing for the last seven years'.[115] One of these scientists, Hussein Kamel al-Majid, had run Iraq's weapons development programmes, and had explained all this when he defected in 1995, but his reports were ignored or 'hushed up'.[116]

The Foreign Affairs Committee inquiry cleared Campbell, stating that Tony Blair's director of communications 'did not exert or seek to exert improper influence' on the drafting of the September 2002 dossier on WMD. But the inquiry was wide of the mark on intelligence, insisting that the intelligence claims made in the September dossier were probably 'well founded'.[117] Remarkably, the Intelligence and Security Committee made the same mistake. These inquiries accelerated the protracted war between Campbell and the BBC, with different elements in the intelligence services backing opposite sides and foreign secretary Jack Straw visibly running for cover by trying to distance himself from the Downing Street machine. At around this time, Dr David Kelly, a scientific expert under contract to the Ministry of Defence, came forward as one of Gilligan's main sources. In early July, Geoff Hoon, the defence secretary, told Downing Street that Kelly worked with 'Operation Rockingham', a tiny cell in the Defence Intelligence Staff which helped to provide leads for United Nations inspectors in Iraq, and which analysed the material they provided in turn. Kelly's knowledge of Iraqi weapons programmes was excellent, and he testified before the Foreign Affairs Committee on 15 July. Four days later, his body was found in circumstances that suggested suicide, triggering a flurry of conspiracy theories and a further inquiry by Lord Hutton.[118]

Campbell resigned halfway through the Hutton inquiry, and many now considered Blair to be doomed. Blair gloomily complained that 'The trouble with Alastair is that he hates the media'.[119] However, on 28 January 2004, Hutton cleared Downing Street of any direct involvement in Kelly's death. MPs were amazed. Chris Mullin noted that Hutton had instead 'placed a good deal of blame on the BBC'. Suddenly, 'a great cloud lifted', and Blair was 'looking happier than he has done for months'.[120] But the avalanche of material on intelligence revealed by the inquiry provided a forensic field day for the armies of hungry journalists. The WMD dossier increasingly appeared to be a deliberate deception, not least because Hutton revealed that on the eve of its publication Jonathan Powell observed to John Scarlett that it 'does nothing to demonstrate a threat, let alone an imminent threat, from Saddam'.[121]

Hutton also uncovered more dirty tricks. A United Nations weapons inspector, Scott Ritter, told the inquiry about an MI6 propaganda campaign, called 'Operation Mass Appeal', to spread stories about WMD in the British and foreign media. Whitehall later confirmed that MI6 had indeed developed such an operation, intended to gain public support for sanctions and the use of military force in Iraq by placing stories about Saddam Hussein's nerve-gas stocks. Ritter noted that many stories had appeared in the international media about 'secret underground facilities' in Iraq and ongoing nerve-gas programmes, adding: 'All of them were garbage.'[122] In 2004, an inquiry into the intelligence surrounding weapons of mass destruction by Lord Butler, a former cabinet secretary, expressed interest in this operation,[123] which demonstrated that the MI6 information operations capability – long admired by Alastair Campbell – was hard at work.

Was the Iraqi WMD fiasco a product of intelligence failure by the agencies, or deception by politicians and spin-doctors? The answer is both. Having badly underestimated Iraqi WMD stocks prior to the Gulf War in 1991, intelligence officers did not want to be caught out a second time, and so opted for 'worst-case analysis'. In other words, they overcorrected. Moreover, the allies cooperated so closely on WMD estimates that, far from challenging each other's findings, they succumbed to a form of multinational 'groupthink'. Only the Dutch and the Canadian intelligence communities expressed serious doubts. Robin Butler's inquiry revealed that most British intelligence had come from a handful of human agents who were not properly 'validated', and whose material was judged to be mediocre at best.[124] Alongside this intelligence failure, there is also evidence of some political manipulation. Tyler Drumheller, the CIA Europe division chief, who worked closely with MI6, has revealed that Naji Sabri, Iraq's foreign minister, did a deal to disclose Iraq's military secrets. Unfortunately, once policymakers learned what he had to say – that there was no active WMD programme – 'they stopped being interested in the intelligence'.[125]

Major General Michael Laurie was well placed to view the whole landscape. As the director-general of intelligence collection in the Defence Intelligence Staff, he worked closely with not only MI6 and GCHQ, but also the Cabinet Office and the JIC. He recalls the massive effort on the WMD dossier between March and September 2002, adding, 'We were under pressure to find intelligence that could reinforce the case.' His boss,

Joe French, was also 'under pressure', and frequently asked 'whether we were missing something'. However, they could find no evidence of planes, missiles or equipment that related to WMD, generally concluding that they must have been dismantled, buried or taken abroad. He observed:

> There has probably never been a greater detailed scrutiny of every piece of ground in any country. During the drafting of the final Dossier, every fact was managed to make it as strong as possible, the final statements reaching beyond the conclusions intelligence assessments would normally draw from such facts. It was clear to me that there was direction and pressure being applied on the JIC and its drafters.[126]

Despite all this excruciating effort, the Downing Street dossier on WMD of September 2002 was dull rather than misleading. It proved little. It said that some intelligence suggested that the Iraqis might have hidden some old biological or chemical stocks from 1991. This was true, but these weapons were unlikely to be usable, and were at most of academic interest. There was also some evidence that Iraq continued to seek nuclear components on the world market, and had nurtured future ambitions. This was also true, but no one thought for a moment that Iraq had got far with reconstituting its nuclear programme. The important claim was that Iraq was engaged in 'continued' production of WMD. This assertion was only made forcibly by the prime minister in his personal foreword to the dossier.

There was no evidence for it.[127] Later Blair assured the House of Commons that the intelligence was 'extensive, detailed, authoritative' – yet, as Robin Butler has demonstrated, this was not the case at all.[128] Indeed, Butler has since acknowledged that the British public had 'every right to feel misled by their prime minister'.[129] Blair did believe the weapons existed, but he was dishonest about the quality of the intelligence that underpinned it. His hasty decision to release intelligence in a 'dossier' to the public in the countdown to war was unprecedented, controversial, and ultimately highly toxic.

Tony Blair was an incompetent intelligence consumer and a poor manager of secret service. Essentially, he did not understand intelligence, and committed the schoolboy error of believing that 'top secret' meant 'accurate and true'. Robin Butler fingered Downing Street culture as the main culprit for the WMD fiasco. Blair had corroded the established decision-making process, and evaded the challenge traditionally provided by cabinet subcommittees. The boundaries were so thin that, when interviewed, neither Jack Straw nor Geoff Hoon knew who had written the WMD dossier, and they could not defend the Downing Street line that it was led by John Scarlett. MI6 was admired most by Blair's inner circle for its 'media operations', and had been turned into a machine for providing policy advice rather than truth.[130] Despite the fact that secret matters were discussed so furiously and so publicly, intelligence under Blair remains opaque. This is partly because Downing Street often confused intelligence with information warfare. Blair's team fought several simultaneous information wars: one against Britain's declared enemies overseas, another against neutrals in the United Nations, another against the British public and press.

Intelligence continued to dominate the headlines. Terrorist attacks on the London transport system killed fifty-two people in July 2005. The new director-general of MI5, Eliza Manningham-Buller, had told a group of Labour Party whips just the day before that there was no reason to believe an attack was imminent. Inevitably, questions were asked about potential intelligence failures, although the Intelligence and Security Committee pointed the finger at lack of resources rather than poor judgement. Blair warned that the 'rules of the game' had changed. Suddenly, cooperation between MI5, MI6, GCHQ and the police deepened impressively. Budgets rose, and new technology developed by GCHQ came online.[131]

Meanwhile, a vicious insurgency had been accelerating in Iraq. Blair had been given several intelligence warnings about this. Two months before the invasion, Admiral Sir Michael Boyce, Chief of the Defence Staff, had told him, 'the Americans felt they would be seen as liberators. It just wasn't so. They would be resented.'[132] In February 2003, the JIC warned of the unpredictable security and political consequences of invasion. The following month the committee put the issue bluntly: 'The Iraqi population will blame the coalition if progress is slow. Resentment could lead to violence.' These intelligence assessments reached the prime minister, but planning remained underdeveloped, and there was an assumption the Americans would provide it.[133] In Washington, the British ambassador Christopher Meyer had watched Ahmed Chalabi, leader of the exiled Iraqi National Congress, sell the idea of easy regime change 'skilfully and assiduously' over a decade. His constant theme was that Iraq was ripe for rebellion, and with a small push from outside the Iraqis would rise up and get rid of Saddam. Despite the failure of a CIA-backed rising in 1996, the

Washington hawks, who had known him for years, were 'eternally vulner-able to Chalabi', and believed the West would be welcomed.[134] British troops in Basra and Baghdad were on the receiving end of this confidence trick for eight years following the invasion.

In the twilight months of Blair's government, the focus shifted to secret CIA prisons, rendition flights and torture. Many European countries, including Britain, had cooperated with renditions on the condition that they would remain secret. But as one former senior Downing Street offi-cial has remarked, 'America is the most secretive country in the world – and also the most incompetently secretive.'[135] By early 2006, the story that the CIA had run secret prisons in Europe was emerging in detail, and by 2007, British involvement in a hidden empire of clandestine flights and detention sites was beginning to seep out. But Blair was now departing from Downing Street, and this toxic legacy was left for his successors.

18

Gordon Brown
(2007–2010)

We condemn torture without reservation. We do not torture,
and we do not ask others to do so on our behalf.
GORDON BROWN[1]

Gordon Brown waited longer than he wished to become prime minister. Instinctively, on arriving at 10 Downing Street in June 2007 he sought to distance himself from the record of his predecessor, especially on Iraq and the WMD intelligence débâcle. Brown had been notable for his silence on this subject, recognising that it was problematic not only for Tony Blair, but also for the government and the Labour Party. 'It's a question of trust,' he said, 'and not finding those weapons has caused us big problems, because that's why we went to war.' When former *Daily Mirror* editor Piers Morgan attended a press conference in the latter part of the Blair period, he took mischievous pleasure in asking Brown if he thought, with hindsight, that it had been a good idea to go to war with Iraq, 'because you seem to have been rather quiet on the matter of late'. Brown looked at him and smiled 'like a KGB spy smiles just before he injects you with cyanide'. He then made a quick joke, and 'ignored the Iraq question altogether'.[2]

However, as prime minister it was impossible for Brown to escape the shadow of Blair's engagement with the secret world. So much intelligence business was a toxic legacy from the last administration. Brown inherited four wars, each with a strong intelligence dimension: the ongoing conflicts in Iraq and Afghanistan, a global war against terrorism, and a revived Cold War with Russia. These simultaneous conflicts required his government to confront not only issues of espionage, but also interrogation, torture, covert action and even assassination. Brown attempted to push back by instigating yet another inquiry into Iraq, no less than the fifth intelligence-related inquisition in a decade. He also asked the Intelligence and Security Committee to consider British involvement in CIA secret renditions, and to publish new guidelines for MI5 and MI6 in an attempt to show that Britain did not condone torture. But Downing Street was losing its customary monopoly over secret service. Judges decided that they now owned intelligence oversight, and a mighty struggle followed as the courts tried to acquire top-secret material, convinced that officials had lied to cover up British complicity with the American mechanisms of torture.

Tony Blair and Gordon Brown were both control freaks, but they were also polar opposites. Blair was confident about taking big decisions quickly, while Brown hesitated over small ones. Blair was content to allow his ministers to take routine decisions, while Brown wanted to micro-manage everything. Blair's 'sofa government' disappeared, and Brown took comfort in planning papers and more elaborate machinery. Notoriously, Brown adored Cobra, the top-secret Cabinet Office Briefing Room which brought together the intelligence and policy worlds in times of crisis. 'He really does have a passion for COBRA,' observed Admiral Alan West, his minister for security and counter-terrorism, adding, 'It's not some magic place. It's just a room really.' Nothing made Brown happier than the BBC news reporting that he had just chaired a meeting of Cobra. This was less about Cobra's mystique and danger, and more about its ability to suggest that the prime minister was doing something – when in reality he was often racked with indecision.[3]

Cobra could be a negative asset. Although it made Brown look competent, at times it actually degraded the operational response at moments of crisis, since the security chiefs were often sitting in a row outside the Cobra room waiting to brief politicians, rather than doing their jobs.[4] The wider national security machinery functioned rather better; but Brown was less interested in this. He used it rarely, and what meetings did take place became somewhat perfunctory. The JIC lacked impact, and Brown seemingly paid it little attention, rarely offering feedback. Unlike Blair, the prime minister's heart was not in it unless it related to a specific set of negotiations.[5] Nevertheless, in his first few months of office the intelligence issues piled up. Difficult decisions had to be taken.

The decade following 9/11 was an era of intrigue and assassination, and Gordon Brown had to confront numerous conspiracies – some more real than others. Within weeks of his becoming prime minister, MI5 believed it had thwarted a Russian plot to assassinate the prominent British-based

Russian dissident Boris Berezovksy. In response, Downing Street ordered a major review of the security situation created by wealthy Russian exiles in London, and of ways in which the capital had become a battleground for different Russian factions with plenty of resources but scant respect for the law. The following year, MI5 significantly increased the number of officers dedicated to watching Russian activities.[6]

This flurry of activity followed the high-profile assassination of the Russian journalist and former security officer Alexander Litvinenko in London in November 2006, after exposure to the radioactive substance polonium 210. The following May, the Crown Prosecution Service demanded the extradition to London of the prime suspect for Litvinenko's murder, Andrei Lugovoy. Moscow rejected this, taunting Gordon Brown by flaunting Lugovoy on Russian state-controlled television, where he alleged that Litvinenko was a British spy killed by MI6 in an intelligence operation that went wrong.[7] Litvinenko had indeed worked for MI6: intelligence officials told Brown that since his arrival in the UK in 2000 he had acted as a consultant for MI6 working through a dedicated handler called 'Martin', and been paid £2,000 a month for information. Litvinenko's intelligence included information on Sergei Ivanov, a close confidant of Vladimir Putin, who visited London in the autumn of 2000 to promote stronger Anglo–Russian intelligence cooperation in the war on drugs.[8] Both Litvinenko and Lugovoy had served in the KGB prior to 1989, and had remained in service with its domestic successor, the FSB, after the end of the Cold War.

In retaliation for the failure to extradite Lugovoy, Brown reluctantly embraced a new Cold War by expelling four Russian intelligence officers from Moscow's London embassy. He explained: 'When a murder takes place, when a number of innocent civilians were put at risk as a result of that murder, and when an independent prosecuting authority makes it absolutely clear what is in the interests of justice, and there is no forthcoming co-operation, then action has to be taken.' David Miliband, the foreign secretary, was equally tough, declaring that he wanted to send Russia 'a clear and proportionate signal'.[9] Although Moscow threatened 'serious consequences', Gordon Brown continued to press the Russians at the G8 summit in July 2008.

Alexander Litvinenko was almost certainly murdered because of his growing dissident status and his relationship with British intelligence. Although he undoubtedly annoyed Putin, MI6 thought that ex-KGB officers were responsible for the assassination. It was an honour killing under the old KGB code: if you encounter a traitor you must liquidate him

as a patriotic duty. The public assassination served to send an unambiguous message that traitors would never be forgotten or forgiven.[10] Litvinenko
died a slow, agonising death, with the best hospitals powerless to save him.
The order, however, likely came from the Kremlin. A 2016 public inquiry
pointed the finger at the FSB and concluded that the assassination 'was
probably approved' by Putin himself.[11]

It is often with assassination that the secret service becomes rather
personal for prime ministers. Only fourteen months before the killing of
Litvinenko, Vladimir Putin had been standing in Cobra alongside Britain's
security chiefs. It had been decided that he would be briefed on the 7/7
London bombings, and Andy Hayman, the head of special operations at
the Metropolitan Police, met Eliza Manningham-Buller at MI5 headquarters in Thames House to plan the meeting. Hayman entered her austere
wood-panelled office, knowing that her staff would have been told to
plump the cushions in the seating area beforehand – 'It was one of her
foibles.' They agreed that MI5 would talk to Putin about intelligence, after
which Hayman would demonstrate a mock-up that had been made of one
of the 7/7 rucksack bombs. 'It was one of the few times a foreign leader
had been allowed into this underground cellar in the bowels of Whitehall,'
and Hayman read this as 'a sign of the prime minister's commitment to
close partnership and even friendship with the Russians.'[12]

On the day of the meeting, Manningham-Buller and Hayman arrived
in Cobra first. Hayman had brought his rucksack, and sat there, slightly
nervous, 'the dummy bomb beside me on the floor'.

> The prime minister swept in with President Putin – I was surprised
> to see how short he was … Putin was immaculately dressed and
> courteous, though he wore a steely expression that he would only
> drop once during the meeting … Thirty or forty minutes into the
> meeting he began to speak … he talked about the horrific siege at
> the school in Beslan in the North Caucasus … His fury and disgust
> with the rebels was visible.

Hayman thought it had been a good meeting, but after the killing of
Litvinenko he looked back on it with 'scepticism and bewilderment'.
Relations between politicians, diplomats and the secret services had now
deteriorated 'to such an extent' that it resembled the old Cold War stand-
off. 'The bizarre and torturously slow murder of the Russian dissident
Alexander Litvinenko was at the heart of the freeze.'[13]

The freeze became colder as British intelligence uncovered another assassin operating in the UK. The intelligence community devised a scheme 'putting our best assets' on standby 'to follow the assassin covertly'. They saw this as the least risky approach, since it promised to uncover others working with him and point to plots they were developing. It was a classic intelligence-led 'watch and wait approach'. But in the corridors of Westminster and Whitehall 'it caused uproar'. Hayman recalls that the politicians and the diplomats 'went bonkers at the idea'. After a meeting at Downing Street the political directive was to 'intervene early'. The suspects were arrested, interrogated for two days and then deported.[14]

Although the Litvinenko plot featured a form of death so twisted it might have been borrowed from *film noir*, death squads were busy everywhere even as Gordon Brown arrived in Downing Street. On the other side of the Atlantic, President George W. Bush became increasingly associated with efforts by special forces hit teams to remove al-Qaeda leaders – dead or alive. Barack Obama accelerated this once he arrived in office in January 2009. Word of this was leaking out, and later in Brown's tenure it was even reported that CIA agents and employees of the American private security firm Blackwater had tried to kill a German-Syrian terror suspect on the streets of Hamburg. European politicians were amazed, and remarked that it sounded 'like a thriller novel'. In the public mind, twenty-first-century intelligence was no longer about analysts patiently counting the numbers of enemy missiles, but more about covert action.[15]

This febrile climate fuelled some secret-service conspiracy theories that were patently absurd. Brown had to oversee attempts to dispel the most persistent of them all – that Princess Diana had been murdered a decade earlier. An inquest under Lord Justice Scott Baker reached its height during the first year of Brown's government. Although the Metropolitan Police had already examined many of the issues under 'Operation Paget', the conspiracy theories had been lent a whiff of credibility by an MI6 officer's allegations that an assassination plot against Slobodan Milošević, former president of Serbia, planned to use a bright flashing light to cause his car to crash. Scott Baker considered if any such flash of light had contributed to the crash that killed Diana, and by extension, whether the British (or any other) security services had any involvement.[16]

Keen to crush the conspiracies, Richard Dearlove appeared before the court. Director of operations at MI6 during the time of Diana's death, he was a credible and pugnacious witness, and he bluntly dismissed the various allegations as inconceivable, absurd and utterly ridiculous. He categorically refused to entertain the idea that Prince Philip, 'establishment figures', MI6, freelancers or the French intelligence services had had anything to do with the crash. Remarkably, though, he did confirm that MI6 had a 'licence to kill'. It did not conduct assassinations, but it did have the power to use 'lethal force' where this was required to defend the realm. Dearlove added, however, that he had never seen this exercised during his entire career. He admitted that a junior MI6 officer in the Balkans had proposed killing a local warlord in the 1990s, but line managers had vetoed it as 'out of touch with service practice'.[17]

Summing up on 31 March 2008, Scott Baker concluded that there was 'not a shred of evidence' that Diana's death had been ordered by the Duke of Edinburgh or organised by the security services. A week later the jury concluded that Diana had been unlawfully killed by the grossly negligent driving of Ritz Hotel employee Henri Paul and the unknown drivers of other vehicles.[18] The hearing cost the taxpayer an estimated £12.5 million, in a complex process in which the jurors heard from 278 witnesses. The following month, Gordon Brown exhorted the public to 'draw a line' under Princess Diana's death and accept the inquest's definitive verdict. He added, 'Princes William and Harry have spoken for the whole country, and it is time to bring this to an end.'[19] While Brown and Dearlove attempted to see off these conspiracy theories, the slightly less illusory matter of the so-called 'war on terror' ground on.

When Gordon Brown entered 10 Downing Street, he assumed that there would be further terrorist 'spectaculars'. Only a year earlier, al-Qaeda had attempted to bring down four airliners flying out of Heathrow using ingenious 'liquid bombs', a plot for which eight men from High Wycombe would eventually receive life sentences.[20] Brown did not have to wait long for attacks to materialise on his watch. Early on the morning of Friday, 29 June 2007, two car bombs failed to explode in London's West End. An equally unsuccessful – if more dramatic – attack on Glasgow airport took place the following day. Because of their multiple nature, experts assumed that these attacks formed part of another attempted al-Qaeda spectacular, on the scale of the High Wycombe airliner plot. Brown braced himself for further attacks as the national threat level was raised to 'critical'. Outwardly, the prime minister seemed self-assured. Speaking from Downing Street, he urged the nation to be 'vigilant', and to support the police and the security services. 'I know', he added, 'that the British people will stand together, united, resolute and strong.'

Privately, Brown was rattled. He did not have the sort of smooth security team that had surrounded Tony Blair as prime minister. Because the two car bombs were defused by experts before they detonated, Downing Street officials decided not to disturb Brown in the middle of the night. Although his home secretary, Jacqui Smith, had been woken and informed, the prime minister only found out from the radio news at 5.30 a.m. He stormed down from the flat in Number 10 in an angry mood. 'Why wasn't I told?' he demanded. Gordon Brown in a bad mood was never a pleasant sight, and this event triggered all his neuralgic instincts about the need for control.[21]

Although the only casualties were the would-be bombers in Glasgow, the attacks had had the potential to kill many, and Brown's new terrorism adviser, Lord Stevens, asserted that they signalled 'a major escalation by Islamic terrorists'.[22] In fact, the exact opposite was true. Al-Qaeda had been crushed by five years of punitive measures, including CIA drone strikes in Afghanistan and Pakistan. Most of its proficient bomb-makers and operatives had been either rounded up and placed in detention or killed. Whatever the long-term consequences of this unrelenting campaign – which the CIA termed 'find, fix and finish' – in the short term the command and control systems of the Islamic militants had been broken up. As a result, 2007 saw a major change in the style of terrorist acts in Britain. Without instructions or support from abroad, amateurish militants did what they could locally. The botched attack on Glasgow, in which one assailant inadvertently set himself on fire, later dying of his injuries, underlined the absence of professional organisation and expertise with explosives.[23]

Brown launched a review, asking Admiral Alan West, the security and counter-terrorism minister, to investigate the security of Britain's protected places, transport infrastructure and critical national infrastructure. West's review was not published, but when discussing it in Parliament, Brown publicly praised the vigilance and courage of MI5 and pressed for improved security at railway stations, airports and ports, especially against vehicle bombs.[24] Surveillance expanded hugely, and Brown publicly emphasised the importance of GCHQ's new technical capabilities in rooting out terrorism.[25] The changes David Omand instigated in his role as Cabinet Office security and intelligence adviser began to pay off. Britain now boasted an all-source terrorism fusion centre, created in 2003 and housed within MI5, known as the Joint Terrorism Analysis Centre, or JTAC. Brown announced a 10 per cent increase in its resources in 2008.[26]

There was also a robust counter-terrorism strategy called 'CONTEST', which was eventually adopted with little change by all of Europe. The Home Office had vast new resources for an Office of Security and Counter-Terrorism, created in 2007, with perhaps six hundred people engaged on work that only a dozen people had been doing five years previously. It aimed to coordinate the counter-terrorism drive. Each region now had a dedicated Counter-Terrorism Unit, with not only special police but also MI5, MI6 and army officers attached. All this paid dividends. In March 2009, Brown praised Britain's counter-terrorism planning, and observed that everyone had become an amateur intelligence officer. 'Tens of thousands of men and women throughout Britain, from security guards to store managers,' he said, 'have now been trained and equipped to deal with an incident and know what to watch for as people go about their daily business in crowded places such as stations, airports, shopping centres and sports grounds.'[27]

But a growing climate of snooping and suspicion had its price, and Brown presided over a period of fear and farcical false alarms. On 14 May 2008, Nottingham University postgraduate student Rizwaan Sabir and his friend Hicham Yezza were arrested on suspicion of terrorism. Sabir had been studying for an MA in international security and terrorism, and had printed off material for his dissertation. The pair were arrested for possessing an al-Qaeda 'training manual', but this document was later found to be available in the university library. Both were released without charge six days later. In September, Oxford graduate Stephen Clarke was arrested after someone reported seeing him taking a photograph of a sealed manhole cover outside the Central Reference Library in Manchester. He was arrested under Section 41 of the Terrorism Act 2000, held for thirty-six hours while his house and computer were searched, and then released without charge. Both events caused considerable adverse comment.

Gordon Brown's problem was not a wave of terrorism. Instead, and despite the climate of self-perpetuating fear, he faced a wave of public anxiety about increased surveillance and counter-terrorism. Even before 9/11, members of the British general public were surprisingly unconcerned about increased security powers. Politicians who dared to question counter-terrorism legislation received a striking amount of hate mail from their constituents – one MP noted dolefully that 'most of them would happily boil alleged terrorists in oil on the word of a single police officer'.[28] But among the chattering classes and the broadsheet-reading public there was growing concern about civil liberties. It was against this background that Brown officially proposed new anti-terror legislation to Parliament in early 2008. It included a fifty-six-day detention period without charge to allow questioning of terrorist suspects.

Just weeks after coming to power, Brown had spoken of the need to extend pre-charge detention. He urged David Cameron, the leader of the opposition, to put the national interest ahead of party politics, arguing that 'We are in a new world.'[29] Although Brown's preferred limit seemed to be fifty-six days,[30] the head of the Metropolitan Police, Sir Ian Blair, told MPs that terror suspects might need to be held for up to ninety days without charge. Concerned at the implications for civil liberties, select committees took detailed evidence and concluded that there was nothing to suggest the law needed to be changed from the existing twenty-eight days. As a compromise, the final Bill proposed extending pre-charge detention to forty-two days in exceptional circumstances. Other measures included the use of intercept evidence in certain terrorism trials (which caused much concern within the intelligence community), and the power to bar the public from a coroner's inquest in the interests of national security. Despite personally speaking with potential rebels, Brown suffered a backbench rebellion by his own party, and the Bill squeaked through the Commons by just nine votes with the assistance of the Democratic Unionists. As the Tories and Lib Dems howled 'You've been bought!' at the DUP benches, Brown must have known he lacked a decent mandate.[31]

Brown's nemesis was the former director-general of MI5. Eliza Manningham-Buller used her first speech as a member of the House of Lords to savage the government's plans on detention, insisting that they were wrong in principle and in practice. With over thirty years' experience in counter-intelligence and counter-terrorism, she was listened to carefully by the lords. She reminded them that there 'is no such thing as complete security', and that 'our hard-won civil liberties' were paramount. In any case, she continued, lengthy pre-charge detention was likely to be counter-productive, as it might prejudice any subsequent trial. It was not only a bad idea in principle, she insisted, it was also unworkable. Similarly, Dame Pauline Neville-Jones, former chair of the JIC, lambasted the plan as 'unnecessary, undesirable and unworkable'. Lord Falconer, the Labour lord chancellor under Blair, agreed, as did Lord Goldsmith, the former Labour attorney general. The government defeat was massive, the lords voting by 309 to 118 to include an amendment to the Bill stopping the extension of pre-charge detention beyond the existing twenty-eight days.[32] From Downing Street the bruised prime minister urged, 'I think the

House of Lords should take the advice of the House of Commons on this matter.'[33] He dropped the issue shortly afterwards.

A month later, in November 2008, terrorists mounted a major attack on Mumbai. In an extraordinary episode that lasted over four days Lashkar-e-Taiba, a terrorist organisation focused on Kashmir, coordinated a series of twelve shooting and bombing attacks which killed or wounded five hundred people. Brown was horrified, observing that the attack 'raises huge questions about how the world addresses violent extremism'.[34] Privately, the incident resolved him to continue to harden Britain's counter-terrorist defences. But this was less about intelligence than about special forces. Mumbai posed the difficult question of how the British police would respond to a dozen people firing AK-47s and throwing grenades in one of Britain's cities. The answer was to give them more powerful guns and to designate a number of regional SAS-type military units to be on standby to support them.[35] In 2015, Brown's successor as prime minister, David Cameron, went further yet, and announced an SAS-style unit inside Scotland Yard.[36]

In November 2009, an angry President Obama threatened the Brown government with a suspension of intelligence links over the release of the convicted Libyan Lockerbie bomber Abdelbaset al-Megrahi. American intelligence believed that Brown had released a terrorist who had killed many Americans in return for an oil and gas deal worth a potential £15 billion.[37] With the American intelligence community seething, the controversial decision was followed by Brown's failure to appease the Americans over Gary McKinnon, a British Asperger's sufferer who illegally accessed US military computers while looking for evidence of UFOs.[38]

All three of Britain's intelligence and security agencies had cooperated closely with the Americans since 9/11. This encompassed some highly sensitive counter-terrorism operations, including secret rendition flights and drone strikes. Unfortunately, because America had over a million people with a top-secret security clearance, it was prone to leaks. What was 'above top secret' on a Tuesday was often on the front page of the *Washington Post* on a Thursday. In Britain, backbench MPs, human rights campaigners and international lawyers avidly read international newspapers and hoovered these secrets up. This spelled trouble.

Even Americans were surprised by the CIA's activities. In January 2008, Obama's new CIA director, Leon Panetta, arrived at the agency's Langley headquarters. Previously a successful head of budget under

President Clinton, he had relatively little experience of intelligence, and expected to take over an organisation devoted to information-gathering and analysis. However, when his predecessor General Michael Hayden gave him a handover briefing, held deep inside a sensitive compartmentalised intelligence facility, Panetta was taken aback. 'What really staggered me,' he recalls, 'were his revelations about the CIA's growing involvement in the effort to locate senior members of Al Qaeda.' These were kill missions, and Panetta suddenly realised that he was to be 'the combatant commander in the war on terrorism'. In early 2009, he visited Tel Aviv for a conference with Meir Dagan, the long-serving and much-respected chief of Mossad, held at its base in a series of low-slung fortified metal buildings on the Israeli coast. Panetta asked Dagan for his advice on the right approach to al-Qaeda. 'I'd kill them,' he said. 'And then I'd kill their families.'[39]

Barack Obama accelerated the killings and backed away from torture. But his decision to make public the CIA's previous directives on torture caused outrage in Washington and discomfited its allies, including MI6. As Panetta rightly notes, the debate was highly polarised, with some asserting as a matter of faith that no good intelligence could ever come from torture, and their opponents seeing practices such as waterboarding almost as a test of national resolve in the war on terror. The truth was somewhere in between, and although some useful scraps of intelligence had been gleaned from torture, many officials, including Bob Mueller, the distinguished head of the FBI, believed that only sympathetic interrogation ever produced worthwhile results. Either way, the spilling of more and more secrets on this subject, almost a monthly event, vexed both Downing Street and MI6, who simply wanted the awkward subject to be forgotten as soon as possible.[40]

Ironically, it was the Americans who harangued the British about spilling secrets. In addition to being angry about al-Megrahi's release, Obama also threatened to suspend intelligence cooperation as a result of a British court case in which judges had allowed revelations about CIA torture to be made public. The case involved Binyam Mohamed, a British citizen granted asylum from Ethiopia in 1994. He was rounded up on the Afghan–Pakistan border in 2002, and then spent seven years inside 'black hole prisons' that were part of the US-run rendition programme for terror suspects. Eventually, he reached the detention camp at Guantánamo Bay. After a lengthy campaign by his supporters, in February 2009 Mohamed was released from Guantánamo. From May of that year, government lawyers fought to prevent senior judges from disclosing a seven-paragraph summary of how the CIA had treated him.

In October, the High Court in London ordered the release of CIA material relating to cooperation with MI5 over Mohamed's interrogation in Pakistan in 2002. The judge did not believe the testimony of an MI5 officer who had been present, and wanted to release no fewer than forty-two classified CIA documents that had been handed to him before he travelled to Pakistan.[41] On hearing the decision, Obama rang Gordon Brown. The CIA followed this up with a letter to MI6 which warned: 'If it is determined that your Service is unable to protect information we provide to you even if that inability is caused by your judicial system, we will necessarily have to review with the greatest care the sensitivity of information we can provide in future.'[42] In response, David Miliband fought an ineffective campaign to convey to the judges that disclosing US intelligence would 'endanger future co-operation between London and Washington'. Meanwhile, and to make matters worse, judges accused several branches of the British government of systematically covering up their involvement in the American torture of suspects. Lord Neuberger, for example, accused MI5 of a 'culture of suppression'. Remarkably for such a senior judge, he warned that the public and the courts could not trust any assurances that the Foreign Office made about human rights. On Obama's threat, the judges rightly concluded the Americans were blustering, and that the risk to national security was 'not a serious one'. It was clear that MI5 had been aware that Mohamed, a British citizen, was kept chained up and deliberately deprived of sleep, something which the JIC considered to be torture. He had also been made to think he might 'disappear'.[43]

In February 2010, the Court of Appeal compelled the government to release seven key paragraphs from the documents and reveal MI5 complicity in Mohamed's treatment. Reluctantly published by the Foreign Office, they confirmed that: 'The treatment reported, if it had been administered on behalf of the United Kingdom, would clearly have been in breach of the undertakings given by the United Kingdom in 1972. Although it is not necessary for us to categorise the treatment reported, it could readily be contended to be at the very least cruel, inhuman and degrading treatment by the United States authorities.'[44] The American director of national intelligence warned that the decision created 'additional challenges' for the Anglo–American intelligence relationship, and that he had heard the court's decision with 'deep regret'.[45] Miliband swiftly phoned secretary of state Hillary Clinton to smooth things over.[46]

Binyam Mohamed's own account is frightening. Kept in an underground prison in Morocco, he was beaten, scalded with boiling water and had his testicles cut with a scalpel. While he was there he realised that 'the people who were torturing me were receiving questions and materials from British intelligence'. These claims are unlikely ever to be fully substantiated, but documents do show that an MI5 officer visited Morocco three times during the period Mohamed claimed to be detained and tortured. In 2010 the British government announced compensation payouts to sixteen detainees from Guantánamo and a further inquiry into the torture allegations.[47]

Brown continued to fight the courts, and struck a defiant tone. He said that he had spoken to Jonathan Evans, the new MI5 director-general, to thank him for the work his service did protecting the public. 'The United Kingdom has the finest intelligence services in the world,' the prime minister argued, adding that he had seen for himself their 'immense bravery'. He assured the public: 'We condemn torture. We are clear that officials must not be complicit in mistreatment of detainees.' The government, he continued, would be publishing its revised guidelines for the intelligence agencies on the treatment of detainees held overseas; but he noted, 'It is the nature of the work of the intelligence services that they cannot defend themselves against many of the allegations that have been made. But I can – and I have every confidence that their work does not undermine the principles and values that are the best guarantee of our future security.'[48] In practice, Brown dragged his heels. This did not go unnoticed by the Intelligence and Security Committee.[49]

Behind the scenes, the prime minister's intervention was more strategic. He assured Obama that such a release of CIA material would not happen again, and set about implementing that assurance. His objective was nothing less than a readjustment of the balance of power between the executive and the judiciary, to make sure that judges could not put CIA documents in the public domain. Whitehall civil servants began preparing legislation for the establishment of closed material procedures and to prevent the making of court orders for the disclosure of what the government deemed to be sensitive information. Brown extracted further reassurances from Obama about the American press and the need to keep British secrets safe.[50]

By 2007, the long, arduous peace process in Northern Ireland had paid dividends. Whitehall had finally learned an unpleasant but fundamental truth: that terrorism is essentially communication with violence, and it is therefore important to keep the channels open. Although Margaret Thatcher had assured the House of Commons that Britain did not talk to terrorists, MI6 had long patiently reminded the IRA that there was an alternative political route. This persistence finally paid off. Under Brown, the British government was having similar thoughts about Afghanistan, which was rapidly turning into a rerun of Vietnam. British casualties had been minimal until the 2006 redeployment to Helmand province. In 2009, there were 108 British deaths, more than twice as many as in the year before, and questions were being asked. In a precise parallel to the Vietnam conflict, defence intelligence believed that the British forces in Helmand were making progress, while the civilian intelligence agencies, including MI6, thought they were losing.[51]

MI6 had often played the role of quasi-diplomats in dangerous places. In the 1960s and 1970s, when Britain had no diplomatic relations with North Vietnam, MI6 officers ran a precarious two-person outpost in Hanoi from which they talked to the Viet Cong leadership and to senior Russian generals, even while American bombs rained down from B-52s above them.[52] Both the CIA and later MI6 had located training missions with the PLO headquarters down the years, in the hope of facilitating change.[53] In the 1990s, Alastair Crooke, a former MI6 officer, arrived in Jerusalem to establish a link with Hamas. These missions had not always been successful, but Britain had long persevered in even the most unpromising circumstances.[54]

Brown, never comfortable playing the warrior, was keen to draw down Britain's military commitments overseas. Meanwhile, David Miliband grew optimistic about the possibility of splitting away some elements of the enemy in Afghanistan. Negotiations were never admitted to, but they were an implicit part of a broader strategy which included isolating the Taliban, encouraging low-ranking militants to switch sides, increasing aid and tackling opium-poppy production. On 12 December 2007, Brown defiantly declared to the House of Commons that 'We are isolating and eliminating the leadership of the Taliban; we are not negotiating with them.' A few minutes later he repeated: 'I make it clear that we will not enter into any negotiations with these people.'[55]

In reality, Brown and Miliband disagreed violently over the idea of talks with the Taliban,[56] but Miliband was allowed to go ahead with secret attempts to split the moderate Taliban away. The secret lasted only a few weeks. On Boxing Day, the *Daily Telegraph* broke the story that MI6 had entered into secret talks with Taliban leaders, and the prime minister found himself under pressure to return to Parliament and reveal exactly why discussions were ongoing with various groups of Taliban fighters. The opposition insisted that MI6 should not be talking to the Taliban while they were killing British troops. Shadow defence secretary Liam Fox warned that 'The prime minister will have some explaining to do to the British public.'[57] Was Gordon Brown secretly suing for peace with the Taliban?

Privately, senior military figures knew that the situation was much more complex. Each region of Afghanistan was ruled by a mixture of tribes and ethnicities. The Taliban were not one group, and it was possible to split some of them away and at least render them neutral. Under direct instructions from London, MI6 officers attempted this by holding a series of *jirgas*, or discussions with key figures, in Helmand over the summer of 2007. This meant getting together with some of President Hamid Karzai's most deadly enemies, so he was not informed even by his own intelligence chief. But Karzai had his own sources spying on his own spies. Now two British 'diplomats', Mervyn Patterson, a political officer advising the UN mission in Kabul, and Michael Semple, the Irish-born acting head of the EU mission, had been arrested in Helmand, and were being expelled for their pains. A retired Afghan air force general who had been working with them had been fiercely interrogated and thrown into prison in Lashkar Gah.[58]

Karzai nurtured a black-and-white view of the world. He believed that hiding behind the Taliban was Pakistan, and behind Pakistan was the Directorate for Inter-Services Intelligence, or ISI, its intelligence agency. He also thought Gordon Brown was colluding secretly with Pakistan to control Afghanistan. Remarkably, in the words of Britain's long-suffering ambassador in Kabul, Sherard Cowper-Coles, Karzai had long been convinced that MI6 had 'especially close' ties to Pakistan, and operated in Afghanistan on Pakistan's behalf. Britain had been working on a programme to resettle and retrain former Taliban fighters, which had been approved by some of Karzai's entourage. Again, Karzai had not been told about this; for him all Taliban were anathema. MI6 used this as a cover to develop conversations with moderate Taliban.[59]

To make things worse, MI6 was also at loggerheads with the Americans. Like Karzai, the CIA believed the only good Taliban was a dead Taliban, and its philosophy was 'Kill, kill, kill,' using an ever more sophisticated combination of special forces and high technology. It had gradually extended these missions inside Pakistan, which had not endeared it to the Islamabad government. The CIA stations in Pakistan were like sealed fortresses, and MI6 stayed well away. Later, the Chairman of the US Joint Chiefs of Staff said publicly what Washington privately knew – that one of the main Taliban factions fighting the Americans, the Haqqani network, was a 'veritable arm of Pakistan's Inter-Services Intelligence Agency'. The American embassy in Kabul saw MI6 as part of the problem and not part of the solution, so the CIA was delighted when in 2008 MI6 was caught with its trousers down talking to the Taliban.[60]

Cowper-Coles, the inimitable British ambassador, decided to raise flagging spirits amongst the British official community in Kabul by bringing in his friend 'Kit', an expert in 'outrageously camp satirical cabaret', to mount the first embassy pantomime. Skilful in 'social intelligence', Kit first spoke to everyone in the mission, 'pulling as many skeletons out of cupboards as he could'. The resulting production, 'A Lad in Kabul', was a thinly veiled parody of recent events, and focused on a British assault by 'the Queen's Own Penpushers', who were trying to force the Taliban into submission by bombarding them with draft strategies. This irreverent version of Britain's recent efforts to love its enemies to death, spearheaded by the Department for International Development, or DFID, included a troupe of tree-huggers who marched onto the stage during a number entitled 'The Day of the DFIDs'. The prickly American ambassador was lampooned as 'Chemical Bill'. As Cowper-Coles noted, beneath all the fun lay some 'darker truths'.[61]

During 2009, Brown tried an alternative strategy of putting more pressure on the Afghan government to engage Taliban leaders. The assumption was that with Western forces beginning to consider departure, Karzai would have no choice but to talk to the enemy. This new strategy of wider reconciliation was developed by MI6, Sherard Cowper-Coles, now the government's special representative for Afghanistan and Pakistan, and Lieutenant General Graeme Lamb, former director of special forces and now Britain's senior military officer in Kabul.

Brown had changed his mind, and was now keener on talking to the Taliban too. He summoned Lamb for a meeting, and asked if this would be possible. Lamb said it would. He wisely believed that while war is an extension of politics by other means, it must always return to politics. He did warn, however, that it would be difficult to know who to talk to, and recommended establishing a high council, including former mujahideen, to bypass Karzai. The prime minister then sent him to Afghanistan with the difficult mission of persuading insurgents to give up the path of armed resistance. Lamb thought there was still a long way to go, given that many rank-and-file fighters felt aggrieved, and their leaders regarded it as only a matter of time before the Americans departed, leaving Karzai exposed.[62]

Cowper-Coles worked on the Americans, trying to persuade them that being nice to Karzai in private, while haranguing him in public, was exactly the wrong strategy. In April 2009, he persuaded his opposite number, the veteran American diplomat Richard Holbrooke, to delay an evening at the theatre in London with the financier George Soros to attend a top-level briefing on the Taliban at Vauxhall Cross, MI6's riverside headquarters. John Scarlett, chief of MI6, produced his veteran Afghan experts, and Holbrooke was enthralled, staying for three hours. Cowper-Coles recalled, 'It was SIS at its very best.' At the end, Holbrooke remembered his social engagements and produced three mobile phones from his pocket, to the considerable consternation of MI6 security staff.[63] Secretary of state Hillary Clinton and Holbrooke were increasingly willing to look at negotiation. But Barack Obama, the Pentagon and the CIA continued to back the 'Fight first, talk later' strategy.[64]

David Miliband and MI6 wanted the reconciled Taliban to be removed from the UN sanctions list. They sought to weaken and divide the Taliban so the insurgency could be reduced to a level with which the new Afghan security forces could cope. This approach was classic carrot and stick, as in Northern Ireland. It combined military and intelligence pressure with the offer of talks and an 'honourable exit'. By 2009, MI6 was proposing something much more radical, not only splitting away many of the friendly Taliban in Afghanistan but also reaching a settlement with the Taliban leaders in neighbouring Pakistan. Publicly, Brown would only talk of 'tactical' reconciliation that involved reintegrating footsoldiers and their immediate commanders back into society. Echoing Miliband's calls to talk to more moderate members, the prime minister spoke of a broader strategy to 'try to bring over those elements that can now work with the democratic process'. But in reality, London wanted a shift in power towards district governors who could make reliable deals, rather than the hopeless Karzai government in Kabul.[65]

In 2010, MI6's efforts imploded. Pursuing its strategic objective of a regional deal, it had brought in a senior Taliban commander, Mullah Akhtar Mohammad Mansour, for discussions. 'Some captured Taliban

fighters reportedly were shown a photograph and confirmed his identity.'
Hillary Clinton thought this 'an exciting prospect'.[66] By November,
however, Mansour had been exposed as a sham, dealing a blow to the
credibility of MI6. This episode highlighted just one of the difficulties in
talking to terrorists, but to be fair to MI6, if it waited for 100 per cent
certainty that each person was genuine, it would never talk to anyone.
Despite meeting Karzai and receiving an estimated half a million dollars,
Mansour is now thought to have been a shopkeeper, or simply a well-
connected fraudster, from the town of Quetta in northern Pakistan.[67] One
senior official conceded: 'The truth is we can't really communicate with
the Taliban. We don't even really know who they are.' By now Brown's time
in office was drawing to a close.[68]

Gordon Brown's period as prime minister was dominated by the financial
meltdown of 2008. While Britain was fortunate to have a leader with the
financial acumen to play at being chancellor of the world,[69] the fact that
two key G20 summit meetings took place in London during that year gave
it other notable advantages, as GCHQ was able to monitor computers and
intercept phone calls to a degree that was much harder overseas. Moreover,
remarkable new technologies came on stream that harnessed the power of
the internet. GCHQ's coverage of the Maastricht Treaty negotiations in the
1990s had been good, but now its ability to follow a major summit was
remarkable. One of the most effective techniques was to use internet cafés
as a front for British intelligence. This allowed GCHQ to harvest passwords and examine email traffic not only during the summits, but long
afterward.

Britain was spying on allies with the help of allies. GCHQ worked with
its larger American sister organisation, the National Security Agency, and
also smaller Canadian, Australian and New Zealand agencies which then
shared data. They jointly targeted NATO countries such as Turkey, and
Commonwealth countries including South Africa. GCHQ's espionage
operation was incredibly complex, needing to follow the business of
twenty delegations all at once. To complicate matters further, the five
'UKUSA' countries sharing the product were by no means in step in terms
of their political objectives. Sharing, therefore, could never be complete.
But although Britain and the United States had different agendas, they did
agree on certain key priorities. The leader of the Russian delegation,
Dmitry Medvedev, sat on top of this list. The NSA's largest overseas intelligence station, based at Menwith Hill in North Yorkshire, targeted phone

calls from London to Moscow by Russian delegates. Turkey was another key target, as a booming economy on the periphery of Europe whose willingness to cooperate with the rest of the G20 nations was uncertain.[70]

Material recently leaked by the CIA whistleblower Edward Snowden shows that by 2009, Gordon Brown and his ministers were supported by radical new espionage techniques. Not only did GCHQ use key-logging software to access the email of summit delegates, it also used devices that looked like modified BlackBerrys to distribute the product to its customers in real time. An army of more than forty analysts sat in a back room at GCHQ, firstly trying to make head or tail of all the data they had harvested, and secondly deciding what was important enough to be forwarded to customers. Political aides who accompanied Brown to G8 and G20 summits emphasised that this was a constant war of electronic offence and defence. They knew that all the other countries also engaged in espionage, and so were advised 'not to plug in our laptops, use photocopiers, wi-fi or our usual BlackBerrys'. Meanwhile, GCHQ busily worked on developing special secure phones and laptops to be used only for the duration of a summit.[71]

'We spy on other countries,' recalls Damian McBride, 'because they are routinely spying on us. Everyone is at it.'[72] Head of strategic planning in Downing Street, McBride was one of Brown's 'shadowy henchpersons'.[73] Formerly head of communications at the Treasury, one of his tasks was storing up unpleasant information on people and then threatening to use it in negative briefings. The majority of MPs have something to hide, so the technique was frighteningly effective. Moving in circles of journalists who thrived on beer, sport and macho male activities, McBride was used to brief against David Miliband as early as the summer of 2008, and acquired the nicknames 'McPoison' and 'Mad Dog'.[74]

McBride was one of the most senior amongst the teams of special political advisers and policy wonks that thronged around the prime minister. Oddly, given that they thrived on risky political espionage, none of these people had been properly trained in either the use of intelligence or proper communications security. They were told 'very seriously' not to use mobiles in Downing Street, because the Chinese and the Russians were routinely intercepting conversations. 'Not that anyone obeyed,' McBride tellingly noted. The intelligence community also warned Brown's advisers that the Chinese could 'use live mobile phones inside No. 10 and No. 11 to hack into nearby computers'. The staff inside Number 10 found all this stuff close to science fiction, and almost beyond belief.[75]

Overseas, Brown's entourage were routinely issued with special secure phones. Security teams ordered them not to switch on their normal BlackBerrys, because the various hostile security agencies would hack them. Anything they left in their hotel rooms, they were told, would automatically be examined and copied, especially in China. In late January 2008, Brown led a delegation to China with a focus on trade. He also took the opportunity to have discussions with senior figures in the Chinese administration, intended to curb the vast money-laundering by terrorists and criminal gangs in China. He then headed on to India to sign a deal bringing Delhi into the Financial Action Taskforce, an international organisation that tackled money-laundering across the globe.[76]

About twenty Downing Street staff accompanied the prime minister. They included senior advisers on foreign policy, the environment and trade. Around twenty-five business leaders, such as Adrian Montague, the chairman of British Energy, Arun Sarin, then chief executive of Vodafone, and Sir Richard Branson, the Virgin boss, also joined Brown.[77] Damian McBride recalls:

> One night in Shanghai, while at a launch party for Richard Branson's new Virgin airline service to the city, our small gaggle of mostly male Downing Street staff and accompanying journalists found ourselves accosted on one side by a beautiful posse of Chinese girls and on the other side by an equivalent group of Russian blondes. Even before our resident security expert could warn us that their interest was not to be taken at face value, we looked up and saw one of our number disappearing up the stairs to the exit with one of the girls, beaming back at us and doing a 'Chelsea dagger' dance as though he had won the lottery.

This person was a senior policy adviser to Brown. Predictably, he woke up in the morning 'minus his BlackBerry and half the contents of his briefcase'. He also had a very bad headache, owing to the Mickey Finn nightcap his overnight companion had administered to him in his hotel room.[78]

Concerted attention from hordes of female spies was not unusual when attending summits. 'At times it felt like I was an extra in an Austin Powers film,' recalled one adviser. Two libidinous members of Brown's entourage decided to take advantage of this, going so far as to prepare bogus phones and intelligence files as 'dangles' for eager female spies when visiting summits abroad, in order to ensure that they had suitable material to 'lose' when honeytrapped. They created plausible documents covered with impressive security classifications denoting eye-watering secrecy. The core of this material actually came from commercially confidential, but unclassified, reports, provided with covers suggesting they were JIC papers on the long-term future of Chinese trade policy and oil in Kazakhstan. Remarkably, when their ruse became known to British security the advisers were asked to desist, on the grounds that they might cut across genuine deceptive material that was being put in the way of the Chinese by MI6. In other words, it was feared that this phoney amateur deception might impede Britain's real deception.[79]

Brown was a great fan of electronic monitoring in support of negotiation. He was also keen to keep it quiet. Although unhappy about Iraq and being tainted by association with the George W. Bush administration, he was serious about counter-terrorism, and about any intelligence instruments that might protect Britain. But electronic espionage unnerved some of his colleagues. Mervyn King, governor of the Bank of England, had got cold feet and announced to the prime minister that he felt a duty to go public about the scale of electronic monitoring. Brown was horrified. He quietly told everyone else in the room to leave, then 'unleashed a volcanic tirade at Mervyn', telling him that to speak out would put counter-terrorism operations at risk, and would do the same to Britain's relationship with America. Rather unfairly, he also said that King was talking 'fucking bullshit', and accused him of disregarding his national duty and being motivated by 'fucking ego'.[80] The truth about mass electronic collection had been gradually leaking throughout the years after 9/11, and Brown knew that it would eventually come out. To his relief, the dam finally burst on David Cameron's watch.

19

David Cameron
(2010–)

I love watching crime dramas on television, as I should
probably stop telling people. There is hardly a crime
drama where the crime is solved without using the
data from a mobile communications device.
DAVID CAMERON[1]

David Cameron entered Downing Street at dusk on 11 May 2010.[2] It must
have been a bittersweet victory, for he did so as the first prime minister
since Winston Churchill to head a coalition, having failed to secure a
majority and so formed a government in partnership with Nick Clegg's
Liberal Democrats. In his mid-forties, Cameron was the youngest prime
minister since 1812, and had only been a Member of Parliament for nine
years. He had never served in government. Consequently, unlike Churchill,
the new prime minister lacked prior experience in dealing with intelligence. He did, however, enjoy regularly recounting a story about KGB
agents trying to recruit him as a nineteen-year-old when he was on
gap-year travels around the Soviet Union. Moscow has since dismissed
this, countering that the young Cameron was merely the target of an
attempted gay pick-up.[3]

Nor did Cameron share Churchill's voracious appetite for raw intelligence and impulsive personal intervention. Operating more in the mould
of Stanley Baldwin, he proudly accentuated his collegiate approach to
leadership, allowing ministers to run their own departments. In fact, he
demonstrated such a hands-off approach that critics accused him of
spending more time 'chillaxing' on the tennis court, on numerous holidays
and playing video games, than actually running the government – a far cry
from the Anthony Eden model of neurotic meddling. Cameron was a 'big
picture' prime minister, rather like Tony Blair; but in contrast to Blair he

adopted a more inclusive 'chairman of the board' approach, rather than surrounding himself with cronies. Keen to make quick decisions, he lacked interest in the minutiae of raw intelligence, and preferred briefings directly from the chairman of the JIC and within the structures of his newly created National Security Council.

Nonetheless, Cameron was regarded as a diligent consumer of intelligence. He enjoyed working with the intelligence agencies, and continued Blair's innovation of having the intelligence community prepare a daily 'Highlights of Intelligence' summary for him as an easily digestible package.[4] Like Alec Douglas-Home, another Old Etonian, David Cameron had a ruthlessness and steely determination behind the apparently charming 'call-me-Dave' exterior. Nowhere was this more evident than when he dealt with the secret state.

Economic austerity defined David Cameron's coalition government, with the result that his initial priorities were overwhelmingly domestic, focusing on vigorous retrenchment and halting spiralling debt. This agenda did not preclude him from turning almost immediately to issues of national security. In some ways, Cameron's austerity actually shaped approaches to intelligence. The economic crisis forced Britain to require 'smaller, cheaper and less ambitious armed forces'.[5] At the same time, Cameron was adamant that Britain would not see any shrinkage in its global role. Like his predecessors, he desperately wanted to retain a place at the top table. Once more, the fancy footwork of intelligence was required to bridge the gap between Britain's global ambitions and the sober realities of economic decline.

Intelligence is a force multiplier. It is a special kind of information that not only provides warning, but also allows more effective action. It enables states to punch above their weight and make the most of whatever material assets they have at their disposal. By predicting crises around the globe, intelligence can, in theory at least, also pave the way for diplomatic or humanitarian action to prevent a threat from developing. Accurate intelligence also permits the swift, surgical and selective use of military force. Similarly, the targeted use of special forces, guided by intelligence, is far less costly and controversial than open warfare. Even more discreetly, intelligence allows MI6 to engage in what it politely refers to as 'event shaping'. On all these fronts Cameron delivered. Although he cut defence more severely than any other area of his budget, his National Security Strategy and Strategic Defence and Security Review emphasised the importance of intelligence and special forces, ensuring that they would be saved from the swingeing cuts imposed elsewhere across Whitehall.

A conscious attempt to learn from Tony Blair's painful and public mistakes also drove Cameron's approach to intelligence. Despite once styling himself 'the heir to Blair', Cameron was, like Gordon Brown, desperate to distance himself from the former prime minister's notoriously informal style of decision-making. As soon as he entered Number 10, he institutionalised his relationship with the three intelligence chiefs. He had long trumpeted a National Security Council (NSC), and wasting no time at all, he convened the new NSC for the first time on 12 May 2010 – less than a week after the general election – to discuss Afghanistan, Pakistan and the terrorist threat. It met on a practically daily basis to discuss Afghanistan during the first weeks of the new government.[6] Cameron chaired every meeting when he was able. The NSC quickly became an influential body. Because the prime minister was ever-present, the secretaries of state also attended, as did the intelligence chiefs. This is how Whitehall works: when the prime minister puts energy into something, everybody starts paying attention and turning up to meetings. As one member recalled, a summons to the NSC demanded 'a command performance'.[7] With the intelligence chiefs and other senior ministers present, many decisions relating to national security were made within the NSC forum rather than at cabinet level.[8] It was also inclusive, drawing in bodies such as the National Crime Agency, which now held responsibility for undercover work against transnational organised crime. This was a vast improvement; the relationship between intelligence and Number 10, started in 1909, had reached its apotheosis 101 years later.

In some senses Cameron's changes merely enhanced existing Cabinet Office machinery and accelerated those begun by Brown. Blair had underused the cabinet committee system, famously preferring his sofa style of government, and so often lacked good advice. Brown then tinkered with the various committees and subcommittees constituting the joint intelligence machinery. Cameron had simply developed Brown's bureaucracy amidst much fanfare.[9] He also displayed more enthusiasm than Brown, who some felt lacked interest, and was merely going through the motions with his meetings.[10]

There were two other fundamental differences which had a significant impact on the relationship between the prime minister and the intelligence agencies. Firstly, the NSC met weekly, after the initial flurry of more regular meetings, in the highly secure Cobra room, which was equipped with all manner of screens and communications technology to bring intelligence direct to the prime minister from around the world, rather than on an *ad hoc* basis as previous systems had. Like Brown, Cameron loved using Cobra. Secondly, and most importantly, the heads of all three intelligence agencies and the chair of the JIC attended the meetings. The latter, Alex Allan, began each meeting with a briefing on the latest intelligence. Distancing himself from Blair's informality, Cameron was therefore able to take opinion from all quarters, including the intelligence agencies.[11] He was a disciplined chair, asking the intelligence chiefs and the chief of the defence staff to speak first, before inviting ministerial comment.

Cameron's reforms instantly created a different kind of regular contact between the prime minister and intelligence chiefs. For the first time ever, the prime minister met his intelligence chiefs together every Tuesday morning, so long as they were all in London, in the company of key decision-makers. This was a far cry from the informal, personality-driven arrangements of the past. For every Clement Attlee and Percy Sillitoe, who represented close and regular contact, there was a James Callaghan and Michael Hanley, who represented the opposite. At a stroke, Cameron had created a formal mechanism to force interaction between intelligence leaders and the most senior policymakers in the land. John Sawers, chief of SIS, now possessed a powerful – if often cautious – voice around the table.[12] Cameron's reforms also brought Iain Lobban, the head of GCHQ and based in Cheltenham, closer to Number 10. Waxing lyrical, Lobban believes the NSC is 'one of the best things this government has done', because it 'takes the sentiment in the room and translates it into tasking for each organisation'. It is '*Civis Britannicus sum*. Brilliant.'[13] Not since Churchill's war cabinet has a prime minister interacted with all his intelligence leaders as frequently as David Cameron.[14]

The NSC sits at the heart of the Whitehall intelligence and security world. It drives the intelligence community's work and, symptomatic of the growing centrality of intelligence over the past decades, offers an unparalleled interaction with policy. Unfortunately, the new system also posed serious problems. It brought intelligence perilously close to the policymaking process, and in doing so potentially allowed Cameron to abuse it. This alarmed one of Whitehall's most experienced observers. From the House of Lords, Peter Hennessy worried about intelligence falling 'into the trap either of advocacy or of telling their customers what they wish to hear'. Some have suggested that Cameron's new system created confusion regarding the role of the JIC: the new behemoth threatened to marginalise a long-standing and successful Whitehall institution.[15] It has certainly opened the door to more active overseas secret operations, since problems are now reported in an environment in which the agencies can be readily, almost instantly, tasked with 'disrupting' a threat.[16] Some of the original authors of the system worry that Cameron was inclined to use it too tactically.[17]

Concerned that his flagship idea was having teething problems, Cameron ordered a speedy review in January 2011. It soon became clear, however, that the intelligence community – in the form of the JIC – had an enviable position tied to the country's most senior policymakers, including the prime minister. Working just below the level of Cameron's weekly meetings with principals, the JIC generated intelligence reviews, while a group called the National Security Council (Official) pulled together senior civil servants who came up with options ready for the Tuesday meeting with Cameron. The whole machine bore an uncanny resemblance to the way the chiefs of staff ran the Second World War. Unlike under Blair, and indeed Chamberlain and Eden long before him, intelligence was now more relevant, and enjoyed a sophisticated audience. It informed policy in a collegiate way at the highest levels.[18] The system seemed to be working well. It would not be long until it faced its first real test.

David Cameron did not expect to intervene in an Arab country quite so quickly. Although far from an isolationist, the new prime minister had no innate desire to enmesh his impecunious nation in messy foreign conflicts. Unlike Blair, he was not a liberal with a gun, driven by an ideological fervour for imposing democracy from the outside. Having seen how the toxic legacy of Iraq had lingered over Blair, Cameron was determined to avoid foreign entanglements, and especially military incursions. He was suspicious of the neoconservatives who continued to run the Pentagon under Barack Obama, and even approached humanitarian intervention with caution, wary of being perceived as crusading.[19]

Instead, his coalition's entire *raison d'être* was economic recovery. The so-called 'big society' and reform of the public services featured next on Cameron's priority list.[20] His early foreign policy, insofar as it existed at all, centred on improving trade links with emerging economies.[21] Britain was for sale. In one somewhat unfortunate example, Cameron's government promoted the sale of sniper rifles to Libya just weeks before the Arab Spring.[22] When he did think about foreign intervention, he consistently emphasised both the need for countries to work together and the idea of 'liberal conservatism'.[23] Even before coming to power, he had secretly agreed with his chancellor George Osborne to withdraw from Afghanistan, which as far as Osborne was concerned could not happen soon enough. In June 2010, Cameron hosted a summit at Chequers on the subject, and after exposing his military chiefs to some speakers with more radical views, whom he dubbed 'the wild men', about possible political negotiations with the Taliban, he discussed an exit strategy with service chiefs and 'the spooks'.[24]

British prime ministers are eternally fated to rediscover the truth of the old adage, 'You may not be interested in war – but war is interested in you.' On 17 December 2010, a young vegetable trader set himself on fire in Tunisia. It was a desperate and dramatic response to an alleged slap across the face by a strict female market inspector, symbolising frustration with a corrupt and authoritarian regime. Protests swept across Tunisia and into Egypt, Yemen, Libya and Syria, and became known as the Arab Spring. Ordinary people came out of their houses and filled the squares to chant for democracy. Nick Clegg, Cameron's deputy, found the turbulence 'incredibly exciting'.[25] As for the prime minister, he did little other than offer supportive words. With instability spreading across the region, he keenly hoped that democracy would develop smoothly within these countries, thereby avoiding the need to support it from outside with force.[26] He was, however, optimistic and excited about the future. John Sawers urged caution, warning the prime minister that the wave of middle-class protest did not necessarily indicate the beginnings of a broader popular revolution.[27]

Dictators often fight back. Leading the charge was Libya's notorious Colonel Muammar Gaddafi. A man roundly regarded by Syrian President Bashar al-Assad, the late Yasser Arafat, long-time leader of the Palestinians, and almost every other regional leader as 'the mad dog of the Middle East', Gaddafi had no intention of rolling over. Instantly recognisable as a deranged dictator who demanded obedience, he was a mercurial character known as much for his all-female security team, elaborate taste in gold ornaments and travelling in a Bedouin tent as for his brutal repression. Since coming to power in 1969, he had attempted to export revolution by supporting terrorism. Now he launched a merciless crackdown on the protesters.

By early 2011, Libya had reached a bloody stalemate. Civilians, dissidents and rebels alike were dying at the hands of the government's brutal security forces. Cameron's anti-interventionist instincts could only hold out so long. Tony Blair might have come to an accommodation with Gaddafi, but the Conservatives had unfinished business with him stretching back to the 1980s. Alongside the French president, Nicolas Sarkozy, Cameron sought to aid the rebel groups in Libya. He had long harboured a 'visceral dislike' of Gaddafi, and was revolted by Blair's decision to deal with him.[28] He received support from hawkish neoconservative colleagues such as Michael Gove, the education secretary, and George Osborne.

The prime minister turned to the professionals for help, but was disappointed. MI6 did not support him, and Sawers opposed the idea of intervening in Libya altogether, whether overtly or covertly. He had a similar reception from David Richards, Chief of the Defence Staff and another NSC regular. In the words of one prime ministerial ally, Cameron sensed that Sawers and Richards were thinking, 'Here we go again, another prime minister with a hare-brained war he wants to fight.'[29] On one occasion Sawers even told the prime minister that intervention would not be in the national interest. Intelligence and defence officials worried that Cameron had not thought things through properly.[30] Shaped by the horrors of Srebrenica in their formative years, and having not been directly involved in Iraq, Cameron and his youngish team were deemed 'twenty years out of date when it comes to dealing with conflict'.[31]

Cameron was not the first prime minister to be disappointed when calling on the secret cohorts of MI6 or the SAS for immediate action. It is not unreasonable, however, for the chief of MI6 to offer a professional judgement and be cautious about such activity. And Cameron did apparently come up with at least one half-baked plan which would have drawn on MI6's particular set of skills. He proposed dropping two hundred million unused Libyan banknotes, worth £1 billion, into the country to help the rebels. Dominic Grieve, the attorney general, had to veto the idea, pointing out that it breached a UN freeze on all Libyan assets, and that the prime minister could be sent to jail. It was also probably illegal under international law. Cameron was furious.[32]

In the end, 'Cameron's decision was a lonely one.'[33] By 19 March 2011, British forces were involved in Libya, knocking out air defences and attempting to 'squeeze' Gaddafi. Britain had intervened in yet another Middle Eastern state. The very next day, Cameron created a war cabinet – the NSC(L), or National Security Council (Libya). Chaired by the prime minister, the new body ran the campaign and met some sixty times. The intelligence heads, the chief of the Defence Staff and the attorney general all attended when necessary and available. Cameron enjoyed having all the practitioners around the table, relying on the official machine, and making quick decisions based on advice from every quarter. According to one insider, he was 'very good at spotting when officials slope shoulders'. He would 'poke and poke at questions', but knew when to back off. He did not want to 'brutalise people'.[34] George Osborne, although without a directly relevant portfolio, proved to be an equally effective interrogator.[35]

Real-time intelligence was crucial if the war cabinet was to work effectively: Cameron needed information upon which to base his decisions. Immediate military, intelligence and diplomatic assessments from the theatre gave the prime minister and his colleagues an understanding of the detailed context – vital as they battled with the pressures of both tactical and strategic matters in the context of the twenty-four-hour media world.[36] Accordingly, the JIC chair, Alex Allan, a colourful character who had once windsurfed up the Thames to work during a train strike,[37] began each meeting by briefing Cameron and other senior ministers on the current intelligence picture. It was an intense period, with Allan arriving at work at 5.30 every morning to be ready for the daily 8 a.m. meeting. Whitehall's Joint Intelligence Organisation had been working through the night.[38] This daily update was supplemented by comments from Sawers and Lobban, alongside assessments from the chief of defence intelligence.[39] In short, Cameron received an abundance of material. It was perhaps too overwhelming and disjointed for such an inexperienced prime minister to digest. Peter Ricketts, Cameron's national security adviser, seems to have thought so. He later suggested that a single briefing integrating all the diplomatic, intelligence, humanitarian and military aspects would have sufficed, and would have freed up the senior intelligence officials for their more pressing tasks.[40]

Despite the barrage of briefings, Cameron's intelligence was not always particularly solid. It was often out of date, and lacked detail. Perhaps Gaddafi's so-called 'deal in the desert' with Tony Blair in 2004 brought about a lowering of MI6 focus on Libya. In any case, in the words of one defence intelligence analyst working in the region, the country was 'an intelligence black hole'. There was little coverage on the ground, and the only material available was imagery intelligence sent to a British base in Cyprus.[41] MI6 had to quickly ramp up its coverage as soon as the Arab Spring began.[42] Embarrassingly, at one point foreign secretary William Hague was left spreading a false rumour that Gaddafi had fled to Venezuela, claiming to have 'information that suggests he is on his way there at the moment'.[43] Once bombing got under way, the lack of intelligence meant that analysts found it difficult to distinguish between loyalist and rebel forces on the front line. In early April 2011, allied air strikes accidentally bombed a rebel column. It soon became clear that Britain needed eyes on the ground in order to direct air strikes and prevent such incidents from happening again.[44]

Cameron faced other problems. Intelligence often presents awkward choices between ethics and action. Even when it could guide air strikes against Gaddafi, the bombs had little impact. Unbeknownst to the prime minister, his defence secretary, Liam Fox, refused to sanction any strikes where there was even the slightest risk of collateral damage or civilian casualties, unilaterally setting a computer model which calculated approved levels of collateral damage to zero. Cameron fumed that this was 'fucking ridiculous'.[45]

Cameron approved increased MI6 and special forces activity inside Libya.[46] Unfortunately, his first foray into the world of secret warfare got off to a shaky start. In March 2011, an undercover team was, in the euphemistic words of officialdom, 'withdrawn after a serious misunderstanding about its role, leading to its temporary detention'.[47] In reality, this was a classic farce that was more Dad's Army than James Bond. MI6 planners had chosen to use a sensitive special forces team, known as 'E Squadron', to escort its officers deep inside Libya. Established in the early 2000s and operating at the disposal of MI6 and the director of special forces, E Squadron was an elite within an elite, with members drawn from the SAS, the SBS and the Special Reconnaissance Regiment.[48]

MI6 had hoped to establish secure communications with the rebels, and a potential base for British diplomats in the Benghazi area. Dressed in black, the group, led by a young MI6 Middle Eastern specialist, flew a clandestine route via Malta and Crete in a special forces Chinook helicopter so as to avoid being stopped at the border. But their landing in a Libyan farmyard in the early hours of 4 March aroused local suspicion. Fearing that the helicopter was carrying pro-regime mercenaries, the farmers fired shots before roughing up the Brits, binding them with plastic cuffs and handing them to the opposition forces. The Foreign Office frantically faxed a note on headed paper to confirm the identities of the 'diplomatic mission', whose members were swiftly deported amid much unwelcome publicity.[49]

Approval for the bungled mission came from the top. John Sawers was fully briefed, and William Hague, who took a close interest in MI6's work, had approved the operation as foreign secretary. A Number 10 spokesman confirmed that the prime minister was in constant contact with Hague, but it is impossible to say for sure whether Cameron knew of the operation in advance.[50] Either way, the incident damaged – temporarily at least – British relations with the rebels. The political fallout also put some inside the NSC off the idea of covert intervention, and hampered MI6 plans to turn some of Gaddafi's inner circle.[51]

The mission was also a security failure. The rebels allegedly managed to seize a range of high-tech spy paraphernalia, including GPS trackers, maps marked with landing and extraction points, passports (including three for the same man), credit cards, satellite telephones, guns, portable welding machines and shortwave radios. Perhaps more alarmingly, the special forces team had also apparently been carrying scraps of paper containing user names and passwords for secret computer systems. The press had a field day; the prime minister, apparently, was furious.[52]

For a while, Cameron confined MI6 to less dramatic operations. One, devised by Alan Duncan, operated out of disused rooms on the top floor of the Foreign and Commonwealth Office. In conjunction with officials from the Foreign Office and the Ministry of Defence, it formed the top-secret Libyan Oil Cell. Its mission: to make sure the sanctions placed on Gaddafi's regime worked. This was easier said than done. Duncan, a former oil trader turned international development minister, had informed Cameron that, as was so often the case with sanctions, the measures had ended up hurting the rebels but failing to impact the regime. Had he been alive, Harold Wilson would surely have sympathised. On 5 May, with the backing of the prime minister and Peter Ricketts, the new team set to work. The cell was initially led by Rear Admiral Neil Morisetti, before a senior Ministry of Defence and National Security Secretariat official, Nicholas Beadle, took over. Drawing on a wide range of tricks associated with covert economic warfare, such as assisting a blockade of Gaddafi-held ports, identifying tankers supplying the government, and spotting overland smugglers' routes, it attempted to starve Gaddafi's war effort.

At the same time, the Libyan Oil Cell helped to ensure that fuel reached rebels in the east of Libya by asking Lloyd's of London to grant insurance for ships heading to Benghazi. It also sought to help rebels sell oil for cash, and set up meetings with companies that were prepared to supply oil without an upfront payment. Furthermore, it provided intelligence to advise the rebels on cutting a particular oil pipeline so as to impede Gaddafi's forces after taking control of the Nafusa mountains outside Tripoli.[53]

MI6 also became involved in drawing up an exit strategy for Gaddafi. The Libyan leader knew too much, and London feared the possibility of his telling his story, including his links to MI6, in front of an international court. With the political situation delicate, Cameron hoped to keep his options regarding the eventual resolution of hostilities open. MI6 and relevant Cabinet Office personnel therefore plotted how to spirit Gaddafi into Equatorial Guinea to serve out his enforced retirement if necessary. The rich, corrupt West African nation would have been ideal – not least because it did not recognise the International Criminal Court.[54] This plan was not ultimately required, but it is always wise to have contingencies.

Bloody stalemate continued. As the conflict dragged on, it became increasingly apparent that intelligence and special forces teams needed to be on the ground directly assisting the rebels. With some reluctance, Cameron eventually sanctioned another operation. Alongside similar teams from France, Qatar and the UAE, MI6 and SAS personnel trained locals in the art of insurgency. This included weapons-handling, street-fighting and sabotage. From April 2011, unarmed British officers in Benghazi aimed to coordinate the amateurish and excitable rebels, more used to speeding around dusty streets in beaten-up trucks firing dramatically into the air than planning an organised military offensive. The international covert force also smuggled hundreds of weapons into Libya, with Britain apparently supplying a thousand sets of body armour. MI6 and the SAS, working closely together, offered advice on local plans to take Tripoli, and by August 2011 more than two hundred Libyan rebels had entered the capital, either from the coast disguised as fishermen or via the western mountains.[55]

Back in London, Sawers and his military counterparts advised Cameron to switch his attention from Benghazi to the west of Libya. The prime minister agreed, and consented to a new plan coordinated by a special operations cell based in Paris. Allied special forces and intelligence teams travelled to western Libya to assist rebel activity, offer tactical advice and gather much-needed intelligence. They dressed as Libyans and blended in with local rebel units. Although backing this shift in focus, senior MI6 officers were hesitant, fearing that the plan was not decisive enough. Whitehall's covert planners have long felt that rebels should only be helped if they can achieve decisive victory, recognising that prolonged stalemate would damage the country concerned and risk political capital for nothing. Sawers also worried about what would happen after the intervention had ended, and about the West's inability to control or manage the Arab

Spring.[56] But Cameron took the risk to commit forces, and it marked a turning point in the campaign.[57]

On 20 October, Gaddafi was killed. He had been fleeing Sirte, his birthplace and stronghold on the Libyan coast, when a NATO strike hit his convoy. On foot, the beleaguered dictator escaped across fields and into a drainage pipe filled with rubbish underneath a major road. That was where local militia found him, took his golden pistol and executed him. It was an ignominious death – his body was dragged through the streets and filmed. Three days later, the rebels declared victory. George Osborne rewarded each member of Cameron's war cabinet with a commemorative set of dinar coins.[58] Such triumphalism was short-lived. Libya remained in turmoil, and Sawers later said publicly that 'If you decide not to [rebuild], as we did in Libya, partly because of the scars from Iraq, then you topple the government and you end up having nothing in its place.'[59] Another member of the NSC concedes that 'In retrospect we were arguably too focused on the short term ... We may have given some warnings about the instabilities that would follow but I don't think we predicted anything like what has emerged.'[60]

Libya was a country in which MI6 had long experience and personal contacts. For that reason Cameron found himself gradually drawn towards the Blairite tendency of relying on MI6 stocktaking papers and single-service private briefings. Whenever this happened, it irked the JIC chairman, Alex Allan, who felt the intelligence agencies were sending their juiciest raw intelligence direct to Number 10, which left it to Cameron's private office to determine what to show the prime minister and what caveats to offer.[61] But in contrast to 2003, the whole intelligence community now understood that this was bad for business: the problem, once uncovered, caused temporary outrage and was soon corrected. But broadly speaking the NSC delivered well, with the JIC undertaking appreciations and the official level of the NSC providing the prime minister and his immediate circle with options that could be discussed with the principals present. The NSC seemed to provide what Tony Blair had never wanted: an objective analysis of the intelligence, a wide range of options, and an open debate about the best course of action.[62]

Both Cameron and Obama saw Libya as an intelligence opportunity. Alarmed by the reversals of some of their staunchest covert allies in the region, including the formidable intelligence service of Egypt, they were looking to establish a new beachhead. After the Libyan revolution, both the CIA and MI6 increased their covert presence in Benghazi and across eastern Libya. This was an ideal point from which to monitor radical groups that pledged allegiance to al-Qaeda in the Maghreb. Western diplomatic facilities were quickly opened; their declared tasks included collecting vast quantities of arms that had flooded the country during the war, in some cases literally buying them with suitcases of cash. About a hundred intelligence and special forces operators from as many as a dozen different units thronged eastern Libya by the summer of 2012. One of their main purposes was to smuggle weapons from Libya to anti-Assad rebels in Syria. The US government denied that the CIA was sending weapons to Syria, but refused to comment on the activities of other US covert units. Or those of their allies.[63]

British and American efforts were being watched by hostile elements. On 11 June 2012, the British ambassador to Libya, Dominic Asquith, great-grandson of Herbert, was returning from a meeting. As his convoy approached the consular office it was hit by a rocket-propelled grenade. Asquith survived because he had recently switched vehicles, but two British protection officers were injured.[64] Thereafter, regular British diplomats were withdrawn from Benghazi, while a remaining security team quartered their vehicles and weapons in the nearby US embassy compound.[65] Worse was to come. On the evening of 11 September, the anniversary of the 9/11 attacks, radicals launched military assaults on two separate US compounds. Just before ten in the evening, over a hundred men, some with heavy machine-guns and artillery mounted on gun trucks, launched a ferocious attack on the US embassy. Shouting 'Allahu Akbar,' they threw grenades over the wall and were soon inside the compound. Remarkably, most of the diplomatic security service agents did not have their weapons to hand. Ambassador J. Christopher Stevens just made it to the safe room, but this was set on fire and he died of asphyxiation while attempting to escape. CIA officers and special forces were located at a second compound a mile away, and attempted a rescue. But just after midnight this was also attacked. After hours of ferocious fighting, mortars were brought to bear and two CIA officers were killed as the second compound was overrun.[66]

In January 2013, it was Britain's turn again. The prime minister summoned his director of special forces to Whitehall for an emergency meeting. Cameron had heard that terrorists had seized a large number of hostages, including Britons, at a gas plant in Algeria, and had placed explosive belts around their necks. Hours later an SAS unit secretly headed off to Cyprus, ready for a daring rescue mission in the Algerian desert. In the end, the Algerian government opted to use its own security forces, and the ensuing operation resulted in bloodshed, with about forty hostages losing their lives. After this litany of unpredictable events, the prime minister, like so many of his predecessors, had learned to value special forces and promised to further increase their funding, protecting them from falling defence spending.[67]

In 2011, David Cameron had never heard of Edward Snowden. And there is no reason why he should have. Back then Snowden was a belligerent, opinionated and self-important young American computer genius busy posting messages in online chatrooms under the alias of 'TheTrueHOOHA'. He had previously worked for the CIA, but had since taken up a position as a contractor for the NSA, taking full advantage of the post-9/11 boom in security consultancy when Michael Hayden, then director of the NSA, had privatised many of the agency's back-office services in an effort to harness the dynamism of the global computer industry. In through this back door stepped Edward Snowden. By 2012, he had moved to a new NSA job, this time in Hawaii, a key nodal point in the worldwide listening chain run by the NSA, GCHQ and their allies. It gave him access to thousands of documents showing how the West undertook top-secret signals intelligence in the Twitter age. The NSA was up to all sorts of twenty-first-century wizardry; from mass collection to bugging foreign leaders' phones, from infiltrating video games to manipulating new medical and automotive technologies. The more Snowden read, the more he became concerned about the NSA's invasion of privacy. He was a committed libertarian who hailed from the American right, and as such was a whistleblower, or a traitor, in waiting, depending on your point of view.[68]

The Snowden revelations broke in early summer 2013. On 6 June, *Guardian* journalist Glenn Greenwald reported that the NSA routinely collected the telephone records of millions of customers of the American telecommunications company Verizon. It was the scoop of his life. Although the US government blocked attempts to review these matters in the courts, Snowden had revealed what top American academic lawyers at Harvard and Yale judged to be illegal and unconstitutional activities. This story was swiftly followed by details of another top-secret operation, known as 'PRISM', in which the NSA accessed systems owned by internet giants such as Facebook, Yahoo, Microsoft and Skype. President Obama instantly went on the defensive, justifying the programmes while attempting to soothe American concerns. It soon became clear, however, that Snowden had stolen far more than documents relating to one or two mass-collection programmes. Moving far beyond his grievances about citizen privacy, he revealed thousands of documents relating to all aspects of NSA – and GCHQ – activity. Publicly America's top intelligence chiefs were robust in defending their programmes; privately they were aghast at having exposed the parallel activities of their partner British agency, GCHQ.[69]

Cameron valued GCHQ extremely highly, and knew of the critical contribution made by its powerful American partner. In recent months the two agencies had worked together on what they called 'high-priority surges' around many current world events, and Downing Street was the beneficiary of this stream of real-time intelligence. Troubled relations with Iran offered but one example. In the last year, GCHQ and the NSA had worked together to provide sigint on the ransacking of the British embassy in Tehran by a mob of protesters, on Iran's discovery of the FLAME computer virus, and had supported policymakers during the multiple rounds of negotiations over Iran's nuclear power programme. The NSA had especially admired GCHQ's efforts to involve other partners in sigint in Afghanistan, although it remained divided over exactly how closely it wished to work with the Israelis across the region.[70]

Yet curiously, at the outset David Cameron did not take much interest in the Snowden story. As self-proclaimed 'minister for the intelligence services', he made some brief remarks about intelligence oversight in response to the PRISM revelations.[71] A couple of weeks later, his relaxed attitude was shown to be misjudged. A sensational *Guardian* story revealed how Gordon Brown had authorised GCHQ to bug foreign leaders at two G20 meetings in London back in 2009. The timing of this story unsettled his successor, for Cameron was about to host a G8 summit in Northern Ireland. It was a prestigious event, with the British prime minister cast as international statesman. The likes of Vladimir Putin, Barack Obama and Angela Merkel would all be present. Like Anthony Eden at the height of the Cold War, Cameron did not want his moment in the spotlight to be marred by intelligence controversies, but Snowden's revelations raised an obvious question: what had the prime minister authorised GCHQ to do against his professed friends with whom he was now sharing a podium? The media loved the sense of personal animosity, and every newspaper carried a photograph of an anxious Merkel talking on her ever-present mobile phone.[72]

So began a bitter struggle between the prime minister and the *Guardian*. Although they were both the product of private schooling and Oxbridge,

Cameron had never enjoyed a particularly warm relationship with the newspaper's left-wing editor, Alan Rusbridger. Unlike Cameron's personal friendships with, and attempts to cosy up to, other press leaders, he and Rusbridger had spent very little time together.[73] From the summer of 2013, however, the relationship became increasingly hostile. Against the backdrop of a recent inquiry into phone hacking by the tabloid press, the struggle climaxed with Cameron ordering the destruction of *Guardian* computer hard drives containing much of Snowden's material.

Air Vice Marshal Andrew Vallance was the secretary of the DA-Notice Committee – the successor of the D-Notice, making Vallance the modern-day Sammy Lohan and broker of gentlemen's agreements. He phoned the *Guardian* to politely complain about not having been consulted over the G20 story. Around the same time, with Cameron playing world leader in Northern Ireland, his press officer, Craig Oliver, also found a quiet moment to call Rusbridger. With national security adviser Kim Darroch at his side, Oliver warned that the story risked causing 'inadvertent damage' to national security, and ominously added that certain unnamed government officials wanted to throw the editor in jail. After the G8 guests had left, Oliver and Darroch fully briefed the prime minister on Snowden. They left him, according to Oliver, 'concerned'.[74]

Cameron now took action, and despatched Jeremy Heywood, the cabinet secretary, to visit the *Guardian*. Britain's most senior civil servant arrived at the newspaper's offices at 8.30 a.m. on 21 June. Visibly irritated, he reiterated that the prime minister was 'deeply concerned' about the Snowden material, warned about dangers to national security, and argued that further revelations would endanger MI5 agents, help paedophiles, and make the *Guardian* a target for foreign espionage. 'We can't,' he continued, 'have a drip drip drip of this material into the public domain.' The *Guardian* had succeeded in provoking debate, and should now stop. If this was not clear enough, Heywood then raised the threat of legal action.[75]

The visit did not work, and Heywood reappeared at the *Guardian*'s offices on 12 July. With Craig Oliver at his side, he demanded that the paper now hand back the GCHQ files. They were, after all, stolen government property. Rusbridger refused. Three days later, Oliver texted the editor: 'You've had your fun. Now it's time to hand the files back.' Cameron had initially been slow to react to the story, but things were heating up. Shortly afterwards, two men from GCHQ – nicknamed 'the hobbits' by the newspaper's journalists – arrived to discuss destruction of the hard drives. On 20 July, they returned with a degausser to destroy magnetic fields, and headed down to a stuffy, windowless basement deep beneath the *Guardian*'s offices. The hobbits watched as the paper's staff took drills and angle-grinders to the hardware. Sparks flew.[76]

The whole event was something of a charade – at best a symbolic protest. But it was not without precedent. In 1983, with similar self-conscious theatricality, Margaret Thatcher had sent 'men in masks' into the offices of the publisher The Bodley Head to confiscate a rogue memoir by a GCHQ operative, Jock Kane.[77] She had also despatched Robert Armstrong to Australia in an attempt to draw a very public line in the sand against Peter Wright in 1986 – with disastrous results. Cameron found Heywood to be similarly ineffective against the *Guardian*. He surely knew that the files were held both electronically and at other locations around the world. Smashing the paper's computer hard drives made no difference at all to the control of information. Cameron felt powerless, since his legal advisers told him that any attempt to prosecute would be defeated by the likelihood that a jury would refuse to convict. But on some level, perhaps, the futile gesture made the prime minister feel better.

President Obama, bound by the First Amendment guaranteeing free speech, could not act against the American press, and distanced himself from Cameron's confrontation with journalists. Instead, he focused his fire on the whistleblowers themselves, prosecuting more leakers than all previous American presidents combined. As for Cameron, various European Union organisations and the UN's independent expert on freedom of expression condemned his draconian response. In February 2014, press freedom groups would write to Cameron urging him to distance himself from the campaign against the *Guardian*. As one *Guardian* journalist put it, Cameron did not want a debate; instead he opted to shoot the messenger.[78]

In August 2013, police detained Greenwald's partner, David Miranda, at Heathrow under terrorism laws. Holding him for nine hours, they seized his mobile phone, laptop and DVDs. Embarrassingly for Cameron, a White House press secretary asserted that the 'British government', rather than specific security authorities, had decided to detain Miranda. Downing Street denied any political involvement in the decision but acknowledged that Cameron had received advance warning of it, and had been 'kept abreast of the operation'. He therefore had ample chance to offer guidance or to intervene. Failure to do so effectively amounted to the prime minister's tacit approval. Moreover, Cameron's personal involvement in the destruction of the *Guardian* hard drives does raise questions about political motivation behind Miranda's arrest, and a desire to intimidate a national newspaper.[79] Overall, the prime minister was roundly frustrated by his inability to control the flow of information.

On 16 October 2013, Cameron launched a stinging public criticism of the *Guardian* in the House of Commons. At a volatile prime minister's questions, he argued that 'what has happened has damaged national security'. As he spoke, it became apparent that smashing the newspaper's computers was not merely about making Cameron feel better. He cleverly spun it to represent an admission of guilt by the paper. 'In many ways,' he spuriously claimed, 'the *Guardian* themselves admitted that when they agreed, when asked politely, by my national security adviser and cabinet secretary, to destroy the files.' He insisted that this was confirmed by the fact that the paper 'went ahead and destroyed those files'. 'So,' he dubiously concluded, 'they know that what they are dealing with is dangerous for security.'[80] This was a sleight of hand. Rusbridger agreed to destroy the hard drives because he knew full well that other copies of the Snowden material existed outside the *Guardian* basement. Changing tone, Cameron grew threatening. 'I do not want to have to use injunctions, D notices, or other, tougher measures'; however, he added, 'If they do not demonstrate some social responsibility, it will be very difficult for the Government to stand back and not to act.'[81]

Cameron's speech was incompetent. It displayed ignorance over how the Defence Advisory system operates. It is some twenty years since 'D-Notices' were replaced by Defence Advisory Notices, or 'DA-Notices'. Moreover, as Rusbridger pointed out, the prime minister had 'talked about threatening people with DA-Notices. That is not how it works.'[82] It is a voluntary and advisory system. Even if Cameron did secure a DA-Notice, it would have had no legal standing. Rusbridger remained free to accept or reject Vallance's – and ultimately Cameron's – concerns. What Cameron was trying to cover up was that he had considered the possibility of prosecution under the Official Secrets Act, but had funked the option of trying to jail the editor of a leading newspaper. Rusbridger had second-guessed Cameron's thinking, and had realised he was effectively bulletproof.[83]

In fact, Rusbridger *had* spoken at length with Vallance – he had allowed him to visit the *Guardian* and talk to reporters on a number of occasions. According to Rusbridger, Vallance was 'quite explicit that nothing we had seen contravened national security in terms of risking life'. Vallance acknowledged that much of the Snowden material was 'politically embarrassing', but it did not risk national security in the way that Cameron alleged. Rusbridger felt that Cameron was deliberately trying to intimidate the *Guardian*.[84] Vallance recognised that much of the damage had already been done by both the *Guardian* and the American media. The cat was now largely out of the bag.

In reality, the biggest security issues were twofold. First, the general impact of Snowden's revelations on the communications practices of both transnational criminals and terrorists. In the short term, they stayed away from their electronic devices; in the long term they sought better encryption. Second, countries as diverse as Kyrgyzstan and Brazil now realised the new opportunities that electronic surveillance technology offered for spying on their citizens, and began queuing up to buy monitoring equipment from enterprising software firms. This was not perhaps Snowden's original intention.[85]

Cameron also failed to appreciate the complexity of the problem. As the NSA and GCHQ had shifted their focus from states to problematic people, and spying now depended upon supermarket loyalty cards as much as secret services, it was no longer possible to have a serious public debate about civil liberties without giving away some information about sources and methods that could be useful to terrorists. Snowden was therefore, at one and the same time, hero and villain. Cameron and his foreign secretary William Hague were wrong in their assertions that GCHQ had done nothing unlawful. After complex inquiries that took over a year, the Interception of Communications Tribunal declared that the GCHQ–NSA surveillance regime had indeed been illegal.[86]

Unlike Harold Wilson and the D-Notice affair in 1967, the rest of the press did not rally around the targeted newspaper. This was in part simple journalistic envy. The *Guardian* itself had become the story, and was, they felt, getting too much media coverage. Moreover, it was the *Guardian* that had exposed the hacking scandal which led to the trial and imprisonment of a number of tabloid journalists, the closure of the *News of the World*, and the imposition of new guidelines on the press. Other editors toed the government line, and received copious backstairs briefings. In addition, the relationship between the government, the secret services and some of the expert media commentators had grown quite cosy. Accordingly, much of the press broadly followed the government's request not to follow up *Guardian* reports, and in particular not to draw out sensitive details that had been overlooked.[87] Specialist media outlets and foreign journalists continued to mine the Snowden material, however, gradually exposing, for example, GCHQ's cable-tapping station at Masirah Island off the coast of Oman.[88]

Belatedly, Cameron received private advice from friendly sections of the press, and as a result he reversed his approach and tried to downplay Snowden's impact. His language took a dismissive turn as he accused the *Guardian* of 'endlessly dallying' in the issue. He continued, 'I think that the public reaction, as I judge it, has not been one of shock-horror; it has been much more along the lines of "The intelligence agencies carry out intelligence work. Good."' He was right when he observed, 'I don't think Snowden's had an enormous public impact.' In Britain, the revelations had not ignited mass public debate, as they had in America and Germany. Cameron continued this matter-of-fact approach in front of Parliament's National Security Strategy Committee by describing his tastes in TV viewing: 'I love watching crime dramas on television, as I should probably stop telling people. There is hardly a crime drama where the crime is solved without using the data from a mobile communications device. That is not about the content.'[89]

Cameron's throwaway remark about television flagged up a crucial issue. Former GCHQ officials insisted that mass access to personal data was not the same as mass surveillance. In any case, much of the security agencies' interest was in geographical data, call patterns and social networks – not call content. A great deal of this work was conducted anonymously by computers, and therefore no spies were watching all of Britain's citizens. By contrast, what Snowden and the *Guardian* found most frightening was the artificial intelligence aspect of the story, with its overtones of the *Terminator* films. What actually constituted intrusive surveillance was now up for debate – and was very much in the eye of the beholder.

By the summer of 2014, Cameron had finally realised GCHQ's main failing. For years it had simply refused to explain itself. While MI5 and MI6 had recently opted to open their archives to independent historians, GCHQ refused to go down this path. Even its American equivalent, the NSA, had released a four-volume history. GCHQ's press office was a mess, with one of the press officers, Alfred Bacchus, trying to sue it for racial discrimination.[90] Former directors of GCHQ like David Omand had joined the debate and made important contributions, but GCHQ itself was conspicuous by its absence from the public discourse.

Cameron now stepped in, and made a dramatic gesture. As the new director of GCHQ he appointed Robert Hannigan, who had never previously worked in an intelligence agency. Hannigan had begun his career in a public relations firm, before joining the press team at the Northern Ireland Office. Promoted rapidly after his boss left to join Alastair Campbell's media unit at Downing Street, his main expertise was in communications. It was rare for someone who had never served in one of the three intelligence agencies to be appointed to such a position, and it signalled Cameron's determination for change. Not entirely trusting the agencies to handle their own publicity, he also created a new press section within the central intelligence machinery in Downing Street to begin the fightback against what he saw as a group of determinedly anti-intelligence journalists.[91] He asserted that, as prime minister, 'I am the minister for the security services ... I feel I have a responsibility to stand up for them publicly because they cannot be thanked as other emergency services are. I need to try to explain what they do and I have done some of that.'[92]

When the Snowden story broke in June 2013, David Cameron was about to host the G8 summit at the Lough Erne Resort, a five-star hotel and golf resort in County Fermanagh, Northern Ireland, and had bigger things on his mind than the exposure of GCHQ's surveillance techniques. The conflict in Syria, the latest iteration of the Arab Spring, was becoming increasingly protracted, and the JIC gloomily predicted 'a long-running civil war', followed by the slow emergence of a fractious coalition. Foreign Secretary William Hague thought that the 'only hope' of resolving the situation was 'a defection of Alawite generals and an assassination'.[93] Cameron also wanted President Assad's regime to fall quickly. As with Gaddafi in Libya, Assad's forces had launched a brutal crackdown on the rebels, creating a humanitarian disaster in the process. Unlike Gaddafi, Syria still had an active chemical warfare capability, which might fall into unsafe hands if his regime collapsed. To complicate matters further, the rebel groups were fractured, disorganised, and included extremist elements affiliated to al-Qaeda – and secretly supported by Turkey and Saudi Arabia, two of the West's key regional allies.[94]

Cameron had already met Russia's President Putin at Downing Street to discuss the Syrian quagmire. After a 'difficult' private meeting, Putin publicly lectured Cameron at the subsequent press conference: 'One does not really need to support the people who not only kill their enemies, but open up their bodies, eat their intestines in front of the public and cameras. Are these the people you want to support?' He added that this was rather out of step with the 'humanitarian values that have been preached in

Europe for hundreds of years'. By contrast, Cameron was keen to intervene in Syria. President Obama had deliberately allowed the British and the French to lead the operations in Libya, and Cameron felt buoyed by their success. Since entering Downing Street in 2010, he had warmed to the prime minister's international role, and indeed to the possibilities of quietly shaping events using special forces. Within the NSC, he had already debated the pros and cons of training the Syrian rebels. He did, however, reject an ambitious military plan to create a 'Syrian army in exile', leaving David Richards, chief of the Defence Staff, frustrated.[95] Richards later vented: 'If they'd had the balls, they would have gone through with it … if they'd done what I argued, they wouldn't be where they are with ISIS.'[96] Nonetheless, Cameron still wanted to do something, and broached the issue again at the G8. But over a working dinner of beef followed by apple crumble, he found his fellow leaders less than willing to act.[97]

Seeing the intelligence agencies as a potential silver bullet, Cameron initially turned to GCHQ to 'influence the outcome in Syria' through online covert action. Alongside mass collection, signals intelligence actors were developing a remarkable range of tools to influence the real world, in effect the ability to infiltrate the computers of opponents and carry out disruption. Unfortunately for Cameron, this achieved little 'beyond messaging and limited online effects operations'; not least, according to the American NSA, because of GCHQ's 'limited resources', which hampered Britain's ability 'to contribute significantly' to the overall Syria sigint effort. The prime minister needed larger-scale military, rather than intelligence, action.[98]

Two months later, Cameron sensed a renewed opportunity when Assad crossed one of President Obama's 'red lines' set down the previous year. On the morning of 21 August, an indiscriminate chemical attack killed scores of civilians – perhaps over a thousand – in a suburb of eastern Damascus called Ghoutta. Cameron pointed the finger at Assad, citing credible evidence from the JIC. Highlighting the messiness of the conflict, he also worried about chemical weapons falling into the hands of al-Qaeda and other extremist groups. 'This is the picture', he said, 'described to me by the Joint Intelligence Committee, and I always choose my words on this subject very carefully because of the issues that there have been in the past.'[99]

He pressed for immediate action together with the Americans. Both he and Obama wanted air strikes and a no-fly zone. Cameron knew that this would mostly be targeted against WMD, but it could also be quietly used to tip the balance of power towards the rebels. Richards worked on this with John Sawers, but disliked Cameron's preference for an American-led multinational bombing campaign. Looking for something decisive but more controllable, Richards and Sawers considered a plan to arm and train a rebel force of 100,000, using clandestine assets with help from the Israelis and Americans. This would allow the West more traction over which specific opposition groups took power after Assad fell. In fact this was a larger-scale version of the secret operation in Libya in 2011, when MI6 and the SAS provided training to rebel groups and called in close air support as they marched on Tripoli, protected by a Western no-fly zone. MI6 desperately wanted to boost the moderates before the opposition became dominated by hard-line Islamists.[100]

Both Richards and Sawers, however, were less than optimistic about yet another adventure in the Middle East. They feared that the Cameron option might eventually mean British boots on the ground. The suave demeanour and good looks of Sawers often prompted the media to compare him to James Bond, but in contrast to the fictional character's recklessness, the MI6 chief counselled Cameron to proceed with caution.[101] But after the August chemical attack and an intelligence briefing from the new JIC chair, Jon Day, Cameron persuaded the NSC that action had to be taken. Obama too was pressing for air strikes to be launched within days. Cameron knew he had to carry the public and Parliament with him against the background of a decade of perceived foreign misadventure in Iraq.

The prime minister now faced what some of his intelligence officials called 'a Tony Blair situation'. Cameron was deeply conscious of the precedents as he sought to intervene in a Middle Eastern country, deploying intelligence material as evidence to persuade MPs of the existence of weapons of mass destruction. It was a risky manoeuvre, since whatever the objective nature of the evidence, the determining factor was the shadow of Iraq and the visceral sentiment this generated in the House of Commons. Cameron was anxious to learn from Blair's mistakes. He believed that by approaching the problem differently, with dispassionate documents and detachment, he could persuade his audience. Yet, in his heart he knew that a war-weary population would be suspicious of any talk of 'intelligence assessments'.

Cameron recalled MPs from their summer holidays for a crucial vote on the principle of military intervention. Labour leader Ed Miliband demanded that 'the evidence has to be clear'.[102] Like Tony Blair, the prime minister placed sanitised intelligence material before the House of

Commons. MPs clamoured for as much information as possible upon which to base their decision.[103] Cameron acknowledged, 'We must recognise the scepticism and concerns that many people in the country will have after Iraq.'[104] He explained that the JIC thought it was 'highly likely' that the Syrian regime was responsible for the chemical weapons attack on its own citizens.[105] At first glance, the debate smacked of Groundhog Day: another war, another dossier. Cameron, though, had learned from his ill-fated predecessor. Jon Day too had thought long and hard over how to handle the intelligence this time around.[106] They made sure that the document was not introduced by a prime ministerial foreword full of hyperbole; instead, Day wrote a simple covering letter, as an indication that the intelligence was issued by the JIC, rather than with prime ministerial authority.[107] Cameron emphasised this early on in the Commons debate: 'We have the key *independent* judgements of the Joint Intelligence Committee.'[108]

But Cameron failed to convince the House. There were few secrets to see, since the JIC material amounted to a brief two-page analysis, no reports were declassified, and no raw material was released. Instead, the prime minister urged his audience to look elsewhere, saying, 'There is an enormous amount of open-source reporting, including videos that we can all see.'[109] He conceded that all this involved a degree of political judgement in a world where 'in the end there is no 100% certainty about who is responsible'.[110] But when asked about Assad's motives he had no answer, simply responding that 'If my hon. friend reads the JIC conclusions, he will see that this is where it finds the greatest difficulty – ascribing motives', before again pointing to the need to 'make a judgement'.[111] Intelligence, he went on to argue, 'is part of this picture, but let us not pretend that there is one smoking piece of intelligence that can solve the whole problem. This is a judgement issue; hon. Members will have to make a judgement.'[112] He explicitly stated that he did not want to raise the status of individual pieces of intelligence 'into some sort of quasi-religious cult', as had happened with Iraq.[113]

But intelligence is all about bits and pieces. Behind the scenes, MI6 was concerned about the information it had on Syria. The bits did not fit together well. MI6 knew that Turkey's new leader, Recep Erdoğan, was secretly supporting the al-Nusra Front, a jihadist group within the opposition. Some in MI6 suspected that rebel groups were trying to provoke Obama into greater intervention by simulating a government sarin attack inside Syria. They reasoned that, in terms of motivation, it made sense for the opposition to perpetrate this deception. It was hard to explain why Assad would use chemical weapons, given that Obama's 'red line threat' was public, and after all, Assad's military position was better now than it had been a year before. Moreover, in early May 2013, when a dozen members of the al-Nusra Front were rounded up, local police told the press that they had found a quantity of sarin – although Turkish government officials later denied this.[114] Even before the parliamentary vote, Ban Ki-moon, the UN secretary general, had insisted that his weapons inspectors had not yet completed their evidence-gathering.[115]

The truth is that we will never have a definitive judgement on the perpetrator of the dreadful attack on Ghoutta. UN inspectors were allowed to visit the sites of the attack, but were cautious: 'the locations have been well travelled by other individuals prior to the arrival of the Mission'. Even while the inspectors were present, 'individuals arrived carrying other suspected munitions indicating that such potential evidence is being moved and possibly manipulated'. Unlike those of Britain and the United States, their conclusions were limited to the nature of the attack, and they were clear that the authors remained hard to identify.[116]

Like Blair, Cameron also misled the public through oversimplification. He gave no indication of the fervent debate over culpability that was going on behind the scenes. Away from Westminster, the prime minister moved well beyond the JIC line by stating that Assad was definitely responsible – in July, for example, he publicly referred to 'appalling behaviour from this dreadful regime using chemical weapons'.[117] By August, Cameron and Obama were both freely asserting that Assad was to blame.[118] Typically, the prime minister stated unequivocally: 'What we've seen in Syria are appalling scenes of death and suffering because of the use of chemical weapons by the Assad regime.'[119] In reality, over half of JIC assertions had some sort of qualifying statement attached, as did the Hansard briefings.[120]

Cameron lost the vote in the House of Commons. Rightly, he conceded that: 'There is never one piece, or several pieces of intelligence, that can give you absolute certainty.'[121] But in the wake of Iraq, most MPs wanted near-certainty, and sought a threshold that was impossible to meet. More than thirty Conservatives rebelled, citing too many uncertainties around intelligence or doubts about the strategic case for war.[122] In a humiliating blow to the prime minister's authority, the House rejected Cameron's plea for military intervention in principle. The heavy shadow of Blair will hang over Westminster for years to come, and future prime ministers will always struggle when drumming up support for war.[123]

Much more was going on behind the scenes than Downing Street was prepared to admit, and eventually WMD intelligence had proved to be as perplexing for Cameron as it had for Blair. All the time MI6 was quietly working with Porton Down, the secret defence laboratory in Wiltshire which for more than a century had been Britain's main chemical and biological weapons centre. British intelligence had obtained a small example of the sarin used in the attack on Ghoutta, and to its surprise the gas did not look like the materials kept by the Syrian army's chemical weapons unit, samples of which had been passed to MI6 by a Syrian officer (although these too could have been a deception). The unwelcome news was relayed to the White House, and was one of the factors that paused Obama's own attack.[124]

News was beginning to leak out. On 6 September 2013, a respected group of retired US intelligence officers claimed that privately, American intelligence community officials disagreed with the White House assessment. CIA analyst Ray McGovern, who had chaired the National Intelligence Estimates Board and who had served in the community for twenty-seven years, said that his colleagues were telling him 'categorically' that, contrary to the claims of the White House: 'The most reliable intelligence shows that Bashar al-Assad was NOT responsible for the chemical incident that killed and injured Syrian civilians on August 21, and that British intelligence officials also know this.'[125]

In reality, no one really knew what to believe. Russian intelligence also claimed to have secured samples of the chemical weapons used at Ghoutta, and shared them with the British. But MI6 feared a Russian deception, since it was in Putin's interest to support Assad and blame the rebels. Some of the samples indicated an amateur cocktail of various toxic agents, which would point to the rebels. But the types of weapons used to deliver the gas pointed to the Syrian army. Each analyst had a different appreciation and a different theory. No one could be sure of the true story, but it was certainly more complex than the narrative offered in Jon Day's two-page letter to Cameron.[126]

Cameron had also failed to admit that the principle of intervention would lead to a proposed strike which was part of a bigger plan to smash the Syrian government. America was to lead with a 'shock and awe' campaign led by a fleet of B-52s armed with 2,000-pound bombs intended to penetrate Assad's safest command bunker. French air power was also to be involved. Even as Parliament rejected Cameron's proposals, the RAF was arming Typhoon fighter jets in Cyprus, while the Royal Navy had despatched a submarine with Cruise missiles. But by early September, some senior CIA officials feared that they were being set up by the rebel opposition. When the air attack was cancelled, Obama told Congress it was because of a fear that it might increase instability in the region. In fact it reflected a ferocious and unresolved debate over the Ghoutta attack, made worse by the knowledge that the Western intelligence community had called it wrong a decade before.

By late 2013, MI6 had got its way. The West was moving towards increasing supplies to selected groups amongst the rebel opposition. This was difficult, since the CIA, Mossad, Turkey's fearsome MIT and the security agencies of Saudi Arabia and Qatar were all assisting different rebel factions in Syria, working together in a fractious pattern of competitive cooperation. MI6's key role was to organise a major consignment of small arms from Libya. American diplomatic and CIA facilities in Libya had been attacked the previous year, so the British role was yet more important. On 13 September 2013, with British and American air strikes off, Obama proudly announced that the first CIA-trained rebel unit was about to join fighting against the Assad regime – but this was not by any means the full story.[127] As for David Cameron, his position on the global stage had been 'fatally undermined'.[128]

Turmoil in the Middle East continued. The rise of the so-called Islamic State, or ISIS, now dominated security discussions in both the media and Number 10. Having emerged from a union of al-Qaeda in Iraq and various Islamist fighters in Syria, ISIS now controlled territory spanning both countries, and was known for its spectacular barbarity, conducting multiple beheadings alongside other, even more brutal, executions, gruesome videos of which it then broadcast for propaganda purposes. In September 2014, one of these videos dramatically caught the attention of British observers, as it featured a knife-wielding executioner with a British accent. The press dubbed him 'Jihadi John'.

After beheading a British hostage, Jihadi John delivered a message for the prime minister: 'This British man has to pay the price for your promise Cameron to arm the Peshmerga against the Islamic State,' before warning, 'Playing the role of the obedient lapdog Cameron will only drag you and your people into another bloody and unwinnable war.'[129] Weeks later, another video emerged of Jihadi John beheading a further British hostage.

Cameron summoned his intelligence chiefs to his country residence, Chequers, and told them to locate Jihadi John – who had since been unmasked as Mohammed Emwazi, born in Kuwait but who had lived in

London for most of his life – so he could send in the SAS to capture or kill him.[130] He paid close attention to MI5's reporting on domestic plots, especially those emanating from British Muslims returning from Syria. He constantly pressed for more information, asked where the agencies had gaps in their capabilities, and pressed to give them more powers, including access to encrypted communications often found in social media apps such as WhatsApp. Cameron now took an 'obsessive interest' in intelligence. Like Thatcher before him, he paid extra attention to any classified papers in his prime minister's box.[131] After the terrorist attack on the satirical magazine *Charlie Hebdo*'s offices in Paris in January 2015, he agreed for the heads of MI5 and MI6 to brief both him and Angela Merkel (who was in London on a visit) together. He knew how easily a similar attack could happen in Britain.[132]

Cameron's close interest in the secret world continued to grow after his re-election as prime minister in May 2015. He sanctioned a new 'proactive' special forces approach to ISIS, apparently giving the SAS 'carte blanche' to launch raids inside Syria and Iraq, and made it clear that Britain had a 'kill list', approved by the NSC.[133] These individuals, including some British citizens, among them the notorious Jihadi John, would be targeted 'as a last resort' by armed drones guided by intelligence – in November 2015 it was reported that Jihadi John had been killed by such a drone strike.[134] In the run-up to the 2015 autumn defence review, the prime minister again stressed the need to increase spending on special forces, and on intelligence more broadly, as a key means of countering terrorism.[135] Despite his initial inexperience, five years of fast-paced events had taught David Cameron a great deal about the power of intelligence.

Conclusion:
Prime Ministers and the Future
of Intelligence

Are we going to allow a means of communications
which it simply isn't possible to read? My answer to
that question is: 'No we must not.'
DAVID CAMERON[1]

Winston Churchill and Clement Attlee were an unlikely double act. Yet,
together, they revolutionised the relationship between intelligence and
Number 10, creating a new approach to British statecraft. Although some
of their successors may have proved more adept users than others, intelligence has moved from the shadows to centre stage, and has become something no current or future prime minister is able to ignore. David Cameron
has accelerated this by creating the National Security Council. His successors will rely on intelligence and other forms of clandestine activity even
more, because a globalised world is a machine for springing constant
surprises upon decision-makers. Moreover, as each prime minister enters
the latter part of his or her term of office, confidence grows and the itch
for secret intervention increases. Accordingly, the relationship between
prime ministers and the secret services will become more important, more
complex – and more challenging.[2]

'Intelligence is a ceaseless underground struggle to protect British interests,' observed Percy Cradock, the doyen of JIC chairs.[3] Prime ministers
have long used intelligence to sustain Britain's global role. As Cradock also
observed, Britain's steady decline over decades has 'increased pretence and
posturing'. Successive governments have attempted to 'make up for declining material assets by manipulating the symbols of power, nuclear status,
the special relationship, diplomatic finesse, the outer forms rather than the
substance'.[4] There is no doubt that intelligence has played its part in this,
and constitutes a form of power akin to economic or military might.[5] It is

'a valuable form of capital in a complex and competitive world', allowing prime ministers to uphold the top-table charade.[6] Remarkably, since the 1980s, successive British leaders have arrested the notions of constant British decline. London is emblematic of this resurgence, perhaps the pre-eminent world capital, with more billionaires than any other metropolis. Part of the reason for that peculiar reversal of British fortune is the fact that its spying agencies are the envy of the world – fearsome to Britain's many enemies, but not much feared by its own citizens. Efforts to sustain a global role into the future will require more of this fancy footwork; not least because the rising powers of Brazil, Russia, India and China are also avid intelligence enthusiasts, and boast their own clandestine cultures.[7]

Intelligence is also about personal survival. In the public mind, assassination attempts against prime ministers are associated with terrorist organisations, like the triple mortar attack on John Major in 1991. But privately, even as that attack took place, Britain was expelling members of the Iraqi secret service whom it thought might perpetrate similar attacks or worse. No prime minister has faced more assassination attempts than Winston Churchill, but since the war the divide between extremism, terrorism and state-sponsored attacks has become ever more blurred. For some countries, liquidating one's enemies is simply part of everyday politics. Harold Macmillan recorded in his diary the uncontrollable mirth of Khrushchev and Bulganin when someone sat in the chair of Beria, the KGB chief whom they had ordered to be shot only a few weeks earlier. They 'could not contain themselves', and 'shook with amusement'. Macmillan recorded: 'a somewhat grim sense of humour'.[8] Tony Blair and then Gordon Brown had the unnerving experience of meeting Russian President Vladimir Putin while dealing with the aftermath of the poisoning in London of Alexander Litvinenko. No occupant of Number 10 wants to be seen as soft on terrorism, but some of the foreign secret services that prime ministers have had to confront make the terrorists look almost mild by comparison.

At least during the Cold War, a prime minister knew who the spies were: there were three iconic organisations, MI5, MI6 and GCHQ. Once in power, they learned the importance of smaller, specialist organisations like the Information Research Department and the SAS. The names of the KGB and the CIA appeared on the prime minister's desk with surprising frequency, while Mossad, BOSS and the French DGSE lurked just offstage, and had mostly walk-on parts in the spy war drama. The British intelligence and security agencies are still there – but they no longer own all of intelligence. The new spies are every organisation that collects data on people: the airlines, the banks, the supermarkets and the ISP providers. Every mobile phone is a mini Bletchley Park. After any terrorist attack, the material collected by an army of bystanders on their iPhones and androids forms some of the best intelligence sources: shortly after the Boston Marathon bombing in 2013 people began to share photos of possible suspects taken on their phones, and to put names to faces. Soon there was a mob outside the house of the main suspect. Alarmingly, this citizen-led exercise in 'Spies 'R Us' got the wrong man.[9]

Advances in real-time communications have brought intelligence to the heart of Downing Street. 'Actionable' intelligence has long been a wartime staple, but developments in technology increase prime ministerial involvement. David Cameron's interest in Libya, for example, demonstrated prime ministerial appetite for operational intelligence direct from war zones, and opened the Pandora's Box of real-time special operations being directed from Number 10. Future prime ministers will not only be expected to keep abreast of 'big picture' developments, but also to digest the details of various battles from a command centre thousands of miles away, where events are mapped second by second. Even the sharpest of minds would struggle with this, not helped by the added stress of those around the table demanding decisive leadership. Winston Churchill would have loved the opportunity to meddle in operational detail, but this pressure-cooker environment has sent at least one recent prime minister into a meltdown.[10] Meanwhile, intelligence has become less passive, and MI6 is more an enforcer or a fixer, taking on more controversial roles which require approval at the highest level.[11] Prime ministers will increasingly rely on special forces, enabled by intelligence fed directly from national assets, to transgress traditional boundaries and reach deniable targets.[12] Balancing dramatic operations against dirtier targets with the demands for more transparency and an ethical foreign policy will be difficult, perhaps impossible.[13]

Intelligence in the Twitter age is a formidable challenge for a prime minister. Senior policymakers have long bemoaned excessive volumes of information, and now labour long into the night to defend premiers from the digital onslaught. Bombarded with fresh information every hour, on an increasing range of national security issues – which now embrace not only risk but even the public fear of risk – prime ministers might miss a key detail, or simply be behind the curve on a new idea.[14] The digital age has made matters worse. Downing Street is now deluged with material, and despite the employment of eager graduates as 'horizon scanners' who compete with secret intelligence, it is hard to keep up.[15] Intelligence will increasingly include overt material, protected personal information taken from flight records and immigration databases, and ever more data gleaned from mass surveillance.[16] Private companies will hold more personal information than the government, leaving Google, Tesco or HSBC as quasi-intelligence actors. As the privatised age of 'knowledge-intensive security' creates ever bigger haystacks, future prime ministers will have to rely even more on assessed all-source intelligence briefings.[17] They will be presented with almost perfect knowledge of the world in real time. Will they be able to match this with appropriate responses? Will they resist the tendency, like Neville Chamberlain and Tony Blair, to use it as a menu for choice, picking out a few tasty morsels that suit their particular predilections and prejudices?

The world of 'big data' is the biggest challenge for future prime ministers. Increasing surveillance in Britain is not being driven by spies, but by our love of gadgets. By 2025, everything we buy in a shop that costs more than £10 will likely have an IP address and will contain a small computer. Our delightful new purchases will gather data all around us 24/7, and will be connected to the web, creating 'the internet of things'. In the near future, one of the other 'things' that will be connected to the internet will be us, creating 'the internet of people', because tele-health monitoring will be widespread in developed countries. Even now there are a million cattle in Europe that contain a SIM card, and in ten years' time many people will have joined the herd. We will surrender much of our privacy willingly, because the health benefits alone from such connectivity are simply enormous.[18]

Getting this right is a huge challenge for Downing Street. If the ownership of individual data is well-managed, relatively flat and transparent, the benefits will be considerable, as will be the political rewards for our leaders. If structures are opaque and hierarchical, governed by ill-thought-out legislation emanating from faceless figures in the Home Office, it will be a disaster. Clement Attlee understood the importance of the delicate balance between security and liberty, and for that reason saw the director-general of MI5 more often than any prime minister before or since, perhaps with the exception of David Cameron. But back in 1950, security was mostly about files and flat-footed spies treading the pavement. Alas, few people in government now understand the digital world and the nature of the trade-offs between security, privacy, convenience and luxury. Government has tried to protect the prime minister by appointing what some on the inside call a 'minister for cyber-disasters' based in the Cabinet Office, knowing that the government's record with large IT projects is appalling, ranging from the failed £14 billion NHS database to the notorious Cabinet Office 'Scope 2' system, that was supposed to distribute intelligence securely around Whitehall. Britain's record in protecting the private information of citizens is even worse. Because central government knows so little, the tendency has been to outsource these issues, but when everything goes wrong, the awkward questions will nevertheless land on the desk of the prime minister.[19]

For premiers, the erosion of privacy is a two-way street. 'Big data' means not only the end of privacy for ordinary individuals, it might also mean the end of secrecy for the powerful. In the late twentieth century, leakers needed twenty-four-hour access to a photocopier, and some big shopping bags, to steal secrets from their department. In a future world in which whistleblowers can leak a million documents with a single pen-drive, it will be difficult for corporations to hide their tax-avoidance arrangements, or to behave unethically. It will also be harder for governments to build secret prisons or to commit torture. In Whitehall and Washington, civil servants are panicking as their empire of secrecy visibly shrinks in size. Governments, corporations, citizens and spies may all find themselves living in a transparent society, and they will find it a strange place.[20]

Regulation by revelations is already here. Global civil society and human rights campaigners have transformed the accountability and transparency of intelligence since 9/11. As globally connected whistleblowers and intrepid investigative journalists, often working in cooperation with judges and EU inquiries, continue to shine a bright light into the darkest corners of the secret state, future prime ministers will have to publicly discuss their intelligence services. They will face greater public scrutiny, and as intelligence actors embark on ever more controversial operations, will have difficult questions to answer. One of the hard lessons Downing Street had to learn during the Blair era was that nothing is non-disclosable. The website of the Hutton Inquiry, investigating the death of Dr David Kelly, carried emails written by the Cabinet Office only months before that contained profanities. Future prime ministers must learn the delicate skills of conducting secret business with the ever-present knowledge that at any moment it may be made non-secret. Each incumbent of Downing Street will have to ask, 'Can I look a camera in the eye and justify the covert action that I am now signing off? Or will this bring my government down?' Secrecy has evaporated for the White House, replaced by mere delayed disclosure. The same phenomenon is heading for Westminster.[21]

Prime ministers know that sometimes circumstances demand executive action. In February 2006, Chris Mullin, a Labour MP with an impeccable reputation for campaigning on behalf of victims of injustice, was on a tour of northern Uganda to find out about the long and bitter war against the Lord's Resistance Army led by Joseph Kony. This guerrilla group operated like a plague of locusts, kidnapping children and turning them into soldiers. Although it was a beautiful region, with fine views of the River Nile and Lake Kyoga, everywhere were villages abandoned to the 'Great Terror'. Mullin's main impression was of exhaustion and quiet desperation. Most of the inhabitants, even the local bishop, spoke in slow whispers, pausing frequently to rub their eyes. The nightmare had been going on for more than twenty years, and they felt abandoned by both their own government and the international community. 'Much talk of the need to negotiate,' Mullin noted, 'but what is there to negotiate about?' The more he listened, the more he felt that, as with Jonas Savimbi, the leader of the protracted guerrilla struggle in Angola, 'one bullet in the head of Joseph Kony is all it would take to bring this madness to an end'. But who, he asked, was 'to administer the *coup de grâce*'? If one of Britain's nicest MPs occasionally thinks such dark thoughts, how often must prime ministers have wished for a silver bullet to solve their problems?[22] In an era of delayed disclosure, doing so will be even more difficult than in the past.

In the darkest matters of secrecy, Downing Street does not control the agenda. The most alarming intelligence scandals of recent times – ranging from secret prisons to Edward Snowden – have emanated from Washington, not Whitehall or Westminster. How to deal with the vexations of the CIA and the NSA, or indeed the secret armies of the Pentagon? Historically, Britain and its closest intelligence allies have often operated at cross-purposes, especially in the Third World. The CIA has at various times offered arms, training, money, even life-saving medical assistance to an international cast of characters that includes Ho Chi Minh, Mohammed Mossadeq, Nasser, the Marxist supporter of national liberation movements Frantz Fanon, and initially even Fidel Castro. Especially during the 1980s, when the CIA was locked down by congressional inquiries, Britain offered America a handy covert action cut-out. Chris Patten, a cabinet minister under both Margaret Thatcher and John Major, reflected, 'We have access to intelligence, particularly through global eavesdropping, which would otherwise be denied us, and who knows what errands we perform in return?'[23]

Sir Crispin Tickell, an adviser to Thatcher, Major and Blair in turn, and also Britain's ambassador at the UN, notes that the CIA is an independent actor. Moreover, 'Washington is usually riven between the Agencies – the White House, State Department, CIA ...' These 'battles' make it hard for a British prime minister to track what is happening in American policy. Tickell recalls that one of his colleagues once said to him, 'The Americans were like a kind of brain-damaged giant who did not entirely understand what was going on, but eventually agreed or disagreed. Most of the time no one objected, but people did object when the brain-damaged giant started to break up the furniture.'[24]

Doubtless the CIA would respond that Britain shared some of the responsibility for 'blowback', and that during the 1990s, Osama bin Laden's main operating base was London, together with some of the most vicious North African terrorists. The debate over whose covert operations contributed most to accelerating the activities of the Taliban and al-Qaeda has kept many a veteran case officer arguing late into the night.[25] American intelligence has tried to bully some British prime ministers, and has caused red-faced embarrassment to others, most recently David Cameron. Their private response has usually been robust; few can compete with Margaret Thatcher's record for sequentially 'handbagging' Al Haig, Caspar Weinberger and Bill Casey. But in an era of increasing public exposure, British prime ministers will frequently be required to address the secret misdeeds of American operatives and their British helpers.

We now inhabit a globalised world, characterised by fragility and fear.[26] Downing Street understands this, and the 2010 Strategic Defence and Security Review identified a bewildering range of threats to Britain's well-being, ranging, in the words of one senior intelligence adviser, 'from sunspot activity to banana skins on the pavement'.[27] Gus O'Donnell, a recent cabinet secretary, once remarked that he was more worried by rainfall than by al-Qaeda. Even though we know that future threats will include pandemics, poverty and climate change, how to use intelligence to defeat them is puzzling.[28] The primacy of nation states is being challenged by messianic religions, economic oligarchs, the rise of mega-cities, and the emergence of new empires based on organised crime.[29] It is a globalised environment in which traditional intelligence bureaucracies move more clumsily than their opponents, and the expectations of intelligence may have to be revised downwards. By the time prime ministers know what they need to know, it will likely be too late.[30] As Henry Kissinger once remarked, 'I don't know what kind of intelligence I want, but I know when I get it.'[31]

As a result of globalisation, 'big data', technology and challenges to secrecy, the prime ministerial burden will surely increase. Future prime ministers will therefore need to be good consumers of intelligence. The best among them will possess three core qualities: experience, judgement and character, together with a crucial ability to build a strong relationship with intelligence leaders.

Experience is helpful, but not always possible. Post-war prime ministers who served under Churchill in his wartime government appreciated the value intelligence could play, and understood its integration into policy or strategy. Later prime ministers, such as James Callaghan, who had served in the highest cabinet positions before assuming office, were also at an advantage, and able to approach the secret world in a level-headed manner. These things, however, are often accidents of history. Tony Blair and his first cabinet, members of a party that had been in opposition for seventeen years, could field almost no one with ministerial experience. But prime ministers are getting younger: Churchill and Callaghan first entered Downing Street in their mid-sixties; Blair and Cameron both took office at the tender age of forty-three.[32]

Experience, though, can only carry a prime minister so far. The realities of the job bring unique pressures. In January 2003, the Labour MP Bruce George told Tony Blair that on issues of the use of military force, 'The buck stops with you,' adding, 'You will ultimately decide.'[33] This is equally true of intelligence, which is peculiarly intertwined with the premiership, and little can prepare someone for taking decisions which might involve authorising a deniable operation using human agents launched from a submarine on the other side of the world. Judgement and a constructive but critical attitude are everything. A good consumer is interested in intelligence, but also, like Harold Macmillan, able to remain detached and maintain a sense of perspective. During his early years in Number 10 Tony Blair demonstrated an impressive attitude, drawing on his legal training to carefully cross-examine intelligence assessments. Similarly, a good consumer does not become mesmerised or bamboozled by the secret world. Churchill was a wonderful innovator who, more than anyone else, created the modern British intelligence community; yet for all his strengths, he often allowed boyish enthusiasm to get the better of him. Above all, prime ministers must not interpret 'top secret' as meaning 'true', 'important' or even 'useful' – a trap into which Margaret Thatcher occasionally fell. Her staff sometimes inserted non-secret material into her box of specially selected intelligence highlights, simply to ensure that it got read.[34] This will increasingly be the case in the future, as intelligence blurs with an infinite world of digital information.[35]

Intelligence at the top is currently handled by David Cameron's National Security Council, perhaps the best mechanism for integrating secret material with high policy that has existed in a century. Judgement increasingly exists within this context. Cabinet ministers have to confront awkward operational decisions that relate to intelligence on a weekly basis. Should Britain share intelligence with countries like Russia or China, which have the death penalty for kidnapping, or chemical castration for sex offenders? The agonies are considerable, and are debated at the highest level, often in emotional terms.[36] In 1916, Maurice Hankey evaded the challenge of connecting the secret world with cabinet machinery for reasons that remain mysterious, leaving government without a central brain for secret matters for two decades. Churchill's energetic innovations addressed this, and Clement Attlee completed the task, leaving an orderly central intelligence machine in place by the early 1950s. Since then the addition of further key figures, including a second cabinet secretary to handle intelligence matters, signalled the growing importance of intelligence within the core executive.[37]

Orderly systems and bureaucratic routines provide leaders with a comfortable safety blanket, but in a crisis prime ministerial character comes to the fore.[38] Prime ministers gasp as their best-laid plans collapse and unravel around them. It is at such times that some of the more improbable figures perform well. Alec Douglas-Home, John Major and indeed Tony Blair were unflappable, and proved able to absorb a fantastic flow of information under pressure. Churchill and Thatcher were enthusiastic, but volatile and too close to the operational detail. Gordon Brown was perhaps the worst example, desperate to manage the smallest decision personally, yet unable to deal with the deluge of data. For Brown, convening Cobra offered a semblance of command but masked chronic indecision. After leaving Downing Street, his impressive performance in the run-up to the 2014 Scottish independence referendum privately frustrated some of those who had worked under him as prime minister. How they had longed for a similar show of character when he was actually in charge.[39]

A prime minister's character is integral to resolving four intelligence dilemmas. First, if a prime minister is too dogmatic he or she will not be open to new ideas, and will interpret intelligence accordingly; yet being too open-minded creates confusion. Prime ministers must be able to tolerate the ambiguity which is integral to all assessments: as Michael Hayden, former head of the CIA, once remarked, 'If it was a fact it would not be called intelligence.'[40] Second, they must also be comfortable with intelligence estimates that implicitly challenge their own policies and plans, some of which may have required months of development. In certain cases, such as that of Neville Chamberlain, challenging intelligence can create a sense of persecution, even martyrdom, on the part of an intelligence chief.[41] Third, if prime ministers spend too much time looking at raw data, they risk becoming their own DIY analysts. This is a growing danger in the era of the multi-level secure online database. Prime ministers are, by their nature, driven people, and often become more impulsive and controlling with the passing years – as both Thatcher and Blair demonstrated. Yet they need to have some familiarity with the raw material if they are to get a feel for intelligence work, or to demand it if they are required to launch covert action. Fourth, if a prime minister has too much information, he or she will lack the time to study it properly; yet too little intelligence undermines the decision-making process. The issue of sources will become increasingly difficult in a digital future in which Downing Street may enjoy almost theological omniscience. To resolve these dilemmas leaders need, as Clausewitz put it, 'sensitive and discriminatory judgement.'[42]

In addition to these personal characteristics, history tells us that prime ministers must have a good working relationship with their intelligence chiefs. This, perhaps, is the most important aspect of all. Trust becomes even more crucial if the prime minister lacks experience in dealing with the secret world. Without a strong relationship, the relevance and impact of the intelligence community will quickly diminish.[43] The relationship must be based on dependability, mutual respect and a degree of familiarity. Under what Peter Hennessy has called 'the Napoleonic premiership', Tony Blair was criticised for 'getting too close' to senior figures in MI6 – but this reflects a misunderstanding. One of the great strengths of the current British system is the orderly nature of political approval for secret operations, and the lack of 'rogue elephants' or independent activity by the agencies, even if it is only verbal.[44]

Conversely, many of the problems of the 1960s and 1970s were caused by undue distance and excessive secrecy within government. Stella Rimington, former director-general of MI5, eloquently describes a world in which intelligence leaders were poor communicators who avoided their political masters, while Downing Street sometimes did not want to know what was afoot. This was a recipe for paranoia and distrust.[45] Clement Attlee, who astutely regularised the British intelligence community in mid-century, adopted precisely the opposite approach, meeting Percy Sillitoe with remarkable frequency. Margaret Thatcher had an excellent relationship with her JIC chair and policy adviser, Percy Cradock, because he was perhaps even more acerbic than her. Equally, the director of the SAS, Peter de la Billière, was relished by Thatcher precisely because he spoke frankly and, in the words of one insider, admitted 'when things are fucked up'.[46]

Famously, Tony Blair's government and MI6 seemed to court each other. Although criticised for the démodé dress sense – 'dark suits and ... battered briefcases', which Alastair Campbell felt indicated a generation gap – of what they called 'the spooks', Downing Street under Blair was nevertheless fascinated by them.[47] Increasingly, it has become the trend for spy chiefs to go on the road with their leaders: as we have seen, Richard Dearlove, chief of MI6, joined Blair and Campbell on a world tour of counter-terrorist diplomacy in late 2001. The Chilcot Inquiry into the Iraq War, which has still to report at the time of writing in early 2016, has spent much time puzzling over the question of the correct distance between the prime minister and the chief of MI6. Some former officers have thought the relationship was too close, but others have said that proximity is essential in a world in which secret services provide event-shaping operations as well as information. This was a veiled reference to the bugging, blackmail and bribery that accompanied some of the fraught diplomacy around the UN during the run-up to the Iraq War in 2003. 'The pressure is very intense and the warnings are real', commented one Mexican diplomat. In a world in which international courts and UN 'rapporteurs' wait to pounce on any transgressor, it would be a brave intelligence chief who embarked on a major operation without being sure that Downing Street had given its blessing.[48]

The relationship between Number 10 and intelligence involves other, unseen, actors. For more than a century the cabinet secretary has served as the key interlocutor in a highly secret system. Rarely seen in public, he has directly shaped how prime ministers have used intelligence, and have also managed the community and its budgets. Maurice Hankey, the first incumbent, vehemently opposed any central intelligence machinery, and despite offering good personal advice to David Lloyd George, left an alarming analytical vacuum that would not be filled until the Second World War. Initially, encouraged by Attlee, successive cabinet secretaries including Edward Bridges, Norman Brook and Burke Trend developed a secretive but effective planning machine that allowed the key permanent secretaries to manage the secret world on behalf of the prime minister. Robert Armstrong, cabinet secretary under Thatcher, remembers how 'The cabinet secretary was the prime minister's principal adviser on intelligence and security matters.'[49] The most delicate task during his era was to manage the interface between secrecy and publicity, and his physical confrontation with a journalist at Heathrow airport while travelling to the ill-fated *Spycatcher* trial in Australia was symbolic of a wider failure.[50] While Andrew Turnbull, who served under Blair, saw the position as 'the pinnacle of the intelligence and security system', he was largely invisible during the trials and tribulations of WMD.[51] Perhaps this was because by then a second cabinet secretary, David Omand, had been appointed to preside over Intelligence, Security and Resilience.

Omand represented the ultimate intelligence singularity. Known as the cabinet intelligence and security adviser, the post was perhaps at its most important at the time of the 7/7 bombings in London in 2005, when Britain needed to develop an entire new counter-terrorism architecture. Omand was the incumbent, and the counter-terrorism strategy he created, known as 'CONTEST', was widely admired and copied around the world, not least by the European Union. Few individuals have the capacity to handle all these complex tasks, and what Omand did with fifty civil servants is now done by the Office of Security and Counter-Terrorism in the Home Office, with a team of several hundred. The core business, including advising the prime minister and overseeing the Single Intelligence Account, has transferred to the new national security adviser.[52] This system is now perhaps rather more dispersed than it was a decade ago under Omand. Nonetheless, whether the prime minister is dealing with the intelligence chiefs, the chair of the JIC, the cabinet secretary, the national security adviser or the burgeoning empire of security in the Home Office, the most important qualities remain trust and the ability to have a frank conversation.[53]

What can history tell us about how future prime ministers might relate to spy chiefs? Does the past offer any sort of reliable guide to an alarming future in which the very concept of 'secret intelligence' might vanish, overtaken by 'big data' owned by airlines, banks and even supermarkets? Douglas Hurd once referred to the sort of people who have written this book as 'the professors of hindsight', a cruel but largely accurate observation.[54] In retrospect, and viewing events in the rear-view mirror of the archives, it is easy to sit and offer persuasive judgements at leisure upon people who were forced to take decisions under high pressure, with imperfect knowledge. Mellow wisdom about experience, judgement and character is easy to dispense, but hard to practise on the slippery terrain of secret service. Yet, because leaders use recent history to guide their decisions, the future will always contain the past. In the world of intelligence, covert action, and even national security more generally, policymakers navigate in part by a collective memory of previous events, seeking to apply what went well and to avoid what failed. In the early twenty-first century, the shadow of the past is especially heavy in the realm of intelligence, including matters such as WMD dossiers, secret prisons and Edward Snowden.[55]

Few can approach Downing Street without feeling an all-pervasive sense of the past. In the summer of 2003, the CIA despatched one of its most distinguished officers to London. Michael Morell's task was to work with the UK's Assessments Staff, who were preparing between two and four intelligence reports a week for Tony Blair. Morell was also conscious of the weight of history, observing that Britain had developed its central intelligence apparatus over more than half a century. He praised the Joint Intelligence Committee, 'an institution in the British government since 1936', adding that it still constituted the 'door that the analysts had to pass through to get their assessments to the Prime Minister'. The JIC could approve a paper, send it back for more work, or 'kill it outright'. He clearly admired this well-oiled machine, adding enviously: 'We did not have anything like this in the United States.'[56] But as we have seen, this was not the whole story. In fact, Blair tended to develop his own relationships with the secret state, blurring assessment with policy advice and preferring personal stock-taking papers. Indeed, it is rather ironic that Morell's tenure in London, tinged with historical envy, coincided with what Lord Butler has described as an unprecedented decline in the traditional British cabinet committee system and its ability to offer objective, independent and critical advice.[57]

We are currently on the run from the informality of Tony Blair in his boxer shorts and his 'sofa government'. On entering Downing Street, both Gordon Brown and David Cameron declared that they wanted more structure, less intervention and a less presidential-style foreign policy. It is rather curious that in pursuit of this goal, they have created an American-style National Security Council with a strong whiff of the 'West Wing' about it. In reality, Britain's intelligence machinery owes much of its character to who is in charge and how they choose to use their power. Whether they display Churchill's impulsiveness or the procedure and processes of Attlee, the new system at least contains the possibility to further institutionalise the prime minister's relationship with the secret world in a measured way. However, it also opens up the possibility of more secret foreign policy driven by special forces, covert action and disruption. It will be intriguing to see where this will lead. Either way, Gus O'Donnell, cabinet secretary under Blair, Brown and Cameron, believes that the new approach is here to stay.[58] Meanwhile, for over half a century, prime ministers have realised that intelligence is something they cannot ignore. Some may embrace it more naturally than others, but all future occupants of Number 10 will wrestle with its dilemmas and its dangers from behind the Black Door.

Appendix I:
Key Officials Since 1909

Cabinet Secretary
Maurice Hankey, 1916–1938
Edward Bridges, 1938–1946
Norman Brook, 1947–1962
Burke Trend, 1963–1973
John Hunt, 1973–1979
Robert Armstrong, 1979–1987
Robin Butler, 1988–1998
Richard Wilson, 1998–2002
Andrew Turnbull, 2002–2005
Gus O'Donnell, 2005–2012
Jeremy Heywood, 2012–

Principal Private Secretary
Vaughan Nash, 1905–1911
Maurice Bonham Carter, 1911–1916
John Davies, 1916–1922
Edward Grigg, 1921–1922
Ronald Waterhouse, 1922–1928
Robert Vansittart, 1928–1930
Alan Barlow, 1933–1934
Osmund Cleverly, 1936–1939
Arthur Rucker, 1939–1940
Eric Seal, 1940–1941
John Miller Martin, 1941–1945
Leslie Rowan, 1945–1947
Laurence Helsby, 1947–1950
Denis Rickett, 1950–1951

John Colville, 1951–1955
David Pitblado, 1951–1956
Frederick Bishop, 1956–1959
Timothy Bligh, 1959–1964
Derek Mitchell, 1964–1966
Arthur Halls, 1966–1970
Alexander Isserlis, 1970
Robert Armstrong, 1970–1975
Kenneth Stowe, 1975–1977
Clive Whitmore, 1977–1979
Robin Butler, 1979–1985
Nigel Wicks, 1985–1988
Andrew Turnbull, 1988–1992
Alex Allan, 1992–1997
John Holmes, 1997–1999
Jeremy Heywood, 1999–2003
Ivan Rogers, 2003–2006
Oliver Robbins, 2006–2007
Tom Scholar, 2007–2008
Jeremy Heywood, 2008–2010
James Bowler, 2010–2012
Chris Martin, 2012–2015
Simon Case 2015–

JIC Chair
Desmond Anderson, 1936–1937
Roger Evans, 1938
Frederick Beaumont-Nesbitt, 1938–1939
Ralph Stevenson, 1939
Victor Cavendish-Bentinck, 1939–1945
Harold Caccia, 1945–1948
William Hayter, 1949–1950
Patrick Reilly, 1950–1953
Patrick Dean, 1953–1960
Hugh Stevenson, 1960–1963
Bernard Burrows, 1963–1966
Denis Greenhill, 1966–1968
Edward Peck, 1968–1970
Stewart Crawford, 1970–1973

Geoffrey Arthur, 1973–1975
Antony Duff, 1975–1979
Antony Acland, 1979–1982
Patrick Wright, 1982–1984
Percy Cradock, 1985–1992
Rodric Braithwaite, 1992–1993
Pauline Neville-Jones, 1993–1994
Paul Lever, 1994–1996
Colin Budd, 1996–1997
Michael Pakenham, 1997–2000
Peter Ricketts, 2000–2001
John Scarlett, 2001–2004
William Ehrman, 2004–2005
Richard Mottram, 2005–2007
Alex Allan, 2007–2012
Jon Day, 2012–2015
Charles Farr, 2015–

Intelligence Coordinator
Dick White, 1968–1972
Peter Wilkinson, 1972–1973
Joe Hooper, 1973–1978
Brooks Richards, 1978–1980
Antony Duff, 1980–1985
Colin Figures, 1985–1989
Christopher Curwen, 1989–1991
Gerry Warner, 1991–1996
John Alpass, 1996–1998
Michael Pakenham, 1999–2000
Peter Ricketts, 2000–2001

Intelligence and Security Coordinator
David Omand, 2002–2005
Bill Jeffrey, 2005

Permanent Secretary, Security, Intelligence and Resilience
Richard Mottram, 2005–2007

Head of Security, Intelligence and Resilience
Robert Hannigan, 2007–2010

Deputy National Security Adviser, Security, Intelligence and Resilience
Oliver Robbins, 2010–2014

Director-General of MI5
Vernon Kell, 1909–1940
Oswald Allen Harker, 1940–1941
David Petrie, 1941–1946
Percy Sillitoe, 1946–1953
Dick White, 1953–1956
Roger Hollis, 1956–1965
Martin Furnival Jones, 1965–1971
Michael Hanley, 1971–1978
Howard Smith, 1978–1981
John Jones, 1981–1985
Antony Duff, 1985–1987
Patrick Walker, 1987–1992
Stella Rimington, 1992–1996
Stephen Lander, 1996–2002
Eliza Manningham-Buller, 2002–2007
Jonathan Evans, 2007–2013
Andrew Parker, 2013–

Chief of MI6
Mansfield Smith-Cumming, 1909–1923
Hugh Sinclair, 1923–1939
Stewart Menzies, 1939–1952
John Sinclair, 1953–1956
Dick White, 1956–1968
John Rennie, 1968–1973
Maurice Oldfield, 1973–1978
Arthur (Dickie) Franks, 1979–1982
Colin Figures, 1982–1985
Christopher Curwen, 1985–1989
Colin McColl, 1989–1994
David Spedding, 1994–1999

Richard Dearlove, 1999–2004
John Scarlett, 2004–2009
John Sawers, 2009–2014
Alex Younger, 2014–

Director of GCHQ
Alastair Denniston, 1921–1942
Edward Travis, 1942–1952
Eric Jones, 1952–1960
Clive Loehnis, 1960–1964
Joe Hooper, 1965–1973
Arthur Bonsall, 1973–1978
Brian John Maynard Tovey, 1978–1983
Peter Marychurch, 1983–1989
John Anthony Adye, 1989–1996
David Omand, 1996–1997
Kevin Tebbit, 1998
Francis Richards, 1998–2003
David Pepper, 2003–2008
Iain Lobban, 2008–2014
Robert Hannigan, 2014–

Appendix II:
Key Intelligence and Security Machinery

1909: Security Service Bureau, SSB. The predecessor to MI5 and MI6

1912–1993: D-Notice system. Voluntary relationship between the media and the government to prevent coverage from harming national security

1919–1946: Government Code & Cypher School, GC&CS. To provide signals intelligence

1931–1939: Industrial Intelligence Centre, IIC. To provide all-source intelligence assessment of economic and production matters

1936–present: Joint Intelligence Committee, JIC. To provide all-source intelligence assessment

1946–1964: Joint Intelligence Bureau, JIB. Responsible for economic, logistic, scientific and technical intelligence

1946–present: Government Communications Headquarters, GCHQ. Replacing GC&CS

1948–1977: Information Research Department, IRD. Foreign Office department conducting unattributable propaganda

1949–1951: Permanent Under-Secretary's Committee, PUSC. To ensure strategic thinking and planning in the Foreign Office

1949–1998: Permanent Under-Secretary's Department, PUSD. Foreign Office department liaising with defence, intelligence and security actors

1949–c.1951: Ministerial Committee on Communism, AC(M). To coordinate anti-Communist activity

1949–1956: Official Committee on Communism (Overseas), AC(O). To coordinate anti-Communist activity overseas

1951–c.1962: Official Committee on Communism (Home), AC(H). To coordinate anti-Communist activity domestically

1951–2010: Permanent Secretaries Committee on the Intelligence Services, PSIS. To oversee the development of the intelligence community

1961–c.1970: Counter-Subversion Committee. To counter Communist and nationalist subversion overseas

1963–2007: Defence and Overseas Policy Committee. Keeping defence and foreign policy under review

1964–c.mid-1970s: Joint Action Committee. To coordinate covert action and special operations interdepartmentally

1964–2010: Security Commission. To investigate breaches of security

1964–2009: Defence Intelligence Staff, DIS. Replacing the JIB

1968–1974: Joint Intelligence Committee (B), JIC(B). To provide all-source intelligence assessment of economic, technical and scientific matters

1972–c.1978: Subversion in Public Life, SPL. To oversee intelligence on subversion and industrial unrest

1993–2015: Defence, Press and Broadcasting Advisory Committee, or DA-Notice. Replacing the D-Notice system

1994–present: Intelligence and Security Committee. To provide oversight

2009: Defence Intelligence, DI. Replacing DIS

2007–2010: National Security, International Relations and Development Committee, NSID. Replacing DOPC

2010–present: National Security Council, NSC. To coordinate discussion of national security issues, chaired by the prime minister, replacing NSID

2015–present: Defence and Security Media Advisory Notice System. Replacing the DA-Notice system

'Eat Before Reading':
A Short Essay on Methodology

'I was cleared to see some intelligence. It would arrive in locked boxes with ferocious instructions – eat before reading.' So recalls James Callaghan's special adviser David Lipsey in his wonderful memoir *In the Corridors of Power*. 'Never having been handy with locks and keys,' he added, 'I soon abandoned the unequal struggle.' It is a telling remark, that captures the character of intelligence at the summit of British government. Accessing the history of intelligence here has also been a difficult task. The corridor connecting Downing Street and the dark world of intelligence is so intensely secret that shedding some light on it has presented the authors with special challenges.

We have been greatly helped by the existence of that odd thing, the Official Secrets Act. No single piece of legislation captures the British class system more completely. Passed into law in 1911, after just twenty minutes of discussion by a House of Commons foaming with fear about 'the spies of the Kaiser', it is surely one of Britain's most 'medieval' statutes. Despite some notable failures to prosecute or extradite using the Official Secrets Act, each 'reform' has made it more fearsome. In 1978, David Owen, then foreign secretary, confessed that officials had disregarded the demands of ministers to liberalise the Act, and instead sought to make it even more regressive and vindictive. As a result, yet another attempt to reform it was abandoned. In the 1990s, further changes ensured that no person prosecuted under the Act could even breathe a word alluding to the possibility of acting in the public interest during their trial. Public interest is now denied as a valid defence, riding roughshod over rights to freedom of expression enshrined in Article 10 of the European Convention on Human Rights.

Yet there are special persons who are above the law. GCHQ translators may be prosecuted for revealing a single email, but prime ministers have long considered themselves immune from mere statutes. From Winston Churchill to Tony Blair, they have been handsomely paid for literary productions that parade state secrets with each turn of the page. Anthony Eden was paid the current equivalent of £9 million just for serial rights to his memoirs by *The Times*. Hairy SAS corporals may be arraigned before the courts for writing their memoirs, but their commanding officers, once knighted and equipped with the epaulettes of a general, feel free to write best-selling autobiographies. The domestic peace of journalists may be disrupted by dawn raids and their papers carried off by Special Branch, but prime ministerial press officers somehow escape this treatment with the Houdini-like flourish of a book contract. In short, while retired secret servants rarely breathe a word about intelligence, by contrast, Britain's political class is splendidly indiscreet. This is partly why it has been possible to write this book – and we thank them all.

Political diaries are best. If the diarists are contemporary chroniclers, they capture what people thought about at the time. Alastair Campbell wrote more than 4,000 pages of diaries during his days in Downing Street. All the while, top security officials watched him nervously. On 28 August 2003, Sir David Omand, Britain's most distinguished secret servant, who was then the cabinet intelligence and security coordinator, warned him: 'I hope you have all your diaries safely locked up somewhere – otherwise the men in black might come looking for them.' Campbell noted, 'I was not entirely sure whether he was joking or not. Probably not.' Like animals in the jungle, diarists have a supernatural awareness of other diarists moving in the undergrowth. Earlier that year, on 27 March, Chris Mullin MP, one of the most delightful observers of the Blair years, bumped into Anji Hunter, Blair's personal assistant and also an old friend of the prime minister. She revealed that Alastair Campbell was keeping a regular diary 'in tiny writing', covering three or four pages of foolscap paper every day. Mullin was thrilled to hear this, noting joyfully, 'At last, an eyewitness.'

Diarists have shed invaluable light on earlier prime ministers too. Guy Liddell, former deputy director of MI5, kept a meticulous record of his experiences during the Second World War and the early Cold War. These were regarded as so secret that they had their own codename – 'Wallflowers' – and were hidden, until recently, deep in the personal safe of MI5's director-general. Their matter-of-fact style belies the turbulence of an era characterised by intrigue, traitors and subversion. Importantly, Liddell probably never expected them to be pored over by curious historians. Other diarists are particularly useful too: Harold Macmillan, for example, kept a reasonably close account of his time in office, including reference to secret affairs and intelligence scandals. And then there are the likes of Richard Crossman and Barbara Castle, avid chroniclers of the Harold Wilson era. These offer fascinating personal insight, but come with a caution. Any historian over-reliant on such sources will leave such characters a greater voice in history than they actually had.

Failing diaries, memoirs can also be useful. Liable to a convenient reordering of events, they nevertheless capture mature retrospective reflections over time on issues of secret service, and even occasional recantation. Blair's public self-flagellation over the introduction of the Freedom of Information Act is a classic example. Even those with a reputation for turgidity can produce the odd gem. Edward Heath's recollections, for example, offer personal details on MI5 and the deportation of KGB spies. John Major's memoirs allude gently to spying and the Maastricht negotiations. That said, historians must approach them cynically. It is human nature to exaggerate one's achievements when writing history. Former MI6 officer Monty Woodhouse's self-effacing memoir, for example, can paradoxically be accused of overplaying MI6's hand in the Iranian coup of 1953. The original title of Tony Blair's autobiography, *The Journey*, smacks of a certain apostolic grandeur, while Denis Healey has been accused of intellectual one-upmanship. And then there are those with apparently explosive revelations, such as Peter Wright's *Spycatcher*, which upon closer inspection turn out to be, at least in part, inaccurate vendetta-fuelled speculation. Memoirs of secret service – like walk-in defectors – need to be vetted carefully by historians; but some, like the thoughtful observations of Stella Rimington, can prove to be pure gold.

So how do we know if and when these diarists and autobiographers are telling the truth? We have spent many hours in the archives, where diaries can be triangulated and cross-compared with the written record. The glories of Britain's 'PREM' files – the papers of the prime minister's office – make up much of the substance of this book, capturing the secretive scribbling of an army of prime ministerial private secretaries, the steely centre of Britain's core executive. In some ways they are the most important intelligence records, since they reveal the linkage between the prime minister's office and the engine room of the British intelligence community. The records of the JIC may have been released to great fanfare – but rather more intriguing is what the incumbents of Number 10 actually made of all this stuff. Often this is not recorded, and therefore the tiny scraps of writing by Harold Wilson or Edward Heath on the edge of a JIC paper resemble nothing so much as the magical 'No more twist' in a Beatrix Potter story. They are the golden threads that run through the very tapestry of a secret world that stretches from Downing Street to MI6 headquarters, and onwards to secret agents spying on the farthest fringes of empire. Files can also be cross-referenced with private papers, taking intrepid historians on a pilgrimage to archives across the country and beyond. Here lie letters and diaries sometimes overlooked by the government weeders. It takes patience to unravel a once-secret narrative, but it can be done.

Acknowledgements

We have received fabulous assistance from many people and places, and it is wonderful to be able to thank them here. Although we are told that the food in Belmarsh prison is quite good, we have nevertheless vowed not to transgress the Official Secrets Act until we are both safely in the House of Lords. Accordingly, this study has been compiled from open sources, and no classified material has been utilised. Mistakes remain our own, and given that we are describing secret things from unsecret sources, errors are unavoidable. Please write to us with comments or corrections at r.j.aldrich@warwick.ac.uk or rory.cormac@nottingham.ac.uk.

So many friends and colleagues offered advice, information or have arranged colloquia from which we have benefited. We would particularly like to thank Christian Bak, Huw Bennett, Hans Born, Peter Catterall, Gordon Corera, Alex Danchev, Philip Davies, Andrew Defty, Stephen Dorril, Rob Dover, Huw Dylan, David Easter, David Edgerton, Geoffrey Elliott, Paul Elston, Ralph Erskine, Rob Evans, John Ferris, Stevyn Gibson, Roy Giles, David Gill, Peter Gill, David Gioe, Michael Goodman, Andrew Hammond, Max Hastings, Michael Herman, Gerry Hughes, Peter Jackson, Keith Jeffery, Rhodri Jeffreys-Jones, Clive Jones, Matthew Jones, John Kasuku, Sheila Kerr, Dan Larsen, Paul Lashmar, Ian Leigh, Julian Lewis, Svetlana Lokhova, W. Scott Lucas, Paul McGarr, Ben Macintyre, Paul Maddrell, Tom Maguire, Carsten Maple, Peter Martland, Paul Mercer, Kaeten Mistry, Andrew Mumford, Philip Murphy, David Omand, Mark Phythian, Dina Rezk, Len Scott, Mark Seaman, Zakia Shiraz, Michael Smith, David Stafford, Mark Stout, Phil Tinline, Karina Urbach, Damien Van Puyvelde, Calder Walton, Wesley K. Wark, Michael Warner, Tim Watson, Cees Weibes, Mark Wilkinson, Simon Willmetts, Aidan Wills and John W. Young. We also enjoy the company of a number of very talented research students and research fellows at both Nottingham and Warwick, an elite unit who specialise in night raids. They know who they are.

Departmental record officers and official historians are wonderful. We are grateful to the many individuals who have declassified materials for us and allowed sight of documents down the years. We would like to thank Christopher Simpson at the attorney general's office; Alan Glennie, Brian Hogan and Shumailla Moinuddin at the Cabinet Office; Gill Bennett, Lynsey Hughes, Janet James, Penny Prior, Duncan Stewart, Stuart Taylor and Stephen Twigge at the Foreign and Commonwealth Office; Iain Goode, Simon Marsh and Steve Roper at the Ministry of Defence; Rosemary Banner, Ashley Britten, Darren Creamer, Francis Houston, Kate Jenkins and Sean Molloy at the Treasury; Patrick Driscoll at Treasury Solicitors. A number of record-keepers and historians at the three agencies have also been helpful.

Armies of archivists and librarians – tireless in their efforts – have extended their kindness, and cannot all be named here. We had much assistance from the presidential libraries of the United States, which are almost prime ministerial libraries once removed. In Washington we would like to mention Nicholas Scheetz at the Special Collections Center, the Lauinger Library at Georgetown University; Jeffrey M. Flannery at the Library of Congress together with Dane Hartgrove, Will Mahoney, Kathy McCastro, Ed Reese and the legendary late John E. Taylor at NARA. The Archives Centre at Churchill College Cambridge has been especially important to us, and unfailingly helpful. But mostly it is the staff of the UK National Archives, overworked and often confronted with two irascible researchers, but unfailingly courteous and helpful, who have facilitated this book. The Universities of Nottingham and Warwick have provided wonderful environments during the years over which this book was written, and study leave generously offered by both institutions at the same time allowed its completion.

There are a few individuals to whom we owe a particularly heavy debt of gratitude. Our literary agent, Andrew Lownie, was especially important in developing this idea. Martin Redfern, Arabella Pike and Stephen Guise at HarperCollins have been wonderful to work with. Robert Lacey has run his formidable expert eye over advanced drafts. James Aldrich read the proofs with scary efficiency. Christopher Andrew, Peter Hennessy and Christopher Moran have offered crucial assistance and constant inspiration. Above all, we owe an enormous debt to our families for their encouragement over the years. Libby, Nicholas and Harriet have endured many weeks of separation imposed by the archive trail in North America with good grace. They have provided endless happy diversions: music, dance and theatre trump historical writing every time as artistic endeavours. Joanne has been a constant source of support, from providing a sounding board for prime ministerial anecdotes to standing just off-camera, waving cheat sheets, during televisual debuts. She is a good egg. Thank you.

Notes

Introduction

1. Churchill, 'My Spy Story', *Thoughts and Adventures*, p.85
2. Laqueur, *A World of Secrets*, p.90
3. Churchill, *The World Crisis*, Part 1, p.193
4. Reynolds, *In Command of History*, pp.36–7
5. Hastings, *The Secret War*, pp.13, 17, 70, 80. Hastings offers the supreme account of intelligence in the Second World War
6. Anglim, *Orde Wingate*, pp.13–14
7. Walton, *Empire of Secrets*, p.334
8. Goodman, *Joint Intelligence Committee*, p.80
9. Bennett, *Morton*, p.266
10. Goodman, *Joint Intelligence Committee*, pp.80, 329; Hennessy, *The Prime Minister*, pp.152–5; Hennessy, *Secret State*, pp.95–7
11. Barker, *British Policy in South-East Europe*, p.141
12. Michaels, 'Heyday of Britain's Cold War Think Tank', pp.152–4
13. David Cameron, 'Minutes of Evidence Taken Before the Joint Committee on the National Security Strategy', 20 January 2014, HC.1040
14. Aldrich, 'Policing the Past', p.923; Moran, *Classified*, pp.22–54; Murphy, 'Whitehall, Intelligence and Official History', pp.236–50
15. Entry for 29 September 1977, Donoughue, *Downing Street Diary*, p.241
16. Entry for 11 December 1996, Mullin, *Decline and Fall*, p.205; Aldrich, *Hidden Hand*, pp.354–6; private information
17. Straw, *Last Man Standing*, pp.98–102
18. Entry for 10 March 1976, Benn, *Against the Tide*, p.532
19. 'Security: Tony Benn, Energy Secretary: access to SIGINT material', PREM 16/1863; also private information
20. Entry for 23 February 1977, Donoughue, *Downing Street Diary*, pp.152–3;

Christopher Leake, 'The day Britain's top civil servant rolled naked on the floor ranting about the end of the world', *Daily Mail*, 20 September 2008
21. M. Oliver, 'Blair avoids questions over British spy ring', *Guardian*, 23 January 2006
22. Chairman of the JIC (Ref: Jp 115) to prime minister, 'Syria: Reported Chemical Weapons Use', 29 August 2013. https://www.gov.uk/government/publications/syria-reported-chemical-weapons-use-joint-intelligence-committee-letter
23. Charlotte McDonald-Gibson, 'David Cameron defends Britain's spy services as anger mounts in Europe over US and UK state surveillance', *Independent*, 26 October 2013
24. Entry for 7 January 1976, Benn, *Against the Tide*, p.492
25. Levitt, *Hezbollah*, p.306; Duncan Gardham, 'Former soldiers shackled and shot by kidnappers, inquest hears', *Daily Telegraph*, 22 June 2011; Kim Sengupta, 'Peter Moore: "I feel guilty I'm the only one alive"', *Independent*, 14 February 2012
26. BBC News, 'Margaret Thatcher "Negotiated with IRA"', http://www.bbc.co.uk/news/uk-northern-ireland-16366413, 30 December 2011
27. Entry for 12 October 1984, Clark, *In Power*, pp.99, 138
28. 'Wilson blocked plans for barriers outside No. 10', *Huddersfield Daily Examiner*, 28 December 2007
29. The full details are now available in 'Project Pindar: refurbishment of accommodation beneath the South Citadel, Main Building', Cm 46/26
30. Entry for 11 October 2001, Campbell, *Burden of Power*, p.49
31. Entry for 15 October 2001, ibid., p.55

32. Sean O'Neill and Duncan Gardham, 'Terror Suspect "Discussed Syria and Buying Firearm"', *The Times*, 17 October 2014

33. Duncan Gardham, '"Al-Qaeda in Britain" leader who threatened Gordon Brown and Tony Blair pleads guilty', *Daily Telegraph*, 10 May 2010

34. Private information

35. 'Pacifist Sentenced', *Sydney Morning Herald*, 12 September 1939

36. Wigg, *Churchill and Spain*, pp.12–15

37. Ben Macintyre, 'How we won the war', *The Times*, 24 May 2013

38. Paul Callan, 'Adolf Hitler's orders: Kill Winston Churchill', *Daily Express*, 21 July 2012

Chapter 1: Herbert Asquith, David Lloyd George and Andrew Bonar Law (1908–1923)

1. Lloyd George, *War Memoirs 1915–16*, p.60

2. Thomas, *Empires of Intelligence*

3. Satya, *Spies of Arabia*, pp.34–5

4. Walton, *Empire of Secrets*, pp.2–4; Bayly, *Empire and Information*, pp.3–14

5. Porter, *Vigilant State*

6. Shpayer-Makov, *Ascent of the Detective*, pp.2–7

7. J.C. Wood, review of ibid., http://www.history.ac.uk/reviews/review/1409

8. Porter, *Vigilant State*, pp.131–3

9. Moran and Johnson, 'In the Service of Empire', pp.9–10

10. Satya, *Spies of Arabia*, pp.17–18

11. Moran and Johnson, 'In the Service of Empire', pp.9–10

12. Ibid., pp.1–2

13. Le Queux, *The Invasion of 1910*, pp.vi, 1–5

14. Moran and Johnson, 'In the Service of Empire', pp.9–10, 14; Andrew, *Secret Service*, pp.39–40

15. Boghardt, *Spies of the Kaiser*, pp.23–5

16. Porter, *Vigilant State*, pp.186–8; Macenczak, *German Enemy Aliens*, pp.13–15

17. Stafford, 'Spies and Gentlemen', p.505

18. Hiley, 'The Failure of British Counter-Espionage', p.844

19. 'The Spy Mania', *The Times*, 21 August 1908, quoted in Macenczak, *German Enemy Aliens*, p.15

20. Moran and Johnson, 'In the Service of Empire', pp.14–15

21. Ibid., p.16

22. Boghardt, *Spies of the Kaiser*, pp.28–31; Hiley, 'The Failure of British Counter-Espionage', pp.838–40

23. Andrew, *Defence of the Realm*, p.9

24. See Sub-Committee of Committee of Imperial Defence, 'Foreign Espionage in the United Kingdom: Report and Proceedings', 1909, CAB 16/8

25. Andrew, *Secret Service*, pp.58–60

26. 'Formation of SS Bureau: meeting at Scotland Yard; findings of The Committee For Imperial Defence (CID) Sub-Committee on Foreign Espionage', 26 August 1909, KV 1/3; Walton, *Empire of Secrets*, pp.6–7; Richelson, *Century of Spies*, pp.10–11

27. Porter, *Plots and Paranoia*, pp.119–21; Andrew, *Secret Service*, pp.60–1

28. Moran, *Classified*, p.71

29. Panayi, *German Immigrants in Britain*, pp.248–51; Stibbe, 'A Question of Retaliation?', pp.23–4

30. Seligmann, *Spies in Uniform*, pp.2–29; Richelson, *Century of Spies*, pp.10–12; Andrew, *Secret Service*, pp.81–2

31. George Riley (Scotland Yard), 'Suffragettes', 27 September 1909, HO/144/1709/425859

32. Anon to Gladstone, 27 September 1909, HO/144/1709/425859; Maev Kennedy, 'Suffragettes plotted to assassinate Herbert Asquith', *Guardian*, 26 September 2006

33. Webb, *The Suffragette Bombers*, pp.1–17

34. Sellers, *Shot in the Tower*, pp.11–35

35. Moran and Johnson, 'In the Service of Empire', p.13

36. Kate Williams, 'The Fateful Year: England 1914, by Mark Bostridge', *Independent*, 17 January 2014; de Courcy, *Margot at War*, pp.221–2

37. Cresswell, *Living With the Wire*, pp.2–4

38. Panayi, 'An Intolerant Act by an Intolerant Society', p.58

39. Andrew, *Defence of the Realm*, pp.3–5; Jeffery, *MI6*, pp.11–16; Walton, *Empire of Secrets*, pp.8–9

40. Quinlan, *The Secret War*, pp.3–4

41. Popplewell, *Intelligence and Imperial Defence*, pp.219–22

42. Aldrich, *GCHQ*, pp.14–19

43. Brock and Brock (eds), *Margot Asquith's Great War Diary 1914–1916*, pp.2–24

44. McMahon, *British Spies and Irish Rebels*, pp.18–19

45. Andrew, *Defence of the Realm*, p.86

46. McMahon, *British Spies and Irish Rebels*, p.19

47. Andrew, *Defence of the Realm*, pp.86–9

48. Foy and Barton, *The Easter Rising*, p.57

49. McMahon, *British Spies and Irish Rebels*, pp.20–1

50. BOD: Asquith to Sylvia Henley, 26 April 1916, MS. Eng. lett. c.542/3, fols.640v–641r
51. BOD: Margot Asquith's Diary, Easter 1916, MS. Eng. d.3214, fols.396v–397r
52. H.C.G. Matthew, 'Asquith, Herbert Henry, First Earl of Oxford and Asquith (1852–1928)', *Oxford Dictionary of National Biography*, Oxford University Press, 2004, online edn
53. Foy and Barton, *The Easter Rising*, p.286, 322
54. Andrew, *Defence of the Realm*, pp.85–92
55. Cassar, *Asquith as War Leader*, pp.122–3
56. Naylor, *A Man and an Institution*, pp.11–19
57. Larsen, 'The First Intelligence Prime Minister', p.1
58. Hiley, 'Internal Security in Wartime', pp.395–415
59. Lloyd George, *War Memoirs 1915–16*, p.60
60. Larsen, 'War Pessimism'
61. Richards, *Secret Flotillas*, pp.16–17
62. Naylor, *A Man and an Institution*, pp.27–8
63. Turner, *Lloyd George's Secretariat*, p.19
64. Ibid., p.3
65. Naylor, *A Man and an Institution*, pp.21–6, 61–4
66. Larsen, 'The First Intelligence Prime Minister', pp.5–6
67. Budiansky, *Battle of Wits*, p.28
68. Lloyd George, *War Memoirs 1915–16*, p.988
69. Satya, *Spies of Arabia*, pp.10–11
70. J.C. Wood, review of *Ascent of the Detective*, http://www.history.ac.uk/reviews/review/1409
71. Andrew, *Defence of the Realm*, pp.107–9
72. Richelson, *Century of Spies*, pp.64–5; Naylor, *A Man and an Institution*, pp.21–6, 61–4
73. Quinlan, *The Secret War*, pp.22–3
74. Andrew, *Secret Service*; Jeffery, *MI6*, pp.211–12
75. Crosby, *The Unknown David Lloyd George*, pp.271–9
76. Ibid.
77. Bar-Joseph, *Intelligence and Intervention*, pp.278–80; Ullman, *Anglo–Soviet Relations*, pp.280–7
78. Bar-Joseph, *Intelligence and Intervention*, pp.285–6
79. Ibid., pp.286–7; Ullman, *Anglo–Soviet Relations*, p.290
80. Crosby, *The Unknown David Lloyd George*, pp.280–1
81. Service, *Spies and Commissars*, p.124
82. Bar-Joseph, *Intelligence and Intervention*, pp.290–6; Andrew, *Secret Service*, pp.272–4
83. Larsen, 'The First Intelligence Prime Minister', pp.7–8
84. Richards, *Secret Flotillas*, pp.16–18
85. Quinlan, *The Secret War*, pp.19–22
86. This is captured in the delightful essay Jeffery and Sharp, 'Lord Curzon and Secret Intelligence', pp.103–27
87. Best, *British Intelligence and the Japanese Challenge*, pp.44–6
88. McMahon, *British Spies and Irish Rebels*, pp.56–64
89. Ibid., pp.78–80
90. Naylor, *A Man and an Institution*, p.121
91. Satya, *Spies of Arabia*, pp.13–14
92. Lloyd George, *War Memoirs 1915–16*, p.988; Moran, *Classified*, pp.69–73

Chapter 2: Stanley Baldwin and Ramsay MacDonald (1923–1937)

1. Bennett, *A Most Extraordinary and Mysterious Business*, p.73
2. Hansard, Baldwin, 22 May 1935, vol. 302
3. Jenkins, *Baldwin*, p.65
4. Ibid., p.63
5. Marquand, *Ramsay MacDonald*, pp.6, 69; Pearce and Goodlad, *British Prime Ministers*, p.91; Neilson and Otte, *The Permanent Under-Secretary for Foreign Affairs*, p.207
6. Andrew, *Defence of the Realm*, p.151
7. Pearce and Goodlad, *British Prime Ministers*, p.97
8. Andrew, *Secret Service*, p.298; Andrew, *Defence of the Realm*, p.146; Bennett, *Churchill's Man of Mystery*, p.79
9. Andrew, *Defence of the Realm*, pp.146, 129–30
10. Andrew, *Secret Service*, pp.298–9
11. Rose, 'Vansittart, Robert Gilbert, Baron Vansittart (1881–1957)', *Oxford Dictionary of National Biography*, Oxford University Press, 2004, online edn
12. Ferris, 'Indulged in all too Little', pp.50–1
13. Bennett, *Churchill's Man of Mystery*, p.127
14. Andrew, *Secret Service*, p.300
15. Quoted in Madeira, *Britannia and the Bear*, p.121
16. Ibid., pp.120–1, 190
17. One of the first things George Brown wanted to do when he became foreign secretary in August 1966 was to track down who had authorised the publication of the Zinoviev letter. He issued instructions to find the draft and see where it was initialled. Anxious officials

searched the archives for the draft, but couldn't find it. One junior Foreign Office official recalled that the 'search was so desperate' that they even came up to his small room in the Northern Department of the Foreign Office, which had been responsible for Russia in 1924, 'and searched all the cupboards … just in case the draft happened to be lying around in the pile of papers preserved forty years later by some accident of history'. Predictably, they didn't find it. BDOHP, Sir Brian Lee Crowe, 15 October 2003

18. Marquand, *Ramsay MacDonald*, pp.381, 383

19. Bennett, *A Most Extraordinary and Mysterious Business*, Annex A: The Zinoviev Letter, 15 September 1924, pp.93–5

20. Henderson to Lord Stamfordham, 26 August 1924, PREM 1/45

21. Handwritten note by MacDonald, 13 September 1924, PREM 1/45; handwritten note by MacDonald on a letter addressed to the Home Office, 20 August 1924, ibid.; note to the Attorney General, 23 August 1924, ibid.

22. Jeffery, *MI6*, p.216

23. Bennett, *A Most Extraordinary and Mysterious Business*, pp.88, 92; Smith, *Six*, p.309

24. Bennett, *A Most Extraordinary and Mysterious Business*, pp.84, 91–2

25. Richard Orange, 'Revealed: the dark past of "Outcast", MI6's top wartime double agent', *Observer*, 10 October 2015

26. Jeffery, *MI6*, pp.218–19

27. Ibid., p.216; Bennett, *A Most Extraordinary and Mysterious Business*, pp.34–5

28. 'History of the Zinoviev Incident', November 1924, PRO 30/69/234; Bennett, *A Most Extraordinary and Mysterious Business*, p.37; Bennett, *Churchill's Man of Mystery*, p.52

29. 'History of the Zinoviev Incident', November 1924, CAB 24/168/87

30. Quoted in Marquand, *Ramsay MacDonald*, p.383

31. Bennett, *A Most Extraordinary and Mysterious Business*, p.40

32. Bennett, *Churchill's Man of Mystery*, p.82

33. Bennett, *A Most Extraordinary and Mysterious Business*, pp.82–3; Smith, *Six*, p.310; Bennett, *Churchill's Man of Mystery*, p.83

34. Bennett, *A Most Extraordinary and Mysterious Business*, pp.44, 28

35. Andrew, *Secret Service*, pp.339–40; Bennett, *Churchill's Man of Mystery*, pp.126–7; Ball, *Portrait of a Party*, p.448

36. Jeffery, *MI6*, p.222

37. Andrew, *Defence of the Realm*, pp.148–50; Bennett, *A Most Extraordinary and Mysterious Business*, p.45; Bennett, *Churchill's Man of Mystery*, p.80

38. McMahon, *British Spies and Irish Rebels*, pp.189–90

39. MacDonald quoted in 'History of the Zinoviev Incident', November 1924, PRO 30/69/234

40. 'History of the Zinoviev Incident', November 1924, PRO 30/69/234

41. Marquand, *Ramsay MacDonald*, pp.384, 387; Bennett, *A Most Extraordinary and Mysterious Business*, p.52

42. Marquand, *Ramsay MacDonald*, p.384

43. Ibid.

44. 'History of the Zinoviev Incident', November 1924, PRO 30/69/234

45. Quoted in Marquand, *Ramsay MacDonald*, p.386; Bennett, *A Most Extraordinary and Mysterious Business*, p.72

46. Marquand, *Ramsay MacDonald*, pp.386–7; Bennett, *A Most Extraordinary and Mysterious Business*, p.73

47. Bennett, *A Most Extraordinary and Mysterious Business*, p.73

48. 'The Zinoviev Letter: Report of Cabinet Committee', 4 November 1924, CAB 27/254; Marquand, *Ramsay MacDonald*, p.388

49. Bennett, *Churchill's Man of Mystery*, p.88; Jeffery, *MI6*, pp.222, 224–5

50. Jeffery, *MI6*, p.228

51. Perkins, *Baldwin*, pp.52–64

52. 'The Soviet Trading Organisation in London', March 1927, KV 2/818

53. Smith, *Six*, p.318; Andrew, *Defence of the Realm*, p.153

54. Kell, 'Arcos: A Chronological Note of Events', 14 May 1927, KV 3/15; Bennett, *Churchill's Man of Mystery*, pp.97–8; Andrew, *Defence of the Realm*, p.154; Madeira, *Britannia and the Bear*, pp.163–4

55. Madeira, *Britannia and the Bear*, p.190; Clayton, 'The Life and Career of Sir William Joynson-Hicks', p.19

56. Madeira, *Britannia and the Bear*, p.242, n44

57. Bennett, *Churchill's Man of Mystery*, p.99

58. Smith, *Six*, p.319

59. Ibid.; West, *MI5*, pp.66–7

60. Bennett, *Churchill's Man of Mystery*, p.95

61. Smith, *Six*, p.318

62. Hansard, Mr Thurtle MP, 24 May 1927, vol. 206 cc1808

63. Note in catalogue of documents found during the raid, 1927, KV 3/35

64. Cabinet Minutes, 32(27)2, 20 May 1927, CAB 13/55/3

65. Ibid.; Andrew, *Defence of the Realm*, p.155

66. Hansard, Baldwin, 24 May 1927, vol. 206 c1845

67. Ibid., c1849; Andrew, *Defence of the Realm*, p.155

68. 'Documents Illustrating the Hostile Activities of the Soviet Government and Third International Against Great Britain', cm 2874, 1927, KV 3/15

69. Andrew, *Defence of the Realm*, p.155

70. West, *Mask*, p.2

71. Smith, *Six*, p.320

72. Aldrich, *GCHQ*, p.19

73. Madeira, *Britannia and the Bear*, p.180

74. Jeffery, *MI6*, p.229

75. Cave Brown, *'C'*, p.146

76. Andrew, *Secret Service*, p.333

77. Cabinet Minutes, 32(27)2, 20 May 1927, CAB 13/55/3

78. Andrew, *Secret Service*, p.332

79. Cave Brown, *'C'*, p.147

80. Smith, *The Bletchley Park Codebreakers*

81. Entry for 30 November 1978, Benn, *Conflicts of Interest*, p.405

82. Churchill, *The Gathering Storm*, p.107

83. McMahon, *British Spies and Irish Rebels*, pp.223, 233–9

84. Best, *British Intelligence and the Japanese Challenge*, pp.69–71, 83

85. Ferris, 'Now that the Milk is Spilt', pp.544–5

86. Bennett, *Churchill's Man of Mystery*, p.163; Ferris, *Intelligence and Strategy*, p.70; Dilks, 'Appeasement and Intelligence', p.144

87. Stuart Ball, 'Baldwin, Stanley, First Earl Baldwin of Bewdley (1867–1947)', *Oxford Dictionary of National Biography*, Oxford University Press, 2004, online edn

88. Wark, *The Ultimate Enemy*, p.47; Perkins, *Baldwin*, pp.100, 103; Pearce and Goodlad, *British Prime Ministers*, pp.78–9; Ball, 'Baldwin'

89. Walton, *Challenges in Intelligence Analysis*, pp.75–6; Dilks, 'Appeasement and Intelligence', p.140

90. Ferris, 'The Road to Bletchley Park', p.87

91. Quoted in Dilks, 'Appeasement and Intelligence', p.142

92. Andrew, *Secret Service*, pp.340–1; Morrow, 'States and Strategic Airpower', pp.48–9

93. Walton, *Challenges in Intelligence Analysis*, p.71

94. Wark, *The Ultimate Enemy*, p.47

95. Wark, 'British Intelligence on the German Air Force and Aircraft Industry', p.630

96. Ferris, 'Now that the Milk is Spilt', p.543

97. Wark, 'British Intelligence on the German Air Force and Aircraft Industry', p.631

98. See Committee of Imperial Defence Minutes, CID(28) 238th meeting, 8 November 1928, CAB 2/5; Ferris, 'Now that the Milk is Spilt'; Bennett, *Churchill's Man of Mystery*, p.135; see also Goodman, 'Learning to Walk', p.42

99. Bennett, *Churchill's Man of Mystery*, pp.187, 163

100. Dilks, 'Appeasement and Intelligence', p.142

101. Wark, 'British Intelligence on the German Air Force and Aircraft Industry', pp.627–48

102. Churchill, *The Gathering Storm*, p.105

103. Quoted in ibid., p.107

104. Wark, *The Ultimate Enemy*, p.43

105. Hansard, Baldwin, 22 May 1935, vol. 302 (emphasis added)

106. Pearce and Goodlad, *British Prime Ministers*, pp.71, 76

107. Wark, *The Ultimate Enemy*, p.44

108. Ibid.

109. Wark, 'British Intelligence on the German Air Force and Aircraft Industry', pp.632, 638; Walton, *Challenges in Intelligence Analysis*, pp.70, 72, 75

110. Dilks, 'Appeasement and Intelligence', p.169

111. Ferris, 'Now that the Milk is Spilt', p.557

112. Marquand, *Ramsay MacDonald*, pp.700–1

113. Wilson, *Nazi Princess*, pp.100–2

114. Perkins, *Baldwin*, pp.109–18; Pearce and Goodlad, *British Prime Ministers*, p.80

115. Hansard, Baldwin, cm 2190, 10 December 1936, CAB 21/4100/1; Horace Wilson, 'King Edward VIII', undated, CAB 127/157

116. Hansard, Baldwin, cm 2191, 10 December 1936, CAB 21/4100/1; H.C.G. Matthew, 'Edward VIII [later Prince Edward, Duke of Windsor] (1894–1972)', *Oxford Dictionary of National Biography*, Oxford University Press, 2004, online edn

117. Williams and Baldwin, *Baldwin Papers*, p.338

118. Curry, *The Security Service 1908–1945*, p.60; Elliott, *Gentleman Spymaster*, p.84

119. Curry, *The Security Service 1908–1945*, p.60; Elliott, *Gentleman Spymaster*, pp.83, 84; Caroline Davies et al., 'Mrs Simpson

had secret affair with car salesman', *Daily Telegraph*, 30 January 2003, p.1; West, 'Review of *Defence of the Realm*', p.770; West, 'To Defend the Realm', *Sunday Telegraph*, 27 September 2009, p.18

120. Letter from Home Office to Sir Thomas Gardiner, 5 December 1936, CAB 301/101
121. Elliott, *Gentleman Spymaster*, p.84
122. Cahal Milmo, 'National archives reveal MI5 bugged Edward VIII's phone calls', *Independent*, 23 May 2013
123. Hansard, Baldwin, 10 December 1936, cm 2186, CAB 21/4100/1
124. 'Scenes in the Streets', *The Times*, 11 December 1936, CAB 21/4100/1

Chapter 3: Neville Chamberlain (1937–1940)
1. Chamberlain to Hilda Chamberlain, 27 August 1939, in Self (ed.), *The Neville Chamberlain Diary Letters, 1934–1940*, pp.440–2
2. Typically, R.A.C. Parker's dominant book on Chamberlain has no reference to intelligence or secret service in its index. Robert Self, *Chamberlain*, only mentions intelligence twice before the outbreak of war, but the works by Frank McDonough and David Faber are more interested in secret service
3. There is an important specialist literature. The pathbreaking essay is Dilks, 'Appeasement and Intelligence'. The most important literature is Wark, *Ultimate Enemy*, Ferris, *Intelligence and Strategy*, and Keren Yarhi-Milo, 'In the Eye of the Beholder'. Andrew's *Secret Service* and *Defence of the Realm*, together with Jeffery, *MI6*, give Chamberlain strong coverage
4. Best, 'The Japanese Threat to British Interests', p.92
5. Groth and Froeliger, 'Unheeded Warnings', p.335; see also Weinberg, *Hitler's Foreign Policy*, pp.112–13
6. Layne, 'Security Studies', p.402
7. Ferris, 'The Road to Bletchley Park', pp.67–70; Best, *British Intelligence and the Japanese Challenge*, pp.136–8
8. 'C', 'Memorandum on Secret Service Funds', C/39, 9 October 1935. CAB 127/371, quoted in Goodman, *Joint Intelligence Committee*, pp.45–6
9. Faber, *Munich*, p.128
10. Wark, *The Ultimate Enemy*, pp.5–18
11. Goodman, *Joint Intelligence Committee*, pp.11–12, 45–6; Crowson, *Facing Fascism*, p.140
12. Goodman, *Joint Intelligence Committee*, pp.12–13

13. Crowson, *Facing Fascism*, p.188
14. Faber, *Munich*, p.85
15. Cockett, 'Ball, Chamberlain and "Truth"', pp.131–2
16. Mills, 'The "Secret Channel" to Italy', pp.286, 292. Mills has conducted extraordinary historical detective work to uncover the trail of Joseph Ball
17. Faber, *Munich*, p.85
18. Parker, *Chamberlain*, p.121
19. Mills, 'The "Secret Channel" to Italy', pp.297, 300
20. Marsh, *The Chamberlain Litany*, pp.292–4
21. Ibid., p.303
22. Self, *The Neville Chamberlain Diary Letters 1934–1940*, p.432
23. Mills, 'The "Secret Channel" to Italy', p.304; Cockett, 'Ball, Chamberlain and "Truth"', pp.131–4
24. Dilks, 'Flashes of Intelligence', pp.101–26
25. Mills, 'The "Secret Channel" to Italy', p.306
26. Watt, *How War Came*, p.95
27. Giorgio Peresso, 'Major Adrian Dingli, éminence grise of Anglo-Italian diplomacy in 1930s', *Times of Malta*, 30 September 2012
28. Mills, 'The "Secret Channel" to Italy', pp.313–14
29. Faber, *Munich*, p.177
30. Beck, *Scoring for Britain*, pp.1–3
31. Andrew, *Defence of the Realm*, pp.197–204; Ferris, 'Indulged in all too Little', pp.125–7
32. Self (ed.), *The Neville Chamberlain Diary Letters, 1934–1940*, p.292
33. Minutes of 6 May 1933, Vnst 2/3, Vansittart MSS, CCC
34. Ferris, 'Indulged in all too Little', pp.129–30, 138–9
35. Richards, *Secret Flotillas*, pp.18–21
36. Faber, *Munich*, pp.227–9; Jeffery, *MI6*, pp.299–303
37. Ferris, 'Indulged in all too Little', pp.142–4
38. Jeffery, *MI6*, p.303; Ferris, 'Indulged in all too Little', pp.160–2
39. Andrew, *Defence of the Realm*, pp.202–4; Faber, *Munich*, pp.224–6
40. Watt, *How War Came*, p.613; Neville, 'Henderson, Sir Nevile Meyrick (1882–1942)', *Oxford Dictionary of National Biography*, Oxford University Press, 2004, online edn
41. Yarhi-Milo, 'In the Eye of the Beholder', pp.39–42
42. Ferris, 'Indulged in all too Little', pp.167–8
43. Best, 'The Japanese Threat to British Interests', p.93

44. Chamberlain to Ida Chamberlain, 6 October 1938, Chamberlain Papers 18/1/1071, Birmingham University Library

45. Mills, 'The "Secret Channel" to Italy', p.306

46. Andrew, *Defence of the Realm*, pp.206–7

47. Andrew, 'Churchill and Intelligence', p.181

48. Thorpe, *Supermac*, pp.133–5; Faber, *Munich*, pp.433–4

49. Andrew, *Defence of the Realm*, pp.202–3

50. Yarhi-Milo, 'In the Eye of the Beholder', pp.42–4

51. Andrew, *Defence of the Realm*, p.205

52. Andrew, 'Secret Intelligence and British Foreign Policy', p.24; Richards, *Secret Flotillas*, pp.19–20

53. Goodman, *Joint Intelligence Committee*, p.46

54. Ferris, 'The Road to Bletchley Park', p.68

55. Andrew, *Defence of the Realm*, pp.205–10; Yarhi-Milo, 'In the Eye of the Beholder', pp.42–4

56. Watt, *How War Came*, pp.208, 214

57. Andrew, *Defence of the Realm*, p.208

58. Wark, 'Something Very Stern', p.150

59. Gerrard, *The Foreign Office and Finland*, pp.17, 22, 26, 58

60. Watt, 'Intelligence Surprise', p.512

61. Goodman, *Joint Intelligence Committee*, pp.52–4

62. Watt, *How War Came*, pp.440–1; Self, *Chamberlain*, p.374

63. Roberts, *Holy Fox*, p.170

64. Goodman, *Joint Intelligence Committee*, pp.53–4

65. Ibid., pp.64–6

66. Ferris, 'Intelligence and Diplomatic Signalling', p.688

67. Self, *Chamberlain*, p.402

68. Jeffery, *MI6*, pp.382–3

69. Richards, *Secret Flotillas*, pp.19–21

70. Self, *Chamberlain*, p.396

71. Duncan Gardham, 'Ballet dancing agent leaked battle plans to Nazis', *Daily Telegraph*, 26 August 2010, p.5

72. Jeffery, *MI6*, p.345

73. Goodman, *Joint Intelligence Committee*, pp.71–5

74. Wark, 'Williamson Murray's Wars', pp.472–81; Peden, *Rearmament and the Treasury*, pp.13–15

75. Goodman, *Joint Intelligence Committee*, p.51

76. Ferris, 'The Road to Bletchley Park', p.74

Chapter 4: Winston Churchill (1940–1941)

1. Churchill, *Their Finest Hour*, p.342

2. Bennett, *Churchill's Man of Mystery*, p.234

3. Morton to Thompson, 6 September 1960, Thompson, *Churchill and Morton*, p.89

4. Andrew, 'Churchill and Intelligence', pp.180–2

5. Ibid., pp.189–90

6. Hinsley, 'Churchill and Special Intelligence', p.412

7. Ibid., p.408; Goodman, *Joint Intelligence Committee*, pp.71–2

8. Hinsley, 'Churchill and Special Intelligence', p.409

9. Hinsley, *British Intelligence*, Vol. 1, p.295

10. Jablonsky, *The Great Game*, p.157

11. Entry for 22 February 1945, Dilks (ed.), *Cadogan Diary*, pp.719–20

12. McMahon, *British Spies and Irish Rebels*, pp.1–3

13. Hull, *Irish Secrets*, pp.301–4; Bowyer Bell, *Secret Army*, pp.157–8; O'Halpin, *Spying on Ireland*, pp.39–42

14. McMahon, *British Spies and Irish Rebels*, pp.259–68

15. O'Halpin, *Spying on Ireland*, pp.48–52; McMahon, *British Spies and Irish Rebels*, pp.262–70

16. McMahon, *British Spies and Irish Rebels*, pp.268–72

17. MI6 messages, 8 and 16 December 1941, KV 2/1321; Stephenson to MI6, 12 September 1941, KV 2/1321

18. Hull, *Irish Secrets*, pp.341–3

19. Hermann Goertz document, December 1944 (MI5 translation), KV 2/1322

20. Entry for 6 January 1942, 'The Diaries of Guy Liddell', KV 8/189

21. O'Halpin, *Spying on Ireland*, pp.26–7

22. Hull, *Irish Secrets*, pp.341–3; McMahon, *British Spies and Irish Rebels*, pp.307, 322–3

23. Richard, *Secret Flotillas*, p.5

24. Ben Macintyre, 'Britain is not Immune from the Enemy Within', *The Times*, 28 February 2014

25. Andrew, *Defence of the Realm*, p.223

26. Rebecca Maksel, 'Spy Pigeons: Unlikely soldiers during World War II: more than 250,000 pigeons were deployed by the British', *Smithsonian Air and Space Magazine*, 18 December 2012

27. McMahon, *British Spies and Irish Rebels*, pp.305–6

28. Kershaw, *Making Friends With Hitler*; Max Hastings, 'When the Nazis came round to play golf', *Daily Telegraph*, 28 December 2004

29. Interrogation of Tyler Kent by Captain Maxwell Knight, 20 May 1940, KV 2/543;

Statement of Captain Maxwell Knight to Special Branch, 24 May 1940, ibid.

30. Quinlan, *The Secret War*, p.137
31. Andrew, *Defence of the Realm*, p.225; Bearse, *Conspirator*, p.265
32. Anon, 'Tales of Internment', *Daily Telegraph*, 6 December 2006
33. Stafford, *Churchill and Secret Service*, p.181
34. Andrew, *Defence of the Realm*, p.231; Lafitte, *Internment of Aliens*, p.201
35. Ibid., p.222
36. Ibid., p.227
37. Warren Manger, 'Secret files reveal mystery MI5 genius who foiled British Nazi spy network with fake Iron Crosses', *Daily Mirror*, 27 February 2014
38. Stafford, *European Resistance*
39. Bennett, *Churchill's Man of Mystery*, pp.259–60
40. Stafford, *Churchill and Secret Service*, pp.185–8
41. Keene, *Cloak of Enemies*, p.73
42. Bennett, *Churchill's Man of Mystery*, p.261
43. Greenwood, *Titan at the Foreign Office*, p.103
44. Bennett, *Churchill's Man of Mystery*, pp.249–52
45. Ibid., pp.249–50
46. Jablonsky, *The Great Game*, p.15
47. Ben Macintyre, 'How Hitler's inner circle was penetrated by an MI6 agent', *The Times*, 13 February 2010, pp.34–5
48. R.V. Jones, *Most Secret War*, pp.102–5; Churchill, *Their Finest Hour*, pp.383–5
49. Stafford, *Churchill and Secret Service*, pp.194–5
50. Hodges, *Turing*, pp.219–22
51. Winks, 'Winston Churchill, Intelligence and Fiction', p.7
52. Jablonsky, *The Great Game*, p.157
53. Correspondence between Sempill and Toyoda, KV 2/871
54. Larry Getlen, 'The traitor of Pearl Harbor', *New York Post*, 27 May 2012; Paul Lashmar and Andrew Mullins, 'Churchill protected Scottish peer suspected of spying for Japan', *Independent*, 24 August 1998
55. Churchill, *Grand Alliance*, pp.317–20
56. Ibid.
57. Hinsley, 'Churchill and Special Intelligence', p.421
58. Hinsley, *British Intelligence*, Vol. 1, pp.59–60
59. Murphy, *What Stalin Knew*, pp.120–34
60. Gorodetsky, *Grand Delusion*, pp.120, 232, 316

61. Churchill to Eden, 13 May 1941, PREM 3/219/7
62. Churchill to Eden, 30 March 1941, PREM 3/510/11
63. Churchill to Stalin, 3 April 1941, FO 371/29479/N1366
64. *Documents on German Foreign Policy*, Series D, Vol. 12, pp.604–5
65. Gorodetsky, 'Churchill's warnings to Stalin', p.979; see also Kimball, *The Juggler*, p.209
66. Churchill to Eden and Beaverbrook, 14 October 1941, PREM 3/403
67. Jablonsky, *Great Game*, p.161
68. Christopher Andrew and Vasili Mitrokhin, *The Mitrokhin Archive*, p.150
69. Reppetto, *Battleground New York*, pp.168–70
70. Bratzel and Rout, 'Pearl Harbor, Microdots, and J. Edgar Hoover', pp.1342–51, 953–60
71. Winks, 'Winston Churchill, Intelligence and Fiction', p.10
72. Charlotte McDonald-Gibson, 'David Cameron defends Britain's spy services as anger mounts in Europe over US and UK state surveillance', *Independent*, 26 October 2013
73. Bennett, *Churchill's Man of Mystery*, p.253
74. Cull, *Selling War*, p.145
75. Entry for 4 March 1940, Berle Diary, reel 2, frame 03093, FDR Library, Hyde Park, New York
76. Berle to Hull, 5 September 1941, Berle Diary, reel 3, frame 0308, FDR Library, Hyde Park, New York
77. Bratzel and Rout, 'FDR and the "Secret Map"', pp.167–73
78. See also his 'Will Hitler Take Ireland?', *Nation*, 31 January 1942, Shirer papers, George T. Henry College Archives, Stewart Memorial Library, Coe College
79. West, *Counterfeit Spies*; Cull, *Selling War*
80. Paul Fussell argues that it was penned at the New York publisher Harcourt, Brace. Fussell, *Wartime*, p.166
81. Holliday, *Children in the Holocaust*, pp.33–54
82. Cull, *Selling War*, p.4
83. Ben Macintyre, 'How we won the war: bugging, burglary, bribes; the defectors, double agents and saboteurs who outfoxed Nazi Germany met their match in the Soviet Union', *The Times*, 24 May 2014
84. Stafford, *Churchill and Secret Service*, pp.198–202

Chapter 5: Winston Churchill (1942–1945)
1. Rose, *The Literary Churchill*, p.122
2. Colville, *Fringes of Power*, pp.124–5
3. Minute by Churchill, 11 March 1944, F1176/66/61, FO371/41723
4. Hinsley and Stripp (eds), *Codebreakers*, pp.4–7
5. Hinsley, 'Churchill and Special Intelligence', pp.422–4
6. Andrew, *Defence of the Realm*, p.289
7. Ben Macintyre, 'How we won the war: bugging, burglary, bribes', *The Times*, 24 May 2013
8. Andrew, *Defence of the Realm*, p.239
9. Ibid., p.289
10. Record of a meeting at 10 Downing Street, 'War Cabinet Committee on "Overlord" Preparations', 8 March 1944, CAB 98/40
11. Macintyre, *Operation Mincemeat*, pp.122–9
12. Andrew, *Defence of the Realm*, p.287
13. Cave Brown, 'C', pp.317–18
14. Jablonsky, *Great Game*, pp.160–1
15. Aldrich, *GCHQ*, pp.55–6
16. Davies, *MI6*, pp.187, 238
17. Paul Callan, 'Adolf Hitler's orders: Kill Winston Churchill', *Daily Express*, 21 July 2012
18. CSS No. 635, 'Triangle', 30 May 1943, HW 1/1709
19. Payn and Morley (eds), *The Noël Coward Diaries*, p.21
20. John Mitchell diary, 2–4 June 1943, MISC 59, CCC, pp.15–17
21. McJimsey, *Harry Hopkins*, p.454, n34
22. O'Sullivan, *Dealing With the Devil*, pp.201–3
23. O'Sullivan, *Nazi Secret Warfare*, pp.222–3
24. Skorzeny, *Meine Kommandounternehmen*, pp.189–93
25. Rezun, *The Soviet Union and Iran*, pp.362–4
26. Erickson, *The Road to Berlin*, pp.153–4
27. O'Sullivan, *Dealing With the Devil*, pp.201–3; see also West, *Historical Dictionary of World War II Intelligence*, pp.140–1
28. Vaughan, *Sleeping With the Enemy*, pp.204–8. Chanel paid for the support of his family after the war, and for his funeral in 1952
29. Picardie, *Coco Chanel*, pp.126–37; Doerries, *Hitler's Intelligence Chief*, pp.165–7
30. Kern, 'How "Uncle Joe" Bugged FDR'
31. Gregory Vartanyan obituary, *Daily Telegraph*, 11 January 2012
32. Duncan Gardham, 'MI5 files: Zionist terrorist plotted to kill Winston Churchill', *Daily Telegraph*, 3 April 2011
33. John Mitchell diary, 25 December 1944, MISC 59, CCC, pp.15–17
34. Cahal Milmo, 'Rommel plot revealed: Plan to assassinate the Desert Fox – and why MI6 abandoned it', *Independent*, 23 May 2013
35. Seaman, *Operation Foxley*; Rigden, *Kill the Führer*
36. John Keegan quoted in Stafford, 'Churchill and SOE', pp.47–8
37. Max Hastings, 'Winston Churchill the terrorist', *Daily Mail*, 24 August 2009; see also Hastings, *Finest Years*, pp.451–76
38. Stafford, 'Churchill and SOE', pp.48–56
39. Van Creveld, *Hitler's Strategy*, pp.5–9
40. Martin, *The Web of Disinformation*, pp.52–75
41. Roberts, *Tito, Mihailović, and the Allies*, pp.131–2
42. Frank McLynn, 'Sir Fitzroy Maclean Bt', obituary, *Independent*, 19 June 1996
43. Lindsay, *Beacons in the Night*, p.235; Maclean, *Eastern Approaches*, pp.319–21
44. Randolph Churchill to Fitzroy Maclean, 9 November 1944, WO 202/283
45. Entry for Friday, 27 October 1944, Davie (ed.), Waugh diary
46. Randolph Churchill, HQ Croatia, to PM, 12 April 1944, PREM 3/511/12
47. Diamond, *Wingate*, pp.2–7
48. Mountbatten, *Report to the Combined Chiefs of Staff*, p.173; Cruickshank, *SOE in the Far East*, pp.184–5
49. Cruickshank, *SOE in the Far East*, pp.189–90
50. Stopford to Browning, 21 July 1945, WO 203/4398; see also 'Note of Operation Character up to 25 April 1945', WO 203/54
51. Churchill's remarks reported in Martin to Harvey, 12 June 1942, F4097/2878/40, FO 371/31866
52. Garden to Ripley, 'Long Range Intelligence in Thailand', 13 April 1945, File 3469, Box 250, Entry 146, RG 226, NARA
53. Aldrich, *Intelligence and the War Against Japan*, pp.119–23
54. Entry for 23 February 1945, Colville, *Fringes of Power*, p.563
55. Downes, *Scarlet Thread*, p.31
56. MacDonald, *Undercover Girl*, p.121
57. 'Report on American activities in Bombay', by O.C. Censor Station, 15 March 1943, and note by Chief Censor India to DMI, 27 March 1943, WO 208/816
58. Interview with Ralph Block (OWI India), May 1967, Oral History collection, Harry

S. Truman Library, Independence, Missouri

59. Stafford, *Roosevelt and Churchill*, p.256
60. R. Aldrich interview with Colin Mackenzie, Special Forces Club, London, April 1985
61. Bartholomew-Feis, *The OSS and Ho Chi Minh*, pp.203–8
62. Air Vice Marshal Harcourt Smith to Air Vice Marshal Whitworth Jones, DO/GHS, 22 February 1945, MBI/C42/66/4, Mountbatten papers, Southampton University Library
63. Stafford, *Roosevelt and Churchill*, pp.182–9
64. Thorne, *Allies of a Kind*, p.266
65. Entry for 15 March 1943, 'Interview with prime minister', Wilkinson, Diary, 1/2, 2, CCC. The authorities swooped on this MI6 diary in 1998 and closed it, but this attempt to police the past was thwarted, since copies exist in the Anthony Cave Brown papers, Lauinger Library
66. Entry for 26 May 1942, Danchev and Todd (eds), *Alanbrooke: War Diary*
67. Entry for 22 March 1943, Wilkinson, Diary, 1/2, 2, CCC
68. Wilkinson (BSC) to Sir George Sansom, 28 December 1944, Box 1, 4, Wilkinson papers, CCC
69. See Zamir, *The Secret Anglo–French War*
70. Killearn (Cairo) to Cavendish-Bentinck, 8 June 1945, HF/EP (1154/1/45G), E4569/1630/65, FO 371/45272
71. Selborne to Churchill, 'Armistice and Post-war Committee', 27 April 1944, SOE main office files. We are most grateful to the SOE adviser Duncan Stewart for providing us with a copy of this document, which was in the process of being released to the TNA
72. Zamir, 'The "Missing Dimension"', pp.791–899
73. Churchill quoted in Colville to Hollis, 18 April 1945, CAB 120/827
74. Lynch (London) to Hoover (FBI), 12 July 1945, Donovan papers, US Army War College, Carlisle
75. Donovan to Truman, 31 August 1945, Box 15, Conway files, Harry S. Truman Library
76. Churchill to Eden, M537/4, 8 May 1944, Eden papers, Pol 44/90, FO 954/20A/169
77. Entry for 23 February 1945, Colville, *Fringes of Power*, p.563
78. A careful account is offered in the second edition of Lewis, *Changing Direction*, pp.xxxvi–xlvi
79. *Guardian*, 2 October 1998. We are indebted to Gary Rawnsley for this

reference. 'Operation Unthinkable', 22 May 1945 (Final), CAB 120/691
80. PM to Ismay, 10 June 1945, CAB 120/691; Bryant, *Triumph in the West*, pp.469–70; Lewis, *Changing Direction*, pp.242–3. For Churchill and Truman on this see Bryden, *Best-Kept Secret*, pp.262–4
81. Goodman, *Joint Intelligence Committee*, p.144
82. JIC (44) 467 (0), 'Russia's Strategic Interest and Intentions from the Point of View of her Security', N678/20/38, FO 371/47860; JIC (45) 163 (0), Revised Final, 'Relations with the Russians', 23 May 1946, CAB 81/129
83. Jon Ungoed-Thomas, 'Attlee Feared Atom Bomb Armageddon', *Sunday Times*, 4 November 2007, p.11
84. Eden to Churchill, P.P./44/1, 4 January 1944, CAB 120/827; Churchill to Ismay, D.41/4, 10 February 1944, ibid.
85. Entry for Saturday, 20 January 1945, 'The Diaries of Guy Liddell', fos.59–60, KV 4/196
86. Denning to Cavendish-Bentinck No.11519, 11 May 1945, fo.1025, WO 203/5625
87. Penney to Sinclair, 2 May 1945, 5/21, Penney papers, Liddell Hart Centre for Military Archives
88. Reynolds, *In Command of History*; Clarke, *Mr Churchill's Profession*; Goodchild, *R. V. Jones*, p.8
89. Brook to Churchill, 4 June 1948, CAB 21/3749; Brook to Menzies, 8 November 1948, ibid.; Churchill to Brook, 7 June 1948, ibid.; Menzies to Brook, C/1438, 29 September 1948, ibid.

Chapter 6: Clement Attlee (1945–1951)

1. Attlee scribbled note on memorandum from Strang to Attlee, 26 March 1949, FO 800/437
2. Attlee to Swinton, 8 April 1950, Attlee dep.100, fol.12, Bodleian Library, Oxford
3. Bastable, *Prime Ministers*, p.102. He was challenged as an MP by an Italian captain
4. Jeffery, *MI6*, p.619
5. Schlaepfer, 'Signals Intelligence and British Counter-Subversion', p.3
6. 'C' to deputy prime minister, 'Boniface', C/5249, 29 December 1943, HW 1/2308
7. Ismay to Attlee, 3 January 1944, CAB 120/827; also Jacob to Attlee, 1 December 1943, ibid.
8. Attlee, *As it Happened*, p.151; Scowcroft, *Attlee's War*, p.51

9. Hennessy, *The Prime Minister*, p.152
10. Jeffery, *MI6*, pp.649, 751
11. Attlee was Churchill's deputy in the War Cabinet and on the Defence Committee, and spoke for the coalition government in Parliament when Churchill was away. He was Lord Privy Seal in 1940, and assumed the newly created post of deputy prime minister in 1942
12. Entry for 25 May 1940, 'The Diaries of Guy Liddell', KV 4/186
13. Lomas, 'The Defence of the Realm and Nothing Else', p.16
14. Walton, 'British Intelligence and Threats to British National Security', p.45
15. Entry for 1 January 1949, 'The Diaries of Guy Liddell', KV 4/471
16. Toye, 'Winston Churchill's Crazy Broadcast', pp.655–80
17. Winston Churchill quoted in Francis Beckett, *Clem Attlee*, p.213; Gilbert, *Never Despair*, pp.32–5; see also Colville, *Fringes of Power*, p.612
18. Andrew, *Defence of the Realm*, p.382
19. Entry for 18 October 1945, 'The Diaries of Guy Liddell', KV 4/466
20. Entry for 28 June 1946, ibid., KV 4/467; see also entries for 10 May and 2 July 1946, ibid.
21. Lomas, 'Labour Ministers, Intelligence and Domestic Anti-Communism', p.115
22. Entry for 19 November 1946, 'The Diaries of Guy Liddell', KV 4/468
23. Entry for 1 January 1946, ibid., KV 4/467
24. Entry for 20 February 1946, ibid.
25. Andrew, *Defence of the Realm*, pp.321, 323; Sillitoe, *Cloak Without Dagger*, p.176
26. Andrew, *Defence of the Realm*, p.323; Andrew, *Secret Service*, p.489: Jones, *Reflections*, p.21
27. Entries for 17 and 31 December 1945, 'The Diaries of Guy Liddell', KV 4/467
28. R.W. Johnson, 'Find the Birch Sticks', *London Review of Books*, 27/17 (2005), p.17
29. Lownie, *Burgess*, pp.289–91
30. Lycett, *Fleming*, pp.251–310
31. Entry for 4 March 1950, 'The Diaries of Guy Liddell', KV 4/472
32. Theakston, 'Brook, Norman Craven, Baron Normanbrook (1902–1967)', *Oxford Dictionary of National Biography*, Oxford University Press, 2004, online edn
33. Attlee to Swinton, 8 April 1950, Attlee dep.100, fol.12, Bodleian Library, Oxford
34. Turchetti, *The Pontecorvo Affair*, pp.81–98
35. Andrew, *Defence of the Realm*, pp.382, 369; Jeffery, *MI6*, p.657
36. On the latter see 'Letter from prime minister to prime ministers of Canada, Australia, New Zealand and South Africa on discussion of security at autumn conference: counter-action of Soviet infiltration methods', 1947–1951, PREM 8/1343
37. Hennessy, *Secret State*, pp.87, 89; Andrew, *Defence of the Realm*, p.383; minute by Attlee, 21 December 1947, CAB 130/20
38. Schlaepfer, 'Signals Intelligence', p.13
39. Hennessy and Brownfeld, 'Cold War Security Purge'
40. Entry for 25 March 1948, 'The Diaries of Guy Liddell', KV 4/469
41. Entry for 14 April 1948, ibid.
42. Entries for 22 February and 16 March 1949, ibid., KV 4/471
43. Clement Attlee, 3 July 1949, Attlee dep.85, fols.110–47, Bodleian Library, Oxford
44. Deery, 'A Very Present Menace', pp.70–2
45. Ibid.
46. Andrew, *Defence of the Realm*, p.324
47. Ibid., p.837
48. Entry for 19 November 1946, 'The Diaries of Guy Liddell', KV 4/468
49. 'Communism in the United Kingdom: Note by the Official Committee', 16 December 1950, attached to 'Communism in the United Kingdom: Note by the Secretary', AC(M)(51)1, 19 January 1951, CAB 134/2
50. Correspondence of 25 October 1950, ED 34/135
51. 'Official Committee on Communism (Home): Constitution and Terms of Reference of the Committee', AC(H)(51)1, 7 June 1951, CAB 134/2
52. See Maguire, 'Counter-Subversion in Early Cold War Britain', pp.1–30
53. Clement Attlee, 'Russian Infiltration', attached to letter from Attlee to the leaders of Canada, Australia, New Zealand and South Africa, July 1948, PREM 8/1343
54. Ibid.
55. Clement Attlee, 'Foreword' in Percy Sillitoe, *Cloak Without Dagger*, p.v; Aldrich, *Hidden Hand*, p.425
56. Hennessy, *Secret State*, p.92
57. Hoover to Souers, 18 June 1951, Box 169, PSF Files, Harry S. Truman Library, Independence, Missouri
58. Hennessy and Brownfeld, 'Cold War Security Purge', pp.969–73
59. John Crossland, 'Attlee sought answers about Burgess and Maclean', *The Times*, 2 April 2007, p.7

60. Robert Verkaik, 'Revealed: Attlee's ignorance of the Cambridge spies who defected', *Independent*, 3 January 2007, p.14

61. Rossiter, *The Spy Who Changed the World*, pp.57, 145, 212, 295

62. Goodman, 'Who is Trying to Keep What Secret from Whom and Why?', pp.99–109

63. Quoted in Rossiter, *The Spy Who Changed the World*, p.296

64. Bower, *The Perfect English Spy*, p.97

65. Entry for 3 March 1950, 'The Diaries of Guy Liddell', KV 4/472

66. Goodman and Pincher, 'Research Note: Clement Attlee, Percy Sillitoe and the Security Aspect of the Fuchs Case', p.69

67. Ibid., p.68

68. Ibid., p.69; Hennessey and Thomas, *Spooks*, p.75

69. Memorandum from Sillitoe to Attlee, 'Klaus Fuchs', 7 February 1950, PREM 8/1279

70. Hennessey and Thomas, *Spooks*, p.81

71. Memorandum from Sillitoe to Attlee, 'Klaus Fuchs', 7 February 1950, PREM 8/1279; Goodman and Pincher, 'Research Note', p.70

72. Roger Hollis quoted in Hennessy and Thomas, *Spooks*, p.80

73. Goodman and Pincher, 'Research Note', pp.70–1

74. 'Extract from Prime Minister's Speech in the Debate on the Address: Official Report 6 March 1950. Cols 71–2', attached to note from Ministry of Supply to 10 Downing Street, 13 March 1950, PREM 8/1279

75. Memorandum from Sillitoe to Attlee, 'Klaus Fuchs', 7 February 1950, PREM 8/1279

76. Moran, *Classified*, p.114

77. 'Extract from Prime Minister's Speech in the Debate on the Address: Official Report 6 March 1950. Cols 71–2', attached to note from Ministry of Supply to 10 Downing Street, 13 March 1950, PREM 8/1279

78. Attlee, *As it Happened*, p.162

79. Goodman, 'Who is Trying to Keep What Secret from Whom and Why?', pp.99–109

80. Entry for 17 March 1950, 'The Diaries of Guy Liddell', KV 4/472

81. Brown, *Bernal*, p.330

82. Close, *Half Life*, p.205

83. Turchetti, *The Pontecorvo Affair*, p.124

84. Quoted in ibid., p.135

85. Skinner to Perrin, 13 June 1951, J1117/11, Cherwell papers, Nuffield College, Oxford

86. On the 'Cold Warrior' debate see Smith and Zametica, 'The Cold Warrior', p.241

87. Peter Hennessy, *The Prime Minister*, pp.166–7; Phythian, *The Labour Party, War and International Relations*, p.25

88. Young, *Masters of Indecision*, p.15

89. Ian Cobain, 'Special report: How T-Force abducted Germany's best brains for Britain: Secret papers reveal post-war campaign to loot military and commercial assets', *Guardian*, 29 August 2007, p.12

90. Beckett, *Clem Attlee*, p.231; Pearce, *Attlee*, p.164

91. Lucas and Morris, 'A Very British Crusade', pp.85–90

92. 'Extract from the Conclusions of the 78th Meeting of the Cabinet held on Wednesday, 14 August 1946', FO 945/400

93. Attlee to McNeil, April 1947, PREM 8/624

94. 'Propaganda to Jews in Europe', GEN.180/4, 2 June 1947, CAB 130/20

95. For details of the operations see Jeffery, *MI6*, pp.689–94

96. Interview, David Smiley, London, May 1999

97. Jeffery, *MI6*, pp.689–94; West, *Friends*, pp.33–40; Dorril, *MI6*, pp.545–9

98. Jeffery, *MI6*, p.712

99. Vickers, *The Labour Party*, p.186; Bullock, *Bevin*, p.78

100. Jeffery, *MI6*, p.714

101. Attlee scribbled note on memorandum from Strang to Attlee, 26 March 1949, FO 800/437

102. Memorandum from Strang to Attlee, 5 April 1949, FO 800/437

103. Ibid.

104. 'Conversations Between Bevin and Acheson on Albania', 14 September 1949, Box 312, Records of Post CFM meetings, RG 49, NARA

105. John Ward to Air Marshal William Elliott, 20 February 1950, attached: '"Deception" Organisation', DEFE 28/1

106. 'Composition and Terms of Reference', AC(M)(49)1, 31 December 1949, CAB 21/2992

107. Gwinnett, 'Attlee, Bevin and Political Warfare'

108. Cliffe, 'Anti-Communist Activities in Europe', AC(M)(50)2, 22 December 1950, PREM 8/1365

109. 'Proposed Activities behind the Iron Curtain', AC(O)(50)52 (Third Revise), November 1950, CAB 21/2750

110. Brook to Attlee, 'Meeting of the Ministerial Committee on Communism, 21 December 1950', 20 December 1950, PREM 8/1365

111. Aldrich, *Hidden Hand*, pp.468–9

112. Jackson to Keating (AIOC), 6 August 1951, Box 52, CD Jackson Papers, Dwight D. Eisenhower Library, Kansas

113. David Howell, 'Morrison, Herbert Stanley', *Oxford Dictionary of National Biography*, Oxford University Press, 2004, online edn. The quote was from Hugh Gaitskell

114. Attlee, *As it Happened*, pp.176–7

115. Goodman, *Joint Intelligence Committee*, p.358

116. EP 1531/674 and FO 371/91550, EP 15331/713, FO 371/91548, cited in Dorril, *MI6*, pp.562–3

117. Smiley, *Albanian Assignment*, p.161; Bethell, *Great Betrayal*, pp.71, 137–9; Lapping, *End of Empire*, p.215; interview, David Smiley, London, May 1999

118. Louis, 'Britain and the Overthrow of the Mossadeq Government', p.132

119. Swinton to Attlee, 5 April 1950, SWIN III, ACC 313, 4/1, Swinton papers, CCC

120. Ibid.

121. Attlee to Swinton, 8 April 1950, ibid.

122. Swinton to Attlee, 18 May 1950, ibid.

123. Herman, 'The Postwar Organisation of Intelligence', pp.11–35

124. Goodman, *Spying on the Nuclear Bear*, pp.36–56

125. Cabinet Office correspondence with the authors, 16 August 2011

126. DJWR to Attlee, 25 October 1950, enclosing Brook minute to Attlee, PREM 8/1527. We are especially grateful to Daniel Lomas for sight of this document

127. In December 1951 GEN 374 was wound up and reconstituted as PSIS

128. Chiefs of Staff (52) 152nd meeting (1), Confidential Annex, 4 November 1952, DEFE 11/350

129. Swinton to Maude, 15 June 1951, SWIN III, ACC 313, 4/1, Swinton papers, CCC

130. Maude to Swinton, 19 June 1951, ibid.

131. Mistry, 'Illusions of Coherence', pp.39–66

132. Mason to Greenhough, 19 October 1951, LAB 13/697

Chapter 7: Winston Churchill (1951–1955)

1. Wilford, *America's Great Game*, p.193

2. Young, *Winston Churchill's Last Campaign*, pp.12–52

3. Theakston, 'Baron Normanbrook (1902–1967)', *Oxford Dictionary of National Biography*, Oxford University Press, 2004, online edn

4. Jenkins, *Churchill*, pp.492–3

5. Entry for 3 May 1953, Dixon diary, in Carlton, *Churchill and the Soviet Union*, p.183

6. Hennessy, *The Prime Minister*, p.183

7. Entry for 31 July 1954, Catterall (ed.), *Macmillan Diaries*, Vol. I, pp.351–3

8. Hennessy, *The Prime Minister*, p.185

9. Entry for 31 July 1954, Catterall (ed.), *Macmillan Diaries*, Vol. I, pp.351–3

10. Whitehead, 'Intelligence archive: Churchill and Stalin's boozy meeting', *Daily Telegraph*, 23 May 2013

11. Montague Brown, *Long Sunset*, p.133

12. Andrew, 'Churchill and Intelligence', p.182

13. Montague Brown, *Long Sunset*, pp.133–4

14. Dorril, *MI6*, p.494. The quotes are from George Blake and Kim Philby respectively

15. Stafford, *Churchill and Secret Service*, p.393

16. Aldrich, *Hidden Hand*, pp.315–42

17. Entries for 13 and 14 March 1953, 'The Diaries of Guy Liddell', KV 4/475

18. Stafford, *Churchill and Secret Service*, p.391; Colville, *The Churchillians*, p.60

19. Bower, *Perfect English Spy*, p.146

20. Stafford, *Churchill and Secret Service*, p.390

21. Aldrich, *Hidden Hand*, p.440; Andrew, *Defence of the Realm*, pp.155, 224, 229

22. Entry for 17 November 1951, 'The Diaries of Guy Liddell', KV 4/473

23. Simkins, 'Sillitoe, Sir Percy Joseph (1888–1962)', *Oxford Dictionary of National Biography*, Oxford University Press, 2004, online edn

24. Stafford, *Churchill and Secret Service*, pp.391–2

25. Entry for 7 December 1951, 'The Diaries of Guy Liddell', KV 4/473; Page, Leitch and Knightley, *Philby Conspiracy*

26. Entry for 12 December 1951, 'The Diaries of Guy Liddell', KV 4/473

27. Bower, *Perfect English Spy*, p.146

28. Ibid.

29. Stafford, *Churchill and Secret Service*, p.390

30. Entry for 22 February 1952, 'The Diaries of Guy Liddell', KV 4/474

31. Dutton, 'Fyfe, David Patrick Maxwell, Earl of Kilmuir (1900–1967)', *Oxford Dictionary of National Biography*, Oxford University Press, 2004, online edn

32. Entries for 22 February and 3 March 1952, 'The Diaries of Guy Liddell', KV 4/474; Andrew, *Defence of the Realm*, p.324

33. Entries for 22 February and 17 March 1952, 'The Diaries of Guy Liddell', KV 4/474

34. Stafford, *Churchill and Secret Service*, p.390

35. Entry for 16 December 1952, 'The Diaries of Guy Liddell', KV 4/474
36. Entry for 17 November 1951, ibid., KV 4/473
37. Entry for 7 December 1951, ibid.
38. Entry for 16 June 1952, ibid., KV 4/474; Dick White, untitled, 16 June 1952, KV 2/1367
39. Entry for 1 January 1953, 'The Diaries of Guy Liddell', KV 4/475
40. Dick White, untitled, 16 June 1952, KV 2/1367
41. Entry for 16 June 1952, 'The Diaries of Guy Liddell', KV 4/474; Dick White, untitled, 16 June 1952, KV 4/474
42. Entry for 23 June 1952, 'The Diaries of Guy Liddell', KV 4/474
43. Prime Minister to SoS for Air, M.412/52, J122/131, Cherwell papers, Nuffield College, Oxford; Air Ministry to Churchill, 9 August 1952, ibid.
44. Young, 'Churchill's bid for peace with Moscow, 1954', p.445
45. Gervase Cowell in Andrew and Aldrich (eds), 'Intelligence Service in the Second World War', p.163
46. 'Record of Meeting between Churchill, Nutting, Rennie, Kirkpatrick', 1 May 1954, PREM 11/773
47. Khokhlov quoted in 'I led KGB Hit Squad', Daily Mirror, 21 July 2007; 'The Khokhlov Case: A Russian Secret Agent's Fantastic Weapons', Illustrated London News, 1 May 1954, p.719; Brook-Shepherd, The Storm Birds
48. Churchill to Nutting and Kirkpatrick, 14 May 1954, PREM 11/773
49. Lloyd to Churchill, 15 May 1954, ibid.
50. CAB 195/13/6, Cabinet Minutes, 8 December 1954, Cabinet Secretary's Notebook; CAB 128/27, Cabinet Conclusions, 8 December 1954, CC(54) 84th Conclusions; CAB 128/8, Cabinet Conclusions, 20 January 1955, CC(55) 5th Conclusions. For legal and other advice see LO 2/937/LCO 2/5190
51. Stafford, 'Churchill and SOE', pp.47–8
52. Braden to Bedell Smith, 28 December 1949, Box 4, ACUE, Bedell Smith papers, Dwight D. Eisenhower Library, Kansas; see also Aldrich, Hidden Hand, pp.342–70
53. Reilly minute, 3 April 1952, ZC.52/54, DEFE 11/433
54. Entry for 1 February 1951, Catterall (ed.), Macmillan Diaries: The Cabinet Years, pp.50–1
55. Entry for 10 August 1951, ibid., pp.94–5; see also p.123

56. Shuckburgh, Descent to Suez, 27 August 1953
57. Defty, Britain, America and Anti-Communist Propaganda, pp.193–4
58. Robert Joyce, 'Final Meeting in London with British Foreign Office and SIS Representatives', 20 December 1951, Executive Secretariat, PSB Working File, 1951–53, Box 6, RG59, NARA. We are indebted to Thomas Maguire for this file
59. Dorril, MI6, p.489; Young, Winston Churchill's Last Campaign, pp.37, 70, 85; Young, 'The British Foreign Office and Cold War Fighting', pp.1–8
60. Young, Winston Churchill's Last Campaign, p.37; Corke, US Covert Operations, pp.153–5; Larres, Churchill's Cold War, pp.163–7
61. Louis, 'The Significance of Muhammad Mossadegh', Times Literary Supplement, 27 June 2012
62. Mawby, 'The Clandestine Defence of Empire', p.105
63. Battersby, 'Sir Winston Churchill's family begged him not to convert to Islam, letter reveals', Independent, 28 December 2014
64. Montague Brown, Long Sunset, p.164
65. Stafford, Churchill and Secret Service, p.397
66. Kinzer, All the Shah's Men, pp.144–7
67. Wilford, America's Great Game, pp.162–9
68. Eisenhower to Churchill, 5 May 1953, in Boyle (ed.), Churchill–Eisenhower Correspondence, p.52
69. Woodhouse to Amery, 13 February 1952, Julian Amery papers, 1/2/93, CCC
70. Thomas to Greenhough, 28 July 1952 (No Circulation), LAB 13/1069
71. Woodhouse, 'Iran 1950–53', 16 August 1976, Woodhouse 8/1, p.5, LHCMA
72. Dorril, MI6, p.581
73. Churchill to Bedell Smith, T.96/53, 15 April 1953, PREM 11/515. We are indebted to Dina Rezk for bringing this file to our attention
74. Top-secret minute to Churchill on discussions with John Foster Dulles, New York, 7 January 1953, ibid.
75. Woodhouse, 'Iran 1950–53', 16 August 1976, Woodhouse 8/1, p.12, 16, LHCMA
76. Montague Brown, Long Sunset, pp.132, 166
77. Andrew, 'Churchill and Intelligence', p.182
78. Molotsky, 'Kermit Roosevelt, Leader of C.I.A. Coup in Iran, Dies at 84', New York Times, 11 June 2000; Anon., 'Kermit Roosevelt; Arranged Iran Coup', Los Angeles Times, 11 June 2000

79. CIA Clandestine Services History, 'Overthrow of Premier Mossadegh of Iran', March 1954, pp.31–8, 54–63
80. Stafford, *Churchill and Secret Service*, pp.401–2
81. Roosevelt, *Countercoup*, p.207; Mokhtari, 'Iran's 1953 Coup Revisited', p.477
82. Wilber, *Regime Change in Iran*, pp.61, 81
83. Ibid., pp.79–80
84. CIA History Staff, *The Battle for Iran*, c.mid-1970s, p.71
85. Wilber, *Regime Change in Iran*, pp.81–3
86. Eubank (COS) to Rowlands (MoS), 31 January 1952, DEFE 11/350; Eubank to DPRC, 31 January 1952, ibid.; COS (52) 152nd mtg (1), Confidential Annex, 4 November 1952, ibid.
87. Cathcart, *Test of Greatness*, p.51
88. Lashmar, *Spy Flights*, p.72
89. Aldrich, *Hidden Hand*, p.394
90. Remarks by Saunders at RAF Historical Branch conference on Cold War intelligence gathering, RAF Hendon, 18 April 2000
91. Lashmar, *Spy Flights*, pp.64–87
92. Aldrich, *GCHQ*, pp.123–4
93. Ibid.
94. Stafford, *Spies Beneath Berlin*, p.108; Maddrell, 'British–American scientific intelligence collaboration', p.88
95. Aldrich, *GCHQ*, pp.177–8; private information
96. Evans, 'MI6 pays out over secret LSD mind control tests', *Guardian*, 24 February 2006
97. Shawcross, *Queen and Country*, p.51

Chapter 8: Anthony Eden (1955–1957)
1. Fred Emery, 'Lord Avon denies "Kill Nasser" Story', *The Times*, 18 June 1975
2. Karen McVeigh, 'How PM and Successor Clashed', *Guardian*, 4 February 2008, p.6
3. *Colville Diary*, p.706
4. Robert Blake, 'Late Deceiver', *London Review of Books*, 17 September 1981
5. Bower, *Perfect English Spy*, p.177; Hennessy, *The Prime Minister*, pp.208–14
6. Entry for 7 December 1951, Catterall (ed.), *Macmillan Diaries: Vol. I*, p.122
7. Hennessy, *The Prime Minister*, p.213
8. Paul Lashmar and Peter Day, 'Wodehouse secretly in pay of the Nazis, say MI5 files', *Daily Telegraph*, 17 September 1999
9. Faber, *Speaking for England*, p.532
10. Entries for 28 September and 3 October 1944, Duff Cooper, *Diaries*, pp.324–5
11. Eden to Churchill, 29 November 1944, AP 20/11/743, Avon papers, Birmingham

University Library; Churchill to Eden, 'Wodehouse', 20 December 1944, AP20/12/679, M/1193/4, ibid.
12. Beevor and Cooper, *Paris*, pp.74–6
13. Eden to Churchill, 6 February 1944, PM/44/45, AP20/11/45, Avon papers, Birmingham University Library
14. Eden to Churchill, 2 June 1944, PM4/402, AP20/11/401, ibid.
15. Andrew, *Defence of the Realm*, p.310
16. Thorpe, *Eden*, p.362
17. Wright, *Spycatcher*
18. Andrew Lownie, 'Unmasked: SIXTH man in Cambridge spy ring sent nuclear secrets to the KGB allowing Russia to develop their own atom bomb', *Mail on Sunday*, 6 September 2015
19. Lownie, *Stalin's Englishman*, pp.266–7
20. Ibid., pp.268–9
21. Hansard, HC Deb, 25 October 1955, vol. 545 cc28–9
22. Macintyre, *A Spy Among Friends*, p.186
23. Pincher, *Treachery*, pp.410–11
24. Hansard, HC Deb, 7 November 1955, vol. 545 cc1483–1611, 1532–3, 1535, 1599, 1604
25. Entries for 19 and 21 September and 20 October 1955, Catterall (ed.), *Macmillan Diaries: The Cabinet Years*, pp.478–9, 493
26. Hansard, HC Deb, 7 November 1955, vol. 545 c1497
27. Macintyre, *A Spy Among Friends*, p.192
28. Ibid., p.178
29. Bower, *Perfect English Spy*, pp.152–3
30. Thorpe, *Eden*, pp.446, 463
31. Andrew, *Defence of the Realm*, pp.408–9
32. Bower, *Perfect English Spy*, p.159
33. Kapitonova, 'Visit of Soviet leaders', p.2
34. Corera, *Art of Betrayal*, p.76; Bridges min., 18 May 1956, PREM 11/2077
35. Aldrich, *GCHQ*, p.178
36. Goodman, 'Covering up Spying in the "Buster" Crabb Affair', p.769
37. Westell, *Inside Story*, pp.88–9; Taubman, *Khrushchev*, pp.370–1; private information
38. Kapitonova, 'Visit of Soviet leaders', p.11
39. Private information
40. Macintyre, *A Spy Among Friends*, p.194
41. Ibid., pp.194–5
42. Moran, *Classified*, p.122
43. Macintyre, *A Spy Among Friends*, p.195
44. Ibid., pp.193–5
45. Kapitonova, 'Visit of Soviet leaders', p.1
46. Goodman, 'Covering up Spying in the "Buster" Crabb Affair', p.769
47. Bower, *Perfect English Spy*, pp.160–1
48. Moran, 'Intelligence and the Media', p.694; Macintyre, *A Spy Among Friends*, p.199

49. Goodman, 'Covering up Spying in the "Buster" Crabb Affair', p.773
50. Ibid.; Macintyre, *A Spy Among Friends*, p.196
51. Bower, *Perfect English Spy*, p.160
52. Although he was treated kindly and in fact promoted: McDermott, *Eden Legacy*, p.129
53. Thorpe, *Eden*, p.472
54. Goodman, 'Covering up Spying in the "Buster" Crabb Affair', p.778
55. Corera, *Art of Betrayal*, p.77
56. Andrew, *Defence of the Realm*, p.328
57. Bower, *Perfect English Spy*, p.186
58. Ibid., p.162
59. West, *The A to Z of British Intelligence*, p.578
60. Hansard, HC Deb, 9 May 1956, vol. 552 cc1220–3
61. Ibid., cc1220–1
62. 'From the archive, 19 January 1963: Editorial: The death of Hugh Gaitskell', *Guardian*, January 2015
63. Hansard, HC Deb, 14 May 1956, vol. 552 cc1751–87, 1751–61
64. Moran, 'Intelligence and the Media', p.685
65. McDermott, *The Eden Legacy*, p.130
66. Hailsham, *A Sparrow's Flight*, p.281
67. Moran, 'Intelligence and the Media', p.694
68. Elliott, *With My Little Eye*, p.25
69. Ibid., p.26
70. Ibid., p.24
71. Macintyre, *A Spy Among Friends*, p.7
72. Ibid., p.201
73. David Williams, 'Cold War mystery solved? I killed Buster Crabb says Russian frogman', *Daily Mail*, 16 November 2007
74. Hutton, *The Fake Defector*, pp.1–21
75. Macintyre, *A Spy Among Friends*, p.201
76. Eden to Bridges, 9 May 1956, M.104/56, AP20/21/228, Avon papers, Birmingham University Library
77. Bridges, 'Report of an Enquiry on an Intelligence Operation against Russian Warships', 18 May 1956, para 9, CAB301/121
78. Moran, 'Intelligence and the Media', pp.694–5
79. Eden to MoD, 22 December 1956, AP20/21/228, Avon papers, Birmingham University Library
80. Aldrich, *GCHQ*, pp.141–3; Aldrich, *Hidden Hand*, p.526
81. Woodhouse, 'Iran 1950–53', p.12, 16 August 1976, Woodhouse 8/1, LHCMA
82. McDermott, *The Eden Legacy*, p.133
83. Bower, *Perfect English Spy*, p.196
84. Goodman, *Joint Intelligence Committee*, p.379
85. Ibid., p.386; Campbell, 'Dean, Patrick', *Oxford Dictionary of National Biography*, Oxford University Press, 2004, online edn
86. McDermott, *The Eden Legacy*, p.137
87. Hennessy, *The Prime Minister*, p.228
88. Walton, *Empire of Secrets*, p.299; Rezk, *Western Intelligence and the Arab World*, pp.2–23
89. Goodman, *Joint Intelligence Committee*, p.382
90. Hennessy, *The Prime Minister*, pp.230–2
91. Cradock, *Know Your Enemy*, p.173
92. 'Egyptian Nationalisation of the Suez Canal Company', 10 August 1956, JIC (56)80, CAB 158/35
93. Cradock, *Know Your Enemy*, p.133
94. Goodman, *Joint Intelligence Committee*, p.409
95. Reiter, 'The Weight of the Shadow of the Past', pp.490–526
96. Braun, 'Suez Reconsidered', p.548
97. Ibid., pp.547, 553
98. Cradock, *Know Your Enemy*, p.116
99. Quoted in Walton, *Empire of Secrets*, p.301
100. Ibid., pp.300–1
101. Dulles to Phleger, 11 May 1964, File 31, Box 53, Dulles papers, Seeley G. Mudd Library, Princeton
102. McDermott, *The Eden Legacy*, p.159; private information
103. Bower, *Perfect English Spy*, p.176
104. Ibid., p.177
105. Eden, 'Counter-Subversion', 10 December 1955, PREM 11/1582
106. Brook to Eden, 28 November 1955, PREM 11/1582
107. Curtis, *Secret Affairs*, p.71; see also Lloyd to Eden, 15 March 1956, FO371/121858
108. Lucas, *Divided We Stand*, p.117
109. Gerolymatos, *Castles Made of Sand*, p.14
110. Goodman, *Joint Intelligence Committee*, p.378
111. Ibid.
112. Ibid., p.387
113. Lucas, *Divided We Stand*, p.194; Gerolymatos, *Castles Made of Sand*, p.14; Dodds-Parker, *Political Eunuch*, p.102; Cradock, *Know Your Enemy*, p.117
114. Eden to Lloyd, M.95/96, 4 May 1956, AP20/21/94, Avon papers, Birmingham University Library
115. Aldrich, *Hidden Hand*, pp.481–2; Bower, *Perfect English Spy*, p.200; Lucas, *Divided We Stand*, p.101; Scott Lucas, 'Suez – The Missing Dimension', BBC Radio 4, 28 October 2006; Gerolymatos, *Castles Made*

of Sand, pp.13–14; 'Interview with Julian Amery conducted by Anthony Gorst and W. Scott Lucas 12 June 1989', SUEZ Oral History Project, SUEZOHP1:AMERY, LHCMA

116. Hennessy, *The Prime Minister*, p.215

117. Goodman, *Joint Intelligence Committee*, pp.378, 408

118. Quoted in 'British Rift Causes new Suez Crisis', *Michigan Daily*, 7 January 1953

119. Richelson, 'When Kindness Fails', p.251

120. Dorril reviews the evidence carefully in *MI6*; see also Bower, *Perfect English Spy*, p.195

121. Blake, *No Other Choice*, p.157; West, *Secret Service*, p.65

122. Young, *Who is My Liege*, pp.79–80

123. Bower, *Perfect English Spy*, pp.185–6

124. Corera, *Art of Betrayal*, pp.79–80

125. Simon Usborne, 'Top Secret: A Century of British Espionage', *Independent*, 6 October 2009

126. Aldrich, *Hidden Hand*, p.480

127. Ibid.; Bower, *Perfect English Spy*, p.192; Dorril, *MI6*, pp.633–4; Simon Usborne, 'Top Secret: A Century of British Espionage', *Independent*, 6 October 2009

128. Gerolymatos, *Castles Made of Sand*, p.10

129. Dorril, *MI6*, p.633

130. Curtis, *Secret Affairs*, pp.62–3; Kyle, *Suez*, p.555

131. Bower, *Perfect English Spy*, p.192; Dorril, *MI6*, p.639

132. Dorril, *MI6*, p.633; John McGlashan obituary, *Daily Telegraph*, 10 September 2010; and private information

133. 'Egypt Demands Death for "Spies"', *Daily Telegraph*, 5 February 1957

134. John Stanley obituary, *Daily Telegraph*, 18 August 2000. For their detention in Cairo see FO 371/125612/1691/2

135. Dorril, *MI6*, pp.631–3

136. Verrier, *Through the Looking Glass*, p.147

137. Bower, *Perfect English Spy*, p.196

138. Aldrich, *Hidden Hand*, p.479

139. Lucas, *Divided We Stand*, p.196

140. Kyle, *Suez*, p.555

141. Fred Emery, 'Lord Avon Denies "Kill Nasser" Story', *The Times*, 18 June 1975

142. Copeland to Avon, 25 June 1975, Folder 117, Box 544, Buckley papers, Yale University Library

143. Goodman, *Joint Intelligence Committee*, pp.403–4

144. Hennessy, *The Prime Minister*, pp.237, 242

145. 'Exclusive extracts from the memoirs of Clarissa Eden', *Daily Telegraph*, 19 October 2007

Chapter 9: Harold Macmillan (1957–1963)

1. Entry for 15 March 1963, Catterall (ed.), *Macmillan Diaries*, Vol. II, p.549

2. Hennessy, *The Prime Minister*, p.249

3. Entry for 23 October 1962, Catterall (ed.), *Macmillan Diaries*, Vol. II, p.510

4. Macmillan to Foreign Secretary, 1 August 1960, PREM 11/4721

5. Macmillan, *At the End of the Day*, p.422

6. Entry for 23 May 1962, Catterall (ed.), *Macmillan Diaries*, Vol. II, p.472

7. Entry for 4 March 1959, ibid., p.198

8. JHR to Bligh, 25 October 1960, PREM 11/4721

9. 'Meeting at No. 10 Downing Street to Discuss Intelligence and Intelligence Targets', 25 November 1959, PREM 11/3101

10. Cradock, *Know Your Enemy*, p.298

11. Entries for 11 and 21 July 1963, Catterall (ed.), *Macmillan Diaries*, Vol. II, pp.575, 579. There are many discreet references to intercepts in his diary – see for example on Rhodesia, 26 February 1962, ibid., p.452

12. Drew Pearson article quoted in Reilly to FCO, No.830, 14 June 1960, NS1381/82, FO 371/152002

13. Entry for 6 September 1961, Catterall (ed.), *Macmillan Diaries*, Vol. II, p.409; see also Macmillan to Foreign Secretary, 1 August 1960, PREM 11/4721

14. Horne, *Macmillan*, p.457; Thorpe, *Supermac*, p.310

15. Entries for 16 November 1962 and 19 February 1963, Catterall (ed.), *Macmillan Diaries*, Vol. II, pp.520, 542; also p.579, n89

16. Entries for 18 and 19 March 1958, Catterall (ed.), *Macmillan Diaries*, Vol. II, pp.374–5

17. Hart-Davis, *The War that Never Was*, pp.34–5

18. Horne, *Macmillan*, p.457; Bower, *Perfect English Spy*, p.258; Ring, *We Come Unseen*

19. Hermiston, *The Greatest Traitor*, pp.229–31; Johnson, *Thwarting Enemies*, pp.150–2

20. Horne, *Macmillan*, p.457; Grant, *Jeremy Hutchinson's Case Histories*, pp.23–4

21. Entries for 4 and 14 May 1961, Catterall (ed.), *Macmillan Diaries*, Vol. II, pp.380–2

22. Quoted in Moran, *Classified*, p.129

23. Ibid., p.131; Catterall (ed.), *Macmillan Diaries*, Vol. II, p.451; Thorpe, *Supermac*, p.527

24. Thorpe, *Supermac*, p.527

25. Bower, *Perfect English Spy*, p.294; Martland, 'Vassall'

26. BDOHP interview, Dennis Amy, 19 March 1998

27. Andrew and Mitrokhin, *The Sword and the Shield*, pp.406–8
28. Andrew, *Defence of the Realm*, p.493
29. Horne, *Macmillan*, p.461
30. Ibid., p.461 and n32
31. Bower, *Perfect English Spy*, pp.294–5
32. Horne, *Macmillan*, p.467; Andrew, *Defence of the Realm*, p.483
33. Minutes of the First Meeting, Radcliffe Inquiry, 25 October 1962, TS 58/658
34. Purvis and Hulbert, *When Reporters Cross the Line*
35. Lamb, *Macmillan Years*, pp.452–3
36. Macmillan to Home Secretary, 5 November 1962, PREM 11/3975
37. 'The Vassall Case', notes on a meeting between Prime Minister, Defence Minister, Brook, and First Lord of the Admiralty, 28 September 1962, ibid.
38. Macmillan to Carrington, 5 November 1962, ibid.
39. Andrew and Mitrokhin, *The Mitrokhin Archive: The KGB in Europe and the West*, pp.366–7
40. Norman Brook to PM, 25 April 1962, and attached memo on Golitsyn, PREM 11/4463. On the agenda one session is denoted 'The Prime Minister and President will talk alone', Shuckburgh to Hood, 19 April 1962, CAB 21/5558
41. Kennedy to Macmillan, 21 October 1962, PREM 11/3689; see also Macmillan, *At the End of the Day*, pp.180–3
42. Macmillan to Kennedy, 22 October 1962, PREM 11/4052
43. Cooper, *The Lion's Last Roar*, p.260; Scott, *Macmillan, Kennedy and the Cuban Missile Crisis*, p.50
44. Scott, *Macmillan, Kennedy and the Cuban Missile Crisis*, pp.46, 50; Catterall (ed.), *Macmillan Diaries*, Vol. II, pp.508–10; Macmillan, *At the End of the Day*, pp.184–7
45. British Ambassador (Washington) to Macmillan, 22 October 1962, PREM 11/3689
46. Hart, *The CIA's Russians*, p.59
47. See Scott, *Macmillan, Kennedy and the Cuban Missile Crisis*, p.120
48. Hennessy, *The Prime Minister*, p.128; Horne, *Macmillan*, pp.369–70
49. Andrew, *Defence of the Realm*, p.493
50. Bower, *Perfect English Spy*, p.280
51. Aldrich, *GCHQ*, pp.322–3
52. Macmillan, *At the End of the Day*, p.187
53. J.F. Kennedy–Macmillan phone call, 24 December 1962, PREM 11/3690; Macmillan to Kennedy, 25 October 1962,

PREM 11/3690; also quoted in Thorpe, *Supermac*, p.532
54. Macmillan, *At the End of the Day*, p.197; Scott, *Macmillan, Kennedy and the Cuban Missile Crisis*, pp.83, 117–18
55. Ormsby-Gore to Home, 12 November 1962, No.135, AK 1261/526/G, CAB 21/5581
56. Hennessy, *The Prime Minister*, p.132
57. Thorpe, *Supermac*, p.533
58. Macmillan to Randolph Churchill, 29 October 1962, Macmillan Dep.334, fol.19, Bodleian Library
59. Lord Harlech (William David Ormsby-Gore), Oral History Interview – JFK#1, 03/12/1965, p.50, JFK Library, Boston
60. Scott, *Macmillan, Kennedy and the Cuban Missile Crisis*, p.186; Thorpe, *Supermac*, p.529
61. Aldrich, 'Whitehall Wiring', p.11
62. YP4/19 'Emergency Communication with HM Ambassador, Washington, and with US Secretary of State', 14 November 1963, FO 850/321
63. Reed to Cabinet Office, 'Defence Inter-Departmental Teleprinter network', 1 July 1963, CAB 21/5429
64. Note by Woodhouse, 2 December 1954, Woodhouse 8/1, LHCMA; Note by Woodhouse, 10 December 1954, ibid.
65. Macmillan to Eden, 19 October 1955, PREM 11/1582, TNA; Macmillan to Eden, 19 October 1955, Macmillan Dep.31, fols. 386–92, Bodleian Library
66. Hennessy, *The Prime Minister*, p.264; Jones, 'Anglo–American Relations After Suez', p.51
67. Entry for 17 November 1960, Catterall (ed.), *Macmillan Diaries*, Vol. II, p.338
68. De Zulueta to Macmillan, 1 November 1961; de Zulueta to Macmillan, 2 November 1961; Macmillan to Dulles, 3 November 1961, PREM 11/4591
69. Britain also used its embassy personnel in Havana to advise on promoting the overthrow of Castro during late 1962: Ormsby-Gore to Kennedy, 31 October 1962, President's Office Files. Countries. United Kingdom: Security, 1962: October–December, JFK Library, Boston
70. On Congo see Cabinet Conclusions, 15 September 1960, CC(60) 50th Conclusions, CAB 128/34; Corera, *Art of Betrayal*, p.121; Davies, *MI6*, p.227. On British Guiana see Macmillan quoted in Walton, *Empire of Secrets*, p.161; Curtis, *Unpeople*, p.279; see also Andrew, *Defence of the Realm*, pp.477–80. On Nasser see

Dorril, *MI6*, p.652. On Syria see Jones, 'Preferred Plan', pp.401-15

71. McDermott, *The Eden Legacy*, pp.170-1
72. Jones, 'Joint Plan'; see also discussion between Dick White and the Chiefs of Staff on 'certain proposals dealing with the situation in Syria', COS (57) 74th mtg, 25 September 1957, DEFE 32/5
73. J.F. Dulles to Macmillan, 5 September 1957, Syria file (3), Box 43, Ann Whitman international series, Dwight D. Eisenhower Library, Abilene
74. Scott to Macmillan, 12 December 1957, FO 371/129531
75. CoS Minutes, 'Confidential Annex' to CoS (58) 34th mtg, 15 April 1958, FO 371/135878
76. Aldrich, *Hidden Hand*, p.587
77. Private information
78. Notes for discussion of Indonesia in Cabinet, South-East Asia Department, 5 February 1956, FO 371/135847. The document is dated 1956, but seems to relate to discussions from February 1958
79. Aldrich, *Hidden Hand*, p.587; Jones, 'Maximum Disavowable Aid', p.1994
80. Entry for 24 March 1958, Catterall (ed.), *Macmillan Diaries*, Vol. II, p.105; see also Curtis, *Unpeople*, p.193; Kahin, *Subversion as Foreign Policy*, p.156
81. Brook to Macmillan, 2 June 1958, enclosing 'Indonesia', PREM 11/2324
82. See also Brook to Macmillan, 2 June 1958, enclosing 'Propaganda/Counter-Subversion', and 'Propaganda', PREM 11/2324
83. Lord Harlech (William David Ormsby-Gore), Oral History Interview – JFK#1, 03/12/1965, p.29, JFK Library, Boston
84. Caccia to Home, 'President Kennedy's Difficulties with the United States Press', 14 June 1961, CAB 21/5133. We are indebted to Christopher Moran for this document
85. Roland Challis, 'Our Dirty Secret Behind Indonesia's Coup', *Sunday Times*, 29 July 2001
86. Easter, 'British and Malaysian Covert Support for the Rebel Movements in Indonesia during the "Confrontation", 1963–66', pp.195–8; de Zulueta to Macmillan, 27 December 1962, PREM 11/4346; 'Extract from Record of Conversation at HM Embassy Washington', 26 November 1963, PREM 11/4905
87. Mawby, 'The Clandestine Defence of Empire', pp.105-17

88. Bower, *Perfect English Spy*, pp.245-8
89. Cormac, *Confronting the Colonies*, pp.139, 142
90. Colonel Neil McLean, 'Report on a visit to the Yemen and the Middle East', 1 March–8 April 1963, AME 1/7/3, Julian Amery papers, CCC; Munro to Amery, 9 July 1963, ibid.
91. Bower, *Perfect English Spy*, pp.245-8
92. Ibid., pp.219, 252
93. Mawby, 'The Clandestine Defence of Empire', pp.109-14, 117-18; Mawby, *British Policy in Aden and the Protectorates*, p.140; Cormac, *Confronting the Colonies*, p.145
94. Mawby, 'Clandestine Defence of Empire', p.119
95. Fielding, *One Man in His Time*, p.156
96. Andrew, *Defence of the Realm*, p.494
97. Vernon Bogdanor, '"A Racy Read" on the Profumo Affair', *New Statesman*, 3 January 2013; Mort, *Capital Affairs*, p.322
98. Denning, *The Scandal of Christine Keeler, 1963*, pp.2–3
99. Horne, *Macmillan*, p.457
100. Entries for 15 and 22 March 1962, Catterall (ed.), *Macmillan Diaries*, Vol. II, pp.548–9, 552
101. Andrew, *Defence of the Realm*, p.495; Catterall (ed.), *Macmillan Diaries*, Vol. II, p.549, n40; Thorpe, *Supermac*, p.541
102. Entry for 19 September 1963, Catterall (ed.), *Macmillan Diaries*, Vol. II, p.595; private information
103. Aldrich, *Hidden Hand*, p.629; Andrew, *Defence of the Realm*, pp.495–6; Lamb, *Macmillan Years*, pp.455–6
104. Shepherd, *Iain Macleod*, pp.294–6, 305; see also Davenport-Hines, *An English Affair*, pp.274–5
105. Thorpe, *Supermac*, p.544
106. Horne, *Macmillan*, p.477
107. Chapman Pincher to Paddy Menaul, 27 March 1982, 11/205/6, Menaul papers, LHCMA
108. Scott and Twigge, *Planning Armageddon*
109. R. Aldrich, conversation with Chapman Pincher, 27 November 2007
110. Telephone Recordings: Dictation Belt 15B.1. Prospective Posting to Latin America for Samuel H. Beer; Schlesinger Trip to England; Profumo Scandal, Presidential Papers. President's Office Files, 22 March 1963, JFK Library, Boston
111. Dallek, *John F. Kennedy*; see also entry for 4 March 1963, Catterall (ed.), *Macmillan Diaries*, Vol. II, p.543
112. Peres, *Battling for Peace*, p.259

113. Knightley and Kennedy, *An Affair of State*, pp.206–7
114. Summer and Dorril, *The Secret Worlds of Stephen Ward*, pp.267–76
115. Entry for 17 November 1960, Catterall (ed.), *Macmillan Diaries*, Vol. II, pp.337–8
116. Meeting between Wilson and Macmillan, 1 May 1963, PREM 11/5092
117. Lamb, *Macmillan Years*, p.467
118. Ibid., pp.468–9
119. Horne, *Macmillan*, p.478
120. Entry for 30 May 1963, Catterall (ed.), *Macmillan Diaries*, Vol. II, p.569
121. Entry for 7 July 1963, ibid., p.571; Mort, *Capital Affairs*, p.323
122. Hansard, 'Security (Mr. Profumo's Resignation)', HC Deb, 17 June 1963, vol. 679 cc34–176; Lamb, *Macmillan Years*, pp.474–5; Horne, *Macmillan*, pp.480–1
123. Hansard, 'Security (Mr. Profumo's Resignation)', HC Deb, 17 June 1963, vol. 679 cc34–176; Lamb, *Macmillan Years*, pp.474–5; Horne, *Macmillan*, pp.480–1
124. Shepherd, *Iain Macleod*, p.298
125. Sam Marsden, 'The Profumo Affair secrets will be told; we may just have to wait another 50 years after inquiry files are given preserved status', *Daily Telegraph*, 2 January 2014, p.13
126. Bligh to PM, 23 November 1963, PREM 11/4472; see also Trend to PM, 22 November 1963, ibid.
127. Denning, *The Scandal of Christine Keeler*, p.115
128. Horne, *Macmillan*, p.492
129. Macmillan to Helsby, 'Lord Radcliffe's Proposal', M.168/63, 8 April 1963, PREM 11/5092
130. Ibid.; entry for 16 November 1962, Catterall (ed.), *Macmillan Diaries*, Vol. II, p.521
131. David Keys, 'The Real Profumo Scandal: Book Claims Russian Spy "Photographed Top Secret Documents"', *Independent*, 14 August 2015
132. Ormsby-Gore to Home, 'Defector Leak', 15 July 1963, PREM 11/5090; see also Mangold, *Cold Warrior*, p.101
133. Entries for 21 February, 28 May and 23 July 1963, Catterall (ed.), *Macmillan Diaries*, Vol. II, pp.543, 569, 580
134. Macmillan had resigned due to ill-health by the time White's working party reported in the negative: Andrew, *Defence of the Realm*, p.500; Thorpe, *Supermac*, p.545; Alan Hamilton and Sam Coates, 'Macmillan, the Queen and the Profumo Affair', *The Times*, 7 March 2003, p.4

135. Entry for 21 September 1963, Catterall (ed.), *Macmillan Diaries*, Vol. II, pp.596–7
136. The full correspondence is in the file 'Downing Street and Treasury, Whitehall, London: reconstruction', 1963 Jan 01–1963 Dec 31, Cm 23/211
137. Thorpe, *Supermac*, pp.479–80; Richard Norton-Taylor, 'MI5 bugged cabinet room at No 10, says historian', *Guardian*, 19 April 2010, p.9
138. Biffen, *Semi-Detached*, p.209
139. Shawcross, *Queen and Country*, p.84; also entry for 21 July 1963, Catterall (ed.), *Macmillan Diaries*, Vol. II, p.579

Chapter 10: Alec Douglas-Home (1963–1964)

1. Callaghan quoting Douglas-Home, Hansard, HL Deb, 9 December 1993, vol. 550 cc1023–79
2. Dutton, *Douglas-Home*, p.31; Pike, *Britain's Prime Ministers*, p.463
3. Hennessy, *The Prime Minister*, pp.274, 278, 280
4. Le Bailly, 'Reflections: The Development of Defence Intelligence Staff: Stage II, 1970–75', p.4, Box 7 (6), Le Bailly papers, CCC
5. Hughes, 'Giving the Russians a Bloody Nose', p.236
6. Thorpe, *Alec Douglas-Home*, p.322; Harrison, 'J.C. Masterman and the Security Service, 1940–72', pp.790–1
7. Hansard, Douglas-Home, 16 December 1963, vol. 686 col.858
8. Bulloch, *MI5*. He had also co-authored a book about the Portland spy ring in 1961
9. Masterman to Swinton, 20 April 1961, Swin III, Acc.313, 4/4, Swinton papers, CCC; Masterman to Hollis, 20 April 1961, ibid.
10. Hansard, Douglas-Home, 16 December 1963, vol. 686 col.858
11. Ibid.
12. Ibid.
13. Ibid., col.861
14. Ibid.
15. Helmsby to Trend, 3 November 1964, CAB 21/6031
16. Trend to Helmsby, 22 November 1962, T216/1005; Winn to PM, 25 June 1965
17. Davies, 'Britain's Machinery of Intelligence Accountability', pp.148–9; 'Fathers' rights protester scales Buckingham Palace', *Guardian*, 13 September 2004
18. Hughes, *Britain, Germany and the Cold War*, pp.67–71; Aldrich, *GCHQ*, pp.178–83; Macmillan to Kennedy, 28 April 1961, PREM 11/4052

19. Horne, *Macmillan*, pp.246–7, 265–8
20. Thorpe, *Supermac*, p.379
21. Jones, *No. 10 Downing Street*, p.155
22. Bourne (ACA.I) to Johnson (AS.31), 'Reconciliation Statement – Be No.20 and 22', 19 November 1962, Appendix G. Downing Street/Treasury: Strikes, Withdrawal of Labour etc', WORK12/575
23. Warwicker, *An Outsider Inside No. 10*, pp.85–6
24. Rothwell (Superintending Architect) memo, 'Downing Street Treasury Reconstruction', 29 August 1962, WORK 12/571
25. Jason Lewis and Tom Harper, 'Revealed: How MI5 bugged 10 Downing Street, the cabinet and at least five prime ministers for 15 YEARS', *Daily Mail*, 18 April 2010
26. Ibid.
27. Memorandum of a conversation between Kissinger, Schlesinger, Colby, Areeda, Silberman and Scowcroft, 'Investigation of Allegations of CIA Domestic Activities', 20 February 1975, NARA online release, document 1552858. We are indebted to Simon Willmetts for this reference
28. Barell (Erith's Architects) to Davey (site quantity surveyor), 21 February 1963, WORK 12/572; see also Climon to Deputy Secretary, 'Downing Street and Treasury Report 4', 3 May 1962, WORK 12/601
29. Gay (A.S.31) to Lightman (A.S.8.(L)), AR.3001/112 Pt.II, 23 April 1963, WORK 12/602
30. Memo to Gay (A.S.31), 'Downing Street and Treasury Reconstruction', AOV/Y/478, April 1963, fol.21, WORK 12/576
31. Perry, *Last of the Cold War Spies*, pp.290–2
32. Andrew, *Defence of the Realm*, pp.436–7
33. Entries for 21 July and 2 August 1963, Catterall (ed.), *Macmillan Diaries*, Vol. II, pp.579, 583
34. Andrew and Mitrokhin, *The Sword and the Shield*, pp.63–5
35. Wright, *Spycatcher*, pp.213–15
36. The matter of who took the lead on Blunt's immunity and who was told is disputed: see Carter, *Anthony Blunt*, pp.664–5; Bower, *Perfect English Spy*, pp.325–6
37. Andrew, *Defence of the Realm*, pp.437–8
38. Entry for 16 December 1986, Curtis (ed.), *The Journals of Woodrow Wyatt*, pp.248–9
39. Andrew, *Defence of the Realm*, p.507
40. Pincher, *Treachery*, p.75
41. See the case of Jane Archer in O'Halpin, *Spying on Ireland*, p.219; Pincher, *Treachery*, pp.97, 163
42. Bower, *Perfect English Spy*, p.325

43. Entry for 13 July 1951, 'The Diary of Guy Liddell', KV 4/472
44. Hugh Trevor-Roper, *Sunday Times*, 25 November 1979; John Costello, *Mask of Treachery*, pp.452–7
45. A forensic account of the visits is offered by Urbach, *Go-Betweens for Hitler*, pp.212–14
46. Carter, *Anthony Blunt*, pp.449–50; Perry, *Last of the Cold War Spies*, p.291
47. Andrew, *Defence of the Realm*, p.501
48. Thatcher Archive Online, 'The Diary of Lord Hailsham', 9 January 1977
49. Andrew Pierce, 'How Alec Douglas-Home foiled student kidnappers with beer', *Daily Telegraph*, 14 April 2008
50. Thatcher Archive Online, 'The Diary of Lord Hailsham', 9 January 1977
51. Mawby, 'Clandestine Defence of Empire', p.120
52. Cabinet Conclusions, CC(60)50th Conclusions, 15 September 1960, CAB 128/34; Corera, *Art of Betrayal*, p.121; Davies, *MI6*, p.227
53. Corera, *Art of Betrayal*, p.125
54. HFT Smith minute, 'The Congo', 28 September 1960, FO 371/146650
55. Kelly, *America's Tyrant*, p.71
56. Caroline Alexander letter recounting her 1988 interview, *London Review of Books*, Vol.35, No.11, 6 June 2013
57. McIndoe to Wright, 23 April 1964, enclosing 'Draft Letter to the Nigerian Prime Minister from the Prime Minister', CAB 21/6007
58. Lacouture, *Charles de Gaulle*, pp.275–9
59. Douglas-Home, *The Way the Wind Blows*, pp.197–8
60. Sir Alec Douglas-Home Oral History Interview – RFK#1, 3/17/1965, John F. Kennedy Library, Boston
61. Easter, 'British and Malaysian Covert Support', p.198
62. Jones, *Britain and the Yemen Civil War*, pp.75–6
63. Jones, 'Where the State Feared to Tread', pp.724, 726
64. Amery to Douglas-Home, 16 December 1964, AMEJ, 1/2/7, Julian Amery papers, CCC
65. Jones, *Britain and the Yemen Civil War*, p.78
66. Ibid., p.100
67. Quoted in Dorril, *MI6*, p.691
68. Many of these are preserved in the papers of Julian Amery; see for example 'Report on Visit to Aden and Saudi Arabia', January 1964, AMEJ, 1/2/7, Julian Amery papers, CCC

69. Greenwood to Amery, 23 December 1964, ibid.
70. Bower, *Perfect English Spy*, pp.248–52
71. Note from Prime Minister to Foreign Secretary, 8 March 1964, PREM 11/4678; handwritten note by Prime Minister to Foreign Secretary, 20 March 1964, 'The Yemen and South Arabian Federation', ibid.; Foreign Secretary to Prime Minister, 'The Yemen and South Arabian Federation', 20 March 1964, ibid.
72. Komer to Bundy, 21 April 1964, Box 213, NSF Country Files: Yemen, Lyndon B. Johnson Library, Austin, Texas. Bob Komer was a veteran CIA officer seconded to the NSC
73. Memo of a conversation between Butler and Bundy, 'Countering UAR Pressure Against the British Position in Aden', 27 April 1964, ibid.
74. Komer to Bundy, 28 April 1964, ibid.
75. Note from Douglas-Home to Butler, 20 July 1964, DEFE 13/570; Jones, *Britain and the Yemen Civil War*, p.111
76. Thorpe, *Alec Douglas-Home*, p.326
77. 'Brief for Chairman JIC – 29 October', 28 October 1964, CAB 163/130
78. FOI Request, 'Composition and Terms of Reference: Joint Action Committee', 13 August 1964, JA(64)1
79. FOI Request, JAC Minutes, 23 September 1964, JAC(64) 2nd Meeting
80. FOI Request, JAC Minutes, 8 September 1964, JA(64) 1st Meeting
81. FOI Request, 'The MI6 Role and Relationships with Departments of State and the Armed Services in the Conduct of Deniable Operations in Conditions Short of War', 2 November 1964, JA(64)3
82. Hansard, Douglas-Home, 21 July 1964, vol.699 cc267–9, 268
83. Curtis, *Unpeople*, p.297
84. Cooper, *One of the Originals*, pp.172–8
85. Jones, *Britain and the Yemen Civil War*, pp.154–6
86. Quoted in Curtis, *Unpeople*, p.298
87. Cormac, *Confronting the Colonies*, p.147
88. Mawby, 'Clandestine Defence of Empire', p.123
89. Jones, *Britain and the Yemen Civil War*, p.87
90. Bower, *Perfect English Spy*, p.253; private information
91. Mawby, 'Clandestine Defence of Empire', pp.119–20, 124
92. Quoted in Easter, 'British and Malaysian Covert Support', p.199
93. Ibid., pp.199–200
94. Quoted in Holt, *The Foreign Policy of the Douglas-Home Government*, p.115
95. Quoted in Easter, 'British and Malaysian Covert Support', p.200
96. Ibid.
97. Jones, *Conflict and Confrontation*, pp.128–9
98. Wright to Douglas-Home, 20 January 1964, PREM 11/5197
99. Bernard Burrows, 'Supplementary Briefs for Talks with Mr McCone: Indonesia–Malaysia', 21 January 1964, ibid.
100. 'Record of Conversation between the Prime Minister and Mr John McCone at 4.00pm on Tuesday, January 21 at 10 Downing Street', 21 January 1964, ibid. This was not the only time Douglas-Home met McCone during his brief stint as prime minister. The two met again in September 1964. This time McCone came with cryptic warnings wrapped up in 'rather elaborate secrecy'. He tried to warn Douglas-Home off collaborating with the French on Concorde, and spoke of 'exceedingly serious' 'new and unexpected problems', as well as risks that the British did not know they were undertaking. Burke Trend was suspicious, fearing that the Americans sought an excuse to send over advisers in an underhand attempt to gain details of the project. During the meeting, Douglas-Home simply sat quietly and listened. Trend to Prime Minister, 'Mr McCone's Visit', 18 September 1964, ibid.; 'Record of a Conversation between the Prime Minister and the Head of the Central Intelligence Agency of the United States, Mr J.J. McCone, at No. 10 Downing Street, at 3.30 pm, on Monday September 21 1964', ibid.
101. Jones, *Conflict and Confrontation*, pp.41, 260–2
102. 'Indonesian Confrontation of Malaya', extract of note of meeting held 14 July 1964, DEFE 25/158
103. Easter, 'British and Malaysian Covert Support', p.201
104. Holt, *The Foreign Policy of the Douglas-Home Government*, pp.116, 117
105. Private information
106. MoD memo, 'The Counter-Subversion Committee', Annex to COS.1593/10/3/63, Top Secret – Very Restricted Circulation, 10 March 1964, CAB 21/6006
107. SV (65) 3, 'Summary of recent activities by working groups', 8 February 1965, CAB 134/2544

Chapter 11: Harold Wilson (1964–1970)

1. Jenkins, 'Wilson, (James) Harold', *Oxford Dictionary of National Biography*
2. Hennessy, *The Prime Minister*, p.287
3. Ibid., pp.287–8, 291–2; Andrew, *Defence of the Realm*, p.526
4. Wilson, *The Labour Government*, pp.2–3
5. Hennessy, *The Prime Minister*, p.292; Andrew, *Defence of the Realm*, p.526
6. Mangold, *Cold Warrior*, p.91
7. Hailsham, *A Sparrow's Flight*, p.331
8. Wyatt, 'Wigg, George', *Oxford Dictionary of National Biography*; 'Extract of a Note of Meeting on 17 November', attached to Wigg to Wilson, 21 December 1965, PREM 13/3471; Moran, *Classified*, p.138
9. Andrew, *Defence of the Realm*, pp.522–3
10. Trend to Wilson, 'Security', 17 October 1964, PREM 13/3471
11. Trend to Wilson, 21 October 1964, PREM 13/352
12. Trend to Wilson, 'Security', 17 October 1964, PREM 13/3471
13. Quoted in Young, 'George Wigg, the Wilson Government and the 1966 Report into Security in the Diplomatic Service and GCHQ', p.199
14. Note attached to Trend to Wilson, 'Security', 17 October 1964, PREM 13/3471
15. Helmsby to Trend, S50/114, 3 November 1964, enclosing minute to Wilson, CAB 21/6031; Anson to McIndoe, 17 November 1964, ibid.
16. Mitchell to Wigg, 15 December 1965, PREM 13/3471; Wigg to Wilson, 20 December 1965, ibid.
17. The outcome, it seems, was that the home secretary could be bypassed if the director-general came to Wilson directly – but not the other way around. 'Note for the Record', 27 July 1969, ibid.
18. Wilson, *The Labour Government*, pp.302–3
19. Young, 'George Wigg, the Wilson Government and the 1966 Report into Security in the Diplomatic Service and GCHQ', p.199
20. Wilson minute on JIC Special Assessment on Indonesia, 5 October 1965, PREM 13/2718; Wilson minute on JIC(A) 74(17), 10 May 1974
21. See 'Aden and the Federation: Ministerial Meeting held at No. 10 Downing Street at 11.30 am on Wednesday, November 25, 1964', DEFE13/404; Trend to PM, 'Malaysia', 23 February 1965, PREM 13/430
22. Hayes, *Queen of Spies*, p.198
23. Kaunda to Wilson, T764/65, 24 February 1965, CAB 21/5568; Wilson to Kaunda, T.97.65, 12 March 1965, ibid.
24. Wilson, *The Labour Government*, pp.116–17
25. Wood, *A Matter of Weeks Rather Than Months*, pp.1–5
26. Watts, 'Killing Kith and Kin', p.413; Pimlott, *Harold Wilson*, pp.375–6; Cradock, *Know Your Enemy*, p.232
27. Castle, *The Castle Diaries*, p.68
28. Palliser to D. Day (FCO), 'Avon Engines for Rhodesia', 21 May 1968, DEFE 13/713; D. Morphet (FCO) to Palliser, 'Avon Engines for Rhodesia', 24 May 1968, ibid.; D. Andrews to Morphet, 4 June 1968, ibid.; see also Cormac, 'Secret Intelligence and Economic Security', p.109
29. Quoted in Cradock, *Know Your Enemy*, p.232
30. Wood, *A Matter of Weeks Rather Than Months*, p.54; Moorcraft, 'Rhodesia's War of Independence'
31. Wood, *A Matter of Weeks Rather Than Months*, p.22
32. White, *Unpopular Sovereignty*, pp.126, 132
33. JIC (6) 19 Final, 'Rhodesia and Zambia: the Present Position and Forward Look', 2 March 1966, CAB 159/61
34. Pimlott, *Harold Wilson*, p.377
35. Palliser, 'Note for the Record', 2 August 1967, PREM 13/2688
36. Trend to Helmsby, 10 June 1967, T 216/1017–8; J 82/793; MAF2345.67, 9 June 1967, LO 2/375
37. Report of the Security Commission, June 1967, 'Report relating to Helen Mary Keenan', Cmnd.3365
38. Ken Flower, *Serving Secretly*
39. Trend to Wilson, 10 February 1966, PREM 13/1116, cited in Coggins, 'The British Government and Rhodesian UDI', in Kandiah (ed.), *Rhodesian UDI*, p.21
40. Sneling to Hughes, 9 March 1966, covering 'Plan A; A Rhodesian Coup', March 1966, PREM 13/1117
41. Johnson to Wilson, 23 April 1966, Smith (ed.), *The Wilson–Johnson Correspondence*, pp.140–1; Wilson to Johnson, 24 April 1966, Johnson to Wilson, 27 April 1966, ibid., pp.142–3
42. Wood, *A Matter of Weeks Rather Than Months*, p.67
43. Coggins, 'Wilson and Rhodesia'
44. Wood, *A Matter of Weeks Rather Than Months*, p.496
45. Wilson, *The Labour Government*, p.42
46. 'British Policy Towards Indonesia', JAC(65)9, February 1965, FO 371/181503;

see also Trend to PM, 'Malaysia', 23
February 1965, PREM 13/430

47. 'British Policy Towards Indonesia',
JAC(65)9, February 1965, FO 371/181503

48. Trend to PM, 'Malaysia', 23 February 1965,
PREM 13/430

49. Desmond Seward, 'John Colvin: Colourful
British diplomat on watch in the world's
troublespots', *Guardian*, 15 October 2003

50. Burrows, 'Supplementary Brief for Talks
with Mr McCone: Indonesia–Malaysia', 21
January 1964, PREM 11/5197

51. Hughes, *Harold Wilson's Cold War*, pp.86–8

52. Elson, *Suharto*, pp.88–91

53. Wilson to Johnson, 29 January 1965,
No.669, Prime Minister's Personal
Telegram, T.40/W, PREM 13/2718

54. Myles Maxfield and Edward G. Greger,
'VIP Health Watch', *Studies in Intelligence*,
pp.53–62, CIA NND 947003

55. Easter, 'British Intelligence and
Propaganda during the "Confrontation"'

56. Elson, *Suharto*, pp.97–8

57. Hunter, *Sukarno and the Indonesian Coup*,
pp.125–7

58. Bittman, *The Deception Game*, pp.107–18,
119–20; Conboy, *Intel: Inside Indonesia's
Intelligence Service*, p.47, n22

59. Kahin, *Southeast Asia: A Testament*,
pp.156–7

60. Myles Maxfield and Edward G. Greger,
'VIP Health Watch', *Studies in Intelligence*,
pp.53–62, CIA NND 947003

61. Ibid.

62. JIC/796/65, 'Special Assessment:
Indonesia' (TRINE), 4 October 1968,
PREM 13/2718

63. Jones and McGarr, 'Real Substance', pp.81–9

64. Office of the Political Advisor to the
Commander-In-Chief (Far East) to FO, 5
October 1965, FO 371/180317; see also
Easter, 'British Intelligence and
Propaganda', pp.95–9

65. Curtis, *Web of Deceit*, pp.392–3

66. Bittman, *The Deception Game*, pp.107–9

67. DD/S CIA, Diary Notes, 27 January 1965,
CREST CIA-RDP76-
00183R000500050054-7, NARA

68. Entry for 11 December 1929, Pimlott
(ed.), *The Political Diary of Hugh Dalton*

69. Easter, 'British Intelligence and
Propaganda during the "Confrontation"'

70. SO (PM) (64) 38, 'Instructions for the Use
of the Marking "Guard"', 30 April 1964,
CAB 21/5246

71. Hawkes to Green, discussing JIC (54) 74
and JIC (57) 44, SY/POL.145/3, 4
November 1965, CAB 21/5346

72. Heaton to Joy, 15 October 1965, CAB
21/5246

73. Aldrich, *GCHQ*, pp.222–3

74. See 1965 report, DEFE 31/47

75. COS (56) 94th mtg, 'American
representation at Operation Grapple',
DEFE 32/5

76. Matthew Aid and Jeffrey T. Richelson,
'U.S. Intelligence and China: Collection,
Analysis, and Covert Action', *National
Security Archive*, p.6

77. Wolf, 'This Secret Town'

78. Aldrich, 'The Value of Residual Empire',
pp.226–58

79. Wolf, 'This Secret Town'

80. Ibid.; Bill Collier, *Diplomatic Wanderings:
From Saigon to the South Seas*, p.29

81. J.C. Pratt (ed.), *Vietnam Voices: Perspectives
on the War Years, 1941–1975*, pp.266–9

82. Palliser to Wilson, 5 January 1967, PREM
13/1917

83. Ibid.

84. Dumbrell and Ellis, 'British Involvement
in Vietnam Peace Initiatives', p.114

85. 'Record of a Conversation between the
Prime Minister and Mr Kosygin at 3.30 on
Monday', 6 February 1967, PREM
13/1917; see also Shah, 'This Secret Town'

86. Wolf, 'This Secret Town'

87. Ken Hughes, *Chasing Shadows*

88. Helms to Bundy, 30 November 1964, Box
208, NSF Country Files, Lyndon B.
Johnson Library, Austin, Texas; see also
Coleman, *A Special Relationship?*, p.33;
Pimlott, *Harold Wilson*, pp.366–7

89. Andrew, *Defence of the Realm*, p.416

90. Ibid.

91. Pimlott, *Harold Wilson*, p.705

92. Andrew, *Defence of the Realm*, p.526

93. Corera, *Art of Betrayal*, p.208; Mangold,
Cold Warrior, p.96

94. Andrew, *Mitrokhin Archive*, pp.528–9

95. Pimlott, *Harold Wilson*, pp.703–4

96. Hayes, *Queen of Spies*, p.194

97. Ibid., p.705

98. Mangold, *Cold Warrior*, pp.94–6

99. Thorpe, 'The "Juggernaut Method"', p.483

100. Andrew, *Defence of the Realm*, pp.528–9;
private information

101. Wilson, *The Labour Government*, p.236;
Andrew, *Defence of the Realm*, pp.529–30

102. Andrew, *Defence of the Realm*, pp.529–30

103. Wilson, *The Labour Government*, p.238

104. Quoted in Andrew, *Defence of the Realm*,
p.528

105. Dorril and Ramsey, *Smear*, p.131

106. Ibid., p.132; Pimlott, *Harold Wilson*, p.407

107. Wilson, *The Labour Government*, p.236

108. Moran, *Classified*, p.136
109. Wilson, *The Labour Government*, p.373
110. Chapman Pincher obituary, *Daily Telegraph*, 6 August 2014
111. Moran, *Classified*, p.137; Aldrich, *GCHQ*, p.238
112. Creevy, 'A Critical Review of the Wilson Government's Handling of the D-Notice Affair', pp.212–13
113. Andrew, *Defence of the Realm*, p.531
114. Moran, *Classified*, pp.140, 142
115. Travis, 'How Wilson Hounded the Colonel', *Guardian*, 13 April 1999
116. Pimlott, *Harold Wilson*, p.444; Moran, *Classified*, p.153
117. Moran, *Classified*, pp.141–2; Andrew, *Defence of the Realm*, p.532
118. Wilson, *The Labour Government*, p.375
119. Moran, *Classified*, pp.146–7
120. Wilson, *The Labour Government*, pp.374–5
121. Ibid.
122. Crossman, *The Diaries of a Cabinet Minister, Volume 2*, p.254
123. Wilson, *The Labour Government*, p.376
124. Wilkinson, *Secrecy and the Media*, p.292; Moran, *Classified*, p.147
125. Wilson, 'Statement by the Prime Minister', 25 February 1967, PREM 13/1816
126. Andrew, *Defence of the Realm*, p.531
127. Wilson, *The Labour Government*, p.375
128. Lee Howard (*Mirror* editor) to Lohan, 24 February 1967, PREM 13/1816
129. Moran, *Classified*, p.147
130. Ibid., p.149; Creevy, 'A Critical Review of the Wilson Government's Handling of the D-Notice Affair', pp.209, 216; Wilkinson, *Secrecy and the Media*, pp.303–4
131. Moran, *Classified*, p.150
132. Aldrich, *GCHQ*, p.240
133. Moran, *Classified*, p.151
134. Ibid., pp.152, 155; Creevy, 'A Critical Review of the Wilson Government's Handling of the D-Notice Affair', p.221
135. Quoted in Creevy, 'A Critical Review of the Wilson Government's Handling of the D-Notice Affair', p.218
136. Hennessy, *The Prime Minister*, p.312
137. Pimlott, *Harold Wilson*, p.445; Wilkinson, *Secrecy and the Media*, p.310
138. Crossman, *The Diaries of a Cabinet Minister, Volume 2*, p.394; Castle, *The Castle Diaries*, p.270
139. Hansard, Wilson, 22 June 1971, cm 2008–2095
140. Castle, *The Castle Diaries*, p.270
141. Crossman, *The Diaries of a Cabinet Minister, Volume 2*, p.394; Castle, *The Castle Diaries*, p.270
142. Wilson to Chief Whip, 10 July 1967, PREM 13/1328
143. Pincher to Arthur Lewis MP, 24 July 1967, PREM 13/1641
144. Wigg to Arthur Lewis MP, 5 September 1967, ibid.
145. Pincher to Arthur Lewis MP, 9 October 1967, ibid.
146. Wilson to Wigg, 3 September 1967, ibid.
147. Young, 'The Wilson Government's Reform of Intelligence Co-ordination, 1967–68', pp.133–51
148. John Young, 'The Wilson Government'; O'Halpin, 'The British Joint Intelligence Committee and Ireland'
149. Poulden to Stewart, D/8987/1402/37, 'JIC (A) Sub-Committee on Automatic Data Processing', 29 September 1969, CAB 163/119
150. File: Sigint: enquiry into cost, funding and scope for economy, 24 June–13 December 1968, CAB 163/79. This file is currently closed to public inspection
151. Young, 'The Wilson Government's Reform of Intelligence Co-ordination, 1967–68', pp.133–51
152. Hastie-Smith to Thomas, 'Third Intelligence Methods Conference', 25 October 1966, enclosing address by Healey, 13 September 1966, DEFE 13/923
153. Chapman, 'Change in the Civil Service', pp.599–610. We are indebted to Christopher Moran for observations on the Fulton Review
154. Goodman, 'The Dog that Didn't Bark', pp.529–51
155. Le Bailly to Butler, 9 December 1993, Box 21 (5), Le Bailly papers, CCC; see also Dorril, *M16*, p.727; Cradock, *Know Your Enemy*, p.249
156. Dunnett to CDS, PUS/68/151/32/1/10, n.d. 1968, DEFE 13/923
157. Earle to Healey, 20 September 1967, ibid.
158. Wilson, *The Labour Government*, p.375
159. Stewart to Wilson, 'Soviet Intelligence Activities in this Country', 27 September 1968, PREM, 13/2009; M. Palliser to FCO, 21 October 1968, ibid.
160. Stewart, circular cypher, 11 November 1968, ibid.
161. Home Office to Halls, 10 October 1968, ibid.
162. Michael Stewart to Wilson, 'Soviet Intelligence Activities in this Country', 27 September 1968, ibid.
163. Home Office to Halls, 10 October 1968, ibid.

164. The best account is in Davies, *MI6*, pp.275–9

Chapter 12: Edward Heath (1970–1974)

1. Heath, *The Course of My Life*, pp.475–80
2. Private information
3. Vague, *The Great British Mistake*, p.84
4. Heath, *The Course of My Life*, p.474
5. Hugh Trevor-Roper, 'Sir Dick White, 1906–1993: A Personal Memoir', in Harrison (ed.), *The Secret World*, pp.155–8
6. Campbell, *Heath*, pp.492–3; Beevor and Cooper, *Paris*, pp.74–6
7. Kenneth Rose, 'Rothschild, (Nathaniel Mayer) Victor, Third Baron Rothschild (1910–1990)', rev. *Oxford Dictionary of National Biography*, Oxford University Press, 2004; online edn
8. L. Baston and A. Seldon, 'Number 10 Under Edward Heath', p.68
9. Record of a meeting in Harold Wilson's room, House of Commons, 31 October 1966, PREM 13/952
10. Wilson to Heath, 16 March 1970, DEFE 23/107
11. Heath to Wilson, 17 April 1970, ibid.
12. Trend to Heath, 'Official History of Intelligence in the Second World War', 16 November 1970, ibid. By this stage Professor Michael Howard, Charles Stewart and Donald McLachlan were also being spoken of as possible authors; Trend to Heath, 1 March 1971, ibid.; Hooper to Trend, 14 May 1971, ibid.; McIndoe to Lohan, 19 November 1966, CAB 21/5865; Moran, *Classified*, pp.278–80. As Moran shows, one or two historians had uncovered the secret but were persuaded to stay silent
13. Transcript of an interview with Detective Sergeant Roy Cremer of the Metropolitan Police Special Branch, December 2002, in Carr, *The Angry Brigade*, pp.189–91; also private information
14. Jonathon Green, 'The urban guerrillas Britain forgot', *Spectator*, 27 August 2001
15. Hoefferle, *British Student Activism in the Long Sixties*, pp.177–9
16. Cormac, 'Much Ado About Nothing', p.478
17. Andrew, *Defence of the Realm*, p.609
18. Zein Rifai to Heath, 17 December 1971, PREM 15/1053; Heath to Rifai, 15 December 1971, ibid.
19. Bridges memo, 12 September 1972, and Cradock to Bridges (Downing Street), 26 September 1972, ibid.
20. Heath minute, 28 December 1971 on JIC (71) (WSI Supplement) 88, 22 December

1971, PREM 15/1053; also Moon to Nortbury, 30 December 1971, ibid.
21. Angel to Meadway, 14 January 1972, PREM 15/1053
22. Neil Tweedie and Peter Day, '1973: A Year of Conflict and Scandal', *Daily Telegraph*, 1 January 2004, p.4
23. Andrew, *Defence of the Realm*, pp.615–16
24. Ibid.
25. Hughes, 'Skyjackers, jackals and soldiers', pp.1019–22
26. Aspin, *The Kovacs Contract*, pp.105–7, 144
27. Mumford, *The Counter-Insurgency Myth*
28. Armstrong to Neil Cairncross, 7 August 1972, CJ 4/261
29. Quoted in Mike Thomson, 'Britain's Propaganda War During the Troubles', BBC News, 22 March 2010
30. Donald Maitland to Edward Heath, 4 November 1971, document released through the Bloody Sunday Inquiry, http://www.webarchive.nationalarchives. gov.uk/20101103103930/http:/bloody-sunday-inquiry.org/
31. Trend to PM, 'Northern Ireland', 29 October 1971, document released through the Bloody Sunday Inquiry, ibid.
32. Armstrong to Neil Cairncross (NIO), 7 August 1972, CJ 4/261
33. Ibid.
34. Chris West, 'Army Warned Against Internment', BBC News, 1 January 2002; Andrew Sparrow, 'Heath Stands by Internment Move', *Daily Telegraph*, 2 January 2002
35. Heath, *The Course of My Life*, pp.429–30
36. Richard Popplewell, 'British intelligence in Mesopotamia', pp.139–72
37. Additional information kindly supplied by Richard Popplewell; see also Rejali, *Torture and Democracy*, pp.329–30
38. This was JIC (65) 15, 'Joint Directive on Military Interrogation in Internal Security Operations Overseas', 17 February 1965, PREM 15/485. Known as 'The Bible', it was subsequently widely circulated as JIC/108/65, 3 February 1965, CAB 163/171
39. In reality, other *ad hoc* techniques were sometimes used. In the late 1970s it was not unusual for detainees to be threatened with being dropped from helicopters. Private information
40. Nicholson, 'Report on Operation Calaba – August 1971', CAB 163/173. The technical staff were responsible for the installation and maintenance of tape recorders and noise generators. See 'Standing Order

No.3: Order for Technical Staff', 1971, CAB 163/171

41. Compton to Allen (Home Office), 13 October 1971, CAB 163/171

42. 'How Ulster internees are made to talk', *Sunday Times*, 17 October 1971

43. Lewis (BGS Int DIS), 'The Noise Machine: Sound Level Measurements Conducted at Ashford on 24 November 1971', BGS (Int)/1/16, 25 November 1971, CAB 163/172

44. Heath (PM) to Trend (Cab Sec), M66/79, PREM 15/485

45. Transcript of Radio 4 *Today* programme with John Timpson, 17 November 1971, 'The Compton Report', CAB 163/171

46. Trend to Armstrong, 'Interrogation Procedures', A0697, 7 November 1971, PREM 15/485. The request came from cabinet subcommittee GEN 47

47. Stewart, 'Report on Interrogation Methods Used in Northern Ireland', draft, October 1971, CAB 163/171

48. Report by Intelligence Co-ordinator, 'Prisoner handling in Interrogation centres in Northern Ireland', 4 November 1971, PREM 15/485. A further copy is at CAB 163/171

49. White to Dunnett, 2 December 1971, CAB 163/172

50. 'Report of the Committee on Interrogation procedures', 31 January 1972, CAB 163/189. This was published in March 1972 as *Report of the Committee of Privy Councillors appointed to consider authorised procedures for the interrogation of persons suspected of terrorism*, Cmnd. 4901 (London: HMSO, 1972)

51. Trend to Herman, A01791, 8 May 1972, CAB 163/189

52. JIC, 'Joint Directive on interrogation in Operations by the Armed Forces', 3rd Draft, 17 April 1972, CAB 163/189. This later became JIC (A) 72 (21) (Final), 'Directive on Interrogation by the Armed Forces in Internal Security Operations', 29 June 1972, WO 32/21726

53. Herman to Trend, 'JIC (A) Directive on Interrogation', 12 May 1972, CAB 163/189

54. GOC Northern Ireland, to Rees, 16 April 1974, DEFE 13/838

55. Donelly, min, 'Settlements in Deep Interrogation Cases', 17 December 1974, FCO 87/410

56. Sanders and Wood, *Times of Troubles*, p.252

57. Andrew and Gordievsky, *KGB*, pp.435–6; Walden, *Lucky George*, pp.144–8

58. Hughes, 'Giving the Russians a Bloody Nose', pp.229–35

59. Heath, *My Life*, pp.249, 468, 474

60. Andrew and Mitrokhin, *The Sword and the Shield*, pp.381–4

61. Davies, *MI6*, p.277

62. West, *The A to Z of Sexspionage*, pp.165–6

63. Andrew, *Defence of the Realm*, pp.569–71

64. Record of a meeting in the PUS's Office, 25 May 1971, in *DBPO*, Series II, Vol.1, Doc. 66, pp.339–43; see also Bennett, *Six Moments*, pp.123–5

65. Heath, *Course of My Life*, pp.475–80

66. Andrew, *Defence of the Realm*, pp.566–7

67. Trend to Palliser (Private Secretary to PM), 29 September 1968, PREM 13/2405; see also Hughes, 'Giving the Russians a Bloody Nose', p.243

68. Bennett, *Six Moments*, p.125

69. Ibid., pp.123–5, 127

70. Ibid., p.144

71. Ziegler, *Edward Heath*, p.399

72. Nicholson, *Activities Incompatible*, p.171

73. Heath quoted in Ziegler, *Edward Heath*, p.399

74. Andrew and Mitrokhin, *Mitrokhin Archive*, p.543

75. Andrew, *Defence of the Realm*, p.574

76. Walden, *Lucky George*, p.148

77. Heath, *Course of My Life*, p.476

78. Ibid., pp.473–4

79. Andrew, *Defence of the Realm*, pp.588–9

80. Ibid., pp.590–1

81. Ibid., pp.594–5

82. 'Former NUM chief was police informer', BBC News, 24 October 2002; private information

83. 'Former NUM chief was police informer', BBC News, 24 October 2002

84. Private information

85. Rawlinson, Secretary BAT, 'Economic League', memo to Chairman's Policy Committee, 6 September 1972, BAT papers, Special Collections, University of California San Francisco. BAT had funded the Economic League since at least 1952 – see Notes of Chairman's Committee 1956, 3 January 1956, doc.201059121, ibid.

86. Andrew, *Defence of the Realm*, pp.547–8; private information

87. Sir Michael Hanley obituary, *Daily Telegraph*, 8 January 2001; private information

88. Andrew, *Defence of the Realm*, pp.547–8

89. Ibid., pp.596–7

90. Neil Tweedie and Peter Day, '1973: A Year of Conflict and Scandal', *Daily Telegraph*, 1 January 2004, p.4

91. Heath to Trend, PM Personal minute, M.84/73, 21 August 1973, PREM 15/2130
92. Trend to Heath, A05194, 21 September 1973, ibid.
93. Armstrong PPS to Hunt, 'Industrial Assessment', A05446, 24 October 1973
94. Armstrong to Dawe, 17 December 1973, ibid.
95. Hunt to Heath, A05854, 18 December 1973, ibid.
96. Hunt to Heath, 'Your speech tomorrow: Subversion', A06972, 8 January 1974, ibid.
97. Andrew, *Defence of the Realm*, p.599

Chapter 13: Harold Wilson (1974–1976)

1. Warwicker, *An Outsider Inside No. 10*, p.77
2. Quoted in Wheen, *Strange Days Indeed*, p.9
3. Entries for 16 September 1975 and 6 January 1976, Benn, *Against the Tide*, pp.440–1, 492
4. Rimington, *Open Secret*, pp.118–19
5. Andrew, *Defence of the Realm*, p.633
6. Haines, *Glimmers of Twilight*, p.44
7. Taylor, *Brits*, p.110
8. Coogan, *The Troubles*, pp.174–5
9. Craig, 'From Backdoors and Back Lanes to Backchannels', p.104; Taylor, *Brits*, p.111
10. Mumford, 'Covert Peacekeeping', p.637
11. Haines, *Glimmers of Twilight*, p.64
12. Cowper-Coles, 'Anxious for Peace', pp.228–9
13. Powell, *Great Hatred, Little Room*, p.67
14. Craig, 'From Backdoors and Back Lanes to Backchannels', p.110; Cowper-Coles, 'Anxious for Peace', p.228; Andrew, *Defence of the Realm*, pp.641, 625; Mumford, 'Covert Peacekeeping', p.642
15. Powell, *Great Hatred, Little Room*, pp.67–9
16. Craig, 'From Backdoors and Back Lanes to Backchannels', p.110; Cowper-Coles, 'Anxious for Peace', p.228
17. Craig, 'From Backdoors and Back Lanes to Backchannels', p.110; Cowper-Coles, 'Anxious for Peace', p.228; Andrew, *Defence of the Realm*, p.626
18. Nigel Wicks to PM, 18 December 1975, PREM 16/676; Bill Innes (HO) to Nigel W (No10), 19 December 1975, ibid.; Duncan Gardham, 'Queen's art gallery on IRA death list, secret files show', *Daily Telegraph*, 28 October 2009, p.4
19. Private information
20. Andrew, *Defence of the Realm*, p.626
21. Hughes, 'Model Campaign', pp.277, 287, 294; Worrall, *Statebuilding and Counterinsurgency in Oman*, p.204

22. Grob-Fitzgibbon, 'Those Who Dared', pp.11, 16
23. Ibid., p.17
24. Hansard, Wilson, 12 January 1976, cm 28
25. Wilson, *Final Term*, p.209
26. Geraghty, *Who Dares Wins*, p.138
27. Grob-Fitzgibbon, 'Those Who Dared', p.17; Taylor, *Brits*, p.190; O'Leary, 'Northern Ireland', p.249
28. Wilson, *Final Term*, p.209
29. Hansard, Fitt, 12 January 1976, cm 37–38
30. Hansard, Wilson, 12 January 1976, cm 38–39
31. Ibid.
32. Entry for 13 January 1976, Donoughue, *Downing Street Diary*, p.628
33. Urban, *Big Boys' Rules*, p.7
34. MacKenzie, *Special Force*, p.239; see also Urban, *Big Boys' Rules*
35. Haines, *Glimmers of Twilight*, p.84; Anthony Bevins, 'Wilson Wanted to Assassinate Amin', *Independent*, 18 September 1996
36. Haines, *Glimmers of Twilight*, pp.84–5
37. Sir Maurice Oldfield obituary, *New York Times*, 12 March 1981
38. Owen, 'Diseased, Demented, Depressed: Serious Illness in Heads of State', p.326; Ingram, *Obote*, pp.142–5
39. Andrew, *Defence of the Realm*, p.534
40. Pincher to le Bailly, 15 September 1981, le Bailly papers, 8 (2), CCC; see also Chapman Pincher, 'How the MI5 Chief lied', *Daily Mail*, 27 March 1982
41. Rimington, *Open Secret*, p.116
42. Andrew, *Defence of the Realm*, pp.534–5; Martland, 'Hanley, Sir Michael Bowen'
43. Sandbrook, *Seasons in the Sun*, p.74
44. Ibid., p.449
45. Entry for 2 February 1976, Donoughue, *Downing Street Diary*, p.653
46. Wheen, *Strange Days Indeed*, p.264
47. Bridges to PM, 17 September 1974, PREM 16/273; Bill Mumford (MoD) to Tom Bridges, 12 September 1974, ibid.
48. Ibid.
49. Hennessy, *The Secret State*
50. Warwicker, *An Outsider Inside No. 10*, p.35
51. Ibid., p.121
52. Ibid., pp.29, 118
53. T(75)1, 'The Responsibility for Approving the Overall Security of Secure Telephone Schemes', note by MI5, 4 February 1975, CAB 134/3967; see also Aldrich, 'Whitehall Wiring', pp.19–34
54. Para 190, 'Potential eavesdropping on telecommunications equipment', in *Report*

on the Security of the Cabinet Office, 1965, CAB 21/6078
55. Ziegler, *Wilson*, p.477, 478
56. Entry for 1 April 1974, Donoughue, *Downing Street Diary*, p.85
57. Andrew, *Defence of the Realm*, pp.637–8
58. Entry for 18 February 1976, Donoughue, *Downing Street Diary*, p.670
59. Private information
60. Aldrich, *GCHQ*, p.357; Hughes, 'Soldiers of Misfortune', p.15
61. Hunt to Wright, 12 March 1976, PREM 16/1151; Wright to Wilson, 12 March 1976, ibid.; Hunt to Wilson, 'Visit of Mr George Bush', 24 March 1976, ibid.
62. Dorril and Ramsey, *Smear*, pp.302–3
63. Steiner, *The Last Adventurer*, pp.57–93
64. Hughes, 'Soldiers of Misfortune', pp.10, 15
65. Sanders, *Apartheid's Friends*, pp.62, 121
66. Quoted in Ziegler, *Wilson*, p.478
67. Bush to Wilson, 28 March 1976, PREM 16/1151
68. Entry for 18 July 1975, Benn, *Against the Tide*, pp.420–1; private information
69. Corera, *Art of Betrayal*, p.213
70. Rimington, *Open Secret*, pp.197–9
71. Hansard, HL Deb, 9 December 1993, vol. 550 cc1023–79
72. Rimington, *Open Secret*, pp.197–9
73. Hansard, HL Deb, 9 December 1993, vol. 550 cc1023–79
74. Ibid.
75. Rimington, *Open Secret*, pp.197–9
76. Ibid., pp.98–105
77. Entry for 31 October 2001, Mullin, *A View From the Foothills*, p.234
78. Entry for 19 January 1976, Donoughue, *Downing Street Diary*, p.634
79. Pimlott, *Harold Wilson*
80. Moran, 'Conspiracy and Contemporary History', p.162
81. Ibid., pp.167–8
82. Sandbrook, *Seasons in the Sun*, p.70
83. Rimington, *Open Secret*, pp.99–102
84. Wright, *Spycatcher*, p.369
85. Ziegler, *Wilson*, p.476
86. Pimlott, *Harold Wilson*, p.698; Rimington, *Open Secret*
87. Quoted in Moran, 'Conspiracy and Contemporary History', p.172
88. Pimlott, *Harold Wilson*, p.713; quoted in Dillon, *The Dirty War*, p.201; Coogan, *The Troubles*, p.242; Cadwallader, *Lethal Allies*, p.166; Dorril and Ramsey, *Smear*, p.258
89. Urban, *Big Boys' Rules*, p.77
90. Hansard, HL Deb, 9 December 1993, vol. 550 cc1023–79

91. Foot, *Who Framed Colin Wallace?*, pp.45–7, 50–2, 58–63, 73–9, 176–80
92. Ibid., pp.94–100, 179, 370
93. Quoted in Pimlott, *Harold Wilson*, p.714; Cavendish, *Inside Intelligence*, p.171
94. Pimlott, *Harold Wilson*, p.714
95. Quoted in ibid., p.718
96. Sandbrook, *Seasons in the Sun*, p.67
97. Wright, *Spycatcher*, p.369; West, *Historical Dictionary of British Intelligence*, p.323
98. Cudlipp, *Walking on the Water*, pp.324–5
99. Ibid., p.326
100. Ziegler, *Mountbatten*, p.660
101. Gupta, 'The Mountbatten Saga', p.297
102. Ziegler, *Mountbatten*, p.662
103. Ziegler, *Wilson*, pp.501–2
104. Wheen, *Strange Days Indeed*, p.254
105. Bennett and Cormac, 'General Sir Frank Kitson as Warrior Scholar'
106. Quoted in Dorril and Ramsey, *Smear*, p.286
107. Sandbrook, *Seasons in the Sun*, p.135
108. Ibid., pp.136–7
109. Routledge, *Public Servant*, p.270
110. Jonathan Freedland, 'Enough of the Cover-up: the Wilson Plot was our Watergate', *Guardian*, 15 March 2006, p.29
111. Mason to Wilson, 2 September 1974, PREM 16/450
112. Entry for 9 February 1976, Donoughue, *Downing Street Diary*, p.659
113. Ziegler, *Wilson*, p.475
114. Moran, 'Conspiracy and Contemporary History', p.167
115. Rimington, *Open Secret*, p.101
116. Entry for 5 February 1976, Donoughue, *Downing Street Diary*, p.657

Chapter 14: James Callaghan (1976–1979)
1. Entry for 25 October 1978, Benn, *Conflicts of Interest*, p.379
2. Morgan, *Callaghan*, pp.47–9, 608; Walden, *Lucky George*, p.191; private information
3. 'Final Report of the Select Committee to Study Governmental Operations with Respect to Intelligence Activities, United States Senate (Church Committee), 26 April 1976, US Government Printing Office
4. Carl Bernstein, 'Watergate reporter: Nixon is still tricky after all these years', *New York Times*, 24 July 2015. Many of these things have only come to light recently as a result of the policies of the enlightened Nixon Librarian, Timothy Naftali
5. Wright, BIS (Washington) to Turner (FCO), 'Northern Ireland: Special Air Service', 9 January 1976, FCO 87/582

6. Private information. Callaghan was preoccupied with IMF negotiations over that weekend

7. Wheen, *Strange Days Indeed*, pp.268–72

8. Entry for 17 July 1977, Donoughue, *Downing Street Diary*, pp.222–3

9. Entries for 3 August 1977 and 2 February 1978, Benn, *Conflicts of Interest*, pp.222–3, 273–4

10. Andrew, *Defence of the Realm*, pp.638–42

11. Morgan, *Callaghan*, pp.609–12; private information

12. Andrew, *Defence of the Realm*, p.440

13. Entries for 8 and 20 September 1977, Donoughue, *Downing Street Diary*, pp.234, 238

14. Entry for 17 November 1978, ibid., p.391

15. Armstrong (HO) to Hunt, 'ABC Trial', 28 November 1979, DEFE 47/34; Hunt to Armstrong (HO), 28 November 1978, ibid.

16. Diplock to Callaghan, 'Security Commission: Crispin Aubrey, John Berry, Duncan Campbell', 14 March 1979, PREM 16/2240; Callaghan to Thatcher, 21 March 1979, ibid.; Thatcher to Callaghan, 21 March 1979, ibid.

17. Thatcher to Callaghan, 26 April 1978, DEFE 47/34

18. For more details see John Rosselli, 'Mark Arnold-Forster', *Oxford Dictionary of National Biography*

19. Entry for 24 December 1976, Benn, *Against the Tide*, pp.691–2

20. Ibid.; entry for 2 February 1976, ibid., p.310; also private information

21. Entry for 18 May 1977, Benn, *Conflicts of Interest*, p.141; Jenkins, *All Against the Collar*, pp.35–87, 163–4

22. Entry for 29 July 1977, Benn, *Conflicts of Interest*, pp.202–3

23. Andrew, *Defence of the Realm*, pp.656–7

24. Ibid., pp.657–9

25. Ted Grant obituary, *Daily Telegraph*, 27 July 2006

26. Entry for 25 May 1977, Benn, *Conflicts of Interest*, pp.150–1

27. Andrew, *Defence of the Realm*, pp.663–4

28. Entry for 2 March 1977, Donoughue, *Downing Street Diary*, p.155; private information

29. Jimmy Carter, 'Statement on the Appointment of the New Members of the Intelligence Oversight Board', 5 May 1977, *Public Papers of the Presidents, Jimmy Carter 1977: Book I*

30. Entries for 24 November 1977 and 29 October 1978, Benn, *Conflicts of Interest*,

31. Entries for 11 September, 18 and 25 October 1978, Benn, *Conflicts of Interest*, pp.336–7, 371, 376–9

32. Lipsey, *In the Corridors of Power*, pp.114–15

33. Benn, 'Civil Liberties and the Security Service: the case for an inquiry', 17 October 1978, PREM 16/1862

34. Minute by Hunt to Callaghan, A08150, 24 October 1978, enclosing 'Procedures for Control of United Kingdom Intelligence Activities', PREM 16/1862

35. Ibid.; see also Sloan to Morris, 27 October 1978, ibid.

36. Lipsey, *In the Corridors of Power*, pp.130–1

37. Morgan, *Callaghan*, p.612; private information

38. The current scholarship suggests that Callaghan's claim to have despatched a warning to the Argentines via MI6 is correct: see Hayes, *Queen of Spies*, p.194

39. Entry for 30 November 1978, Benn, *Conflicts of Interest*, pp.403–4

40. Owen to Callaghan, PM 78/49, 13 June 1978, CAB 103/717. We are indebted to Dina Rezk for bringing this file to our attention

41. Andrew, *Defence of the Realm*, pp.552–5

42. Albert Buckley, 'Obituary: Sir Howard Smith', *Independent*, 10 May 1996

43. Nicholson, *Activities Incompatible*, p.55

44. Entry for 25 October 1978, Benn, *Conflicts of Interest*, p.452

45. Andrew, *Defence of the Realm*, pp.553–5

46. 'C' to Palliser, C/4886, 8 July 1977, CAB 103/706. He added: 'You may like to recall the amount of trouble we ran into over Michael Foot's book on SOE in France.' See also Hooper to Dick White, Jf.0639/J.425, 18 July 1975, ibid. We are indebted to Dina Rezk for bringing this file to our attention

47. 'Official History of British intelligence in the Second World War', A05289, mins. mtg. 21 July 1977, ibid.

48. Callaghan to Thatcher, 14 July 1978, ibid.; Thatcher to Callaghan, 17 July 1978, ibid.

49. Meadway to Rotherham, 8 December 1976, WLN042/1, FCO 87/582

50. Cragg to Meadway, 'The SAS and the Special Reconnaissance Unit (SRU) in Northern Ireland', 20 September 1976, MO19/3/15, FCO 87/582

51. Merlyn Rees to Callaghan, 'The SAS – Special Reconnaissance Unit in Northern

Ireland', 21 September 1976, NLU062/1, FCO 87/582

52. Geraghty, *The Irish War*, p.119

53. Taylor, *Brits*, pp.192–3

54. Entry for 17 February 1977, Donoughue, *Downing Street Diary*, pp.148–9

55. Private information

56. Whitmore to Morland, 'The Lufthansa Hijacking', 26 October 1977, FCO 33/3186

57. Entry for 18 October 1977, Donoughue, *Downing Street Diary*, pp.248

58. Davies, *Fire Magic*, pp.4–6

59. Ibid., pp.7–8; private information

60. Davies, *Fire Magic*; telephone calls 14 and 16 October 1977, Box 33, Callaghan papers, Bodleian Library

61. Davies, *Fire Magic*, pp.86–98

62. Entry for 18 October 1977, Donoughue, *Downing Street Diary*, pp.248

63. Entry for 22 September 1977, Benn, *Conflicts of Interest*, pp.219–20

64. Hunt to Callaghan, A056701, 10 October 1977, PREM 16/1456

65. Hunt to Callaghan, A05696, 'Plot to Assassinate the President of Togo', 10 October 1977, PREM 16/1456; Callaghan minute, 10 October 1977

66. Owen, *Time to Declare*, pp.386–7

67. Ibid.; Cowper-Coles, *Ever the Diplomat*, pp.51–3

68. Abrahamian, 'Mass Protests in the Iranian Revolutions', pp.162–9

69. Entries for 12 and 19 July 1978, Radji, *In the Service of the Peacock Throne*, pp.17–20

70. Entries for 22 November and 1 December 1978, ibid., pp.263–4, 270–1

71. Entry for 14 September 1978, Benn, *Conflicts of Interest*, p.339

72. Kuzichkin, *Inside the KGB*, pp.101–4, 197–201; Andrew, *Mitrokhin II*, pp.191–2

73. Sreberny and Torfeh, *Persian Service*, pp.78–83, 92, 99, 113

74. Owen, *Time to Declare*, p.390

75. Lebovic, 'Why Intelligence Fails' (review of Kane, *The Negative Asset*)

76. Neil Tweedie, 'National Archives: British ambassador to Iran failed to predict downfall of Shah', *Daily Telegraph*, 29 December 2008

77. 'Declassified diplomacy: Washington's hesitant plans for a military coup in pre-revolution Iran', *Guardian*, 11 February 2015

78. Neil Tweedie, 'National Archives: British ambassador to Iran failed to predict downfall of Shah', *Daily Telegraph*, 29 December 2008

79. Bar-Joseph, 'Forecasting a Hurricane', pp.15–17; Owen, *Time to Declare*, pp.391–2

80. Callaghan to the Shah, 14 September 1978, FCO 8/3185

81. Harney, *The Priest and the King*, pp.17, 65

82. Owen, *Time to Declare*, pp.391–2

83. 'Declassified diplomacy: Washington's hesitant plans for a military coup in pre-revolution Iran', *Guardian*, 11 February 2015; entry for 8 January 1979, Radji, *In the Service of the Peacock Throne*, pp.306–7

84. Petersen, *Anglo–American Policy Toward the Persian Gulf*, pp.64–9

85. Shawcross, *The Shah's Last Ride*, pp.219–23; Owen, *In Sickness and in Power*, pp.202–10

86. Entry for 3 November 1976, Donoughue, *Downing Street Diary*, pp.92–3

87. Entry for 25 October 1978, Benn, *Conflicts of Interest*, p.378

88. Barder (FCO) to Allinson and PUSD, 'Allegations of South African Security Services Activity in Britain', 13 October 1980, FCO 105/480; Allinson minute, 16 October 1980, ibid.

89. Winter, *Inside BOSS*, pp.452–3

90. Hervey (PUSD) memo, 'Activities of Arab Intelligence Services in the UK', 26 July 1978, FCO 76/1875

91. Andrew, *Defence of the Realm*, pp.650–1

92. Entry for 25 January 1979, Jenkins, *European Diary*, pp.389–90

93. Cartledge, 'Protection of UK Head of Mission in Brussels', 19 February 1979, PREM 16/2244; Lever (FCO) to Cartledge (PM/PS), 'Bomb attacks in France and Possible Threat to British Targets in Belgium', 12 February 1979, ibid.

94. Hervey to FO, 23 March 1979, PREM 16/2244; private information

95. BDOHP Interview, 'Colin Munro', p.23, CCC. Others suggest the target was John Killick, British ambassador to NATO – see entry for 23 March 1979, Jenkins, *European Diary*, p.430

96. Ferris, 'Head of Mission Cars' draft, 16 June 1979, FCO 33/3848; entry for 3 December 1980, Jenkins, *European Diary*, p.651

97. Hervey to FCO, 20 April 1979, FCO 87/906

98. Private information

99. Prior, *A Balance of Power*, p.99

100. Entry for 27 November: 1979, Clark, *Into Politics*, p.139

101. West, *At Her Majesty's Secret Service*, p.197

102. Lipsey, *In the Corridors of Power*, pp.126–7

Chapter 15: Margaret Thatcher (1979–1990)

1. Hansard, HC Deb, 26 March 1981, cc1/1079–85
2. Lawson, *The View From No. 11*, p.314
3. Thatcher to Acland, 5 March 1980, THCR 3/2/22 (156), Thatcher MSS, CCC
4. BDOHP interview, Sir Antony Acland, CCC
5. Hilaire Barnett, *Britain Unwrapped*, pp.72–6; Urban, *UK Eyes Alpha*
6. Carrington to UK Missions and Embassies, 'Security Coordinator in Northern Ireland', 2 October 1979, PREM 19/82
7. Entries for 20 and 23 April 1987, Curtis (ed.), *Journals of Woodrow Wyatt*, Vol.1, pp.333–5
8. Ibid., p.236
9. Campbell, *Margaret Thatcher, Volume Two: The Iron Lady*, p.385
10. BDOHP interview, Sir Antony Acland, CCC
11. Collin, *Altered State*, pp.99–100
12. Crozier, *Free Agent*, p.198
13. Ibid., pp.127–8
14. 'Note of a telephone conversation between prime minister and Mr Nicholas Elliott on 13 August 1979', 15 August 1979, PREM 19/10. The conversation concerned Smith's distrust of the UK Foreign Office and secret diplomacy between the United States, Rhodesia and South Africa
15. Crozier, *Free Agent*, pp.244–5, 250–1
16. Private information
17. Entry for 30 November 1990, Clark, *In Power*, p.373, also p.369 n; entry for 5 May 1981, Clark, *Into Politics*, p.225
18. Crozier, *Free Agent*, pp.131–3
19. Andrew, *Defence of the Realm*, pp.670–1
20. Between 1977 and 1980 BAT doubled its contribution to the Economic League to about £20,000 at current values: Dennis (Secretary BAT), 'Economic League', memo to Chairman's Policy Committee, 2 April 1980, doc.201033297, British American Tobacco papers, Special Collections, University of California San Francisco
21. Andrew, *Defence of the Realm*, p.674
22. Confidential interview
23. Hurd, *Memoirs*, p.284
24. Ingham, *Kill the Messenger*, pp.362–3
25. Private information
26. Andrew and Mitrokhin, *Mitrokhin II*, pp.393–404; Diamond, *The CIA and the Culture of Failure*, pp.59–72; Haslam, *Near and Far Enemy*, pp.244–5
27. Record of a meeting between the PM and the President of the US, Mr Jimmy Carter, at the White House on 17 December 1979 at 10.30, part IV, PREM 19/127
28. PM's personal message T180A/79T, telephone conversation between Thatcher and Carter, Friday, 28 December 1979, THCR 3/1/4, Thatcher MSS, CCC
29. Campbell, *Iron Lady*, pp.141–2
30. PM/80/1, Carrington memo to Thatcher, 'Iran and Afghanistan', 2 January 1980, PREM 19/273
31. Letter from Carter to Thatcher handed over by Warren Christopher on 14 January 1980, THCR 3/1/5 f.33, Thatcher MSS, CCC
32. Thatcher to Carter, 26 January 1980, THCR 3/1/5 f.84, Thatcher MSS, CCC
33. PM/80/5, Carrington to PM memo, 'Afghanistan', 19 January 1980, PREM 19/135
34. Martin Beckford, 'Britain agreed secret deal to back Mujahideen', *Guardian*, 30 December 2010
35. PM/80/8, Carrington to Thatcher, 'Afghanistan: The Next Steps', PREM 19/136
36. Carter to Thatcher, 15 October 1980, Prime Minister's personal message series No. T202/80, THCR 3/1/10 f66, Thatcher MSS, CCC
37. Casey to Meese, 23 December 1985, CREST CIA-RDP88B00443R001804410033-1, NARA
38. Speech to the veterans of the Office of Strategic Services, 28 February 1981, Thatcher Archive, document 104584
39. Entry for 28 February 1981, Henderson, *Mandarin*, pp.385–7. Denis Thatcher was moved to tears
40. Purvis and Hulbert, *When Reporters Cross the Line*, pp.248–9
41. Crile, *Charlie Wilson's War*, pp.199–203; private information
42. Private information
43. Crile, *Charlie Wilson's War*, p.201
44. Connor, *Ghost Force*, pp.419–20; Cooley, *Unholy Wars*, pp.74–7
45. Purvis and Hulbert, *When Reporters Cross the Line*, pp.249–53
46. Crile, *Charlie Wilson's War*, pp.199–203; see also Corera, *Art of Betrayal*, p.305
47. Purvis and Hulbert, *When Reporters Cross the Line*, pp.254–5
48. Woodrow Wilson International Center for Scholars, 'The KGB in Afghanistan: Defector's Documents Shed New Light on Soviet War', 25 February 2002
49. Carrington, *Reflections*, p.285

50. See the material on the Central Policy Review Staff (CPRS) review of the Information Research Department (IRD) at FCO 79/498

51. Renwick, *Margaret Thatcher*, pp.13–14

52. Diary entry for 28 January 1981, reproduced in G.R. Urban, *Diplomacy and Disillusion: At the Court of Margaret Thatcher: An Insider's View*, pp.28–36

53. Ibid.; see also discussion on paper by Urban, 'Case for a Western information policy', January 1982, George Urban memo, Churchill/URBN 1, CCC

54. See the extensive correspondence in files 53–55, AMEJ 1/10, Amery papers, CCC

55. Walden, *Lucky George*, pp.252–3

56. Ash, *The Polish Revolution: Solidarity*, p.45; Prados, *How the Cold War Ended*, p.26

57. Prados, *How the Cold War Ended*, p.99

58. Moran, *Classified*, pp.324–5

59. Ingham, *Kill the Messenger*; Moran, *Classified*, pp.320–4

60. Entry for 21 November 1979, Clark, *Into Politics*, p.138

61. Entry for 19 March 1981, Clark, *Into Politics*, p.217; Andrew, *Defence of the Realm*, p.754

62. Pincher to le Bailly, 15 September 1981, le Bailly papers, 8 (2), CCC; see also Chapman Pincher, 'How the MI5 Chief lied', *Daily Mail*, 27 March 1981

63. The exception is perhaps Gordievsky, for whom she clearly had a 'high regard': Thatcher, *Downing Street Years*, p.470

64. Thatcher to Callaghan, 7 August 1980, THCR 3/2/34 (57), Thatcher MSS, CCC. Remarkably, one of these volumes was written by Michael Howard, the Chichelle Professor of Military History at Oxford, who was even at that moment serving as an informal adviser to Thatcher on Cold War tactics

65. Vincent, *Culture of Secrecy*, p.262

66. Moran, *Classified*, pp.336–8

67. Armstrong to Whitmore, 'Civil Service manpower: GCHQ', A03229, 14 October 1980, PREM 19/152

68. Entry for 24 November 1986, Curtis (ed.), *Journals of Woodrow Wyatt*, p.229

69. Luke Jones, 'The time when spy agencies officially didn't exist', *BBC News Magazine*, 8 November 2014

70. Moran, *Classified*, p.337

71. Entry for 24 November 1986, Curtis (ed.), *Journals of Woodrow Wyatt*, pp.229, 236

72. Hurd, *Memoirs*, p.325

73. Ingham, *Kill the Messenger*, p.284

74. Goodman, 'The Dog that Didn't Bark', pp.529–35

75. Aldrich, *GCHQ*, pp.396–9

76. Ibid.

77. Ibid.; Duff to le Bailly, Jf 0154, 12 May 1982, Le Bailly papers, 9 (3), CCC; see also Wallace Turner, 'Adm. Inman says U.S. Has Intelligence Gaps', *International Herald Tribune*, 29 April 1982; author interview with Inman, May 2002, Austin, Texas

78. Ingham, *Kill the Messenger*, pp.284–5

79. Prior, *Balance of Power*, p.147

80. Faber, *Speaking for England*, p.532

81. Fowler, *Ministers Decide*, p.155

82. Baker, *The Turbulent Years*, p.67

83. Briefing by Lt Gen Glove, Deputy Chief of the Defence Staff (Intelligence) to COS 3rd mtg./82, 3 April 1982, FCO 7/4472

84. Renwick, *Margaret Thatcher*, pp.47, 53; private information

85. Private information

86. Prebble, *Secrets of the Conqueror*, pp.108–10

87. Freedman, *Falklands Campaign*, pp.242–52

88. FCO notes of 51st Meeting/82 of Chiefs of Staff Committee, Section (a) 'Exocet', FCO 7/4474

89. Neil Tweedie, 'Thatcher's blistering attack on French over Exocets during Falklands', *Daily Telegraph*, 28 December 2012

90. Ibid.

91. Private information

92. John Follain, 'The Sphinx and the curious case of the Iron Lady's H-bomb', *Sunday Times*, 20 November 2005; also private information

93. Gordievsky, *Next Stop Execution*, pp.353–5

94. John Barron, *Operation Solo*, pp.318–60

95. Barrass, *The Great Cold War*, p.320

96. Prados, *How the Cold War Ended*, pp.167–80

97. Barrass, *The Great Cold War*, p.397

98. Ibid., p.382

99. DNSA: President's Foreign Intelligence Board, *The Soviet 'War Scare'*, 15 February 1990

100. Barrass, *The Great Cold War*, p.299

101. Prados, *How the Cold War Ended*, pp.188–9; private information

102. Thatcher, *Downing Street Years*, p.463

103. Cahal Milmo, 'Ronald Reagan Prepared for Historic Cold War Meeting by Reading Tom Clancy Thriller', *Independent*, 30 December 2015

104. Thatcher, *Downing Street Years*, pp.450–3

105. Aldous, *Reagan and Thatcher*, p.160
106. Corera, *Art of Betrayal*, p.272
107. Walden, *Lucky George*, pp.223–5
108. Corera, *Art of Betrayal*, p.277
109. Private information
110. BDOHP interview, Sir Bryan George Cartledge, 14 November 2007
111. Cowper-Coles, *Ever the Diplomat*, pp.89–92
112. Diamond, *The CIA and the Culture of Failure*, p.467; Cherkashin and Feifer, *Spy Handler*, p.25
113. Barrass, *The Great Cold War*, p.397, also p.449, n27
114. Thatcher, *Downing Street Years*, pp.773–4
115. Bergman, *The Secret War With Iran*, pp.124–6; private information
116. Bergman, *The Secret War With Iran*, pp.97–8
117. Levitt, *Hezbollah*, p.38
118. Ibid.
119. Peter Taylor, 'Six Days that Shook Britain', *Guardian*, 24 July 2002
120. Walter Pincus and David Ottaway, 'Poindexter Assured British on US Policy', *Washington Post*, 23 November 1986
121. Hansard, HC Deb, 16 April 1986, vol. 95 cc875–962
122. Aldous, *Reagan and Thatcher*, pp.225–8; Wroe, *Lives, Lies and the Iran–Contra Affair*, p.165; private information
123. Curtis, *Secret Affairs*, pp.161–3
124. Walter Pincus and David Ottaway, 'Poindexter Assured British on US Policy', *Washington Post*, 23 November 1986
125. Wroe, *Lives, Lies and the Iran–Contra Affair*, pp.286–7
126. Waldegrave, *A Different Kind of Weather*, pp.256–7
127. Report of the Congressional Committees Investigating the Iran/Contra Affair, pp.317–19; Bergman, *The Secret War With Iran*, pp.127–8
128. Aldous, *Reagan and Thatcher*, pp.225–8; Campbell, *Margaret Thatcher*, pp.267–8
129. David Rogers, 'UK Security Firm with Thatcher Ties had Role in Contra Aid, Data Indicate', *Wall Street Journal*, 25 March 1987
130. Entry for 16 December 1983, Clark, *In Power*, p.57
131. 'IRA Says it Attacked Lawmaker', *Washington Post*, 1 August 1990

Chapter 16: John Major (1990–1997)

1. Major, *Autobiography*, p.114
2. Barrass, *The Great Cold War*, pp.382–3
3. See Aldrich, Cormac and Goodman, *Spying on the World*, pp.380–1
4. Barrass, *The Great Cold War*, pp.363–5, 368
5. Urban, *UK Eyes Alpha*, pp.189–91
6. Barrass, *The Great Cold War*, pp.363–5, 368
7. Private information
8. Renwick, *Margaret Thatcher*, p.239; Waldegrave, *A Different Kind of Weather*, p.255
9. Vladimir Pasechnik obituary, *Daily Telegraph*, 29 November 2001; Mangold and Goldberg, *Plague Wars*, pp.167–8; Barrass, *The Great Cold War*, p.408
10. Hennessy, *The Prime Minister*, p.440
11. Private information
12. Private information
13. Private information
14. Malcolm McBain interview with Percy Cradock BDOHP, CCC
15. Private information
16. Parris, *Chance Witness*, pp.403–5
17. Lawson, *The View From No. 11*, p.314
18. See Report by Sir Michael Quinlan, 'Review of Intelligence Requirements and Resources, Part 1: Processes for Handling', 23 November 1993. Professor Peter Hennessy obtained this document under FOIA, and we are most indebted to him for sight of it; GCSF Annual Report 2005, pp.24–5, GCHQ-UR, MSS.384/3/37, WMRC; Urban, *UK Eyes Alpha*, pp.258–9; Aitken, *Pride and Perjury*, pp.4–7; Andrew, *Defence of the Realm*, p.781
19. Lustgarten and Leigh, *In From the Cold*, pp.393–4
20. Andrew, *Defence of the Realm*, pp.788–9
21. Aldrich, Cormac and Goodman, *Spying on the World*, p.382
22. Private information
23. Private information
24. Andrew, *Defence of the Realm*, pp.776–8; private information
25. Entry for 31 October 2001, Mullin, *A View From the Foothills*, pp.234–5; private information
26. Robertson, 'Recent Reform of Intelligence in the UK', pp.144–58; Gill, 'Reasserting Control', pp.313–15
27. Cradock, *In Pursuit of British Interests*, p.45
28. Entry for 2 March 1999, Mullin, *Walk-On Part*, p.425
29. Urban, *UK Eyes Alpha*, pp.143–8; C. Powell, 'Reading behind the lines', *Spectator*, 2 March 2002
30. Freedman, *A Choice of Enemies*, p.219

31. Baker, *Politics of Diplomacy*, p.274
32. Hurd, *Memoirs*, p.390
33. Hennessy, *The Prime Minister*, p.443
34. Major, *Autobiography*, p.221
35. Ibid., pp.222–3
36. Ibid., pp.223–4; 'He Should be Shot', *Newsweek*, 14 January 1991; Atkinson, *Crusade*, p.153
37. Cradock, *In Pursuit of British Interests*, p.39
38. Major, *Autobiography*, p.234
39. Gillespie, *Desert Fire*, p.119; J. Fullerton, 'British Ruse Held Iraqis' Attention While Real Invasion Came Elsewhere', *Philadelphia Inquirer*, 3 March 1991
40. Entry for 13 March 1991, Currie, *Diaries*, p.24
41. Private information
42. Private information
43. Private information
44. Urban, *UK Eyes Alpha*, pp.166–8
45. Sir Percy Cradock obituary, *Daily Telegraph*, 28 January 2010
46. Major, *Autobiography*, pp.224–5, 432
47. Entry for 7 November 1984, Clark, *In Power*, p.99
48. Butler (Cab Sec) to Whitmore (HO), 'Review of Security Arrangements for Public Figures', AO90/2395, 12 October 1990, Cm 44/34; Home Office, 'Review of Security Arrangements for Public Figures', section on 'Technical Protection', pp.30–41, September 1990, ibid.
49. Lamont, *In Office*, p.48
50. Waldegrave, *A Different Kind of Weather*, p.210
51. Major, *Autobiography*, p.432; Taylor, *Brits*, p.323; private information
52. Andrew, *Defence of the Realm*, pp.773–6
53. Ibid., pp.773–4
54. Ibid., p.785
55. Taylor, *Brits*, p.318; Powell, *Great Hatred*, pp.66–8
56. Powell, *Great Hatred*, p.71
57. Taylor, *Talking to Terrorists*, pp.33–5. Oatley's work was continued by a retired MI6 officer re-employed by MI5
58. Andrew, *Defence of the Realm*, p.783
59. Major, *Autobiography*, pp.444–5; Taylor, *Talking to Terrorists*, pp.33–5
60. Hansard, HC Deb, 1 November 1993, vol. 231 cc19–37, cm 34
61. Major, *Autobiography*, p.447
62. Ibid., p.446
63. Powell, *Great Hatred*, p.72
64. Entry for 1 May 1996, Morgan, *The Insider*, p.115
65. Private information
66. Andrew, *Defence of the Realm*, p.786
67. Taylor, *Brits*, p.338
68. Major, *Autobiography*, pp.446–7
69. Powell, *Great Hatred*, pp.72–3
70. Hansard, HL Deb, 9 December 1993, vol. 528, cc1–12, cm 1039–40
71. Cormac, 'Secret Intelligence and Economic Security', p.99
72. Entry for 6 August 1999, Mullin, *A View From the Foothills*, p.11
73. Cradock, *In Pursuit of British Interests*, p.136
74. Private information
75. Major, *Autobiography*, pp.266–7
76. Private information
77. Shashank Joshi, 'France should remember its own history before complaining too much about American espionage', *Daily Telegraph*, 1 July 2013; private information
78. Major, *Autobiography*, pp.271–85; private information
79. Major, *Autobiography*, p.267
80. Kevin Toolis, 'The Man Behind Iraq's Supergun', *New York Times*, 26 August 1990
81. Lang, *Blue Remembered Years*, pp.286–7
82. Phythian, 'A Tale of Two Inquiries', p.162
83. Norton-Taylor, *Truth is a Difficult Concept*, pp.68, 100
84. Hansard, HC Deb, 23 November 1992, vol. 214 cc.631–712, cm 638
85. Urban, *UK Eyes Alpha*, pp.119–24
86. Barker, 'Practising to Deceive', pp.41–2
87. Scott Inquiry, D8.16
88. Urban, *UK Eyes Alpha*, pp.126–8
89. Scott Inquiry, G5.41
90. Lang, *Blue Remembered Years*, pp.270–1
91. Hansard, HC Deb, 24 May 1994, vol. 244 c102W
92. Major, *Autobiography*, p.559–61
93. Butler to Le Bailly, AO93/3693, 14 December 1993, Le Bailly papers, 21 (5), CCC
94. Thatcher, evidence to the Scott Inquiry (Arms for Iraq), 8 December 1993, document 110798, Thatcher Archive, CCC
95. Powell, *A Soldier's War*, pp.309–10
96. Renwick, *Margaret Thatcher*, p.232
97. Cahal Milmo, 'Why Britain backed down on banning Saddam Hussein's chemical weapons during Iran war', *Independent*, 3 July 2015
98. Patrick Cockburn, 'MI6 in plot to kill Saddam', *Independent*, 17 February 1998
99. Lang, *Blue Remembered Years*, p.269
100. Entry for 15 February 1996, Mullin, *Decline and Fall*, p.147
101. Paul Vallely, 'The Scott Report', *Independent*, 15 February 1996

102. Major, *Autobiography*, p.565

Chapter 17: Tony Blair (1997–2007)
1. Entry for 4 June 2003, Mullin, *A View From the Foothills*, p.413
2. Lanning and Norton-Taylor, *Conflict of Loyalties*, p.204; Grindley to Blair, 28 July 1992, MSS.384/3/49, GCHQ-UR, Warwick Modern Record Centre; Blair to Grindley, 14 August 1992, ibid.; Brown to Grindley (GCHQ TU), 18 June and 19 August 1992, ibid.
3. Entry for 29 July 1998, Mullin, *Decline and Fall*, p.363
4. MacKenzie, *Special Force*, pp.225–8
5. Rawnsley, *The End of the Party*, p.4
6. Private information
7. 'Telcon with British Prime Minister Blair', 16 August 1998, National Security Council and Records Management Office, 'Declassified documents concerning Tony Blair', Clinton Digital Library
8. N. Rufford, 'Blair's Spy Summit on Red Mafia', *Sunday Times*, 5 December 1999; also private information
9. Andrew, *Defence of the Realm*, p.793
10. Alex Baker, 'Gordon Brown's "internal market" for MI6', *Financial Times*, 25 January 2011
11. SIS5, evidence to Iraq inquiry, p.11
12. Jonathan Powell, *The New Machiavelli*, p.286
13. SIS1, evidence to Iraq inquiry, p.64
14. Even in 2008 there were still some WMD true believers in MI6: see entry for 29 October 2008, Mullin, *Decline and Fall*, p.387
15. Aldrich, Cormac and Goodman, *Spying on the World*, p.410; private information
16. Corera, *Art of Betrayal*, p.334
17. Private information
18. Entries for 5 June and 26 July 1999, ibid., pp.42, 91
19. Entry for14 September 1999, ibid., pp.109–11
20. Entries for 25 January and 22 February 2000, ibid., pp.218–19, 242–3
21. Ibid.
22. Andrew, *Defence of the Realm*, p.793
23. Ibid., pp.811–12, 846
24. Ibid., p.797
25. Private information
26. Andrew, *Defence of the Realm*, p.797
27. Powell, *Great Hatred, Little Room*, p.16
28. Jonathan Powell, 'A moment in history: sitting down to talk with Adams and McGuinness', *Guardian*, 17 March 2008
29. Ibid.

30. Entry for 31 March 1999, Campbell, *The Blair Years*, p.375
31. 'How Britain Eavesdropped on Dublin', *Independent*, 16 July 1999; see also Laura Friel, 'Spying on the border', *An Phoblacht* Republican News, 21 December 2000
32. Powell, *Great Hatred, Little Room*, p.19
33. In 2003 Liam Clarke, a journalist on the *Sunday Times*, was arrested after he included transcripts from a bugging operation codenamed 'Narcotic1' in a biography of Martin McGuinness: 'Editor arrested over "phone tap"', *Sunday Times*, 1 May 2003
34. Private information
35. Powell, *The New Machiavelli*, pp.54–5
36. Andrew, *Defence of the Realm*, p.798
37. Entry for 14 January 1999, Mullin, *Decline and Fall*, p.404
38. Entry for 24 January 2000, Morgan, *The Insider*, p.249; see also Morell, *The Great War of Our Time*, p.22
39. Coll, *The Bin Ladens*, p.468
40. Entry for 21 October 2001, Campbell, *Burden of Power*, p.61
41. Rawnsley, *The End of the Party*, p.89
42. Ibid., p.21
43. Ibid., pp.24, 33
44. Entry for 13 March 2003, Morgan, *The Insider*, p.383
45. David Leppard, 'Blair gets gas-proof armoured Jaguar', *Sunday Times*, 9 March 2003
46. Entries for 21 October, 7 and 14 November 2002, Campbell, *Burden of Power*, pp.334, 355–6, 364
47. Entry for 6 November 2008, Mullin, *Decline and Fall*, p.283; Blair, *Speaking for Myself*, p.307
48. Clarke, *Against All Enemies*, pp.30–1
49. Entries for 11–14 September 2001, Campbell, *Burden of Power*, pp.5–11
50. Entry for 20 September 2001, ibid., pp.23–5
51. Private information
52. Seldon, *Blair Unbound*, p.61
53. Entries for 4 and 5 October 2001, Campbell, *Burden of Power*, pp.36, 39
54. Entries for 10, 11 and 21 October 2001, ibid., pp.48–9, 61
55. Ibid.; see also entry for 3 March 2002, Morgan, *The Insider*, p.322
56. Evidence from SIS4, Iraq inquiry, http://www.iraqinquiry.org.uk/media/50700/SIS4-part-1.pdf
57. Dearlove's Private Secretary to Manning, Appendix 1, SIS4, 3 December 2001, http://www.iraqinquiry.org.uk/transcripts/declassified-documents.aspx

58. Entry for 14 November 2001, Campbell, *Burden of Power*, p.89
59. Urban, *Task Force Black*, p.8
60. Private information
61. Entry for 7 January 2002, Campbell, *Burden of Power*, p.135
62. Entry for 7 March 2002, ibid., pp.183–5
63. Entry for 2 April 2002, ibid., p.198; also private information
64. Jonathan Owen, 'Tony Blair and Iraq: The damning evidence', *Independent*, 7 April 2013
65. Campbell at Camp David talked of 'poodle-ology gone mad'
66. Bryan Burrough et al., 'The path to war', *Vanity Fair*, May 2004, p.110
67. Taken from http://www.number10.gov.uk/Page1712 on 6 January 2010
68. Powell to Bush, 'Your Meeting with the UK Prime Minister Tony Blair', 2 April 2002. The document was leaked to the *Mail on Sunday* and published in full on 17 October 2015
69. Jonathan Owen, 'Tony Blair and Iraq: The damning evidence', *Independent*, 7 April 2013
70. Entries for 3–5 September 2002, Campbell, *Burden of Power*, pp.291–3 and n1; Aldrich, Cormac and Goodman, *Spying on the World*, p.390
71. Entries for 5 and 9 September 2002, Campbell, *Burden of Power*, pp.293, 297
72. Rawnsley, *The End of the Party*, p.111
73. Corera, *Art of Betrayal*, p.361
74. Simon Jeffery, 'Julian Miller: Head of the Cabinet Office unit responsible for providing classified assessments to the joint intelligence committee (JIC)', *Guardian*, 20 August 2003
75. Kampfner, *Blair's Wars*, p.204
76. Entries for 12, 13 and 18 September 2002, Campbell, *Burden of Power*, pp.300–3
77. Entries for 24 and 25 September 2002, ibid., p.309
78. Blix, *Disarming Iraq*, p.128
79. Entry for 5 November 2002, Campbell, *Burden of Power*, p.354
80. 'Blair Says Iraq Could Launch Chemical Warheads in Minutes', *New York Times*, 25 September 2002
81. 'Some Evidence on Iraq Called Fake: UN Inspector says Documents on Purchases were Forged', *Washington Post*, 8 March 2003; S.M. Hersh, 'The Stovepipe: How conflicts between the Bush Administration and the intelligence community marred the reporting on Iraq's weapons', *New Yorker*, 27 October 2003
82. Steven R. Weisman with Felicity Barringer, 'U.S. Seeks 9 Votes From U.N. Council to Confront Iraq', *New York Times*, 21 February 2003
83. Lagos, *The Southern Tiger*, pp.217–19
84. S. Shane and A. Sabar, 'Alleged NSA memo details U.S. eavesdropping at UN', *Baltimore Sun*, 4 March 2003
85. The nature of American policy towards the coup is still disputed – see Gustafson, *Hostile Intent*, pp.3–12
86. M. Bright, E. Vulliamy and P. Beaumont, 'UN launches inquiry into American spying', *Observer*, 9 March 2003; private information
87. Nicholas Watt, 'Top civil servant tells Short to shut up', *Guardian*, 1 March 2004
88. Entry for 26 February 2003, Mullin, *A View From the Foothills*, p.455
89. Select Committee on Foreign Affairs Ninth Report, 'The Decision to go to War in Iraq', 7 July 2003, HC813–1, para.129
90. Ibid., para.135
91. Entry for 7 February 2003, Campbell, *Burden of Power*, pp.451–2
92. Entry for 3 March 2003, Mullin, *A View From the Foothills*, p.372
93. Entry for 11 February 2003, Campbell, *Burden of Power*, p.456
94. Entry for 12 March 2003, Stothard, *30 Days*, p.30
95. Jonathan Owen, 'Tony Blair and Iraq: The damning evidence', *Independent*, 7 April 2013
96. Entry for 5 February 2003, Campbell, *Burden of Power*, p.448
97. Entries for 10 and 29 April 2003, ibid., pp.542, 554
98. BBC Radio 4 *Today* programme, 29 May 2003, 6.07 a.m. *Today* timeline at http://www.bbc.co.uk/radio4/today/reports/politics/hutton_audio_timeline_20040128.shtml
99. Ibid., 7.32 a.m.
100. Private information
101. Entry for 1 June 2003, Campbell, *Burden of Power*, p.592
102. Entry for 9 June 2003, ibid., p.601
103. Entries for 29 and 30 May 2003, ibid., p.589
104. Rawnsley, *End of the Party*, p.204
105. Entry for 1 June 2003, Campbell, *Burden of Power*, p.592
106. Segal, *Axis of Evil*, p.241; see also entry for 27 June 2003, Morgan, *The Insider*, p.407
107. Entry for 4 June 2003, Mullin, *A View From the Foothills*, p.413

108. George Jones and Toby Helm, 'No 10 fails to endorse Reid claim', *Daily Telegraph*, 5 June 2003

109. Rawnsley, *End of the Party*, p.207

110. Danchev, 'Story Development'. CIC contained a five-person team called the 'Strategic Story Development Unit'

111. Entry for 4 June 2003, Campbell, *Burden of Power*, p.596

112. Entry for 4 June 2003, Mullin, *A View From the Foothills*, p.413

113. Seldon, *Blair Unbound*, p.138

114. Corera, *Art of Betrayal*, p.362

115. Entries for 2 and 7 September 2003, Mullin, *A View From the Foothills*, pp.424–5

116. John Barry, 'The Defector's Secrets', *Newsweek*, 3 March 2003

117. Hansard, HC 813-I, 'The decision to go to war with Iraq', 9, paragraph 8. However, opinion varies as to the extent to which the IISS has drawn on informal assistance from Whitehall

118. Entry for 1 July 2003, Campbell, *Burden of Power*, p.625

119. Rawnsley, *End of the Party*, p.206

120. Entry for 28 January 2004, Mullin, *A View From the Foothills*, p.447

121. Email from Jonathan Powell to John Scarlett, 17 September 2002; Hutton inquiry evidence, CAB/11/69

122. Nicholas Rufford, 'Revealed: how MI6 sold the Iraq war', *Sunday Times*, 28 December 2003; see also Mackay, *The War on Truth*, pp.104–6; Ritter, *Iraq Confidential*, pp.280–1

123. Hansard, 41HC 898, Butler, 120, paragraph 485

124. Aldrich, 'Four Enquiries', pp.74–7

125. Tyler Drumheller, *60 Minutes*, CBS News, 23 April 2006

126. Michael Laurie, Statement to the Iraq inquiry, http://www.iraqinquiry.org.uk/media/52051/Laurie-statement-FINAL.pdf

127. Aldrich, 'Four Enquiries', pp.73–5, 81

128. Seldon, *Blair Unbound*, p.140

129. Lord Butler quoted in Peter Taylor, 'Iraq: The spies who fooled the world', BBC News website, 18 March 2013

130. Entry for 8 July 2003, Campbell, *Burden of Power*, p.634

131. Ewen MacAskill and Ian Cobain, '7/7 Seemed to Herald a New Era of Terror on UK Soil – One that did not Materialise', *Guardian*, 7 July 2015

132. Entry for 30 January 2003, Campbell, *Burden of Power*, p.438

133. Aldrich, Cormac and Goodman, *Spying on the World*, pp.399–402

134. Meyer, *DC Confidential*, pp.229–30

135. Private information

Chapter 18: Gordon Brown (2007–2010)

1. 'Gordon Brown: Britain is not involved in torture', *Daily Telegraph*, 26 February 2010

2. Entry for 7 April 2004, Morgan, *The Insider*, p.447

3. Rawnsley, *End of the Party*, pp.467, 522–3

4. Hayman, *Terrorist Hunters*, p.305

5. Private information

6. 'Russia "backed Litvinenko murder"', BBC, 8 July 2008; private information

7. Owen, *Litvinenko Inquiry*, para.9.17

8. J. Blitz and N. Buckley, 'Moscow envoys expelled in spy row', *Financial Times*, 17 July 2007

9. Eastern Dept to Moscow, FCO Tel. No. 448, 'Subject: Russia: Visit By Sergei Ivanov: Overview', 2 November 2000, http://www.Cryptome.Org/Fco-Ivanov.Htm

10. Sixsmith, *The Litvinenko File*, pp.299–303

11. Owen, *Litvinenko Inquiry*, para.9.215

12. Hayman, *Terrorist Hunters*, pp.227–30

13. Ibid., pp.229–30

14. Ibid., pp.241–4, 308–10

15. Florian Gathmann and Veit Medick, 'Magazine Report Angers Politicians: Did the CIA Plot to Kill German Citizen?', *Der Spiegel*, 5 January 2010

16. Tomlinson, *Big Breach*, p.98

17. Richard Dearlove, Evidence to the Scott Baker Inquiry into the Deaths of Diana, Princess of Wales, and Mr Dodi al Fayed, 20 February 2008, http://www.webarchive.nationalarchives.gov.uk/20090607230252/http://www.scottbaker-inquests.gov.uk/hearing_transcripts/index.htm

18. Rebecca English, 'Ex-MI6 chief admits agents do have a licence to kill but denies executing Diana', *Daily Mail*, 21 February 2008

19. Peter Walker, 'Brown calls for line to be drawn under Diana death', *Guardian*, 8 April 2008

20. Duncan Gardham, 'Eight life sentences at the end of trans-Atlantic terrorist plot intended to eclipse 9/11', *Daily Telegraph*, 13 July 2010

21. Rawnsley, *End of the Party*, p.466

22. Mark Townsend, Jo Revill and Paul Kelbie, 'Terror threat "critical" as Glasgow attacked', *Observer*, 1 July 2007

23. Herrington, 'British Islamic Extremist Terrorism', pp.16–35

24. Hansard, Gordon Brown, 'National Security', 14 November 2007, cm 667
25. Hansard, Gordon Brown, 'National Security Strategy', 19 March 2008, cm 926
26. Ibid.
27. Gordon Brown quoted in IISS, 'UK Rethink on Counter-Terrorism', p.1
28. Entry for 26 August 1998, Mullin, *Walk-On Part*, p.367
29. Matthew Weaver, 'Brown considering 56-day terror suspect detention limit, reports say', *Guardian*, 25 July 2007
30. Gordon Brown, 'In Full: Brown Speech on Liberty', BBC News, 25 October 2007
31. BBC, 'Brown Wins Crunch Vote on 42 Days', BBC News, 11 June 2008
32. James Kirkup, 'Eliza Manningham-Buller, former MI5 chief, savages 42-day detention plan', *Daily Telegraph*, 8 July 2008; Rosa Prince, 'Terror bill: 42-day detention rejected by House of Lords', *Daily Telegraph*, 13 October 2008
33. Rosa Prince, 'Terror bill: 42-day detention rejected by House of Lords', *Daily Telegraph*, 13 October 2008
34. Damien McElroy, Rahul Bedi and Andrew Alderson, 'Mumbai attacks: 300 feared dead as full horror of the terrorist attacks emerges', *Daily Telegraph*, 29 November 2008
35. Private information
36. Vikram Dodd, 'Scotland Yard creates SAS-style unit to counter threat of terrorist gun attack', *Guardian*, 29 June 2015
37. Rawnsley, *End of the Party*, p.663
38. David Leigh, 'WikiLeaks cables: US spurned Gary McKinnon plea from Gordon Brown', *Guardian*, 30 November 2010
39. Panetta, *Worthy Fights*, pp.204–5, 272–3
40. Ibid., pp.199–226, 293; private information
41. Richard Norton-Taylor and Ian Cobain, 'Top judge: Binyam Mohamed case shows MI5 to be devious, dishonest and complicit in torture', *Guardian*, 10 February 2010
42. Intelligence and Security Committee, Annual Report 2009–2010, p.18
43. Gordon Rayner and Duncan Gardham, 'Binyam Mohamed: release of secrets will harm relations with Britain, warns US', *Daily Telegraph*, 11 February 2010
44. US Government, 'Binyam Mohamed: read the secret torture evidence', *Guardian*, 10 February 2010
45. Intelligence and Security Committee, Annual Report 2009–2010, p.19
46. Richard Norton-Taylor, 'Binyam Mohamed torture evidence must be revealed, judges rule', *Guardian*, 10 February 2010
47. 'Binyam Mohamed: the torture allegations', *Daily Telegraph*, 12 January 2012
48. 'Gordon Brown: Britain is not involved in torture', *Daily Telegraph*, 26 February 2010
49. Intelligence and Security Committee, Annual Report 2008–2009 (2009), p.44
50. Private information
51. Cowper-Coles, *Cables From Kabul*, pp.53–5; Ford, *The CIA and Vietnam*, pp.75–89
52. Wolf, 'This Secret Town', p.556
53. Elaine Sciolino, 'Violence Thwarts C.I.A. Director's Unusual Diplomatic Role in Middle Eastern Peacemaking', *New York Times*, 13 November 2000; Chris McGreal, 'UK recalls MI6 link to Palestinian militants', *Guardian*, 24 September 2003; private information
54. Scott, 'Secret Intelligence, Covert Action and Clandestine Diplomacy', pp.322–41
55. Hansard, Gordon Brown, 12 December 2007, cm 303–5
56. Seldon and Lodge, *Brown at No. 10*, pp.410–12
57. Robert Winnett, 'Gordon Brown called to explain Taliban talks', *Daily Telegraph*, 27 December 2007
58. Ibid.
59. Cowper-Coles, *Cables From Kabul*, pp.68–9, 125–32
60. Ibid., p.134; Panetta, *Worthy Fights*, pp.204–5, 378–9; private information
61. Cowper-Coles, *Cables From Kabul*, pp.133–4
62. Private information
63. Cowper-Coles, *Cables From Kabul*, pp.221–2
64. Clinton, *Hard Choices*, pp.154–8
65. Richard Norton-Taylor, 'UK pressing Karzai to negotiate with Taliban', *Guardian*, 13 November 2009; James Kirkup, 'Gordon Brown Signals End to Afghanistan Offensive', *Daily Telegraph*, 27 July 2009
66. Clinton, *Hard Choices*, p.155
67. Tom Coghlan, Michael Evans and Daniel Lloyd, 'How MI6 was fooled by Taleban impostor', *The Times*, 26 November 2010; private information
68. Seldon and Lodge, *Brown at No. 10*, p.411
69. Rawnsley, *End of the Party*, p.634
70. Ewen MacAskill, Nick Davies, Nick Hopkins, Julian Borger and James Ball, 'GCHQ intercepted foreign politicians'

communications at G20 summits', *Guardian*, 17 June 2013

71. Nigel Morris and Andrew Grice, 'G20 summit: Britain plunged into diplomatic row over claims GCHQ spied on foreign politicians', *Independent*, 18 June 2013; also private information

72. McBride, *Power Trip*, p.121

73. Entry for 12 April 2008, Mullin, *Decline and Fall*, p.319

74. Seldon and Lodge, *Brown at No. 10*, pp.243–8

75. McBride, *Power Trip*, p.121

76. Andrew Porter, 'Gordon Brown's historic trade deal with China', *Daily Telegraph*, 18 January 2008

77. David Leppard and Claire Newell, 'Gordon Brown aide a victim of "Honeytrap" operation by Chinese', *Sunday Times*, 20 July 2008

78. McBride, *Power Trip*, pp.119–27

79. Private information

80. McBride, *Power Trip*, pp.124–6

Chapter 19: David Cameron (2010–)

1. David Cameron, 'Minutes of Evidence Taken Before the Joint Committee on the National Security Strategy', 20 January 2014, HC1040

2. See Seldon and Snowdon, *Cameron at 10*, pp.1–2

3. Michael Wilkinson, 'KGB spies who "tried to recruit" David Cameron were just a "gay pick-up"', *Daily Telegraph*, 30 July 2015

4. Hennessy, *Distilling the Frenzy*, p.96. On Cameron's leadership style see Theakston, 'David Cameron as prime minister', pp.194, 203, 205–7

5. Beech and Oliver, 'Humanitarian Intervention and Foreign Policy in the Conservative-led Coalition', p.11

6. Seldon and Snowdon, *Cameron at 10*, p.62

7. Private information

8. Theakston, 'David Cameron as prime minister', p.202

9. Davies, *Intelligence and Government*, p.307

10. Private information

11. Honeyman, 'Foreign Policy', p.124

12. Seldon and Snowdon, *Cameron at 10*, p.62

13. Iain Lobban, quoted in Charles Moore, 'GCHQ: "This is not Blitz Britain. We sure as hell can't lick terrorism on our own"', *Daily Telegraph*, 11 October 2014

14. Hennessy, *Distilling the Frenzy*, p.96

15. Aldrich, Cormac and Goodman, *Spying on the World*, pp.412–13

16. Personal information

17. Personal information

18. Aldrich, Cormac and Goodman, *Spying on the World*, pp.412–13

19. Honeyman, 'Foreign Policy', pp.122–4; Daddow and Schnapper, 'Liberal Intervention in the Foreign Policy Thinking of Tony Blair and David Cameron', p.335

20. D'Ancona, *In it Together*, pp.160–1

21. Daddow and Schnapper, 'Liberal Intervention in the Foreign Policy Thinking of Tony Blair and David Cameron', p.332

22. Colin Freeman and Patrick Sawer, 'UK Promoted Sale of Sniper Rifles to Gaddafi just Weeks before Uprising Began', *Daily Telegraph*, 11 September 2011

23. Honeyman, 'Foreign Policy', pp.122–4; Daddow and Schnapper, 'Liberal Intervention in the Foreign Policy Thinking of Tony Blair and David Cameron', p.335

24. Seldon and Snowdon, *Cameron at 10*, p.59

25. Tom Whitehead, 'Arab Spring provided new breeding ground for British terrorists – spy chief', *Daily Telegraph*, 25 June 2012

26. Honeyman, 'Foreign Policy', pp.124–5

27. Seldon and Snowdon, *Cameron at 10*, p.97

28. Ibid., pp.98–9

29. Quoted in D'Ancona, *In it Together*, p.167

30. Seldon and Snowdon, *Cameron at 10*, p.103

31. Ibid., p.102

32. D'Ancona, *In it Together*, p.172

33. Ibid., p.168

34. Quoted in Hennessy, *Distilling the Frenzy*, p.96

35. Private information

36. National Security Adviser, 'Libya Crisis', pp.3, 19

37. 'Profile: Spy Chief Alex Allan', BBC News website, 4 July 2008

38. Private information

39. National Security Adviser, 'Libya Crisis', p.7

40. Ibid., p.20

41. Private information

42. Private information

43. Gaskarth, *British Foreign Policy: Crises, Conflicts, and Future Challenges*, p.30

44. Mark Urban, 'Inside Story of the UK's Secret Mission to Beat Gaddafi', BBC News, 19 January 2012

45. Quoted in D'Ancona, *In it Together*, p.177

46. Quintana, 'The War from the Air', pp.32–7

47. National Security Adviser, 'Libya Crisis', p.9

48. Mark Urban, 'Inside Story of the UK's Secret Mission to Beat Gaddafi', BBC News, 19 January 2012

49. Hala Jaber, 'SAS had Secret Computer Codes in their Pockets', *Sunday Times*, 13 March 2011, p.4

50. Patrick Wintour, 'William Hague Approved Botched Libya Mission, PM's Office Says', *Guardian*, 7 March 2011

51. Mark Urban, 'Inside Story of the UK's Secret Mission to Beat Gaddafi', BBC News, 19 January 2012

52. Hala Jaber, 'SAS had Secret Computer Codes in their Pockets', *Sunday Times*, 13 March 2011, p.4

53. Sam Coates, 'How the UK Waged a Secret Oil War in Libya', *The Times*, 1 September 2011; James Landale, 'How UK Starved Gaddafi of Fuel', BBC News, 31 August 2011; 'Supplementary Written evidence from Rt Hon William Hague MP, Secretary of State for Foreign and Commonwealth Affairs', 26 September 2011

54. D'Ancona, *In it Together*, p.178

55. Sean Rayment, 'How SAS Brought a New Dawn to the Mermaid of the Med', *Sunday Telegraph*, 28 August 2011, p.5; Mark Urban, 'Inside Story of the UK's Secret Mission to Beat Gaddafi', BBC News, 19 January 2012

56. Lionel Barber, 'Lunch with the *FT*: Sir John Sawers', *Financial Times*, 19 September 2014

57. D'Ancona, *In it Together*, p.178

58. Ibid., p.184

59. Lionel Barber, 'Lunch with the *FT*: Sir John Sawers', *Financial Times*, 19 September 2014

60. Private information

61. Private information

62. Private information

63. J. Risen, M. Mazzetti, M. Schmidt, 'U.S.-Approved Arms for Libya Rebels Fell Into Jihadis' Hands', *New York Times*, 5 December 2012; E. Schmitt, H. Cooper, M. Schmidt, 'Deadly Attack in Libya Was Major Blow to CIA Efforts', *New York Times*, 23 September 2012; 'Syrian rebels squabble over weapons as biggest shipload arrives from Libya', *The Times*, 14 September 2012; D. McElroy, 'CIA "running arms smuggling team in Benghazi when consulate was attacked"', *Daily Telegraph*, 2 August 2013; S. Hersh, 'The Red Line and the Rat Line', *London Review of Books*, 7 April 2014

64. 'British ambassador to Libya escapes uninjured after his convoy is hit by rocket-propelled grenade', *Daily Mail*, 12 June 2012

65. Raf Sanchez, 'Foreign Office admits British guns lost during Benghazi attack', *Daily Telegraph*, 7 February 2013

66. E. Schmitt, H. Cooper, M. Schmidt, 'Deadly Attack in Libya Was Major Blow to CIA Efforts, *New York Times*, 23 September 2012; Murphy and Webb, *Benghazi*, pp.25–58

67. Con Coughlin, 'The SAS: A Very Special Force', *Daily Telegraph*, 31 January 2013, p.21; James Kirkup and Tim Ross, 'Special Forces will go to Mali, says Cameron', *Daily Telegraph*, 22 January 2013, p.4

68. Harding, *The Snowden Files*, pp.37–9

69. Private information

70. NSA, 'VISIT PRÉCIS: Sir Iain Lobban, KCMG, CB, Director, Government Communications Headquarters (GCHQ), 30 April 2013–1 May 2013', National Security Archive online

71. Rowena Mason, 'David Cameron: We Can be Sure British Spies Keep Within the Law', *Daily Telegraph*, 10 June 1013

72. Harding, *The Snowden Files*, p.177

73. Ibid., p.178

74. Ibid., pp.178–80

75. Ibid., pp.182–3

76. Ibid., pp.191–2

77. Private information; the staff of The Bodley Head still recall the masks

78. Harding, *The Snowden Files*, pp.280, 320; Roy Greenslade, 'Press Freedom Groups Urge David Cameron to Lay off the *Guardian*', *Guardian*, 18 February 2014

79. Tim Ross, 'Cameron "sanctioned" destruction of paper's hard drives', *Daily Telegraph*, 21 August 2013, p.10; Nicholas Watt, 'David Cameron had advance warning of Miranda Detention, No. 10 Confirms', *Guardian*, 20 August 2013

80. Cameron quoted in 'David Cameron Criticised the *Guardian* for Publishing Snowden Data', BBC, 16 October 2013

81. Hansard, David Cameron, Prime Minister's Questions, 28 October 2013, cm 666–7

82. Alan Rusbridger, 'Oral Evidence Taken Before the Home Affairs Committee: Counter Terrorism', Home Affairs Committee – Minutes of Evidence, HC231-iv, 3 December 2013

83. Private information

84. Alan Rusbridger, 'Oral Evidence Taken Before the Home Affairs Committee:

Counter Terrorism', Home Affairs Committee – Minutes of Evidence, HC231–iv, 3 December 2013
85. Private information
86. See Owen Bowcott, 'UK–US surveillance regime was unlawful "for seven years"', *Guardian*, 6 February 2015
87. Private information
88. See for example the work of Duncan Campbell
89. David Cameron, 'Minutes of Evidence Taken Before the Joint Committee on the National Security Strategy', 20 January 2014, HC1040
90. 'Racism is rife at GCHQ, says officer suing for bullying', *Daily Telegraph*, 23 April 2012
91. Private information
92. David Cameron, 'Minutes of Evidence Taken Before the Joint Committee on the National Security Strategy', 20 January 2014, HC1040
93. Entry for 19 January 2013, Carr, *Diary of a Foreign Minister*, p.277
94. Private information
95. Seldon and Snowdon, *Cameron at 10*, p.327
96. Quoted ibid.
97. D'Ancona, *In it Together*, pp.357–8
98. NSA, 'VISIT PRÉCIS: Sir Iain Lobban, KCMG, CB, Director, Government Communications Headquarters (GCHQ), 30 April 2013–1 May 2013', National Security Archive online
99. Patrick Wintour, 'Syrian Regime Used Sarin Against Opposition at Least Twice, Says Cameron', *Guardian*, 14 June 2013
100. Richard Spencer, 'Britain drew up plans to build 100,000-strong Syrian rebel army', *Daily Telegraph*, 4 July 2014
101. Con Coughlin, 'How Coalition Came Close to Involving Itself in an Open-Ended Middle East Conflict', *Daily Telegraph*, 5 July 2014, p.18
102. Quoted in Seldon and Snowdon, *Cameron at 10*, p.344
103. Bochel, Defty and Kirkpatrick, *Watching the Watchers*, p.1
104. Aldrich, Cormac and Goodman, *Spying on the World*, p.418
105. Ibid., pp.418–19
106. Private information
107. Aldrich, Cormac and Goodman, *Spying on the World*, p.418
108. Hansard, David Cameron MP, 29 August 2013, cm 1426 (emphasis added)
109. Ibid., cm 1437
110. Ibid., cm 1432
111. Ibid., cm 1433
112. Ibid., cm 1437
113. Aldrich, Cormac and Goodman, *Spying on the World*, p.419
114. 'Turkey arrests 12 in raids on terrorist organization', Reuters, 30 May 2013
115. Seldon and Snowdon, *Cameron at 10*, p.337
116. Nafeez Mosaddeq Ahmed, 'Special report: fixing intelligence on Syria?', *Le Monde*, September 2013
117. Philip Sherwell and Rowena Mason, 'Syria's civil war could last for years, says US official, and is reviving Al Qaeda in Iraq', *Daily Telegraph*, 21 July 2013
118. Alex Delmar-Morgan and Jane Merrick, 'Special report: Syria to allow UN to inspect site of alleged chemical attack as David Cameron and Barack Obama warn Assad that military action looms closer', *Independent*, 25 August 2013; Martin Chulov and Toby Helm, 'Cameron and Obama on the brink of Syria intervention', *Observer*, 25 August 2013, p.1
119. David Cameron, 'Syria: transcript of PM's interview', 27 August 2013, https://www.gov.uk/government/speeches/syria-transcript-of-pms-interview
120. Dudley, *Understanding the UK Parliament's Decision*, pp.55–6
121. David Cameron, 'Syria: Transcript of PM's interview', 27 August 2013, https://www.gov.uk/government/speeches/syria-transcript-of-pms-interview
122. Dudley, *Understanding the UK Parliament's Decision*
123. Adam Withnall, 'Syria Crisis', *Independent*, 3 September 2013
124. Seymour M. Hersh, 'The Red Line and the Rat Line', *London Review of Books*, 17 April 2014, pp.21–4
125. Nafeez Mosaddeq Ahmed, 'Special report: fixing intelligence on Syria?', *Le Monde*, September 2013
126. Private information
127. Private information
128. Seldon and Snowdon, *Cameron at 10*, p.345
129. Quoted in ibid., p.471
130. Richard Kerbaj, 'PM Orders Spy Chiefs to Find Jihadi John', *Sunday Times*, 5 October 2014
131. Seldon and Snowdon, *Cameron at 10*, pp.471–2
132. Ibid., pp.475–6
133. Mark Hookham, 'SAS gets "carte blanche" on Isis', *Sunday Times*, 5 July 2015, p.13

134. Peter Dominiczak, 'SAS "beefed up" to take fight to Isil', *Daily Telegraph*, 4 October 2015

135. Peter Dominiczak and Ben Riley-Smith, 'Britain's Special Forces will be increased ahead of fresh assault on Isil', *Daily Telegraph*, 12 July 2015

Conclusion: Prime Ministers and the Future of Intelligence

1. Christopher Hope, 'Spies should be able to monitor all online messaging, says David Cameron', *Daily Telegraph*, 15 January 2015

2. Daddow and Schnapper, 'Liberal Intervention in the Foreign Policy Thinking of Tony Blair and David Cameron', pp.330–49

3. Cradock quoted approvingly by Daphne Park, Hansard, HL Deb, 9 December 1993, vol. 550 cc1023–79

4. Cradock, *Know Your Enemy*, p.299

5. Herman, *Intelligence Power in Peace and War*, p.1

6. Handel, 'The Politics of Intelligence', p.7

7. Inkster, 'Chinese Intelligence in the Cyber Age', pp.45–54

8. Entry for 5 June 1959, Catterall (ed.), *Macmillan Diaries*, Vol. II, p.221

9. Starbird, 'Rumors, False Flags, and Digital Vigilantes'

10. Private information

11. Aldrich, 'Beyond the Vigilant State', p.891

12. Finlan, 'The (Arrested) Development of UK Special Forces', pp.971–82

13. Omand, 'The Future of Intelligence', p.15

14. Laqueur, *A World of Secrets*, p.97

15. Teitelbaum, *The Impact of the Information Revolution on Policymakers' Use of Intelligence Analysis*, p.76

16. Omand, 'The Future of Intelligence', p.16

17. Gibson, 'Future Roles of the UK Intelligence System', p.919

18. Moore, 'Real-time syndrome surveillance', pp.3–11

19. Field, 'Tracking terrorist networks', pp.997–1009

20. Aldrich, 'Beyond the Vigilant State', p.892

21. Phythian, 'Hutton and Scott', pp.124–37

22. Entry for 27 February 2006, Mullin, *Decline and Fall*, p.81

23. Patten, *Not Quite the Diplomat*, p.97

24. BDOHP interview, Sir Crispin Tickell, 28 January 1999, CCC

25. Coll, *The Bin Ladens*, pp.464–6

26. Beck, *World Risk Society*

27. Private information

28. Treverton, 'The Future of Intelligence', p.29

29. See Barber, *If Mayors Ruled the World*; John Milbank, 'British Foreign Policy: An Alternative Future', talk at the University of Nottingham, 2015

30. Treverton, *Reshaping National Intelligence*, p.179

31. Kissinger in Betts, 'Analysis: War and Decision', p.118

32. Asa Bennett, 'Today's prime ministers are younger than ever', *Daily Telegraph*, 1 April 2015

33. Hennessy, 'Rulers and Servants of the State', p.15

34. Private information

35. Gazit, 'Intelligence Estimates and the Decision Maker', p.262; Handel, 'The Politics of Intelligence', p.14; Lowenthal, *Intelligence*, p.147

36. Private information

37. Goodman, *Joint Intelligence Committee*, pp.3–15

38. Kaarbo, 'Prime Minister Leadership Styles in Foreign Policy Decision-Making', p.573

39. Private information

40. Evan Thomas, 'I haven't suffered doubt', *Newsweek*, 26 April 2004, pp.22–6

41. Hughes, *The Fate of Facts in the World of Men*, p.20

42. Handel, 'Leaders and Intelligence', pp.5–6

43. Ibid., p.35

44. Hennessy, 'Rulers and Servants of the State', p.15

45. Rimington, *Open Secret*, pp.190–1

46. Private information

47. Entry for 15 December 2001, Campbell, *Burden of Power*, p.14

48. Dafna Linzer, 'U.S. officials go to Security Council capitals in diplomatic drive for Iraq support', Associated Press, 24 February 2003

49. Lord Armstrong, interview with Lord Hennessy, *Men of Secrets*, November 2012, Mile End Group, QMU

50. 'The fall guy for Thatcher's "economy with the truth"', *New Straits Times*, 14 May 1989

51. Lord Turnbull, interview with Lord Hennessy, *Men of Secrets*, January 2013, Mile End Group, QMU

52. Cabinet Office, *National Intelligence Machinery*, p.21

53. Davies, 'UK Intelligence'

54. Hurd, *Memoirs*, p.vii

55. Reiter, 'The Weight of the Shadow of the Past', pp.490–526

56. Morell, *The Great War of Our Time*, p.115

57. Lord Butler, 'Review of Intelligence on Weapons of Mass Destruction, Report of a Committee of Privy Councillors', HC 898, 2004

58. Lord O'Donnell, interview with Lord Hennessy, *Men of Secrets: The Cabinet Secretaries* (February 2013), Mile End Group, QMU

Bibliography

There are many books on British intelligence over the last hundred years, and even more on prime ministers. We have only referenced those that we have used extensively or quoted. All books referred to in the bibliography are published in London unless otherwise stated. All references to primary documents in the endnotes are to the UK National Archives at Kew unless otherwise stated.

Manuscripts and Private Papers
Julian Amery papers, Churchill Archives, Churchill College Cambridge
Lord Attlee papers, Bodleian Library Oxford
Lord Attlee papers, Churchill Archives, Churchill College Cambridge
Lord Avon, Foreign Secretary, Birmingham University Library
Patrick Beesly and other Ultra historians, Churchill Archives, Churchill College Cambridge
British-American Tobacco papers, Special Collections, University of California San Francisco
William Bundy, Seeley G. Mudd Library, Princeton University
Sir Alexander Cadogan, Churchill Archives, Churchill College Cambridge
Jimmy Carter, Jimmy Carter Library, Atlanta, Georgia
Anthony Cave Brown papers, Special Collections, Lauinger Library, Georgetown University
Lord Cherwell papers, Nuffield College Oxford
Sir Winston Churchill, Churchill Archives, Churchill College Cambridge
William Colby, Princeton University
Sir Andrew Cunningham, British Library
William Donovan papers, US Military Institute, Carlisle Barracks, Pennsylvania
Alec Douglas-Home, Scottish Record Office
Allen Dulles, Seeley G. Mudd Library, Princeton University
Dwight D. Eisenhower, Dwight D. Eisenhower Library, Abilene, Kansas
GCHQ Trade Union records, Warwick Modern Records Centre (WMRC)
General Sir Hastings Ismay, Liddell Hart Centre for Military Archives, King's College London
Lyndon B. Johnson, Lyndon B. Johnson Library, Austin, Texas
Admiral Louis Le Bailly, Churchill Archives, Churchill College Cambridge
Selwyn Lloyd, Churchill Archives, Churchill College Cambridge
Clare Booth Luce, Library of Congress
John McCone, Bancroft Library, University of California, Berkeley
Harold Macmillan papers, Bodleian Library, Oxford University
Cord Meyer papers, Library of Congress
John Mitchell papers, Churchill Archives, Churchill College Cambridge
Sir Walter Monckton, Bodleian Library, Oxford University
Field Marshal Lord Montgomery of Alamein, Imperial War Museum
Admiral Lord Mountbatten, University of Southampton

General William Odom, Library of Congress
Franklin D. Roosevelt, Franklin D. Roosevelt Library, Hyde Park, New York
Vice Admiral Gerard Rushbrooke, Imperial War Museum
Duncan Sandys, Churchill Archives, Churchill College Cambridge
Arthur Schlesinger, New York Public Library
William Shirer papers, Stewart Memorial Library, Coe College
Lord Strang, Churchill Archives, Churchill College Cambridge
Lord Swinton, Churchill Archives, Churchill College Cambridge
Harry S. Truman, Harry S. Truman Library, Independence, Missouri
Robert Vansittart papers, Churchill College Cambridge
Gerald Wilkinson papers, Churchill Archives, Churchill College Cambridge

Oral History Projects and Digital Archives
British Diplomatic Oral History Project (BDOHP), Churchill College Cambridge
Digital National Security Archive (DNSA)
Foreign Affairs Oral History Project, Special Collections, Lauinger Library, Georgetown
    University
Suez Oral History Project, Liddell Hart Centre for Military Archives, King's College London

Memoirs, Diaries, Published Documents and Reports
Aitken, J., *Pride and Perjury: An Autobiography* (HarperCollins, 2000)
Aspin, L., *The Kovacs Contract: The Autobiography of the Notorious Master Mercenary* (Everest
    Books, 1976)
Attlee, C., *As it Happened* (Heinemann, 1954)
Bagley, T.H., *Spy Wars: Moles, Mysteries, and Deadly Games* (New Haven: Yale UP, 2007)
Baker, K., *The Turbulent Years: My Life in Politics* (Faber & Faber, 1993)
Benn, T., *Out of the Wilderness, Diaries 1963–67* (Hutchinson, 1987)
_____, *Office Without Power, Diaries 1968–72* (Hutchinson, 1988)
_____, *Against the Tide, Diaries 1973–76* (Hutchinson, 1990)
_____, *Conflicts of Interest, Diaries 1977–80* (Arrow, 1991)
Benson, R.L. and Warner, R., *Venona: Soviet Espionage and the American Response, 1939–57*
    (Menlo Park: Aegean Park Press, 1997)
Biffen, J., *Semi-Detached* (Biteback, 2013)
Bittman, L., *The Deception Game* (NY: Ballantine, 1981)
Blair, C., *Speaking for Myself* (Little, Brown, 2008)
Blair, T., *A Journey* (Hutchinson, 2010)
Blake, G., *No Other Choice: An Autobiography* (Jonathan Cape, 1990)
Blix, H., *Disarming Iraq: The Search for Weapons of Mass Destruction* (NY: Pantheon, 2004)
Blunkett, D., *The Blunkett Tapes: My Life in the Bear Pit* (Bloomsbury, 2006)
Boyle, P. (ed.), *The Churchill–Eisenhower Correspondence, 1953–56* (Chapel Hill: University of
    North Carolina Press, 1990)
Brock, M. and Brock, E., *Margot Asquith's Great War Diary, 1914–1916: The View From Downing
    Street* (Oxford UP, 2014)
Cabinet Office, *National Intelligence Machinery* (HMSO, 2010)
Callaghan, J., *Time and Chance* (Collins, 1987)
Campbell, A., *Prelude to Power: The Alastair Campbell Diaries, Vol. 1, 1994–97* (Hutchinson,
    2010)
_____, *The Power and the People: The Alastair Campbell Diaries, Vol. 2, 1997–99* (Hutchinson,
    2011)
_____, *Power and Responsibility: The Alastair Campbell Diaries, Vol. 3, 1999–2001* (Hutchinson,
    2011)
_____, *Burden of Power – Countdown to Iraq: The Alastair Campbell Diaries, Vol. 4, 2001–03*
    (Hutchinson, 2012)
_____, *The Blair Years: Extracts From the Alastair Campbell Diaries* (Arrow, 2008)
Carr, B., *Diary of a Foreign Minister* (Sydney: NewSouth, 2014)
Carrington, Lord, *Reflections on Things Past: The Memoirs of Lord Carrington* (Collins, 1988)
Castle, B., *The Castle Diaries 1964–70* (Weidenfeld & Nicolson, 1984)
Catterall, P., *The Macmillan Diaries, Vol. I, The Cabinet Years* (Macmillan, 2003)

____, *The Macmillan Diaries, Vol. II, Prime Minister and After* (Macmillan, 2011)

Cavendish, A., *Inside Intelligence* (HarperCollins, 1990)

Cherkashin, V. and Feifer, G., *Spy Handler: Memoir of a KGB Officer – The True Story of the Man Who Recruited Robert Hanssen and Aldrich Ames* (NY: Basic Books, 2005)

Churchill, W., *The Second World War: Vol. 1, The Gathering Storm* (Penguin, 2005)

____, *The Second World War: Vol. 2, Their Finest Hour* (Penguin, 2005)

____, *The Second World War: Vol. 3, The Grand Alliance* (Penguin, 2005)

CIA History Staff, *The Battle for Iran*, mid-1970s, web access

Clark, A., *Diaries: Into Politics, 1972–1982* (Weidenfeld & Nicolson, 2000)

____, *Diaries: In Power, 1983–1992* (Weidenfeld & Nicolson, 1993)

____, *Diaries: The Last Diaries, 1993–1999* (Weidenfeld & Nicolson, 2002)

Clinton, H., *Hard Choices* (NY: Simon & Schuster, 2014)

Collier, B., *Diplomatic Wanderings: From Saigon to the South Seas* (Radcliffe, 2003)

Colville, J., *The Fringes of Power: Downing Street Diaries 1939–1955* (Hodder & Stoughton, 1985)

Cooper, C., *The Lion's Last Roar: Suez, 1956* (Collins, 1978)

Cooper, D., *The Duff Cooper Diaries: 1915–1951* (Weidenfeld & Nicolson, 2006)

Cooper, J., *One of the Originals: The Story of a Founder Member of the SAS* (Pan, 1991)

Cowper-Coles, S., *Cables From Kabul: The Inside Story of the West's Afghanistan Campaign* (HarperCollins, 2011)

____, *Ever the Diplomat: Confessions of a Foreign Office Mandarin* (HarperCollins, 2013)

Cradock, P., *In Pursuit of British Interests: Reflections on Foreign Policy Under Margaret Thatcher and John Major* (John Murray, 1997)

Crossman, R., *The Diaries of a Cabinet Minister: Vol. 1, 1964–66* (Hamish Hamilton/Jonathan Cape, 1976)

____, *The Diaries of a Cabinet Minister: Vol. 2, 1966–68* (Hamish Hamilton/Jonathan Cape, 1976)

Crozier, B., *Free Agent: The Unseen War, 1941–91* (HarperCollins, 1993)

Cudlipp, H., *Walking on the Water: An Autobiography* (The Bodley Head, 1976)

Currie, E., *Diaries, 1987–92* (Little, Brown, 2002)

Curtis, S. (ed.), *The Journals of Woodrow Wyatt* (Macmillan, 1988)

Davie, M., (ed) *The Diaries of Evelyn Waugh* (Weidenfeld & Nicolson, 1976)

Davies, B., *Fire Magic: Hijack at Mogadishu* (Bloomsbury, 1994)

Denning, A., *The Scandal of Christine Keeler and John Profumo: Lord Denning's Report, 1963* (Tim Coates, 2003)

Documents on British Policy Overseas (HMSO, 1984–)

Documents on German Foreign Policy, 1918–1945 (HMSO, 1951–58)

Dodds-Parker, D., *Political Eunuch* (Springwood, 1986)

Donoughue, B., *Downing Street Diary: Vol. 1, With Harold Wilson in No. 10* (Pimlico, 2006)

____, *Downing Street Diary: Vol. 2, With James Callaghan in No. 10* (Pimlico, 2009)

Douglas-Home, A., *The Way the Wind Blows: An Autobiography* (Collins, 1976)

Downes, D., *Scarlet Thread: Adventures in Wartime Espionage* (NY: Verschoyle, 1953)

Elliott, N., *With My Little Eye* (Michael Russell, 1993)

Flower, K., *Serving Secretly – An Intelligence Chief on Record: Rhodesia into Zimbabwe, 1964–81* (John Murray, 1987)

Fowler, N., *Ministers Decide: A Personal Memoir of the Thatcher Years* (Chapmans, 1991)

Gates, R., *From the Shadows: The Ultimate Insider's Story of Five Presidents and How They Won the Cold War* (NY: Simon & Schuster, 2006)

Gillespie, A., *Desert Fire: The Diary of a Gulf War Gunner* (Pen and Sword, 2001)

Gordievsky, O., *Next Stop Execution: The Autobiography of Oleg Gordievsky* (Macmillan, 1995)

Hailsham, Lord, *A Sparrow's Flight: Memoirs* (HarperCollins, 1990)

Haines, J., *Glimmers of Twilight: Harold Wilson in Decline* (Politico's, 2003)

Harney, D., *The Priest and the King: Eyewitness Account of the Iranian Revolution* (I.B. Tauris, 1998)

Hayman, A. with Gilmore, M., *The Terrorist Hunters: The Ultimate Inside Story of Britain's Fight Against Terror* (Corgi, 2010)

Heath, E., *The Course of My Life: The Autobiography of Edward Heath* (Hodder & Stoughton, 1998)

Helms, R. and Hood, W., *A Look Over My Shoulder: A Life in the Central Intelligence Agency* (NY: Random House, 2004)

Henderson, N., *Mandarin: The Diaries of Nicholas Henderson* (Weidenfeld & Nicolson, 1994)

Hennessy, P., *Distilling the Frenzy: Writing the History of One's Own Times* (Biteback, 2013)

Heseltine, M., *Life in the Jungle: My Autobiography* (Hodder & Stoughton, 2000)

Howe, G., *Conflict of Loyalty* (Macmillan, 1994)

Hurd, D., *Memoirs* (Little, Brown, 2003)

Hutton, J.B., *The Fake Defector* (Howard Baker, 1970)

Ingham, B., *Kill the Messenger* (HarperCollins, 1991)

Intelligence and Security Committee, Annual Report 2009–2010 (HMSO, 2010)

____, Annual Report 2008–2009 (HMSO, 2009)

Jenkins, C., *Life Against the Collar* (Methuen, 1990)

Jenkins, R., *Life at the Centre* (Macmillan, 1991)

____, *European Diary 1977–1981* (HarperCollins, 1989)

Jones, R.V., *Most Secret War* (Hamish Hamilton, 1978)

____, *Reflections on Intelligence* (Heinemann, 1989)

King, C.H., *The Cecil King Diary, 1965–1970* (Jonathan Cape, 1972)

Lagos, R., *The Southern Tiger: Chile's Fight for a Democratic and Prosperous Future* (NY: St Martin's Press, 2012)

Lamont, N., *In Office* (Little, Brown, 1999)

____, *The View From No. 11: Memoirs of a Tory Radical* (Heinemann, 1992)

Lang, I., *Blue Remembered Years: A Political Memoir* (Politico's, 2002)

Lee, R.E., *The London Observer: The Journal of General Raymond E. Lee, 1940–1941* (Hutchinson, 1972)

Lindsay, F., *Beacons in the Night: With the OSS and Tito's Partisans in Wartime Yugoslavia* (NY: Stanford UP, 1993)

Lipsey, D., *In the Corridors of Power: An Autobiography* (Biteback, 2012)

Lloyd George, D., *War Memoirs*, 2 vols (Odhams Press, 1938)

McBride, D., *Power Trip: A Decade of Policy, Plots and Spin* (Biteback, 2014)

McDermott, G., *The Eden Legacy and the Decline of British Diplomacy* (Leslie Frewin, 1969)

MacDonald, E.P., *Undercover Girl* (Macmillan, 1947)

Maclean, F., *Eastern Approaches* (Jonathan Cape, 1949)

Macmillan, H., *At the End of the Day, 1961–1963* (Macmillan, 1973)

Machon, A., *Spies, Lies and Whistleblowers: MI5, MI6 and the Shayler Affair* (Lewes: The Book Guild, 2005)

Major, J., *The Autobiography* (HarperCollins, 1999)

Meyer, C., *DC Confidential* (Weidenfeld & Nicolson, 2005)

Montague Brown, A., *Long Sunset: Memoirs of Winston Churchill's Last Private Secretary* (Cassell, 1995)

Moore, R., *My Word is My Bond* (Michael O'Mara, 2009)

Morell, M., *The Great War of Our Time: The CIA's Fight Against Terrorism from Al-Qaida to ISIS* (Twelve, 2015)

Morgan, P., *The Insider: The Private Diaries of a Scandalous Decade* (Ebury, 2005)

Mountbatten, Earl, *Report to the Combined Chiefs of Staff by the Supreme Allied Commander South-East Asia, 1943–1945* (HMSO, 1951)

Mullin, C., *A View From the Foothills: The Diaries of Chris Mullin* (Profile, 2009)

____, *Decline and Fall: Diaries 2005–2010* (Profile, 2010)

____, *A Walk-On Part: Diaries 1994–1999* (Profile, 2011)

National Security Adviser, 'Libya Crisis: National Security Adviser's Review of Central Co-ordination and Lessons Learned', Prime Minister's Office (29 April 2013) https://www.gov.uk/government/uploads/system/uploads/attachment_data/file/193145/Lessons-Learned–30-Nov.pdf

Nicholson, M., *Activities Incompatible: Memoirs of a Kremlinologist and a Family Man 1963–1971* (self-published, 2013)

Nott, J., *Here Today, Gone Tomorrow: Recollections of an Errant Politician* (Politico's, 2002)

Nutting, A., *No End of a Lesson: The Story of Suez* (NY: C.N. Potter, 1967)

Owen, D., *Time to Declare* (Michael Joseph, 1991)

Owen, R., *The Litvinenko Inquiry: Report into the Death of Alexander Litvinenko* (Crown, 2016)

Panetta, L. with Newton, J., *Worthy Fights: A Memoir of Leadership in War and Peace* (Penguin, 2014)

Parris, M., *Chance Witness: An Outsider's Life in Politics* (Penguin, 2013)

Patten, C., *Not Quite the Diplomat: Home Truths About World Affairs* (Allen Lane, 2005)

Payn, G. and Morley, S. (eds), *The Noël Coward Diaries* (Macmillan, 1982)

Penkovsky, O.V., *The Penkovsky Papers* (Collins, 1966)

Peres, S., *Battling for Peace: Memoirs* (Weidenfeld & Nicolson, 1995)

Philby, K., *My Silent War: The Autobiography of a Spy* (MacGibbon & Key, 1968)

Pimlott, B. (ed.), *The Political Diary of Hugh Dalton, 1918–1940, 1945–60* (Jonathan Cape, 1987)

Powell, C., *A Soldier's Way: An Autobiography* (Hutchinson, 1995)

Powell, J., *Great Hatred, Little Room: Making Peace in Northern Ireland* (The Bodley Head, 2008)

____, *The New Machiavelli: How to Wield Power in the Modern World* (Vintage, 2011)

Prescott, J., *Prezza – My Story: Pulling No Punches* (Headline Review, 2008)

Prior, J., *A Balance of Power* (Hamish Hamilton, 1986)

Radji, P.C., *In the Service of the Peacock Throne: The Diaries of the Shah's Last Ambassador to London* (Hamish Hamilton, 1983)

Renwick, R., *Margaret Thatcher: Foreign Policy Under the Iron Lady* (Biteback, 2013)

Report of the Security Commission, May 1983, Cmnd 8876 (HMSO, 1983)

Report of the Security Commission, October 1986, Cmnd 9923 (HMSO, 1986)

Rimington, S., *Open Secret* (Arrow, 2002)

Robertson, G., *The Justice Game* (Chatto & Windus, 1998)

Roosevelt, K., *Countercoup: The Struggle for the Control of Iran* (McGraw Hill, 1979)

Scott, R., *Report of the inquiry into the export of defence equipment and dual-use goods to Iraq and related prosecutions (The Scott Inquiry)* (HMSO, 1996)

Self, R. (ed.), *The Neville Chamberlain Diary Letters, 1934–1940* (Ashgate, 2005)

Shuckburgh, E. and Charmley, J., *Descent to Suez: Diaries, 1951–56* (NY: Norton, 1987)

Sillitoe, P., *Cloak Without Dagger* (Cassell, 1955)

Skorzeny, O., *Meine Kommandounternehmen* (Dresden: Winkelried, 2007)

Smiley, D., *Albanian Assignment* (Chatto & Windus, 1984)

Smith, S. (ed.), *The Wilson–Johnson Correspondence, 1964–69* (Ashgate, 2015)

Steiner, R., *The Last Adventurer* (Weidenfeld & Nicolson, 1978)

Stothard, P., *30 Days: A Month at the Heart of Blair's War* (HarperCollins, 2003)

Straw, J., *Last Man Standing: Memoirs of a Political Survivor* (Macmillan, 2012)

Thatcher, C., *Below the Parapet: A Biography of Denis Thatcher* (HarperCollins, 1994)

Thatcher, M., *The Downing Street Years* (HarperCollins, 1993)

Thompson, R.W., *Churchill and Morton: Correspondence Between Major Sir Desmond Morton and R.W. Thompson* (Hodder & Stoughton, 1976)

Tomlinson, R., *The Big Breach: From Top Secret to Maximum Security* (Edinburgh: Cutting Edge, 2001)

Urban, G.R., *Diplomacy and Disillusion: At the Court of Margaret Thatcher – An Insider's View* (I.B. Tauris, 1996)

Verrier, A., *Through the Looking Glass: British Foreign Policy in an Age of Illusions* (Jonathan Cape, 1983)

Walden, G., *Lucky George: Memoirs of an Anti-Politician* (Allen Lane, 1999)

Warwicker, J., *An Outsider Inside No. 10: Protecting the Prime Ministers, 1974–79* (History Press, 2015)

Watson, T. and Hickman, M., *Dial M for Murdoch: News Corporation and the Corruption of Britain* (Allen Lane, 2012)

Westell, A., *The Inside Story: A Life in Journalism* (Dundurn, 2002)

Wilber, D., *Regime Change in Iran* (Spokesman, 2006)

Williamson, P. and Baldwin, E. (eds), *Baldwin Papers: A Conservative Statesman, 1908–1947* (Cambridge UP, 2009)

Wilson, H., *The Labour Government 1964–1970: A Personal Record* (Michael Joseph, 1971)

____, *Final Term: The Labour Government 1974–1976* (Weidenfeld & Nicolson, 1979)

Winter, G., *Inside BOSS: South Africa's Secret Police* (Allen Lane, 1981)

Wright, P., *Spycatcher: The Candid Autobiography of a Senior Intelligence Officer* (NY: Viking, 1987)

Wyatt, W., *Confessions of an Optimist* (Collins, 1985)

Young, G.K., *Masters of Indecision: An Inquiry into the Political Process* (Methuen, 1962)

____, *Who is My Liege? A Study of Loyalty and Betrayal in Our Time* (Gentry, 1972)

Books and Theses

Adams, J., *Tony Benn: A Biography* (Biteback, 2011)

Agee, P. and Wolff, L., *Dirty Work: The CIA in Western Europe* (Zed Press, 1981)

Aid, M., *The Secret Sentry: The Untold History of the National Security Agency* (NY: Bloomsbury Press, 2010)

——, *Intel Wars: The Secret History of the Fight Against Terror* (NY: Bloomsbury Press, 2012)

Aid, M. and Wiebes, C. (eds), *Secrets of Signals Intelligence During the Cold War and Beyond* (Frank Cass, 2001)

Albright, J. and Kunstel, M., *Bombshell: The Secret Story of America's Unknown Atomic Spy Conspiracy* (NY: Time Books, 1997)

Aldous, R., *Reagan and Thatcher: A Difficult Relationship* (Random House, 2012)

Aldrich, R.J. (ed.), *British Intelligence, Strategy and the Cold War, 1945–51* (Routledge, 1992)

—— (ed.), *Espionage, Security and Intelligence in Britain, 1945–70* (Manchester UP, 1998)

——, *Intelligence and the War Against Japan: Britain, America and the Politics of Secret Service* (Cambridge UP, 1999)

——, *The Hidden Hand: Britain, America and Cold War Secret Intelligence* (John Murray, 2002)

——, *GCHQ: The Uncensored Story of Britain's Most Secret Intelligence Agency* (HarperPress, 2010)

Aldrich, R.J., Cormac, R. and Goodman, M., *Spying on the World: The Declassified Documents of the Joint Intelligence Committee, 1936–2013* (Edinburgh UP, 2014)

Aldrich, R.J. and Hopkins, M.F. (eds), *Intelligence, Defence and Diplomacy: British Policy in the Post-War World* (Frank Cass, 1994)

Aldrich, R.J., Rawnsley, G. and Rawnsley, M.Y. (eds), *The Clandestine Cold War in Asia, 1945–65* (Frank Cass, 1999)

Ambrose, S., *Ike's Spies: Eisenhower and the Espionage Establishment* (NY: Doubleday, 1981)

Andrew, C.M., *Secret Service: The Making of the British Intelligence Community* (Heinemann, 1985)

——, *For the President's Eyes Only: Secret Intelligence and the American Presidency From Washington to Bush* (HarperCollins, 1995)

——, *The Defence of the Realm: The Authorized History of MI5* (Allen Lane, 2009)

Andrew, C.M. and Dilks, D. (eds), *The Missing Dimension: Governments and Intelligence Communities in the Twentieth Century* (Macmillan, 1982)

Andrew, C.M. and Gordievsky, O., *KGB: The Inside Story* (Hodder & Stoughton, 1990)

Andrew, C.M. and Mitrokhin, V., *The Sword and the Shield: The Mitrokhin Archive and the Secret History of the KGB* (NY: Basic Books, 1999)

——, *The Mitrokhin Archive: The KGB in Europe and the West* (Penguin, 2000)

——, *The World Was Going Our Way: The KGB and the Battle for the Third World* (NY: Basic Books, 2005)

Anglim, S., *Orde Wingate and the British Army, 1922–1944* (Routledge, 2015)

Ball, S., *Portrait of a Party: The Conservative Party in Britain 1918–1945* (Oxford UP, 2013)

Bamford, J., *The Puzzle Palace: America's National Security Agency and its Special Relationship With GCHQ* (Sidgwick & Jackson, 1983)

——, *Body of Secrets: How NSA and Britain's GCHQ Eavesdrop on the World* (NY: Doubleday, 2001)

——, *The Shadow Factory: The Ultra-Secret NSA From 9/11 to Eavesdropping on America* (NY: Doubleday, 2008)

Barber, B., *If Mayors Ruled the World: Dysfunctional Nations, Rising Cities* (New Haven, CT: Yale UP, 2014)

Bar-Joseph, U., *Intelligence Intervention in the Politics of the Democratic States: The United States, Israel, and Britain* (Pennsylvania State UP, 1995)

Barker, E., *British Policy in South-East Europe in the Second World War* (Macmillan, 1976)

Barnett, H., *Britain Unwrapped: Government and Constitution Explained* (Penguin, 2002)

Barrass, G., *The Great Cold War: A Journey Through the Hall of Mirrors* (NY: Stanford UP, 2009)

Barron, J., *Operation Solo: The FBI's Man in the Kremlin* (Robert Hale, 1997)

Bartholomew-Feis, D., *The OSS and Ho Chi Minh: Unexpected Allies in the War Against Japan* (Lawrence, Kansas: UP of Kansas, 2006)

Bastable, J., *British Prime Ministers* (David & Charles, 2011)

Bayly, C., *Empire and Information: Intelligence Gathering and Social Communication in India, 1780–1870* (Cambridge UP, 2000)

Bearse, R., *Conspirator: The Untold Story of Tyler Kent* (Macmillan, 1991)

Beck, P.J., *Scoring for Britain: International Football and International Politics, 1900–1939* (Routledge, 2013)

Beck, U., *World Risk Society* (Polity, 1999)

Beckett, F., *Clem Attlee* (Politico's, 2007)

Beesly, P., *Room 40: British Naval Intelligence, 1914–1918* (Hamish Hamilton, 1982)

Beevor, A. and Cooper, A., *Paris After Liberation, 1944–49* (Allen Lane, 2004)

Bennett, G., *A Most Extraordinary and Mysterious Business: The Zinoviev Letter of 1924* (Foreign and Commonwealth Office, 1999)

____, *Churchill's Man of Mystery: Desmond Morton and the World of Intelligence* (Routledge, 2009)

____, *Six Moments of Crisis: Inside British Foreign Policy* (Oxford UP, 2014)

Bennett, R., *Ultra in the West: The Normandy Campaign of 1944–45* (Hutchinson, 1979)

____, *Behind the Battle: Intelligence in the War With Germany* (Sinclair Stevenson, 1994)

Bergman, R., *The Secret War With Iran: The Thirty-Year Covert Struggle for Control of a Rogue State* (Oneworld, 2009)

Beschloss, M.R., *Mayday: Eisenhower, Khrushchev and the U-2 Affair* (NY: Harper & Row, 1986)

Best, A., *British Intelligence and the Japanese Challenge in Asia, 1914–41* (Palgrave Macmillan, 2002)

Bethell, N., *The Great Betrayal: The Untold Story of Kim Philby's Biggest Coup* (Hodder & Stoughton, 1984)

Bicheno, H., *Razor's Edge: The Unofficial History of the Falklands War* (Weidenfeld & Nicolson, 2006)

Bochel, H., Defty, A. and Kirkpatrick, J., *Watching the Watchers: Parliament and the Intelligence Services* (Palgrave, 2014)

Booth, C. and Haste, C., *The Goldfish Bowl: Married to the Prime Minister, 1955–1997* (Chatto & Windus, 2004)

Bower, T., *The Perfect English Spy* (Heinemann, 1995)

Bowyer Bell, J., *Secret Army: The IRA* (Transaction, 1997)

Boyce, R. and Maiolo, J.A., *The Origins of World War II: The Debate Continues* (Palgrave, 2003)

Breindel, E. and Romerstein, H., *The Venona Secrets: The Soviet Union's World War II Espionage Campaign Against the United States and how America Fought Back* (NY: Basic Books, 2000)

Brook-Shepherd, G., *The Storm Birds: Soviet Postwar Defectors* (Weidenfeld & Nicolson, 1989)

Brown, A., *J.D. Bernal: The Sage of Science* (Oxford UP, 2005)

Bryant, A., *Triumph in the West, 1943–1946* (Collins, 1959)

Bryden, J., *Best-Kept Secret: Canadian Secret Intelligence in the Second World War* (Lester, 1993)

Budiansky, S., *Battle of Wits: The Complete Story of Codebreaking in World War II* (NY: Free Press, 2000)

Bulloch, J., *M.I.5: Origin and History of British Counter Espionage* (Arthur Baker, 1963)

Bullock, A., *Ernest Bevin: Foreign Secretary, 1945–1951* (Oxford UP, 1985)

Cadwallader, A., *Lethal Allies: British Collusion in Ireland* (Cork: Mercier Press, 2013)

Callanan, J., *Covert Action in the Cold War: US Policy, Intelligence and CIA Operations* (I.B. Tauris, 2010)

Calvocoressi, P., *Top Secret Ultra* (Cassell, 1980)

Campbell, D., *The Unsinkable Aircraft Carrier* (Michael Joseph, 1984)

____, *Surveillance électronique planétaire* (Paris: Editions Allia, 2001)

Campbell, J., *Margaret Thatcher: Vol. 2, The Iron Lady* (Jonathan Cape, 2007)

____, *Edward Heath: A Biography* (Jonathan Cape, 1993)

Carlton, D., *Churchill and the Soviet Union* (Manchester UP, 2000)

Carr, G., *The Angry Brigade: A History of Britain's First Urban Guerilla Group* (PM Press, 2011)

Carter, M., *Anthony Blunt: His Lives* (Macmillan, 2002)

Cassar, G.H., *Asquith as War Leader* (Hambledon, 1994)

Cathcart, B., *Test of Greatness: Britain's Struggle for the Atomic Bomb* (John Murray, 1994)

Cave Brown, A., *'C': The Secret Life of Sir Stewart Graham Menzies, Spymaster to Winston Churchill* (NY: Macmillan, 1987)

Charmley, J., *Chamberlain and the Lost Peace* (Chicago: Ivan Dee, 1990)

Churchill, W., *The World Crisis, 1911–1918* (Penguin Classics, 2007)

Clarke, P., *Mr Churchill's Profession: Statesman, Orator, Writer* (Bloomsbury, 2000)

Clarke, R., *Against All Enemies: Inside America's War on Terror* (Simon & Schuster, 2004)

Close, F., *Half Life: The Divided Life of Bruno Pontecorvo, Physicist or Spy* (Oneworld, 2015)

Coll, S., *The Bin Ladens: The Story of a Family and its Fortune* (Allen Lane, 2008)
Collin, M., *Altered State: The Story of Ecstasy Culture and Acid House* (Serpent's Tail, 2008)
Colville, J., *The Churchillians* (Littlehampton, 1981)
Conant, J., *The Irregulars: Roald Dahl and the British Spy Ring in Wartime Washington* (NY: Simon & Schuster, 2008)
Connor, K., *Ghost Force: The Secret History of the SAS* (Orion, 1999)
Coogan, T.P., *The Troubles: Ireland's Ordeal, 1969–96, and the Search for Peace* (Arrow, 1996)
Cooley, J., *Unholy Wars: Afghanistan, America and International Terrorism* (Pluto, 2002)
Corera, G., *The Art of Betrayal: The Secret History of MI6* (Pegasus Books, 2013)
Corke, S.J., *US Covert Operations and Cold War Strategy: Truman, Secret Warfare and the CIA, 1945–1953* (Routledge, 2007)
Cormac, R., *Confronting the Colonies: British Intelligence and Counterinsurgency* (NY: Oxford UP, 2014)
Cradock, P., *Know Your Enemy: How the Joint Intelligence Committee Saw the World* (John Murray, 2002)
Cresswell, Y.M., *Living With the Wire: Civilian Internment on the Isle of Man During the Two World Wars* (Douglas: Manx National Heritage, 1994)
Crile, G., *Charlie Wilson's War: The Extraordinary Story of How the Wildest Man in Congress and a Rogue CIA Agent Changed the History of Our Time* (Atlantic, 2007)
Crosby, T.L., *The Unknown David Lloyd George: A Statesman in Conflict* (I.B. Tauris, 2014)
Crowson, N., *Facing Fascism: The Conservative Party and the European Dictators 1935–1940* (Routledge, 1999)
Cruickshank, C., *SOE in the Far East* (Oxford UP, 1983)
Cull, N.J., *Selling War: The British Propaganda Campaign Against American Neutrality in World War II* (NY: Oxford UP, 1995)
Curry, J., *The Security Service 1908–1945: The Official History* (PRO Publications, 1999)
Curtis, M., *Unpeople: Britain's Secret Human Rights Abuses* (Vintage, 2004)
_____, *Secret Affairs: Britain's Collusion With Radical Islam* (Serpent's Tail, 2012)
Daddow, O., *Harold Wilson and European Integration* (Routledge, 2002)
Dallek, R., *An Unfinished Life: John F. Kennedy 1917–1963* (Allen Lane, 2003)
D'Ancona, M., *In it Together: The Inside Story of the Coalition Government* (Penguin, 2014)
Davenport-Hines, R., *An English Affair: Sex, Class and Power in the Age of Profumo* (HarperPress, 2013)
Davies, P.H.J., *MI6 and the Machinery of Spying* (Frank Cass, 2004)
_____, *Intelligence and Government in Britain and the United States: A Comparative Perspective, Vols 1 & 2* (Praeger, 2012)
de Courcy, A., *Margot at War: Love and Betrayal in Downing Street* (Weidenfeld & Nicolson, 2014)
Deighton, A., *The Impossible Peace: Germany* (Oxford: Clarendon Press, 1988)
Denniston, R., *Churchill's Secret War: Diplomatic Decrypts, the Foreign Office and Turkey, 1942–44* (Stroud: Alan Sutton, 1997)
Diamond, J., *The CIA and the Culture of Failure: US Intelligence From the End of the Cold War to the Invasion of Iraq* (Stanford UP, 2008)
_____, *Orde Wingate* (Osprey, 2012)
Dilks, D., *Churchill and Company: Allies and Rivals in War and Peace* (I.B. Tauris, 2012)
Dillon, M., *The Dirty War* (Arrow, 1991)
Doerries, R.R., *Hitler's Intelligence Chief: Walter Schellenberg* (Routledge, 2007)
Dorril, S., *MI6: Fifty Years of Special Operations* (Fourth Estate, 2000)
Dorril, S. and Ramsey, R., *Smear!: Wilson and the Secret State* (HarperCollins 1992, new edn)
Dover, R. and Goodman, M. (eds), *Spinning Intelligence: Why Intelligence Needs the Media, Why the Media Needs Intelligence* (NY: Columbia UP, 2009)
_____, *Learning From the Secret Past: Cases in British Intelligence History* (Washington DC: Georgetown UP, 2011)
Dudley, C., *Understanding the UK Parliament's Decision to Vote Against the Possibility of Intervention in the Syrian Conflict, August 29th 2013* (University of Nottingham: MA thesis, 2014)
Dutton, D., *Neville Chamberlain* (Arnold, 2001)
_____, *Douglas-Home* (Haus, 2006)
Elliott, G., *Gentleman Spymaster: How Lt. Col. Tommy 'Tar' Robertson Double-Crossed the Nazis* (Methuen, 2011)

Elson, R., *Suharto: A Political Biography* (Cambridge UP, 2008)

Erikson, J., *The Road to Berlin: Stalin's War With Germany* (Weidenfeld & Nicolson, 1983)

Faber, D., *Speaking for England: Leo, Julian and John Amery – The Tragedy of a Political Family* (NY: Free Press, 2003)

____, *Munich, 1938: Appeasement and World War II* (NY: Simon & Schuster, 2009)

Fielding, X., *One Man in his Time: The Life of Billy McLean* (Macmillan, 1990)

Foot, P., *Who Framed Colin Wallace?* (Pan, 1974)

Ford, H., *The CIA and the Vietnam Policymakers: Three Episodes, 1962–1968* (Military Bookshop, 2011)

Foy, M. and Barton, B., *The Easter Rising* (The History Press, 2011)

Freedman, L., *The Official History of the Falklands Campaign, Vols 1 & 2* (Routledge, 2005)

____, *A Choice of Enemies: America Confronts the Middle East* (Public Affairs, 2008)

Freedman, L. and Gamba-Stonehouse, V., *Signals of War: The Falklands Conflict of 1982* (Princeton, NJ: Princeton UP, 1991)

Fussell, P., *Wartime: Understanding and Behavior in the Second World War* (NY: Oxford UP, 1989)

Garton Ash, T., *The Polish Revolution: Solidarity* (NY: Scribner's, 1984)

Gaskarth, J., *British Foreign Policy: Crises, Conflicts, and Future Challenges* (Polity, 2013)

Geraghty, T., *Who Dares Wins: The History of the Special Air Service* (Fontana Press, 1983)

Gerolymatos, A., *Castles Made of Sand: A Century of Anglo–American Espionage and Intervention in the Middle East* (Thomas Dunne Books, 2010)

Gerrard, C., *The Foreign Office and Finland: Diplomatic Sideshow* (Routledge, 2004)

Gilbert, M., *Winston S. Churchill: Vol. 7, The Road to Victory, 1941–45* (Orion, 1986)

____, *Winston S. Churchill: Vol. 8, Never Despair, 1945–65* (Orion, 1988)

Gill, D.J., *Britain and the Bomb: Nuclear Diplomacy, 1964–1970* (Stanford UP, 2014)

Gill, P., *Policing Politics: Security Intelligence and the Liberal Democratic State* (Frank Cass, 1994)

Goodman, M.S., *Spying on the Nuclear Bear: Anglo–American Intelligence and the Soviet Bomb* (NY: Stanford UP, 2007)

____, *The Official History of the Joint Intelligence Committee: Vol. 1, From the Approach of the Second World War to the Suez Crisis* (Routledge, 2014)

Gorodetsky, G., *Grand Delusion: Stalin and the German Invasion of Russia* (New Haven: Yale UP, 1999)

Grant, T., *Jeremy Hutchinson's Case Histories: From Lady Chatterley's Lover to Howard Marks* (John Murray, 2016)

Greenwood, S., *Titan at the Foreign Office: Gladwyn Jebb and the Shaping of the Modern World* (The Hague: Martinus Nijhoff Publishers, 2008)

Grob-Fitzgibbon, B., *Imperial Endgame: Britain's Dirty Wars and the End of Empire* (Palgrave Macmillan, 2011)

Gustafson, K., *Hostile Intent: US Covert Operations in Chile, 1964–1974* (Washington DC: Potomac Books, 2008)

Harding, L., *The Snowden Files: The Inside Story of the World's Most Wanted Man* (Guardian/Faber, 2014)

Harrison, E.D.R. (ed.), *The Secret World: Behind the Curtain of British Intelligence in World War II and the Cold War by Hugh Trevor-Roper* (I.B. Tauris, 2014)

Hart, J.L., *The CIA's Russians* (Annapolis, MD: Naval Institute Press, 2003)

Hart-Davis, D., *The War that Never Was* (Arrow, 2012)

Haslam, J., *Near and Distant Neighbours: A New History of Soviet Intelligence* (NY: Oxford UP, 2015)

Hastings, M., *The Secret War: Spies, Codes and Guerrillas, 1939–1945* (William Collins, 2015)

Hastings, M. and Jenkins, S., *The Battle for the Falklands* (Pan, 1997)

Hayes, P., *Queen of Spies: Daphne Park, Britain's Cold War Spy Master* (Duckworth, 2015)

Haynes, J.E. and Klehr, H., *Venona: Decoding Soviet Espionage in America* (New Haven: Yale UP, 1999)

Hennessey, T. and Thomas, C., *Spooks: The Unofficial History of MI5 From the First Atom Spy to 7/7, 1945–2009* (Stroud: Amberley, 2009)

Hennessy, P., *Whitehall* (NY: Free Press, 1989)

____, *Never Again: Britain 1945–51* (Vintage, 1993)

____, *The Prime Minister: The Office and its Holders Since 1945* (Allen Lane, 2000)

____, *The Secret State: Whitehall and the Cold War* (Allen Lane, 2002)

____, *The New Protective State* (Continuum, 2007)

Herman, M., *Intelligence Power in Peace and War* (Cambridge UP, 1992)

_____, *Intelligence Services in the Information Age* (Frank Cass, 2001)

Hermiston, R., *The Greatest Traitor: The Secret Lives of Agent George Blake* (Aurum, 2014)

Hinsley, F.H. et al., *British Intelligence in the Second World War, Vols 1–4* (HMSO, 1979–83)

Hinsley, F.H. and Stripp, A. (eds), *Codebreakers: The Inside Story of Bletchley Park* (Oxford UP, 1993)

Hodges, A., *Turing: The Enigma* (Vintage, 1992)

Hoefferle, C., *British Student Activism in the Long Sixties* (Routledge, 2012)

Holliday, L., *Children in the Holocaust and World War II: Their Secret Diaries* (NY: Washington Square Books, 1995)

Holt, A., *The Foreign Policy of the Douglas-Home Government* (Palgrave, 2015)

Horne, A., *Macmillan 1957–1986: Vol. 2 of the Official Biography* (Macmillan, 1989)

Howarth, P., *Intelligence Chief Extraordinary* (The Bodley Head, 1986)

Hughes, K., *Chasing Shadows: The Nixon Tapes, the Chennault Affair, and the Origins of Watergate* (Charlottesville, VA: University of Virginia Press, 2015)

Hughes, R.G., *Harold Wilson's Cold War: The Labour Government and East–West Politics, 1964–1970* (Boydell Press, 2009)

_____, *Britain, Germany and the Cold War: The Search for a European Détente 1949–1967* (Routledge, 2007)

Hughes, R.G., Jackson, P. and Scott, L.V., *Exploring Intelligence Archives: Enquiries Into the Secret State* (Routledge, 2008)

Hughes, T., *The Fate of Facts in a World of Men: Foreign Policy and Intelligence-Making* (Foreign Policy Association, 1976)

Hull, M., *Irish Secrets: German Espionage in Wartime Ireland 1939–1945* (Dublin: Irish Academic Press, 2004)

Hunter, H., *Sukarno and the Indonesian Coup: The Untold Story* (Praeger, 2007)

Ingram, K., *Obote: A Political Biography* (Routledge, 2013)

Jablonsky, D., *Churchill, the Great Game, and Total War* (Routledge, 1991)

Jakub, J., *Spies and Saboteurs: Anglo–American Collaboration and Rivalry in Human Intelligence Collection and Special Operations, 1940–45* (Macmillan, 1999)

Jeffery, K., *The Secret History of MI6* (NY: Penguin Press, 2010)

Jenkins, R., *Asquith* (HarperPress, 1986, 3rd edn)

_____, *Baldwin* (Collins, 1987)

Johnson, W., *Thwarting Enemies at Home and Abroad: How to be a Counterintelligence Officer* (Washington DC: Georgetown UP, 2009)

Jones, C., *Britain and the Yemen Civil War 1962–1965: Ministers, Mercenaries and Mandarins: Foreign Policy and the Limits of Covert Action* (Brighton: Sussex Academic Press, 2004)

Jones, K., *Number 10 Downing Street: The Story of a House* (BBC Books, 1985)

Jones, M., *Conflict and Confrontation in South East Asia, 1961–1965: Britain, the United States, Indonesia and the Creation of Malaysia* (Cambridge UP, 2012)

Kahin, A. and Kahin, G., *Subversion as Foreign Policy: Secret Eisenhower and Dulles Debacle in Indonesia* (NY: The New Press, 1995)

Kahin, G., *Southeast Asia: A Testament* (Routledge, 2002)

Kahn, D., *The Reader of Other Gentlemen's Mail: Herbert O. Yardley and the Birth of American Codebreaking* (New Haven: Yale UP, 2004)

Kampfner, J., *Blair's Wars* (Free Press, 2004)

Karatzogianni, A., *Firebrand Waves of Digital Activism 1994–2014: Studies on the Rise and Spread of Hacktivism and Cyberconflict* (Palgrave Macmillan, 2015)

Keene, J., *Cloak of Enemies: Churchill's SOE, Enemies at Home and the 'Cockleshell Heroes'* (Spellmount, 2012)

Kelly, S., *America's Tyrant: The CIA and Mobutu of Zaire* (Washington DC: The American University Press, 1993)

Kennedy-Pipe, C., *Stalin's Cold War: Soviet Strategies in Europe* (Manchester UP, 1995)

Kershaw, I., *Making Friends With Hitler: Lord Londonderry and Britain's Road to War* (Allen Lane, 2005)

Kimball, W.F., *The Juggler: Franklin Roosevelt as Wartime Statesman* (Princeton, NJ: Princeton UP, 1991)

Kinzer, S., *All the Shah's Men: An American Coup and the Roots of Middle East Terror* (John Wiley & Sons, 2008)

Kiras, J.D., *Special Operations and Strategy: From World War II to the War on Terrorism* (Routledge, 2006)

Knightley, P. and Kennedy, C., *An Affair of State: The Profumo Case and the Framing of Stephen Ward* (Jonathan Cape, 1987)

Kyle, K., *Suez: Britain's End of Empire in the Middle East* (Weidenfeld & Nicolson, 1991)

Lacouture, J., *Charles de Gaulle: Le Souverain 1959–1970* (Paris: Editions du Seuil, 1986)

Lafitte, F., *The Internment of Aliens* (Penguin, 1940)

Lamb, R., *Macmillan Years 1957–63: The Emerging Truth* (John Murray, 1995)

Lapping, B., *End of Empire* (St Martin's Press, 1985)

Laqueur, W., *World of Secrets: The Uses and Limits of Intelligence* (Basic Books, 1985)

Larres, K., *Churchill's Cold War: The Politics of Personal Diplomacy* (New Haven: Yale UP, 2002)

Lashmar, P., *Spy Flights of the Cold War* (Stroud: Sutton, 1996)

Lashmar, P. and Oliver, J., *Britain's Secret Propaganda War: The Foreign Office and the Cold War, 1948–1977* (Stroud: Sutton, 1998)

Le Queux, W., *The Invasion of 1910: With a Full Account of the Siege of London* (Everleigh & Nash, 1906)

____, *Spies of the Kaiser: Plotting the Downfall of England* (Hurst & Blackett, 1909)

Levitt, M., *Hezbollah: The Global Footprint of Lebanon's Party of God* (Hurst, 2013)

Lewin, R., *Ultra Goes to War: The Secret Story* (Hutchinson, 1978)

Lewis, J., *Changing Direction: British Military Planning for Post-War Strategic Defence, 1942–47* (Frank Cass, 2003, 2nd edn)

Lownie, A., *Stalin's Englishman: Guy Burgess* (Hodder & Stoughton, 2015)

Lucas, W.S., *Divided We Stand: Britain, the US and the Suez Crisis* (Hodder & Stoughton, 1991)

Lustgarten, L. and Leigh, I., *In From the Cold: National Security and Democracy* (Oxford UP, 1994)

Lycett, A., *Ian Fleming* (Weidenfeld & Nicolson, 1996)

MacDonnell, F., *Insidious Foes: The Axis Fifth Column and the American Home Front* (NY: Oxford UP, 1995)

McDonough, F., *Neville Chamberlain, Appeasement and the British Road to War* (Manchester UP, 1998)

____, *Hitler, Chamberlain and Appeasement* (Cambridge UP, 2001)

Macintyre, B., *Operation Mincemeat: The True Spy Story that Changed the Course of World War II* (Bloomsbury, 2010)

____, *A Spy Among Friends: Kim Philby and the Great Betrayal* (Bloomsbury, 2014)

McJimsey, G.T., *Harry Hopkins: Ally of the Poor and Defender of Democracy* (Cambridge, Mass.: Harvard UP, 1987)

Mackay, N., *The War on Truth* (Glasgow: Sunday Herald Books, 2006)

MacKenzie, A., *Special Force: The Untold Story of 22nd Special Air Service Regiment* (I.B. Tauris, 2011)

McMahon, P., *British Spies and Irish Rebels: British Intelligence and Ireland, 1916–1945* (Boydell Press, 2008)

Macenczak, A., *German Enemy Aliens and the Decline of British Liberalism in World War I* (MA thesis, Louisiana State University and Agricultural and Mechanical College, 2010)

Maddrell, P., *Spying on Science: Western Intelligence in Divided Germany, 1945–61* (Oxford UP, 2006)

Madeira, V., *Britannia and the Bear: The Anglo–Russian Intelligence Wars, 1917–1929* (Boydell & Brewer, 2014)

Mahl, T.E., *Desperate Deception: British Covert Operations in the United States* (Brassey's, 1998)

Maiolo, J., *Cry Havoc: The Arms Race and the Second World War, 1931–1941* (John Murray, 2011)

Mangold, T., *Cold Warrior: The CIA's Master Spy Hunter* (Simon & Schuster, 1991)

Mangold, T. and Goldberg, J., *Plague Wars: The Terrifying Reality of Biological Warfare* (NY: St Martin's Press, 2000)

Marquand, D., *Ramsay MacDonald: A Biography* (Jonathan Cape, 1977)

Martin, D., *The Web of Disinformation: Churchill's Yugoslav Blunder* (NY: Harcourt, Brace, Jovanovich, 1990)

Mawby, S., *British Policy in Aden and the Protectorates, 1955–67: Last Outpost of a Middle East Empire* (Routledge, 2005)

May, E.R. (ed.), *Knowing One's Enemies: Intelligence Assessment Before the Two World Wars* (Princeton, NJ: Princeton UP, 1984)

Milne, T., *Kim Philby: The Unknown Story of the KGB's Master Spy* (Biteback, 2014)

Montgomery Hyde, H., *George Blake: Superspy* (Futura, 1987)

Moore, R., *Task Force Dagger: The Hunt for Bin Laden* (Random House, 2002)

Moran, C., *Classified: Secrecy and the State in Modern Britain* (Cambridge UP, 2012)

_____, *Company Confessions, Secrets, Memoirs and the CIA* (NY: St Martin's Press, 2015)

Morgan, K., *Callaghan: A Life* (Oxford UP, 1997)

Mort, F., *Capital Affairs: The Making of the Permissive Society* (New Haven: Yale UP, 2010)

Mumford, A., *The Counter-Insurgency Myth: The British Experience of Irregular Warfare* (Routledge, 2011)

Murphy, D.E., *What Stalin Knew: The Enigma of Barbarossa* (New Haven: Yale UP, 2005)

Murray, W., *The Change in the European Balance of Power, 1938–1939* (Princeton, NJ: Princeton UP, 1984)

Murray, W. and Millet, A.R., *Calculations: Net Assessment and the Coming of World War Two* (NY: Free Press, 1992)

Naylor, J.F., *A Man and an Institution: Sir Maurice Hankey, the Cabinet Secretariat and the Custody of Cabinet Secrecy* (Cambridge UP, 2009)

Neilson, K. and Otte, T., *The Permanent Under-Secretary for Foreign Affairs, 1854–1946* (Routledge, 2008)

Nichols, D.A., *Eisenhower 1956: The President's Year of Crisis: Suez and the Brink of War* (NY: Simon & Schuster, 2011)

Nickles, D.P., *Under the Wire: How the Telegraph Changed Diplomacy* (Cambridge, Mass.: Harvard UP, 2003)

Norton-Taylor, R., *Truth is a Difficult Concept: Inside the Scott Inquiry* (Fourth Estate, 1995)

O'Halpin, E., *Spying on Ireland: British Intelligence and Irish Neutrality During the Second World War* (Oxford UP, 2008)

Omand, D., *Securing the State* (Hurst, 2010)

Osman, A.H., *Pigeons in the Great War: A Complete History of the Carrier Pigeon Service* (Racing Pigeon, 1929)

O'Sullivan, D., *Dealing With the Devil: Anglo–Soviet Intelligence Cooperation During the Second World War* (Peter Lang, 2010)

Owen, D., *In Sickness and in Power: Illness in Heads of Government During the Last 100 Years* (Methuen, 2014)

Page, P., Leitch, B. and Knightley, D., *The Philby Conspiracy* (Doubleday, 1968)

Panayi, P., *The Enemy in Our Midst: Germans in Britain During the First World War* (Oxford UP, 1991)

_____, *German Immigrants in Britain During the Nineteenth Century, 1815–1914* (Berg, 1995)

Parker, R.A.C., *Chamberlain and Appeasement: British Policy and the Coming of the Second World War* (Palgrave, 1995)

Pearce, R., *Attlee* (Essex: Longman, 1997)

Pearce, R. and Goodlad, G., *British Prime Ministers From Balfour to Brown* (Routledge, 2013)

Peden, G., *British Rearmament and the Treasury, 1932–1939* (Scottish Academic Press, 1979)

Perkins, A., *Baldwin* (Haus, 2005)

Perry, M., *Last of the Cold War Spies: The Life of Michael Straight, the Only American in the Cambridge Spy Ring* (Da Capo Press, 2005)

Petersen, T.T., *Anglo–American Policy Toward the Persian Gulf, 1978–1985: Power, Influence and Restraint* (Brighton: Sussex Academic Press, 2014)

Phythian, M., *The Labour Party, War and International Relations, 1945–2006* (Routledge, 2007)

Picardie, J., *Coco Chanel: The Legend and the Life* (HarperCollins, 2011)

Pike, R., *Britain's Prime Ministers From Walpole to Wilson* (Odhams, 1968)

Pimlott, B., *Harold Wilson* (HarperCollins, 1992)

Pincher, C., *Too Secret Too Long* (Sidgwick & Jackson, 1984)

_____, *Traitors: Labyrinths of Treason* (Sidgwick & Jackson, 1987)

_____, *Treachery: Betrayals, Blunders, and Cover-Ups – Six Decades of Espionage* (Mainstream, 2012)

Popplewell, R., *Intelligence and Imperial Defence: British Intelligence and the Defence of the Indian Empire 1904–1924* (Frank Cass, 1994)

Porter, B., *The Origins of the Vigilant State* (Weidenfeld & Nicolson, 1987)
____, *Plots and Paranoia: History of Political Espionage in Britain, 1790–1988* (Routledge, 1989)
Powers, T., *The Man Who Kept the Secrets: Richard Helms and the CIA* (Weidenfeld & Nicolson, 1979)
Prados, J., *Presidents' Secret Wars: CIA and Pentagon Covert Operations From World War II Through the Persian Gulf Wars* (Ivan Dee, 1996)
____, *How the Cold War Ended: Debating and Doing History* (Potomac, 2010)
Prebble, S., *The Secrets of the* Conqueror: *The Untold Story of Britain's Most Famous Submarine* (Faber & Faber, 2012)
Punch, M., *State Violence, Collusion and the Troubles: Counter-Insurgency, Government Deviance and Northern Ireland* (Pluto, 2012)
Purvis, S. and Hulbert, J., *When Reporters Cross the Line: The Heroes, the Villains, the Hackers and the Spies* (Biteback, 2013)
Quinlan, K., *The Secret War Between the Wars: MI5 in the 1920s and the 1930s* (Bowyer, 2014)
Ranelagh, J., *The Agency: The Rise and Decline of the CIA* (Weidenfeld & Nicolson, 1986)
Rankin, N., *Ian Fleming's Commandos: The Story of 30 Assault Unit in World War II* (Faber & Faber, 2011)
Rawnsley, A., *The End of the Party: The Rise and Fall of New Labour* (Allen Lane, 2010)
Rejali, D., *Torture and Democracy* (Princeton, NJ: Princeton UP, 2009)
Reppetto, T.A., *Battleground New York City: Countering Spies, Saboteurs, and Terrorists Since 1861* (NY: Potomac, 2012)
Reynolds, D., *In Command of History: Churchill Fighting and Writing the Second World War* (Allen Lane, 2005)
Rezk, D., *Western Intelligence and the Arab World: Analysing the Middle East, 1956–1981* (Edinburgh UP, 2016)
Rezun, M., *The Soviet Union and Iran: Soviet Policy in Iran From the Beginnings of the Pahlavi Dynasty Until the Soviet Invasion in 1941* (Geneva: Institut Universitaire de Hautes Études Internationales/Kluwer, 1981)
Richelson, J., *The US Intelligence Community* (NY: Ballinger, 1989)
____, *A Century of Spies: Intelligence in the Twentieth Century* (NY: Oxford UP, 1995)
____, *The Wizards of Langley: Inside the CIA's Directorate of Science and Technology* (Boulder, CO: Westview, 2001)
Richelson, J. and Ball, D., *Ties that Bind: Intelligence Co-operation between the UKUSA Countries* (Boston: Allen & Unwin, 1985)
Rigden, D., *Kill the Führer: Section X and Operation Foxley* (Stroud: Sutton, 1999)
Ring, J., *We Come Unseen: The Untold Story of Britain's Cold War Submariners* (Faber & Faber, 2011)
Ritchie, S., *Our Man in Yugoslavia: The Story of a Secret Service Operative* (Frank Cass, 2004)
Ritter, S., *Iraq Confidential: The Untold Story of America's Intelligence Conspiracy* (I.B. Tauris, 2005)
Roberts, A., *The Holy Fox: The Life of Lord Halifax* (Head of Zeus, 2014)
Roberts, W., *Tito, Mihailović, and the Allies* (Durham, NC: Duke UP, 1987)
Rose, J., *The Literary Churchill: Author, Reader, Actor* (New Haven: Yale UP, 2014)
Rossiter, M., *The Spy Who Changed the World: Klaus Fuchs and the Secrets of the Nuclear Bomb* (Headline, 2014)
Routledge, P., *Public Servant, Secret Agent: The Elusive Life and Violent Death of Airey Neave* (Fourth Estate, 2002)
Sandbrook, D., *State of Emergency: The Way We Were: Britain 1970–1974* (Allen Lane, 2011)
____, *Seasons in the Sun: The Battle for Britain, 1974–1979* (Penguin, 2013)
Sanders, E. and Wood, I.S., *Times of Troubles: Britain's War in Northern Ireland* (Edinburgh UP, 2012)
Sanders, J., *Apartheid's Friends: The Rise and Fall of South Africa's Secret Service* (John Murray, 2006)
Satya, P., *Spies in Arabia: The Great War and the Cultural Foundations of Britain's Covert Empire in the Middle East* (Oxford UP, 2009)
Schecter, J.L. and Deriabin, P.S., *The Spy Who Saved the World* (NY: Scribner's, 1992)
Scott, L.V., *Macmillan, Kennedy and the Cuban Missile Crisis: Political, Military and Intelligence Aspects* (Macmillan, 1999)

Scott, L.V. and Twigge, S., *Planning Armageddon: Britain, the United States, and Command of Western Nuclear Forces, 1945–1964* (Routledge, 2015)

Scowcroft, R., *Attlee's War: World War II and the Making of a Labour Leader* (I.B. Tauris, 2011)

Seaman, M. (ed.), *Operation Foxley: The British Plan to Kill Hitler* (PRO, 1998)

Seldon, A., *Major: A Political Life* (Weidenfeld & Nicolson, 1997)

_____, *Blair Unbound* (Pocket Books, 2008)

Seldon, A. and Lodge, G., *Brown at No. 10* (Biteback, 2010)

Seldon, A. and Snowdon, P., *Cameron at No. 10: The Inside Story 2010–2015* (William Collins, 2015)

Self, R., *Neville Chamberlain: A Biography* (Aldershot: Ashgate, 2006)

Seligmann, M., *Spies in Uniform: British Military and Naval Intelligence on the Eve of the First World War* (Oxford UP, 2006)

Sellers, L., *Shot in the Tower: The Story of the Spies Executed in the Tower of London During the First World War* (Pen and Sword, 2009)

Service, R., *Spies and Commissars: Bolshevik Russia and the West* (Macmillan, 2011)

Shawcross, W., *The Shah's Last Ride* (Chatto & Windus, 1988)

_____, *Queen and Country: The Fifty-Year Reign of Elizabeth II* (NY: Simon & Schuster, 2008)

Shepherd, R., *Iain Macleod: A Biography* (Hutchinson, 1994)

Shpayer-Makov, H., *Ascent of the Detective: Police Sleuths in Victorian and Edwardian England* (Oxford UP, 2012)

Sixsmith, M., *The Litvinenko File: A True Story of a Death Foretold* (Macmillan, 2007)

Smith, B.F., *The Ultra-Magic Deals and the Most Secret Special Relationship, 1940–1946* (Shrewsbury: Airlife Publishing, 1993)

_____, *Sharing Secrets With Stalin: How the Allies Traded Intelligence, 1941–5* (Kansas: University of Kansas Press, 1996)

Smith, M., *New Cloak, Old Dagger: How Britain's Spies Came in From the Cold* (Victor Gollancz, 1996)

_____, *Station X: The Codebreakers of Bletchley Park* (Channel 4 Books, 1998)

_____, *The Emperor's Codes: Bletchley Park and the Breaking of Japan's Secret Ciphers* (Bantam, 2000)

_____, *The Spying Game: A Secret History of British Espionage* (Politico's, 2003)

_____, *Six: The Real James Bonds 1909–1939* (Biteback, 2011)

Smith, M. and Erskine, R. (eds), *Action This Day: Bletchley Park From the Breaking of the Enigma Code to the Birth of the Modern Computer* (Bantam, 2001)

Soldatov, A. and Borogan, I., *The Red Web: The Struggle Between Russia's Digital Dictators and the New Online Revolutionaries* (Public Affairs, 2015)

Sreberny, A. and Torfeh, M., *Persian Service: The BBC and British Interests in Iran* (I.B. Tauris, 2014)

Stafford, D., *Churchill and Secret Service* (John Murray, 1997)

_____, *Roosevelt and Churchill: Men of Secrets* (Abacus, 2000)

_____, *Spies Beneath Berlin* (John Murray, 2002, 2nd edn)

_____, *Britain and European Resistance 1940–1945: A Survey of the Special Operations Executive With Documents* (Thistle Publishing, 2013)

Stewart, G., *Burying Caesar: Churchill, Chamberlain, and the Battle for the Tory Party* (Phoenix, 2000)

Summer, A. and Dorril, S., *The Secret Worlds of Stephen Ward* (Headline, 2013)

Svendsen, A.D.M., *Intelligence Cooperation and the 'War on Terror': Anglo–American Security Relations after 9/11* (Routledge/Studies in Intelligence, 2009)

Taubman, W., *Khrushchev: The Man and His Era* (NY: W.W. Norton, 2004)

Taylor, P., *Brits: The War Against the IRA* (Bloomsbury, 2002)

_____, *Talking to Terrorists: Face to Face With the Enemy* (HarperPress, 2011)

Teitelbaum, L., *The Impact of the Information Revolution on Policymakers' Use of Intelligence* (Santa Monica, CA: Rand, 2005)

Thomas, M., *Empires of Intelligence* (Berkeley, CA: University of California Press, 2008)

Thorne, C., *Allies of a Kind: The United States, Britain, and the War Against Japan, 1941–1945* (Hamish Hamilton, 1979)

Thorpe, D.R., *Eden: The Life and Times of Anthony Eden, First Earl of Avon, 1897–1977* (Chatto & Windus, 2003)

_____, *Alec Douglas-Home* (Sinclair-Stevenson, 1996)

_____, *Supermac: The Life of Harold Macmillan* (Pimlico, 2011)

Treverton, G., *Reshaping National Intelligence for an Age of Information* (Cambridge UP, 2001)

Turchetti, S., *The Pontecorvo Affair: A Cold War Defection and Nuclear Physics* (University of Chicago Press, 2012)

Turner, J., *Lloyd George's Secretariat* (Cambridge UP, 1980)

Ullman, R.H., *Anglo–Soviet Relations, 1917–1921: Vol. 3, The Anglo–Soviet Accord* (Princeton, NJ: Princeton UP, 1972)

Urbach, K., *Go-Betweens for Hitler* (Oxford UP, 2015)

Urban, M., *Big Boys' Rules: The Secret Struggle Against the IRA* (Faber & Faber, 1992)

_____, *UK Eyes Alpha: The Inside Story of British Intelligence* (Faber & Faber, 1996)

_____, *Task Force Black: The Explosive True Story of the SAS and the Secret War in Iraq* (Abacus, 2011)

Vague, T., *The Great British Mistake: Vague 1977–92* (AK Press, 1994)

Van Creveld, M., *Hitler's Strategy 1940–1941: The Balkan Clue* (Cambridge UP, 2008)

Van der Bijl, N., *Operation Banner: The British Army in Northern Ireland 1969–2007* (Pen and Sword, 2007)

Vaughan, H., *Sleeping With the Enemy: Coco Chanel's Secret War* (NY: Alfred A. Knopf, 2011)

Vickers, R., *The Labour Party and the World: Vol. 1, The Evolution of Labour's Foreign Policy, 1900–51* (Manchester UP, 2004)

Vincent, D., *The Culture of Secrecy: Britain, 1832–1998* (Oxford UP, 1998)

Walker, J., *Aden Insurgency: The Savage War in Yemen 1962–67* (History Press, 2004)

Walton, C., *Empire of Secrets: British Intelligence, the Cold War and the Twilight of Empire* (HarperPress, 2013)

Walton, T., *Challenges in Intelligence Analysis: Lessons from 1300 BCE to the Present* (Cambridge UP, 2010)

Wark, W., *The Ultimate Enemy: British Intelligence and Nazi Germany, 1933–39* (I.B. Tauris, 1985)

Warner, M., *The Rise and Fall of Intelligence: An International Security History* (Washington DC: Georgetown UP, 2014)

Watt, D.C., *How War Came: The Immediate Origins of the Second World War, 1938–1939* (Heinemann, 1989)

Watts, C., *The Rhodesian Crisis in British International Politics, 1964–1965* (University of Birmingham Ph.D., 2006)

Webb, S., *The Suffragette Bombers: Britain's Forgotten Terrorists* (Pen and Sword, 2014)

Weinberg, G., *Hitler's Foreign Policy, 1933–1939: The Road to World War II* (Enigma Books, 2010)

West, N., *A Matter of Trust: MI5, 1945–72* (Weidenfeld & Nicolson, 1982)

_____, *GCHQ: The Secret Wireless War, 1900–86* (Weidenfeld & Nicolson, 1986)

_____, *The Friends: Britain's Post-War Secret Intelligence Operations* (Weidenfeld & Nicolson, 1988)

_____, *The Secret War for the Falklands* (Little, Brown, 1997)

_____, *Counterfeit Spies* (Little, Brown, 1998)

_____, *Venona: The Greatest Secret of the Cold War* (HarperCollins, 1999)

_____, *Historical Dictionary of British Intelligence* (Scarecrow, 2005)

_____, *At Her Majesty's Secret Service: The Chiefs of Britain's Intelligence Agency, MI6* (Greenhill, 2006)

_____, *Historical Dictionary of World War II Intelligence* (Scarecrow, 2008)

_____, *The A–Z of British Intelligence* (Scarecrow, 2009)

_____, *Mask: MI5's Penetration of the Communist Party of Great Britain* (Routledge, 2012)

West, N. and Tsarev, O., *The Crown Jewels: The British Secrets at the Heart of the KGB Archives* (New Haven: Yale UP, 1999)

Westlake, M., *Kinnock: The Biography* (Little, Brown, 2001)

Wheen, F., *Strange Days Indeed: The Golden Age of Paranoia* (Fourth Estate, 2010)

Wigg, R., *Churchill and Spain: The Survival of the Franco Regime, 1940–1945* (Routledge, 2005)

Wilford, H., *America's Great Game: The CIA's Secret Arabists and the Shaping of the Modern Middle East* (NY: Basic Books, 2013)

Wilkinson, N.J., *Secrecy and the Media: The Official History of the United Kingdom's D-Notice System* (Routledge, 2009)

Wilkinson, P. and Bright Astley, J., *Gubbins and SOE* (Pen and Sword, 2010)

Wilson, J., *Nazi Princess: Hitler, Lord Rothermere and Princess Stephanie von Hohenlohe* (The History Press, 2011)

Winterbotham, F.W., *The Ultra Secret* (Weidenfeld & Nicolson, 1974)

Wood, J.R.T., *A Matter of Weeks Rather Than Months: The Impasse Between Harold Wilson and Ian Smith* (Trafford, 2012)

Woodward, B., *Veil: The Secret Wars of the CIA, 1981–1987* (NY: Simon & Schuster, 2005)

Worrall, J., *Statebuilding and Counterinsurgency in Oman: Political, Military and Diplomatic Relations at the End of Empire* (I.B. Tauris, 2012)

Wroe, A., *Lives, Lies and the Iran–Contra Affair* (I.B. Tauris, 1991)

Young, J., *Winston Churchill's Last Campaign: Britain and the Cold War 1951–1955* (Oxford UP, 1996)

_____, *The Labour Governments, 1964–1970: International Policy* (Manchester UP, 2003)

Young, J. and Kent, J., *International Relations Since 1945* (Oxford UP, 2004)

Zamir, M., *The Secret Anglo–French War in the Middle East: Intelligence and Decolonisation, 1940–48* (Abingdon: Routledge, 2015)

Ziegler, P., *Mountbatten: The Official Biography* (Collins, 1985)

_____, *Wilson: The Authorised Life* (Weidenfeld & Nicolson, 1993)

_____, *Edward Heath: The Authorised Biography* (HarperPress, 2011)

Secondary Works: Chapters, Journal Articles and Papers

Abrahamian, E., 'Mass Protests in the Iranian Revolutions, 1977–79', in Roberts, A. and Garton Ash, T. (eds), *Civil Resistance and Power Politics: The Experience of Non-Violent Action From Gandhi to the Present* (Oxford UP, 2011), 62–79

Aldrich, R.J., 'Secret Intelligence for a Post War World', in Aldrich, R.J. (ed.), *British Intelligence, Strategy and the Cold War* (Routledge, 1992), 15–49

_____, 'The Value of Residual Empire: Anglo–American Intelligence Cooperation in Asia After 1945', in Aldrich, R. and Hopkins, M. (eds), *Intelligence, Defence and Diplomacy: British Policy in the Post-War World* (Routledge, 1994)

_____, 'GCHQ and Sigint in the Early Cold War 1945–70', *I&NS*, 16/1 (2001): 67–96

_____, 'Policing the Past: Official History, Secrecy, and British Intelligence since 1945', *English Historical Review*, 11/483 (2004): 922–53

_____, 'Whitehall and the Iraq War: The UK's Four Intelligence Enquiries', *Irish Studies in International Affairs*, 16 (2005): 73–88

_____, 'British Intelligence, Security and Western Co-operation in Cold War Germany: The Ostpolitik Years', in de Graaf, B., de Jong, B. and Platje, W. (eds), *Battleground Western Europe: Intelligence Operations in Germany and the Netherlands in the Twentieth Century* (Amsterdam: Uitgeverij Het Spinhuis, 2007)

_____, 'Beyond the Vigilant State: Globalisation and Intelligence', *Review of International Studies*, 35/4 (2009): 889–902

_____, 'Whitehall Wiring: The Communications-Electronics Security Group and the Struggle for Secure Speech', *Public Policy and Administration*, 28/2 (2013): 178–195

Aldrich, R.J. and Coleman, M., 'The Cold War, the JIC and British Signals Intelligence, 1948', *I&NS*, 4/3 (1989): 535–49

Alvarez, D., 'Behind Venona: American Signals Intelligence in the Early Cold War', *I&NS*, 14/2 (1999): 179–86

Andrew, C.M., 'Gordon Welchman, Sir Peter Marychurch and the "Birth of Ultra"', *I&NS*, 1/2 (1986): 277–81

_____, 'The Growth of Intelligence Collaboration in the English Speaking World', *Wilson Center Working Paper*, 83 (November 1987)

_____, 'Churchill and Intelligence', *I&NS*, 3/3 (1988): 181–94

_____, 'The Growth of the Australian Intelligence Community and the Anglo–American Connection', *I&NS*, 4/2 (1989): 213–57

_____, 'Intelligence Collaboration Between Britain and the United States During the Second World War', in Hitchcock, W.T. (ed.), *The Intelligence Revolution: A Historical Perspective* (Washington DC: US Air Force Academy, 1991): 111–23

_____, 'The Making of the Anglo–American SIGINT Alliance', in Peake, H. and Halperin, S. (eds), *In the Name of Intelligence* (Washington DC: NIBC Press, 1994): 95–109

_____, 'Intelligence and International Relations in the Early Cold War', *Review of International Studies*, 24/3 (1998): 321–30

_____, 'The Venona Secret', in Robertson, K. (ed.), *War, Diplomacy and Intelligence* (Macmillan, 2002): 203–25

Andrew, C.M. and Aldrich, R.J. (eds), 'The Intelligence Services in the Second World War', *Contemporary British History*, 13/4 (1999): 130–69

Ball, S., 'Baldwin, Stanley, First Earl Baldwin of Bewdley (1867–1947)', *Oxford Dictionary of National Biography* (Oxford UP, 2004)

Bar-Joseph, U., 'Forecasting a Hurricane: Israeli and American Estimations of the Khomeini Revolution', *Journal of Strategic Studies*, 36/5 (2013): 718–42

Barker, A., 'Practising to Deceive: Whitehall, Arms Exports and the Scott Inquiry', *Political Quarterly*, 68/1 (1997): 41–9

Baston, L. and Seldon, A., 'Number 10 Under Edward Heath', in Ball, S. and Seldon, A. (eds), *The Heath Government 1970–74: A Reappraisal* (Longman, 1996): 47–74

Beech, M. and Oliver, T., 'Humanitarian Intervention and Foreign Policy in the Conservative-Led Coalition', *Parliamentary Affairs* (2013): doi: 10.1093/pa/gst02

Bennett, H. and Cormac, R., 'Low intensity operations in theory and practice: General Sir Frank Kitson as warrior-scholar', in Mumford, A. and Reis, B. (eds), *The Theory and Practice of Irregular Warfare: Warrior-Scholarship in Counter-Insurgency* (Routledge, 2013): 105–24

Best, A., 'Intelligence, Diplomacy and the Japanese Threat to British Interests, 1914–41, *I&NS*, 17/1 (2002): 85–100

Betts, R., 'Analysis, War, and Decision: Why Intelligence Failures are Inevitable', *World Politics*, 31/1 (1978): 61–89

Bratzel, J.F. and Rout Jr, L.B., 'Pearl Harbor, Microdots, and J. Edgar Hoover', *American Historical Review*, 87 (1982): 1342–51

_____, 'Once More: Pearl Harbor, Microdots, and J. Edgar Hoover', *American Historical Review*, 88 (1983): 953–60

_____, 'FDR and the "Secret Map"', *Wilson Quarterly*, New Year's (1985): 167–73

Braun, L.F., 'Suez Reconsidered: Anthony Eden's Orientalism and the Suez Crisis', *Historian*, 65/3 (2003): 535–61

Brown, K., 'Churchill's Golden Eggs – British Interception of US and French Communications', unpublished paper given in London, 3 October 1994

_____, 'The Interplay of Information and Mind in Decision-Making: Signals Intelligence and Franklin D. Roosevelt's Policy-Shift on Indochina', *I&NS*, 13/1 (1998): 109–31

Bruce-Briggs, B., 'Another Ride on Tricycle', *I&NS*, 7/2 (1992): 77–100

Budiansky, S., 'The Difficult Beginnings of US–British Codebreaking Cooperation', *I&NS*, 15/2 (2000): 49–73

Chapman, R., 'Change in the Civil Service: A Traditional View in a Period of Change', *Public Administration*, 72 (1994): 599–610

Clayton, H., 'The Life and Career of Sir William Joynson-Hicks, 1865–1932: A Reassessment', *Journal of Historical Biography*, 8 (2010): 1–38

Cockett, R.B., 'Ball, Chamberlain and "Truth"', *Historical Journal*, 33/1 (1990): 131–42

Cogan, C., 'From the Politics of Lying to the Farce at Suez: What the US Knew', *I&NS*, 13/2 (1998): 100–22

Coggins, R., 'Wilson and Rhodesia: UDI and British Policy Towards Africa', *Contemporary British History*, 20/3 (2006): 363–81

_____, 'The British Government and Rhodesian UDI' in Kandiah, M. (ed.), *Rhodesian UDI* (ICBH, 2000): 13–23

Cormac, R., 'Secret Intelligence and Economic Security: The Exploitation of a Critical Asset in an Increasingly Prominent Sphere', *I&NS*, 29/1 (2014): 99–121

_____, 'Much Ado About Nothing: Terrorism, Intelligence and the Mechanics of Threat Exaggeration', *Terrorism and Political Violence*, 25/3 (2013): 476–93

Cowper-Coles, F., '"Anxious for Peace": The Provisional IRA in Dialogue with the British Government, 1972–75', *Irish Studies Review*, 20/3 (2012): 223–42

Craig, T., 'From Backdoors and Back Lanes to Backchannels: Reappraising British Talks with the Provisional IRA, 1970–74', *Contemporary British History*, 26/1 (2012): 97–117

Creevy, M., 'A Critical Review of the Wilson Government's Handling of the D-Notice Affair in 1967', *I&NS*, 14/3 (1999): 209–27

Daddow, O. and Schnapper, P., 'Liberal Intervention in the Foreign Policy Thinking of Tony Blair and David Cameron', *Cambridge Review of International Affairs*, 26/2 (2013): 330–49

Danchev, A., 'Story Development, or Walter Mitty the Undefeated', in Danchev, A. and Macmillan, J. (eds), *The Iraq War and Democratic Politics* (Routledge, 2004)

Davies, P.H.J., 'Organizational Politics and the Development of British Intelligence Producer/Consumer Interfaces', *I&NS*, 10/4 (1995): 113–32

_____, 'Britain's Machinery of Intelligence Accountability: Realistic Oversight in the Absence of Moral Panic', in Baldino, D. (ed.), *Democratic Oversight of Intelligence Services* (New South Wales: Federation Press, 2010): 133–60

Deery, P., '"A Very Present Menace"? Attlee, Communism and the Cold War', *Australian Journal of Politics and History*, 44/1 (1998): 69–93

Defty, A., Bochel, H. and Kirkpatrick, J., 'Tapping the Telephones of Members of Parliament: The "Wilson Doctrine" and Parliamentary Privilege', *I&NS*, 29/5 (2014): 675–97

Denniston, A.G., 'The Government Code and Cypher School between the Wars', *I&NS*, 1/1 (1986): 48–70

Dilks, D.N., 'Appeasement Revisited', *University of Leeds Review*, 15 (1972): 28–56

_____, 'Appeasement and "Intelligence"', in Dilks, D. (ed.), *Retreat From Power: 1906–1939* (Macmillan, 1981): 139–69

_____, 'Flashes of Intelligence: The Foreign Office, the SIS and Security Before the Second World War', in Andrew, C. and Dilks, D. (eds), *The Missing Dimension: Governments and Intelligence Communities in the Twentieth Century* (Macmillan, 1982): 101–25

_____, '"We Must Hope for the Best and Prepare for the Worst": The Prime Minister, the Cabinet, and Hitler's Germany, 1937–9', *Proceedings of the British Academy*, 73 (1987): 309–52

Donovan, M., 'National Intelligence and the Iranian Revolution', *I&NS*, 12/1 (1997): 143–63

Dorey, P., 'The Fall of the Wilson Government, 1970', in Heppell, T. and Theakston, K. (eds), *How Labour Governments Fall: From Ramsay MacDonald to Gordon Brown* (Palgrave, 2013): 83–112

Dumbrell, J. and Ellis, S., 'British Involvement in Vietnam Peace Initiatives, 1966–1967: Marigolds, Sunflowers and "Kosygin" Week', *Diplomatic History*, 27/1 (2003): 113–49

Dutton, D.J., 'Fyfe, David Patrick Maxwell, Earl of Kilmuir (1900–1967)', *Oxford Dictionary of National Biography* (Oxford UP, 2004)

Easter, D., 'British and Malaysian Covert Support for the Rebel Movements in Indonesia During the "Confrontation", 1963–66', *I&NS*, 14/4 (1999): 195–208

_____, 'British Intelligence and Propaganda During the "Confrontation", 1963–1966', *I&NS*, 16/2 (2001): 83–102

_____, 'GCHQ and British External Policy in the 1960s', *I&NS*, 23/5 (2008): 681–706

Erskine, R., 'Churchill and the Start of the Ultra–Magic Deals', *International Journal of Intelligence and Counterintelligence*, 10/1 (1997): 57–74

_____, 'The 1944 Naval BRUSA Agreement and its Aftermath', *Cryptologia*, 30/1 (2006): 1–22

_____, 'The Holden Agreement on Naval Sigint: The First BRUSA?', *I&NS*, 14/2 (1999): 187–97

_____, 'William Friedman's Bletchley Park Diary: A Different View', *I&NS*, 22/3 (2007): 367–79

Ferris, J., '"Now that the Milk is Spilt": Appeasement and the Archive on Intelligence', *Diplomacy and Statecraft*, 19/3 (2008): 527–65

_____, 'Intelligence and Diplomatic Signalling During Crises: The British Experiences of 1877–78, 1922, and 1938', *I&NS*, 21/5 (2006): 675–96

_____, 'The Road to Bletchley Park: The British Experience with Signals Intelligence, 1892–1945', *I&NS*, 17/1 (2002): 53–84

_____, '"Indulged in all too Little"? Vansittart, Intelligence and Appeasement', in Ferris, J. (ed.), *Intelligence and Strategy: Selected Essays* (Routledge, 2005): 45–98

Field, A., 'Tracking Terrorist Networks: Problems of Intelligence Sharing Within the UK Intelligence Community', *Review of International Studies*, 35/4 (2009): 997–1009

_____, 'The "New Terrorism": Revolution or Evolution?', *Political Studies Review*, 7/2 (2009): 195–207

Finlan, A., 'The (Arrested) Development of UK Special Forces and the Global War on Terror', *Review of International Studies*, 35/4 (2009): 971–82

Fischer, Benjamin B., 'Anglo–American Intelligence and the Soviet War Scare: The Untold Story', *I&NS*, 27/1 (2012): 75–92

French, D., 'Spy Fever in Britain, 1900–1915', *Historical Journal*, 21/2 (1978): 355–70

Fussell, P., 'Writing in Wartime: The Uses of Innocence', in Fussell, P. (ed.), *Thank God for the Atom Bomb and Other Essays* (NY: Summit, 1989): 53–81

Gaddis, J.L., 'Intelligence, Espionage and Cold War Origins', *Diplomatic History*, 13/2 (1989): 191–213

Gasiorowski, M.J., 'The 1953 Coup d'Etat in Iran', *International Journal of Middle East Studies*, 19/3 (1987): 261–86

Gazit, S., 'Intelligence Estimates and the Decision Maker', *I&NS*, 3/3 (1988): 261–87

Gibson, S., 'Future Roles of the UK Intelligence System', *Review of International Studies*, 35/4 (2009): 917–28

Gill, P., 'Reasserting Control: Recent Changes in the Oversight of the UK Intelligence Community', *I&NS*, 11/2 (1996): 313–31

Goodman, M., 'Who is Trying to Keep What Secret from Whom and Why? MI5–FBI Relations and the Klaus Fuchs Case', *Journal of Cold War Studies*, 7/3 (2005): 124–46

_____, 'The Dog that Didn't Bark: The Joint Intelligence Committee and the Warning of Aggression', *Cold War History*, 7/4 (2007): 38–42

_____, 'Learning to Walk: The Origins of the UK's Joint Intelligence Committee', *International Journal of Intelligence and Counterintelligence*, 21/1 (2007): 40–56

_____, 'The Tentacles of Failure: British Intelligence, Whitehall and the Buster Crabb Affair', *International Historical Review*, 30/4 (2008): 768–84

_____, 'Covering up Spying in the "Buster" Crabb Affair: A Note', *International History Review*, 30/4 (2008): 768–84

Goodman, M. and Pincher, C., 'Research Note: Clement Attlee, Percy Sillitoe and the Security Aspect of the Fuchs Case', *Contemporary British History*, 19/1 (2005): 67–77

Gorodetsky, G., 'Churchill's Warnings to Stalin: A Reappraisal', *Historical Journal*, 29/4 (1986): 979–90

Gorst, A. and Lucas, W.S., 'The Other Collusion: Operation Straggle and Anglo–American Intervention in Syria, 1955–56', *I&NS*, 4/3 (2008): 576–95

Grob-Fitzgibbon, B., 'Those Who Dared: A Reappraisal of Britain's SAS, 1950–80', *International History Review*, iFirst (2014)

Groth, A.J. and Froeliger, J.D., 'Unheeded Warnings: Some Intelligence Lessons of the 1930s and 1940s', *Comparative Strategy*, 10/4 (1991): 331–46

Gupta, S.R., 'The Mountbatten Saga: Myths, Images, and Facts of Current History', *International Studies*, 23/3 (1986): 287–300

Gwinnett, G., 'Attlee, Bevin and Political Warfare', *International History Review* (2016)

Hammond, A. and Aldrich, R.J., 'Securing Freedom: Obama, the NSA and American Foreign Policy', in Parmar, I., Miller, L.B. and Ledwidge, M. (eds), *Obama and the World: New Directions in US Foreign Policy* (Routledge, 2014, 2nd edn): 303–14

Handel, M., 'The Politics of Intelligence', *I&NS*, 2/4 (1987): 5–46

Harrison, E., 'J.C. Masterman and the Security Service, 1940–72', *I&NS*, 24/6 (2009): 769–804

Hennessy, P., 'Rulers and Servants of the State: The Blair Style of Government 1997–2004', *Parliamentary Affairs*, 58/1 (2005): 6–16

Hennessy, P. and Brownfeld, G., 'Britain's Cold War Security Purge: The Origins of Positive Vetting', *Historical Journal*, 25/4 (1982): 965–73

Herman, M., 'Up from the Country: Cabinet Office Impressions 1972–75', *Contemporary British History*, 11/1 (1997): 83–97

_____, 'The Postwar Organisation of Intelligence: The January 1947 Report to the Joint Intelligence Committee on the Intelligence Machine', in Dover, R. and Goodman, M. (eds), *Learning From the Secret Past: Cases in British Intelligence History* (Washington DC: Georgetown UP, 2011): 11–35

_____, 'What Difference did it Make?', in Herman, M. and Hughes, G. (eds), *Intelligence in the Cold War: What Difference did it Make?* (Routledge, 2013): 159–63

Herrington, L., 'British Islamic Extremist Terrorism: The Declining Significance of Al-Qaeda and Pakistan', *International Affairs*, 91/1 (2015): 16–35

Hiley, N., 'Internal Security in Wartime: The Rise and Fall of P.M.S.2, 1915–1917', *I&NS*, 1/3 (1986): 395–415

_____, 'The Failure of British Counter-Espionage Against Germany, 1907–1914', *Historical Journal*, 28/4 (1985): 835–62

Hinsley, F.H., 'British Intelligence in the Second World War', in Andrew, C. and Noakes, J. (eds), *Intelligence and International Relations* (Exeter: Exeter Studies in History No.15, 1989): 209–18

——, 'British Intelligence and Barbarossa', in Erickson, J. and Dilks, D. (eds), *Barbarossa: The Axis and the Allies* (Edinburgh UP, 1994): 43–75

——, 'Churchill and the Use of Special Intelligence', in Blake, R. and Louis, W.R. (eds), *Churchill* (Oxford UP, 1996): 275–90

Hoggarth, D., 'Post-Colonial Market-Building: The Rise of Islamic Finance in Central Asia', *International Affairs*, 92/1 (2016): 116–36

Honeyman, V., 'Foreign Policy', in Heppell, T. and Seawright, D. (eds), *Cameron and the Conservatives: The Transition to Coalition Government* (Palgrave, 2012): 121–35

Hughes, G., '"Giving the Russians a Bloody Nose": Operation Foot and Soviet Espionage in the United Kingdom, 1964–1971', *Cold War History*, 6/2 (2006): 229–49

——, 'Britain, the Transatlantic Alliance and the Arab–Israeli War of 1973', *Journal of Cold War Studies*, 10/2 (2008): 3–40

——, 'A "Model Campaign" Reappraised: The Counter-Insurgency War in Dhofar, Oman, 1965–1975', *Journal of Strategic Studies*, 32/2 (2009): 271–305

——, 'Soldiers of Misfortune: The Angolan Civil War, the British Mercenary Intervention, and the UK Policy Towards South Africa, 1975–6', *International History Review*, 36/3 (2014): 493–512

——, 'Skyjackers, jackals and soldiers: British planning for international terrorist incidents during the 1970s', *International Affairs*, 90/5 (2014): 1013–31

IISS, 'UK Rethink on Counter-Terrorism: Contest II Places Greater Focus on Tackling the Causes of Extremism', *Strategic Comments*, 15/2 (2009): 1–2

Inkster, N., 'Chinese Intelligence in the Cyber Age', *Survival*, 55/1 (2013): 45–66

Iourdanou, I., 'What News on the Rialto? The Trade of Information and Early Modern Venice's Centralized Intelligence Organization', *I&NS*, 31/3 (2016)

Jeffery, K. and Sharp, A., 'Lord Curzon and Secret Intelligence', in Andrew, C. and Noakes, J. (eds), *Intelligence and International Relations, 1900–1945* (Exeter: Exeter Studies in History No.15, 1987): 103–27

Jeffreys-Jones, R., 'The Role of British Intelligence in the Mythologies Underpinning the OSS and Early CIA', *I&NS*, 15/2 (2000): 5–19

——, 'The End of an Exclusive Special Intelligence Relationship: British–American Intelligence Co-operation Before, During and After the 1960s', *I&NS*, 27/5 (2012): 707–21

Jenkins, R., 'Churchill: The Government of 1951–1955', in Blake, R. and Louis, W.R. (eds), *Churchill* (Oxford UP, 1996): 491–503

——, 'Wilson (James) Harold, Baron Wilson of Rievaulx (1916–1995)', *Oxford Dictionary of National Biography* (Oxford UP, 2004)

Jervis, R., 'Reports, Politics and Intelligence Failures: The Case of Iraq', *Journal of Strategic Studies*, 29/1 (2002): 3–52

Jones, C., '"Where the State Feared to Tread": Britain, Britons, Covert Action and the Yemen Civil War, 1962–64', *I&NS*, 21/5 (2006): 717–37

Jones, M., '"Maximum Disavowable Aid": Britain, the United States and the Indonesian Rebellion, 1957–58', *English Historical Review*, 114/459 (1999): 1179–216

——, 'Anglo–American Relations After Suez, the Rise and Decline of the Working Group Experiment, and the French Challenge to NATO, 1957–59', *Diplomacy and Statecraft*, 14/1 (2003): 77–99

——, 'The "Preferred Plan": The Anglo–American Working Group Report on Covert Action in Syria, 1957', *I&NS*, 19/3 (2004): 401–15

Jones, M. and McGarr, P., 'Real Substance, Not Just Symbolism? The CIA and the Representation of Covert Operations in the Foreign Relations of the United States Series', in Moran, C. and Murphy, C. (eds), *Intelligence Studies in Britain and the US: Historiography Since 1945* (Edinburgh UP, 2013): 65–89

Kaarbo, J., 'Prime Minister Leadership Styles in Foreign Policy Decision-Making: A Framework for Research', *Political Psychology*, 18/3 (1997): 553–81

Kahn, D., 'Codebreaking in World War I and II: The Major Successes and Failures, Their Causes and Their Effects', *Historical Journal*, 23/3 (1980): 617–39

——, 'Soviet Comint in the Cold War', *Cryptologia*, 22/1 (1998): 1–24

Kapitonova, N., 'Visit of Soviet leaders Nikita Khrushchev and Nicholas Bulganin to Britain in April 1956', *Cold War History*, 14/1 (2014): 127–52

Karatzogianni, A., 'The Politics of Cyberconflict', *Journal of Politics*, 24/1 (2004): 46–55

Kern, G., 'How "Uncle Joe" Bugged FDR: The Lessons of History', *Studies in Intelligence*, 47/1 (2007)

Larsen, D., 'British Intelligence and the 1916 Mediation Mission of Colonel Edward M. House', *I&NS*, 25/5 (2010): 682–704

____, 'War Pessimism in Britain and an American Peace in Early 1916', *International History Review*, 34/4 (2012): 795–817

____, 'The First Intelligence Prime Minister: David Lloyd George (1916–1922)', *UK Cabinet Office* (8 February 2013)

____, 'Abandoning Democracy: Woodrow Wilson and Promoting German Democracy', *Diplomatic History*, 37/3 (2013): 476–508

____, 'Intelligence in the First World War: The State of the Field', *I&NS*, 29/2 (2014), 282–302

Lashmar, P., 'Canberras over the USSR', *Aeroplane Monthly*, 23/2 (1995): 32–5

Layne, C., 'Security Studies and the Use of History: Neville Chamberlain's Grand Strategy Revisited', *Security Studies*, 17/3 (2008): 397–437

Lebovic, J., 'Why Intelligence Fails: Lessons from the Iranian Revolution and the Iraq War', *Critical Dialogue*, 8/4 (2010): 1167–9

Lomas, D., 'Labour Ministers, Intelligence and Domestic Anti-Communism, 1945–1951', *Journal of Intelligence History*, 12: 2 (2013): 113–33

____, '"… the Defence of the Realm and Nothing Else": Sir Findlater Stewart, Labour Ministers and the Security Service', *I&NS* (iFirst, 2014): 1–24

Louis, W.R., 'Britain and the Overthrow of the Mossadeq Government', in Gasirowski, M. and Byrne, M. (eds), *Mohammed Mossadeq and the 1953 Coup in Iran* (NY: Syracuse UP, 2004): 126–78

Lucas, S. and Morey, A., 'The Hidden "Alliance": The CIA and MI6 Before and After Suez', *I&NS*, 15/2 (2008): 95–120

Lucas, S. and Morris, C., 'A Very British Crusade: The Information Research Department and the Beginning of the Cold War', in Aldrich, R. (ed.), *British Intelligence, Strategy and the Cold War, 1945–51* (Routledge, 1992): 85–110

Maddrell, P., 'British–American Scientific Intelligence Collaboration During the Occupation of Germany', *I&NS*, 15/2 (2000): 74–94

Maguire, T., 'Counter-Subversion in Early Cold War Britain: The Official Committee on Communism (Home), the Information Research Department, and "State-Private Networks"', *I&NS* (iFirst, 2014)

Martland, P., 'Vassall, (William) John Christopher (1924–1996)', *Oxford Dictionary of National Biography* (Oxford UP, 2004)

____, 'Hanley, Sir Michael Bowen (1918–2011)', *Oxford Dictionary of National Biography* (Oxford UP, 2005)

Matthew, H.C.G., 'Edward VIII [*later* Prince Edward, Duke of Windsor] (1894–1972)', *Oxford Dictionary of National Biography* (Oxford UP, 2004)

Mawby, S., 'The Clandestine Defence of Empire: British Special Operations in Yemen, 1951–64', *I&NS*, 17/3 (2002): 105–30

Michaels, J.H., 'Heyday of Britain's Cold War Think Tank: Brian Crozier and the Institute for the Study of Conflict', in van Dongen, L., Roulin, S. and Scott-Smith, G. (eds), *Transnational Anti-Communism and the Cold War: Agents, Activities, and Networks* (Palgrave, 2015): 146–66

Mills, W.C., 'Sir Joseph Ball, Adrian Dingli, and Neville Chamberlain's "Secret Channel" to Italy, 1937–1940', *International History Review*, 24/2 (2002): 278–317

Milner-Barry, S., '"Action This Day": The Letter from Bletchley Park Cryptanalysts to the Prime Minister, 21 October 1941', *I&NS*, 1/2 (1986): 272–6

Mistry, K., 'Illusions of Coherence: George F. Kennan, US Strategy and Political Warfare in the Early Cold War, 1946–1950', *Diplomatic History*, 33/1 (2009): 39–66

Mokhtari, F., 'Iran's 1953 Coup Revisited, Internal Dynamics versus External Intrigue', *Middle East Journal*, 62/3 (2008): 457–86

Moorcraft, P., 'Rhodesia's War of Independence', *History Today*, 40/9 (1990)

Moore, K., 'Real-Time Syndrome Surveillance in Ontario, Canada: The Potential Use of Emergency Departments and Telehealth', *European Journal of Emergency Medicine*, 11/1 (2004): 3–11

Moran, C., 'Intelligence and the Media: The Press, Government Secrecy and the "Buster" Crabb Affair', *I&NS*, 26/5 (2011): 676–700

Moran, C. and Johnson, R., 'In the Service of Empire: Imperialism and the British Spy Thriller 1901–1914', *Studies in Intelligence*, 54/2 (2010): 1–22

Moran, C. and Willmetts, S., 'Filming Treachery: British Cinema and Television's Fascination with the Cambridge Five', *Journal of British Cinema and Television*, 10/1 (2013): 49–70

Moran, J., 'Conspiracy and Contemporary History: Revisiting MI5 and the Wilson Plot[s]', *Journal of Intelligence History*, 13/2 (2014): 161–75

Morrow, J., 'States and Strategic Airpower: Continuity and Change, 1906–1939', in Higham, R. and Parillo, M. (eds), *The Influence of Airpower Upon History: Statesmanship, Diplomacy and Foreign Policy Since 1903* (Lexington, KY: UP of Kentucky, 2013)

Mumford, A., 'Covert Peacekeeping: Clandestine Negotiations and Backchannels with the Provisional IRA During the Early "Troubles", 1972–76', *Journal of Imperial and Commonwealth History*, 39/4 (2011): 633–48

Murphy, C., 'Whitehall, Intelligence and Official History: Editing SOE in France', in Moran, C. and Murphy, C. (eds), *Intelligence Studies in Britain and the US: Historiography Since 1945* (Edinburgh: Edinburgh UP, 2013)

Nagyfejeo, E., 'Transatlantic collaboration in countering cyberterrorism', in Jarvis, L. and MacDonald, S. (eds), *Terrorism Online: Politics, Law and Technology* (Routledge, 2015): 144–72

O'Halpin, E., 'The British Joint Intelligence Committee and Ireland, 1965–1972', *IIIS Discussion Paper*, 211 (2007)

O'Leary, B., 'Northern Ireland', in Hickson, K. and Seldon, A. (eds), *New Labour, Old Labour: The Wilson and Callaghan Governments 1974–1979* (Routledge, 2004): 240–59

Omand, D., 'The Future of Intelligence: What are the Threats, the Challenges, and the Opportunities?', in Duyvesteyn, I., de Jong, B. and Van Reijn, J. (eds), *The Future of Intelligence: Challenges in the 21st Century* (Routledge, 2014): 14–26

Owen, D., 'Diseased, Demented, Depressed: Serious Illness in Heads of State', *QJM: An International Journal of Medicine*, 96/5 (2003): 325–36

Palmer, A., 'The History of the D-Notice Committee', in Andrew, C. and Dilks, D. (eds), *The Missing Dimension: Governments and Intelligence Communities in the Twentieth Century* (Macmillan, 1984): 227–49

Panayi, P., 'An Intolerable Act by an Intolerable Society: The Internment of Germans in Britain During the First World War', in Cesarani, D. and Kushner, T. (eds), *The Internment of Aliens in Twentieth Century Britain* (Frank Cass, 1993): 53–75

Phimister, I., 'Smith, Ian Douglas (1919–2007)', *Oxford Dictionary of National Biography* (Oxford UP, 2011)

Phythian, M., 'Hutton and Scott: A Tale of Two Inquiries', *Parliamentary Affairs*, 58/1 (2005): 124–37

Popplewell, R., 'British Intelligence in Mesopotamia 1914–16', *I&NS*, 5/2 (1990): 139–72

Price, E., 'Interview: Lord Carrington', *Country Life* (30 August 2007)

Pronay, N. and Taylor, P.M., '"An Improper Use of Broadcasting": The British Government and Clandestine Radio Propaganda Operations Against Germany During the Munich Crisis and After', *Journal of Contemporary History*, 19/1 (1984): 357–84

Quintana, E., 'The War from the Air', in Johnson, A. and Mueen, S. (eds), *Short War, Long Shadow: The Political and Military Legacies of the 2011 Libya Campaign* (RUSI, 2012): 33–4

Reiter, D., 'Learning, Realism, and Alliances: The Weight of the Shadow of the Past', *World Politics*, 46/4 (1994): 490–526

Rentola, K., 'Intelligence and Stalin's Two Crucial Decisions in the Winter War, 1939–40', *International History Review*, 35/5 (2013): 1089–112

Rezk, D., 'Seeing Sadat, Thinking Nasser', in Freedman, L. and Michaels, J.H. (eds), *Scripting Middle East Leaders: The Impact of Leadership Perceptions on US and UK Foreign Policy* (NY: Bloomsbury, 2013): 63–82

———, 'Orientalism and Analysis: Notions of Arab "Otherness" in Anglo–American Intelligence', *I&NS*, 30/4 (2015)

Richelson, J., 'When Kindness Fails: Assassination as a National Security Option', *International Journal of Intelligence and Counterintelligence*, 15/2 (2010): 243–79

Robertson, K., 'Recent Reform of Intelligence in the UK: Democratization or Risk Management?', *I&NS*, 13/2 (1998): 144–58

Rose, K., 'Rothschild, (Nathaniel Mayer) Victor, Third Baron Rothschild (1910–1990)', *Oxford Dictionary of National Biography* (Oxford UP, 2004)

Rosselli, J., 'Forster, Mark Arnold (1920–1981)', *Oxford Dictionary of National Biography* (Oxford UP, 2004)

Schlaepfer, C., 'Signals Intelligence and British Counter-Subversion in the Early Cold War', *I&NS* (iFirst, 2012)

Scott, L., 'Espionage and the Cold War: Oleg Penkovsky and the Cuban Missile Crisis', *I&NS*, 14/4 (1999): 23–48

____, 'Secret Intelligence, Covert Action and Clandestine Diplomacy', *I&NS*, 19/2 (2004): 322–41

Shiraz, Z., 'Drugs and Dirty Wars: Intelligence Cooperation in the Global South', *Third World Quarterly*, 34/10 (2013): 1749–67

Simkins, A., 'Sillitoe, Sir Percy Joseph (1888–1962)', *Oxford Dictionary of National Biography* (Oxford UP, 2004)

Smith, R. and Zametica, J., 'The Cold Warrior: Clement Attlee Reconsidered, 1945–7', *International Affairs*, 61/2 (1985): 237–52

Spelling, A., '"Recrimination and Reconciliation": Anglo–American Relations and the Yom Kippur War', *Cold War History*, 13/4 (2013): 485–506

Stafford, D., 'Spies and Gentlemen: The Birth of the British Spy Novel, 1893–1914', *Victorian Studies*, 24/4 (1981): 489–509

____, 'Churchill and SOE', in Seaman, M. (ed.), *Special Operations Executive: A New Instrument of War* (Routledge, 2006): 47–60

Starbird, K. et al., 'Rumors, False Flags, and Digital Vigilantes: Misinformation on Twitter After the 2013 Boston Marathon Bombing', *Ideals* (2014), https://www.ideals.illinois.edu/handle/2142/47257

Stibbe, M., 'A Question of Retaliation? The Internment of British Civilians in Germany in November 1914', *Immigration and Minorities*, 23/1 (2005): 1–29

Strang, B., 'Once More Unto the Breach: Britain's Guarantee to Poland, March 1939', *Journal of Contemporary History*, 31/4 (1996): 721–52

Theakston, K., 'Brook, Norman Craven, Baron Normanbrook (1902–1967)', *Oxford Dictionary of National Biography* (Oxford UP, 2004)

____, 'David Cameron as Prime Minister', in Heppell, T. and Seawright, D. (eds), *Cameron and the Conservatives: The Transition to Coalition Government* (Palgrave, 2012): 194–209

Thorpe, K., 'The "Juggernaut Method": The 1966 State of Emergency and the Wilson Government's Response to the Seamen's Strike', *Twentieth Century British History*, 12/4 (2001): 462–85

Toye, R., 'Winston Churchill's "Crazy Broadcast": Party, Nation, and the 1945 Gestapo Speech', *Journal of British Studies*, 49/3 (2010): 655–80

Treverton, G., 'The Future of Intelligence: Changing Threats, Evolving Methods', in Duyvesteyn, I., de Jong, B. and Van Reijn, J. (eds), *The Future of Intelligence: Challenges in the 21st Century* (Routledge, 2014)

Troy, T.F., 'The British Assault on J. Edgar Hoover: The Tricycle Case', *International Journal of Intelligence and Counterintelligence*, 3/2 (1989): 169–209

Walton, C., 'British Intelligence and Threats to British National Security After the Second World War', in Grant, M. (ed.), *The British Way in Cold Warfare: Intelligence, Diplomacy and the Bomb, 1945–1975* (Continuum, 2009): 141–59

Wark, W.K., 'British Intelligence on the German Air Force and Aircraft Industry, 1933–39', *Historical Journal*, 25/3 (1982): 627–48

____, 'British Military and Economic Intelligence Assessments of Nazi Germany Before the Second World War', in Andrew, C. and Dilks, D. (eds), *The Missing Dimension: Governments and Intelligence Communities in the Twentieth Century* (Macmillan, 1982): 78–100

____, 'Williamson Murray's Wars', *I&NS*, 1/3 (1986): 472–81

____, 'Something Very Stern: British Political Intelligence, Moralism, and Grand Strategy in 1939', *I&NS*, 5/1 (1990): 150–70

____, 'In Never Never Land? The British Archives on Intelligence', *Historical Journal*, 35/1 (1992): 196–203

Watt, D.C., 'British Intelligence and the Coming of the Second World War in Europe', in May, E.R. (ed.), *Knowing One's Enemies: Intelligence Assessment Before the Two World Wars* (Princeton, NJ: Princeton UP, 1984): 237–40

_____, 'An Intelligence Surprise: The Failure of the Foreign Office to Anticipate the Nazi–Soviet Pact', *I&NS*, 4/3 (1989): 512–34

Watts, C., 'Killing Kith and Kin: The Viability of British Military Intervention in Rhodesia, 1964–5', *Twentieth Century British History*, 16/4 (2005): 382–415

West, N., 'Defending Whom?', *International Journal of Intelligence and Counterintelligence*, 23/4 (2010): 776–83

Willmetts, S., 'The Burgeoning Fissures of Dissent: Allen Dulles and the Selling of the CIA in the Aftermath of the Bay of Pigs', *History*, 100/340 (2015): 167–88

Winks, R., 'Winston Churchill, Intelligence and Fiction: Mysteries Inside Enigmas', lecture at Yale University (2 April 1995), http://www2.westminster-mo.edu/cm/scholar/021995.pdf

Wolf, N., '"This Secret Town": MI6 Officers in Hanoi During the Vietnam War', *International History Review* (2016)

Wyatt, W., 'Wigg, George Edward Cecil, Baron Wigg (1900–1983)', *Oxford Dictionary of National Biography* (Oxford UP, 2004)

Yarhi-Milo, K., 'In the Eye of the Beholder: How Leaders and Intelligence Communities Assess the Intentions of Adversaries', *International Security*, 38/1 (2013): 7–51

Young, J., 'Churchill's Bid for Peace with Moscow, 1954', *History*, 73/239 (1988): 425–48

_____, 'The British Foreign Office and Cold War Fighting in the Early 1950s: PUSC(51)16 and the 1952 Sore Spots Memorandum', *University of Leicester Discussion Papers in Politics*, P95/2 (University of Leicester, 1995)

_____, 'George Wigg, the Wilson Government and the 1966 Report into Security in the Diplomatic Service and GCHQ', *I&NS*, 14/3 (1999): 198–209

_____, 'Britain and LBJ's War, 1964–8', *Cold War History*, 2/3 (2002): 63–92

Zamir, M., 'The "Missing Dimension": Britain's Secret War Against France in Syria and Lebanon, 1942–45 – Part II', *Middle Eastern Studies*, 46/6 (2010): 791–899

Index